Drohitchin Memorial (Yizkor) Book
500 years of Jewish Life
(Drohiczyn, Belarus)

Translation of

Drohitchin - finf hundert yor yidish lebn

Original Edited by: Dov Warshawsky, Book Committee Drohiczyn

Originally Published in Yiddish in Chicago, 1958

Editor: Florence Schumacher

Published by JewishGen

**An Affiliate of the Museum of Jewish Heritage - A Living Memorial to the Holocaust
New York**

Drohitchin Memorial (Yizkor) Book 500 years of Jewish Life (Drohiczyn, Belarus)
Translation of *Drohitchin; finf hundert yor yidish lebn*

Copyright © 2014 by JewishGen, Inc.
All rights reserved.
First Printing: March 2014, Adar Sheni' 5774
Second Printing: August 2019, Av 5779

Editor: Florence Schumacher
Translator: David Goldman
Layout: Joel Alpert
Image Editor: Dr.Larry Gaum
Cover Design: Jan R. Fine
Publicity: Sandra Hirschhorn
Yiddish and Hebrew Consultant: Josef Rosin
Indexing: Bena Shklyanoy

Translation Project Coordinator: Glen David Strauss

Published by JewishGen, Inc.
An Affiliate of the Museum of Jewish Heritage
A Living Memorial to the Holocaust
36 Battery Place, New York, NY 10280

Digital images of the original book's contents can be seen online at the New York Public Library Web site: http://yizkor.nypl.org/index.php?id=2116

The mission of the JewishGen organization is to produce a translation of the original work and we cannot verify the accuracy of statements or alter facts cited.

Printed in the United States of America by Lightning Source, Inc.
Library of Congress Control Number (LCCN): 2014902044
ISBN: 978-1-939561-16-9 (hard cover: 744 pages, alk. paper)

Cover Credits: From the cover of the original Yiddish book

JewishGen and the Yizkor-Books-in-Print Project

This book has been published by the **Yizkor-Books-in-Print Project,** as part of the **Yizkor Book Project** of **JewishGen, Inc**.

JewishGen, Inc. is a non-profit organization founded in 1987 as a resource for Jewish genealogy. Its website [www.jewishgen.org] serves as an international clearinghouse and resource center to assist individuals who are researching the history of their Jewish families and the places where they lived. JewishGen provides databases, facilitates discussion groups, and coordinates projects relating to Jewish genealogy and the history of the Jewish people. In 2003, JewishGen became an affiliate of the **Museum of Jewish Heritage - A Living Memorial to the Holocaust** in New York.

The **JewishGen Yizkor Book Project** was organized to make more widely known the existence of Yizkor (Memorial) Books written by survivors and former residents of various Jewish communities throughout the world. Later, volunteers connected to the different destroyed communities began cooperating to have these books translated from the original language—usually Hebrew or Yiddish—into English, thus enabling a wider audience to have access to the valuable information contained within them. As each chapter of these books was translated, it was posted on the JewishGen website and made available to the general public.

The **Yizkor-Books-in-Print Project** began in 2011 as an initiative to print and publish Yizkor Books that had been fully translated, so that hard copies would be available for purchase by the descendants of these communities and also by scholars, universities, synagogues, libraries, and museums.

These Yizkor books have been produced almost entirely through the volunteer effort of researchers from around the world, assisted by donations from private individuals. The books are printed and sold at near cost, so as to make them as affordable as possible. Our goal is to make this important genre of Jewish literature and history available in English in book form, so that people can have the personal histories of their ancestral towns on their bookshelves for themselves and for their children and grandchildren.

A list of all published translated Yizkor Books can be found at:
http://www.jewishgen.org/Yizkor/ybip.html

Lance Ackerfeld, Yizkor Book Project Manager

Joel Alpert, Yizkor-Book-in-Print Project Coordinator

JewishGen
Yizkor Book Project

This book is presented by the
Yizkor Books in Print Project
Project Coordinator: Joel Alpert

Part of the
Yizkor Books Project of JewishGen, Inc.
Project Manager: Lance Ackerfeld

These books have been produced solely through volunteer effort
of individuals from around the world. The books are printed and
sold at near cost, so as to make them as affordable as possible.

Our goal is to make this history and important genre of Jewish
literature available in English in book form so that people can have
the near-personal histories of their ancestral towns on their bookshelves for themselves and for their children and grandchildren.

Any donations to the Yizkor Books Project are appreciated.

Please send donations to:
Yizkor Book Project
JewishGen
36 Battery Place
New York, NY 10280

JewishGen, Inc. is an affiliate of the
Museum of Jewish Heritage
A Living Memorial to the Holocaust

MEMORIAL BOOK DROHICHYN

1 9 5 8

בית־הדפוס של בן־ציון לעווקאוויטש

אינטערנעשיאנאל טייפסעטטינג קאמפאני

204 סאוט קעדזי עוועניו

שיקאגע. 12, אילינאיס

Title Page of Original Yiddish Book

דראָהיטשין

פינף הונדערט יאָר ייִדיש־לעבן

באַאַרבעט און רעדאַקטירט
פון
הרב דוב ב. וואַרשאַווסקי

לזכרין נאָך די פינף טויזנט ייִדישע נפֿשות פֿון דראָהיטשין, וועלכע זיינען געוואָרן

אומגעבראַכט פֿון די מערדערישע דייטשן
אין צוויי מאָסן־שחיטות

יא אב תש״ב — 25 יולי 1942   17 אָקט. 1942 — 1 חשון תש״ג

אַרויסגעגעבן פֿון בוך־קאָמיטעט "דראָהיטשין"
תש״ה   •   שיקאַגאָ   •   1958

גדליה קאַפּלאַן
מאַטעריאַל־זאַמלער

זלמן שעווינסקי
איניציאַטאָר פֿון בוך

דוד אייזענשטיין   •   לייזער וואַרשאַווסקי   •   הערש ליב אייזענשטיין   •   זלמן שעווינסקי
פֿאָרזיצער   וויצע פֿאָרזיצער   קאַסירער   סעקרעטאַר

אברהם אייזענשטיין   •   ישראל ברוך אייזענשטיין   •   הרב יהודה דוד גאָלדמאַן   •   בלומע גוטאַוו
אברהם גראַטש   •   יוסף גראַטש   •   שלום גראַטש   •   חיים ליב גראַסמאַן   •   חיים האָפֿמאַן
באַנטשע וואַסערמאַן   •   זיידל וויינמאַן   •   בען טעפּער   •   רחל מאָזורסקי   •   טודרוס ליב מילנער
יוסף פֿעלדמאַן   •   יוסף קאָלען   •   גדליה קאַפּלאַן   •   מעקס קלאַר   •   יוסף שיב   •   הערי שקאַלניק
אַדוואָקאַט שלמה שקאַלניק   •   הרב דוב ב. וואַרשאַווסקי רעדאַקטער

Translation of the Title Page of Original Yiddish Book

DROHITCHIN

FIVE HUNDRED YEARS OF JEWISH LIFE

REVISED AND EDITED

BY

RABBI DOV B. WARSHAVSKY

In memory of the five thousand Jewish souls from Drohitchin who perished in two
massacres at the hands of the murderous Germans

October 17, 1942   July 25, 1942

PUBLISHED BY THE DROHITCHIN YIZKOR BOOK COMMITTEE

Chicago, 1958

Zalman Shevinsky- Originator
Gedaliah Kaplan-Researcher

Dovid Eisenstein - Chairman
Leizer Warshavsky - Vice President

Hersh Leib Eisenstein - Treasurer
Zalman Shevinsky - Secretary

ABRAHAM EISENSTEIN * YISROEL BARUCH EISENSTEIN * RABBI YEHUDA
DOVID GOLDMAN * BLUMA GUTAV * ABRAHAM GRATCH * YOSEF GRATCH *
SHOLOM GRATCH * CHAIM LEIB GROSSMAN * CHAIM HOFFMAN * BONCHE
WASSERMAN * ZEIDEL WEISSMAN * BEN TEPER * ROCHEL MAZURSKY *
TODROS LEIB MILNER * YOSEF FELDMAN * YOSEF KOLEN * GEDALIA
KAPLAN * MAX KLAR * YOSEF SHUB * HARRY SHKOLNICK * SHLOMO
SHKOLNICK, ESQ. * RABBI DOV B. WARSHOVSKY, Editor

FOREWARD FOR PUBLICATION OF THE TRANSLATION

The original Drohitchin Yizkor Book, published in Yiddish in 1958, was a wonderful memorial tribute, but it was accessible only to people who could read Yiddish. There also were only a limited number of copies of the book, now typically owned by the descendants of people who had bought the original book.

In the mid 1990s, JewishGen, the major web portal for Jewish genealogy, made a huge contribution to genealogy researchers when it created the Yizkor Book translation project, which now has completely translated 90 books, and over 700 are in the process of being translated. Thanks to Glenn Strauss, who became the project leader to translate the Drohitchin Yizkor Book, and to all those who contributed funds to pay for the translation, the translated book was posted on the JewishGen.org website. The content became available at no cost to anyone who visited the website. This was a major step forward in making this invaluable genealogy resource available to all researchers.

JewishGen's most recent advance in 2011, the publication of the translated Yizkor books, makes the printed hardcover versions of these books available to a much broader audience. Joel Alpert created this project for JewishGen and with the help of dozens of volunteers, 24 books have been published as of January 2014. These Yizkor books are now more widely available to people interested in learning about their family history and the history of the towns from which their ancestors came.

This project is personal for me. I became aware of the Drohitchin Yizkor Book when I first started researching my family's history more than 20 years ago. Two cousins owned the original Yiddish Yizkor book, but my basic Yiddish skills were not advanced enough for me to read it. All I could do was copy the page about my Hausman/Hoizman family and have my mother translate it. About 10 years ago, I was thrilled to discover the Drohitchin book was online at JewishGen. I immediately downloaded many of the pages and learned much more about my family's story and the community from which they came. When I heard about the publication project last year, I asked Joel if the Drohitchin book could be published, so I -- and others -- could read about the history of the entire Jewish town where our families originated. Even more importantly, I could pass the book along to my sons, so they could learn their grandmother's history. To make this happen, I agreed to be the volunteer editor and convinced Joel that there would be interest in this book. He approved the project and took on the leadership to make it happen, including the difficult task of laying out the text and inserting all the photos from the original book.

All of us, especially Drohitchin descendents, owe a debt of gratitude not only to JewishGen but also to Glenn Strauss and Joel Alpert for their volunteer efforts. Their commitment to genealogy research made this publication possible. Your job now, dear reader, is to pass on to your own family the legacy of Drohitchin, the vibrant Jewish world that was eliminated so brutally in 1942.

Florence Schumacher, Editor
January 2014

Acknowledgements

Special thanks to the National Yiddish Book Center in Amherst, Massachusetts and the New York Public Library for supplying the high resolution images used in this book.

Our sincere appreciation to Walter Warshawsky, David Warshawsky, Ann Warshawsky and Judith Warshawsky for providing this material to JewishGen, Inc.

Notes to the Reader

Within the text the reader will note "{34}" standing ahead of a paragraph. This indicates that the material translated below was on page 34 of the original book. However, when a paragraph was split between two pages in the original book, the marker is placed in this book after the end of the paragraph for ease of reading.

All references within the text of the book to page numbers, refer to the page numbers of the original Yizkor Book.

The original book can be seen online at the NY Public Library site:
http://yizkor.nypl.org/index.php?id=2116

The Table of Contents in the original Yizkor Books was much more detailed than the Table of Contents in this translation, so the reader is urged to peruse the original Table of Contents at the very end of the book to find specific people of interest such as a relative. Then the reader can find the proper page by finding the original page number as represented by [page 234] in the left column on many pages in this translation.

Location of Drahichyn in Belarus Today

Map by Jan R. Fine

Geopolitical Information

Political locations in recent times:

	Town	District	Province	Country
Before WWI (c. 1900):	Drogichin	Kobrin	Grodno	Russian Empire
Between the wars (c. 1930):	Drohiczyn	Drohiczyn	Polesie	Poland
After WWII (c. 1950):	Drogichin			Soviet Union
Today (c. 2000):	Drahichyn			Belarus

Drohitchin is located at 52°11' North Latitude and 25°09'East Longitude

40 miles W of Pinsk, 33 miles E of Kobryn, 16 miles E of Antopol.
[Not to be confused with the smaller town of Drohiczyn, Poland, 49 miles WNW of Brest].

Other close towns:
       Simonovichi 7 miles NNW
       Yakovleva 8 miles E
       Khomsk 11 miles NNE
       Antopol 16 miles W
       Ivanava 17 miles ESE
       Haradzets 20 miles W
       Motol 21 miles ENE
       Byaroza 25 miles NNW
       Velikaya Glusha, Ukraine 26 miles S
       Pyershamayskaya 26 miles NNW
       Malaya Glusha, Ukraine 27 miles SSW
       Malech 28 miles NW
       Divin 28 miles WSW
       Syalyets 30 miles NNW

Alternate names for the town: Drahichyn [Belarussian], Drogichin [Russsian], Drohiczyn [Polish], Drohitchin [Yiddish], Drahitschyn [German], Drogičinas [Lithuanian], Drohichin, Drohiczyn Poleski, Drahičyn, Dorohiczyn

Region: Grodno

A Brief History of Drohitchin

Drohitchin lies between the Bug and Dneiper Rivers, one of the great swamp areas of Europe, known as the Polesia, in what today is the country of Belarus. The town is between Pinsk, 40 miles (70 killometers) to the west, and Brest-Litovsk, 60 miles (105 killometers) to the east, and there were several smaller villages nearby. Do not confuse this town with still another, smaller town, Drohiczyn, with the same name located in Poland, 49 miles WNW of Brest.

Drohitchin is the Yiddish spelling for the town, which today is spelled *Drahichyn.* It has variously been known as *Drohiczyn* (Polish), *Drogichin* (Russian), and *Drahitschyn* (German), as well as *Drohichin* and *Drohicyn Poleski.* This Yizkor book uses the Yiddish spelling of the original book.

The Drohitchin Yizkor Book describes a flourishing Jewish community almost 500 years old before it was destroyed in 1942. The swamps served to protect the town from the armies of King Karl XII of Sweden, Napoleon Bonaparte, and the Germans in World War I. The area's forests and rivers were a good source of fish and lumber for the town's major businesses.

The earliest reference to Jews from the town is found in the records of the Grand Duke of Lithuania. Jews farmed some significant plots in the area during 1463-1494, according to these records. The town was created in 1623 in what was then part of Lithuania. The 1766 census counted 510 Jews in the town. In 1897, according to the official census, there were 843 Jews, 46% of the population. The economic conditions of the area improved in the early part of the twentieth century with the opening of a railroad station nearby and the construction of a road from the station to Drohitchin. In 1921, there were 1521 Jews, 77% of the population, and by 1939 there were nearly 5,000.

Jews were traders, craftsmen, artisans, and they even owned a few big businesses. Most of the population sustained itself with small gardens and a few animals. Drohitchin was a marketplace town, drawing trade from nearby villages. The intellectual and cultural life centered on the houses of study, and the rabbi was the unofficial head of the community.

Religious life and religious education were very important, with several synagogues and four houses of study before 1914. The town was a center for Cabalism. In the late part of the eighteenth century, Reb Dovid Yafa (Jaffee, Yaffe) was one of the prominent rabbis and also a Cabalist. Legend has it that he created a golem. Later the Chassidic Movement influenced the town. There even was a yeshiva from 1905–1914. The Yizkor Book describes the biographies and work of the many rabbis in the town, including the popular Kholozhin rebbe (the blacksmith).

World War I brought the fighting among the Russians, the Germans, and the Poles to Drohitchin. The population suffered greatly as the various armies occupied the town. It was bombed, and most of the buildings later were burned. There was a typhus epidemic in 1915 causing many deaths.

As the town was recovering from World War I, the Polish-Russian War in 1921 brought more hardship as the two countries fought for control of the area. The Poles controlled the town between the world wars. The Jews of Drohitchin formed a vigilante group before World War II, allowing them to stand up against the growing anti-Semitism. There were no pogroms during that time thanks to the proud and defiant attitude of the Jews.

During the Second World War, the Germans occupied Drohitchin in June, 1941. They established two ghettos, and Jews from nearby villages also were brought to these ghettos. Two mass slaughters on October 17 and July 25, 1942 killed 4,700 Jews in Drohitchin. Some extraordinarily brave survivors escaped to the nearby Svaritsvitch Forest joining other partisans or were hidden by Christians until the Russians liberated the town in 1944. They tell the haunting story of this time in this Yizkor Book. Among the amazing accounts, read about Chava Feldman, who lived in a pit for three years, Chaya Rieder, who was hidden in a neighbor's house for two years, and Bashka Fialkov, who with her two children, aged 14 and nine, fled the massacre in the ghetto and hid in the swamp until they found their way to the partisans in the forest.

Emigration to the United States from Drohitchin began in the 1880's, and it continued intensely until World War I began in 1914. After the war, in 1920, it resumed until 1924, when the United States severely restricted immigration. People then went to Argentina, Cuba, Palestine, and Canada. Chicago, New York, and Palestine became three major centers for Drohitchin residents. The Yizkor Book describes the many activities of these centers -- forming synagogues, cemeteries and *landsman* societies -- as well as the biographies of Drohitchin immigrants who became prominent in their new countries.

Florence Schumacher, Editor

Table of Contents

Drohitchin Yizkor Book

Drohitchin Worldwide
Part Seven: pp. 633 - 716

Family Notes

FOREWORD

Finally, after years of exhaustive and intensive work, we present the Drohitchin Yizkor Book to our esteemed friends and readers. This book should serve as a memorial to the holy community of Drohitchin. Our parents are no more. Our brothers and sisters are no more. Drohitchin - where the elderly lived in peace and quiet, and where children laughed and played in the streets - is no more. The sweet voices of the children will never be heard again, and our joy will be consumed by fury and suffering.

Drohitchin, our dear hometown, the place where our cradles stood, the place where our mothers used to lull us to sleep with melodies of Jewish hopes and fears. Drohitchin, the beloved hometown of our youth, where we soaked in the Jewish *oy!* and *krechts* (groan), is silent. Together with millions of Jewish martyrs who were put to death by the German murderers, approximately five thousand Drohitchin Jews were killed to sanctify the name of G-d. May G-d avenge their deaths!

Those of us who were witnesses to the enormous catastrophe have no strength to measure and make sense of the great disaster and the enormity of the tragedy. This is because we were too close to the misfortune that befell us. We became accustomed to the cries of the Jewish children in the gas chambers and their laments in the crematoria. Perhaps the following generations will have the strength to get a feeling of the gruesome tragedy that overtook our generation.

However, to remain silent and not tell our children and the world what the Germans did to us and refrain from immortalizing the holy memory of our loved ones from Drohitchin would be a crime against G-d and the martyrs. In just a few decades, the memory of Drohitchin would have totally been forgotten.

This, then, is the goal of the *Drohitchin Book:* to describe for future generations the joys and sorrows of approximately 500 years of the Jewish community in Drohitchin and to provide a gravestone in words and pictures for our *shtetl* and its martyrs.

There can be no better and enduring monument than this Yizkor Book. It is a gravestone of holy letters that can never be erased. Gravestones of wood and stones are not immortal. Wood rots and burns; stones can be dug up and broken off. A gravestone of letters, however, lives forever. Many stone and wooden monuments remain, but what about the butchery that Jews have endured in just the last couple of hundred years? If we do something about material conditions, this is due to the monuments of the written word. It suffices, for example, to mention the book by Rabbi Notta Hanover (who died on July 14, 1683), *Yavan Metsulah [Deep Mire],* which is an immortal historical document and a monument for approximately a half million Jews who fell victim to Bogdan Chmielnitski's Cossacks in 1648-49.

Furthermore, a stone or wooden monument cannot move; it is mute and lifeless. It cannot speak; it says nothing. It is merely an ornament for a few people who live around it. However, a monument of a Yizkor Book gets distributed all over the world and says to every individual, "Look at me; read me; look and remember."

When the Romans wrapped him in a Torah scroll and burned him in an *auto-de-fé*, the great sage of the Talmud, Rabbi Chaninah ben Tardion, said:

[*Page VII*]

"The parchment burns, but the letters rise heavenward." (Tractate *Avoda Zarah,* 18).

The German murderers killed and burned the holy martyrs in order to hide all traces of their butchery. Those martyrs didn't even get a grave, but our "Scroll of Fire," written in letters of fire will soar across the whole world; from the ash, from the extinguished sparks, shall arise *esh* [the Hebrew word for 'fire']. The burned bodies of the martyrs will turn into fiery, glowing and flying images and strike the minds of their murderers with the pointers the rabbis taught the alphabet to the children in the *cheders* (religious elementary schools).

Even if hundreds of years from now there only exists only a single copy of the Drohitchin Book in some far away museum, archive or library, the exterminated Jewish community of Drohitchin will live forever in history.

We realize that there is repetition of information in the Yizkor Book. We intentionally left it in because we specifically wanted to immortalize the various versions that were provided by several individuals in their descriptions of the Holocaust and who survived the slaughter and hell of the Germans. This is because each version makes a unique contribution. We believe that every single letter, groan and cry that is put to paper at the feverish moment of suffering and rage is history itself. It reflects the very survival of the moment described. The truth is that none of the contributors could have expressed their survival in as such a strong way as the way we have expressed it in this book. Therefore, we have immortalized every written description and document that is even remotely related to Drohitchin.

We also realize that not everything that could, or should, be written about Drohitchin has been described in this book, and the opposite is also true. However, even the small amount described in this book arrived with great difficulty. The most difficult job was the revising, assembling and editing of the material, which was in extremely raw condition. In addition, most of the articles had to be revised both in style and form, and recreated, giving them life and spirit. Afterwards, we had to correct and classify the material, break up and layout the pages, and read the corrected versions (dozens of times). This was all done and written by one person. It's no wonder that it has taken so long to publish this book.

   We should mention Zalman Shevinsky, the originator of the book, and Gedaliah Kaplan, who assembled part of the original unedited material and photos. We extend heartfelt congratulations to the administrative committee and everyone else who participated in getting the Yizkor Book published. We did the work; now the Drohitchin Book belongs to our esteemed readers and friends. It's now up to critics and historians to judge it.

15 Shvat 5714
Rabbi Dov B. Warshavsky
January 19, 1954 – Tu Bishvat
With G-d's Help.
Printed on 15 Shvat 5718
February 5, 1958 – Tu Bishvat

[*Page VIII*]
[*Page 10*]

Map of Drohitchin and Environs

DROHITCHIN
Historical Overview
by E. Ben Ezra (New York)

[Page 11]

A.
POLESIA

Polesia is renowned as one of the swamp areas of Europe, extending from the middle of the Bug River on one side to the Dneiper River on the other. The area used to belong to Russia. After the Riga Treaty of 1921, the entire Grodno gubernia (province) and smaller areas of Minsk gubernia, including large areas of Polesia, were transferred to Poland.

The swamps of Polesia covered almost half of the whole area. The Polesia swamps were responsible for halting the armies of the Swedish king, Karl the Twelfth. His armies got bogged down in the marshlands of Pinsk (1706). Napoleon Bonaparte was forced to avoid the swamps (1812), and in 1915, the Germans were forced to stop at the marshlands of Pinsk.

A large portion of Polesia is also made up of sand and clay. Between the swamp and the sandy areas, there are pine forests, as well as many lakes, rivers and streams in which a variety of fish can be found. These fish provided a good source of income for the inhabitants of Polesia.

Great numbers of wolves, foxes, bears, deer, and other such animals once lived in the Polesia woods, and very often they would attack the villages. The swamps also provided nests for a variety of wild fowl. In the last few hundred years, during which time great areas of the forest were cut down, the number of wild animals and birds has decreased, and as a result the danger to the villages has also decreased.

The inhabitants of Polesia are mostly White Russians, who can be divided into two groups: the White Russians of the areas of Kobrin, Kosov, Luninets, and Pruzhan, and Polish culture that had a great influence on these people. The other group is composed of White Russians from Minsk and Mogilev, and they were greatly influenced by Russian language and culture. In addition to the White Russians in Polesia, there are also Poles, Jews, Russians, Germans, Hungarians, and Gypsies. The Poles comprise almost 10 percent of the total population, and a few Poles, who formed the nobility, owned large tracts of land. Many years ago, the nobles were the undisputed rulers of Polesia. Until the German hordes exterminated them, the Jewish communities in Polesia formed approximately nine percent of the entire population. The majority of them lived in cities or villages and occupied themselves with business or trade. Only a small number of them were involved in farming. This is why their cultural level was higher than that of the other inhabitants

The soil of Polesia is very good for growing potatoes, peas, cucumbers, carrots, onions etc. Polesian peasants would plant rye, oats, barley, and buckwheat.

The clay of Polesia was good material for making pots, and potmaking was widespread among the landless peasants, who used to sell their pots individually in the market. Sometimes Jewish merchants would buy them up and send them by boat to be sold in the surrounding cities or villages where they were very popular.

[Page12]

One of the main sources of livelihood in Polesia was the lumber business; the wood was furnished by the Polesia forests. Jews controlled this business. They owned forests and hired gentiles to chop down the timber, take it to the river, form it into rafts, and send it up river to Germany. This business provided a livelihood for a large number of both Jews and non-Jews.

Part of Pinsker Street (spared by the fire) during the German occupation in 1916.

B.
THE POLITICAL SITUATION

The town of Drohitchin, which is the subject of this Yizkor Book, is located in this area of Polesia. It is important to emphasize that there is an older Drohitchin, which is located not far from Byalistock. So as not to confuse it with our own town, our Drohitchin, was called The Second Drohitchin, and it was located 70 kilometers from Pinsk, the former capital city of Polesia.

The name Drogitchin (Drohitchin) indicates that the source of the name is the Slavic word *doroga* (road). Perhaps this is because the village lies on the road between Brisk and Pinsk. It is indeed in this way that Drohitchin is identified by Bobrofsky, the chronicler of the Grodno gubernia.

In an old document of the local government of Pinsk (1561-1566), there is mention of a geographical location for the town: "Drohonitsa is near Nagoria." I believe that this is the old name of what would later be called Drohitchin. This particular document indicates that in those days Drohitchin was part of the Duchy of Pinsk, which belonged to the Polish king and Lithuanian Grand Duke, Sigmund August (1548-1572).

Poland and Lithuania were united in 1569, and the Pinsk region remained part of Lithuania. This included Drohitchin, which at that time was only a village. It did not become a small town until 1623.

The Grand Duchy of Lithuania opened its doors to Polish culture and institutions, and especially to Roman Catholic culture. The Roman Catholic Church used all available means to expand its influence in all areas of life, and it was very successful in that effort. The whole territory of Polesia was gradually Polanized. This aroused the wrath of the Cossacks, which expressed itself in the infamous Chmielnicki Massacres (1648).

The Cossacks were aided by the oppressed peasant masses. The Cossacks went on the rampage for two years, and a great deal of Jewish blood was spilled in Polesia until the Polish government vanquished the Cossacks.

In the spring of 1706, under the leadership of Karl the Twelfth, the Swedes launched a war against the Polish government. But thanks to the swamps of Polesia, he had to leave Poland that same year, and Poland remained intact until 1772, when the territory of Poland started to be partitioned. It was at that time that White Russia reverted to Russia, and after the war – from 1793 to 1795 - the gubernias of Minsk, Vilna and Grodno were also taken over by Russia.

[Page 13]

The gubernia of Grodno included the following regions: Grodno, Lida, Novgrudek, Slonim, Volkovisk, Pruzhany, Brisk, and Kobrin. Apparently, Drohitchin was then part of the uyezd (district) of Kobrin.

Before long, Napoleon Bonoparte began his wars against Russia (1812), and the war did not spare Drohitchin. However, because of the Pinsk marshlands, Napoleon was forced to turn back.

The Poles of the area were unhappy with the Russian government and attempted two uprisings against it: in 1830 and in 1863. Both times, however, the Poles were defeated. These rebellions were very bad for the Jews of that area, who suffered at the hands of both sides.

A part of Pinsker Street (spared by the fire) under German occupation in 1916.

The area surrounding Drohitchin was untouched by wars for over 100 years; however, the situation did not remain calm for the local Jews, who remained subjugated by the Czarist government. In 1914, on the ninth of Av, the Jewish day of mourning for the Temple of Jerusalem, the Russian-German war broke out. It was what the history books call World War I.

The Germans entered Drohitchin in September 1915, and remained there until November 1918, when they withdrew back to Germany. The two months from November until the end of 1918, were months of anarchy, when every person did whatever his heart desired. At the end of 1918, the Ukrainians occupied Drohitchin and lorded over it and the whole surrounding area.

The Ukrainians didn't last very long. In January 1919, the Bolsheviks arrived and instituted new rules and regulations. That regime, however, didn't last very long either. In March of 1919, the Polish Legionnaires entered Drohitchin. Their arrival brought about a new era for the whole region. The Polish wanted to take the area by force. Jewish blood was spilled there, and a lot of Jewish property and possessions were plundered.

Things were just beginning to settle down, and the inhabitants of the area were just starting to get their lives back to normal, when the Polish-Bolshevik War broke out in July 1920. At first the Russians were winning and were already at the gates of Warsaw, but their luck ran out, and the Polish army started to drive them back. In the meantime, the volunteer army of General Bulak Balakhovitch, the leader of the White Guards, decided to "help" the Poles. The "help" they offered the Poles is a story in itself, a story written in Jewish history with tears and blood.

The peace treaty between Poland and the Soviet Union was signed in Riga in March 1921 and resulted in Drohitchin and the Pinsk region being annexed to Poland. In 1925 Drohitchin became a separate district, which included Yanove, Khomsk, Motela, and the surrounding villages and hamlets.

The Polish government controlled the area until September 1939, when World War II broke out. The Red Army arrived, took the whole area and instituted the Bolshevik system. The Bolsheviks controlled the area until June of 1941 when the Germans attacked them, took over all of Poland and Ukraine, and almost got to the gates of Leningrad and Moscow.

[Page *14*]

Drohitchin young men, members of the Betar Organization, learning how to shoot.

The bitter wars and the German atrocities during those years of blood and fire will never be erased; they are etched in the minds of everyone, especially in the minds of the Jewish people. Those bloody years, from June 1941 to July 1944, when the Germans annihilated seven million Jews, will never be forgotten! We will only mention those German beasts with a curse on our lips because they wiped out hundreds of Jewish communities without even leaving a trace.

In July 1944, Drohitchin became part of the Soviet Union. Very little is known about the town and its inhabitants: how many there were, their economic condition or their cultural achievements. From then on, a veil has hung over Drohitchin, and only rarely does a ray of sunshine break through to the town, which is now 400 years old.

C.
THE HISTORY OF THE JEWS OF DROHITCHIN

As we have already observed, Drohitchin was already mentioned 400 years ago. Whether Jews were living there at that time is unknown. An old Jewish document tells us that there existed, as early as 1652, a Jewish community in Drohitchin. In the registry book, *The State of Lithuania* of the *Councils of the States of Lithuania,* Drohitchin is mentioned together with Pinsk, Lekhovitz and Khomsk as having to pay 40 shok in taxes. From the registry book, we learn that the Jewish population of Drohitchin was small, but it was large enough not to be ignored.

Another document, dated January 1679, indicates that the Jewish community of Drohitchin was then part of the Jewish community of Pinsk, and from the same source, we learn that there was organized Jewish life in Drohitchin. The Jews of Drohitchin, together with the Jews of 13 other towns that were also part of the greater Pinsk community, promised to be responsible for repayment of 1500 zlotys (Polish currency) borrowed from Kalakovski, the priest of Pinsk, to build a hospital. Evidently, the Jews of Drohitchin also used the hospital.

This event also indicates the level of poverty of the Jews of Drohitchin and the other mentioned 13 Jewish communities, since 13 communities had to co-sign a loan of 1,500 zloty. The document also indicates that if the annual interest charge of 150 zloty was not paid on time, the priest had the right to demand a three-fold increase. He even had the power to jail the Jews of the towns and to keep them there as long as he wanted. He could also confiscate their property until the entire sum was repaid. The Jews didn't even have the right to appeal.

This is how the Jews of that time were virtually enslaved to the Roman-Catholic clergy.

There is another document from July 18th of same year, indicating that the Jews of Drohitchin did not let themselves be exploited. The document states that the tax collector in the District of Pinsk, Michael Botvina, complained that when he came to collect the taxes from a group of Drohitchin Jews, they refused to pay. In addition, they attacked him, tore his clothes and drove him out of town. This example of protesting against the ruling government was a common occurrence among the neighboring gentiles, but it demanded extraordinary courage and bravery for the Drohitchin Jews to stand up to a government official.

We also read of a complaint dated September 13 1698 that was lodged against a Drohitchin Jew named Moshe Polyak, a broker who worked for a nobleman, and who beat some peasants and stole a horse and wagon, some grain and other items for his nobleman. This complaint tells us something about the pride of a Drohitchin Jew.

The tradition of courage and defiance was also transmitted from father to son in later years as well. In correspondence to the journal, *Hamelitz,* (18 Cheshvan, 5643 [October 31, 1882]), we read a letter about a pogrom that occurred in Drohitchin, in which the local Jews defended themselves quite well. The letter states that, on Friday, October 1, 1883 (there is obviously an error in one of these two dates), some drunken gentiles, together with some Russians who built the railroad near Drohitchin, started beating Jews and looting everywhere. The Jews defended themselves, and the conflict turned into a real war that lasted for quite a while.

[*Page 15*]

The Jews were not always successful in defending themselves with force. It was often necessary to pay or bribe someone in order to get a decree rescinded. Another letter in *Hamlitz* (1883) describes such a tactic, which took place during a repeat of the May Decrees of 1882. The letter from Drohitchin stated that in the month of Av (August) of that year, a decree was issued ordering all the Jews living in the villages in the Kobrin region to leave their homes within seven days. Thanks to an "intercession" of a large sum of money, the decree was delayed for a month.

In the same issue of *Hamelitz,* there appeared a letter from someone in Khomsk, a village administered by Drohitchin at that time, who wrote that the Commissioner of Police of Drohitchin assembled all the Jews of the villages surrounding Drohitchin and informed them that he had received a decree from Vilna ordering the expulsion of all the Jews from their villages. It appears, however, that the decree was never put into effect thanks to the implementation of the age-old adage, "money talks."

Sand Alley leading to the hospital.

D.
THE NUMBER OF JEWS IN DROHITCHIN

How many Jews were there in Drohitchin? The number of Jews is not precise and depends on the economic conditions of the town and the surrounding areas.

According to the official census of 1766, there were 510 Jews in Drohitchin. But there is reason to believe that this number is probably incorrect. It is possible that there were many more Jews, but that the Jews lied about their numbers because they had to pay a head tax of two gilders, regardless of sex. The only exception was for children under a year old.

In 1847, there were 843 Jews in Drohitchin. According to my estimate, the Jewish population in Drohitchin began to decline, so around 1889 there were only approximately 500 souls. Another census, in 1897, indicates that at that time the Jewish population of Drohitchin was 784, and the non-Jewish population 923, meaning that the Jewish population was 45.9 percent. Around 1904, the population of Drohitchin was 2660 inhabitants. We can conjecture that the Jewish population then consisted of around 1300 people. Thereafter, the Jewish population started to increase significantly, thanks to the increasingly favorable economic conditions in Drohitchin, a subject we will address later on.

In 1921, the Jewish population reached 1521, and the non-Jewish population 466. In other words, the Jewish population was 76.5 percent. The Jewish population increased threefold, to 4500, in only 18 years. How did this great increase come about?

[*Page 16*]

Drohitchin was on the road that ran from Brisk [*Brest-Litovsk*] to Pinsk. Because of its geographic location, fairs or markets were frequently held in Drohitchin. Even in 1817, there were seven fairs there. When the train station was built near Drohitchin (in Nagoria), transportation became even better. This, in turn, led to more economic opportunities in the town, and, therefore, to the growth in the number of Jews.

As is well known, Drohitchin had many deep marshlands that were difficult to get through, so the local Jews used to wear high boots or galoshes. Over 25 percent of Drohitchin and the surrounding area consisted of marshlands. Wearing boots, however, did not reduce the unpleasantness very much. Wooden sidewalks, built around 1905, did improve the lives of the inhabitants of Drohitchin.

In 1910, a road was built from the train station to the city. This improved transportation to and from town. This development gave rise to a lot of new business activity to town, such as mushrooms and egg businesses that shipped their products to Warsaw.

As the economy grew, a bank became necessary. At the end of the nineteenth century, ICO opened a bank in Drohitchin. Jews bought stock and became investors in the bank. The bank continued to operate even after the First World War. In 1925, the bank had 247 investors. As an ICO report showed, the aforementioned institution sent an agriculture instructor to teach farming to a few Jews from Drohitchin and surrounding villages that he employed.

House of Yudel Ravinsky, Yeshayahu-Ber, Fruma and Yitzchak Kahn.

We should note a few catastrophes that occurred in Drohitchin, specifically the famous Drohitchin fires, based on which Drohitchin Jews dated their ages, marriages and their deaths.

The first big fire occurred around 1873. The elderly spoke about it with trembling and fear. The second fire took place on Hoshana Rabba (the seventh day of the holiday of Sukkot – Friday September 30) in 1904. Approximately 25 homes burned to the ground. The third fire broke out in 1910 on Yom Kippur afternoon, and practically half the town went up in smoke.

There is a Yiddish proverb: "A fire will make you rich." Each fire in Drohitchin provided work for builders, painters and other artisans. Drohitchin was rebuilt, and life continued productively until the next fire broke out.

E.
CULTURAL AND SOCIAL CONDITIONS

Of the rabbis who had lived in Drohitchin, we were most familiar with Reb Dovid Yaffe, of blessed memory, who lived 150 years ago. Reb Dovid was of the family of Reb Mordechai Yaffe, the author of the famous rabbinical work, *Levushim (Garments)*. In addition to being a great rabbi, Reb Dovid was also a great kabbalist. Legend has it that he created a golem, though no one knows the fate of this golem. There is a folk expression, however, about the golem, in reference to an idle person: "He walks around like a Drohitchiner golem." It seems that Drohitchin was a hospitable place for the study of Kabbalah. The great kabbalist, Reb Moshe of Drohitchin also lived there.

In addition to kabbalists, Drohitchin also had a community rabbi, a pioneer, who moved to the Holy Land years before the advent of the Lovers of Zion movement. That rabbi, however, was not the only one who left town and settled there. Inscriptions on tombstones on the Mount of Olives in Jerusalem show that other Drohitchin Jews lived and died in Palestine as early as the 19th century.

The Chassidic movement did not bypass Drohitchin. The Chassidic movement put down roots there too, but the people of Drohitchin were more attracted to the more folksy Chassidism of Kobrin than the more scholarly chassidism of the closer town, Karlin. The Chassidism of Drohitchin also encountered greater opposition from the opponents of Chassidism (called *Mitnagdim*).

There was once also an attempt to establish a yeshiva in Drohitchin for full-time Torah scholars.

[*Page 17*]

This was in 1912, and the idea was initiated by Reb Meir Kaplan (also known as Meir the Borrower) and Reb Benyomin Moshe, the Ritual Slaughterer. This yeshiva did not last very long, however.

Bright young men in Drohitchin would also travel to the nearby Maltch Yeshiva to learn with Reb Zalman Sender, or to the Slobodka Yeshiva, which produced rabbis and scholars. The children of Drohitchin would also attend the Talmud Torah (religious elementary school) of Pinsk, where secular studies were also included in the curriculum. Others studied at the Russian schools in Pinsk.

Traces of the Enlightenment also found their place in Drohitchin. In 1883, through the efforts of Yitskhak Rosenkrantz and Shlomo Shedrovitsky, a group of Drohitchin Jews was granted permission to open a school for Jewish boys, and the government sent them a Russian teacher. The teacher didn't have a stitch of work to do because there was no special building to house the school. It seems that the majority of Jews in Drohitchin still did not think such school was necessary, giving priority instead to the old-fashioned cheders (traditional religious primary schools). Finally, in 1885, a school was opened with 52 boys and quite a large number of girls.

Of the various community organizations that existed in the 1890s, we should note the Free Loan Society founded by Reb Moshe Lobendiker, or as he was called, Moshe Badya's (referring to his mother first name). A large number of Drohitchin Jews belonged to that organization, and each one lent money to the society so that any person in need could obtain an interest-free loan.

Another society that also functioned in Drohitchin in those day was the Care for the Infirm Society (called *Bikkur Kholim* in Orthodox Jewish communities), which would provide the poor with doctors, medicine and nutritious food to eat to help them recover. The Guest Society (Hakhnasat Orkhim) was another organization; it provided housing and food for the poor.

The nearby large city of Pinsk had an influence on the little town of Drohitchin. The Jews of Drohitchin used to travel to Pinsk to buy their merchandise or to visit doctors. They used to bring back big-city manners and secular ideas from Pinsk.

Pinsk had a strong influence on the youth movement in Drohitchin at the time of the first Russian revolution. The Bund and the S.S. of Pinsk were very successful in recruiting members for their organizations in Drohitchin, and there was much excitement in Drohitchin during that time. The youth of Drohitchin organized a vigilante group, and there were no pogroms during those terrible times. The Drohitchin Jews proudly defended their tradition of courage and determination.

Even during the terrible days of German occupation, many Jews of Drohitchin displayed acts of resistance.

Will we ever again hear about the proud Jews of Drohitchin?

Only G-d knows!

SOURCES

A Thousand Years in Pinsk , N.Y., 1941.

The Book of Kobrin , Tel-Aviv, 1981.

Registry Book of the State of Lithuania , p. 115, Berlin, 1921.

[Hebrew:] Hamelitz , 1882, vol.40; 1883, vols. 18, 59, 60; 1885, vols. 10, 81; 1889, vol. 39; 1890, vol. 17.

[Hebrew:] The Portion of the Law Giver vol. 2, pp. 1, 13, 35; vol. 4, p. 44, Jerusalem.

"[Russian:] Documents Issued by the Vilna Commission for the Collection of Old Documents" Vol. 29, pp. 216-218 Vilna, 1902.

[Russian:] *Property Registry,* Vol. 2, pp. 123, 495, Vilna 1874.

Journal of the Ministry of Internal Affairs , Vol. 1, pp. 382, 385, Petersburg 1843.

Bobrovsky, "[Russian:] Material for the Geography and Statistics of Russia, Grodno Gubernia" Vol. 1, p. 215; Vol. 2, p. 386.

"[Russian:] Encyclopedic Dictionary," Vol. 21, p. 170.

"[Russian:] Jewish Encyclopedia," Vol. 5, p. 793; Vol. 7, p. 344; Vol. 9, pp. 575-576.

"[Russian:] *Memorial Book of the Gubernia of Grodno,* " p. 172, Grodno 1905.

"Jewish Colonization Association Report," 1925, 1927, 1930, 1931, (French).

"Zeitschrift" ["Periodical"] Vol. 2-3, pp. 307-378, Minsk, 1928, Zalman Shevinsky and Gedaliah Kaplan.

[*Page 18*]

CORRESPONDENCE ABOUT DROHITCHIN IN *HAMELITZ*

Hamelitz, vol. 40, 18 Cheshvan, 5673 [should be 5643]- 1882
Who By Earthquake
Drohitchin (Kobrin district, Horodna region)

"Suddenly fear gripped our town on Friday, October 1. Groups of gentiles were in the taverns on one of their holidays to enjoy themselves and drink wine along with railway workers who worked on the railroad near town. After they drank themselves into a stupor, they departed at 10 am and approached the store of a Jew, where they began beating him with their fists. As soon as the Jew realized they were finished, he ran outside shouting for help from other Jews in town. The gentiles ran after him and started calling the gentiles. What soon developed was a virtual war: the gentiles came after the Jews with heavy sticks and injured three of them. One man, who came out to look for his son who disappeared during the melee, was grabbed and beaten viciously until he collapsed at their feet. Many of our brethren were lightly injured because the rioters spread through town and struck any Jew they encountered. Unfortunately, we had no police in town because they had all gone off to the nearby town of Khomsk for market day. Thus, the rioters realized they had the opportunity to do anything they wished. The scandal continued until 1 pm, when it subsided because the rioters heard that General Oninikov, who was responsible for the railway, was expected in town. Who knows what would have happened to us otherwise? My fingers tremble from fear as I write these words."

Yechezkel, son of Y. L. Valevelsky

Tordos Leib Milner with his "Hebrew School" before World War I in Drohitchin

Hamelitz, vol. 18, page 282, 1883. Correspondent Valevelsky

"I am complaining about the battle against the situation of the new false messiah (*Shats – abbreviation for Shabtai Zevi*). Every day we hear the sounds of broken window glass. One person who supports the young new messiah with a charming voice, and the other rejects the new one because of devotion to the old one. I am complaining that there is no expert doctor in town." (translator: This appears to be some kind of cryptic message describing the events that occurred between Jews and gentiles).

"Mr. Yechezkel Valevelsky reports that through the efforts of the scholar, Mr. Yitzchak Rosenkrantz, the Jewish residents of the city obtained permission to open a school for Jewish youth." *Hamelitz, Vo. 59, 1883.*

[Page 19] *Hamelitz, Vol. 60, 1883.*

"On the second of the month of Av (August 5, 1883), a decree was issued requiring all Jews who lived in the villages in the district of Kobrin to prepare to leave their homes on the following Sabbath and come to the city. Only with great effort were they able to receive an extension (apparently for about a month). They discovered that there was no truth to the "decree" to expel the Jews because, in fact, they lived in peace with the farmers who were their neighbors, despite arising jealousy and envy about their wealth and businesses. On the contrary, during the days of the pogroms in southern Russia, the gentiles in the villages prided themselves on the fact that their Jewish neighbors enjoyed protected status."

A correspondent from Khomsk reported the following in the same issue of Hamelitz:

"Yesterday the official (policeman) of Drohitchin (to which our city was linked) assembled the Jews who lived in the surrounding villages and announced that he received a decree from the commander of the district on July 20 of this year reporting that the commander had received a directive from the acting governor of Vilna to relocate all the Jews from the villages to the city. This was to include those who owned their own homes for 23 years that were built on land owned by landlords or farmers. The only exceptions were those few who permanently owned land. After intensive weeping and begging, the official agreed to delay the decree for 10 days. (Apparently this decree was based on the May 3 1882 Laws)."

Hamelitz, Vol. 10, 1885 – Correspondent from Rad.

"Two years ago the government agreed to grant the Jews in our town a permit to open a school for Jewish youth (as I reported in *Hamelitz, Vol. 59, 1883*), but for various reasons the plan was not implemented. Our community didn't have the financial means to either build or rent a building for this purpose. It's already been a year that the government sent a Christian teacher here, but he has done nothing because there is no school. This has been a great embarrassment for us among our Christian neighbors who said this proved that we had no desire to educate our children according to the law, and that all we were interested in was economic exploitation. We heard this repeatedly from the government official.

However, now we are overjoyed that a number of our most respected citizens, Mr. Yitzchak Rosenkrantz and Mr. Aharon Drogitchinsky, decided to provide enough money to open the school on the 24th of this month. There were 52 students who started, in addition to quite a few girls. Their fine teacher is T. Iskra."

Hamelitz, Vol. 81, 1885, Correspndent from Drohitchin

"Mr. Yaakov Eliyahu Reichman reports that on Wednesday of last week, the rebbe of Kobrin came to town. One of the rebbe's opponents wrote his family that when the rebbe was walking down the street of the city, he tripped and broke his hand and foot. So his followers rushed here to hear what he would order them to do. The rebbe's family sent his brother here, and thanks G-d, his health is fine now. His opponents then slandered him in a letter to the city official, saying that someone had come to town to fool people into giving him their money. The official hurried over to where the rebbe was staying, but the rebbe slipped away before the official arrived after hearing the story of how he had been slandered."

Hamelitz, Vol. 39, 1889
Receiving Guests in Drohitichin

Someone set up 10 beds in his home and provides meals to the guests." Correspondent Yehoshua, son of Chirkel Yehudah Berg

Hamelitz, Vol. 17, 1890
Drohitchin, Kobrin District, Horodna Region

"The number of families is about 700. The Charity Society was established five years ago by the current director and respected elder, R. Moshe Lebendiker, who is commonly known as R. Mosheka Bodya's. This precious person fulfills the precept, 'actions speak louder than words,' because he has devoted his time and energy in his old age for this charitable work. In addition to the 665 rubles he collected as sacred money from private contributions and the estates of a number of individuals, there are another 400 rubles that were deposited as loans from society members, who have each contributed a sum of money as a loan for a period of time. The fund is available to anyone. They receive 1 ruble per week, and anyone wishing to borrow money from the fund must bring along a co-signer.

Of no less importance is the Society for Visiting the Sick, which was established three years ago. Its goal is to provide medical assistance to poor people who are ill, medications and nutritious food while they are ill until they fully recover. The funds of the society come from contributions from members and totals about 200 rubles annually, in addition to private donations. We wish to publicly pay tribute to our local doctor, Dr. S. Weissman, who made an agreement with the treasurer of the Society to provide assistance and medication to all local poor people for a token monthly contribution. The Hosting Guests Society faithfully fulfills its obligations. Its purpose is to take in poor travelers passing through our city, provide them with a place to stay in a comfortable apartment with freshly made beds and provide them with bread and food offered at the homes of the Society's members."

Yechezkel, son of Y.L. Valevelsky

The gravestones of Drohitichin residents at the Mount of Olives in Jerusalem
Khelkat Hamekhokek, vol. 2, p. 1, 13; vol. 4, p. 44.
"Shaul, son of Yehoshua the Kohen, died in 1869. The respected elder, Zvi Zelig, son of Moshe died on the 15ᵗʰ of Tevet, 5647 (January 11, 1887)"

[*Page 20*]
The corrections to the map are listed below:

The bottom text, which the original translator placed at the top left of the map, is incomplete. Here is the full text:
"This drawing of Drohitchin was made by Zvi Lewak (Los Angeles, California). Even though it is not drawn to scale, it does give an idea about the geographical situation of the town."

Corrections in the Legend:
4) Chassidic *Shtibel* [Small synagogue]
5) Hebrew Secular School
6) Religious Elementary School
8) Fire House [from Russian]
10) Government Office
["cemetery" was misspelled]
20) Steam Mill [from Russian]
22) The Electric Power Station

Corrections on the map:
Lipniber Rd. == Lipnicker Rd. [this may refer to a road leading to a place called Lipnick]
Sacher St. == Sokher Rd. [Sokha in Yiddish means "hook plow" – could also refer to a road leading to a place called Sokha]
Rovener Road [may refer to a road leading to Rovno?]
[very top] Lasintzer Road [a road leading to a place called Lasintz?]
Old Needle St. == Old Power Rd. [Russian]
Nakis St. == Noska's Alley [probably referring to a Jew named Noska]
New St. == New Alley
Right next to the 5 it should say Synagogue Courtyard Street.
Right above 20. it should say "To the Mill"
Path through the fields == Road through the fields
To the right of Train Station, it should also say: "Railroad Line"
Below Train Station, it should say: "Popiner Road [Road leading to Popin?]
Under the railroad line, the handwritten text refers to the paved and unpaved roads that the first translator had placed at the very top, together with the reference to the Polish names.

The Shtetl
Dov B. Warshavsky (Chicago)

[Page 21]

Rabbi Dov. B. Warshavsky

Drohitchin
Introduction

With a feeling of great awe and responsibility, 1 take my pen in hand to record for our generation and for future generations information about the holy community of Drohitchin, which was destroyed by the cruel German murderers, may their names be erased, together with the communities of hundreds of other Jewish towns and villages.

Unfortunately, I have no statistics or historical documentation available to refer to while writing these lines. *Pinkas Drohitchin (Drohitchin Record Book)*, the only historical document describing the events and customs of 150 years of Jewish life in Drohitchin, disappeared during the period of turmoil and extermination and has never been found. Unfortunately, I will have to be satisfied with relying on what I remember about my beloved hometown since childhood and what I heard from the adults and elders of Drohitchin. I have to rely on my imagination and common sense for the rest and, with God's help, hope I don't make any errors. For this reason I am not writing a comprehensive history of the last 500 years of Drohitchin. I will make every effort to describe the recent past, which will thereby indirectly shed light on the more distant past of Drohitchin.

A.

Geographical Layout of Drohitchin

The entire shtetl of Drohitchin (It's possible that it still exists today; however, I speak of the town in the past tense because as a Jewish town it no longer exists.) comprised one long street that wound along the highway running through Drohitichin from Pinsk-Yanov to Antopolia-Kobrin and beyond. Two residential areas fanned out from the center of the shtetl, or street, like propellers on a small steamship: the synagogue courtyard (on the south) and the row of stores (on the north). The synagogue courtyard (the spiritual center) and the market (the economic center) were the two propellers that drove and occupied the life of the Drohitchin Jewish community for hundreds of years.

[Page 22]

There were, of course, other smaller streets such as New Town and Krasna Ulitsa (Red Street), but these were no more than small branches on a large tree. There were also two one-street villages, Zaritchke and Starasilia which bordered the shtetI and which were inhabited exclusively by White Russian peasants.

General Minkov, the noble landowner who owned the shtetl.

Drohitchin actually resembled a ship floating on water because it was surrounded by a body of water, a marsh called "Vion." There were times when, because of driving rain, the water of the Vion would rise; the result was that the entire town turned into a steamship floating on a lake. Therefore, the town of Drohitchin could only expand lengthwise. In later years, the main street extended to a length of over two miles.

Half of the street on the west end was called Kobriner Street, and the other half, Pinsker Street. These two half streets also had other names: Pinsker Street was called "Land of Israel Street," and Kobriner Street was called "Egypt Street." No one knows for sure how these nicknames originated, or who created them. Could it have originated from the fact that more well-bred and wealthy Jews lived on Pinsker Street than on Kobriner Street? If that was the reason, then it isn't a joke. I prefer to accept the hypothesis that Kobriner Street was called Egypt Street because it was on Kobriner Street that the wandering gypsies had their small taverns, where they would eat and get drunk. It was commonly believed that the gypsies were descendants of the ancient Egyptians. Some joker invented the nickname "Egypt Street," and the name remained ever since.

Parallel to the highway next to the shtetl was the Pinsk-Brisk railway line built by the Russians in 1883. However, the Russians removed the train station, and placed it in Nagoria, 7 verst (approximately 5.5 miles; one verst equals 3,500 feet] from Drohitchin. People said that this move was a whim of the chief engineer who built the railway line, and who had expected the town would give him "a little something." Since the Jews pretended not to know anything about it, and because the soil around town was swampy, the engineer had an excuse to build the station seven verst from Drohitchin.

The Shtetl Was Built in a Valley

Why was Drohitchin built right in a valley, in marshlands, even though further out of town, and especially on the sand street, the ground was mountainous and dry? This was probably for two reasons.

First, because the first Jews who settled in Drohitchin wanted to live next to the dirt road near the main road. Secondly, the early local authorities apparently didn't allow the Jews to settle on mountainous, dry land (and perhaps the Jews didn't have enough money to buy better land.) The authorities were seemingly satisfied that Jews settle on marshland and develop and cultivate it.

The old cemetery located at the end of the Vion attests to the fact that years ago the whole town didn't reach the bridge but only extended as far as the church, where the sand street started, and which for years was inhabited by Russian officials and peasants. Only in the latter period did a few Jewish families also tread onto the "sand."

(Years later, when the old cemetery was full, or according to other sources, when the authorities no longer allowed burials there, the community dedicated a new cemetery far from town, on the Bubin [presumably a river] and called it the New Cemetery. In jest people would say, "He is off on the Bubin.")

It can also probably be assumed that the name "Drohitchin" was taken from the Russian "Doroga" or from the Polish "Droga." It is unclear whether the name Drohitchin has a Russian or Polish root. In Russian, the shtetl was called "Drogitchin" because there is no "h" sound in Russian. The White Russian peasants who live in and around Drohitchin pronounce the word "doroha" with an "h", and therefore the name remained Drohitchin with an "h."

[Page 23]
The Jews Received the Land Free - A Theory

Our theory is that the first Jews probably received the Drohitchin marshlands from the landowner free of charge or in lease, so the Jews could cultivate it, as described earlier. Evidence of this is that until World War I the Jews of the shtetl paid *tsinzen,* a kind of land tax, to the landlord or landlady of the nobleman's estate who owned all the land of the shtetl.

The following is a legend from the recent past: The Czarist regime was to give away the nobleman's estate located near Drohitchin, as well as all the land of Drohitchin as a gift to the hero of the Russo-Turkish War in 1877, General Minkov. How was it that the nobleman's estate belonged to the Russian government? The fact is that the nobleman's estate and the Drohitchin area had previously belonged to a Polish nobleman who probably participated in Polish revolts against Russia, such as the 1863 Matiesz uprising and earlier revolts. The Czarist government punished him by confiscating his property, and gave it to General Minkov. This was the same action the Russians had taken against other Polish nobility.

A section of Pinsker Street (spared by the fire) under German occupation in 1916.

So it is more than probable that the ground on which the shtetl stood or still stands was at one time a very deep valley into which the water from the surrounding mountainous fields flowed. Over time, the standing water soaked the ground so much that it turned into a bay and a marsh. Later on, the bay was drained, and a road was built in the middle of it, and right next to the road the Jews built Drohitchin. However, around the shtetl, the bay, which we called Vion, remained untouched. The ditches and the bridges that cut through the shtetl are evidence of this: one is next to the sand, and the other is next to the village of Zaritchka (the name of the village means "over the creek" – "retchka" in Russian means "creek"). Thus, the shtetl served to join the two Vions, so that the water would run from one Vion into the other.

[*Page 24*]

In the springtime, when the ice and snow would melt, and in autumn when the great rains would begin and the water of the Vion reached the houses, the shtetl would look like an island embraced by two great lakes. In the middle of the summer the Vion would dry out a bit, and *tcherot,* moss, reeds, small weeping willows, would grow there. Wagon-drivers' horses from town would also graze there.

The Vion as a place for youth and sports

The Vion in the summer time was one of the greatest attractions and amusement spots for the school children, especially on Fridays, when the children got out of *cheder* around noon. The *cheder* boys would go around barefoot, roll up their pants, and run around in the moss that brushed and tickled the soles of the feet. In certain spots the ground would shake under your feet. This was a sign not to go any further, since if you did, you could sink up to your neck.

We schoolboys took pleasure in goofing off at the Vion. Where else were we as free as at the Vion? We played hide-and-seek in the high moss; we made whistles from young willows or *tcherot;* we would tear the reeds and toss them to the wind like feathers or stick them on each other's collar. We would go out onto the Vion Mountains on the festival of Shavuot and gather moss and spread it around and at home. On the festival of Sukkot, we would cut down branches to cover the tops of sukkahs, willow branches to be joined with the palm branches and additional willows for the last day of Sukkot, *Hoshana Raba* .

In the winter the Vion served as a place to play sports for all the youth of the shtetl. The youth would go sleigh riding with horses on the thick gleaming ice that extended for a square mile, and perhaps even more.

Small fish, porgies, leeches and various other species of creatures creeping animals multiplied. The area was also full of loaches, which the peasants used for their special dishes.

The bridge next to the sand at the edge of town, under German occupation during World War I

At sunset in the summer the songs of the millions of frogs in the Vion was heard throughout the shtetl. Every evening at sunset, one frog would croak, then a second, and then a third, until the whole shtetl was filled with the sounds of croaking and creaking frogs. It was known as the sound of the frogs reciting the bedtime *Kriat Shma (Hear O Israel)* prayers. The frogs used to spend the entire summer in town. We knew that spring was here and summer was on its way as soon as the frogs started croaking at sunset. The croaking of the frogs left me looking forward to the mild, pleasant, and homey summer evenings that lulled me to sleep with sweet dreams.

[*Page 25*]

B.
ECONOMIC CONDITIONS IN DROHITCHIN PRIOR TO 1914

Jewish Occupations

How did Jews earn a living in Drohitchin, and who employed them? The quick answer is that they made their living from the landowner and the peasant. Drohitchin never had any factories or industries. Until World War I, there were only two tanneries in Drohitchin; they tanned rough animal hides, shoe soles and light leather. There was briefly also a small straw factory in town that produced straw bottle covers, and a small oil press that produced seed oil, a product needed by the peasants. Those little factories were destroyed in a fire during World War I, and were never rebuilt.

For several years there existed a small candle factory, which produced wicked candles. That factory was the subject of a story in Drohitchin. In the middle of Yom Kippur in 1910, the candle factory caught fire from a flame that constantly burned there. Due to the fact that it was Yom Kippur, no one wanted to violate the Sabbath laws, and thus let the fire burn. In the meantime, the fire spread to neighboring houses, and it was permitted to put the fire out. However, by that time the fire spread out of control, and the result was that half of the town (starting from the Sand) burned to ashes.

Most Jews in Drohitchin were small traders: storeowners, merchants, and brokers engaged in the animal and horse trade, for example. There were also the artisans and workers, such as bricklayers, carpenters, glaziers, painters, blacksmiths, tailors, shoemakers, quilt makers, saddlers, furriers, bakers, tinsmiths, locksmiths, and watchmakers. There were also a few big businesses engaged in forestry and lumber and ox traders, but they no longer existed in Polish Drohitchin.

Part of Pinsker Street (spared during the fire) under German occupation in 1916

Trading and Stores

Jews used to travel through the villages and buy merchandise from the landowners and peasants: cattle, oxen, calves, sheep, horses, and various agricultural products such as grain, and then sell it in town for local use, or sell it to exporters, who loaded it on to freight wagons and transported it to the large cities. Another well-known occupation was that of the village peddlers, who used to travel through the villages carrying a sack and who traded with the peasants for a *pud* (36 pounds) of seeds, a hen or pig hair, and then sell it in town.

[Page 26]

A large trade fair in Drohitchin after World War I.

Another major source of livelihood was during the large trade fairs, smaller Monday fairs before Passover, and the usual market days. During the large fairs, the entire town was filled with peasants and merchants, who came from the surrounding villages and more distant towns and cities. People were tightly packed back to back. The peasants would come to town to sell animals, calves, horses, hens, eggs, potatoes, corn, oats, millet, barley, seeds (to make oil), mushrooms, pig hair, sheep wool, and homemade flax linen. The peasants had nothing to take back home; they sold off everything to Jewish merchants in Drohitchin and other cities.

The peasants didn't take home the money they made from their produce either because they exchanged it in Jewish stores, which they cleaned out of merchandise. At each fair, the stores had to hire extra help to deal with the demand. The peasants bought up the smallest household items: sewing thread, fabric for clothing, herring, heating oil, candles, mushrooms, salt, fish oil for their boots, and tar for their wagon wheels. They also bought ironware such as scythes, sickles and plows and other implements. The peasant could find everything in any Jewish store, from needles and threads to a pound of tar for greasing their wagon wheels. (You could never even find such an assortment of merchandise and bargains in Woolworth's stores today.)

The bakers and tavern keepers also enjoyed success. The peasants loved to sit down to eat a white bread roll and drink a bottle of kvass (a type of lemonade). This was holiday time for the peasants. They especially enjoyed buying white bread rolls, herring and kvass, which they considered a very tasty combination, for their festivals. There were many treats and gifts during those days. The peasants drank lots of whisky and vodka, but not much beer.

[Page 27]

It was easy for them to drink down a bottle of whisky all at once. By the time a peasant drank half a bottle, he had already forgotten how much it cost him, and he often returned home to the village with empty pockets, after having drunk the value of a horse or other animal.

The Jews storekeepers were able to earn a substantial living during such trade fairs, and have enough money for an extended period.

Craftsmen and Artisans

Sirka Baum, the seamstress, with her workers at her home

The Jewish artisans who had the least direct benefit from the peasants were the second-hand shoemakers, tailors, and furriers. There were times when a White Russian didn't even know about leather boots. Instead, they wore a pair of *Postolas* that were made out of braided *pritlach* with rags around their feet. They also wore a long shirt, a pair of pants (from coarse linen), and a short sweater or goat vest. They dressed that way in winter and summer, and they made their own material for their clothes. They also produced their own linen, cloth and sheep hides. However, when the peasants became more cultivated, they started wearing higher quality clothing. The urban peasants particularly took on the fashions of the times.

The peasant men and women would go to the Jewish shoemaker for a pair of boots and shoes. The truth is that the boots were of cheap quality, large and stiff, made from the coarsest hide leather, with iron bottoms on the heals, which made a strong impression. It was still major progress. The peasants really wanted a Jewish tailor or furrier to make his sweater, goatskin vest, and hat. In later years, there were many peasants who still wanted to have a Jewish tailor make his clothes. The peasant was no expert in either awls or shears.

A blacksmith sets up his wagon to sell merchandise in the market, summer, 1935.

On the other hand, the other Jewish artisans, such as builders, painters, carpenter. and bricklayers couldn't make a livelihood from the peasants, since everyone knew that peasants were experts with axes and saws. The peasants built their own houses and barns out of wood. Many of the peasants even built their own ovens. It was very rare for a peasant to use a Jewish bricklayer or carpenter, and he certainly didn't need a painter. However, the peasants did make use of Jewish glaziers to build their windows. The peasants also had to make use of Jewish blacksmiths to repair their plows or wagon wheels and put shoes on their horses. The Jewish saddlers also made a living from the peasants who took care of the peasant's needs for bridles, reins, saddles, calfskins, and other leather articles.

[*Page 28*]

Drohitchin market, drawn by Elmer Shevinsky.

The old market and wagon wheel stores before the 1915 fire. Drawn by Eliyahu Leib Shevinsky of Chicago.

The Landowner's Estate: A Source of Livelihood

A different source of livelihood for Drohitchin Jews was, as mentioned before, on landowners' estates and manors, such as: Sokha, Roven, Astroveck, Dubovy, Poppina, Khlevishtch, Zakazelia, Liedviana, Smolnick, Cheromkha, Osevitz, Perkovitch, Bilien, Lekhevitch, Balkon, Hutta, and Ozitch. In contrast to the village peasants, the landowners provided the Jewish artisans with quite a bit of work. The landowners trusted the Jewish artisans a great deal, and considered them good workers. The magnates' apartments and animal barns and sheds were all built by Jewish builders, bricklayers, carpenters and painters. Many Jews were even employed as breeders and contractors, and earned a good living by working for the landowners.

The landowner estates were obviously the best customers of Jewish storekeepers, who supplied groceries and food products. The better Jewish tailors and shoemakers also made a good living from the landowners, as did the saddlers. There were also Jews involved in the agricultural activities of the estates. There were Jews who were tenants who managed the estates. These managers were called *possessors* and played a role as important as the landowners themselves.

Jews also leased milk production on the estates and would produce milk products such as butter and cheese at the estate, with the aid of centrifuges and other machinery, and would transport the products in huge barrels to large cities in Russia and abroad. These Jewish businessmen were very wealthy and lived well. Other Jews were involved in managing the orchards of the landowners' manors. Every estate had its own large orchard that produced alot of fruit. The Jewish orchard managers supplied the market with various precious fruit. The Jewish householders were able to have a supply of apples and pears for their fruit compote for the entire year. They were able to make jams and jellies, and used to say, "We just shouldn't need it." It was eaten on the Sabbath following the afternoon nap and offered to guests.

[Page 29]

Gardening and Raising Cattle and Poultry

It should be mentioned that almost 90 percent of the Jews in Drohitchin tended their own or someone else's garden. Everything grew in those gardens: potatoes, cabbage, beans, beets, carrots, cucumbers, scallions, onions, white radishes, red radishes, turnips, green beans, and pumpkins. Many Jewish families had enough vegetables for themselves and to sell to others.

It's interesting that the peasants from the villages were the main buyers of the surplus of cucumbers sold by the Jews. This was the only agricultural product that the peasants didn't grow themselves, because it required alot of patience, work and time, which the peasants didn't have.

The usual custom was to make pickles and sauerkraut, and store it in a barrel or two for the winter. When Jewish women used to get together to help their neighbors pickle cabbage, there was a holiday atmosphere. There was also the custom of filling up the cellar or yard with potatoes bought from the peasants at low prices. Potatoes were one of the main foods of every Jewish family.

Almost every Jewish family also had a cow or two, and were therefore able to produce their own milk, butter and cheese, and some extra to sell. Others raised hens and were thus able to have chicken for the Jewish festivals and fresh eggs for the children. After Sukkot, people would catch geese and fatten them with grain; at Chanukah time they would slaughter the fattened geese; and for Passover they would fry them up with fat. Fried goose skins were also enjoyed during Chanukah.

Home-baked Bread and Challah

Most of the Jewish housewives used to bake black rye bread for the week and white challah for the Sabbath in their own ovens. It was a form of art to create well-baked bread. First, the housewives would leaven flour and water in the leavening trough and let it get it warm and rise. Afterwards, the housewives would knead the dough until it became nice and thick. Then they took pieces of dough and threw it up in the air and started punching it with their hands until it formed a shining smooth loaf of bread, which they then placed into the waiting hot oven to be baked. Two hours later, they removed the freshly baked bread from the oven and would fill the house with its aroma. The rye bread could stay good for weeks, and the older it got, the tastier and more delicious it became.

[*Page 30*]

Left: The new town – S. Feldman, B. Warshavsky, A. Zlotnick
Right: Khomsk Alley, where the post office and the Mechayeh School were located.

Most Jewish families had a sack of white flour and three iceboxes that the deliveryman would bring to the house and would offer credit terms for payment. Thus, it was possible to make bread dough. In addition to a challah for the Sabbath, the housewives used to bake milk and pareve cookies, twisted challah bread and fruit cakes for the festivals; rolls for Rosh Hashanah; ladders for Yom Kippur; hands for Hoshanah Rabba (last day of Sukkot); Hamentashen for Purim, as well as noodles and farfel. Once in a while, people used to go to the baker to buy a couple of fresh bagels for lunch, a buckwheat bun, a cracker or a pure white round bread roll.

Earning Money from Savings

Nowadays, how much money do people make from what they save? If a ceramic or clay cooking pot (most people used clay or ceramic pots) was cracked, no one just threw it out. It was repaired and used over and over again, until the wire started to stick through it because of repeated heating. Those wire pots were very popular in the whole region.

There was also the custom in the summer of preparing a cord of 12 loads of wood for warming the house during the winter. There were no housing problems. Almost every person had his own house, and if anyone had to rent an apartment, he could find it for a pittance.

With the arrival of winter, when the roads were covered in snow, frost burned your eyes, and it was harder to earn a living, or livelihoods were non-existent, you were satisfied with preparing for summer. During the long winter evenings, Jewish fathers would spend a few more hours in the houses of study, while mothers would sit by oil lamps and pluck goose feathers to use to fill new cushions and featherbeds for their families. Sometimes they made them for dowries for their children who were engaged.

Baking Matzah and the Workshops

A couple of weeks before Purim, Drohitchin housewives started getting busy with preparations for Passover. People used to start scraping beets, washing the large clay Passover pots or cupboards, and making brine for Passover. At the same time, they made honey wine for the four cups of Seder wine. Some people made grape wine themselves.

[Page 31]

The workshops were bustling at this time because these workshops were the places where hand-made matzahs were baked. Every person had to have his own assigned place and task in the matzah production process. First, one person set up the baking equipment, then someone else added the measured amount of water to the flour, and a third person started kneading the dough and then turned it over to the person who rolled the dough. After that, someone punched the dough. Jewish women and girls would pull and pound the dough from all sides, and spend the time humming a folksong. The next person would start rapidly poking the matzahs. Finally, a man or woman would use a long stick to slide the matzahs into the glowing hot oven. A while later, that person would place the brown baked matzahs into a basket.

Those workshops had a romantic air about them, a magnetic force that attracted all the children, who jealously watched the kneaders and the rollers do their work. The children just wished they could be right there and participate. It was a real privilege if any of us children was able to participate.

In the final years before World War I, Drohitchin also had a modern matzah factory, which produced machine-made matzahs. Most of the Jews, however, preferred the hand-made ones. After the war, however, almost all the matzah workshops disappeared, and everyone used machine matzahs.

The Saratshick wedding, 1917. The wedding canopy is being brought from Chaikel Milner's house to the synagogue courtyard, accompanied by music.

Every Friday, the air in town was filled with the aroma of freshly baked bread, challahs, pirogues, roast, puddings and fish, which was being cooked and baked in Jewish homes in honor of the Sabbath. Actually, the food of the Jewish Sabbath had the taste of paradise, especially during the long Friday evenings, when the stoves gave off an affable warmth, and the Divine Presence hovered over the Sabbath table.

This is the way things were before World War I (1914), and probably the way things were for hundreds of years before that.

[*Page 32*]

C.
ECONOMIC CONDITIONS UNDER THE POLISH REGIME

Czarist Despotism and Polish Democracy
(We're leaving out the period from 1914-1921 (war years) because others are writing about it later in the book.)

The new municipal building built by the Polish government on the Sand

After Polish authority established itself in Drohitchin, life took on an entirely different character. Life became more concentrated and modernized, but also more difficult. Even though the Czarist regime was despotic and reactionary regime, life in town under it was actually quite flexible and open. This was because apart from the police commissioner, the local governor and a couple of policemen, nobody was around. The fact that the Czarist empire was so large meant that the Czarist iron hand was almost totally unnoticed in the faraway *shtetl* in Polesia. People were able to get the commissioner and the governor to do practically anything they wanted them to do. It was sort of a non-authoritarian situation. On the other hand, under the Polish "democratic" regime, life became restricted, contained and mean. Everybody was under the watchful eye of the Polish officials who watched every Jew with seven eyes and every step a Jew took. There was no more freedom of movement.

Drohitchin Grew and Prospered

During the first years of the Polish regime, the situation was still tolerable. When the town had to stop building its ruins, former residents of Drohitchin in the United States would send money, and craftsmen and storekeepers still made a living – the economy still hummed along.

Later on, in 1925, Drohitchin was promoted to the level of a district (*uyezd*). A local official came to town with a large staff of bureaucrats. Unlike earlier times, when Jews had to travel to the district center of Kobrin to deal with their tax issues, hundreds of people now started coming to the municipal offices in Drohitchin to deal with their tax issues. The municipal officials and the people from the surrounding areas needed places to stay, hotels, food, and clothing. This of course, brought money into town.

[Page 33]

New stores and bakeries opened, and the number of Jewish tailor and shoemaker shops increased. Jewish tailors and shoemakers from Mezeritch, Lyubeshei and other places moved to Drohitichin. The situation caused an increase in the number of Jewish foremen and drivers because the roads carried along more travelers.

From right to left: Moshele Perkovsky, Steinberg, Moshe Porush, Goldberg, Berl Resnick (driver), and others next to Goldberg's house.

The increased traffic of people into town was partly due to the district offices, especially to the Kholozshin Rebbe, who settled in Drohitchin after World War I. Every single day, the roads carried dozens of travelers into town – Jews who came to receive blessings from the Kholozshin Rebbe. Due to the increase in travelers, the Poles moved the train station, known as the *Stantsia-Ravina* station to Drohitchin from Nagoria. The coachmen who drove passengers back and forth on the road in large heavy wagons became urbane; they exchanged their wagons for horse-drawn carriages and ultimately, automobiles, becoming chauffeurs.

As the population increased, the demand for new homes and offices also increased. Suddenly new roads and houses sprung up in town. The little *shtetl* starting growing in all directions and became a city. The Polish government built a large municipal building, as well as a brand new road and houses for city employees. Large parts of the Vion were cleared, and new roads and houses were built in the area of the former bay.

Instead of stores and stalls, fine new hotels were built, and the street was known for its hotels rather than shops. The small dirt alleys were now paved (The Russians had paved the main road earlier.). The entire town was equipped with sidewalks, and an electricity station was built, which provided electric lights on the streets, just like in any other district center.

Hotel Street: The hotel of Asher Siderov and his family – grandson Yossek, Dina (wife),

[*Page 34*]

The funeral of the Kholozshin Rebbe (the blacksmith), and the public who turned out for his burial on October 20, 1932. The house in the background (indicated with an arrow) belongs to the Kholozshin family.

[*Page 35*]

The town had a good fire department that was provided with the latest equipment and machinery. The Polish city authorities were involved with the fire department and provided the instructors. The costs of the machinery were covered by donations. The firemen, who were recruited from among the Jewish men, were volunteers.

It should be mentioned that Drohitchin owned three steam mills (one already existed before World War I) that produced assorted flour and grain for the entire area. Windmills and horse-driven mills used before the war belonged to the past.

Drohitchin even had a printing press, which was a rare commodity in smaller towns. Prior to this time, if someone wanted to get something printed, he had to travel to Pinsk. The new results of civilization and modernity that suddenly flooded Drohitchin were all due to the establishment of the district center. The fact was, however, that the pleasure of having the district government cost a great deal of money. At first it was expected that nearby Yanova would become the district center, but Drohitchin merchants and storekeepers greased some hands along the way, and for a small fortune, they were able to win the prize for Drohitchin. This was how Drohitchin became the regional government center.

First Row, from right: Two Poles, Yonah Sapozhnik and Leibel Gurstein. Second Row: Shinder, Y. Kaminetsky, Shapiro, L. Warshavsky --- Y. Siderov, L. Goldman, B. Schwartz. Third Row: Y. Schwartzberg, Kotak, A. Bliakh, L. Oberman, Kachler, D. Yudelevsky, A. Braverman, M. Kalenkovich, and others.

Poles Start an Anti-Semitic Campaign

Very soon, however, the wheel turned, and the economic situation in town started declining, and each day things went from bad to worse. The reasons causing the economic decline felt in every corner and in every Jewish home were numerous and obvious.

First of all, construction in town quickly came to a halt, and all the Jewish artisans were left without work or an income since a large number of Jewish families had no money for food, which obviously had an effect on the income of shopkeepers and other businessmen. Secondly, the flow of American money that had been sent to Drohitchin in large amounts in the years after World War I was now either held up or stopped. Third, the large landowner estates, which were a source of income for Drohitchin Jewish artisans, merchants and shopkeepers for hundreds of years, were liquidated. The Polish government took over those estates while the owners retreated to Russia with the Czarist army and never returned. Other landowners who did return couldn't administer their estate because of high taxes and had to break them up into small farms and sell them. The result of this was that almost all estates around Drohitchin were parceled out and sold, either through the Polish authorities or the owners themselves.

[Page 36]

The steam mill of Chaikel Miller and Yisrael Elazar Khorsel under German occupation in 1916.

In most cases, the land of the estates was distributed by the Polish government to the Polish legionnaires, the *osadniks*, who were relocated from central Poland. This was done with the express intention of the Polish rulers to transform the Polesia region into a Polish region, since previously it was mostly populated for a number of years by White Russian peasants, Jews and Ukrainians.

Fourth, the Poles started oppressing the population, especially the Jews, with harsh taxes. The tax obligations strangled business, and, therefore, Jewish life. The Poles were simply skinning the flesh of every Jew. Every day, the sorrowful and well-known "Grabsky wagons" would go around Drohitchin, and the tax collectors would confiscate the smallest bags from Jewish homes. Whenever they would see the Grabsky wagons, Jews would turn pale. The tax collectors would confiscate merchandise, furniture, household items, and even the last pair of pants. This writer witnessed such sad events. A tax collector went into the house of the Brisk quilt maker and confiscated his only quilt machine, which was his only source of livelihood. He was a man burdened by many small children. He fell down on the ground and started tearing his hair out.

Fifth, the newly arrived Poles (*osadniks*) immediately started a quiet boycott of Jewish workshops and businesses. The Poles gave no work to Jewish craftsmen, and in contrast to the White Russians, the Poles were good tradesmen and wouldn't get anywhere near the Jewish artisans. The Polish craftsmen even took away the smallest bit of work that a Jew would get from village peasants.

Going from Bad to Worse

The Poles were also experiences merchants, and a Jewish merchant or businessman could do business with the Pole the way he did with with village White Russian peasants. The Poles knew how and when to market their agricultural produce. They weren't fond of the Jewish middleman, and they pushed him out of his position. Later on, when the Polish boycott against the Jews came out in the open, the Poles went ahead and set up their own cooperatives in town and in the villages and incited the peasants to refrain from buying from Jews. The peasants were in any event already impoverished by the high taxes, and their purchasing power was greatly reduced.

[Page 37]

A shortage in heating material also developed because the Polish authorities prohibited cutting down trees and the sale of firewood. For the first time in the history of Drohitchin, people were forced to heat their ovens with coal that a few Drohitchin merchants brought to town from the Polish coalmines. With the ban on firewood, the Polish authorities naturally forced the populace to use as much coal as possible, since coal wasn't selling very well in foreign markets. However, as a result, many Jewish families suffered from the cold because it was impossible to heat large ovens with just a few pounds of coal that amounted to a great deal more that wood, which was bought from Jewish wood merchants or peasants at the market.

Everything together was made even worse by the social problems in the country, which proved fatal to the economic situation in the town. If a Jewish trader took a chance to do business in the villages with a calf or a few pud of grain, a tax collector would follow him and confiscate his bit of merchandise. In addition, such a poor businessman was unable to pay for a tax or a license.

The egg exporters and pig hair traders still had something to sell. Apart from that, however, there was apathy and stagnation in the whole business sector, which was becoming increasingly paralyzed and depressed.

A so-called marshland alley in 1928 reflects the picture of the Vion. This street goes over footbridges and marshes.

[Page 38]
Jews Suffer from Hardship and Hunger

The ban on kosher animal slaughter (thanks to Madame Pristorova), which the Polish parliament legislated throughout the country, broke another branch of Jewish life. In addition to the fact that people longed for a bit of meat, the Jewish butchers and slaughterers were left without a livelihood (Once in a while the government would authorize slaughtering a small calf.).

Many Jewish homes in Drohitchin became impoverished. Never mind the absence of meat or clothing, which was considered a luxury. People didn't even have a piece of dry bread to eat. I don't want to say that there was nothing to eat in Poland. In a country where 70 percent of the population was involved in agriculture, it wasn't possible for there not to be food. There was actually enough to eat, but there wasn't money to buy it. As they saying goes: " An axle for a penny, but no penny to buy it with." What happened to the Jews in "democratic" Poland was no accident. It was a well-conceived plan and agreement with the a formulated "social" policy of the Polish "democratic" regime, whose prime minister, General Skladowski, proclaimed, "Hit Jews – No! Boycott – Yes!" The intention of the policy was clear and obvious: to get the Jews out of business until they would eventually leave the country.

I don't know why anyone would be nostalgic about the former Polish "democratic" regime. We Jews certainly have nothing to be nostalgic about, but maybe there are a few.

Funeral of Moshe Naftali Bronner. From right: Kaminitzer (Wisotsky), Leah, Miriam Tsirel's, Dina Kharsal, Shifra and Alter Saratschik, Feitshe and Berl Vichnes, Sarah Kharsal, Moshe Milner, Hershel, et al.

D.
THE STRUCTURE OF THE COMMUNITY

Head of the Community – Community Rabbi

In Drohitchin, just as everywhere in the Polesia area, there was no organized community structure, i.e. a "city hall," under the Czarist regime. The entire intellectual, cultural and social life in the shtetl centered in and around the House of Study. The rabbi served in the unofficial position of community head in the shtetl. All community meetings took place at his home, with him serving as chairman. The rabbi had his own "city council," and advisors, who were recruited from the heads and treasurers of the synagogues and burial society, as well as ordinary disciples and people of influence, with whom the community rabbi discussed and decided on relevant internal and external decisions of his community.

The rabbi was responsible for making sure that his community had a public bath, a ritual bath and a doctor. The rabbi was also responsible for the social well being of his Jews, and he had to make sure that the poor Jews received money for Passover matzah flour, medical and other social assistance that they required. The rabbi was also responsible for the community's vital statistics records, where the births and deaths of the residents were recorded. In addition, the records were handled by a specially appointed "administrative rabbi" (*kozheniy rabbin*).

[*Page 39*]

Under the Polish regime, the official rabbi of the town was also the "administrative rabbi" in relation to outside authorities. The community representative to the city authorities, both under the Russian and Polish regimes, was the Jewish Elder, who was appointed by the community for a specified term of office. The Elder was the liaison between the community and the local government officials.

Under the Polish regime, the Elder was accredited to the city council, which included both Jewish and Christian representatives. Prior to the First World War, there was a *korobka* account (i.e. the city leased all the income from animal slaughter to one of the local businessmen for a specific amount of money). The money contained in the *korobka* account covered the costs of paying slaughterers, and whatever was left was used to pay for other local needs. Under the Polish regime this system was terminated. All income derived from animal slaughter went directly to the slaughterers, who earned a good living until the ban on kosher slaughter.

Seated, from right: Moshe Porush, unknown, L. Mishovsky, A. S. Goldman, Yaakov Rosenstein, Rabbi A. I. Kalenkovitch, Zechariah Schmid, Chaim Volevelsky, Chaikel Milner, Hershel Eisenstein. Standing: Eliyahu Goldman, Nachman Wisotsky, Itshe M. Shavsky, Lipman Feldman, Zemach Odelsky, et al.

[The handwritten text is as is legible:] On the occasion of the journey of our esteemed and honest member who is involved in the community needs of our city, [illegible] Chaikel Milner, to our holy land. As a token of thanks and a souvenir, we are giving him a set of the Talmud from Drohitchin [illegible] and the picture. We bless his and all his family that they merit to witness the arrival of the Messiah speedily in our days.

[Illegible] The Rabbi, [names illegible]

Rabbis and Rabbinical Court Judges in Drohitchin

Unfortunately, we know very little about the men who held the position of community rabbi in Drohitchin over a period of almost 500 years. For example, we know about the kabbalist, Rabbi Dovidel Yaffe, who was the community rabbi of Drohitchin 150 years ago. We also know a few details about rabbis Yisrael Valevelsky and Zvi Eliyahu Reichman who lived a century ago. The following rabbis served in Drohitchin in the last three generations:

Rabbi Menachem Reichman and his son-in-law, R. Isaac Yaakov Kalenkovitch; the rabbinical court judge, Rabbi Yossel Goldman; the scholar, Rabbi David Mordechai Yudovsky, and his son-in-law, R. Noach Kahn, and finally, the rabbinical court judge, Rabbi Velvel Miller. The last community rabbi of Drohitchin was Rabbi Isaac Yaakov Kalenkevitch, may G-d avenge his blood!

[*Page 40*]

The rabbis never received official salaries. Therefore, the town gave the rabbis the authority over the sale of candles and yeast, which provided them with a livelihood, some a greater livelihood and others a smaller one. There were times when a community rabbi and his family experienced hardship, and other times when a rabbi made a good living from the yeast business.

It goes without saying that the rabbi of the town had to be well-learned and well-versed in Jewish law. Due to the important tasks of being a rabbi, answering Jewish legal questions and participating in rabbinical court cases was a daily event. The community rabbi didn't have to be a public speaker. In fact, many rabbis weren't adept at public speaking. The rabbi would speak publicly only twice a year - on the Sabbaths before Passover and Yom Kippur. His speech wasn't supposed to be humorous or to involve storytelling, since his audience was learned Jews themselves who wanted their rabbi to speak about profound, relevant issues. In short, the rabbi of town had to be a great scholar and decisor of Jewish legal problems.

The Reorganized Community

Later on, the Polish government passed a law in the Polish parliament regarding the re-organization of Jewish communities in Poland, including that of Drohitchin, of course, which became an autonomously organized community, with elected Jewish council members and officials who took over the administration of the town. The community council even had the right to impose a tax on the Jews, which was intended to pay for the budget of the community. The re-organized community system, however, wasn't well received in Drohitchin and didn't function the way it supposed to. The attitude of Jews in Drohitchin to the idea of a community organization was one of contempt and mistrust because it meant new officials and positions to fill, which had to be financed. The community council members would hold meetings and vote, but they didn't do much more than that. The administration of the community continued as it had earlier. The rabbi and his advisors exerted more influence than the new officials in town, even though the officials were the legal administrators.

From right: the old House of Study and the new one in 1938.

E.
RELIGIOUS AND SOCIAL LIFE

Everything Centered on the House of Study

(*Trans.* It should be noted that the terms "synagogue" and "House of Study" are historically basically interchangeable. Strictly speaking, however, a synagogue is where only prayers are held, whereas a House of Study is where Jewish men also engage in religious study. Usually a "synagogue" would be furnished with rows of pews, whereas a "House of Study" would have tables and chairs/benches instead.)

Before World War I (1914), there were four Houses of Study in Drohitchin: the old House of Study, the new one, the Scholars' House of Study, the Street House of Study and a chassidic *shtibel* (small one-room synagogue). When the Russians evacuated Drohitchin, they burned down three-quarters of the town, the synagogue courtyard and all four Houses of Study. Only the chassidic remained untouched. After the war, the three Houses of Study were rebuilt, but the Scholars' House of Study was not rebuilt. The version of the prayers in the Houses of Study was *Ashkenaz,* while the Chassidim prayed according to the *Sephard* version. This means that about 80% of the Jews in Drohitchin were not Chassidim. The Drohitchin Chassidim belonged to the Karlin-Kobrin dynasty of rebbes. Every winter, the Kobrin rebbe would come to Drohitchin to stay with his Chassidim for a visit.

The Jews of Drohitchin, as in the rest of Polesia, were very traditionally religious in the Lithuanian manner, and they followed almost the same customs. The population was mostly made up of Jews who were scholarly and householders, while a small number were modernized followers of the Enlightenment. The people spoke Lithuanian Yiddish and wore short jackets. On the Sabbath and the holidays, they would wear long jackets and dress hats. There was no question of "religious and irreligious." All Jews observed the Sabbath and laws of kashruth and family purity (except for a handful of people). All Jewish homes were considered to be properly religious. This is how ordinary Jewish life was ever since the beginning.

[Page 41]

As mentioned, all cultural and social life centered on the Torah and the House of Study. The Houses of Study were always filled with people, especially on the Sabbath. Even young men who worked for a living would come to the House of Study on the Sabbath. Interestingly enough, even the representative of the secular Yiddish Bund would always show up in the synagogue on the Sabbath. Just like any religious Jew, he would carry his tallith under his arm on his way to synagogue (Drohitchin always had an *eruv* – a ritual commingling of domains to allow one to carry on the Sabbath), and walk inside holding his children's hands. I remember how we would point at someone who identified with the Enlightenment and say that he "ate before greeting the Sabbath." That man, however, used to go to synagogue early.

Shakhna Shul-Ruffer, the custodian of the Street House of Study.

The Sabbath in Drohitchin

On Friday afternoons, people would already start thinking about the arrival of the Sabbath. In honor of the Sabbath, Jews would go to the public bath, while the housewives would hurry to prepare the chulent (Sabbath stew) in their ovens. The shopkeepers finished up with their last customers, and the custodian of the synagogue, known as the shul-ruffer (shul-caller), would go around town shortly before candle-lighting time and call the Jews to go to synagogue. Right after that the stores would close up, and a short time thereafter the entire weekday hustle and bustle would come to a standstill. All streets were then empty of toiling and busy people. The Jewish homes shone with the light of the Sabbath candles that glowed through the windows. The calm of the Sabbath covered the town. Fathers and their children, dressed up in the Sabbath finery made their way to the synagogue for Sabbath prayers.

The New House of Study – From right: Yozep Bezdzhesky, the slaughterer R. Yosef David Shub, Moshe Aharon Berg and Tuvia David Lev.

In every House of Study, there was a group of men studying Talmud; every day they studied a page. There were also groups who studied the Mishnah, the anthologies of Eyn Yaakov, the Midrash, the halachic work, Chayei Adam, Bible, and psalms. It was like that a whole week. On the Sabbath it was as busy as a beehive.

People were studying at all the tables – some in groups and others by themselves. Even the mundane conversations of the wagon drivers, who chatted under the Torah reading platform near the stove, was a spiritual pleasure and colored with the imprint of the Sabbath.

All day long on the Sabbath the stores and business were closed up. Even the least religious person didn't dare violate the prohibition. No weekday activity was found occurring on the streets. The peasants knew that they had no reason to come into town on the Sabbath. There was a mysterious calm that hovered over the stones of the bridge. Once every so often, the peasants made a noise or disturbance that broke the Sabbath stillness in Drohitchin. Those quiet streets were used by the Jews going to and from synagogue or going on a stroll on Sabbath afternoons after the chulent stew. This is what a Jewish town looked like there in faraway Polesia. Drohitchin was a miniature Jerusalem.

[*Page 42*]

The Sand Street in 1935. A Sabbath calm covered the stones of the bridge.

Charitable Activities

It was the same thing in the areas of kashruth, family purity and charity. There were no kashruth supervisors, and anyone was able to eat a kosher meal in anyone else's home. Drohitchin Jews also gave a lot of money to charity and provided for the needs of visitors. There was never a Sabbath when there wasn't a preacher or charity collector in town, or even ordinary visitors. Everyone received contributions with a smile.

Shimshon Goldman's family. From right: Mordechai, Henya-Chaya (mother), Shlomo Zelig (son), Esther, Yaakov, Tsippe, Shashke (daughter), Peretz, Esther, Zvi Weingarten (son-in-law), Rachel (daughter-in-law), Hadassah, Yitzchak Goldman (son-in-law).

Every poor person who came to town had his "day" or "Sabbath." A long-standing custom was that the custodian of the synagogue (of each synagogue) sent a "Sabbath note," and each Sabbath a different householder would receive a poor visitor with his note for a meal or meals, or even for a weekday meal. There was also a place where poor visitors were able to sleep at no charge. For many years there was also a respite and health care service that provided assistance with doctors and medicine for those in need. The service also provided the ill with overnight company so they would not be alone, and people also provided anonymous charity so as not to embarrass the recipients.

From left: Avraham Baum, Sheinke Baum-Warshavsky, Odel Eisenstein-Buder and B. Warshavsky near the bridge.

Shimshon Goldman's family. From right: Mordechai, Henie-Chayha (Mother),

Shlomo-Zelig (son), Esther, Ya'akov, Tsipe, Shoshke (daughters), Peretz, Esther,

Tsevi Vaingartn (brother in law), Rachel (sister in law), Hadasah, Yitschak Goldman (brother in law)

[*Page 43*]

F.
EDUCATION AND CULTURE

Education before 1914

The yeshiva in the Street House of Study. The head of the yeshiva, Rabbi Aharon (seated), Rabbi Eliyahu Velvel Altvarg, Zvi Eisenstein, Shakhna Shamash.

For hundreds of years (prior to 1914), education in Drohitchin was based on the kheder. Generations of Drohitchin Jewish boys were educated and trained in the kheder. After finishing the kheder, a certain number of local children also traveled to study in nearby yeshivas. Others continued with their education privately at home. For an extended period of time, there were a Jewish religious elementary school and a yeshiva in Drohitchin, and the yeshiva was filled with students from Drohitchin and other places in the surrounding region.

It should be noted that the percentage of Drohitchin yeshiva students who traveled to study in yeshivas was actually not that large and was smaller than in neighboring towns. This fact is indicated by the small number of rabbis that Drohitchin produced. Before World War I, there were around a dozen yeshiva students, including some outstanding ones from Drohitchin in the large yeshivas. However, except for two or three, none of them remained a student, and this fact can probably be attributed to the war. In the inter-war period, the number of local yeshiva students decreased even further. There were only six students studying in the yeshivas. It is difficult to understand the reasons why parents in Drohitchin, who had great respect for scholars, didn't send their children to study in the yeshivas. Apparently, studying Torah is a very difficult undertaking. In general, I believe that the reason can be attributed to circumstances; the wealthy children didn't want to have to face eating their meals at the homes of strangers as was once the usual custom. The poor children were forced to work with craftsmen to help support their families. We really don't have to speculate and try to give the benefit of the doubt. The fact is that Drohitchin didn't produce many rabbis in relation to the size of the town. Drohitchin did, however, have fine householders. In general, Drohitchin Jews were considered more advanced than those of nearby towns.

[Page 44]

There were also parents from among the wealthiest residents who sent their children to study in the gymnazia high schools and in university. These were very few, however. There was also an attempt by Russian-Jewish secularists to open a Russian school for Jewish children. The school didn't last long, however, and it closed rather quickly.

Just before World War I a group of followers of the Enlightenment wanted to open a modern Hebrew school called Yavneh. Naturally, Russian was held in high esteem, and the school looked like it was going to succeed. Many children from town and surrounding towns started studying there. However, the war intervened, and the school was forced to close.

Rabbis, Religious and Secular Teachers

The well-known rabbis and teachers who educated generations of Jews in Drohitchin were: Chaim Kronstadt, Shimon Appelbaum, the Kaminitzer, and Shmuel Artshes and his son, Hershel Baum. The Talmud instructors were: R. Eliyahu Makhlis Zilbergleit, Mendel Moshe Isser's Kaminetsky, Avraham Shabtai Kapuller, Yosef Shakhat (Yossel Tchernas), Eliezer Adler, R. Moshe Velvel Shkolnick, and others.

The secular teachers who taught the modernized elementary school classes were: Naftali Steinberg, Yehudah Leib Neiditch (the Reciter), Gedaliah Sacker, Yaakov Sidorov, Sender Shapiro (from Odrezshin), Bezalel Wolfson, Zvi Schwartz, and Feigel Steinberg. These are deceased, and the following are still living: Yisrael Baruch Eisenstein, Yisrael Baruch Warshavsky, Todres Leib Milner, Yosef Wasserman, Aharon Kravitsky (from Lekhovitch), Chana Steinberg, and others.

The Moriah School. Teachers from right: Moshe Bezdzhesky, R. Asher Weizel, Remz, Goldstein, Wolfson, Kolnick, Feldman et al. 1931.

Education after World War I

With the assistance of Drohitchin émigrés in America, a building was constructed in Drohitchin after the First World War to house the Hebrew school, Moriah, which took in almost all the children in town. The educational program was the same as in the government schools, but it also offered classes in Yiddish and Hebrew subjects, as well as some Talmud.

The more religious householders in town weren't entirely satisfied with the intellectual orientation of the Moriah school, which was eventually taken over by the Tarbut (secular culture) movement. These religious families, with assistance from Drohitchin émigrés in America, established an elementary school that was run according to an Orthodox orientation.

[Page 45]

A group of Young Judea from the Moriah School, with their teacher Rachel Prishkulnick, in 1937.

The school emphasized the religious subjects, and, of course, the children from this religious elementary school received a balanced elementary education. The administrators of the school were the community rabbi and several distinguished householders in town.

Before the school was established, there was an elementary yeshiva in the Street House of Study (p. 43). A larger number of Jewish children also studied in the government Polish school called Powszechna. Many Jewish children spent a year studying there after completing their studies at the Moriah School in order to cover Polish subjects.

After completing their education in various schools in Drohitchin, a smaller percentage of Jewish children went on to study in gymnazia high schools, and thereafter in teachers' colleges and universities in Pinsk, Brisk, Vilna, Warsaw, and so forth. The majority of Jewish children stayed at home.

The Polish government-run Powszechna School, where a large number of Jewish children studied.

The Polish "Kingdom" elementary school in which many Jewish children studied

[Page 46]

7.
PARTIES, ORGANIZATIONS AND INSTITUTIONS

Tempestuous Times

At the end of the 19th century, when a wave of rebellion against the Czarist regime spread through Russia, the revolutionary spirit came to Drohitchin too. SS (socialist party) and Bund (Jewish Yiddishists) groups were established. Their members referred to each other as "brother: and "sister" and agitated against Czarism.

A large demonstration in Drohitchin in honor of the Balfour Declaration, May 14, 1919.

At the same time, the ideas of the Lovers of Zion movement (Hovevei Zion) spread to Drohitchin, and later on Herzl's political Zionism came on the scene among the Jewish community. A Zionist movement was started in Drohitchin, and Jewish young people would go door-to-door to sell shekels for the Zionist Congress, stamps for the Jewish National Fund and shares in the Palestine Colonial Bank. These causes also had their own charity plates in the synagogues on the eve of Yom Kippur.

The Balfour Declaration – Excitement and Disappointment

Real Zionist activity first started in 1918. Afterwards, the German occupation authorities were dismantled, and people heard about the Balfour Declaration, which people thought meant that the British were giving Palestine to the Jews. Drohitchin Jews were seized with messianic fervor, and everyone, young and old, were overtaken by enthusiasm for the Land of Israel. Then, after having lived through such a difficult and long war with so much suffering and affliction, people thought they were hearing the footsteps of the Messiah. Large demonstrations were held in honor of the Balfour Declaration, and a young man rode through town on a white horse, symbolizing "messiah on his white donkey." The only thing on everyone's mind was Palestine. Everybody's thoughts and discussions were about going to their own country in Palestine as quickly as possible.

[Page 47]

When the first group of pioneers set off for the Land of Israel, the entire town turned out to accompany them with music and song. It was a great moment. Many of the participants were crying with joy, and many Drohitchin families actually started preparing to move to Palestine.

All the Jews in town accompanied the first pioneers on their way to Palestine in 1922.

However, disappointment and emptiness of the messianic dream set in very quickly. Everyone who was prepared to go to Palestine faced great hardships. First of all, they were disappointed by the certificate system that authorized entry into Palestine. Also, it became difficult for families with children to travel. Certificates were made available only to people younger than 35, and the candidate had to promise to undergo training for two to four years in advance. That immigration system immediately dashed the hopes of most of the Drohitchin Jewish families who had long dreamed of reaching the borders of the Land of Israel.

In addition, the terrible news about the Arab pogroms against Jews in Palestine reached Drohitchin, and belief in the Zionist redemption was badly shaken. Instead of excitement and joy, Jews were filled with bitterness, rage and disappointment. The slow process of propaganda, fundraising and anticipation began.

The Growth of Zionist Parties

Zionist organizations and parties began to develop in Drohitchin. The first groups were the General Zionists, the religious Zionists (Mizrachi), Poalei Zion (Workers of Zion), Hechalutz (Pioneers) and Hashomer Hatza'ir (Young Guard). The last two groups operated as national organizations. In the early years, principal Zionist activity was undertaken through the General Zionists and Mizrachi. The Mizrachists were the pioneering experts in fundraising for the various funds. As religious Jews, the Mizrachists had the task of standing up in the synagogues and convincing the synagogue-going Jews (who were the majority) to contribute money for the Zionist project.

[*Page 48*]

The Poalei Zion Party and the Freiheit youth group in 1928.

In approximately 1926, a branch of Jabotinsky's Revisionist Zionists opened in Drohitchin, together with its youth arm, Betar. To offset the Betar youth group, the Poalei Zion created its own group, called Freiheit (Freedom).

From then on, the ideological battle between the Poalei Zion and the Revisionists began, with both sides maneuvering for the best positions in town, and seeking to increase their memberships as much as possible.

There was a radical shift of party power in Drohitchin in 1929. Due to the awful Arab pogroms against Jews in Palestine, a large number of Drohitchin young people and adults overnight switched allegiance to the Revisionists, who advocated a much more drastic approach to the British mandatory government and the Arabs. The balance between the Poalei Zion-Freiheit and the Revisionists-Betar became equalized. The two groups remained the two largest and aggressive forces in town, and the Poalei Zion and Revisionists had the allegiance of 90 percent of the youth in Drohitchin. The politically unaffiliated and inactive Jews also joined up with the two groups. Some joined the Poalei Zion, and others joined the Revisionists. The General Zionists and Mizrachi, because they had no youth wing, remained passive. In many areas, the General Zionists, Mizrachi and Revisionists joined together against the left-wing groups. There were friendly relations among these three groups, and they sought recruits among the same religious element in town.

The Hashomer Hatsa'ir didn't have many members, but it was very popular in town anyway, because it had very energetic and fiery young people. There was never a group of the anti-Zionist Agudath Israel in Drohitchin.

[*Page 49*]

The Revisionist Youth Group, Brit Trumpeldor/Betar.

There were a few Agudah sympathizers, mostly from among the chassidim. There didn't undertake any activity, however. Similarly, there was never any organized Poalei Mizrachi party (labor offshoot of the Mizrachi party). The few people who were supporters did work together with the Mizrachi and supported the Revisionists and Betar.

Socialist Parties

First Row: M. Kalenkevich, Y. Mishovsky, L. Lewak, B. Milner, K. Oberman, S. Slonimsky, S. Milner, M. Kalenkevich, S. Beich.

There was an organized group of the Bund (Yiddishists) in Drohitchin, but it was unnoticed among all the activity of the Zionist parties. The Drohitchin branch of the Bund wasn't as aggressive as branches in other towns. First, because there were no factory workers in Drohitchin, no wage disputes or strikes, or professional unions to provide membership for the Bund. Second, most of the Bund leaders in Drohitchin worked in home workshops and were owners of craft workshops and people who attended synagogue and people who believed in "sinful" Zionism. Drohitchin was, therefore, not a suitable for the Bund's political activity, and the Bund had to limit itself to cultural activities.

There were also some communists in Drohitchin. How likely was it for there to be communists in Poland? Drohitchin was no different than other cities and towns, but since the Communist Party was illegal in Poland, it wasn't possible to know the actual number of communists in town, but the fact is that the communists were involved in underground activity. I remember once that on a Sabbath the Polish police raided the house of the Mezeritch tailor, looking for communist literature. They even tore down pictures off the wall, but they didn't find anything. Later it was discovered that his son had fled to Russia.

Generally speaking, the Polish authorities took harsh measures against the communists. One of the famous cases was that of the revolt of some villages in Polesia against high taxes. The police suspected that the communists were somehow involved. The raided the villages, seized grain from wagons and threw it out onto the street, mixing it with sand and straw. This was to teach all the peasants in the villages the punishment for the sins of a few communists. Naturally, the press didn't write a word about this, but people talked extensively about the revolt of the peasants against the Poles.

Library and Cinema

There was also a well-stocked library that owned hundreds of books covering all Jewish classics. I remember a long time ago the administrators of the library first installed a radio without a loudspeaker in the library, and everyone rushed over in amazement to look at the magical device. The administration of the library created a business with the "magical device," and charged a fee of 10 groschen for a listening session. You put on the earphones and were able to listen in for a few minutes to the magical device's spirit talking over the wire.

[Page 50]

Mention should also be made of the amateur theater group that occasionally gave performances on behalf of charitable causes. Drohitchin was virtually the only small town with a cinema; it showed a few pictures and attracted people from all over the area.

The People's Bank and Charity Fund

The Charity Fund and the Cooperative Fund were the community economic institutions that provided material assistance for all Jews in town and in the surrounding area. A third institution was the People's Bank. Any individual could receive a charitable contribution (interest-free) of up to 20 dollars from the Charity Fund, which could be repaid in installments over many months. Similarly, the People's Bank provided long- and short-term loans of several hundred zlotys at a low percentage rate.

Bank directors. Seated from right: David Warshavsky, the slaughterer Moshe Prager, Yosef Berezovsky, Zechariah Schmid, Moshe David Wasserman, Alter Goldberg. Standing, from right: Beich, David Shushanov, A. Kravetz, Feigel Epstein, M. Auerbach, S. Z. Goldman, A. Saratshik.

The People's Bank, as well as the Charity Fund, were the most important sources of assistance for shopkeepers and businessmen who needed money to buy merchandise or repay a debt, as well as for the ordinary householder or artisan who needed a few hundred zlotys to get through the harsh winter, when there wasn't enough business, until he could repay the loans in the summer.

The People's Bank and the Charity Fund were known for their work as the only community institutions frequently able to save Jewish families from bankruptcy or hunger, especially in the later years when the pressures of poverty among Jews spread significantly. As mentioned previously, the respite and health care service were among the most important forms of assistance to the ill and needy in the form of doctor services, medicine and overnight company at no charge.

In later years the orphan assistance organization made tremendous contributions in Drohitchin. A separate section will be devoted to the work of this organization among the other community institutions.

The Halutz Youth Group, circa 1923.

Left: From right: B. and Fruma-Gittel Warshavsky, Esther Shushanov, Simcha Feldman, A. Zlotnick, and others in Feivel the kvass-maker's yard in 1938.

Right: From right: Freidel Appelbaum and her husband and child, Yenta Goldman, M. Schwartzberg, Rachel and Shmuel Appelbaum, Eliyahu Kalenkovich (in center), and others at the train station in 1939, shortly before the war.

The development of the Charity Fund in Drohitchin, Polesia in numbers
REPORT
For the last five years, from April 1, 1934 to April 1, 1939
[Right side:] Notice how the Charity Fund was able to revive the dead in the last five years.

	1934/35	1935/36	1936/37	1937/38	1938/39
Loans issued	151	208	345	420	445
No. recipients	95	123	207	239	250
Annual loan totals	8,404.31	10,524.11	20,018.70	28,442.33	38,207.14
Bad Accounts from 1927-35	37	40	43	35	45
Totals from bad accounts	1,627.28	1,608.00	1,577.38	908.41	1,274.78
Bad mortgage debt	-------	------	700.00	500.00	590.00
New accounts	29	38	62	61	60
Total borrowers	304	310	355	364	411
Joint and *Tsekava* credit	350.00	1,250.00	2,100.00	3,350.00	4,700.00
Local deposits	41.50	61.25	482.85	1,701.80	1,283.25
Member dues	420.98	515.50	667.00	671.95	793.00
Minor income and charges	7.34	8.47	24.35	49.41	66.01
Community grants	----	-----	-----	50.00	-----
Contributions	-----	-----	------	------	60.00
Administration	486.65	489.91	591.15	703.92	782.71
Losses for obligations	-----	------	--------	------	130.00
Profit	------	34.06	145.45	67.44	6.30
Deficit	65.67	-----	------	----	------
Funds in loans	9,743.19	10,070.10	12,258.92	15,143.20	17,435.79
Capital stock	14,787.71	14,821.77	14,967.22	15,034.66	15,040.96
Annual turnover	25,588.48	40,141.48	46.773.68	64,734.71	83,412.56

[*Page 51*]   **G.**
                                   THE LAST CHAPTER

Drohitchin Jews Wanted to Save Themselves

To summarize: the situation of the Jews under the Polish regime was a sorry one. Soon after their arrival in Drohitchin, the Poles showed their real faces. In their treatment of the so-called "communist *zhids*," the Poles demonstrated arrogance, malice and prejudice more than anything else.

A class from the Moriah School. The teachers, from right: Palevsky, Barantchuk, M. Bezdzhesky, Rabinovich, Wolfson, Kolnick and Hackman.

The Jews knew in advance that their situation under the Poles wouldn't be rosy. People, especially young people, started leaving Drohitchin for understandable reasons and went off into the big world. As long as it was possible, people went to America, and later, when the United States shut its doors, young people started leaving for Palestine. A small number of them were lucky enough too obtain certificates and emigrated there. Others immigrated to other countries, and several dozen emigrated to Cuba, Argentina and Canada, until those countries also closed their doors to Jewish immigration.

Young people who didn't leave Drohitchin remained in town without hopes of a better tomorrow. Each year there were increasing number of young men and women who hung around on the streets without any purpose in life, hoping for some miracle that would allow them to emigrate somewhere. They had no trade, since in any event there wasn't enough work for everyone, and the town didn't need any more shopkeepers. In addition, it became difficult for them to find mates. So the question was, "What shall we eat?"

What were they going to do the day after their wedding? The situation was worse for girls than it was for boys. Fathers were very concerned about their daughters' future, and each parent hoped that a young man would arrive from the United States and take their daughter to the golden country.

The Burial Society, from right: Meir Kaplan (the *Liener*), a colonist, Mordechai Perkovsky and Motya Warshavsky.

It wasn't as if Drohitchin young people squandered their time doing nothing. They were involved in community activities such as political parties, collecting money to send to Palestine and pre-emigration training. Unfortunately, this activity didn't bear any fruit; they couldn't go to Palestine because they couldn't obtain immigrant certificates. So they continued hanging around on the streets of Drohitchin like they were in the twilight zone, embittered and disappointed.

[*Page 53*]

It goes without saying that the Jews of Drohitchin wanted to save but all doors were closed to them. Of course, the friends and former residents of Drohitchin in the United States were thinking about their friends and relatives in Drohitichin and would occasionally send some money, which helped people back home to financially survive.

Funeral of Bobba Grossman, July 28, 1935, followed by her husband Gedaliah and sons Yirmiyahu, Chaim and Zelig.

Pogroms against Jews in Poland

After the ban on kosher slaughtering in 1938 and with the growing boycott by the Poles against Jews, relations between Jews and Poles went from bad to worse. A pogrom spread throughout Poland, breaking out in Pshitick, Tchenstokhov, Brisk, Kobrin and other Jewish communities where Jewish blood flowed and Jewish property was plundered and looted by the raving anti-semitic Polish mobs.

All of Poland was overtaken by pogrom fever. I'll never forget the Friday night when the Polish court convicted the Jews of Pshitick of the "sin" of daring to defend themselves against the Polish mobs. The day turned into a day of mourning for all of Polish Jewry, and a series of court cases began, such as the one where "witnesses testified" against a Jew who was accused of insulting "Polish honor" and sentenced to prison.

The Poles wouldn't let the Jews eat in peace. On the other hand, they wanted to assure that no Jew neglected the sanitation services. Several times a week Jews had to sweep the bridge and courtyards and wash the sidewalks. If someone disobeyed the "law" he had to pay a heavy fine. If someone spit on the street or dropped a streetcar ticket on the ground, he was fined one zloty. They wanted the Jews to be clean, but not to be able to have something to eat.

Between 1931 and 1938, I was in Warsaw, and I was virtually a member of the family at Jewish editorial offices. I had the opportunity to feel the pulse of Jewish life in Poland. I still remember the phone ringing on the day of Pshitick Affair at the offices of *Moment* with the following message that was transmitted throughout the cities of Poland:

"Save us, we're in danger. The mob is going to attack us any moment. Send help!"

[Page 54]

The last road. A casket on the way to the cemetery.

Excerpts from my Diary

For illustrative purposes, I would like to cite a few excerpts from my diary.

26 Tammuz, 5697 - July 5, 1937, Warsaw

"No one believes in a better tomorrow. All Jews have given up. The Jews of Brisk weren't spared taxes. On the contrary, they had to pay even more for damage caused during the pogrom. There was joy in the village of Kanilin. The priest says that it's a historical festive day that the last two Jews were expelled. The Jews of Stavnitz were expelled from the park. The *Goniec Warszawski* writes: 'The Jews have it too good in Poland.' The *Awece* writes: 'In the swamp of the Talmud the Jews are enemies of Poland.' Six Jews were murdered in Kobrin; what did they do to deserve that?"

July 13, 1937, Warsaw

"A ghetto has been set up for the Jews. The *Goniec Warszawski* and *Awece* declare triumphantly that the management of the Katowitz railway has provided separate trains for the Jews."

July 17, 1937, Warsaw

"We're closed off from the world. We don't even know what's going on in nearby towns. The Poles don't allow us to write about the pogroms in the newspapers. I read today in the American newspaper that the Poles have already killed 22 Jews and wounded 400, and destroyed large amounts of Jewish property."

July 21, 1937, Warsaw

"The mobs don't stop. In Gdinia they are going to boycott the Jews. The Poles are doing the work for the Germans."

July 24, 1937, Warsaw

" *Cegerowski* writes: 'The Jews are suffering horribly in Milatin, Galicia. There used to be 50 Jewish families, and now there are only two. Their property was burned, and there remain only three houses. There were three acts of arson in three months."

"Tears flowed from our eyes, and we cried *gevalt!* How do human beings turn into animals like this? Let's get out of here! Let's save ourselves! Every day we hear the words "murdered, beaten and robbed!" I'm scared of taking a step out of the city. I haven't left the Jewish ghetto in Warsaw for two years. I've already forgotten what a field or grass looks like. We live in a wild desert."

July 29, 1937, Warsaw

"They're starting a huge boycott in Brisk. They force the customers out of the Jewish stores. The municipal government told a Jewish delegation that boycotts are permissible."

July 30, 1937, Warsaw

"Anti-semitism is getting worse. The Poles picket stores, and tear out the smallest piece of bread from our mouths. In Lomza and surrounding areas the situation is terrible. The priests incite the people to wickedness and violence. Jews are being beaten on the streets of Warsaw, and Jewish

[Page 55]

young men fight back. Fifteen Jews were arrested for standing up to the hooligans. Jungle justice."

September 1, 1937, Warsaw

"In Bidgoszcz, Stok, Malkyn, Kelc, Stuczyn, Czyzew, Oszmany, Drohobicz, Bryansk and Vilna. Jews are being beaten everywhere! People are crying for help everywhere."

The new cemetery. From right: Hershel Eisenstein (Blumacker), Moshe Leizer Gratch, Yisrael Dovid and Chana Milner. Seated: Chava Milner and her son, Yosef.

This is how things were for Jews during those fateful days. I also experienced Polish hostility. I was beaten twice on the streets of Warsaw by Polish "democratic" mobs, who the Western democrats yearn and grieve over. What a pity.

The situation in Drohitchin was no exception. The mood was very bad in town. One day, some young Poles who worked on the roads started rampaging through town. The Jews in Drohitchin stood up against them and taught the mob a good lesson. Finally, the Polish authorities arrested some Jews and took them into custody. Such was Polish "justice."

This Hitlerian atmosphere existed in Poland even before the German storm troopers even marched into the country. The ghettos were already set up by the Poles. It's no wonder that Poland was the graveyard of European Jewry. It should be emphasized that we have nothing against the country of Poland itself. It was a good and fertile country.

[Page 56]

Over a period of a thousand years, dozens of generations of Jews lived there honorably and comfortably, and Drohitchin provided a true Jewish life. They could have continued to live there for hundreds of years, which would have been a blessing for the country. However, the Poles, who controlled the area, consciously and intentionally sought to impoverish the Jews, and thus brought down the most beautiful and finest Jewish community! They thereby also ruined and devastated their own lives and their own land.

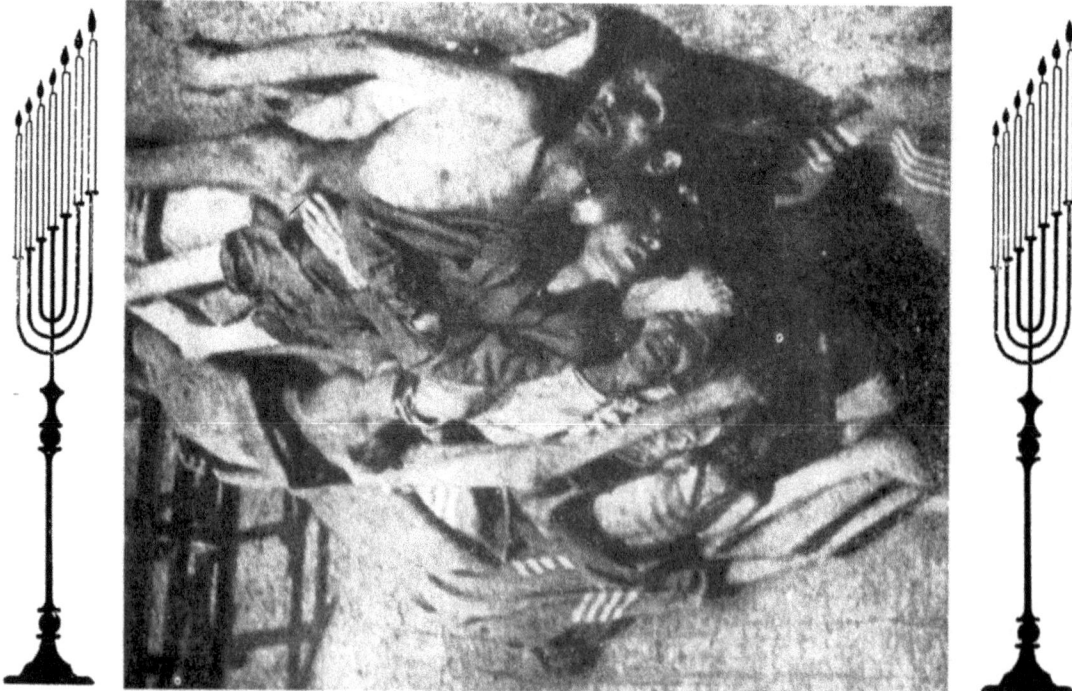

This is what the German murderers did to the men, women and children of Drohitchin.

My Last Look at Drohitchin

On November 1, 1938, I left my hometown and departed for England. Before my departure, I bade an emotional farewell to my dear parents and sister. Other Drohitchin Jews, with tears in their eyes, said, "Don't forget us! Remember us!" I cast my last glance at Drohitchin, and left with the thought that at the first opportunity, I would return to celebrate with my family and visit with my friends and neighbors. Unfortunately, however, my hopes were dashed.

Our parents are no more; our siblings are no more. There's no one left to back to visit. In the same way as the sound of dripping water from a broken water faucet breaks the silence of the night, the dripping of tears and blood from my heart breaks the stillness of the darkness that surrounded their last cries of "Hear O Israel." May the Germans and their friends today never enjoy anything good or pleasurable! They injured us bloodily; we are constantly haunted by them like a plague on our hearts, and we will never be able to forget.

Yes, martyrs of Drohitchin, your will and testament is engraved on my heart with blood and tears. Never will I forget you! I will forever remember you and your murderers, the Germans, may their names be obliterated!

[Page 57]

Yoel Slonim (New York)

Yoel Slonim, who was a famous poet, and for a time a colleague from the New York *Tag* newspaper, in which he published a large number of poems, was born in Drohitchin. We are printing here a few of Slonim's poems that he published in *Tag* following his visit to Drohitchin. Y. Slonim died in 1944. [Editor]

Yoel Slonim

TWICE IN DROHITCHIN

1.

Is this the same stream
where we used to swim, and
where the dogs and bad kids would
stand near the mountain?

Is this the same Vion
where we used to play horses
and think up stories after
finishing *kheder* in the summer evening?

And is this the same garden
where for hours we used to munch
on berries, cherries and little eggs
that we took from the birds' nest?

Is this the same little mountain
where my little army and I
would always conquer the "Philistines"
in pits of mud and snow?

Is this the same field, where through the rye fields,
I used to go with Chaya on the Sabbath?
I never forgot the kisses, and how
the years flew by.

And is this – the huge towers,
the chaos, the wild cries,
the flames spreading out, burning
the dancing heart of Broadway?

And in a riot, did I lose the joy
that was before,
and did I forget the faraway voice
in the flames?

Is this Drohitchin, Drohitchin,
the green island of joy,
when I came from America
with amazement in my eye as a small boy?

That path to the well
was like from a dream,
and every day, far far away from Papa
a hazy hand would lead me.

Don't wonder, my friend, you're now
back in Drohitchin,
back on the streets and alleys
holding onto beautiful memories.

My friend, everything is the way it was,
the forest, the river and the rye;
It's all here like it was before,
but you have changed.

2.

When I came back to Drohitchin,
I didn't recognize it at all;

[*Page 58*]

the streets, houses and people
appeared different and strange.
The streets are paved with cobblestone,
the mud in the market is no more,
no stores in the market, that used to
stand like an old man with a bent neck.
The stores were built from brick,
and their number increased everywhere,
but here and there along Egypt Street,
stood a bent and twisted house.
I went over to the old Synagogue courtyard,
it's now completely changed,
now my school room is a three-story house,
where my childhood is as good as gone.
I went over to the sand by the bridge,
and Chaya wasn't there,
her parents are dead,
and she left, and no one saw her again.
I went over to the sawmill,
that belonged to my grandfather, R. Velvel, long dead.
Where are the landowners from the villages and hamlets,
with their *britschkas* in green and red?
Where are the women in flesh and bone,
the houses with roofs from straw?
Where is the bath house, with the old broken windows,
the poorhouse with loneliness and pain?
Where are the chassidim, in the long drawers and sidecurls ,
the Rebbe, the holy Jew,
the long coats, and the hats?
The happy and calm life.
Where is the long ago old stillness,
the clean, proper times?
It's all gone away, it's all changed.
It's all so far away.

Then I left the *shtetl*, and I
started feeling nostalgic,
my heart was filled with the shadow
of the synagogue courtyard,
and the synagogue's bright light and hanging lamps.
It's either the heaven made of soft blue silk
and a golden chair made ready,
or the earth with a vampire-like
look in the air, and noise everywhere.
Broadway is better, with its bloody beauty,
with souls in a blazing wind,
the flame of sin in New York
is better than half a sin in a little town.
I left the *shtetl*, and then felt a pain
in my heart.
I traveled overseas, magical dreams,
yet still feeling the pain, ashamed.

I FEEL SO NOSTALGIC

There's no limit to what can happen to me,
I often don't even known what can happen to me.
Suddenly it seems as if I'm a child,
back in Drohitchin.
My grandparents came to the train station to meet me,
with Yankel the wagon-driver and two horses.
The horses neighed and wildly stamped their feet,
scratching the muddy ground.
I jumped off the wagon, and ran
around in the high grass.
The horses were panting heavily along
the sand road.
And I fly in the field, as free as a rabbit.
My mother is content, but yells at me,
and R. Yankel warns me about the wolves around.
I laugh cheerfully laugh and say,
"In America every child is a man."
"What a naughty boy, what a naughty boy,"
says my grandfather to me,
and laughs through his beard, and gives me a pinch.
I kiss his hairy mouth, jump off the wagon, running
around in the free summer air.
Everyone comes to grandfather's house
to say hello to the relatives and then leave.
In the courtyard near the barn, there are two dogs,
I get friendly with them and bring them in the house.

[*Page 59*]

I go to the kheder, and study well,
I get pinched on the cheek and get a blessing too.
I'm bored in the class and in synagogue,
I sneak out through a back door.

I play in the rye field, I run around the forest,
I climb up trees, and bang my head.
I look for birds' nests, I just take a look,
I don't move the eggs, I slowly climb down.
I run after animals, I jump on the horses,
How free I feel, never feeling bad,
the herdsmen seem so good,
and wicked Pavliuk even likes me.
I guide the herd back to town,
I make noise with the other kids on the street,
and my mother yells at me, so what?
I know it's just a joke.
I ride on the back of Kashtan,
He barks, and shakes his head cheerfully to me,
And Murza jumps around like a black and white dog,
he looks at me happily, and lets me go first.
I teach the children how to play ball,
and also how to box.
We can even turn the bad kids into a heap.
I sit in New York and smile to myself,
the years fly by so very fast,
I see Drohitchin before my eyes, as clear as can be,
as if it was just last year that I was there as a boy.
My heart gets hot, I am really tired,
and my dry words fly up as if on wings.
It rings with nostalgia, a long-dead poem,
I feel pain, I feel joy.

NEW YORK AND DROHITCHIN

I was in Drohitchin yesterday,
I saw the green Vion again;
the old House of Study and chassidic synagogue too.
The market was filled with peasants,
the blacksmith at the stream, striking up sparks.
The stream was flowing noisily,
and barefoot mothers washing
the hair of their crying babes.
When I left the synagogue courtyard to go to the well,
the trees hid the sun along the road;
when I went to the landlord, into his well,
the forest looked so magical and stood there so fine.
The dogs started barking again,
I just stood still as always.
Suddenly a young Polish fellow arrived,
and took me by the hand.
I later went back to Drohitchin,
along crooked paths, with joy and a gaze;
Worn out women are sitting on *prizvas,*
while the men smoke their pipes next to them.
They tell each other stories of this one or that,
and no one wishes anyone bad or pain.

The moon starts to shine through the trees,
how good is it to be now in Drohitchin.
And here is grandpa, and grandma too,
and here their four-cornered house.
Here is the poplar, the young oak tree,
in the middle a huge oak full of leaves.
I meet the rabbinical judge, I talk with the rabbi,
how warm and friendly, how deep their gaze;
it's all so close to me, so dear,
it's so nice here, I don't want to go back.
As a boy I was here only once,
but every home was open to me.
I think that each flower, each tree
murmured something to me, about calm, about life.
I feel exalted, I feel a faith,
I got rid of the burden that was New York;
Life won't rob me of any dreams,
here is where I will renew my youth.
Here I won't hear any talk that is false,
and not fooled by any of my friends;
no one will hold back my fantasies,
and here my messiah will never be imprisoned.
New York, its towers are trying to pierce the heavens,
and I could never reach them.
I want to forget them, their haunting gaze,
I want to stay here, and never go back.

[Page 61]

Rabbi Mordechai Minkovitch (New York)*

Shops of Esther Yehudith Gratsh at the market in year 1932

A HISTORY CHAPTER
A.

My first Introduction to Drohitchin

I was born in Butan, near Slonim, but I was lucky enough to meet my wife in Drohitchin, and I was therefore connected to life in Drohitchin, where I spent a large part of my life, raised a family and shared all the joys and sorrows of the Jews of Drohitchin.

My first introduction to Drohitchin was as a newlywed in the summer of 1902. The *shtetl* superficially looked like any other town in Polesia but was distinctive in one respect: it didn't have streets paved with cobblestones as did many other towns in the area. Also, the weather in the summer was bearable. You walked in sand and dirt, while the dust blew in your eyes, but it was dry. Therefore, when winter arrived, people were virtually sinking into the mud, and during the winter, both men and women had to wear high boots. Together with everybody else, I had to trek through the deep mud. Only in 1910 when the Russian government put in a sidewalk, did Drohitchin seem like a proper city.

When I arrived in Drohitchin, I met three young newly ordained rabbis who were engaged in Torah study and awaiting appointment to rabbinical positions. One was my brother-in-law, Rabbi Ze'ev Wolf Miller (he was from Kletsk). The second was Rabbi Isaac Yaakov Kalenkovitch, the Rebbe's son-in-law. The third was Rabbi David Mordechai Yudovsky, a non-chassid, who originally came from a small town near Brisk.

Rabbi Yudovsky lived very modestly and spartanly. Most of the time he stayed at home and studied by himself. Whenever I tried to speak with him, I was never successful in doing so. I once found him studying in the New House of Study, and attempted to strike up a conversation with him. However, since I noticed that he was displeased with my questions, as if he suspected me of something, I ended the conversation and left.

In those days Rabbi Menachem Reichman was the community rabbi in Drohitchin. Rabbi Reichman was already quite elderly and very hard of hearing. It was extremely difficult to converse with him. His innocence and honesty was spread across his face. His wife was a real righteous woman. She would go through town and collect money for the poor, and supported a teacher (R. Izik) for the poor children.

B.

Establishment of the Talmud Study Group

Since I was R. Moshe Poritsker's second son-in-law and ordained, my father-in-law purchased a spot for me to study and pray in the Old House of Study.

* These edited excerpts are taken from the family biography of the Author [Editor]

[Page 62]

He probably did this to avoid the Evil Eye by not having both sons-in-law located in the New House of Study. Joining the Old House of Study was very beneficial. After getting to know the householders and scholars of the Old House of Study, I was asked to teach a class in Talmud to the congregants, which I was only happy to do. Until then the late R. Moshe Velvel studied the Jewish legal text, *Chayei Adam,* with a few men. The main founders of the Talmud study group were R. Yisrael Ephraim's (Yisrael Tilles), R. Zalman Bunyes and others. The Old House of Study started to come alive. The Talmud study group steadily grew stronger and larger. Our Talmud class between the afternoon (Minchah) and evening (Ma'ariv) prayers became popular throughout town and always drew more participants.

When we completed our first tractate of the Talmud, we celebrated the occasion with a beautiful meal in R. Yitzchak Avigdor's home. Years later, when we completed the entire Talmud, there was a great celebration in the Old House of Study that lasted a whole week. The synagogue was decorated, and festive meals were served every day, where the appropriate blessings were pronounced. Everybody had a real enjoyable time.

The street after the bridge, leading to the Sand.

The Talmud study group continued during the First World War. After the retreating Russian army burned down all the synagogues, the Talmud study group moved to the only remaining chassidic synagogue. I continued the Talmud study group until I left for the United States in 1924. I gave my final class in my home to an overflow crowd. As the wagons stood on the street ready to depart for the train station, the class participants arrived with copies of the Talmud and lamps. I taught my final page of Talmud to them. The study group then offered me a thank-you letter signed by all of the participants in recognition for my lectures over the previous 23 years. Then the participants started a joyous dance and accompanied me with song all the way to the train station on my way to the United States.

C.
The Rabbinical Disputes

There is an old saying: "Too many isn't healthy." Drohitchin was known as a fine *shtetl* and a quiet place. No one argued, and everyone lived together in peace. However, Satan found an opening to create conflict in the community. The reason was the young ordained rabbis, as mentioned previously, who were waiting for rabbinical positions. What happened was that the elderly rabbi, Rabbi Menachem Reichman, decided to move to Palestine with his wife, and handed over his position to his son-in-law, Rabbi Isaac Yaakov Kalenkovitch. The old rabbi's opponents came out in the open, recommending that the position be filled by the non-chassid, Rabbi David Mordechai. The friends and family of the third ordained rabbi, Rabbi Ze'ev Wolf Miller, suggested a third choice. However, a wise Jew suggested appointing Rabbi Miller as the head rabbinical judge and Rabbi Isaac as the community rabbi. Thus, there were now two groups: one group was with Rabbi Isaac, and the other was for Rabbi David. Since neither side wanted to give in, and each stuck by their candidate, a sharp dispute erupted in Drohitchin, leading to violence and informing to the non-Jewish authorities.

There was a scoffer who gave names to both camps: he called R. Isaac the "Russian rabbi," and R. David Mordechai the "Polish rabbi." This is also how he referred to both groups: the "Russian" group and the "Polish" group – even though all the Jews were Russian Jews. This stayed this way the entire time. The Russian rabbi prayed in the Old House of Study, and the Polish rabbi prayed in the New House of Study. The Polish group had the upper hand, and it never happened that either of the rabbis would end up in the synagogue of the other.

Where did I fit in all this? Even though I was also ordained, I could have had a group of my own in town, but since I was right in the middle of the rabbinical dispute, I gave up the idea of being a rabbi and went into business.

[Page 63]

I remained neutral the whole time, and got along with both sides. This ended up being the best choice, since there were people from both groups at my Talmud class, and there was never any dispute during the class.

Whenever there was a wedding where the groom was from one group and the bride from the other, there was a problem about which rabbi to choose to officiate. Inviting one of the two rabbis could lead to confusion at the wedding; inviting both rabbis was impossible. The two families thus had no way out. Since I was neutral, they decided to invite me to officiate. So the custom was to invite me to officiate at any "mixed marriage." However, I didn't take any money to do this.

It's worth describing a small episode. As mentioned, I decided to go into business instead of the rabbinate and had thought up an idea in opening a leather business. I figured that since members of one group or the other owned the existing leather businesses, mine would be a "neutral" business, and both sides could shop at my store. As soon as I opened the doors of my leather store, shoppers from both camps came by. My plan worked, but I made one mistake. I didn't realize that shoemakers were used to buying on credit. Consequently I myself was forced several weeks later to buy on credit, and thus ended up paying a price for my neutrality!

A large demonstration in Drohitchin in honor of the Balfour Declaration – May 18, 1919.

D.
A Groom Dies Under the Wedding Canopy

In the small towns there was a custom of accompanying the bride and groom with music through the streets of town, all the way to the wedding canopy at the synagogue courtyard. If the two families and the couple were from the "Russian" side, they set up the canopy next to the Old House of Study; if they were from the "Polish" side, they set it up at the New House of Study.

[Page 64]

There was a case where Yaakov Baruch the Peddler made a wedding for one of his sons, and since he was from the "Polish" side, they set up the canopy at the New House of Study, and the officiating rabbi, of course, was the non-chassid, R. David Mordechai. As mentioned, the couple was accompanied by music to the synagogue courtyard, which was filled with guests and curiosity-seekers. The Polish rabbi pronounced the first blessing, and the couple was married. Suddenly, the groom started to fall to the ground, and confusion erupted. At first people thought that the groom fainted, and they tried to revive him, but when they realized that he wasn't regaining consciousness, they rushed to get a doctor, who pronounced the groom dead.

You can imagine what happened under the wedding canopy. Instead of shouting *mazel tov,* everyone started crying. At that very moment I was giving my class in the Old House of Study, and we thought that people were shouting because a fire had broken out somewhere. When we ran outside, we found out what happened. The horrible event brought the entire community to the scene of the tragedy. The groom was laid out on a bench, and he was carried to the house where the wedding was to take place. The guests, who had prepared a welcome for the couple prepared instead a funeral for the dead groom.

The Jews of Drohitchin couldn't forget about the horrible event for a long time. People attributed the tragedy to the rabbinical dispute and saw it as a punishment from heaven for the community dispute. Later they found out that the groom had heart trouble, and the excitement of the wedding hastened his demise. A short time later, the bride had to perform the ceremony releasing her from levirate marriage with the groom's brother (This is required by Jewish law when a childless widow does not marry her husband's brother, called a levirate marriage.). The Russian rabbi officiated at the ceremony in the Old House of Study, and I was also present at the ceremony.

E.
Founding of the Yeshiva

I then became interested in the situation of the religious elementary school, which had three teachers who taught two to three pages of Talmud a week. I found many good students in R. Moshe Velvel's class who knew how to study Talmud and who needed a yeshiva environment.

In 1905, after making the appropriate preparations, we established a yeshiva for older students and appointed R. Eliyahu Machles as head of the yeshiva. He knew how to teach Talmud to older students. We also appointed a yeshiva supervisor who oversaw the yeshiva study program; the yeshiva held classes in the chassidic synagogue. We publicized the yeshiva in surrounding Jewish communities, and we recruited a sufficient number of students. We had enough money to support the yeshiva: the students' parents paid some, and the rest was collected in town and the nearby communities. R. Hershel Chaim Lev, who was a community activist, assisted us considerably.

In the second semester I took over management of the yeshiva, which over time grew significantly. We had students from Khomsk, Yanova, Motele, Antapolia, Kobrin as well as Brisk. The yeshiva classes were moved to House of Study Street, and I taught the children myself every day, and showed them how to learn the Talmud on their own. They had to prepare their studies each day and to study on their own. This gave them a desire to study. The program supervisor was the aged R. Getzel, a highly respected person who assisted the children in preparing their studies. I taught at the yeshiva for three years.

Later, the yeshiva administration appointed Rabbi Yosef David Shub (Binyamin Moshe the Slaughterer's son-in-law). Finally, Rabbi Aharon from Khomsk, a great scholar, joined the yeshiva as its head, and invited Rabbi

Eliyahu Velvel Altvarg (Chaim Ber, the bricklayer's son) to teach at the yeshiva.

The yeshiva, which had good students who later excelled in the large yeshivas, existed from 1905 until the outbreak of World War I in 1914.

F.
My First Trip to America

A few years before World War I, I had the idea to go to the United States. In those early days, a trip to America was easy. All you had to do was think about it, and you went. During the four months I was in the United States, my family wrote me begging me to return home. So one day I just appeared back in Drohitchin. Since people didn't know I left, they also didn't know I had returned. When I went to the Old House of Study, I found the rabbi, R. Isaac, teaching a page of Talmud.

[Page 65]

When the rabbi noticed me, he immediately asked me to read the page out loud. However, I wouldn't let him cut short his class. The next day I started reading the page at the same spot where I was before my trip to America.

Shortly afterwards, Rabbi Ze'ev Wolf Miller, the rabbinical judge in town, left Drohitchin and became a rabbi in Pinsk. The "Polish group" built the non-chassid a house and a House of Study. Most of the householders, however, remained at the synagogues where they were members before. This indicated that the dispute was starting to dissipate.

The teacher, Betzalel Wolfson, with his class before World War I.

A couple of years before World War I, the "Polish" rabbi married off his eldest daughter to a young ordained rabbi. Shortly after his daughter's wedding in 1912, the non-chassid died, and was buried on the second day of Shavuot. The non-chassid's position was filled by his son-in-law, Rabbi Noach Kahn (Rabbi Kahn died in the United States.).

G.
Outbreak of World War I

When World War I broke out, the rabbinical dispute came to an end, and the nicknames "Russian group" and "Polish group" were totally forgotten. Everyone had the sense that bad times were coming, especially for the Jews. Many young men immediately set off for the border areas, just as people did during the Russo-Japanese War, in order to get to the United States. This time, however, they quickly found out that the borders were locked tight.

Businessmen faced tight money, and anyone who had some money hid it. No one paid off their debts, and no loans were available. Thus, the situation progressively deteriorated.

A couple of months later, dozens of Jewish refugee families, who were expelled from towns and cities along the war front, arrived in Drohitchin.

[*Page 66*]

We housed the refugees in the Houses of Study and in private homes and provided them with food and clothing.

The local mayor and police chief started helping the Czarist regime to collect as much money as possible for the war effort. They went from house to house, requiring each person to contribute one to three rubles to the national treasury. The Russian police also went around to local villages and signed up the peasants to pay a monthly contribution. Of course, the Jews paid their promised contributions on time. However, when the police went to collect money from the peasants, the peasants responded, "We don't have any money, so we might as well go to jail."

When the Germans got to Warsaw, the Russian police issued an order to turn over anything made of copper and brass, including brass vessels, at the mayor's house, where everything was listed and registered. People were promised that after the war, the Russian government would pay for the confiscated possessions.

The Germans moved quickly from Warsaw to Brisk. There was a drought that particular summer, which benefited both sides. With dry weather, the Germans were able to advance faster, and the Russians were able to retreat more quickly. The Germans arrived in Brisk very quickly, and the Russians evacuated the entire population of Brisk and burned down the city. Many Jews were stranded in Drohitchin, and many moved further into Russia with the Russian troops.

Jan Meier, Rachel Goldfarb, Aharon Drogitchinsky and Tilla Zucker

Afterwards, as soon as the Germans arrived in Brisk without a shot, they realized that there would be a battle around Drohitchin. The Russians decided to initiate a resistance to give their army time to retreat. All the peasants from around Drohitchin were terrified of the Germans; they abandoned their homes and escaped to Russia with wagons full of grain. The Jews, however, had long experience with Czarist pogroms, and since the Germans were then considered to be the supporters of freedom, the Jews decided to stay put. This was three weeks before Rosh Hashanah, and because of the drought, the Vion, which had been filled with marshland and water, now turned as dry as bone. People decided to build trenches on the Vion so they could hide out of the line of fire until the end of the fighting.

The streets of Drohitchin were filled with retreating Russian soldiers and trucks as day and night they made their way to Pinsk. The deafening noise of the horses and other animals that the Russians soldiers were leading away with them filled the air. Many of the animals died from thirst along the way because of the drought. To make matters worse, thousands of fleeing peasants and their wagons added to the confusion. All the peasants of Zaritshka, Stara-Silia and other villages traveled with the Russian army. Only one gentile, the bathhouse owner, remained, and he ended up being vital for lighting flames on the Sabbath.

Every Jew bought a horse and wagon so that if, at the last minute, the Russians decided to expel the Jews from town, the Jews would have means to escape. Together with another Jew I bought a team of horses. I didn't obviously know how to climb up on a horse. People spent the last couple of days digging. First of all, they buried their few remaining possessions, and then started digging the trenches on the Vion. Everything was ready on the last day, and we waited for the inevitable. The town became filled with Cossacks and Circassians; this was considered a sign that the Germans were close by. Occasionally I saw a line of refugees and their children and bundles on wagons. I looked and them and realized they were Drohitchin Jews from Egypt Street. I ran out of the house and showed them the way. I told them that they shouldn't take such a risk by moving as a group on the road, especially during such a drought when people were falling like flies from thirst. I also told them that they were putting their lives and the lives of their children in danger and that they should return home. I advised them to dig ditches, and G-d would help. Those Jews listened to me and went home. They later thanked me for my advice.

[Page 67]

One Thursday at nightfall, the sky turned red from all the fires started by the Cossacks in the villages around the town. We now realized that this was the last night, and Drohitchin would be next. (By the way, there was an interesting episode: during the day, a German airplane dropped a bomb in Zakazelia that fell right on the large whiskey factory, breaking down some walls. There were some Jews from Valevel and Drohitchin there in the brewery to get some liquor that the Russians had left over in the basins in the ground. Luckily, the bomb didn't injure anyone).

That same Thursday evening, we gathered all of our belongings – some people put them in their wagons, others carried them on their shoulders – and made our way to our trenches on the Vion, where we waited for the assault to begin. Exactly at 12 midnight the Russians started burning the houses in town, and it was like daylight. We all stood and watched their property go up in smoke.

H.
Cannon Bombardments in Drohitchin

They started bombarding Drohitchin on Friday afternoon. The Germans were hiding underground somewhere, and the Russians were in Lipnick. The airplanes flew around the town, and the Jews ran for cover in the trenches that were filled with the elderly and children. We were terrified that an airplane would bomb a trench. Everyone was crying out 'Hear O Israel' throughout the battle.

In the evening at Sabbath candle-lighting time the bombardment died down, and we went out of the trenches to get some fresh air. We ushered in the Sabbath in the trenches and had a Sabbath meal. Around midnight the shooting started again and lasted until dawn. On Saturday morning we left the trenches and held our Sabbath services on the grass. A couple of neighbors and I found a house that the Cossacks didn't completely burn down, and we conducted our prayers as a group and read from a Torah scroll that we had with us. That little house was very good for us since Friday night there was suddenly a tremendous rainfall that flooded our trenches. We were drenched to the bone and ran for shelter in that little house. This was a good thing, since the rain had already caused one trench to collapse on top of a Jewish girl.

From right: Meir Yehuda, Chaya, Leiba and Sheinka Feldman; Velvel, Esther and Leah Beila Mishovsky; and Machlea.

On Saturday afternoon the bombardment started once again, but this time it was much worse. It's impossible to describe the effects of the bombs of both sides of the battle. The little house where we sought shelter shook and bounced like a ball. Then it collapsed on us, and we didn't even have a chance to say 'Hear O Israel' and ask G-d to help us survive the assault. The following morning things calmed down. We went out onto the road and saw a few horses that were hit by shrapnel and were lying dead next to the trenches. Meir the Wagon-Driver was also hit and injured slightly in the hand by shrapnel. Other than that, however, thank G-d no one else was harmed.

It was quiet all day on Sunday, and we all stayed close to the trenches talking. On Sunday night the shooting started again, forcing us back into the trenches where we remained, seized with fear, until Monday morning, when the shooting stopped again. We crawled out of the trenches again into the fresh air, feeling overjoyed and excited. We then saw the first Germans arriving in town, which meant that the battle around Drohitchin was over. We were so overjoyed to see the Germans, that a few Jews ran up to the Germans and kissed them.

[*Page 68*]

I.
Drohitchin Under German Occupation

As soon as the first Germans entered Drohitchin, everyone picked up their bundles and went to look for somewhere to live. Unfortunately, what we saw was that only Red Street (Krasna Ulitsa) and the street next to the bridge leading to the Sand remained untouched. We went to take a look at the non-Jewish street. Anyone who could run fast enough immediately became the owner of a house and a barn filled with grain that were abandoned by the peasants when they fled. In addition, everyone went back to dig up the property they had buried earlier. We also dug up possessions that the peasants had buried.

It's worth noting the tragic case of Moshe Mendel, the cabinetmaker's son-in-law. He went to dig up his possessions that were buried in the oven; the oven collapsed on him and injured him. Using superhuman efforts, we (I was there too) cleared out the heap lying over him and managed to pull him out of the grave in which he was being buried alive. Unfortunately, he lingered for a few days, and then died. He was the first war casualty.

We decided to set up a committee to prevent lawlessness in town; the committee was made up of the following people: Rabbi Isaac Kalenkovitch, Zechariah Schmid, Zalman Bunyes, Chaim Binyamin's, Tuvia David Warshavsky, Hershel Chaim, Zusha Warshavsky, and this writer. The committee notified the German commander of Drohitchin of the committee's existence and that the German authorities should consult with the committee on all local matters.

Shortly afterward, an epidemic of spotted typhus and diphtheria broke out in Drohitchin. The epidemic's victims, both young and old, started dropping on the street like flies. Almost all the refugees who came to Drohitchin from Congress-Poland and Brisk died in the epidemic. They left behind many orphans without anyone to assume guardianship or take care of them. The town committee, naturally, assumed responsibility for those orphans, as well as for the weak and sick who could not provide for themselves.

The committee was also obliged to look after householders whose houses still stood after the fire to make sure that they didn't take advantage of their neighbors who had lost their property in the fire.

In connection with this, it's worthwhile saying a word about something that happened to me. As one of the victims of the fire, I rented an apartment in one of the remaining houses. Since I had to heat the apartment, I borrowed a hatchet from my landlord to chop some wood. Shachna, the synagogue caretaker, asked me to attend a meeting of the town committee. When he saw me chopping wood, he grabbed the hatchet from my hands and wouldn't let me continue to chop. He said that it wasn't right for me to do it and that he would do it himself. Shachna the woodworker simply struck the wood once, and it broke into several pieces. He also hit and broke the hatchet handle. He must have known what this involved and then moved off to the side so he wouldn't get hit.

We didn't have to wait long for my landlord to come along; he started hitting his head in his hands and banging his head on the wall.

Jewish children from Zaritshka Street under German occupation in 1916.

[Page 69]

I evidently ruined him but tried to calm him down by telling him it was a shame for a person to bang his head on the wall, and promised him I would make him a new hatchet for free.

[Photo:] Shachna the Caretaker (who was once a woodcutter), Berl Resnick and another fellow named Berl.

Shachna went off to the committee meeting without me. When he was asked where Mordechai was, he answered, "He's got a problem." Everybody froze when they heard Shachna's answer. They figured that I had suffered the same fate as many other people who went out on the street and fell down dead. They finally calmed down when Shachna told them the story about the hatchet.

I went out on the streets looking for someone who could make a new hatchet, but I soon realized that it wasn't so easy to find someone to construct such a treasured item until G-d sent me a Jew who revealed a secret: somewhere on Egypt Street lived a Jew named Yitzchak Konushkas. He told me to go to Yitzchak, and he would make a new hatchet for me.

When, after alot of searching, I finally found Yitzchak's little house, I could understood why the Cossacks spared that house. There was, however, one thing that I couldn't understand: since Yitzchak was such a skilled individual – virtually the only person in town who could make a hatchet – why did he live in such poverty? This demonstrated the truth of what the Sages said: "No bread for the wise." Yitzchak looked over the hatchet like a professional, and told me it would take him an hour and would cost me 15 kopeks for a new hatchet. Did I ever feel relieved! Not more than 15 kopeks? An hour later I joyfully ran home and handed the new hatchet to my landlord. I noticed how happy he was when he examined the hatchet. He was probably thinking he would like me to break the handle of the new hatchet, but I didn't do him that "favor."

J.
The Jewish Mayor and the Police

After taking power in Drohitchin, the German commander immediately proceeded to install order in town. First, he nominated a mayor, David Chatzkel's son-in-law (from Lodz); Nachum Hershel's son-in-law, Sola, as deputy mayor; and four Jewish policemen. The people in town weren't too happy with the new mayor and deputy. The Jewish policemen, however, were able to gain the sympathy of all Jews in Drohitchin. The commander also established a German patrol, that monitored the town day and night, and Drohitchin also got a German-Jewish doctor named Miller, whose medical assistance was greatly needed. The commander also converted three houses into an interim hospital for patients who were cared for by volunteer nurses.

The population started storing food for the winter, since they knew that the railway wouldn't be able to bring in any supplies. There weren't any food stores, and during the week of Sukkot, people went off into the fields to collect potatoes that the peasants had left in the ground. Only a few people didn't do it, and those people laughed at me for taking my family out to gather potatoes. Later, however, they realized their error and paid for it in high prices.

There was no end to problems. It wasn't enough that the Russians burned down three-fourths of the town, and thousands of Jews were homeless, a fire broke out on the second day of Sukkot in the village of Stara-Silia, now populated only by Jewish families. Everyone lost all his or her possessions in that fire – everything was destroyed. So a second time Jewish victims had to go on the road and spread out in the nearby villages such as Bilinka and others. It was like the saying goes: "A beggar has nothing to lose. If one village burns down, he goes to another one."

[*Page 70*]

The Jewish police, 1915-1918. From right: Itshe Mishovsky, Zeidel Weissman and Yirmiyahu Grossman.

It turned out, however, that the fire in Stara-Silia turned out for the best. The victims of the fire were able to find good places to live in the villages they settled in, with barns filled with grain and potatoes. In addition, they were spared by the epidemic that raged in Drohitchin the entire winter. People weren't allowed to go beyond the town limits. The bridge near the Sand was the boundary – no one could go beyond that limit, and on the "other side" was the war zone. We weren't even allowed to go over to the new cemetery without a special permit from the commander of Drohitchin; thus we had to bury the dead in the old cemetery.

K.
The New City Council

As previously mentioned, the city was unhappy with the mayor, who was from Lodz and an outsider, as far as the Drohitichin Jews were concerned. They sent a request to the German commander to elect a new mayor. The commander, who was a very liberal person, acceded to their request. He called a meeting of local householders and attended the meeting himself.

The commander and his lieutenant went to the meeting, as did the mayor. The commander held separate meetings with each person, and asked each one who he thought should be mayor. Everyone mentioned my name. Finally, the commander told us to choose a delegation of four people from among us to return to him the next day, at which time he would make choice. The next day, Zechariah Schmid, Hershel Chaim Lev, Lipman Ezriel's Feldman, and I went to see the commander, who announced that the mayor who be whoever was the oldest. However, since all the Jews trusted me, he would appoint me as supervisor of finances, i.e. treasurer. The remaining three men would also be members of the committee. The commander then supplied a wagon with sugar and other food, and told the four of us to distribute the sugar and food to all the communities in the city. The commander gave us official documents certifying that we were now the official town committee.

The committee immediately got down to work. We rented a large granary (from Alter the Merchant) to store the sugar, and the first wagon of sugar arrived shortly thereafter. The Jewish committee distributed the sugar to all of the surrounding settlements, and of course, to all the Jews in Drohitchin, based on family size. The town came to life since no one had seen sugar for many months, and nothing to sweeten the drinking water of typhus patients. Now, however, they were able to make life better for the typhus victims with a bit of warmth. The income derived from the committee's sale of sugar was used to support the hospital, which was located in three houses and was filled with patients. It should be mentioned that the chief activist at the hospital was Khasha Levin, the Bronner Lady, the wife of Chaim Hershel Levin. She would tended to the sick and worked with superhuman powers until she ended up as a patient herself. There was also money left over to rebuild the public bath and mikvah (ritual bath), and people even started thinking of building a House of Study.

During the entire period of the German occupation, there were no shops, and the people had to be satisfied with the food that the committee obtained from the commander. To be sure, the committee thanked the commander with gifts and presents. At every opportunity, he had his photograph taken together with the members of the Jewish committee and would send the photos to Berlin to show how "beloved" the German occupation government was among the Jews. Our committee continued its work until the Germans left Drohitchin.

[*Page 71*]

The Jewish committee gives a gift to the German commander in 1916. From right: Zechariah Schmid, mayor (holding the flag), Hershel Chaim Lev, Rabbi Mordechai Minkovitch, Lipman Feldman, Yirmiyahu Grossman and Itsche Mishovsky (last three: policemen).

L.
German Iron Discipline

Slowly but surely, we started getting used to our way of life. The only thing that negatively affected us was German military discipline and forced labor. We felt like prisoners, even worse than slaves: you can't go here; you can't do that. All Jewish young people had to spend months chopping trees in the forest that were then transported to Germany. They took apart the peasants' huts in the villages and used the wood to pave the roads and build sidewalks. The Jewish youths slept in barracks under torrid rainfalls and frost. It was no surprise that after a few weeks of forced labor, they returned home broken down and ill.

No resident of Drohitchin was allowed to go beyond the bridge. If someone wandered a few steps beyond the bridge, the German patrol would tie him up to the bridge and leave him there until nighttime. A German decree allowed each house to light only one oil lamp after dark. On the first Friday night after the decree, when Jewish women had lit Sabbath candles in addition to their oil lamps, German soldiers went from house to house, jotting down people's names. The next day, on Sabbath morning, the Germans brought all the women on their list to the town marketplace, put them in a line and marched them to the bridge; as punishment, made them stand in front of armed German guards for four straight hours. The women stood there, terrified that their husbands might eat up all of the Sabbath cholent stew and leave nothing over for them.

[*Page 72*]

M.
Jews Involved in Agriculture

During the war years, the majority of Jews were involved in agriculture. Every person took over a portion of a field that was abandoned by fleeing peasants and developed the land as if they were experienced farmers. Many of those Jews had enough bread and potatoes for their own needs and surplus to sell. Others who weren't suitable for farming had to pay high prices for a pud (40 Russian pounds) of rye and would often go hungry.

The Jews who cultivated the land also had cows, and, therefore, had supplies of milk, butter and cheese. There was no shortage of pastureland for the cows, but the problem was the shortage of shepherds. There weren't any gentile shepherds, but two Jewish young men took the job of watching the "Jewish" animals.

One Friday I went to take a look at my planted fields, near where our animals were pasturing. I started wondering what a Jewish shepherd was supposed to do on Friday afternoons before the Sabbath. I sat down among stocks of rye and saw the shepherds in the distance. Since the animals were grazing happily and lying on the grass, the shepherds pulled out prayer books from their sacks and started chanting *Song of Songs* with a melody that penetrated every limb. That was what Jewish shepherds were like.

N.
Private Businesses

In the second year of German occupation, life began to get back to normal, and the epidemic began to diminish. Jews slowly started getting involved in business, and people began buying and selling illegally. Jews would bring assorted merchandise – such as leather, produce and dishes – to Drohitchin from Pinsk with a permit from the commander and with a German escort on their wagon. With the silent approval of the escort, they would barter these items for a bag of rye or a few pounds of potatoes, which served as the favorite produce for hungry Pinsk Jews.

People would smuggle mostly produce in wagons from Brisk, Biala, Mezeritch and other cities to Drohitchin, and barter it for grain or other merchandise. Once it was rumored that there was produce available for purchase in the city of Slonim, and Jews, who never knew the meaning of manufacturing, went off to Slonim, bringing back bundles of manufactured goods to Drohitchin. Nobody asked about prices and paid whatever the seller asked. They continued to go to Slonim until supplies there were exhausted.

Later on, the whiskey business started to grow. With a permit from the German commander (in exchange, of course, for nice gifts), some Jews started producing alcohol, which the Russians left over in their distilleries before their retreat. In particular, the whiskey business grew significantly in Zakazelia, and special large machinery was installed there to produce whiskey. Jews from both Drohitchin and Valevel were involved in that, and many Jews became extremely wealthy in the whiskey business.

During the three years of the German occupation, both the German mark and the Russian paper rubles were recognized currency. The Germans had immediately withdrawn the Russian gold rubles from circulation through the use of a trick: they imposed penalties against the civilian population that were payable in Russian gold rubles. Afterwards, new fresh Russian rubles were in circulation, and then later on, the old Russian rubles were no longer usable, and many Jews lost alot of money because of this. Ultimately, however, people started rejecting the new Russian rubles, and Jews started losing money again. No one knew where the hatred of the Russian rubles came from.

O.
The Town Starts Getting Built Up

When Jews saw the Germans chopping down trees in the forests and shipping them off to Germany, the Jews figured they could do the same thing. After making sure to provide "gifts" to the commander, they started going into the forests, chopped down trees, and brought them into town. Whoever had a horse and a wagon did it himself, and whoever didn't have them rented them from someone else who did. There was a real rush to bring the most wood into town. Others traveled to the villages and transported whole peasant houses to town. In the space of a few months, many new houses were thus erected in Drohitchin.

[Page 73]

The old House of Study was rebuilt the same way, as was the Street House of Study. Whoever had a horse and wagon offered to bring wood from the forest. Artisans volunteered their services, while others helped with money. In a short time the Old Synagogue was rebuilt.

P.
The Germans Leave, and the Poles Arrive

After the Germans lost Drohitchin, the city had no civilian government. The town quickly set up a Jewish self-defense unit armed with a few rusty rifles, guarding against attacks from outside of town.

A few weeks later, a group of Bolsheviks came to town, and were well received by the residents of town. People took them in as guests in their homes, providing them with food and drink. For their part, the Bolsheviks were very respectful and made huge promises to the Jews.

First row, from right: Heska Feldman, Velvel Mishovsky, Manya Padarovsky. Second row: Gedaliah Kaplan, Sheinka Feldman, Hersh Leib Eisenstein, Esther Mishkovsky. Third row: Leah Mendelson, Sonia Piasetsky, Hershel Shkolnick and Yosef Feldman.

In the evening, the Bolsheviks left for Antopolia, and the next morning we saw some of them running back to town. In Antopolia the small group of Bolsheviks ran into a larger group of Poles who beat them up.

The same week, the Poles entered Drohitichin, and we had the feeling that the real "owners" of Drohitchin were arriving. The Poles immediately showed us what they were made of. A child died, and was being taken to the cemetery for burial. Some Poles started shooting over the child, and killed the horse. Another lucky day that Jews got through in one piece. In other cities, the Poles showed even greater "bravery" in their relationship to Jews.

The Polish army was well equipped with all types of weaponry and was well clothed. In one single day the Poles were in Drohitchin and grabbed up all the chickens in town. That same evening they left town for Yanovo. They left in town a commander and policemen to maintain order, as well as a Polish court. Aharon Asher Shifra's was appointed as mayor, and life in town started getting back to normal. The Jews started getting their lives back together to the extent where they believed that all their suffering would end.

Q.

The Bolsheviks Drive out the Poles

People were scarcely able to catch their breaths when new trouble arrived. Merely two short months after the Poles took over the Pinsk region, the Bolsheviks drove them out. All the Jews in the cities and towns where the Poles passed through now faced enormous problems. I remember how on the ninth of Av, a fast day and day of mourning, a gang of Poles burst into the chassidic synagogue while we were attending the Minchah [afternoon] Service in stocking feet with phylacteries and prayer shawls. They then proceeded to go after the livestock of the tired Jews and take the animals to Antopolia. This was one of the smaller events to occur. Gangs of armed Poles ran like wild animals from house to house, looting and savagely beating Jews. They grabbed the boots and shoes of every Jewish man and woman, while at night lying in the attic, I could hear terrible wailing from Jewish homes where the Polish gangs were pillaging the helpless Jews.

[Page 74]

One day, a couple of Poles burst into my house and demanded money. They went through my pockets, and when they were dissatisfied with the small amount of money they found, they pointed their guns at me, threatening to shoot me if I didn't show them where my money was hidden. My family started crying, and only with great suffering were we able to get the Poles to leave. The Poles' looting, beating and rape went on for a whole week, until the last Polish thief was chased out of Drohitchin.

When the Bolsheviks arrived in Drohitchin, everyone crawled out of their hiding places and went out on the street with great joy at having gotten rid of the Poles. Small children trailed after the Bolsheviks without any fear, as if they were one of us.

I suffered personal loss at the hands of the Bolsheviks. As is known, the Bolsheviks were starving for leather products and were looking for any valuable item. I was identified as someone who worked in the leather business, and a group of Bolshevik officers came to my house. I gave them all the leather I had. They paid me with their paper money. When the news got around that I had leather, groups of soldiers came to my house, and wouldn't leave until they had taken away the last bit of leather I had buried in my garden.

Apart from that incident, nothing else happened to me. Life was calm in town, and we continued with our usual agricultural work. We were starting to harvest the potato crop, and the Bolsheviks helped us with the work. None of us believed that the Bolsheviks would stay in town forever.

R.
The Poles Drive out the Bolsheviks

In the meantime, the Poles were obtaining assistance from other countries, as well as from debtors and started driving out the Bolsheviks, who were already in Warsaw. When we heard the news that the Bolsheviks were retreating and that we would again have to face suffering from the approaching Poles and their partners, the debtors and murderers, we became terribly frightened. Not long thereafter, just before Rosh Hashanah, we saw the first retreating Bolsheviks soldiers in town. A few days before Yom Kippur Drohitchin was filled with Bolsheviks, and all the Jews from surrounding villages flocked to town because of their fear of the debtors.

I will never forget that Yom Kippur and the fear that fell upon all of us. I led the prayers for the Mussaf services in the chassidic synagogue, and all the women had gone to the old cemetery to "tear up" the graves; their crying and screaming tore the heavens, and we heard it all in the synagogue and started crying together with them. We prayed to G-d to have mercy on us and save us from the murderous debtors.

On the first day of Sukkot, Drohitchin was caught in the crossfire between the Poles and Bolsheviks. Cannon shells from both sides flew over our heads, and many landed in town. The bombardment stopped for just a couple of hours, and things were quiet. We climbed out of the cellars and ditches, and went back to our homes. Looking out through the draped windows we saw Poles marching into town. No one dared stick his head out the door, and we were all terrified about what the next day would bring.

S.
We Were in Danger

When the Poles left for the front in Pinsk, Drohitchin was without any government. There were a couple of gendarmes on the Sand, but they provided little security for the town.

[Page 75]

Gangs of debtors broke away from the Polish army, sneaked into towns and cities and started pillaging and looting. In Kamin-Kashirsk, the debtors carried out frightful killings of 90 Jews, including the ritual slaughterer, who they murdered with his own slaughtering knife.

Large sections of debtors showed up around Drohitchin. We didn't see them during the day, but at night they would sneak into town to loot and plunder. We were living in fear for our lives. A group of young people decided to organize a unit to set large fires in four areas of town: near the Street House of Study; in the market, near Meshel Averbuch; a third was set near the bridge, and a fourth on the Sand. There were plenty around the fires, and both young and old sat near the fires, or walked from one fire to the other. Many

Jews chose their safest place to bed down for the night, near the fires. This technique was successful, and the gangs didn't come into town.

T.
The Debtors Engage in Slaughter in Zakazelia

One day there was a rumor that a large group of debtors was arriving. They stopped at the Bronner courtyard near Drohitchin. While I was standing near Eliyahu Leibka's house, I saw a debtor break into the house. He had the face of a real killer and stopped to pull out a Cossack whip. After waiting for a half hour in Leibka's house, the debtor came out extremely angry, got on his horse and left town.

The news of the arrival of the debtor promised the worst, and the town was seized by fear. All streets were empty of people, and everyone went into hiding. Later, we found out that the debtor was intending to carry out a slaughter in Drohitchin when he arrived at Leibka's house. Through some miracle, we located Pintakowski, the Polish gendarme (of the famous Polish family that had lived in Drohitchin for years). Pintakowski immediately asked the debtor what he was doing in town. Realizing that the debtors wanted to carry out a pogrom in Drohitchin, Pintakowski told him that Pintakowski was appointed by the Polish authorities to ensure the safety of the town, and he ordered the debtor to get out of town. As mentioned, the debtor was forced to leave.

The text of the gravestone of three people who were killed on the 2nd of Cheshvan, 5681 (October 14, 1920) is:

Earth! Earth! Don't cover the blood of our martyrs.

[Right to left:] Honored and Honest Man, Yitzchak Shmuel, son of Ezra His Mother, the Modest Leah, [rest obscured] Her daughter, the Virgin, Toiba, daughter of Ezra

The gravestones of Leah Lev and her children, Shmuel and Toibel (Ezra Mishiver's family), in addition to 14 other people slaughtered by the debtors: 2 Cheshvan 5681, 1921 (This is an error, since the correct date is above).

The victims are buried in the Drohitchin cemetery.

Since they weren't able to do anything in Drohitchin, after that very night the debtors then attacked Zakazelia, where they found a dozen Jewish refugee families, and killed 17 Jews. Ezra Mishiver's son was shot by the bandits while lying sick in bed. His mother, who was taking care of him, was also killed. Her daughter, who escaped and hid in a tree, was found and shot by the bandits.

Having finished their savage work, the group of debtors went on their way to Pinsk.

The Jews of the village of Valivel heard about the massacre that very night and immediately came to Zakazelia, but all that was left for them to do was recite psalms for the victims. The next day they sent someone to inform the Jews of Drohitchin about the dreadful murder. It's impossible to describe the effect the massacre in Zakazelia had on us. It became even more sorrowful when the martyrs of Zakazelia were brought to Drohitchin for burial in our cemetery a few days later. All the Jews in town wept and wailed as they accompanied the 17 victims to their eternal rest.

[Page 76]

The Zakazelia massacre was a warning to all Jews. A decision was made to go to Kobrin, where a Polish commander and many policemen were stationed, to request the commander send police protection to Drohitchin. The question was who ought to be the one to make the trip? Who was going to take the risk to life and limb to make such a long wagon trip to Kobrin? There weren't any trains at that time because the tracks had been destroyed. There was one courageous person who was willing to take the risk and travel to Kobrin – Aharon Asher Tolkovsky. May his memory be blessed!

U.
The Debtors Pillage in Drohitchin

While Aharon Asher was on his way to Kobrin, four Polish soldiers arrived in Drohitchin and were looking for a place to bake bread for the soldiers working on the rail lines. It was decided that they would bake their bread in my house and that of my neighbor, Hershel the Shoemaker. The soldiers also stayed in Hershel's house. We lived together with those several Polish soldiers, and felt safer.

On the third night, around midnight, we suddenly heard banging on the door. From the screaming I realized that it was the debtors. I immediately instructed my wife and children to climb out the window and go over to Hershel's house. When I opened the door, four debtors barged in with revolvers and ordered me to set a table with bread, butter eggs, cheese and milk, and to hand over dollars and jewelry. They warned me that if I didn't do as I was told, they would do to me what they did to the Jews in Kamin-Kashirsk where the debtors had just come from. They then started imitating the way the Jewish women in Kamin-Kashirsk were screaming and crying during the massacre. The bandits sat around the table, and I started placing anything I could find in the house on the table.

While I was involved with the debtors, my wife and children were calling out to Hershel Popinsky at his house and alerted the Polish soldiers. When they heard the word "debtors," the oldest of the soldiers got dressed, grabbed his revolver, and came into my house. The debtors asked him what he was doing here so late at night. The Pole answered that he came to heat up the oven to bake bread for his soldiers. He started to tinker around the oven, which got the "guests" interested. After they finished eating, the debtors ordered me to arrange beds for them to sleep in. Apparently to frighten me, one of the gang pointed his revolver at me the whole time. I wasn't scared by the diabolical behavior, and with total calm and a smile, I took the revolver from his hand. This confused the debtor, who asked whether a Jew shouldn't be scared to hold a revolver. The bandits went to sleep almost immediately. I started to leave the room, and one of the debtors called me in Yiddish. I was taken aback and asked him whether he was a Jew. He told me to be quiet and said that they wouldn't harm me but that they wanted me to give them two thousand marks, and they would leave town.

That same night we heard that a whole brigade of debtors was headed for Drohitchin and would arrive the next morning. You can imagine how we must have felt. In the morning, the new "guests" started arriving in town. All the streets became filled with debtors. I stood up and looked through the window onto the street and noticed a couple of horses and wagons passed quickly in front of my house. There were six Polish gendarmes. One of them stood up in the wagon and waved around a whip, shouting cheerfully. I recognized them. It was our own Aharon Asher, who was returning to Drohitchin with six Polish guards. He intentionally pulled out the whip to show the debtors that the town was no longer out of control. We began to feel much better.

I had to give the four debtors who slept in my house 2000 marks, and they left town. They passed through Lipnik on the way to Yanovo, and went to the home of Shlomo from Lipnik, where they started to act up again. Shlomo's sons started to flee, and the hooligans started shooting and severely wounded one of them (Shlomo's sons, the Gutov brothers, now live in Chicago with their families.).

[Page 77]

On the first day, the commander of the debtors called together a few householders in Drohitchin and to everyone's surprise declared that no one should be afraid and that we would see that things would be peaceful in town and in order. He sent out patrols through all the streets, and any soldier who bothered a Jew was punished. After 6:00 pm not a single soldier was to be on the street. He also promised to provide white flour to bake bread for his soldiers. (Apparently the democrats has found out that enough "communist zhids" had already been killd--ed.).

The commander kept his word. We slept well the next several nights and woke up relaxed. Many Jewish families started baking white bread for the debtors and some challah for themselves. They took the opportunity to bake white (American) buns that hadn't been seen since 1915.

Whenever we heard the debtors sing their well-known pogrom tunes such as, "Russia, Russia, I suffer so because the Jewish commissars are robbing you," a chill ran down our spines. This is how the Russian peasants were poisoned with anti-Semitism (and with white buns – Ed.). It was no wonder that they forgot the rivers of Jewish blood. Thank G-d we didn't suffer from these "guests."

First row, seated from right: Yehudah Zilberstein, Ezra Weissman, Eliyahu Eisenstein, Menachem Averbuch, Avraham Gratch. Standing from right: Shalom Gratch, David Epstein, Yosef Gratch, Tevel Zbar, Itshe Goldman

Before the debtors left Drohitchin, the commander contacted the city householders and requested a signed document that the debtors conducted themselves well while they were in town. Naturally, we gave him that document, which demonstrated that the bloody game of the debtors had come to an end, and that they were going to show a more humane face. (In England and the United States people realized apparently, that there was no way Bolshevism could be defeated if Jewish blood was flowing. – Ed.) As we learned later, the end of the bloody White Guards and all other murderers had arrived!

V.
Drohitchin Under the Polish Regime

After the debtors left Drohitchin, the Polish authorities set up a civilian administration, and created law and order in town. Later, after the Russian-Polish War, aid started arriving from the United States. A few wagonloads of rice, white flour, boxes of clothing as well as money arrived from the United States. R. Eliyahu Eisenstein, who came to Drohitchin as a representative, brought alot of money. Eisenstein also provided money to build a Jewish religious elementary school and to complete the Houses of Study. In particular, aid arrived for women whose husbands were in the United States, and who were in great need and hunger during the war. Shops started opening again as well.

[Page 78]

Nevertheless, we had to endure much suffering from anti-Semitic Poles. In particular, the soldiers of General Haller's army displayed anti-Semitic behavior. (It's interesting that these soldiers were actually recruited in the United States – Ed.). These soldiers tore out the beards of Jewish men, and threw Jews off moving trains. This happened to me personally.

When I once traveled from Warsaw, a gang of General Haller's soldiers from Brisk got onto the train I was on. The conductor, noticing the danger facing us, immediately closed me inside his cubicle. The soldiers started banging on the door until the conductor assured them that no one was in the cubicle. They then left.

Since I felt that Jews weren't going to have a good life under the Polish regime, I started thinking about going to the United States. With G-d's help, my family and I were brought to the United States in 1924 by Drohitchin emigrés, where I served as a rabbi in New York.

Menachem Averbuch (murdered)

SPRINGTIME AT HOME

The calm Polesia shepherds –
A gift.
The heavens are cracking a smile,
like a child just waking from sleep,
dispersing gray thunder,
and bringing in a springtime wind.
Waking up from a long sleep,
the stream opened its eyes wide
next to the road,
and is gone in a flash.
Flocks of birds crying and singing
over pastures, fields, swamps and marshes,
kissing and hugging,
telling secrets in the silence.
Sticking out its green top,
the stalks of rye from its bed;
Makar, the peasant and his horse,
He just plows, he just sees.
The shepherd chases his herd on Friday,
sings and plays a tune,
By twisting and tying,
A shepherd never tires.
In his sack,
a thick slice of bread,
a bottle of milk –
that's his meal.
over pastures, forests and marshes
he strides along with his herd.
Days and weeks, through rain and sun,
the pasture is his home,
even when there's thunder, lightening and rain,
his only shelter – a tree!
When the sun sets in the forest,
shadows fall down to earth,
the shepherd leads his herd back home,
fattened cows and horses.
Shepherd tunes are his company,
full of sadness, a bad mood,
because the fields are sparse
and gardens small.
Because his hut is small and poor,
because there is no joy there,
because the youth have gone away,
and old age has now arrived.
This is what the children of Polesia sing,
about the poor homeland,
where G-d has struck with a full hand,
forests and marshes.

Voices from Pinsk, Bug Canal, 1939

[*Page 79*]
Yisrael Baruch Warshavsky (New York)

Yisrael Baruch Warshavsky (Warsaw)

HISTORICAL NOTES
My Memoirs
Written at the end of World War I

I am going to start my memoirs with the events we lived through in the World War (1914). As of this writing, the war has been going on for four years, and we still don't know where things are at, whether we are at the end of the war, or just in the beginning. We hope that the war is coming to an end, but in the meantime we are living through an extremely critical period. Nobody knows whether we'll be able to get through it. Therefore, I am writing my memoirs for my children, who are living through this awful time together with us. They are, however, still too small to be able to appreciate what is going on around them.

A.
The Situation of the Jews in Russia before the War

After the reactionary Czarist regime put down the Revolution of 1905 in a river of blood, it started oppressing the Jews. Decrees after decrees were issued to embitter Jewish life, and whoever oppressed the Jews more was rewarded with a higher position from the Czarist regime.

The reactionary press thundered against the Jews, and the regime had its black undercover agents, the "Black Magnikas," in all gangs and bands that were involved in theft and murder. There were bloody pogroms in Kishinev, Gomel, Bialistock and many other cities. The Jews increasingly lived in fear of their lives.

In Drohitchin we also lived through this fear and the pogroms. Once there was a rumor in town that the peasants were preparing to carry out a pogrom against the Jews, and the local gentiles in town already had their share in Jewish homes and property. The pogrom was supposed to take place on a market day. The Jews, however, found about the danger, and paid off the local police chief and the district policeman. The entire police force of the district (uyezd) were called to the market fair and arrived with loaded guns. The peasants, who came to the fair with bags and hatchets, were disappointed and left the fair with empty sacks. It was the police chief and policeman who made out the best at the fair. As far as they were concerned, Drohitchin was a milk cow, and they had a personal interest in preventing pogroms in town.

B.
The Autbreak of World War I

While the Russian government was involved with the Jews and did so energetically, Germany was making its plans to dominate the world, and especially Russia. It had to happen sooner or later. The murder of the Austrian crown prince in Sarajevo was the first spark in the worldwide blaze. This happened in the summer of 1914. Austria's move against Serbia served as a sign of bloody things to come. Soon thereafter, Russia mobilized, and the world started flowing with blood.

[Page 80]

Seated, from right: David Epstein, Yosef Feldman, Velvel Mishovsky and Meir Meyerovich as students in the Russian high school.

We heard about the first announcement of the mobilization on Friday, July 31, 1915 (This is an error, and should be 1914]. It's impossible to describe how we felt on that Sabbath, when many young men suddenly had to leave their families and go to war. On Sunday morning, the Fast of the Ninth of Av, we mournfully accompanied the unfortunate boys; we all walked along, weeping and sobbing silently, wiping our eyes. We then hugged and kissed each other, fainted and said goodbye to the poor boys. They then left for the train, and their relatives departed like mourners, returning to the synagogue to recite the laments for the fast day.

Shortly thereafter, we heard a rumor that the Germans had gone on and taken Kalisch and Tchenstechov. The turmoil in Poland got stronger, and new families arrived every day to stay with their relatives in Drohitchin, while others traveled further on. There was alot of movement, and our hearts and minds were only absorbed in the war; we would get up early in the morning just to hear the news from new arrivals. As soon as a train arrived, people would surround the cars from all sides, asking questions about everything happening in other places. Afterwards, people would congregate in the House of Study to talk about the political situation. People offered various opinions and assessments about the Germans' intentions and plans. Some people were amazed at the Germans, while others believed that the Germans were very good to the Jews. They referred to Kaiser Wilhelm as "R. Velvel," and that he was good to the Jews and would therefore be successful. It was argued that life would become unbearable if the Germans didn't arrive.

Everywhere two people stood together, and as soon as shopkeepers closed their stores, crowds congregated to talk about what the *Blatt* newspaper was saying, and what travelers were reporting. If the paper wrote about great victories by the Russians, people had doubts, thinking this wasn't true. When they read about the cruelty of the Germans, no one believed it. No one believed this about a "civilized people" like the Germans. Throughout the winter, the Russians pushed back the Germans and marched into Galicia and eastern Prussia.

C.
The Fall of the Czarist Army

We felt the same about the fall of the Czarist army as we did about the fall of the Russian reactionary regime. The more frequent the failures of the Czarist army, the quicker the end of the Russian reactionary regime was expected to come. The first summer wasn't very good for the Russians. The Germans were able to route the Russians from Galicia and East Prussia, which was followed by a series of Russian retreats. The Germans got progressively stronger and marched on, while the Russians put up little resistance. The population of Poland was evacuated, and more of them became homeless. Thousands of families of German settlers were expelled from the Chelm and Lublin gubernias. Some traveled on peasant wagons, while others traveled on their own wagons. Kettles of hot tea and bread were provided to the refugees, while many of them died along the way. The wave of homeless refugees kept growing, like birds flying ahead of a storm. This is how they were fleeing eastward. They included wealthy people, bureaucrats, and Russian peasants.

[*Page 81*]

[Handwritten lines:] On the first day of Passover, I was photographed together with twelve of my friends [illegible] who spent our youth together joyfully, with love and brotherhood in my hometown of Drohitchin before my trip to America. 1904. David Goldman

There was no shortage of Jewish suffering at the hands of the reactionaries, who provoked the killing of many Jews. The Russian regime spread false rumors that the Jews were responsible for their failures and that the Jews were collaborating with the Germans. The Russian newspapers spread lies and slander that the Jews were shipping off their gold to Germany in stuffed geese. Such stories and lies about the Jews were used by the Black Magnikas to deflect the people's anger at their own failures.

Considered a dangerous element, thousands of Jews were evacuated from the war fronts. They were ruined and became totally dependent on the rest of the Jews. The Jews, in fact, played a major role in the war, both with money and manpower, for the benefit of the Russians.

This kind of behavior of the Russian authorities toward their subjects provoked hatred in response on the part of the Jews.

D.
The Russians Lose Drohitichin

When the Germans were closing in on Brest-Litovsk, everyone, including the Russian press, was saying that Brest-Litovsk had to be defended and that the Germans had to be stopped. We thought that Brisk was secure and that the Germans wouldn't be able to take Brisk so easily, especially since for an entire year, thousands of people were taken to work at the Brisk fortress. To our surprise, however, the opposite happened. The Germans simply had to act as if they were going to Brisk, and immediately the rumor spread that they had taken it. No one believed that the rumors would be confirmed. People said the Germans had almost arrived in Kobrin. In Drohitchin, the commotion got worse. Everyone started packing, bought horses and wagons, and if possible, got ready to leave town. Whoever was unable to leave buried all of his valuables. The town was filled with soldiers on their way to and from the front. The noise and banging of the carts and wagons continued unceasingly. There was a shortage of water because the wells were dried up, and it was only possible to get some water early in the morning.

[Page 82]
People were going thirsty the whole day.

Cossacks and Circassians showed up in town. They were running around like wild tigers. The stores were closed, and at night the town was pitch dark. No flames were lit in the houses, in order not to provide any signs to the Cossacks and Circassians.

One evening, a girl who was a neighbor ran over to our house in tears, telling us that the Cossacks were robbing her house. I stepped outside and noticed two Circassians coming right in my direction, and I closed the door. The women closed themselves in a separate room. When the Circassians saw the door was locked, they started banging loudly on the door. I feared they were going to break the door down, so I opened the door and went outside. They cursed and threatened me with their daggers. They started poking me with the daggers, but luckily a policeman came by and took them away.

From right: Berl Lechovitsky, Isser Zlotnick, Moshe Kravetz, Yaakov Siderov, a man from Yanova, Dov Warshavsky and Yitzchak Kahn (New York) next to David Warshavsky's house in August, 1932.

The soldiers all said that wherever an army withdraws, it had to destroy everything first. This made us feel very depressed, and we just kept thinking about staying alive and trying to save as much of our belongings as possible. The wagons were ready, and as soon as the army started to burn the town, we would make our way behind the town to the trenches that we had prepared earlier.

The Russian headquarters was in Drohitchin, as were the district treasury offices. The Christian population was evacuated to Russia, and they sold their livestock (cows, horses and pigs) at the district treasury offices, where the Christians got money in exchange.

The Jewish population wasn't forced to leave town, and whatever people could take along they did, destroying the rest. Thus, people destroyed the alcohol produced in the brewery by pouring it out on the ground. The Russians took away all the copper and metal and also wanted to take the livestock, but they didn't have a chance to do it.

On the last Thursday morning (a week before Rosh Hashanah) when I went to pray in synagogue, I noticed a group of Cossacks riding around in town, looking around and tearing off locks and emptying stores of anything that the owners hadn't had a chance to remove. The Cossacks worked very quietly and methodically. When they passed the pharmacy, I saw a group of soldiers go inside and steal. An army officer dispersed the soldiers and told me to lock the door again.

That evening, someone reported that they were breaking into the pharmacy again. I went together with a Cossack who had come to my house to ask me to make him some powdered milk. When we opened the door, we saw a group of soldiers shaking all the drawers and stuffing their pockets with whatever they could get their hands on. The Cossack, who was with me, screamed at the soldiers to leave, telling them they were touching poison, and would be poisoned. The soldiers ran out of the store and I locked the door again.

E.
The Town Burns

The military headquarters moved out of Drohitchin. Soldiers repeatedly told us that the town would be burned that night. Everyone was ready for that and buried as much as they could, while loading the rest onto the wagons. Some left for Pinsk, and a few others moved out of town. In our case, everything was packed on a wagon. The house was upside down, and everybody was sitting around with hanging heads. The windows were closed and the drapes drawn. Every so often we would step outside to see whether the fires had begun. We could see a red sky in the distance, which indicated another nearby location that was going up in flames. We could tell that the train station was being burned, as well as the courtyard near town.

[Page 83]

Looking around, we could see a small fire burning on some side street. It was a weak fire and could be put out easily. Then we saw a fire on the street of the House of Study, then another fire, and yet a third. The fires became larger and jumped from one side to the other. The two sides then joined together as one large flame. Behind the flames we could see the retreating Russian army. It was almost as if the flames wanted to serve as torches to show us their withdrawal.

When we saw that the town was burning from all sides, we moved out of the house. The horse was harnessed, but because of the delay in soldiers' departure, we couldn't leave. Some of them would go into a house looking for something or to get a piece of bread. Others looked for an empty bed to sleep in. With great effort, we got away from the fire, going behind the house and garden and then to the Vion.

We could see men standing around. They were soldiers and Cossacks, and we wondered what would become of us. We were all alone, since everybody else had already moved to the other side of town. Our hair stood on end, and we started crying out " O, G-d, answer us in our time of trouble!" We screamed with all our strength. The fire raged, dancing like demons from one rooftop to the next. We suddenly heard Jewish voices. They were those of a few Jewish families and their wagons. This helped us relax a bit and gave us courage. Our situation was just like being in a desert, when suddenly a person happens along an oasis. We spent the whole night talking about the fire, watching how everything was burning to ashes. The next morning, we took our belongings and went over the other side of the Vion with the rest of the populace.

The town was almost entirely destroyed. Only a few houses were spared on Pinsk Street and in back alleys. Their owners paid off the bandits not to burn their houses. On the other side of town, on the Vion, all of our wagons and carts stood, together with the nervous animals that were tied to them.

In the morning, the town looked like a cemetery. There was a deathly silence everywhere; no wagons, no Cossacks. Was it all over? The Russians had left. Were the Germans going to arrive? No, it was only the calm before the storm. Crouching soldiers were heading towards the train tracks where their trenches were. It was Friday afternoon, and the weather was nice. Everybody was sitting out on the open grass; some were sleeping and others were cooking over a fire, while yet others were reciting psalms.

From right: Zelig Hausman, Berl Resnick, Herman Grossman (New York), Motya Yachnes, Feldman, and others.

Summer of 1937.

F.
The Three-Day Battle in Drohitchin

Suddenly, everyone started looking up at the sky. A German airplane was surveying the area; it flew over the town and then disappeared. We all became frightened and ran for the trenches. German and Russian shells started whistling by over our heads. We heard a bang in one direction and saw above us a red line moving through the air and sounding like a mournful whistle. It then went a little further and landed in pieces with a bang.

Our trenches were dug very deep, covered on top with wood and earth. The women and children were the first to go into the trenches, which were extremely crowded and stuffy. It was extremely dangerous, and people were pushing and making noise, arguing for a better spot. Some brought along bundles or a chicken that they remembered to salvage, figuring they'd need something to live on if necessary.

[Page 84]

The men started to gradually get used to the sounds of the explosions and remained above ground. The cannons stopped at night, and only the machinegun fire continued. It looked like fried potatoes. This didn't frighten us and remained above ground. From time to time we were alarmed by the appearance of a Cossack, but we calmed down when he disappeared.

From left, A. Zlotnick, Leon Michaels (New York), Yossel Burstein, Yossel Lieberman, and others. August 1932.

The next morning, on the Sabbath, cannon fire resumed, and that day it rained heavily. The trenches were crowded and wet, so we moved over to a nearby house that had not been destroyed in the fire. We stayed there overnight. It was very crowded in there, and we sat on the floor the whole night, because we couldn't lie down and sleep. During the night we heard the machine gun fire, and on Sunday morning it rained heavily again, and it was impossible to go back into the trenches. We stayed in the house, while the cannon fire continued a whole night. In the evening we were especially frightened by the cannon shells that fell near the house where we were staying. We dashed out of the house and ran back to the trenches. My wife and I ran to the trenches as I carried our one-year old daughter. The trenches were already as packed as a chicken coop and appeared like huge graves with people buried alive. I made an enormous effort to make some room for my wife and daughter in one of the trenches, while I remained hunched over at the entrance to the trench.

It was dark outside, and the cannon fire didn't stop. Searchlights illuminated the entire area, and machine gun fire started again. Hand grenades were thrown over our trenches, thundering and blazing. We were certain it was only a matter of time before they hit our trenches and killed us. It was a horrible time as we wondered whether we would live or die.

Then the noise gradually started to die down. The grenades flew over our trenches, and the searchlights illuminated the east, on the other side of town. Apparently, the Russians had completely withdrawn, and the town had fallen into the hands of the Germans, since the silence had grown in the distance until it was totally quiet.

Everyone else remained in the trenches, but my wife and I, with our sleeping baby, made our way to a nearby little house that was still standing. In that house I found R. Yossel, the rabbinical judge of Drohitchin, and his wife. He hadn't been able to find a spot in the trenches; he lied down and went outside. He was sick, and the next day he left. In the morning, I went out onto the street, where I saw a small group of wet Russian soldiers running without weapons. Apparently they had run late and were now trapped. When the sun came out and everyone came out of the trenches, the Germans were arriving.

G.

The Germans March into Drohitchin

The storm moved further and further away, and like ocean waves that sweep away everything in their path, the groups of German cavalry and infantry carried away thousands of wagons that remained in Drohitchin. Then they started requisitioning other items: a horse, a cow or even just a good object. They took it and often gave out signed notes in exchange.

On the road we saw a very tragic event: a Jew who was traveling with his wagon had small children sitting on it, while the adults walked along very weakly. It was a Jewish family that was returning home after the Germans arrived in Pinsk. A unit of German soldiers passed them by, and yelled out: "Jews, stop!" The Jew stopped, and without a word, the German harnessed the horse. The desperate Jew fell at the feet of the German while his whole family broke down and cried.

[Page 85]

The German took a skinny weak horse and gave it to the Jew, saying "Well, Jew, here's a better horse." The Germans then left. The Jew harnessed up this old horse and his family got into the wagon. But since they realized the Germans wouldn't give them another horse, they just left the wagon, and each member of the family took what he could and continued by foot.

When we got out of the trenches everyone ran over to the peasants' house and moved in. They didn't find anything to eat; whoever had some food had something to eat, and whoever didn't had anything and went hungry. Whoever had some bread felt very lucky – just like Robinson Crusoe on the deserted island. Everything had to be made from scratch. The peasants had already brought grain into the barns, and we had the opportunity to use it to make bread, until the Germans, who stood with their wagons, were able to take away everything they could find, using the barns for their horses. We all then went off to the nearby villages, threshed the grain and brought it back to town.

Germans confiscating cows and horses from the local population during World War I.

These were days when everybody was out for himself. Sometimes the Germans would grab some item that someone had dug up, and sometimes one Jew would even do the same to another. We also saw the true faces of some people who wore a mask until life started getting back to normal.

Those times were also auspicious for cholera outbreaks. Small children, adults and families died in every dark corner without any assistance whatsoever. The German doctor didn't even bother to continue to register the deaths.

During the Jewish holidays we would have to sneak out of synagogue after services to go home, since the Germans grabbed any hungry person to dig graves and bury horses who died, as well as other types of work. They didn't pay any money and demanded the people to work for free. People would never even dare to ask why they should be forced to work this way, since they valued their lives.

[Page 86]

H.
Jewish Officials

In the evening, around sunset, bats always come out and fly around in the darkness; it was the same for us Jews. The Jewish officials would turn up and fly around in the dark, so to speak, feeling very much at home. They hoped that the night would never end. The poor Jewish residents had a lot to put up with, with those "officials" who were used by the Germans to squeeze blood out of the Jews.

Jews were actually more scared of the Jewish officials than of the non-Jews. If a person ever fell into the clutches of the Jewish officials, he could never get rid of them. This situation occurred in Drohitchin too. Whenever the residents dared to protest against those who took power, the latter responded that they were powerless in the face of all the pressure because the German authorities supported all the lowlifes who were of great use to them. The following incident is an illustration that I witnessed myself.

It happened on one Sabbath. Everyone was agitated and went to a meeting to protest against those were taking over, and they asked the commander to allow them to elect a mayor. As usual, everyone made their claims and came to agreements. Thereafter, we began the afternoon Minchah prayer services. Even before the end of the service, a German sergeant came into the house and started yelling, "What kind of meeting is this?" He immediately started striking people over the head with a cane, and didn't even spare old men. Everyone just barely managed to get out of there in time, and never again were there any protests against the mayor. We just kept quiet and put up with him.

First row, from right: Rachel Epstein, Hershenhaus, Chana Greenstein, Beila Milner, Naomi Wasserman. Second row: Esther Goldberg, Chaytshe Andrinovsky, Slonimsky, Valevelsky, Yentel Wasserman, Schwartz. Third row: Kobrinsky, Baum and others.

I.
The Iron Hand of the German Authorities

The Germans made order in town, and commanders were assigned throughout the occupied area. The residents were under the authority of these commanders, and the occupied areas were divided up into various administrative district. Each commander did whatever he wanted. If he was a good person, he worked like a good person. If, however, he was a tyrant, he behaved tyrannically, and no one could level any accusations against him.

The locale closest to the administrative authorities was referred to as the administrator's territory, and the commanders in those areas enjoyed unlimited power over the civilian population. They could use people for any kind of work without compensation. Therefore, the commander wanted to make sure that the population never went hungry and that they had food supplies. The situation wasn't as good in places further away from the front.

The concern wasn't the same everywhere and depended on the discretion of the commander. If he was good, the people lived pretty well, and if he was bad, he took everything away and gave it to whomever he wanted, according to the German system. If someone had 40 pounds of rye put away, he had to have hidden it very well. Discipline in the administrative centers was much stricter than in other areas. As soon as nightfall arrived, everybody had to remain at home. Lamps had to be extinguished at the prescribed time. Movement between administrative districts could only take place with a permit and with a military escort. If someone wanted to come into town to shop, he had to first get a travel permit from the commander. This meant that a person had to know his reasons for traveling ahead of time, such as going to a doctor, buying shoes, or other things. When the commander was in a good mood, he gave out the permit together with a military escort (the permit was at most only for one day). If the commander was in a bad mood, he could make life difficult. If someone so much as committed "a sin," the entire village or town would be locked for a month, and no one could obtain a travel permit. If someone wanted to travel from the administrative district to an outlying district, he had to first submit a request to the district inspector, which took a very long time. Later on, things got even stricter. In order to get a travel permit – even within the same district – you had to obtain a special permit from the authorities.

[Page 87]

If somebody became ill, he could already be dead by the time he got his travel permit. Each governor made very sure that nothing would be exported from his district. On the other hand, however, he was pleased whenever something was illegally imported into his district. Although discipline in the administrative districts was unproductive, many Jews lived well thanks to butter and eggs, which even the strictest German couldn't resist. Anyone could get a permit for butter and eggs, engage in smuggling and go from one district to the other, thereby not having to engage in forced labor.

Gradually the Germans also got used to bribery, and the iron hand of the Germans was powerless against life, which broke down any iron wall in its path.

J.
The Typhus Epidemic

After the holidays in 1915, my brother David, sister Toiba and I, together with other Jews, left town and went to the village of Horvacha. My wife and daughter stayed in town. Unfortunately, a typhus epidemic started to go around, and Drohitchin was closed. No one could enter or leave. Occasionally we heard bad news: someone died, and someone else was on his deathbed. I was cut off from my family, and I couldn't stop worrying about what might have happened to them, and they had no livelihood. I started trying to bring them to the village. At first, the commander told me this was impossible. Later on, however, a number of us received permission to go to Drohitchin, and I was able to bring my wife and child to the village.

I was indescribably happy, and I hoped that I would be saving my family from the fire of the epidemic, as well from hunger and want. We left with two wagons. A non-commissioned officer rode along on his horse, and a soldier sat on the wagon. The road wasn't too good, and it rained all night. The next morning the weather cleared up, and we saw the sun rising over the horizon. The two horses were harnessed side by side and started running along. The officer, a brave and precise German, rode along and sang a patriotic German song. Above us, we could see an airplane flying in the direction of the railroad, and the German told us that it was a Russian airplane. In a couple of hours we were already at the entry to town. We were first met by the local patrol, walking with their rifles on their shoulders. They looked at us with malicious eyes, and asked us, "Where are you going, Jews?"

From left, Gedaliah Kaplan (as policeman). He was a male nurse in 1918. The other man is Yaakov Einbinder.

Our escort exchanged greetings with the patrol and asked for the commander. He stopped our wagons, and went in to talk to the commander. The secretary told him that going in and out of Drohitchin was prohibited, and the officer ordered the soldier to keep the wagons where they were, and keep an eye on us so we wouldn't go into town. The officer himself went to shop in town, and was allowed access. We couldn't see any Jews on the street in town; we only saw a Red Cross nurse go by. She didn't even stop to speak to us.

A lieutenant was walking by the commander. He was tall and had a sympathetic

[Page 88]

face. He walked slowly, and his dog was running in front of him. The dog kept stopping, standing on both front legs, and looked straight into the face of the lieutenant. The lieutenant petted the dog and had tremendous pleasure from it, just like from a naughty child, and he didn't even pay any attention to the fact that the secretary was trying to make sure the lieutenant heard him speak about us. The lieutenant just ignored it, walking and petting the dog. Soon, the officer came back and told us to go back.

Anyone can understand the suffering we went through. We invested alot of effort to obtain the permit, and now, when we were already in town, we had to go back. My situation was utterly desperate. Everyone in town was lying in the hospital; people were dropping like flies, and here I was about to be able to save my family from the horrible fire. Who could imagine how this all would end? The German wouldn't give in and told us to go back. By the time we started back, it was already dark. The officer rode on his horse and sang a song from his homeland. The soldier sat on the wagon and accompanied the officer in song. They both made fun of us. On the horizon I could see the moon. The horses started galloping, panting and going faster.

From left, Zechariah Schmid, the director of the People's Bank, and others, standing next to the bank.

The horses let us know how they were affected by the journey and by the man's cruelty. We, however, told them that we weren't guilty; we had our own problems. When I came home, I couldn't settle down. My imagination produced sorrowful pictures. The idea that I could lose my family didn't give me a moment's rest. For a long time I couldn't even work. Later on, I received a permit to bring them to the village. This time I was successful. It wasn't until the winter that the epidemic subsided, and I was then able to bring them out.

K.
Drohitchin Jews in the Village of Horbacha

In the village of Horbacha, two miles from Drohitchin, we were a few dozen Jewish families from Drohitchin and other villages and town during the war years. Among the Jews were the Kholozshin Rebbe and his family.

The peasants in the village were evacuated to Russia. Their grain was moved into the barns, and potatoes were planted. The Jews had food to live on. The commander stayed in the village of Vartzavich; the first commander was Commander Romm. He was of average height, wasn't a bad person, but was whimsical. He never had any strong views about anything. If at one moment he refused a permit, the next minute he could change his mind and give one. When we would go to him to request a permit to go to town, we would hang around his courtyard and had the same feeling we would have about a dangerous dog. Many times the commander would jump up just like a dog, hitting and shouting curses like "You lazy fools!" Soon, however, he cooled down and finally gave us the permits.

When my mother, Gittel, died in the winter of 1916 in Horbacha, the commander didn't allow her to be buried in the Drohitchin cemetery. He told us to bury her in the village, and we persuaded him to let us bury her in a colony.

The German commander made sure that everyone was working, and he had alot of work to do: in the "horse hospital" and field work, picking nettle, raking hay, and tearing down old houses so that they could use the wood for fuel.

On the first Purim, after we finished our prayers and came home, we saw patrol soldiers standing next to every house, with soldiers going from house to house to record how much grain each person owned.

[Page 89]

German forced labor during World War I. Young children were forced to engage in heavy labor.

We were told that they would take our grain and distribute it according to the German system that was used by other German commanders. Fortunately, we got away with just being scared about it, since the plan was never carried out, and we held onto our grain.

As soon as spring arrived, we started working in the fields with zest, and we realized instinctively that only the soil could save us from hunger. The commander did everything possible to assist us with our work in the fields. We got some horses from the military hospital and sometimes (*nasiniya*) as well.

L.
German Forced Labor and Slavery

The first commander was gone and was replaced by a new one who was not at all a friendly person. He wanted to make sure that Jews were not idle. He would oversee the work himself and make sure no one cheated, for which he would make us pay a heavy price. I remember how once in the summer he stood by the worksite and watched us like a hawk and wouldn't even let us take a break, calling us a lazy bunch, while he would hit people with his whip. If someone asked him if it would be all right to put on a coat because of the cold, he refused to permit it. It was under such conditions that we had to work until nightfall.

The same commander made sure that the chickens were registered and that no Jew would "cheat" him. He would go through the village and record the chickens. If a Jewish woman did try to trick him, saying she didn't have more than three chickens and that the others he saw weren't hers, the cunning knew he had her in his hands, and responded, "Oh, the damn woman wanted to cheat me."

On one Sabbath morning, we suddenly heard knocking on the door, and yelling at the windows. "Jews, get out of the house." We quickly got dressed and ran outside to see what had happened.

[*Page 90*]

The Germans had canes and were running from house to house, and they were sadistically chasing Jews out of their homes onto the street. No one was spared. They even ordered the old rebbe out of his house. The Germans divided the men into groups and sent them off to work in the fields. I was in a group that had to shovel hay. When we arrived behind the village, the commander ordered us to start shoveling hay. We told him that until now we hadn't worked on the Sabbath and we weren't going to do so from now on either. He started making faces and slapped me on the face with a wet rod. Suddenly, as if to spite him, rain started falling, and we went home. I was lucky not to have to violate the Sabbath.

We later found out that it was punishment because a Jew in the village of Vortzevich, where the commander lived, was discovered with a few pounds of grain he got from some stalks while he was working in the field with the Germans. Therefore, the Germans penalized all the Jews, forcing them to work on the Sabbath.

First row, from right: Aharon Lasovsky, Dr. Goldstein, Tevel and Freidel Zbar, Tanya Gratch, Yosef Berezovsky, Yirmiyahu Grossman. Second row: Chaika Lasovsky, Alter Saratchik, Mrs. Goldstein, Rachel and Shlomo Zelig Goldman, Dora Grossman. Bottom: Avraham Gratch and Chaim (Herman) Grossman, in 1927.

In the autumn the Germans took small children, eight to ten years old, to plant potatoes and other vegetables. It was extremely hard work. If the soldier was a decent person, the work was bearable. However, if he was mean, he would persecute people and report to the commander that they didn't want to work.

This type of situation occurred once on the day before Rosh Hashanah. I remember that day very well. Another fellow and I were forced to plant potatoes. Our work was overseen by a Polish-German soldier, a Jew-hater, who persecuted us while we worked, watching us like a hawk and not giving us a moment's rest. The other fellow, a frail person, was too slow and drew the attention of the soldier when he said that we were doing enough work for the money we were getting. A minute later, the commander showed up, riding his horse. As he approached us, he expressed his dissatisfaction with our work and insulted us by calling us a "damned lazy bunch," even though this time we were working quite well. The soldier told the commander what my friend told him. The guard became upset, turned swiftly and headed toward my friend. He rewarded my friend with a strike of his whip over his head, promising to punish him even further. We had to work until late that evening, and by the time we got home, people were already coming home from synagogue.

I remember that we had very bad weather on the day before the festival of Sukkot. It was raining and a cold wind was blowing. There was no way we could work in the fields, but the commander would even release the children from work. The next day, when we went to synagogue, the children were taken to work. They weren't let go, not on Yomtof and not on the Sabbath, until they had finished digging up the potatoes.

In the second winter, in 1917, the labor got even worse. The Germans were getting increasingly nervous, and they persecuted us even more. Once they had us hunt hares. It was a cold frosty day, and the snow was very deep. The Germans and we lined up to go hunting for hares, but the hares went into hiding, and we wasted our time moving around the forest, sinking in the deep snow. That evening, when we went back to the wagons that were waiting for us, we heard the commander yell out, " That no good lazy bunch!"

[Page 91]

You lost everything!" This was all we "earned" for a whole day's work. When I went home, my foot felt frostbitten, and I had to spend five weeks in bed.

In the summer of 1917, our situation worsened. Commander Romm left, and he was replaced by the horse hospital veterinarian serving at the military headquarters. He turned over power to the low-level Germans, who did what they wanted.

The commander in the village was the ruler over the whole village. The Jews got him used to accepting bribes to exempt them from working. Later on, he began demanding butter, eggs and cheese, and would persecute anyone who refused his request.

The so-called representatives of "culture" around the world had the impression that Germany was greater than any country, and the Germans were better than anybody else, especially the "damnable Jews," who turned into slaves for those representatives of "culture," and who performed all types of slave labor in the forests and fields. Jews built wagons, sidewalks, all the while suffering from cold and hunger. We were tortured like slaves for months and years. Just like in Egypt! The Germans forced both young and old into slave labor, even small children. When someone would try to encourage the children to go to school, he would get this answer from the Germans: "It's wartime; they don't have to study." The so-called representatives of "culture" would call us the "damnable Jews" and "lazy bunch."

M.
The Peace Treaty in Brisk [Brest-Litovsk]

Winter 1918. When the Germans and the Bolsheviks began their peace talks, we hoped that slowly but surely we would be liberated from the Germans and our troubles. However, what turned out was that the Bolsheviks retreated from their front and allowed the Germans to go wherever they wanted. The Germans penetrated Ukraine and were in a rush to take out of Russia whatever they could. They made sure to carry off timber, using civilians as slaves who worked without pay under the worst conditions.

Nevertheless, even the iron discipline of the Germans loosened up a bit, and we were able to breath easier, but we were then faced with a new threat on the horizon – hunger. After the Germans invaded far into Russian, the fleeing peasants started returning to the villages. We learned that hunger started to spread in Russia, and we, too, started to experience hunger. The Germans grabbed the last drop of milk from our children and took eggs and fowl, and demanded cattle as well. The Jewish families gradually returned to town from the village in order to make room for the arriving peasants. We left the village of Horbacha and returned to Drohitchin.

N.
The Germans Depart Drohitchin, and the Ukrainians Arrive

Summer, 1918. The Germans were finally defeated by the Allies, and began retreating from Russia.

The German withdrawal proceeded slowly and methodically. Whatever they could take along with them, they took, and whatever they couldn't, they sold. Every German tried to make as much money as he could.

In Poland, Pilsudski had already organized his legions to repel the German retreat through Poland. The Germans, therefore, did everything possible to evacuate through Lithuania to West Prussia.

Even before the Germans had lost Ukraine and Byelorussia, they had already arranged a successor to take over their government, which allowed for an independent Ukraine. As far as possible, they appointed Ukrainian commissars in every city and town to take power immediately after the German withdrawal. A Ukrainian commissar was also appointed in Drohitchin. As soon as the Germans left town, he organized a militia-police made up of village peasants, and proclaimed himself the head of the Ukrainian government. He ordered storeowners to obtain licenses for their stores, and began distributing Ukrainian currency, called *karvontsas* (I think the correct term may be the same term used in the 1990s, *karbovantsi*).

[*Page 92*]

His government didn't last very long, however. Rumors circulated that the Poles were moving from the west, and the Bolsheviks from the east. Suddenly, on one fine morning, the Ukrainian commissar disappeared.

For a brief time Drohitchin was without a government, and the people were in great peril. A local committee was established and organized a militia of Jewish young men, who were required to maintain order in town and to serve as a defense force against any outside attacks.

From right, Menachem Auerbuch, Moshe Mendel Milner and Avraham Kravetz.

O.
The Polish-Bolshevik War

The rumors that the Poles and Bolsheviks were going to face each other were confirmed. The Poles were in Kobrin, and the Bolsheviks were in Pinsk. One day, a horseman - a Bolshevik military scout - arrived in Drohitchin. He gave a speech to the assembled crowd in the marketplace, and he explained that the Bolsheviks would be arriving shortly and would bring freedom and justice for everyone. As soon as he finished speaking, he rode off.

Shortly thereafter in the middle of the night, a group of Polish soldiers arrived in Drohitchin and created chaos in town. They cursed out the town committee and went off to Kobrin with the militia leader in custody. They made their way back to Kobrin, and things were again quiet in Drohitchin, though not for long.

The Bolsheviks kept their word. A few days later they began marching from Pinsk to face the Poles. The traveled on Polish wagons that they obtained from nearby villages. It wasn't a regular army, however, and was composed of several hundred men and young men dressed in civilian clothes with rifles over their shoulders.

When they got to Horodetz-Antopolia on the way to Kobrin, the two hostile camps faced each other. The Poles, with an organized army and supported by the Allies, attacked the Bolsheviks with the newest weaponry and outnumbered the Bolsheviks. The Bolsheviks concentrated their forces on other fronts against the Byelorussian gangs that were supported by the Allies.

The retreating Bolsheviks stopped in Drohitchin. One officer, who fell in battle, was buried in the middle of the marketplace with a military parade. The Poles, who came into town afterwards, covered the grave over with dirt to remove any sign of it. It was a painful sight.

During the battle, a few young men from Pinsk, who had joined the Bolsheviks, were captured by the Poles and shot after being forced to dig their own graves.

[*Page 93*]

P.
The Poles Take Drohitchin

After the retreat of the Bolsheviks, the Polish army encountered no uprisings on the part of the Bolsheviks who fled without interruption.

"Remember what Amalek did to you (Biblical verse)!" The Poles, who were overcome with hatred of Jews, now had an opportunity to take revenge against the Jews. They cut and tore off beards together with flesh! Jews were scared to travel by train because there were many cases of encounters with Polish soldiers, called *Poznantschiks,* who threw Jews out of windows of moving trains.

We Drohitchin Jews suffered enough from Poles who would break into Jewish homes, cursing, "Dirty Jew. Give us milk, eggs and butter!" They demanded more and more. If someone didn't give them what they demanded, he was struck by a rifle butt. The Poles behaved like coarse hooligans, and if all this wasn't enough, they called Jews "Jew-Bolshevik!" This meant that they could do anything they wanted with a Bolshevik without legal process.

The Poles believed that if a Jew's oven was heated up and producing smoke, this indicated some kind of a signal to the Bolsheviks. Many Jews went through these experiences. There was also the dreadful case of the rabbi of Plotsk, and in Pinsk dozens of Jews were brutally shot. We were afraid for our very lives!

From right: Yaakov Warshavsky, , Yisrael Schmid, Moshe Altvarg, Leibe Oberman, Yeshayahu B., Fruma-Gittel Warshavsky, Yitzchak Kahn, Leizer Warshavsky, Baum and others. August 1932.

Q.
Material Aid from the United States

After the Poles had established civil order in Drohitchin, the local Jews suffered very hard times. Many people were suffering from hunger and were searching everywhere for a morsel of bread. As stated previously, under the German regime the Jews became involved in agricultural work. Each Jewish family worked on a small plot and barely had enough grain, potatoes and other vegetable for themselves. However, afterwards, when the peasants returned from Russia, the Jews no longer had any land to cultivate, and the Polish authorities settled Poles on the open land around Drohitchin. This created a very bitter situation for the town's Jews, who the Polish government cared little for.

Those who hadn't prepared any provisions had nothing to use to buy anything with, because the money issued by the Germans was worthless. There were Russians snapping "hundreds" (known as *Yekaterinkas*), which were first made from linen. From what people were saying, this was the work of the Germans. This type of "currency" had to be handled very carefully so that they didn't get crumpled. The purchaser would have to hold the "hundred" up to the sun to see if there were any punctures or pins in it because if there were, they wouldn't use the money. You couldn't buy anything with it, not even a bag of garlic. Therefore, when anyone would sell something, he would first announce that he was offering a "snap."

If someone had something to sell, or if he did a job, he requested merchandise, such as grain or potatoes in exchange, since they had greater value than gold has for us today.

People sold off anything they had, such as jewelry, household items and clothes in order to buy a pood (40 pounds) of potatoes or grain to stave off hunger. Women whose husbands were in America and who couldn't help them suffered more than anyone.

(I shouldn't forget to mention unforgettable people such as my sister Toiba Kahn and my sister-in-law Freidel Eisenstein. Both used the last bit of strength they had to provide for their children. But just before assistance became available, they passed away in their best years. They died from typhus. The first to die was my sister Toiba, just after Passover, 1919. Both my brother, David, and I became very ill with the same illness at the same time as Toiba. When I recovered, I found out that my sister had succumbed. The disease didn't even spare my wife and children. Then my sister-in-law, Freidel, became very sick and died a few days before Shavuot. That summer my dear and unforgettable friend, Yaakov Sidorov, also died from typhus.)

[Page 94]

Finally, the long-awaited aid arrived from the United States, starting with aid through the Joint, which provided food and clothes and also opened soup kitchens for children. This was followed by visits from émigrés from Drohitchin in the United States who brought money from relatives in the United States and especially from men for their wives. Eliyahu Eisenstein from Chicago brought money twice from relatives in the United States. This saved many families from hunger who also had the opportunity to emigrate to the United States.

R.
The Poles Run Back In and Destroy the Town

In the summer of 1920, rumors circulated that the Bolsheviks were pushing the Poles back. This was noticeable in the attitude of the Poles, who had lost their arrogance and pride. It didn't take long for the retreating Polish forces to show up in Drohitchin as they fled to Warsaw. The civil administration had already lost Drohitchin, and the Polish military authorities then took over. The Poles were able to do whatever they wanted, including taking Jews into forced labor, robbing and expropriating horses, cattle, household items, and anything else they could get their hands on. People immediately started burying valuable possessions in the ground, and men fled to the forest. Only women and small children stayed at home.

Each retreating group of military forces was followed by huge wagons with ammunition. They would stop over in Drohitchin, and like experienced thieves, the Poles would go through gardens using spears poked the earth in an attempt to find where the Jews had buried their possessions. Whenever they found things, they took them. I had buried all my worldly possessions in my brother David's garden. One early morning I found an empty hole. The Poles had taken everything. Overnight we were as naked and penniless as on the day we were born.

The situation worsened every day. Our house was safer than anywhere else because there was a bakery where soldiers baked their bread, so there was some protection from the robbers. There were also officers stationed in the same alley, at the homes of Chaikel Milner and Yisrael Eliezer Kharsel, and people were hiding out on the Vion for days. However, from time to time, they would sneak into a house to take a look what the family was up to and then run away, since the Poles would take the men away.

On the last night before the Poles left Drohitchin, the situation became very dangerous. None of the men stayed home overnight. People weren't as scared of the thieves because the Poles had already taken everything, but one's life was still in danger. Therefore, with a heavy heart I left my wife and children and went to hide out somewhere in another town. The whole town looked like cemetery. It was covered in darkness. Suddenly there was a light coming from a house; screams of "Help!" could be heard, but it was futile because no help was forthcoming. Every so often there were heartrendering desperate cries breaking the silence of the night, but the Polish thieves kept up their violent actions undisturbed.

At daybreak, I trekked home and found out that the thieves were also in the house I was living in. However, they were disappointed, since they didn't find anything to steal. They cursed and shouted. Finally, they threw cushions at the children, and fled. I then thanked G-d that we got off with only a fright, since later we found out about the destruction that the Polish thieves had perpetrated in town. They robbed and committed violence. They raped and abused many Jewish married women and girls.

S.
The Arrival of the Bolsheviks

After everything we suffered from the Poles, it is understandable how pleased we were to get rid of them. On the same day the Bolsheviks arrived in Drohitchin. Everyone came out of hiding and received the Russians as saviors. It is true that we knew what was to be expected under the Bolshevik regime. First of all, our contact with our relatives in the United States was cut off, but the fear of death that we experienced under the Polish regime caused us to feel happy about the fact that the Poles had left. Unfortunately, we didn't think much about what would happen afterwards.

[Page 95]

This indicates how incapable the Poles were of governing. They led their own citizens to despair. The Poles were their own worst enemy, causing others to hate them and wanting to get rid of them.

The economic situation soon worsened considerably. The United States was closed to us, and no food aid came in. Whoever did have provisions hid them so they wouldn't be confiscated by the Bolsheviks. Life, however, was safe. Military discipline was very strict, and no soldier would dare to enter a house to forcibly take something or cause suffering to anyone.

The following story is rather interesting. One day a Jewish policeman and a soldier came to the house where I was living. The landlady was baking bread that she was going to sale. The soldier (a Bolshevik) asked for bread, but the lady baker told him that she wasn't baking any more bread because she didn't have any more flour. The soldier and the policeman went over to the oven and found bread inside, proving that bread was baking. The bread she was making was actually mine, and I told them so, but it did no good. They needed bread for newly arrived soldiers and would give me a voucher for flour. The Jewish policeman told the soldier that he should leave me one loaf. The soldier, however, who was a gentile, was even more understanding and offered me two loaves, and he also gave me a voucher for flour, which enabled me to obtain a couple of poods (80 pounds) of flour a couple of days later.

The Bolsheviks had arrived at the end of the summer. The army, which was made up of infantry, cavalry and artillery, came through continuously. The Bolsheviks rapidly penetrated into Poland, and it became apparent that they would take over the whole country. However, when they got to Warsaw, they suffered a defeat and were forced to leave Poland. The situation of the Jews of Drohitchin again experienced tough times.

After a brief battle, in which bullets were flying over the heads of the residents, the Bolsheviks withdrew, and the Poles again took control of Drohitchin, and the withdrawal of the Russians took place quietly. This time the Polish army didn't stay in Drohitchin. They only left one unit to protect the railway.

T.
The Bolshevik Murders

Drohitchin remained without any protection. The Poles then had an ally, the White Guards and Bulak Bolokhovitch and his gangs, in their fight against the Bolsheviks. These allies were led around like leashed dogs being led by their masters, the Poles, who let them off their leash to engage in brutal murders of Jews.

At the train station near Drohitchin there was a group of Bolokhovitch's gang, and there was a danger that the bloody hounds would suddenly be let loose in town, which was, as mentioned, defenseless. People paid the Polish unit that was guarding the railway to protect the town. At night we were protected and surrounded from all sides in case they tried to come to town. One night the Bolokhovitch gang broke into the Zakazelia Court near Drohitchin, and slaughtered 17 Jews. We lived in deathly fear until peace talks were held between the Poles and the Bolokhovitch gangs. The war came to a close, and a civilian administration was set up in Drohitchin, which brought some law and order.

Chanukah party of Sheinka Feldman's class. Chana Greenstein, Esther Goldberg and others.

After the peace agreement the Russian government fdemanded that the Bolokhovitch gangs be interned, but the Polish government was slow to do it. In Drohitchin a group of the gangs remained for a couple of months. They were recognizable by their insignias that had a skull on it and which they wore on their fur hats. After a while they underwent drilling and were taught the art of war. For us, however, they were no longer a danger, and looked like beaten down dogs. Finally, the Polish government acceded to the requests of the Moscow and interned the Bolokhovitch gangs.

[*Page 96*]

A large demonstration in honor of the Balfour Declaration in Drohitchin on Lag Ba'Omer, 1919 [Sunday, May 18, 1919].

[*Page 97*]
By Gedaliah Kaplan (New York)

THE TYPHUS EPIDEMIC
1915-1916

Gedaliah Kaplan

Illness and disease always accompany wars and catastrophes. A few weeks after the arrival of the Germans in Drohitchin, a horrible typhus epidemic broke out in town. It spread like wildfire from house to house, and attacked both young and old. The close proximity, and especially the crowding of the homes like sardines, helped the Angel of Death to accomplish his work (one fourth of the city was affected).

The Germans feared for their own lives, and during the first days of the epidemic, they marked the houses where the fatal illness had struck and wouldn't let anyone in or out. However, this was of no use, since the disease spread further each day.

Finally, the German authorities took over three Jewish houses in the alley near the church (that leads toward the new gardens), and set up a temporary field hospital, which was surrounded by a barbed wire fence, and thereby isolated the patients from the outside world.

The hospital staff was headed by Shimon Weissman, Aharon Lasovsky (from Pinsk) as folk surgeons. Solka Weissman, Reizel Baum, Feiga Rachel Warshavsky, Meita Trashinsky and others were the "nurses," as well as several Jewish young men who the Germans brought out from Kobrin to work as medics. Tordos Leib Milner and I were the administrators of the hospital. The German doctor, naturally, had the last word in the hospital, and the rest of us had to follow along.

As stated, the field hospital was isolated and cut off from the town. Without special permission from the Germans, no one dared to leave or enter the hospital. Similarly, no one was allowed into town any further than the bridge. Anyone violating this prohibition was saddled with a large fine. I was an exception, and I could go in and out of town freely because I was responsible for bringing ill people from town to the hospital and for taking the healthy patients home, as well as providing the patients with prescription medicine from the only pharmacy in Telechan.

We made every effort to try to save the typhus sufferers, who arrived every day in greater numbers to the hospital. The Germans didn't care much about human life. If someone didn't show signs of a rapid recovery, the German doctor tried to give the patient a large dose of morphine to shorten his life. We ignored the doctor's orders, however. As soon as the German doctor would leave the hospital, we would go over to the patients whose life the doctor gave up on, and work as long as necessary until the patient opened his eyes.

A similar situation occurred involving Rachel Waldman, who the German doctor wanted to take off to the morgue (located in Naftali Steinberg's house). When the German doctor left the hospital, I and others put Waldman in a hot bath and put ice-cold compresses on her head until Rachel opened her eyes. The next morning, the German doctor was surprised to find Rachel Waldman alive, but he didn't dare to know the secret.

[*Page 98*]

A similar situation occurred with Yaakov Chacham (Rosenstein) who the doctor gave up on. The truth was that Yaakov Chacham was already half-dead, but we didn't give up hope. At night we sent for the doctor, Shimon Weissman and Rosenstein's family. (who we smuggled through the German patrol as patients for the hospital). We worked on the patient all night long, applying ice-cold compresses to his head, wrapping him in sheets, until Rosenstein finally opened his eyes and asked to eat something. This is how we managed to save many Jewish lives from certain death.

The staff of the Isolation Hospital during the typhus epidemic in 1915 in Drohitchin. First row from right: Aharon Lasovsky (folk surgeon), a German doctor, Shimon "the doctor" Weissman and another German. Second row from right to left: Todres Leib Milner, Dora from Brisk, Solka Weissman-Wasserman, Reizel Baum-Shoshanov, Feiga Rachel Warshavsky-Kotler, Meita Trashinsky and Gedaliah Kaplan. Third row, from right: Rosenblatt (a Jewish prisoner-of-war of the Germans), Moshe Perkovitsky, a non-Jewish prisoner-of-war, and Pesach, Berl Rim. [sic] son-in-law.

SEEING DEATH BEFORE OUR EYES

It happened on an early morning in February 1919. A unit of Polish soldiers and officers suddenly arrived and dragged a large number of Jews out of bed, ordering them to start dancing. Afterwards they cruelly beat those Jews to reveal where the Bolsheviks were located. Finally the Poles brought the Jews to Eisenstein's Wall and stood them against the wall to shoot them.

I can still hear the wailing and shouting. Each one of them recited the confessionals, waiting to die in cold blood. I was also standing in the line and survived those awful moments, seeing death before my eyes. However, there was one soldier with a human heart who fell at the feet of the squad-officer and begged him not to shoot innocent people. His pleas did no good. The Polish officers simply wanted to shoot a few hundred Jews.

Suddenly there was a loud crashing sound of a cannon behind the town. The Bolsheviks were attacking. The soldiers became frightened, left us and ran away wherever they could. Miraculously we were saved from an awful death.

A few hours later, the Bolsheviks arrived, took over Drohitchin and brought in law and order. However, they wanted to sentence me to death because I was a representative of the Polish government. There was someone who was my enemy and reported me to the Bolshevik authorities. I fled in the middle of the night through the forests and fields, running for miles until I got to the small town of Khomsk, where some fine people hid me in their attic. I stayed there until the Bolsheviks left Drohitchin. Then after great effort and hardship I arrived in the United States.

Gedaliah Kaplan

David Eisenstein (Chicago)

SELF-DEFENSE
1918

As soon as the German occupation government left Drohitchin in 1918, and the town was left without any civilian government or police, the rabbi and his congregants called a meeting to develop plans to protect Drohitchin from possible attacks from various terror groups, which had started sprouting like mushrooms after a rainfall.A local committee was organized without extensive arguments. It was a type of local government made up of local community businessmen and Rabbi A. Y. Kolenkovich as the chairman. The rabbi took on the responsibility for the local leadership. The meeting was held in the house of Chaikel Miller.

The first task of the committee was to create a Jewish self-defense militia. It wasn't a difficult task at all because every young Jewish man, married and unmarried, felt the duty to serve in the self-defense unit. The Jewish militia, which for all intents and purposes served as a police force, was made up of the following young men: David Eisenstein, Yudel Trashinsky, Asher Schwarzbard, Chaim Lev, Baruch Kakhler and Motya Yakhnes. The headquarters of the self-defense unit was located in the church, and the weapon depot was located at the home of Alter Goldberg, the merchant.

David Eisenstein

The question of money then arose. They needed money to buy weapons and other local needs. The committee imposed a tax on all the Jews in town. Families that had their own son in the self-defense unit paid less than those who weren't participating in it. Everyone had to pay something, however. Actually, in Drohitchin there were enough weapons because of what the Germans had left behind. However, one day a group of Bolsheviks came along and ordered that anyone who had weapons had to bring them to the Bolsheviks, who left a small number of weapons for the self-defense unit. This wasn't sufficient, and we needed money to buy more.

Some well-to-do businessmen wanted to get out of paying the tax, but the committee used their authority to force them to pay their share. It would be useful to recount an event that occurred relating to this. The committee determined that Yankel Chacham (Rosenstein) had to pay a tax of 1000 rubles because no one in his family was serving in the self-defense unit, and because everyone knew he could afford to pay. However, Rosenstein remained obstinate, and refused to pay. One Saturday night a few members of the committee came to Rosenstein's house with the militia and ordered him to pay the tax. Rosenstein broke open a windowpane and screamed. In the meantime, the militia noticed Yankel's daughter running into a room and slamming the door shut.

[*Page 99*]

Actually, in Drohitchin there were enough weapons because of what the Germans had left behind. However, one day a group of Bolsheviks came along and ordered that anyone who had weapons had to bring them to the Bolsheviks, who left a small number of weapons for the self-defense unit. This wasn't sufficient, and we needed money to buy more.

[*Page 100*]

Since she didn't want to open the door, the militiamen had to break it open. They found the entire room filled to the ceiling with wheat. In those days, when it was hard to get hold of a pood of grain for any money, here was a virtual silo full of priceless grain. The committee confiscated 22 bags of wheat, which were valued at 1,250 rubles and which covered the 1,000-ruble tax, plus 150 ruble fine because Rosenstein broke his own window, and 100 additional rubles for creating a public disturbance. The committee sold the wheat to Jews in town to bake Passover matzahs.

The case of Hershel Papinsky was also something worth mentioning. When Hershel started building his house, he mistakenly built on a few meters of property belonging to the widow Zippa Buder. The Buders brought over the rabbi, who, of course, ruled in favor of the Buder family. However, Hershel's workers didn't want to stop working, and the rabbi called for the Jewish militia, who stopped the work. Since he had no choice, Hershel had to pay for the small amount of property he had taken.

One night the rabbi called for me. When I arrived at the rabbi's house, I met Berl Zbar, who told me that a gang of Balokhovitch's men broke into Shmuel Yudel Piasetsky's house (Zbar also lived there.), and demanded they provide women, sugar, etc. so they wouldn't carry out a pogrom in town.

In the meantime, I organized a self-defense group who were secretly waiting near the church for those demons. As soon as the gang rode by horse to the church, the Jewish boys surrounded them and pulled their weapons. The Balokhovitch gang were held prisoner a whole night in the church, and the next day they were sent off to Pinsk after undergoing a lashing. Shortly thereafter when the Germans left Drohitchin, the peasants who had fled to Russia started returning from the surrounding villages. The return of the peasants created a problem for the Jews in town.

As is known, the Germans took over the abandoned houses of the peasants, and they cut down the wood for use on the muddy roads. Many Jews in town took advantage of that situation. Before the Germans could demolish the houses, the Jews took over the houses and moved them to their own locations where their burnt down homes had stood. The returning peasants demanded back their houses. The Lasintz landowner, an anti-Semite, called a meeting of the peasants and incited them to make a pogrom in Drohitchin. The situation in town worsened by the day, and people were terrified of what was in store for them.

At a special meeting of all Jews in town, it was decided that all Jews against whom the peasants had claims should offer the peasants payment for their houses. As far as possible the Jews were to avoid entering into a conflict with the angry peasants. People should be prepared to allow peasants to purchase goods in Jewish stores without payment, and if a pogrom were to break out, the self-defense unit would intervene with its own force. However, this did not take place.

A minor incident did take place in Yossel Shinder's store. A few peasants seized salt, spices, and other items and didn't want to pay. Yossel's wife, Chaya Leah, ran out into the street shouting. At the same time, David Eisenstein, Chaim Lev, Yudel Trashinsky and others from the self-defense unit appeared at the scene. The gentiles, seeing the guns over the boys' shoulders, immediately paid for the merchandise and quickly left.

As mentioned, everyone who was involved in the situation paid the peasants for the houses and barns, and the peasants calmed down.

In general, the Jewish self-defense unit was extremely responsible in their work. Soon the term, "self-defense" aroused fear among the local gentiles and adventurers, who didn't dare attempt any adventures into Drohitchin. This should be remembered for generations to come.

NOTE. On a certain day a person named Vadka appeared in town wearing a Ukrainian uniform, and presented himself as a representative of the Ukrainian government. However, no one believed him. On one occasion, Vadka got drunk, wandered around town shooting off his gun at the ground. He would walk a few meters and then take a shot. As he walked by the house of David Eisenstein, Vadka became frightened of the boys, headed by David Eisenstein. They struck him on the head and removed the revolver from his hand, and gave him a few good punches. Then they let him run away frightened and defeated. We never saw Vadka in Drohitchin again.
[Editor]
Shmuel Fishman (Israel)

[Page 101]

SLAUGHTER IN ZAKAZELIA
October 1920

It happened on a cloudy, windy October morning in 1920, when Zavel, the mason from Zakazelia, ran into Drohitchin, screaming hysterically and carrying the awful news that a gang of Balakhovitch followers broke into Zakazelia at night and killed 17 Jews, among whom wrere: Zavel's wife Breindel, son, daughter, and son-in-law, my dear sister, Batsheva, and her two young daughters, and another 10 Jewish men and women, most of whom were refugees from the town of Libeshei (Lubeshov) in the Pinsk district. These refugees had sought temporary shelter in Count Bobrinsky's good Zakazelia because their hometown was destroyed in battle and its almost 500 Jewish families were dispersed among the towns and villages in the so-called German occupation zone. The dreadful news spread through the Drohitchin Jewish community like wildfire, and everyone was seized with fear.

The war of the Poles and their "Balakhovitch legionnaires" against the Bolsheviks raged with full force, and wherever the Balakhovitchists went, they started a pogrom against the Jews. The robbery, rape and murder, and now, the Zakazelia butchery, cast an indescribable fear on the Jews in the entire region. What would tomorrow bring?

The first that had to be done was to make sure the Zakazelia martyrs were buried in a Jewish cemetery, and the few remaining living Jews were evacuated to Drohitchin. However, the situation became very difficult. First, there was no one who wanted to volunteer to risk his life to travel the dangerous route to Zakazelia, which was 14 viorst (10 miles) away, to determine what could be done for both the dead and the living. Second, no one dared to move the dead until a permit was received from the Polish authorities in Kobrin. In the meantime, however, it was still necessary to arrange to watch the bodies so they wouldn't be desecrated. So who should do this? Since there was no other alternative and out of desperation, I took on the painful and superhuman task of going to Zakazelia, against the protests of my wife and my old, mourning father.

When I arrived in Zakazelia, the valley of death and saw my dearly beloved sister lying there shot dead, and next to her, her two sweet daughters Feigele and Chashele, 12 and 14 years old, with their torn open stomachs and smashed heads, I broke down, and a gruesome lament tore out my heart. A couple of Jews from Zakazelia were already at the spot: R. Zerach Sheinbaum and Pessel, who made every effort to calm me down.

We were all broken up and heart-broken as we went to check up on the other victims: Shmuel Lev, the former mayor of Libeshei (under the German occupation), his sister, Taibel, and their elderly mother. They were a respectable and hard-working family of five people from Libeshei. Also, the wife of Zavel the mason's wife, son, daughter and son-in-law, who were the only long-standing residents of Zakazelia were among the dead. The picture was horrible, and unimaginable by any person. My pen cannot even describe it on paper.

It turned out that a gang of a dozen soldiers belonging to the Balakhovitch unit that was stationed for a few hours at the Nagoria station had broken away and gone into Zakazelia. According to gentile witnesses, they broke into Jewish homes, shooting anyone they could lay their hands on. Later it was discovered that the victims were shot with *dum-dum* bullets, and the murderers quickly returned to their unit at the station after the executions.

[Page 102]

Shmuel Fishman – At the new cemetery in Drohitchln. He is standing near the graves of his sister, Batsheva and her children Feigele, 12, and Chashele, 14, who were brutally murdered together with 14 other Jews by the murderous Balakhovitch gang members (who joined with the Poles to fight the Bolsheviks) in Zakazelia in 1920. May G-d avenge their blood!

If the Polish government at that time had not been saturated by anti-Jewish hatred, they could have easily captured the unit and found out who the people were who were responsible for the massacre. It should be noted as a historical fact, however, that the Polish regime quietly agreed to the behavior of their partners, Batka [Papa] Balakhovitch gangs, who rampaged across Polesia, committing horrific pogroms against the Jewish population and didn't take any action to stop the murderers and punish the guilty. This also occurred to dozens and hundreds Jewish victims who fell to their bloody hands in Pinsk and surrounding areas and many villages between Kamen-Kashirsk (Kovel district) Libeshei and Pinsk.

A large part of the bloody acts that were perpetrated against many Jewish victims was memorialized by the famous Zionist and community activist from Pinsk, R. Avraham Asher Feinstein, under the title, "The Scroll of the Calamity in Pinsk and Surrounding Region during the Balakhovitchist Regime."

Returning to the 17 martyrs of Zakazelia, it took five days to receive the permit from the Polish authorities to bury them in a Jewish cemetery. Three to four Jews from Zakazelia and I didn't leave the victims for a moment during that period. We recited psalms and studied Mishnah, and were overcome with hot tears. This was my "food" during the entire five days.

All of Drohitchin was in deep mourning when the funeral procession of five carts went through the streets on the way to the cemetery. The entire Jewish population, young and old, led by the rabbis, accompanied the dead to their eternal rest with heart-rendering wailing, which must have torn the heavens and risen straight to the Divine Throne. There were 17 eulogies made by rabbis and businessmen. I eulogized the dead with heart-felt words, beginning with the verse from Lamentations, "Woe, G-d, what has happened to us? Look at us and see our shame."

The 17 graves were prepared, and 17 Mourner's Prayers were recited. The entire mournful congregation remained silent and returned home in a tearful mood and with bowed heads, reciting the prayer, "Lord of the Universe, avenge the blood of your servants!"

Who could have thought that 25 years later, the American émigrés from Drohitchin would publish a special Yizkor Book dedicated to the sacred memory of the entire Jewish community of the beloved and dear town of Drohitchin, which was so brutally destroyed in a Sanctification of G-d's Name, together with hundreds of Jewish cities, towns and villages at the hands of the German murderers, whose people descend from Amalek, Pharoah, Haman, Torquemada, Khmelnitsky, Balakhovitch, and many others.

Woe to our People who lived through this!

May these pages, written with pain and blood from my heart, serve as an eternal monument for my dear unforgettable sister, Batsheva, and her two small daughters, blooming flowers, and to the 14 other martyrs of Zakazelia in 1920, as well as to many hundreds of Drohitchin émigrés - men, women and children - who died in the Sanctification of G-d's Name in 1942-43. May G-d avenge their blood!

[Page 103]

THE DEATHS IN OSEVETZ [OSEWEC]
1899

More than half a century ago, in 1899, the Jews in Drohitchin and the surrounding area were shocked by a horrible murder of a Jewish family in the Osevetz forest, 10 kilometers from Drohitchin. Before his death on May 1, 1954, Baruch Feldman (from 1411 S. Kedwill), originally from Osevetz, told us about the horrible murder.

R. Sender (whose last name is unknown), the father of the murdered family, who originated in Antapolia, was a scholarly individual and involved in the lumber business. When the famous Lifshitz family of Antapolia, also in the lumber business, bought the Osevetz forest to cut down timber, they hired R.

Sender as their treasurer and manager of the forest. Sender and his family moved into the office of the Osevetz forest and made a good living.

Sender's son, Yisrael Leib, bought an expensive horse for 100 rubles. This event was a major topic of conversation among the gentiles of the surrounding villages, and eventually became known to the *korpuses*, the famous thieves of Hoteva, who managed to steal the horse. The local Drohitchin police official, Arsim, traveled with Leib to Hoteva, and after an extensive struggle, arrested the thieves. However, the horse was not found, and Sender had to buy a new one.

On the evening of the festival of Shemini Atzeret, according to Feldman, his father went to water the horse in Sender's barn. At the squeak of the key, Sender's children came out of the house and were talking. They led the horse off to overnight lodging, and since they weren't afraid of anything, they just fell asleep. At the same time, however, the thieves were lying in wait among the trees for their victims.

At approximately midnight, the church bells started ringing. It was an alarm that sent everyone running over to the office, which was in flames. Panic set in, and no one knew what was going on. People thought it was just an ordinary fire, but when the fire went out, they found the bodies of Sender and his family. This event was immediately reported to Drohitchin, and the local police official and police chief arrived to look for evidence of the killers. They didn't have to look too far, since the footprints in the dew led them directly to the Hoteva thieves' house. The *korpuses* soon admitted to the murder.

The killers reported that because they had been arrested for stealing the horse, they became very angry with Sender and his family and decided to take revenge against them. On the evening of Yom Kippur they had set out to commit the murder, but because of all the people praying in the office, the thieves became frightened and ran away. On Shemini Atzeret night, they broke into the office and committed the murder using iron bars and crowbars, they murdered everybody: Sender (48 years old) and his wife, Chasha Rivka; his elderly father, Yudel; his children Freidel, Yisrael Leib, Pintsha, David and others. They also killed a Jewish servant girl from Antapolia – a total of 14 people. Only one son, Yaakov Asher, survived. He was away in yeshiva.

After stealing the family's possessions, the killers tried to hide evidence of their break-in and burned down the house together with the dead victims. All of the killers except for one who escaped, named Gartchik, were put on trial in the regional court in Kobrin and were sentenced.

The charred remains of the dead were buried together in a family grave in the old Drohitchin cemetery. The town placed a grave structure over the grave, which was preserved until the destruction of the Jewish community of Drohitchin.

D.W.

[Page 104]
By Yaakov Goldberg (New York)*

Yaakov Goldberg

A POGROM

In 1937, as is known, pogroms were unleashed in the Pshiteck area and in the nearby Brisk region. We in Drohitchin were terribly scared that the Poles were conspiring to ambush the Jews and carry out a pogrom against their businesses, but the chief rabbi of Drohitchin, Rabbi Kalenkovitch, tried to comfort and calm us that G-d would protect us from harm.

One day it was heard that the bishop of Pinsk was coming to bless the Poles to continue with their dark plans to carry out pogroms against Jewish businesses and to do with the Jews as they saw fit. The Poles were overjoyed, and they prepared their arms and weapons of death to carry out the horrible work. On Sunday afternoon, after their religious services at church, the gentiles started gathering in the middle of the market, where the reception for the bishop was to take place. Rabbi Kalenkovitch called the Jews to the synagogue to plead with G-d to perform a miracle and assure the bishop's ceremony would take place peacefully. A delegation was selected made up of Rabbi Kalenkovitch, Dr. Lampa, G. Grossman, Zechariah Schmid, Menachem Auerbach and others to greet the bishop with a Torah scroll and bread and salt.

The bishop passed by, smiled and took the bread and salt from the delegation, and said: "Jews of Drohitchin, I offer you my heartfelt blessings from the Eternal G-d. May you always have two good things, salt and bread, for as long as Drohitchin exists. I ask you to trust each other as the Torah says, 'Love thy brother as thyself.'

[Page 105]

The Bishop of Polesia greets a Jewish delegation.

The Bishop of the Pinsk region receives a Jewish delegation from Drohitchin on August 13, 1937. From right: Zechariah Schmid, Rabbi Kalenkovitch, Dr. Globerson, Gedaliah Grossman and others.

This photo was printed in *Nash Pshegland,* September 20, 1937, Warsaw.

(From Warshavsky's archives).

The esteemed rabbi thanked him for his friendly blessing. The anti-Semites were very disappointed. They never imagined this would happen. The left the market embarrassed and went home without spoils, since the bishop warned the Poles not to harm the Jews of Drohitchin because of the Jews are good citizens of all countries.

These words were like a bright star in a dark night in which we lived in fear. The bishop's speech was soon published in the Polish press, and created confusion in the minds of all the anti-Semites, who constantly embittered the lives of the Jewish population. As a result of the fact that he blessed the Jews and didn't allow any bloodletting, the bishop was removed from his position and sent off to another region.

MY LITTLE TOWN OF DROHITCHIN
Zalman Shevinsky

Drohitchin, my little town of Drohitchin,
You are very holy and dear to me,
Just your name Drohitchin,
burns within me like a flame.
Once upon a time,
I was very far from you
in distance and thought –
I now miss you very much.
I am far away on a far-off road,
I ran away, I flew away, filled with courage.
Now, standing on the mountains,
I see that the youth aren't doing right.
Now my eyes look back,
To take a look at you.
I never saw this before,
how foolish I was in my youth.
I will never forget
Your picture that stands before my eyes.
I get old and forget,
But your name shines like a rainbow.

GREETINGS FROM LITHUANIA AND POLAND

An American citizen who was in the area of World War I (1916) published his impressions in the Tagblatt.

Harry Marcus (a son of Moshe Paritsker Valevelsky from Drohitchin), an American citizen who traveled on a pleasure trip to Russia and was detained because of the war, finally left Europe on the ship New Amsterdam from Rotterdam. Mr. Marcus, who visited other cities and towns in Lithuania and Poland such as Brisk, Kobrin, Antapolia, Drohitchin and Warsaw, described the tragic situation of the Jews on the other side of the ocean to a representative of the *Taglblatt.*

"It is impossible to put into words what I saw with my own eyes in that country that is called Russia," Mr. Marcus said with a tear in his eyes. "I spent two years among the refugees and war victims. Not only did I experience and see their suffering and trouble, but I also survived it. I arrived in Russia exactly one week before the war, and got stuck in Drohitchin, Grodno gubernia. Drohitchin is a small town with 700 Jewish families. Their businesses before the war? The usual ones: shops, small business, timber merchants. Before the war the Jews managed to make a living, but now they suffer from hunger and hardship."

"The Germans arrived there in August 1915. Four days before the Germans arrived, the Russian Cossacks destroyed and annihilated everything they got their hands on and pillaged all the stores. For the entire four days, there was war in Drohitchin. There was an awful battle, and the Germans finally won. Eventually, we the residents remained in trenches that we had dug, and for those four days we didn't even drink a drop of water.

[*Page 106*]

"The Germans arrived, and there was a cholera breakout. Hundreds of Jews died in the epidemic. However, the situation of the survivors ended up being much worse, since every day death stared them in the face. It's interesting that the fire that the Russians started in town didn't provide any benefit because the army that was trying to escape couldn't get out of town because of the fire and were taken prisoner.

" Besides the hunger suffered by the Jewish population, both the Germans and Russians armies took horses and livestock from the Jews. I should give credit to the Russians because whenever they took a horse from a Jews, they would pay for it – perhaps not the full price, but they paid. The Germans took the horses and gave receipts instead of money. We later had to examine the receipts, and most of them carried the following words: 'Nikolai isn't too sick to pay for the horses.'

"Before I left, I visited Brisk. The town became a heap, a ruin, with no Jews because they were expelled. The small towns awaited help from the United States. They live with the hope that you will soon send them aid. Unfortunately, they don't receive anything, and are dying of hunger."

"And what about the efforts of the Relief Committee to send aid?" asked the *Tagblatt* reporter.

"The victims in the military battles never benefited from that aid – not even a glass of water. Simply put, we didn't get a cent from the Relief Committee. Women in Lithuania, whose husbands were in the United States, suffered more than anyone. They don't get anything from their husbands, nor do they get anything from anywhere else. The men whose families are in Russia should send them help as soon as possible; otherwise they'll certainly die of hunger."

By Herman Grossman (New York)

Herman Grossman

GOING HOME

Those sweet little town were greeted,
They swam the seas the you,
Those sweet little town were greeted,
I also came to visit you.
I bring you regards from your children
Who are across the world,
And I come to you from a rich and illuminated country,
Where many of them are living.
We miss your fields,
Where we spent our youth,
We miss your fields,
That stretch across.
We also miss the old cemetery,
Where a multitude floats,
And in the shade of its large trees,
Dreams were fashioned.
In large cities of steel and iron,
Your children work happily,
Hoping and aspiring to show you,
Dear towns, that they will return.
Your trustworthy children surely
Never forget you at any time.
They love you then and now
From near and from far.

                    Printed in *Pinsker Shtima [Voice of Pinsk]*, 1931

[*Page 107*]
By Dov B. Warshavsky

Today's News from **TODAY**
October 6, 1935, Warsaw

SPOILED HOLYDAYS
A.
ROSH HASHANAH

In 1920, during the Polish-Russian War, the residents of Drohitchin lived through unbelievably difficult days. The town went back and forth from one side to the other several times. Only those who lived through those days can have an idea what that meant.

The Jews in Drohitchin lived through fear of their lives for several weeks and months. People usually stayed in hiding in their attics, cellars, going through suffering and torment. At night the town looked like a cemetery, without the slightest ray of light to penetrate the darkness or rustle or move of a single person. All that was heard was the neighing of the horses and the clattering of the military wagons, which occasionally penetrated the silence of the dark night.

Daytime started giving way to evening, another frightening day for the Jews. This time, however, it was Rosh Hashanah, and Jews were praying together. They felt like letting their hearts pour out and weep a little. The holiness of Rosh Hashanah rose above the fear and worry. Here and there a few Jews showed up; they were sneaking around like shadows, headed in the same direction.

There was an old house on a side street. A poor Drohitchin Jew lived there, and all the shadows disappeared inside. His house was used as a makeshift synagogue because the Czar's army was in control of three quarters of Drohitchin and had burned down all four synagogues, so it was in this house that some of the Jews arranged to hold their prayer services. (By the way, to be more exact, this house belonged to Yossel, the wagon driver, at a side street on Kobrin Street).

An hour later a group of Jews stood and prayed. As they went on, the congregants started forgetting about the danger they faced, and they were able to pray earnestly. Their prayers were a huge cry that cast great fear into the stillness of the night. Suddenly, there was total silence. What happened? A group of Bolsheviks surrounded the house, and everybody's hearts pounded from fear. The eldest ordered all Jews to leave the house. Only the cantor remained at his spot with his tallith [prayer shawl] over his head. Apparently the Bolshevik was in awe of him.

On the street the entire congregation was surrounded by armed soldiers who barked out the order, "Get going!" Everyone's knees were shaking from fear, and they were wondering where they were being sent. They were led to a large empty building, Feivel Katz's Wall, and told to carry bricks and clay. This is what happens: the Bolsheviks needed to bake bread, and since Drohitchin didn't have a large oven because all bakeries were destroyed, they came up with the idea that the Jews should build an oven overnight. No appeals and begging about Rosh Hashanah did any good. The Bolsheviks didn't want to hear about it. The Jews had to get to work, some as bricklayers and others as assistants. A couple of dozen Jews, young and old, worked throughout the night until the oven was complete.

The Jews then went back into hiding. For the rest of Rosh Hashanah, no one dared stick his head out the door, but this was still tolerable.

[Page 108]
The Moment, Warsaw
September 26, 1934

B.
SUKKOT

In those uneasy times during the Polish-Russian War in 1920, the Jews hesitated to appear on the streets, and remained in hiding, waiting for the storm to pass.

Finally, the situation improved somewhat just before the eve of the Sukkot holiday. Jews the world over were preparing for the holiday, but in Drohitchin the situation made it virtually impossible to even think about Sukkot. Even though the situation eased a little, everyone remained in hiding and was scared to put their head out because the deathly silence in town cast greater fear in town. However, it was the calm before the storm. There were rumors that trenches were being built behind the town, and that the Bolsheviks were preparing an attack on the Polish army, so that the retreating army could have time to escape. Secondly, people heard that the Czar's general, Bulak Balakhovitch and his army were operating at the Volhyn front near Kovel, and taking revenge on the Jews before anything else. These "guests" were supposed to be visiting Drohitchin. The situation in town was tense.

In the meantime, as mentioned, the town was calm and quiet. A few of the more courageous Jews were wondering what they were going to be doing in the cellars. First of all, it was the eve of Sukkot, they had to build sukkah huts, and were thinking about whether there would be food to eat in the sukkah. Whatever the case, they had to fulfill the commandments of the holyday of Sukkot. So they started to build sukkah huts. Among those courageous Jews was my own father. Half a sukkah was already ready, and then suddenly turmoil, a clamor. What happened?

Apparently a group of Bolshevik soldiers went to the front and were looking for people to show them the way to Somenitscha, which was on the front. Whoever knew had to go into hiding. When the commissar of the group noticed me standing in front of the house (I was a small child at that time), he wanted to take me along as his guide. I ran to my father to hide. In the meantime, the commissar saw my father next to the sukkah, and he went over to him and told my father that he would have to show him the way to the front. We desperately tried to appeal to him, and the commissar waved his hand and left.

After this, all the Jews went back into hiding, and the town seemed like a cemetery. The sukkahs remained standing unfinished. The first night of Sukkot arrived. No one could hear anything. The slightest ray of light shining through a crack in a window disappeared immediately. People were waiting for the next day that would bring some news. As soon as daylight appeared there were sounds of one shot, then another and a third. This was followed a half-hour later by bullets. Shots were fired from both directions, and a large amount of shrapnel tore through town. Dirt and wood was mixed up with smoke, rising several dozen meters into the air. The hum of grenades was deafening. No one could see anything besides earth and fire. Around the middle of the day the situation quieted down, and there were fewer grenades. From our hiding places we could see the Bolsheviks pulling back, and the first Polish soldiers appeared in town, followed by Polish army units.

C.

A few days passed peacefully. We were breathing easier, and we thought that our suffering and difficulties, which lasted for months, would be coming to an end. Unfortunately, we weren't lucky enough to avoid further suffering. The whole time the Poles were in Drohitchin there were ongoing problems. However, as soon as the Polish units went off to the front and the Bolokhov gangs pulled back, everyone became scared for his life. As soon as the Bolokhov gangs passed through, they started with their murderous acts. On every occasion they operated with a revolver. If there were no victims in the first days, this was thanks to the fact that the Jews remained in hiding. The priest decided to invite the rabbi and several householders to listen to a lengthy list of the sins that the town supposedly was engaged in with the Bolsheviks against them. Therefore, he decided to impose a tax in gold, without which a pogrom would be launched in town.

[Page 109]

As it later turned out, the current priest was already in town a few months earlier as the Bolshevik commissar. On the front he was taken prisoner by the Poles and volunteered to join the Bolokhov gangs.

The "priest's" warning made a deep impression on the Jewish delegation. The Jews were sure that he could do it. There was wailing, but they had to come up with the money. No one who had a few rubles refused; others gave a gold watch and other things. They collected quite a bit of money, though not the entire amount demanded. The delegation brought the money to the Bolokhovite, who since the outset was cursing and didn't let anyone speak. At first he refused to accept the smaller amount, but following appeals and begging, he relented and accepted the money.

The Bolokhov gangs left Drohitchin and carried out a massacre in Zakazelia. They went to Zakazelia (10 miles from Drohitchin), rounded up all the Jews and killed them. Seventeen Jews, young and old fell victim at the savage hands of the Bolokhovites, the Russian White Guards. One woman was lucky enough not to be noticed by the killers, but she was worried sick about her husband and took a sum of money to the killers, so they would free her husband. They took the money and then killed the woman along with her husband.

On that gruesome and wild day the only thing people could think about was burying the dead in a Jewish cemetery. The 17 victims were transported in wagons to Drohitchin. No one who saw that scene could ever forget it: a row of five wagons carrying 17 horribly mutilated and murdered victims. All the residents of Drohitchin attended, young and old, attended the funeral, and their wailing rose to the heavens.

If you go to the cemetery in town, you'll see a row of 17 graves, covered over by grass, leaving only the large gravestones describing the horrible event. D. B. W.

Gedalia Kaplan

A PRAYER
With awe and quiet words,
My lips recite a prayer for you.
You, my hometown, I'll always remember,
My heart pines away for you.
I wish I could see you again,
To just get a passing glance of you,
To see your streets, your little houses,
To feel your pure breath and soul.
All my life I dream dreams,
They are dissolved, because I scattered them.
Today they are all broken, crushed,
None of our dear ones remain there.
From "Chicago Periodical" - February, 1951

The wedding of Asher and Dina, son of R. Yoel Moshe, dispatcher of the train station. Top row, standing left to right: three klezmer performers, Leibetshka the Humorist, Pesach Sidorov, two girls from Kobrin, Mordechai Sidorov, Malka Khlevitsch and a klezmerer. Second row, from left: Yaakov Sidorov, Olkhovitch (son), 2 girls from Kobrin, Sarah Yitzchak-Yoel's, Rachel Sidorov, Lieba, Sarah and Mindel from Antapolia, Gittel and Pinya from Perkovitz, Chaya Bloom and Yitzchak Yoel's. Third row, seated from left: Yosef Shaul Olkhovitch and his wife, Dina and Asher Sidorov (bride and groom), Yoel Moshe and Beila Sidorov, the "lady cantor" (the grandmother) and Pinya Sidorov. Seated on the plank, from left: Leizer, Max, Aharon Yosef, Yaakov, Pessel and Lieba Frieda (standing: Yoel Moshe's children), and Freidel (Pinya Sidorov's daughter).

[Page 113]
PART TWO

RABBIS AND RITUAL SLAUGHTERERS
By E. Ben-Ezra (New York)

Rabbi Moshe of Drohitchin
1705-1781

One of the criteria for determining the greatness of a historical personality is the extent of legends that develop about him. A legend reflects how people saw the person, and that individual can be evaluated even though historical information is lacking.

Rabbi Moshe of Drohitchin (as he referred to himself) was just such a person. We never found a single piece of information about his life, so we have to make due with biographical information in legends, and extract the kernels of truth from them.

Apparently, Rabbi Moshe was born in Drohitchin, since in all of his books he signs his name, "Rabbi Moshe of Drohitchin," and in my estimation he was born no later than 1705. His father was Rabbi Yekutiel Zalman, who was a descendant of the family of Rabbi Eliezer Kharif, who was the head of the rabbinical court of Tiktin, and his maternal great-grandfather was the famous eminent scholar, R. Elayakim Getz, who started a chain of ten generations of great rabbinical scholars.

Rabbi Moshe was the head of the rabbinical court of Drohitchin, but no one knows when he started in that position. According to the title page of *Magid Mishnah,* he began the position of rabbi in Pinsk around 1745. Pinsk was where his father-in-law, R. Yehudah lived.

Apparently, Rabbi Moshe did not serve as rabbi in Pinsk for very long, because in 1746 he was appointed head rabbi in Sambar, Galicia. He served in that city as the highly revered head rabbi for about 25 years, if not longer, until he moved to the Holy Land. How did Rabbi Moshe, the rabbi of Drohitchin and Pinsk, become a rabbi in Galicia? What led to it?

In my estimation, Rabbi Moshe moved to Galicia because there were great kabbalists in Galicia, such as: R. Moshe Ostrer, R. Chaim Sanzer of Brody and others. Brody was a kabbalistic center in those days, where many kabbalists lived and studied the kabbalistic method of R. Isaac Luria (known as the *Arizal*) in opposition to the kabbalistic teachings of the messianic pretender, Shabtai Zvi. In Galicia, Rabbi Moshe found his place where he could flower and where he could share the company of rabbis who understood him and appreciated him.

Rabbi Moshe was not a kabbalist with a limited knowledge of the Talmud and decisors of Jewish law. On the contrary, he didn't acknowledge such kabbalists because whoever was not a great scholar in the Talmud and commentaries could never understand the secrets of the *Arizal.* Therefore, he devoted his entire being to such studies. When R. Moshe filled himself with Jewish law and Talmudic debate, he became involved in kabbalah, especially the kabbalistic system of the *Arizal.* This is when he came across the writings of Rabbi Emanuel Chai Riki, one of the commentators of the Lurianic [*Arizal's*] system (1688-1743), especially his book,

[*Page 114*]

Mishnat Chassidim, that was incomprehensible even to experts in kabbalah.

R. Moshe undertook to explain that book to its readers. R. Moshe completed that task with his commentary, *Magid Chassidim,* on the book,

Mishnat Chassidim. He received the approbations for his work from R. Yechezkel Landau, the author of *Nodah Be'Yehudah* as well as other esteemed scholars of that time.

Rabbi Moshe's commentary, *Magid Mishnah,* was very popular, and the Belzer Rebbe, R. Shalom, used to study it daily. Rabbi Moshe wasn't very pleased with his commentary, *Magid Mishnah,* because he felt that there were gaps here and there in the commentary, and in 1765 he published *Kiryat Arba,* a continuation of his earlier book. The second work also received the approbation from none other than the great kabbalist, Rabbi Zvi Hirsh of Zidichov, who praised him repeatedly in his own book, *Pri Kodesh Hillulim.* The book, *Kiryat Arba* was a widely used text, and it went out of print very quickly.

2.

As discussed earlier, R. Moshe studied Jewish law extensively. In this area as well, R. Moshe did not lag behind. He wrote novellae commentaries on difficult sections of the Talmud, and clarified certain difficult sections of the commentaries of *Tosafot* and of Maimonides on the Talmud. His commentaries were published in his book, *Chilukei de-Rabbanan,* to which the greatest rabbis gave their approbations.

The title page of the book indicates a number of significant details about R. Moshe. First of all, two or three years after he published *Kiryat Arba,* (1765) and his other book, *Chilukah de-Rabbanan* (1768), R. Moshe became very ill, and only recovered miraculously. During that illness, he was given the added name of "Yosef." This is certainly a hint to the verse in Isaiah 38:5, *I shall add [yosef] to your days.* Not only did his name change, but he changed as well. The event was an impetus for his to publish his book on Jewish law, *Chilukah de-Rabbanan.*

The same title page indicates that R. Moshe authored a work called *Beit Tefilah,* in which he discussed the importance of prayer according to the Lurianic system. However, the book was never printed. Another of his books that was never printed was *Merkavat Mishnah,* which deals with Jewish law and the writings of Maimonides.

In addition to that halachic work, R. Moshe also had a manuscript of a small treatise called *Mar'eh Ofanim,* in which he dealt with astronomy and the laws regarding the sanctification of the new month according to Maimonides. R. Moshe was very interested in astronomy because it is possible to understand the greatness of G-d through it. The treatise was held in high esteem by rabbis of that period. Nevertheless, only a small part of the *Mar'eh Ofanim* was published.

Rabbi Moshe evidently sought to distance himself from disputes. We don't find him to be involved in the dispute regarding the divorce certificate of Kleva. He was also not among the supporters or opponents of R. Yonatan Eibschutz and R. Yaakov Emden.

Rabbi Moshe was involved in his Talmudic and kabbalistic studies, and therefore stayed away from disputes even when they involved the greatest rabbis of his generation, and who were among his friends and associates.

[Page 115]

3.

I would now like to discuss a few of the legends surrounding R. Moshe, and consider them to be realistic. The famous chassidic leader, Rabbi Elimelech of Lizhensk, once said that R. Moshe's face shone like the Divine Presence. This legend indicates how highly R. Elimelech of Lizhensk and his colleagues respected R. Moshe.

There is also the legend that R. Emanuel Chai Riki, the author of *Mishnat Chassidim,* said that whoever writes a commentary on his book that isn't in consonance with the ideas of R. Emanuel would not live out the year. However, whoever writes a commentary that is in consonance with the ideas of R. Emanuel would merit being buried next to him. Rabbi Moshe lived out the first year after he published *Magid Mishnah,* and thereby understood that his commentary was acceptable. In his old age R. Moshe moved to the Holy Land to die and be buried next to R. Emanuel Chai Riki. The legend goes on to say that after R. Moshe died, people wanted to bury him next to R. Emanuel, but the plot was too narrow. However, as they dug deeper, they found that the spot widened, and they were thus able to bury him there.

In order to clarify the foregoing legend, we should refer to the statement of R. Moshe's son, R. Yitzchak, regarding his father's trip to the Land of Israel. R. Yitzchak wrote that all his life his father regretted that he couldn't travel to the Holy Land and kiss the ground. In his old age, he did get there, and was buried in Safed. It is a historical fact that R. Emanuel Chai Riki's grave is in Zento, Italy.

It is worth mentioning what R. Moshe wrote about himself. When he went to the grave of the Talmudic sage, R. Yehudah son of R. Ilai, located on a high mountain near Safed, R. Moshe didn't want to ride a donkey. However, because he was weak, he couldn't find his way. Then a miracle occurred: like an eagle, a strong wind carried him to the gravesite, where he performed kabbalistic formulae and attained a great spiritual level. Tears started flowing, and he was able to transcend physicality, at which time he was able to perform certain kabbalistic formulae in his study of Torah and in his prayers.

This description shows the great love and faith that R. Moshe had for kabbalah and its masters. R. Moshe went to Safed where the graves of great rabbis are located, and where he was also buried. He died in 1781, and on the 17th of Tammuz of that year, his son R. Yitzchak eulogized him in the new synagogue in Lemberg.

4.

R. Moshe was survived by four sons who became acclaimed for their great erudition and righteousness, as well as for their books, which were known among the rabbis of the generation:

- R. Yitzchak, known as R. Yitzchak Charif, the head of the rabbinical court in Olyanov and Sambar. He was the teacher of the famous kabbalist, Rabbi Zvi Hirsh of Zidichov. R. Yitzchak Charif was the author of *Pnei Yitzchak* (rabbinical responsa on the Code of Jewish Law, Shulchan Aruch), *Ha'Elef Lecha Shlomo,* and *Pnei Yitzchak Apei Zutra* on the Talmud. Yitzchak had four sons who served in rabbinical positions, and included rabbis and authors of important works on Jewish law.
- Rabbi Yehuda, the father-in-law of the Sambar rebbe, R. Moshe.
- Rabbi Yisrael Isser.
- Rabbi Gershon, the head of the rabbinical court in Glino.
  May the memory of R. Moshe of Drohitchin and his family never be forgotten for many many generations.

[*Page 116*]
EB"E

Rabbi Davidel Yaffe
1800
Creator of the Golem (*a man-like speechless creature created by kabbalists*) of Drohitchin
Even in distant past there were stories about how the Talmudic sages, Rabbi Chaninah and Rabbi Oshaya, created a calf. Another sage, Rava, created a man (see tractate Sanhedrin, p. 65). Rav Papa created a golem to act as Rav Papa's servant (tractate Hulin, p. 105). This was also recounted in Spain about the great poet, Shlomo Ibn Gabirol and the great scholar, Avraham Ibn Ezra.

Not only did these stories about golems circulate among Jews, but they circulated among gentiles as well. Such golems were said to have been created by alchemists and wise men (The character of the Frankenstein monster was said to have been modeled on the idea of a Golem.).

The most famous case of a Jewish golem was the one created by the rabbi known as the Maharal of Prague. This golem didn't only serve the Maharal, but also the entire Jewish community of Prague, which the golem saved several times from their enemies.

In Jewish legend there also existed the creature known as the Golem of Chelm, created by the head of the rabbinical court of Chelm, Rabbi Eliyahu, who lived approximately in 1500. It is also recounted that the Ba'al Shem Tov created a golem. The creation of golems was not thought of by kabbalists, but by halachic scholars as well. In Jewish law texts there is discussion of whether such a creature may be included in a prayer quorum (minyan) and other similar topics related to golems.

Therefore, the golem was part of reality, since there was no country where there weren't tales of great kabbalists creating them. One of the most recent golems was known as the Golem of Drohitchin, created by the head of the Drohitchin rabbinical court, Rabbi David Yaffe. We know very little about Rabbi Yaffe beyond the above legend that is known among Drohitchin émigrés and in the Jewish Encyclopedia.

As far as is known, Rabbi Yaffe was a descendant of Rabbi Mordechai Yaffe, the author of the book, *Ba'al Halevushim,* and he lived in approximately 1800. Rabbi David Yaffe was a kabbalist like his ancestor, R. Mordechai Yaffe, went a bit further, and became involved in practical kabbalah by creating a golem.

There are two versions of this golem legend: one is oral, and the other is written. The oral legend states that late every Friday afternoon, Rabbi David created a golem out of clay, which would bring water to the old synagogue and to the rabbi's house. At the end of the Sabbath, the rabbi would pronounce holy names in order to send away the golem. The written legend records that the golem was a type of *shabbos-goy* (*a non-Jew who agrees to perform actions on the Sabbath that Jews are prohibited to perform*) that during the winter Sabbaths the golem would heat ovens in Jewish homes. He wasn't asked to do this on the Sabbath itself, but prior to the Sabbath, in accordance with Jewish law pertaining to asking non-Jews to perform tasks prohibited to Jews on the Sabbath.

Due to a minor error that occurred when the golem was asked to perform a task that caused a fire, the whole town burned down. The story about the fire has a source: there is a tradition in the family of R. David that R. David warned his children that it was better to become involved in a trade rather than the rabbinate. It's possible that this was because of the huge fire that took place in town.

[Page 117]

His two sons, R. Zusha and R. Yeshayahu, heeded his request, as did R. Yeshayahu's two children, who took up trades. One of them became a brick mason and the other a builder. At the same time they changed their family names. One took the name Warshavsky. His descendants were the Warshavskys of Drohitchin; the other took the name Milner. These names were retained up until the present.

R. Yeshayahu's son, R. Yaakov, and his three sons didn't heed the above request. R. Yaakov was a rabbi in Kobrin, and his own son, R. David Yaffe, was a rabbinical judge in Kobrin. His other son, R. Moshe, was a rabbi in Pitshatz (Shedlitz gubernia). The third son, R. Mordechai, was rabbi in Goniadz (Grodno gubernia).

Twenty years ago, R. Hirsh Leib Levy, who was born in Drohitchin, stated that R. Davidel Yaffe left a kabbalah manuscript that is in the possession of one of his grandchildren or great-grandchildren in the United States. It's worth finding that manuscript and publishing it. It should exist as a cultural monument to one of the most eminent rabbis in Drohitchin, about whom we know very little. The Drohitchin émigrés should get involved so that no one should repeat the old saying, "He crawls like Rabbi Yaffe's golem."

R. Davidel Yaffe's grave and structure over the gravesite is still in the old cemetery in Drohitchin. Whenever someone in Drohitchin experienced problems, he would visit the holy man's grave, and light candles for spiritual purposes.

Note from editorial board:

There is a similar story about Rabbi Davidel in the *Yiddish Courier* of March 20, 1941, Chicago. Y.L. Wiecker writes the following:

"The most recent story of the creation of a golem was written to Dr. Davidel Yaffe of Drohitchin, Grodno gubernia in approximately 1800. Rabbi Davidel's golem had a task different from the Maharal's golem. The Maharal's golem had to do his job for six days and rested on the Sabbath. R. Davidel's golem had to work on the Sabbath, effectively serving as the *shabbos-goy*, heating the ovens in Jewish homes and the synagogues. The golem would receive his orders on Friday and performed his duties on time on Sabbath morning. Once someone made a minor error and ordered the golem to do something, which he performed automatically. The whole town went up in smoke." This is the story told in the *Yiddish Courier*.

"Rabbi Yisrael Baruch Warshavsky (Warsaw) of New York wrote us that his family had a tradition from his father, R. Yeshayahu, that R. Davidel had two other children: R. Eliyahu and R. Yoshka. R. Eliyahu had a son named Yisrael Baruch Warshavsky, and the Warshavsky family of Drohitchin was his descendants. Yisrael Baruch had six children: Shmuel Leizer (his children were Tuvia-David and Zusha Warshavsky); Yeshayahu (his children were Yehoshua, Eliyahu, David, Yisrael Baruch and Toiba Warshavsky); Mordechai (his children were Yaakov Zvi, Moshe, David and Faiga Rachel Warshavsky); Chaya Gittel (her children were Eliyahu, Lipman, Yisrael Baruch, Leizer, Avraham and Reichel Eisenstein); Esther Pessel Buder (her children were Eliyahu, Rachel Kotler and Baba Zlotnick); and Leah Fodor.

Yoshka had a son Todres Leib Milner, who was the ancestor of Milner family in Drohitchin. Todres Leib's children were Aharon Yeshayahu, Zadok, Yisrael David and Moshe Mendel Milner.

The description of R. David Yaffe's golem is also in *Hamagid* from 1867, number 42; Stories published by Wolf Pesheles pp. 2-51; Dr. Rubin, *Acts of Deception*, p.117.

[Page 117]
By E. Ben-Ezra (New York)

Rabbi Avraham Eisenstein
1800-1885

Introduction

The Land of Israel was always the dream of the Jewish People. Jews dreamed day and night about going there, and there was almost no generation where there wasn't some group of people moving there.

One of the greatest Jewish personalities who provided an impetus for that activity was Rabbi Eliyahu, known as the Gaon of Vilna. Even though his dream wasn't realized during his lifetime, his students undertook a large-scale immigration to the Land of Israel. Ten years after the death of the Gaon in 1808, the immigration began, and was led by his student, Rabbi Menachem Mendel of Shklov.

R. Menachem Mendel settled in Safed because the Jews of Safed where not as accustomed to the wild behavior of the Arab rulers as were the Jews in Jerusalem. This situation was due to the Jewish tax collector, R. Chaim Parchi, who had great influence over the Pashas of Akko (Acre).

Safed was an ideal place for the students of the Gaon. There were also not many Chassidim there as there were in Tiberias who were in a dominant position in relation to the non-chassidim. Emissaries were sent from Safed to encourage students of the Gaon to move to the Holy Land. This activity had an influence not only on the Gaon's students but also on other scholarly Jews as well. Wherever the emissaries stopped, they were welcomed with great honor, and they received funds for the Jewish community in Palestine.

One of the strongest supporters of the Jewish community in Palestine was R. Chaim, the head of the rabbinical court in Pinsk, and the father-in-law of R. Avraham Eisenstein.

I.

R. Avraham Eisenstein was born in Drohitchin in 1800. His father was named Zvi, but we know little about R. Avraham's youth. Information about him and his work begins when R. Avraham arrived in Palestine. R. Avraham arrived in Palestine with his father-in-law, R. Chaim, in 1826. His voyage took three months, and the travelers had to face seafaring robbers. In addition, the waters were very stormy and the sailboat was thrown from one wave to the next. When he arrived in Constantinople, the travelers had to continue over land, since there were military battles going on at sea.

They soon arrived in Safed, where the Gaon's students were concentrated and who were known as *Perushim (ascetics)*, since they separated themselves from worldly pleasures (such as wealth, business, enjoyment of food). A yeshiva had already been established in Safed years earlier, and where students studied Talmud and the Code of Jewish Law with the commentaries of the Gaon of Vilna.

[Page 119]

Spiritually speaking, Safed was an enjoyable place, but in terms of material comforts, the town wasn't doing well because the residents only received a third of the money collected from abroad. Nevertheless, economic problems did not stifle the growth of the Safed community.

In 1834, Safed experienced several catastrophes: an epidemic, and on the 15th of Iyar, (Saturday, May 24) two earthquakes. R. Avraham didn't leave Safed at that time. Later that year, when there was a pogrom against the Jews of Safed, R. Avraham and his family remained there.

That same year R. Chaim passed away, and R. Avraham was appointed a rabbinical judge in the rabbinical court of the *Perushim* in Safed. However, life did not go easily for him for very long. As if all the suffering and disturbances weren't enough, the great earthquake arrived on Monday, January 30, 1837 and destroyed the entire Jewish community. Only a few individuals survived. Among them were R. Avraham and his young daughter. His wife, son and other daughter were killed. Only then did R. Avraham leave Safed and move to Jerusalem.

2.

When R. Avraham settled in Jerusalem he remarried. His wife was the daughter of the famous community leader, R. Aryeh Ne'eman (Marcus). From then on R. Avraham was known as R. Avraham R. Aryeh's after his father-in-law. R. Avraham became involved in community activity, and there was almost no organization in which R. Avraham didn't take part. There was no public announcement that did not bear R. Avraham's signature. R. Avraham was the heart and soul of Jerusalem institutions that were in very dire straits.

He was then appointed as an emissary to Hungary, and when he organized the financial collection for Palestine, he returned home and put his heart and soul into work on behalf of the Jewish community of Palestine. He was one of the original founders of the Jerusalem charity organizations, and in 1866, when he established the General Community Council to unite all Ashkenazim in Jerusalem – both chassidim and non-chassidim – R. Avraham was the chairman and decision-maker.

R. Avraham sensed intuitively that it wasn't enough that the Ashkenazim of Jerusalem were unified. He sought to unify the Jewish communities of Jerusalem, Hebron, Safed and Tiberias, and purchased land for construction of houses for the poor. R. Avraham did all his work voluntarily, but did so as if he were receiving compensation for his work. Day in and day out he would come to the General Council building and would be among the first there and the last to leave. He behaved this way for 20 years and would even attend meetings when he was already 80 years old.

R. Eliyahu Mordechai, a son of R. Avraham Eisenstein; he was a trustee and treasurer of the Jerusalem rabbi, Shmuel Salant.

He requested that all Hebrew newspapers be available at the Council building. R. Avraham used to say, "The Council building is the heart of Jerusalem, and Jerusalem is the heart of the world. So it's worthwhile for the heart of the world to know what's going on with all its limbs." R. Avraham was also a member of the Jerusalem Chevra Kadisha (burial society), and he would often host the dinners for the Chevra Kadisha in his own home. However, he never took any enjoyment from them.

R. Avraham was also the rabbinical judge in the rabbinical court of the eminent scholar, Rabbi Meir Auerbach, but he did not take any money for his work. So how did R. Avraham support himself? He received a stipend from the Grodno Kollel (in the 19th and early 20th century, a *kollel* were communities of individuals from a particular place abroad who were assisted by individuals in those towns or cities), as well as from good friends who would send him money from time to time. However, in his old age, this source dried up.

[*Page 120*]

A typical market day in town. The new market and stores were rebuilt after the First World War.

3.

Apart from R. Avraham's interest in community issues, he was also interested in publishing manuscripts of famous scholars. When he rewrote them, he wouldn't change anything but would make comments and corrections wherever he felt great knowledge and understanding.

There is a story regarding one particular manuscript of the famous Talmudic commentary *Shita Mekubetzet* on the Talmudic tractate *Kodshim* (that deals with matters relating to the Jerusalem Temple). It is said that for 20 years he worked on that manuscript that he found on an old volume of Talmud in Jerusalem. With G-d's help he rewrote the manuscript, so that when a fire singed the edges of the manuscript, R. Avraham was able to restore it thanks to his great memory.

R. Avraham also published the novellae on the tractate of Rosh Hashanah written by the medieval Spanish Talmudic scholar known as the *Ritva* that R. Avraham obtained from a manuscript that he found in Jerusalem. He also published a manuscript of the commentary, *Ha-Meiri*. R. Avraham was interested in publishing manuscripts even if their contents weren't so important. He thus published novellae of the Spanish commentator known as *Rashba* (Rabbi Shlomo ben Adret) on tractate *Menachot*, even though many scholars have argued that this work was not written by *Rashba*, but by Rabbi Yeshayahu De-Trani.

This was the life of a Drohitchin Jew. He spent 60 of his 86 years in the Holy Land – 60 years of fruitful work, from which many are eating the fruits until today. The text of his gravestone:

Here is buried

Great in Torah and Good Deeds

Rabbi Avraham, son of Zvi Eisenstein,

Died on 6 Elul 5646

A facsimile of the signature of R. Avraham Eisenstein

[Page 121]
Raabis Yisrael Valevelsky and Zvi Eliyahu Reichman

As told by Rabbi Zusha Warshavsky, received from Rabbi Yisrael Be'eri (Kolodner) from the Land of Israel.

More than 100 years ago, Rabbi Yisrael Valevelsky lived in Drohitchin, and because of the small size of Drohitchin, he lived in abject poverty. Rabbi Valevelsky spent some time wandering throughout the country looking for another place to serve as a rabbi and where a community could provide him and his family with a livelihood. Therefore, in every city and town he would give speeches and make a small amount of money.

Rabbi Valevelsky once received an invitation from a town that wanted to offer him the position of town rabbi, and he immediately departed Drohitchin. Before his departure, he told the Drohitchin businessmen that if he didn't return within nine months, they could choose another rabbi. Nine months went by, and Rabbi Valevelsky didn't return. The community waited another two months but heard nothing from him. The community leaders called a meeting of the local community, and a decision was taken to appoint a new rabbi.

There was a large yeshiva in the town of Kossova that counted many scholars among its students. A delegation from Drohitchin traveled to Kossova and asked the local rabbi to recommend a worthy candidate for the position of rabbi of Drohitchin. The rabbi of Kossova paused briefly and then recommended the head of the yeshiva, Rabbi Zvi-Eliyahu, as rabbi of Drohitchin. As soon as the Drohitchin community leaders became acquainted with Rabbi Zvi Eliyahu, who was a real scholar and a pious individual, they sent Rabbi Zvi-Eliyahu a Letter of Appointment, and he became the rabbi of Drohitchin.

One year later the former rabbi, Rabbi Yisrael Valevelsky, came back to Drohitchin totally unexpectedly. He announced that since he didn't fulfill the agreement to return within nine months, he would not be claiming his position as rabbi of Drohitchin.

On the issue of the question of the position of rabbi there were two camps, especially by virtue of the fact that Rabbi Valevelsky had a large family in Drohitchin. A sharp dispute between the sides broke out that even resulted in violence; in one case, someone even hit someone else with a piece of wood. In view of the fact that the rabbinical dispute could lead to tragic results, and since Drohitchin could not support two rabbis, an agreement in Drohitchin was reached to resolve the question in a rabbinical court under the leadership of the rabbi of Slonim, Rabbi Eisel Kharif. The agreement also resolved to accept as rabbi of Drohitchin whomever won in the rabbinical court.

After hearing the claims of the two rabbis, Rabbi Kharif responded, "Both rabbis are correct. I cannot direct or compel either rabbi to leave Drohitchin. We are going to draw lots. Both rabbis will study a section of Talmud, and whoever provides me with three correct answers to my questions will be the rabbi of Drohitchin."

Both rabbis naturally agreed to the proposal, and they looked over the Talmudic material. A while later, Rabbi Zvi-Eliyahu stated that he was prepared to answer Rabbi Kharif's questions. Rabbi Zvi-Eliyahu responded with wisdom and erudition. Rabbi Kharif ruled that Rabbi Zvi-Eliyahu should remain in Drohitchin. Rabbi Valavelsky accepted the outcome and moved from Drohitchin to Yanova. After Rabbi Eliyahu passed away, his son, R.

Menachem, became the rabbi of Drohitchin. After R. Menachem, his own son-in-law, R. Isaac Yaakov Kalenkovich, became the rabbi of Drohitchin and was the last rabbi of Drohitchin.

[Page 122]
By Yosef Kallen (New York)

Rabbi Menachem Reichman

Rabbi Menachem Reichman

He was called "the Old Rabbi" and replaced his father, Rabbi Zvi-Eliyahu Reichman, as the head rabbi of Drohitchin for 40 years until he moved to Palestine. His wife, Riva Mindel, was the daughter of the famous lumber businessman, R. Moshe Hirsh Unterman.

Just like his father, Rabbi Menachem Reichman was the rabbi for everyone in Drohitchin. However, when his son-in-law, Rabbi Isaac Kalenkovich, became rabbi, two camps developed in town. In 1904, R. Menachem moved to Palestine. He arrived in Jerusalem on the day before Rosh Hashanah, and on the following 22 of Kislev, he passed away. His wife, Riva Mindel, died four years later, and both were buried on the Mount of Olives. When the sad news of the death of Rabbi Reichman got to Drohitchin, the community invited the famous preacher, R. Elyakim Getzel, to eulogize the great rabbi. R. Elyakim Getzel eulogized Rabbi Reichman for an entire week. Every day, between the afternoon and evening prayers he offered a two-hour long eulogy that moved everyone listening.

Riva Mindel was a true righteous woman. She devoted her entire life to helping her community, and would go around town collecting contributions. One day she would collect for the children's school; another day she would collect for poor brides. On Fridays she would collect challah for the poor, referred to as "bread for the poor." She supported a teacher for the children of poor parents who couldn't afford tuition.

All children who were born in Drohitchin during the year following Rabbi Reichman's death were named Menachem.

When he died, Rabbi Menachem was 76 years old. He had seven children: Reuven Reichman (a broker and circumcisor in Kiev); Yaakov Mordechai Richman (a tea and coffee wholesaler in Hartford, CT); Avraham Yosef Richman (in Chicago); Shmuel Richman (Chicago); Zvi Eliyahu Reichman (Brisk); Devorah Berman (a wine producer in Brisk), and Chana Yehudit Kalenkovich, the wife of the rabbi of Brisk, Rabbi Isaac Yaakov Kalenkovich, who occupied the position of rabbi in Drohitchin after Rabbi Reichman left for Palestine.

[*Page 123*]

Rabbi Isaac Yaakov Kalenkovich

Rabbi Isaac Yaakov Kalenkovich

The last rabbi of Drohitchin, Rabbi Isaac Yaakov *Kohen* Kalenkovich, was born in 1870 in the town of Klishchel (near Byalistock). His father, R. Yitzchak Shmaryahu Kalenkovich, was a scholar, merchant and community leader. Rabbi Isaac Yaakov's mother, Beila, was a businesswoman. All the landowning nobles of the area would come to shop in their store. Rabbi Isaac Yaakov had four brothers and two sisters. One brother, a rabbi, died very young, and this brother's wife later married the famous Rabbi Yisrael Meir Kagan, known as *Chafetz Chaim*, who raised one of the two remaining orphans.

Rabbi Kalenkovich spent his youth in the yeshivas in Grodno, Lomza, Slabodka and Volozhin. He received ordination from several rabbis including the great rabbinical leader, Rabbi Chaim Ozer Grodzinsky, the rabbi of Vilna.

In 1889, Rabbi Kalenkovich married Chana Yehudit Reichman, the elder daughter of the rabbi of Drohitchin, Rabbi Menachem Reichman. Between 1889-1903, Rabbi Kalenkovich spent his time in yeshiva studies, and his wife (with three small children) ran a small grocery store, which provided them with their livelihood.

In 1903, Rabbi Isaac Y. Kalenkovich officially became rabbi of Drohitchin after his father-in-law moved to Palestine. Rabbi Kalenkovich received no direct income from the community, but in his role as rabbi he had a type of monopoly on the sale of yeast, which provided him with some income. He had to pay rent from this income to the rabbinical judge, Rabbi Ze'ev Miller, the son-in-law of Moshe Poritzker.

Prior to becoming the rabbi of Drohitchin, Rabbi Isaac Yaakov suffered from the same dreadful lung ailment that brought about the sudden death of his brother, the rabbi. The doctors told Rabbi Isaac Yaakov that if he wanted to survive, he would have to be very careful about his health and hygiene. Evidently, this tragic event had a strong influence on the rabbi's way of life and his role as rabbi in the community.

Between 1910-1914 Rabbi Isaac Yaakov initiated the construction of the modern bathhouse and "ultra-modern" mikvah ritual bath in Drohitchin (the first ones of this type in the area). The ritual bath, he insisted, should be built from tile and fresh water provided for each bather. He argued that women couldn't be criticized for not immersing in the mikvah when the water wasn't clean.

Cleanliness and hygiene were of prime important to Rabbi Kalenkovich. He opposed the ritual of metzitzah (whereby the circumcisor removed blood after a circumcision with his mouth) as was the custom. Since he was a skilled circumcisor, he would use special cotton to draw out the blood. He even went further. If a circumcision was to be performed on a Sabbath, he would wash his hands and nails with soap (which is otherwise forbidden on the Sabbath). He also never kissed the Torah scroll when he was called up to the Torah (which occurred frequently because he was a Kohen), and did not kiss the tsitsit (prayer shawl strings).

[Page 124]

His two traditional yearly speeches (on the Sabbath before Yom Kippur and the Sabbath before Passover, as was customary in those days) were timely and consistent, and he dealt with local issues. He also never reported anyone to the gentile authorities, and never instructed women to wear wigs, or men to wear tsitsit because he believed his role as rabbi was to lead in community-wide issues. During the critical years of World War I, he organized citywide committees to assist the poor and needy. He led a struggle against the distillers who used wheat, rye and potatoes to make schnapps at a time when people were suffering from hunger.

Seated, from right to left: Rabbi Menachem and Mrs. Riva Mindel Reichman, Yosef and Sheina Golda Kalenkovich (grandchildren). Standing, from right to left: Rabbi Zvi Eliyahu Reichman, Mrs. Chana Yehudit Kalenkovich, Devorah and Rabbi Reuven Reichman, the children of Rabbi Menachem.

After World War I, Rabbi Isaac Yaakov dedicated all his energy to rebuild the ruined and burned down Drohitchin. With the aid of money from former residents of Drohitchin in the United States, a large synagogue was built on the site of the burned Old House of Study, as were a large religious school, public bath and workshop.

Thanks to his dedication to community issues, the rabbi established many good friendships. His house always a center where people could share their joys and sorrows with him. (A merchant who had a good business approached the rabbi and told him the details about his successful business. Another businessman came to ask the rabbi's advice on how to get out of a bad business arrangement).

The rabbi had a good business sense, which he inherited from his mother. He always gave good business advice. His devoted friends and visitors respected him greatly and were generous with financial contributions they gave him. This was especially true after a fire broke out twice at his house in a brief period, and his friends and supporters from Drohitchin in the United States made sure to provide him the means to build him a new house worthy of his stature.

In 1928, Chana Yehudit died after a brief illness. She was 58 years old. The death of his wife was a major blow to Rabbi Kalenkovich. In addition to having been a devoted wife and mother of her children, she was the family provider. Many years later, Rabbi Isaac Yaakov remarried. His new wife was a highly respected woman from Baranovich named Mrs. Michela Chafetz. She bore him a daughter named Beila.

Rabbi Isaac Yaakov took over the rabbinical position from his father-in-law, R. Menachem. None of Rabbi Isaac Yaakov's sons entered the rabbinate, and the family tradition passed from him to his son-in-law, Rabbi Shoel Margalit, who was a rabbi in Michalova (near Byalistock). Unfortunately, the branches of the tree were cut off. Rabbi Margalit and his family were killed by the German butchers. May G-d avenge their blood!

[Page 125]

Rabbi Isaac Yaakov Kalenkovich died in the ghetto and was fortunate to be buried in a Jewish cemetery (For more information, please see the section on the Holocaust. Ed.) His wife Michela and their daughter Beila were killed. May G-d avenge their blood!

Rabbi Isaac Yaakov had four sons and two daughters: Moshe (killed in Russia); Menachem (killed in Drohitchin with his family); Sheina Golda, Mrs. Margalit and Beila (killed); Yosef (who lives in New York) and Eliyahu (in Israel).

Information from Yosef Kallen

Rabbi Shoel Margalit

Rabbi Shoel Margalit was born in the town of Rotsk, near Suwalki. His father, R. Yehoshua, was an iron dealer, was a learned person and among the honored people in town. Rabbi Shoel was educated in the large Lithuanian yeshivas prior to World War I. He spent several more years in the Slabodka Yeshiva, where he was considered to be one of the outstanding students. In the winter of 1923, he became the son-in-law of the rabbi of Drohitchin, Rabbi A. Y. Kalenkovich. For a short time, until he was appointed the rabbi of

Michelova-Nezbodka, near Byalistock, R. Shoel was a member of his father-in-law's rabbinical court.

Rabbi Margalit, who was known as a great scholar and pious individual, was the only heir of his father-in-law's rabbinical position in Drohitchin. Had events been other than they were, he surely would have become the rabbi of Drohitchin. Unfortunately, Rabbi Shoel, his wife and four children (Shmerel, Rivka, Sara and Chana Yehudit) were killed together with his community. May G-d avenge their blood!

Right: Rabbi Shoel Margalit

Left: Mrs. Sheina Golda Margalit and children. From right: Shmerel, Rivka and Sarah (Chana Yehudit was born later). May G-d avenge their blood!

[*Page 126*]
By Rabbi Yehuda David Goldman (Chicago)

Rabbi Yosef Goldman

Rabbi Yossel, the *Dayan* (Rabbinical Judge)

My grandfather and teacher, Rabbi Yosef Goldman was known as R. Yossel the *Dayan*, from Drohitchin, and was born in Khomsk into a scholarly family in approximately 1825. My great-grandfather, the father of my grandfather, was R. Tzemach, a great Torah scholar. I still have some of his Talmudic writings.

Rabbi Yosef Goldman – R. Yossel the *Dayan*

My grandfather, R. Yossel, once told me that a delegation from Pinsk once offered my great-grandfather the position of head rabbi of Pinsk, but R. Tzemach didn't want to take the position. He justifies his view from the Talmudic maxim: "If a person has lived out most of his allotted years without sinning, he should not then allow himself to sin." As far as R. Tzemach was concerned, since he had reached old age and had not become a rabbi, he therefore did not wish to become one now. He considered himself as one of those who feared instructing others, meaning that he didn't want to take on the responsibility of being an appointed rabbi. It is also told that when the rabbi of Klomsk would travel to visit R. Tzemach to ask him questions relating to Jewish law, R. Tzemach would hide. His wife (my great-grandmother), Nisha Chana, who was known as a righteous woman, would say, "What do you want from him? He doesn't know anything and is unlearned."

My grandfather, R. Yossel, was one of the first students in the newly established Mir Yeshiva, and was known as the Genius of Khomsk. When he got older he became the son-in-law of R. Yudel David Kosovsky of Drohitchin, who I am actually named after, and who was the rabbinical judge of Drohitchin and one of the leaders of the community. When the great scholar and rabbi of Drohitchin, Rabbi Zvi Eliyahu, died, two camps developed in town. One group wanted Rabbi Zvi Eliyahu's son, R. Menachem Reichman, to become the rabbi in town. The other group wanted my grandfather, R. Yossel, to occupy that position. After a rabbinical court case, and the judges ruled in favor of R. Menachem, who became the rabbi of Drohitchin.

I remember that when we were living in Brisk (because my mother, Chaya Liftsha, was from there, and her entire family lived there), a tall Jew with an imposing countenance came to our house from Drohitchin. As soon as the man left, my father said to me, "That Jewish man who was just here was the leader of the group opposed to your grandfather. That man was very arrogant and his group chose him specially so that he could oppose grandfather and make him lose his case."

My grandfather was a rabbinical judge in Drohitchin for over 60 years. He never made much money from that position, so he studied Talmud privately with some older students. His wife, grandmother Esther, had a store at the town market, and was able to make some money that way.

My grandfather had four sons and one daughter. One of the sons was my father, Eliyahu, who was a great scholar and educated in secular subjects as well. My father was considered one of the most respected people in Brisk.

In connection with this, it's worth mentioning the following story: While I wasat the Slabodka Yeshiva, the great rabbinical leader and rabbi of Brisk, Rabbi Chaim Soloveitchik came to the yeshiva for a visit. As was customary, hundreds of students came to visit him at the Dagmar Hotel. When I went there and mentioned my father's name, R. Chaim answered, "Oh, R. Eliyahu, he's a dear person!"

[*Page 127*]

R. Eliyahu Goldman, father of Rabbi Yehuda David Goldman

My grandfather had only one brother, known as Zissel R. Tzemach's. His full name was R. Alexander Ziskind, and he was named after the author of the great scholar from Grodno who wrote *Yesod Shoreseh Ha'avodah [Principles of the Base of Divine Service]*. My grandfather's brother, R. Zissel, was also the father of my father-in-law, Rabbi Mordechai Zundel Rubenstein, who studied together on Volozhin with the great scholars, R. Moshe Mordechai Epstein and my teacher, R. Baruch Ber Leibovitz. My father-in-law was also the author of many books, including *The Jewish Man* and *My Travels in Russia*.

My grandfather, R. Yossel, died at the height of the First World War under a hail of bullets that fell on Drohitchin on the eve of Rosh Hashanah, 1915. Together with the rest of the Jews, my grandfather ran for shelter into the trench on the Vion. On the last night of the battle he left the trench and went into a nearby house (belonging to Sanny the Pot Maker) where he gave up his holy soul. Together with my uncle Yitzchak Efraim's, my father, R. Eliyahu, who was also in Drohitchin at that time, buried my grandfather in the old cemetery near the graves of the martyrs of Osevitz. Later, when my wife, child and I returned from Motele (where we saw the arrival of the Germans), Zeidel Steinberg (the son of Naftali the teacher) and I built a structure over the grave of my grandfather. As mentioned, my uncle Yitzchak Efraim's was known as Yitzchak the Mishiver and was a land tenant. Among other estates, he leased the Stanislav and Rakum estates. Yitzchak Efraim's was a major community leader in Drohitchin.

At his death, my grandfather was about 90 years old and had been in Drohitchin for more than 60 years. He was respected and admired by everyone with mere mention of his name. His photo still hangs in the homes of many Drohitchin Jews living in the United States. He was one of the finest individuals ever produced in the Polesia region. In addition to being a great teacher, he also got along well with people. He had a shining countenance and a constant smile on his face. He never became angry, and always tried to judge people favorably. He was our pride. I remember how on one eve of Yom Kippur, our entire family, young and old, would go to grandfather for a blessing. He would lay his hands on each person's head and would bless us with tears in his eyes.

As stated above, my grandfather had four sons and one daughter, none of who are still living. However, his grandchildren and great-grandchildren currently live in Israel, New York, Philadelphia, Virginia, St. Joseph, Missouri and Chicago. It can be said about our grandfather that the glory of the children is their parents.

[*Page 128*]
By Yisrael Baruch Warshavsky

Rabbi David Mordechai Yudovsky

Rabbi David Mordechai Yudovsky

(Died in 1913)

The great Rabbi David Mordechai Yudovsky died on the first day of Shavuot, at the age of 46. He was a rabbi in Drohitchin for 12 years, and we loved him greatly, because in addition to the fact that he was a great scholar and a famous speaker, he excelled in personal character traits and good deeds. In order to accurately describe Rabbi Yudovsky, I would like to relate his biography.

The great Rabbi David Mordechai Yudovsky was born in Kuznitza, a small town near Grodno, to poor parents. In his youth he already demonstrated great devotion to his religious studies, and when he decided to travel to the Volozhin Yeshiva without any financial means to do so, he decided to walk to Volzhin by foot, without even a morsel of bread to stave off his hunger. When he arrived at the Yeshiva, the head of the school was Rabbi Zvi Leib, and Rabbi Yudovsky became known as the Scholar from Kuznitza.

He arrived in Drohitchin 26 years ago, when he was a newly married young man. At that time no one even knew where he came from or how he ended up in Drohitchin. All we knew was that the "ascetic" (as he was known in town) studied Torah night and day. He had a permanent place to study in the old House of Study near the oven where he studied with intense devotion. Once in a while he would get up and stroll around the House of Study behind the Torah-reading platform and then return to his seat and his books. He would only separate himself from his books during prayer services, at which time he used to stand behind the Torah-reading platform and pray quietly and modestly without anyone even noticing him.

During this 14-year period, his single goal was to absorb as many books as possible without expecting a rabbinical post. People felt that Rabbi Yudovsky himself was a book together with the rest of the books surrounding him. He earned a livelihood from the community and usually lived on the edge of poverty. Then his situation changed, which led to his untimely death.

The old rabbi in town traveled off to Palestine and was replaced by his son-in-law. This led to the community being divided into two camps. One side chose the rabbi's son-in-law as rabbi. The late Rabbi Yudovsky had to put up with a great deal from his own followers who wouldn't stop at anything. In fact, there were even many cases of informing on other Jews to the gentile authorities, and people were feeling intense fear and suffering. However, it soon ended, and even the opponents had to keep quiet; many even eventually became good friends of the rabbi.

[Page 129]

The problems that Rabbi Yudovsky experienced slowly had their effect on his health, and he later became ill with tremendous physical suffering. Three months ago, Rabbi Yudovsky came down with TB, which eventually took his life.

The death of Rabbi David Mordechai Yudovsky was an irreplaceable loss. We lost both a great Torah scholar and a good friend of everybody. He had a place in his heart for everyone, and shared every person's problems. He always offered a consoling word for anybody. Any out-of-town visitor or downtrodden person would find his way to Rabbi Yudovsky, who would never ignore anyone, no matter how unknown that person was to him. He was a person who was willing to give large amounts of charity with a full hand even when he scarcely had enough for himself.

Mrs. Rachel Yudovsky, wife of Rabbi Yudovsky

Rabbi Yudovsky never wavered from the truth, even when it pertained to his own benefit, as the following case illustrates. When he was asked if there was anything that his own family needed, he responded that he didn't need anything, since G-d would not abandon them just like he hadn't abandoned him. When he was asked if his son-in-law was suitable to become a rabbi, he responded that although he was a great scholar and was suitable, he warned that his son-in-law could not become a rabbi without the agreement of the greatest scholars.

(Comments from the editor: Some time later, Rabbi Yudovsky's son-in-law Rabbi Noach Kohn, replaced his father-in-law and assumed the rabbinical post on the "Polish side" in Drohitchin until 1929, when he and his family moved to the United States. Rabbi Yudovsky's wife and two daughters arrived in the United States before World War I and settled in Baltimore. Their only son, Moshe, remained in Poland where he studied in the yeshivas. His last yeshiva was in Vilna, where he shared the fate of the rest of the Jews of Vilna.)

Zalman Shevinsky, a member of the "Polish side," told the following story about Rabbi Yudovsky:

Rabbi Mordechai Yudovsky received a letter of rabbinical appointment from a certain town that wanted to invite him to leave Drohitchin. In cooperation with the business leaders, he called a meeting to discuss the issue. All invited businessmen came to the meeting on time. They were gathered in the synagogue and were waiting for the rabbi to come out of his private room. They continued to sit and wait, but it got late and the rabbi didn't come out. R. Nachum Shevinsky (Zalman's father) and a few other businessmen went into the rabbi's room, where they found him deeply engrossed in his studies, and they asked him, "Rebbe, we came to talk about your issue, so why are you silent and won't come out to meet us?"

Rabbi Yudovsky responded, "I have been thinking over what it would mean if I were to receive a higher income in the other town. Then what? No, I won't go there, I am going to stay here with you. Just fix the roof on the synagogue, and repair the invalid Torah scroll. That's all I ask of you."

Another story: Rabbi Yudovsky drew up a sale certificate for R. Nachum Shevinsky, which took a long time, of course. The rabbi had to check his books and write such-and-such. Shevinsky then offered the rabbi five rubles for his work. Rabbi Yudovsky started to tremble, "G-d forbid that I should take any money from you. You buy yeast from me; that's my fee. It's enough." Rabbi Yudovsky didn't take any money.

The rabbi was entirely unimpeachable, and therefore no other testimony about his honesty and purity is necessary.

[Page 130]

Rabbi Ze'ev Miller

(R. Velvel the *Dayan*)

Rabbi Ze'ev Miller and Mrs. Miriam Miller

Rabbi Ze'ev Miller, known as "Velvel the *dayan* ," was born in 1868 to his father, R. Aharon, a distinguished merchant in Kletsk, and was educated in Kletsk, and later in Volozhin, where he received rabbinical ordination.

In 1890, R. Velvel approached the Drohitchin leader, R. Moshe Poritzker-Valevelsky, to marry his daughter and become R. Velvel's son-in-law. Over a period of several years, R. Velvel settled in town and continued his studies in the House of Study while he waited for an opportunity to obtain a rabbinical post, which soon arrived. When the aged rabbi of Drohitchin, R. Menachem, left for Palestine and turned over his rabbinical post to this son-in-law, Rabbi Isaac Kalenkovitch, Rabbi Miller was appointed rabbinical judge in Rabbi Kalenkovitch's rabbinical court.

In 1911 Rabbi Miller moved to Sernik, near Pinsk, where he served in the post of rabbi until 1940, when he died in a Pinsk hospital after a difficult operation. Rabbi and Mrs. Miller had four sons and three daughters. Of the entire family, only one daughter – Sarah Mirsky – survived because she had left for the United States many years earlier. In addition, one son – R. Hirsh Miller – survived because he escaped the German murderers, and arrived in the United States after going through Russia, Japan and Shanghai. Rabbi Hirsh Miller was the son-in-law of the rabbi of Shanghai, Rabbi Ashkenazi.

Mrs. Miriam Miller and the following children was killed (May G-d avenge their blood!): R. Aharon from Lennen (near Lunenetz); R. Leib, the rabbi of Sernik; R. Menachem, the rabbi of Wisotsk (near Pinsk); and daughters Chana and Perl and their families.

[Page 131]
Rabbi Noach Kohn

Rabbi Noach Kohn

Rabbi Noach Kohn, the rabbi of the "Polish camp" in Drohitchin, was born in 1891 into a rabbinical family in Kamenitz-Litovsk. His father, Rabbi Yeshayahu Kohn, was one of the most highly respected people in town.

When he was still a youngster, Noach demonstrated great enthusiasm in Torah study and attended the yeshiva of Rabbi Baruch Ber Leibovitz in Slobodka. Later he went off to the Volozhin yeshiva, where he studied intensively for many years. In approximately 1913, R. Noach became the son-in-law of R. David Mordechai Yudovsky in Drohitchin.

R. Noach continued his studies for a period of time after his wedding, preparing for a rabbinical post. He was then ordained by Rabbi Rafael of Volozhin and Rabbi Baruch Ber Leibovitz, two of the greatest rabbinical scholars and yeshiva heads. After the death of Rabbi Yudovsky, R. Noach took his father-in-law's place, but he was not able to have an uneventful life, since soon thereafter World War I broke out, bringing in its wake years of suffering and pain. Rabbi Kohn's home and House of Study, together with other Jewish houses, was burned down during the war. Many local businessmen died during the typhus epidemic, though Rabbi Kohn, his wife Etka, and their small children survived fear and hardship.

Despite his personal hardships, Rabbi Kohn often interceded with the German authorities on behalf of the residents of Drohitchin. He was able to win the release of many Jewish men who were given heavy punishments for evading forced labor. After the war, R. Noach Kohn decided to rebuild his house, but he faced great hardship in earning a living, and didn't see a good future for himself in Drohitchin, so he decided to move to the United States.

In 1929, he and his family arrived in Baltimore, where he was accepted as the rabbi of the Tavrig synagogue, *Anshe Emunah. (Men of Faith)*. He and his family felt themselves fortunate when after so much hardship and wandering, things finally became easier. They were provided with income and anticipated a good future for their children. Their older son studied in Rabbi Yitzchak Elchanan's yeshiva in New York (early forerunner of Yeshiva University) and was preparing for ordination. Unfortunately, this son suddenly became gravely ill and died. This misfortune struck a heavy blow to Rabbi Kohn and his own health suffered because of it. In 1938 during the week of Sukkot, R. Noach died suddenly from a heart attack.

He was survived by his wife, Etka, and a son and a daughter, but without any means of support. However, with the assistance of good friends, Etka was able to open a bookstore in Baltimore that was a successful undertaking. The children were soon married; the daughter married a rabbi, and the son remained in the business.

Details are from Y. B. Warshaw

[Page 132]
Rabbi Asher Eisenstein

Rabbi Asher Eisenstein was born in Drohitchin; his parents were R. Berl and Toiva. In Drohitchin, R. Asher was known as "Asher Toiva's" even though he rarely visited Drohitchin.

I first met R. Asher in approximately 1923, when I went to study at the Grodno yeshiva. At that time Rabbi Eisenstein was the head of the elementary school division of the yeshiva, and it goes without saying that Rabbi Eisenstein was extremely kind to me, and I frequently visited him at his home.

R. Asher was educated in the large yeshivas of Slobodka, Volozhin and others, and was ordained into the rabbinate by the great scholars and heads of yeshiva, Rabbi Isser Zalman Meltzer and Rabbi Baruch Ber Leibovitz. In the yeshivas, R. Asher was known as "R. Asher Drohitchiner," and was greatly respected. He was considered a great scholar and a man of great character. It is said that Rabbi Chaim Soloveitchik greatly admired R. Asher, who became very close to Rabbi Soloveitchik. He was especially distinguished at the Grodno yeshiva and held in high esteem by Rabbi Shimon Shkop.

Rabbi Asher Eisenstein

R. Asher was very creative in his Talmudic studies, and he wrote many of his own Torah commentaries, though I don't know if he ever published any of his manuscripts. Rabbi Eisenstein's wife was an attractive and educated woman; she was the daughter of the rabbi of Yashinovka (near Byalistock). Although they had no children, their life together was idyllic and satisfying.

In approximately 1926, Rabbi Eisenstein was selected as the rabbi of Semiatitsch, near Byalistock. A yeshiva student (Chaimovich) and I were selected by the yeshiva administration to accompany R. Asher to Semiatitsch, where R. Asher was welcomed with great respect and affection. Over the years, I lost contact with Rabbi Eisenstein, and never heard from him again. I have heard that he and his wife shared the same fate as the other Jewish martyrs in Poland. Rabbi Eisenstein had a brother, Shimon, a full-time yeshiva student, and one sister. They were all killed, except for two sisters who were in Palestine.

Rabbi Eliyahu V. Altwarg

Rabbi Eliyahu Velvel Altwarg

Rabbi Eliyahu Velvel Altwarg was born in Drohitchin. His father, R. Chaim Ber the glassmaker, was a respected businessman from the Street House of Study, and served as the teacher of the Mishnah study group. Nothing is known about R. Velvel's youth; all that is known is that studied at the Slobodka yeshiva. He married the daughter of a rabbi in Lithuania, and for a few years before World War I, he was the rabbi of Vidz, a town in Lithuania.

When World War I broke out, R. Eliyahu Velvel and his family went to Drohitchin, where he remained thereafter and served unofficially as the rabbi of the Street House of Study. He would give speeches on the holydays and on various other occasions.

Later, when the rabbi of the "Polish side," rabbi Noach Kohn, left for the United States, some Jews from the "Polish side" started buying yeast from Rabbi Altwarg, which stirred opposition from the supporters of the official rabbi, Rabbi Kalenkovitch, who had previously purchased the rights to sell yeast from Rabbi Kohn. These supporters brought the rabbi of Pinsk, Rabbi Aharon Walkin, to Drohitchin to resolve the controversy. Unfortunately, no resolution was attainable, and R. Eliyahu continued selling yeast. His wife helped him in this business, and was a virtuous woman and community leader. R. Eliyahu Velvel had three sons and one daughter.

[Page 133]
His eldest son, Moshe, was a yeshiva student. None of their children survived. May G-d avenge their deaths! R. Eliyahu Velvel's father, R. Chaim Ber, was killed by the Germans near his house, and a gentile neighbor buried him in the neighbor's courtyard. May G-d avenge his death!

Rabbis Yosef David Schub, Yaakov and Hershel Shuster

Rabbi Yosef David Schub

Rabbi Yosef David Schub ("R. Yossel David, the ritual slaughterer" [the letters of the name Schub are an acronym for " *Shochet ve-Bodek – Slaughterer and Examiner*]) was descended from a good scholarly family in Drohitchin. R. Yossel David and his brothers, R. Yekef (Yaakov) and R. Hershel, learned for years in yeshiva and were ordained rabbis. His sister's husband was the son of the rabbi of Ovel, and was a scholar who died young.

R. Yossel David's father, R. Sender Shuster (this was his family name), who sold second-hand boots to the peasants, was an ordinary synagogue-attending person. R. Sender and his wife experienced misfortune in their youth: Zissel, R. Sender's wife, had broken her foot and remained crippled for the rest of her life. Women used to say that because of this misfortune, G-d repaid Zissel with good children. Everyone envied Sender and Zissel's scholarly children.

In 1912 R. Yossel married Mar-Yasha Hoffman, the daughter of R. Binyamin Moshe, the ritual slaughterer of Drohitchin. When his father-in-law died, R. Yossel David became the ritual slaughterer of Drohitchin, and then changed his last name from Shuster to Schub (Slaughterer-Examiner). R. Yossel David was extremely active in Drohitchin community life. His talent as a speaker helped him significantly in his community activities. He was always the lead speaker at community meetings, and taught Talmud in the Old House of Study.

In 1920, his wife, Mar-yasha, passed away, leaving him with two small children, a boy and a girl. He later remarried and had another daughter. His son, Binyamin Moshe, studied in yeshivas, and his daughter, Nechama, eventually married and moved to Kamin-Kashirsk.

R. Yossel David's second brother, R. Yekef, married a woman from Kovel, and his youngest brother, R. Hershel, married a woman from Ruzhinoy. Both remained in those towns. No one of that large family survived. They were all killed. May G-d avenge their blood (See pp. 149-150)!

Rabbi Asher Berzovsky

Rabbi Asher Berzovsky was born in Drohitchin. His father, Yitzchak Berzovsky owned a house near the bridge on Kobrin Street. We have almost no information about Rabbi Berzovsky. We only know that he was a rabbi (after World War I) in some town near Lomza, and I don't remember him ever having visited Drohitchin. Rabbi Berzovsky and his family and community were killed. May G-d avenge their blood!

Rabbi Yitzchak Siddur (Sidorov)

At the beginning of the 19th century there lived in Drohitchin a cantor/ritual slaughterer named R. Yitzchak, son of R. Avraham. We don't know where R. Yitzchak came from, or when he came to Drohitchin. Apparently, one of his sons, Yoel Moshe (born in Kislev, 1818) inherited his position in Drohitchin.

R. Yoel Moshe's position was taken over by his son, R. Yitzchak Siddur (Sidorov) or "the old cantor," the name R. Yitzchak was known by. He was a son-in-law of a distinguished Grodno family. R. Yitzchak was a gifted cantor who was known throughout the region. He died at an advanced age in approximately 1910 and must have been around 90 years old. His wife, Chaya-Gittel, was known as the "cantor's wife," and was a modest woman who was active in community life and very popular in town. (See page 110).

[Page 134]
Rabbi Yehuda David Goldman

Rabbi Yehuda David Goldman

Rabbi Yehuda David Goldman was born in Drohitchin. His father, R. Eliyahu, was a famous scholar and educated man, and was one of four sons of the great Rabbi Yosef Goldman, who was known as R. Yossel the Rabbinical Judge. His mother, Chaya Lifsha, was from a highly respected family in Brisk.

When young Yehuda David was only four years old his parents moved to Brisk from Drohitchin. In Brisk he studied under the finest teachers in town, and after finishing his elementary yeshiva education, where he was able to learn a page of Talmud with *Tosafot* and other commentaries, Yehuda David was then able to study on his own in the *Mishmar* House of Study in Brisk and to attend the classes of the heads of the yeshiva, R. Simcha Zelig and R. Moshe Soloveitchik.

Later, he went to study in the yeshivas of Ludmir (near Kovel) and Lomza, where he was considered one of the best yeshiva students. He also studied Torah and secular subjects for two years in the yeshiva of R. Yitzchak Yaakov Reines, the founder of the religious Zionist Mizrachi movement. Rabbi Goldman also attended the lectures of Rabbi Shlomo Poliatshik and then traveled to the *Knesset Beit Yitzchak* Yeshiva in Slabodka headed by the illustrious Rabbi Baruch Ber Leibovitz, where he studied intensely for three years.

Rabbi Goldman then spent two years at the Ponevezh Yeshiva headed by Rabbi Yitzchak Yaakov Rabinovitch, known as R. Itsele Ponivezher. The Ponevezh Yeshiva was composed of only 12 unmarried boys and eight married young men and was founded and maintained by the famous Wisotzky family.

Rabbi Mordechai Zundel Rubinstein

In 1913, Rabbi Yehudah David Goldman married Sarah Ester, the daughter of rabbi Mordechai Zundel Rubinstein, the author of *Ish Yehudi (Jewish Man), My Travels in Russia* and others. Rabbi Rubinstein, who lived his entire life in Molodetschna (near Vilna), was the son of Rabbi Alexander Ziskind Rubinstein, known as "R. Zissel R. Tzemach's" from Khomsk (near Drohitchin).

After his wedding, R. Yehudah David studied in the Volozhin Yeshiva, where he was ordained in 1914 by the eminent scholar, Rabbi Rafael Volozhiner. Rabbi Goldman remained in Brisk, and when World War I broke out, he moved to Drohitchin. In 1921 he and his family moved to Chicago. In Chicago Rabbi Goldman served as rabbi in the following synagogues: Bais Avraham (3017 South Wabash Avenue) and at the same time led the Pesach Neierman Talmud Torah for ten years, Sha'arei Shalom and Beis Eliezer (Drexel Boulevard). From 1933 to 1954 Rabbi Goldman served as rabbi at the Bais Yisrael-Anshei Yanovo synagogue (3905 14th St.) and finally at the Machzikei Hadat synagogue in place of Rabbi Chaim Mednik, who died on December 31, 1954.

Rabbi Goldman often visited the Louis Institute where he studied English language and literature. He knew Hebrew and occasionally wrote in English and Yiddish in various newspapers and magazines. Rabbi Goldman was the executive director of the Chicago Rabbinical Center; a director of HIAS, the Beit Midrash la-Torah, the Educational Committee, Jewish Parochial School, and Oak Forest. He was the finance secretary of the synagogue division of the Combined Jewish Appeal; secretary of *Keren Hatzolah (Relief Fund,* director of Mizrachi and a local Passover food fund, and secretary of the united committee of the *Beit Elmen's* in Waldheim.

Rabbi and Mrs. Goldman had three sons and one daughter: Alexander Ziskind, a student in the Beit Midrash la-Torah an accountant; Rabbi Eliyahu, the rabbi of the West Oakline Jewish Community Center in Philadelphia; Rabbi Yosef, a rabbi in Norfolk, Va.; and Mrs. Chaya Lifsha (Eileen) Keiths, a social worker and a teacher at the College of Jewish Studies. His son-in-law Nachum (Norman) Keiths is a senior engineer in a large firm, and is a former president and leader of the Zionist Youth Movement in Chicago.

Rabbi Mordechai Minkovitch

Rabbi Mordechai Minkovitch (Minkov) was born in Boten, near Slonim. His father, R. Shalom Shachna, was a distinguished businessman in town who gave his children a genuine Jewish education. Until the age of 12, young Mordechai studied in the Slonim yeshiva, where he entered the Mir yeshiva under the great scholar, Rabbi Chaim Leib a half year later. He also spent some time in the yeshivas of Navardok and Zhaludok. From Zhaludok he went to the eminent Moltsh yeshiva, which was headed by the great Rabbis Zalman Sender and later, Shimon Shkop. Rabbi Minkovitch also studied at the Radin yeshiva and finally, in a yeshiva for married men in Eishishok, where most of the boys and men were involved in teaching as preparation for the rabbinate. It was in Eishishok that Rabbi Minkovitch received his ordination.

After that same year, 1899, when he was ordained, Rabbi Minkovitch married Chana Beila, the young daughter of R. Moshe Poritzker (Valevelsky) of Drohitchin. They had five children – two sons and three daughters. During the time he was living in Drohitchin, he didn't serve as a rabbi and was more interested in his leather business, which he opened and did well in following his wedding. His wife, Chana-Beila, who was a very virtuous woman, was deeply involved in helping him in business. Rabbi Minkovitch was heavily involved in community affairs and taught a Talmud class in the Old House of Study for 23 years. He also led the *Mussaf* prayer services there during the High Holydays. He was involved in many activities and was highly respected.

In 1924, Rabbi Minkovitch and his family arrived in the United States following the suggestion of his friend from the Zhaludok yeshiva, Rabbi Yisrael Rosenberg (president of the Rabbinical Association of the United States). In the United States, R. Mordechai again went into business, and with the assistance of Drohitchin émigrés in New York, he opened a grocery store, which was very successful, as was his wholesale oil business.

R. Mordechai was an unpaid rabbi at the Drohitchin synagogue in New York for three years, and also taught a class at the Yavneh yeshiva. He then served four years as the rabbi in the Volkovisk synagogue (New York) and later in a Bronx synagogue.

His wife, Chana-Beila, suddenly passed away; she was his housewife, and her death was a great blow to R. Mordechai. Some years later he married Rivka, a daughter of Shimon the doctor. When he reached old age, R. Mordechai stopped his community activities, and now his two sons, Yisrael and Michael run his businesses. They follow the path of Judaism and the traditions of their parents. R. Mordechai also had three daughters: Sarah, Yehudit and Esther.

[Page 136]
Rabbi Yisrael Be'eri Koldodner

Rabbi Yisrael Be'eri Kolodner

Rabbi Yisrael Be'eri Kolodner was born in 1911 in Drohitchin. His father, known as "R. Shmuel Getzel's," was from a wonderful family in Antopolia. His mother, Sarah, who died when he was only seven years old, was the daughter of an important Drohitchin businessman, R. Getzel Kaplan, who was the father of two rabbis: Rabbi Shmuel Yisrael Kaplan, the rabbi of Kolna (near Lomza), and Rabbi Avraham Yehuda Kaplan, the rabbinical judge of Yanovo.

R. Shmuel strove to maintain the tradition of the family, and provided his son Yisrael with a sound religious education under the teachers in town. At 17, young Israel was sent to study elsewhere. He spent three years in the Novardok yeshiva, Beit Yosef, in Pinsk (headed by R. Moshe Reiz); six months in the Novardok yeshiva in Byalistock under R. Avraham Yaffen; 10 years in the Kamenitz yeshiva, Knesset Beit-Yitzchak, under Rabbi Baruch Ber Leibovitz and his son-in-law, R. Reuven Grozovsky.

After receiving ordination from Rabbi Baruch Ber and Rabbi Weinstein (who headed Yeshiva Beit Yosef in Pinsk), Rabbi Kolodner moved to Palestine in 1933, where he spent several years studying in the Hevron Yeshiva in Jerusalem. In 1938, R. Yisrael became the son-in-law of the famous Jerusalem rabbi and kabbalist, R. Yaakov Moshe Charlap, and with the help of his wife, Chana Dina, R. Yisrael, was able to devote himself to his studies under his father-in-law.

In 1943, R. Yisrael was appointed a rabbi in the old colony of Nes Ziona, where he excelled in various areas. He taught Talmud to elderly men and was concerned with the education of children. He founded a charity fund for residents of the colony, and created a charity fund for visitors. He also assisted new immigrants to find places to live.

In 1940, he published his first book, *Mishnat Rishonim (Part 1),* which was well received by the press in Palestine. The second part of his book is to be published shortly. Another book, *Higyonei Kedem* is still in manuscript form, and he is working on a fourth book on part of the Shulchan Aruch. R. Yisrael also writes Torah articles in various publications in Israel.

Rabbi Kolodner had four sons and one daughter. Of his large family, only two brothers and one sister survive: Yechezkel in Cuba; Mordechai and Rachel and her husband, Berl Warshavsky, and children in Israel. His father, R. Shmuel died of natural causes in the Drohitchin ghetto.

Rabbi Menachem Memde; Feer

Rabbi Menachem Mendel Feer-Ferkovsky was born in Drohitchin. His parents, R. Yechiel and Slava, gave him a good Jewish upbringing. While still a child, he studied under the teachers, Chaim Michaelsky, Shimon Nohurier, etc. Later he studied Talmud under R. Moshe Velvel Shkolnick, R. Eliyahu Machlis and R. Mordechai Minkovitch at the Drohitchin yeshiva. An outstanding student, he went to study in the Slobodka yeshiva, where he studied intensely until the outbreak of World War I.

In 1920, R. Menachem Mendel (with his parents) came to the United States, where he enrolled in Rabbi Yitzchak Elchanan Yeshiva. As a pious and studious "Slobodka student," R. Menachem Mendel developed a close relationship with the rabbis of the yeshiva. Having received ordination from Rabbis Moshe Mordechai Epstein and Aharon Kotler, R. Menachem Mendel Feer was appointed rabbi in South Ozone Park, Long Island. He is a member of the Rabbinical Association and is also active in the Drohitchin émigré community in New York. He is known for his fear of G-d and care in observing the Torah commandments.

[Page 137]
Rabbi Dov B. Warshavsky

Rabbi Dov Ber Warshavsky was born in Drohitchin to his parents, R. David and Feigel Warshavsky. On his father's side, he was a descendant of the Drohitchin rabbinical judge and kabbalist, R. Dovidel Yaffe. He studied in *kheder* under the best teachers in town. In addition to Torah subjects, Warshavsky also studied secular subjects. He always had the ambition to be the most diligent and best students in class.

At the end of 1921, his father sent him to study out of town. For certain reasons he ended up in the Rameiles Yeshiva in Vilna, which was headed by Rabbi Hirsh Grodzensky, a brother of the great scholar, Rabbi Chaim Ozer Grodzensky. Rabbi Warshavsky spent two years in the Vilna yeshiva, and early on spent time at Gurevitch's seminary.

From 1923 to 1932, Dov studied in the Grodno yeshiva under the esteemed Rabbi and Yeshiva Head, Shimon Yehuda Shkop. During this time he spent a year in the Kobrin yeshiva, where Rabbi Pesach Pruskin headed the Yeshiva. In 1932 he traveled to Warsaw, where he became involved in teaching while briefly running the yeshiva located in the House of Study at 10 Tvarda Street.

In 1933 the following great rabbis ordained R. Dov: Rabbi Shlomo David Kahane (chief rabbi of the Warsaw rabbinate), Rabbi Yitzchak Shuster (Sokolov Rabbi) and Rabbi Yechiel Meir Blumenfeld (head of the middle level school, *Techakmoni*). He also received official government-sponsored Polish-language ordination signed by the rabbis of the Warsaw Rabbinical Court: Rabbis Shlomo David Kahane, M. Kanal, P. Zilberstein and Chaim Posner.

From then on (1932), until he left for England, Rabbi Warshavsky lived in Warsaw. He was the rabbi at the *Brit Hachayal* Synagogue on Elektoralnaya Street. He taught Talmud to older children from the Jewish Folkschule at 14 Tvarda Street and Kupetsky Street.

Since he was very familiar with Warsaw businessmen, Warshavsky was able to provide doctors for many ill Drohitchin patients and free hospital services. Several times a week, Rabbi Warshavsky went to the hospital to visit the sick and bring them food. He also used his connections with political parties to obtain emigration certificates to Palestine and was available to assist anyone from Drohitchin who felt alien and alone in the big city.

On November 15, 1938, he was able to leave Poland and get to England. On April 20, 1939, he married Chana, the daughter of Rabbi Yehoshua and Mrs. Rachel Shpetman of London. During the next eight years, Rabbi Warshavsky was the rabbi of the Teasdale Street Synagogue, where he founded a religious school (Talmud Torah).

On April 21, 1950, Rabbi Warshavsky arrived in the United States with his family and settled in Chicago, where he was a member of the Rabbinical Center; he also served as a congregational rabbi for three years.

Community Activities

It was Rabbi Warshavsky's nature to empathize with Jews experiencing suffering and persecution. From his early youth, he was committed to Zionism. He was an active fundraiser and an energetic participant in building Israel, for which the Zionist Central Office in Warsaw gave him an award.

Later on, as political party disputes grew sharper in the Jewish community, and after the Arab pogroms against Jews in 1929 in Palestine, Rabbi Warshavsky offered his support to Vladimir Jabotinsky's Revisionist movement and was a senior co-founder and secretary of the Revisionists in Drohitchin.

In 1932, Rabbi Warshavsky expanded his work to Warsaw, and in 1933 he was: a member of the administrative committee of the Warsaw religious Revisionist group, *Brit Yeshurun*; a co-founder of the international *Brit Yeshurun* (Covenant of Israel) and *Brit Hashmona'im* (Covenant of the Maccabees) movement; a delegate of *Brit Yeshurun* at the establishment of the New Zionist Organization in Vienna in 1935; a former co-founder (1935) and a director of the *Religious Association*, later known as *Jewish Unity* (which was the merger of *Brit Yeshurun* and groups of Mizrachi and Agudath Israel members) in the New Zionist Organization; a participant in its journals, *Religious Front* and *Jewish Tribune;* the former leader and cultural secretary of the Warsaw region command of *Brit Hachayal (Covenant of the Soldier); and* rabbi of the Warsaw *Brit Hachayal* synagogue; former member of National Jewish Election Committee to the Polish Parliament, 1935; member of the Warsaw Tel-Chai Fund Committee; member of steering committee of the New Zionist Organization in 1937 in Warsaw; former co-founder and close colleague of R. Hillel Zeitlin's *Kol Yisrael* (All Israel) movement; former member of the Central Youth Committee to Protect Jewish Ritual Slaughter in Poland in 1936.

[*Page 138*]

From left, Rabbi Dov Warshavsky, Ze'ev-Zelig, Yehudit-Gittel, David (children), Chana (wife) and Rabbi Y. Shpetman (father-in-law), 1954.

He had planned to organize all Jewish youth organizations into a single self-defense unit to protect the Jews from pogroms by the Poles. Together with his soldiers he was able to strike back at the gangs. He traveled throughout Poland (at his own expense) to speak on behalf of a Jewish State, a Jewish army and a rescue evacuation plan.

When he arrived in England, he resumed the same activities. He built the Revisionist Zionist organization in East London and roused the Jews to save the Jews of Eastern Europe. He also bitterly fought the anti-Semitism of the Polish émigré community and its *moshkas* in England. When Ze'ev (Vladimir) Jabotinsky died and especially after the horrible German murder of Jews, Rabbi Warshavsky underwent an intellectual transformation. He ceased his former activities and devoted himself singularly to create a vengeance organization against the German murderers.

In January 1945 in London, Rabbi Warshavsky organized the *People's Blood Redemption Movement* , the goal of which was "to encourage the people to memorialize the six to seven million Jewish martyrs who were killed by the German murderers in 1940-1945 through a boycott of Germany and Germans." He led a bitter struggle against Victor Golantz and others like him in London who preached forgiveness and pardon of the German murderers, etc. He undertook this vengeance activity with fire and brimstone, in speech and in writing, and continued this in the United States. He was also an uncompromising opponent of the Jewish-German agreement of September 10, 1952, and opposed accepting German restitution payments.

Literary Activities

In addition to his studies and community activities, Rabbi Warshavsky was also active in the literary sphere. As a youngster he wrote fairly good poems. In 1928 his first published work was an article in the Vilna publication, *Dos Vort* (The Word). He also wrote in provincial newspapers, and was the official polemicist on behalf of the Grodno yeshiva in the Grodno press.

When he arrived in Warsaw, he befriended the editor of *Der Moment*, Yosef Heftman-Emanuel, later the editor of *Haboker* (The Morning), and began writing in *Der Moment*. At the same time, he published his literary portraits in the literary supplement of *Unzer Express* (Our Express), headed by Aharon Zeitlin. Warshavsky became part of the writing community located at 13 Tlomotzka Street and later at 6 Granitchna Street. Rabbi Warshavsky became especially close to the great writer and thinker, R. Hillel Zeitlin, and his family. May G-d avenge their blood, whose trust and friendship began from his very first visit to Zeitlin at Zeitlin's home at 60 Shliska Street. Until Warshavsky left Warsaw, he was a member of the family. It was in Zeitlin's home that Warshavsky met his wife and had his engagement ceremony.

From 1936 to the end of 1938, Warshavsky was the editorial secretary of the *Yiddisher Gezelshaftlicher Lexicon* (Jewish Community Handbook) published by Dr. Reuven Feldschuh, Warsaw, 1939. All the material in the handbook was prepared and edited by Warshavsky.

When Warshavsky left for England, the Editor-in-Chief of *Der Moment*, Zvi Prilutsky, made Warshavsky his Western Europe correspondent. In London, Rabbi Warshavsky worked with all Jewish newspapers and magazines, especially *Zeit* (Time) and *Lashon un Leben* (Language and Life). He put out three pamphlets: *I accuse!* (April, 1941), *False Messiahs* (November, 1941) and *Gassen Mentschen* (Street People, (December 1952) He also made plans to produce a *Yiddisher Gezelschaftelecher Lexicon* about Jewish life in London; the war, however, interfered with his plans. From 1939 Warshavsky was a member of the Jewish Writers and Journalists Association of England.

[Page 139]

In Chicago, Rabbi Warshavsky was the publisher and editor of the *Chicager Zeitshrift* (Chicago Periodical from September, 1950); editor of the *Chicago Bulletin* of the Rabbinical Center (1954); he prepared and edited the Drohitchin Yizkor Book; he was the author of the book, *The Book of Eicha (Lamentations) of the Third Destruction* (1952). He also prepared a book of essays (unpublished as of when the yizkor book was published). Rabbi Warshavsky collaborated on and wrote poems, articles, treatises, literary portraits, memoirs, images and essays in the following newspapers: *Dos Vort (Vilna), Grodner Moment (1929), Grodner Express (1930), Dos Yiddishe Tagblatt (Warsaw, 1931), Pinsker Vort (1931-32), Brisker Shtimma (1932), Der Moment (Warsaw, 1932-39), Radio (afternoon edition of Moment), Heint,* and *Heintike Nayes (Warsaw), Unzer Express (Warsaw), Religiezner Front* and *Yiddish*

Tribuna (Warsaw), *Der Nayer Ruf* (Rabbi S. Auerbach, 1939, Warsaw), *Die Zeit* (M. Meyer, London, England), *Die Vachenzeitung* (London), *Kanader Adler* (1941), *Unzer Vort* (Goldenberg, London, 1943), *Lashon un Leben* (poet stencils, London), *Zion in Kampf* (Paris, 1949), *Shul Leben* (A. Reichman, New York, 1955), *Die Yiddishe Shtimme* – Editory Ben-A. Sochotchevsky (London, England). His work was reprinted in *Die Yiddishe Velt* (Philadelphia, Cleveland, 1941), *Yeshurun, Unzer Velt* (Munich, 1948), *Moreh Derech* (Salzburg, 1947), *and Unzer Zil* (Linz).

His parents, David and Feigel Warshavsky, and his sister, Fruma Gittel, were killed. May G-d avenge their blood! The Warshavskys had three children, Yehudit-Gittel, Ze'ev-Zelig and David.

Bibliography
Yiddisher Gezelshaftlicher Lexicon (Biography of Warshavsky, p. 898); Heint (April 7, 1939, Warsaw); Der Moment (May 26, June 20, 1939, Warsaw); Die Vochenzeitung (May 2, December 12, 1941, London); The Jewish Standard (May 2, 1941, London); Polish Jewish Observer (January 8, 1943, London); Tarbut (Journal, 1948, London); Die Zeit (April 13 and 16, 1950, London); Die Yiddishe Shtima (Feb. 6, 1953, London); Sentinel (May 25, 1950, Chicago); Der Morgen Journal (Match 21, 1947, April 25, May 30, June 16, 1950, January 23, 1952, New York); Der Tag (May 3, 1950, November 2 and 23, 1951, New York); Tag Morgen Journal (Feb. 2, Dec. 31, 1953, July 8, 1954, New York); Forverts (April 27, 1950, New York, May 5, June 14, June 18, 1950, Chicago).

The Life and Passing of the Kholozhin Rebbe
Radio (Moment), Warsaw, October 26, 1932

As mentioned earlier, on the 20th of this month, the Kholozhin Rebbe, Rabbi Eliyahu Mordechai Levinovitz died in Drohitchin. Although he was very popular and well known, even outside of Poland, there are actually very few people who knew how to appreciate his greatness, and sanctity.

The Kholozhin Rebbe was a remarkable and friendly person. He wasn't a rebbe with a whole group of Chassidim and ceremonies. He also wasn't such a great scholar and didn't spend his entire day studying. He never even studied in a yeshiva. However, he was a very pious person and a person of action. He always had his head in a book and was always giving charity. He hosted guests and had a fine character. He did things. He hated publicity and always did his work anonymously so no one would find out about him. He lived very modestly, was restrained, and dressed simply. In winter he would wear a peasant coat, with fur on top. Nevertheless, anyone with sensitive hearing could hear him murmur psalms as he banged his hammer on an anvil. A person could tell this wasn't just anybody but rather a hidden and G-d fearing *tsaddik*. People started traveling to him to receive his blessings, and he was implored to reveal himself as a hidden *tsaddik*. R. Eliyahu was born in 1846 in the town of Utian, near Vilna. His father, Yaakov, was a contractor, and was highly regarded in town. At the age of seven, young Eliyahu lost his father, and his mother remarried. Her second husband was someone named David Bashes from Yakovlev, a Jewish colony near Drohitchin.

[Page 140]

R. Eliyahu Mordechai Levinovitz

A few years later, Eliyahu went to learn to be a blacksmith in Drohitchin. Even as a youngster, he showed tremendous fear of G-d. When he got older, he married a girl from Pinsk and settled in the village of Kholozhin, 17 kilometers from Pinsk, and the place that gave him the name, *Kholozhiner.* He opened his own blacksmith shop and hired a teacher to study with him in his free time. He also used to fast frequently, immerse himself in the river (as a mikvah), and invited any guest who happened to come by. Soon there were rumors of marvelous events related to the "blacksmith," and people started coming to him for blessings and advice.

This continued for 42 years, until the outbreak of World War I. Since his village was close to the war front, the rebbe had to move to the village of Horbacha, near Drohitchin. In 1920, he settled in Drohitchin, where he remained until his death. Of course, because of his age, the rebbe was no longer involved in blacksmithing, though his children continued it instead. He didn't even use the money that people gave him for his blessings and advice, but instead he would give it away to yeshivas.

At the end of his life, he became very weak and was almost totally deaf. However, he was still extremely sharp mentally and even continued accepting requests just two hours before he passed away. According to his will and testament, he was buried together with two bags of receipts for contributions he had sent to yeshivas and other worthy institutions.

Dov B. Warshavsky
Correspondent from Drohitchin, writing in the *Pinsker Vort,* April 15, 1932

An American Jew Writes to the Kholozhiner Rebbe

We received a letter this week from the United States addressed to the Kholozhiner. The writer said that he was wanted to request the holy Rebbe to help find Charles Lindberg's kidnapped child. Here is what the letter said:

> "13 Adar, 5692 (March 21, 1932)
>
> Holy Rebbe!
>
> A twenty-month old child was kidnapped from his parents here in the United States, and I would very much like to know whether through you G-d could tell us where the child is located. The child's parents, the Lindbergs, are not Jewish. It's been four weeks, and the child cannot be found. It would be a great honor for the Jewish People in the United States if the child could be found. I hope that through you G-d could locate the whereabouts of the child.
>
> I hope to hear good news from you. Pray to G-d for my family and me.
>
> Yours truly, H. H. Bloom"

This is the entire text of the letter, which also contained five dollars. The Rebbe was extremely interested in the letter. After thinking over the issue for a while, he responded as follows: "The child is ill, but will be found on June 5, 1932." His response was immediately sent to the United States. The letter, and especially the response from the Rebbe, caused a great sensation in Drohitchin. Everyone was dying to know whether his response proved correct.

[Page 141]
By Shmuel Lev (New York)
Rabbi Eliyah Mordechai Levinovitz

1.

Among countless legends there will be a special place in history for the simple though popular village holy man known as the *Kholozhin Blacksmith.* Rabbi Eliyahu Mordechai Levinovitz spent his youth in dire poverty and deprivation. He had to work hard and bitterly in his blacksmith shop in Kholozhin so he could support his wife and children. His wife died suddenly in her youth, and he was forced to serve as mother and father to his small children. Shortly thereafter he remarried. He then started to become a very great person.

The transformation took place slowly and with difficulty. However, his unrelenting dedication served him well, and he was able to personify the maxim of the Talmudic rabbis: "Be as strong as a tiger, as light as an eagle, run like a deer and be as courageous as a lion."

The rebbe asked that his new wife agree to allow him to pursue his new undertaking of Torah study. R. Eliyahu Mordechai Levinovitz realized that he wasn't able to bring a teacher to his village to study with him, so he worked out the following arrangement: on Mondays and Thursdays he traveled to

Pinsk (if I'm not mistaken, a distance of 14 Russian versts [approximately 10 miles]), hired a teacher, and studied intensely as much as he could.

Under all circumstances and in all kinds of weather, the "Kholozhiner Blacksmith" traveled to Pinsk on Mondays and Thursdays after a half-day's work in the blacksmith shop in order to revive his soul with Torah study. When he accomplished more, he couldn't find a study session that was able to provide him with intellectual satisfaction. He derived special and great pleasure from reading books in Yiddish on kabbalah.

In later years, after he became known to people, he owned a set of the Torah anthology, *Chok Le-Yisrael,* the Beit Yehuda Torah commentary (the Rashi Torah commentary in Yiddish translation), and the book, *Sha'arei Zion.* Evidently his primary studies were in Yiddish, rather than Hebrew.

At that time the esteemed scholar, Rabbi Dovidel Karliner lived in the town of Karlin (a part of Pinsk). Rabbi Levinovitz frequently visited that great holy man. Rabbi Dovidel of Karlin noticed how a simple Jew like Rabbi Levinovitz showed such self-sacrifice to study Torah, and drew him close to him. This had an enormous impact on Rabbi Levinovitz's entire way of life. I remember from my youth a legend that Rabbi Dovidel blessed him that because of his self-sacrifice, R. Eliyahu Mordechai would become known throughout the world. And so it was.

2.

The increasing fame of Rabbi Eliyahu Mordechai grew to such an extent that even the name of his village became famous. For miles around just the words "the Kholozhiner" was instantly recognizable. Dozens of stories about him spread among the people, and each story had its own version. This didn't happen only among Jews, but even among Christian neighbors, who knew him as a miracle-maker. The Christians used to tell how their fields would be blessed any time R. Eliyahu Mordechai even approached them.

Jews with suffering hearts (there were no shortage of them) would flock to the Kholozhiner Rebbe by horse, wagon and train. The Yochnovich train station near Pinsk, which was the closest one to Kholozhin, was also a well-known name. If a Jew needed advice in business, he traveled to the Rebbe, and in all likelihood G-d himself helped that Jew to benefit from the Rebbe's blessing or advice. Timber merchants, who couldn't wait for a snowfall to ship off some lumber on the forest railway came to the Rebbe for a blessing for snow to assure a good shipment.

[Page 142]

People always told all kinds of stories and legends in Polesia about various eminent rabbis and kabbalists to whom Jews would go to pour out their hearts in times of trouble. In our area, Rabbi Pinchas Michael from Antopolia and Rabbi Mordechale of Slonim were famous as great scholars and kabbalists. When R. Eliyahu Mordechai became widely known in his area, his fame spread to R. Mordechale in Slonim, who started sending some people who were coming to him to go to R. Eliyahu Mordechai instead. Thanks to R. Mordchale, the fame of the Kholozhiner Blacksmith grew, and Jews from everywhere flocked to him.

3.

It's worth mentioning a few interesting stories that I remember from my childhood. The first was the marriage connection between the villages of Kholozhin (near Pinsk) and Horbacha (near Drohitchin) – the village where I was born.

Rabbi Levinovitz wanted to marry off his daughter to the son of R. Wolfka, the blacksmith of Horbacha. He wanted to do this because of R. Wolfka's illustrious ancestry. Alterka, the eldest son of R. Wolfka, returned home to Horbacha from Russian military service, and his father decided to travel to Rabbi Levinovitz, his old acquaintance, to request advice and a blessing. He was amazed to hear Rabbi Levinovitz say that it was the will of Heaven that they become in-laws. Rabbi Levinovitz didn't want R. Wolfka to think he was fooling Alterka into taking "cheap merchandise," so he introduced his beautiful daughter Fruma as the future wife of Alterka desired by Heaven and extended his wishes for the match to be a success.

The Kholozhiner Rebbe, R. Eliyahu Mordechai Levinovitz

R. Wolfka had no reason to oppose this sudden marriage proposal. On the contrary, he expressed his fondest hopes for it and returned to Horbacha to tell Alterka the good news about the divinely ordained marriage proposal.

As far as I remember, Alterka wasn't all that enthusiastic at the first meeting with Fruma. However, when he eventually became engaged to her, he became an entirely different person. After returning to Horbacha from Kholozhin, he became extremely enthusiastic, lavishing praise upon everything and everyone, and he spent four weeks talking about what he saw and heard in the holy man's house. He recounted to his Jewish neighbors all the miracles that occurred at the home of the Rebbe on the evening of the engagement. One of his stories was as follows:

When the Rebbe called on the deceased relatives of both sides by name to come to him and bless the new couple, a miracle occurred.

[Page 143]

As soon as the Rebbe finished inviting his "guests," the light bulbs in the house burst from joy. This meant that the holy souls participated in the celebration, and gave their approval to it. Some Horbacha Jews wanted to dispute Alterka's miracle stories, but he didn't budge from his claims.

I can still see the interesting scene at the wedding held in Kholozhin. Since we were good neighbors, our family was also invited to that wedding, though I must admit that the trip to Kholozhin scared me a bit. I imagined that since people were traveling to Kholozhin, the Rebbe was a preeminent scholar who would ask me a difficult question about a passage of Talmud that I couldn't answer. I was scared of such an embarrassing situation. I found out, however, that my fears were unfounded.

When we arrived in Kholozhin, we saw the unusual preparations and pageantry for the wedding, and from a distance we could see the entire booth for the large number of expected guests. The beautifully covered booth appeared to my youthful eyes as curtains of the Temple in Jerusalem.

It goes without saying that there were huge numbers of people invited to the wedding. Of all the guests and travelers attending the wedding, I was most impressed with R. Yaakov Ivaniker, known as R. Yankele Ivanik (Ivanik was a Jewish colony near Pinsk). He was a tremendous scholar and very pious, as well as a clever and wise person. His cleverness showed through especially when he became a bit tipsy in honor of the couple. Aside from the fact that he didn't stop studying (He knew writings by heart.), he added his own beautiful sayings and ideas.

For example, let me recount a couple of his maxims that I still recall. He disapproved of mixed dancing and decided to interfere with some boys and girls dancing together by going right in the middle wearing his long *tzitzit*, thereby making the festivities even more enjoyable than usual and causing everyone to break out in laughter. This interference, however, upset one couple, and the young man decided to protest. R. Yankele answered, "Why does it bother you to dance with me, young man? Is it because of my long *tzitzit*? Forgive me, but you are foolish. Whenever Yankele Ivaniker goes into the street wearing his long *tzitzit*, everyone knows that it's Yankele. But when you go out on the street, they say that you are a gentile. You'll then yell out that you're a Jew, but who's going to believe you? You'll have no choice but to undress."

Here's another example of his way of chastising the youth: "The devil knows what's doing with you. On the Fast of Esther you say that you're from Haman's people (so that you don't have to fast), and as soon as you see the Purim dumplings, suddenly you turn into Mordechai's people."

The morning after the wedding, all the guests went to R. Eliyahu Mordechai to get blessings, and as was his custom, he would bless each person with his hand. On the Sabbath of the week of the wedding festivities (*Sheva Brachot* – Seven Blessings), he visited Horbacha, so that Horbacha also benefited from the first Sabbath visit to their town.

4.

Fate ruled that the Rebbe live in Horbacha. On the eve of Yom Kippur, 1914, right after the village of Kholozhin was occupied by the Germans, R. Eliyahu Mordechai decided to remain in the village for the holy day of Yom Kippur without a quorum of ten men for prayers. Wrapped in his white *kittel* gown and tallith, the Rebbe stood in awe and pronounced the prayers of *Kol Nidrei*. Suddenly he saw before his eyes a bright light from the village grain warehouse, which was located close to his house. Some supernatural power pulled him toward that light shining from the warehouse, which was being used to accommodate the Germans for their night lodgings, and he ran out toward the shining warehouse. "Stop! Stop!" shouted the German soldiers at their unexpected guest dressed in white. R. Eliyahu Mordechai, who was already in his 70's and hard of hearing, didn't hear the soldier, and continued rushing in the direction of the bright light. Suddenly a shot range out, and R. Eliyahu Mordechai fell. He was wounded from a bullet in his side.

[*Page 144*]

The Funeral of the Kholozhiner Rebbe

The funeral of the Kholozhiner Rebbe, the Blacksmith, R. Eliyahu Mordechai Levinovitz, who died on October 20, 1932. In the background people are carrying his coffin. The entire town accompanied the deceased to his eternal rest at the New Drohitchin Cemetery.

[*Page 145*]

Later, when, with G-d's help, R. Eliyahu Mordechai recovered from his injuries, he would repeat the curse he made on the Germans: "If you dared to shoot me, you weren't going to go any further and were to remain standing on the hill." In fact, the Germans did remain on the same high position near the Pinsk swamps, letting the Russians lie in the swamps.

When he felt a little better, R. Eliyahu Mordechai realized it was impossible for him to remain in Kholozhin, first, because of the Russian bullets, and second, because of the famine that existed in the areas along the front, the civilian population was forced to evacuate deeper inside Russia. So R. Eliyahu Mordechai was also forced to go to stay with his son-in-law in Horbacha.

5.

With the arrival in the village of a number of Jewish refugees, the education issue surfaced in addition to economic problems. No yeshivas could exist under such circumstances, but the children had to receive an education. With G-d's help there was a famous rabbi among the refugees. He accepted the role of head of the yeshiva for the small number of teenage boys who were able to study but who could not travel to a yeshiva. Some of the students, including me, cleaned and fixed up an abandoned gentile house and turned it into a place to study Torah that also was a jewel for the Jews of Horbacha during the entire period of the German occupation. These little houses also benefited from having R. Eliyahu Mordechai, the Kholozhiner Rebbe, who established his home there.

Since he spent the greater part of the day in a house, all our friends were very interested in observing and learning about his conduct and fine character. Naturally, we realized from the subjects he studied that he was a simple Jew who had to study from Yiddish translations of holy books. However, on each occasion we were able to feel his intellect and intense dedication, especially when he experienced and lamented the suffering of the people. We were especially happy when we were able to explain to him a statement of the Talmudic sages that was difficult to understand.

It didn't take very long for Jews to locate where he lived and start coming to Horbacha to ask him for blessings. One thing was very noticeable – everything he went through had a definite effect on his health. First, he used to complain about feeling cold because of the tragic event that occurred with the Germans when he was wounded and lost alot of blood on Yom Kippur. Second, the summer heat made him feel uncomfortable and nervous. It was in those times that we didn't see the quiet and modest R. Eliyahu Mordechai but instead a stormy fighter for Judaism and traditions. If he suspected anyone of doing something, that person didn't dare show himself to the Rebbe. Many of his Chassidim from just about everywhere knew not to disturb him during the hot summer.

Let me give just a couple of examples: A young man came to visit him during the summer. This fellow came a great distance and insisted that the Rebbe give him a blessing. "What's your name?" asked the Rebbe. "Avraham Yitzchak," answered the young man. "What a nice name, Avraham and Yitzchak," the Rebbe stated impatiently. "Well, tell me something. Do you wear *tzitzit?*" The young man felt he was in trouble and ran for the door, but the Rebbe ran after him with incredible strength, and snapped, "What a *chutzpah.* Coming into my house without a *tzitzit!*"

Then there was another case that I witnessed myself. Rabbi Levinovitz met a young ritual slaughterer (shochet) who settled in our area, and wanted the young fellow to tell him a famous story mentioned in the Talmudic tractate of Bava Batra, 8:1. He pretended to be angry and opened the tractate further on, using difficult Talmudic terminology. The young man didn't do very well, and the Rebbe responded, "Listen. Take a look at him, the big shot. He doesn't deserve a dowry of more than 3000 dollars. Are you worth it? Do you know something?" The young man fled out of the house in shame.

[*Page 146*]

There were dozens of such stories. Whenever the summer months passed, so did his nervousness, and it always appeared as if a stone was removed from the hearts of not only his family but of the entire Jewish community in the area who loved and admired the Rebbe so much. We then had the familiar quiet and modest R. Eliyahu Mordechai.

These events occurred during the little more than three years that he lived in Horbacha, mostly under German rule, with a small break, until some law and order was restored in Poland, and we could then breathe easier. When the Rebbe's youngest son got married right after World War I in Drohitchin, R. Eliyahu Mordechai also moved to Drohitchin, where he lived out his final years in sanctity and honor. He died in 1932, and was buried in the Drohitchin cemetery.

By Yosef Rubinstein (Israel)
My Grandfather, the *Kholozhiner Blacksmith*

My grandfather, known as the "Kholozhiner Blacksmith" became an orphan at seven years old. His sister who lived in Osovetz (a village near Drohitchin) took care of him and sent him to study in a *kheder*, though this didn't last long. As soon as my grandfather learned how to pray, he went to learn a trade. Little Eliyahu Mordechai stood on a bench in the blacksmith shop of R. Zechariah the Blacksmith's father and began hammering an anvil to earn his small piece of bread. At night he would go study Torah in the House of Study.

After his wedding, my grandfather moved to the village of Kholozhin, where he got involved in blacksmithing. On every eve of a new month he would travel by foot to Pinsk (a distance of 17 miles), where he was a frequent visitor of R. Dovidel and R. Eliezer Moshe. A few years later my grandfather's wife died, leaving him with three small orphans to take care of – two girls and a boy. Obviously, he couldn't stay that way for long, and soon thereafter he married a fine woman, Gittel Beila, who was my maternal grandmother, who bore him five children. Their life was very difficult, and my grandfather couldn't earn enough as a blacksmith to support a family of 10 people.

There's a story that my grandfather once hired someone to teach his children Torah. After the end of the period he was hired for, grandfather had no money to pay him. Grandfather was very disappointed – he couldn't pay a poor teacher? At the same time, grandfather had a sheep that had gone off to the field and never returned because a wolf devoured him. The family started wailing: what would they do without milk? Grandfather, however, started dancing and singing. Grandmother asked him what he was so happy about. He responded by saying, "Had I wanted to sell the sheep, you would never have let me do it. Now I'll have Stepan go and sheer the wool off the animal, and you'll have money to pay the teacher." So it was, and the teacher received his entire salary.

Grandmother used to help make ends meet by painting thread and linen for the gentiles. On one occasion before a Jewish holiday, she handed over her last couple of rubles to grandfather so he could go to Pinsk to buy some white flour for challah bread and meat for the children in honor of Rosh Hashanah. The rest of the year they used to serve rye bread on the Sabbath and holidays. So grandfather went off to Pinsk with the couple of rubles. While he was there he met a Jewish man he knew, finding him walking barefoot. Grandfather took the poor Jew to a shoemaker and had him make the poor man a pair of new boots. He paid the shoemaker with the money that Grandmother had given him. The poor Jew protested, but grandfather had already paid for the boots. Afterwards, grandfather traveled back home without any flour or meat. Grandmother then asked him what they were going to do for the holiday, and grandfather responded by telling her not to worry, to take a basket and go into the forest to gather mushrooms, which she would use instead of meat. He said he would go over to Ivan and borrow *garnitz* wheat, grind it with a small hand mill, and make challahs out of it. This was what they ate on the yom tov.

[Page 147]

Before grandfather became famous as a holy man, there was a tragedy in the family. A Jewish neighbor hit one of grandfather's sons; the boy died from the injury. Grandfather remarked that the neighbor would have a bitter end because of what he had done to the boy. Not long thereafter the neighbor went insane and started barking like a dog; his own children started dying also. Only one daughter remained alive, and years later, when grandfather was already in Drohitchin, he once told grandmother to be prepared to give out more pennies than usual for charity because the daughter of that neighbor who was wandering the world would be coming. The door soon opened, and there she was, a poor woman, who announced that she came from Kholozhin. Grandmother understood everything.

It once happened that someone stole grandfather's anvil, and grandfather was left with no way of making a living. Grandfather said that the thief wouldn't benefit from the theft, and that anyone using it would twist his hand. Shortly thereafter, grandfather found out that the gentile blacksmith, who was the person who stole grandfather's anvil, was killed under a wagon carrying coal. The person who bought the anvil from the thief couldn't work with it at all, and ultimately returned the anvil to grandfather.

Grandfather didn't actually work much. Most of the time he studied and prayed, so grandmother was the one most involved in the blacksmith shop, helping the workers hammer the anvil. Later, grandfather used to brag what a great wife he had, since thanks to her making a livelihood, he was able to spend his time studying Torah. Thanks to her, grandfather became a rebbe.

During World War I, when the battlefront approached Kholozhin, grandfather once ran out onto the street on Yom Kippur night to get some fresh air. The German patrol ordered him to halt, but since grandfather didn't hear well, he continued on his way. The Germans shot off two bullets; then they brought two doctors from Berlin who operated on grandfather and saved his life. Unfortunately, he never recovered the strength he had before the event.

Shortly thereafter, Grandfather and his family moved to Horbacha, a village 18 kilometers from Drohitchin. I still remember that in my childhood hundreds of people came from far away to ask Grandfather for advice and blessings. He would open a holy book, look at a page, and then touch the page with his eyes closed. Sometimes he would repeat it three times, opening and closing the book until he found the right verse. Then he pronounced his blessing. His table was covered with various locked charity tin boxes into which he would tell his visitors to drop their charity contributions when they received his blessings.

The funeral of the Kholzhiner Rebbe (the Blacksmith), R. Eliyahu Mordechai Levinovitz. He died on October 20, 1932, and was buried in the new cemetery in Drohitchin.

[Page 148]

On every eve of a new month grandfather would call over one of the ritual slaughterers, sometimes Yosef David Schub, and other times Moshe Prager, and ask them to help him distribute the charity money for yeshivas, elementary religious schools, as well as ordinary needy Jews. Grandfather always required a receipt for the money he received, and he always kept an eye on them.

A fire once broke out in Drohitchin and was headed for the house of Chayka the pharmacist. Chayka went running to grandfather, begging him to save her house. He went to her house stood with his cane at a wall of her house that was starting to get singed. He raised his cane, and the fire stayed in the air and didn't touch Chayka's house. The singed wall remained as a sign of the event for years afterward.

Avraham Baum, son of Shimon the butcher, was going through very difficult times and was unsuccessful in making a living. To make matters worse, the Poles took away much of his livestock, and there was almost no food on the table. Avraham went to ask grandfather his opinion. Grandfather told him to request the government to compensate him for the animals that were taken away. At first Avrahamele didn't want to do it and wondered what would come of this advice. However, when grandfather told him that he would be a partner in the "business," he submitted a request for compensation, which he received. Avrahamele then asked grandfather what portion he deserved as a partner. Grandfather asked him for a glass of wine for Kiddush on Friday night as his portion of the partnership. So Avrahamele provided wine every Sabbath for grandfather's congregation.

Grandfather's son, Yitzchak, had a small soda water company; a tax official found saccharine in the factory, which caused Yitzchak to convicted to several years in jail. Yitzchak went to grandfather to save him from this misfortune. Grandfather threw him out of his room and told Yitzchak that Yitzchak was responsible for his own misfortune, and he would have to suffer for his own sins. Yitzchak didn't give up and engaged the ritual slaughterers, including Gedaliah Grossman, who convinced grandfather to save his own son from misfortune. Grandfather told Yitzchak that before going to court, Yitzchak should say a certain verse, and then look the judge in the eye and not look anywhere else, even if he should hear someone call his name. The result was that the judge freed him.

On Rosh Hashanah 1932, grandfather went home from synagogue and complained that he didn't feel well. The entire family became very worried; he was already in his 80's, and his daughter (my mother) was pregnant with her tenth child, which was also a concern. After Rosh Hashanah, grandfather called for his son and said, "This is a bad month." "Why?" wondered his son, "Do you need money to give charity? I'll lend it to you." "No, that's not what I mean," responded grandfather, who then called for the ritual slaughterer, R. Yosef David Schub and held a long conversation with him. He told Schub that he wanted to be buried with two bags of receipts that he had collected for his charity contributions. The two bags were hanging on the wall right in front of him.

That Sabbath my mother was about to have her baby, and they called for Sarah Pisatesky the midwife. The wagon driver, Berl, however, didn't want to harness his horse. Grandfather then ordered Berl to harness his horse right away and bring the midwife to his daughter. With G-d's help the baby – grandfather's tenth grandchild from his daughter – was born, and grandmother gave him a *mazel tov*. Grandfather said that the new baby boy should be named Eliyahu Mordechai, which caused a stir in the house. Was the baby going to be named for Grandfather himself? It was decided that grandfather's decision should be ignored. However, on the Sabbath, the day of the circumcision ceremony, grandfather surrendered his holy soul.

Grandfather's wish was fulfilled. After the funeral the circumcision was performed, and the grandson was given the name, Eliyahu Mordechai. Hundreds people from the region attended grandfather's funeral, and the newspapers wrote long articles about the funeral and offered praise for the Kholozhiner Blacksmith and Rebbe.

Thursday, Jan. 4, 1951 – Haifa, Israel

[*Page 149*]

Sarah Beila Hoffman   **R. Binyamin Moshe Hoffman, the Ritual Slaughterer**

R. Binyamin Moshe Hoffman

R. Binyamin Moshe Hoffman was born in approximately 1857 in Khomsk (near Drohitchin) to his father, R. Avraham, a religious teacher and scribe in town. He received his education in the House of Study. When he was 16 years old, R. Binyamin married Sarah Beila Lasinsky (the same age as R. Binyamin) from Drohitchin. He returned to study Torah under the old rabbi, R. Menachem, and was certified as a ritual slaughterer. In approximately 1876, R. Binyamin Moshe was hired as the ritual slaughterer of Drohitchin.

R. Binyamin was also a mohel (circumcisor) in town, and his stately appearance earned him respect and honor. He was a devoted Chassid of the Kobrin dynasty, attended the chassidic synagogue his whole life, and he served as cantor, shofar-blower and Torah-reader. He also led the singing in the synagogue.

R. Binyamin, who was more than 40 years old when he became ritual slaughterer and examiner in Drohitchin, came down with typhus during the War, and on the first day of the month of Shvat, 1916, he passed away at the age of 57. Shortly thereafter his wife, Beila fell victim to the same illness, and died on the 23rd of Adar II, 1916.

After the death of R. Binyamin Moshe, the position of ritual slaughterer in Drohitchin was given to his sons-in-law, R. Yossel David Schub and R. Moshe Prager. R. Binyamin Moshe and Sarah Beila Hoffman had four sons and three daughters: Yisrael David and Lazer – who both died in the United States, and whose families live in Chicago; Marisha and Devorah, who died in Drohitchin; Naftali, who was killed with his family in the Byalistock ghetto; Chaim Hoffman and his family, who live in Chicago, and Ethel Goodman who lives in Cleveland.

[Page 150]

R. Moshe Prager

R. Moshe Prager

R. Moshe Prager was born in Brisk into a chassidic family. He received his education in the House of Study and then became the son-in-law of R. Binyamin Moshe, the Ritual Slaughterer. After the death of his father-in-law, R. Moshe Prager became the ritual slaughterer of Drohitchin. As a strict Chassid, R. Moshe Prager prayed at the chassidic synagogue, where he was one of the people who led songs and was one of the distinguished members of the congregation.

In general, R. Moshe was one of the most respected people in town and was involved in community affairs. For a number of years he was a director of the Co-op Bank (Volksbank) and other institutions. In 1937, his beloved wife, Devorah, died and left him with three children: Beiltsha, Berl and Chayale.

Unfortunately, none of his children survived. They were all killed. May G-d avenge their blood!

R. Avraham Asher Kravetz-Kohn

R. Avraham Asher Kravetz-Kohn was born in approximately 1885 in Drohitchin to his parents, R. Yisrael and Esther Rachel. His father, a wealthy businessman, was involved in the masonry business. Avraham Asher studied in the yeshivas of Pohost, Antapolia, Vilna, Slobodka and others. He received certification as a slaughterer from the eminent scholar, Rabbi Chaim Soloveitchik and then married Sarah, the daughter of Pinya the Merchant.

In 1907, R. Avraham Asher and his family left for the United States, where he was a slaughterer for a number of years in a town somewhere in Minnesota.

Rabbi Yosef David Schub standing at the grave of his wife, Miriam (daughter of R. Binyamin Moshe), who died on the second day of Shavuot, 1920 in Otvotsk at the age of 33. She was buried there. [Gravestone:] Here is buried the refined, modest and respected woman, whose hand was always extended to the poor, MRS. MIRIAM, daughter of Binyamin Moshe, and wife of Yosef David SCHUB, from the town of Drohitchin, Polesia. She died in the flower of her youth on the second day of Shavuot, 1920 [rest illegible, then:] May her soul be bound up among the living.

R. Matityahu Warshavsky – R. Shmuel Reichman

R. Velvele the Ritual Slaughterer was involved as a distinguished cantor in local Houses of Study. His son, Matityahu Warshavsky, replaced his father as ritual slaughterer as well as cantor in the New House of Study until 1907, when he left for the United States. For a short time, R. Shmuel also served as ritual slaughterer. He was the son of R. Menachem Reichman. R. Shmuel was the son-in-law of a man in Bereza, and lived there for a while, until left for the United States, where he changed his name to Richman, and spent the rest of his life in Chicago.

[Page 151]

Rabbi Moshe Ze'ev Skolnick and Chava Leah Skolnick

Rabbi Moshe Ze'ev Skolnick

Rabbii Moshe Ze'ev Skolnick, known as "R. Velvel the Teacher," was born in approximately 1860 in Kossovo, near Slonim. At the age of 10, he became an orphan upon the death of his parents and was raised by friends and relatives. Until the age of 13, he studied in the House of Study in town, and later he studied on his own at the yeshivas of Maltsh and Seltz.

At the age of 20, R. Moshe Velvel was ordained as a rabbi and certified as a ritual slaughterer. He didn't earn a living in either field, however. After his wedding, he settled in Drohitchin and taught Talmud. He was very good at teaching and never lacked students. In fact, he taught hundreds of students, many of whom later studied in yeshivas.

R. Moshe Velvel was a rare individual. Besides his erudition in Talmud and the commentaries, he also had fine character traits, and was a talented person who was liked by everyone. He also had a Jewish sense of humor.

Even though he had a seat at the eastern wall of the Old House of Study, he was always found sitting at the table next to the oven, studying a text or engaging in Torah study with someone. Although he was able to give erudite lectures in Talmud for welcome students, he preferred to teach the weekly Torah portion to the simple folk on Friday night, or psalms and abridged halachic texts such as *Chayei Adam* between the afternoon and evening prayer services during the week. He especially enjoyed speaking with people, and in turn, they enjoyed listening to his Torah anecdotes and humor. R. Moshe Velvel also studied regularly on his own between 2 am and the morning prayer service.

R. Moshe Velvel was also a good cantor, Torah reader and shofar blower, and gave charity above his means. As a devoted Zionist, he was one of the first people to buy shares in the Colonial Bank.

[Page 152]

In 1920, R. Moshe Velvel and his family moved to Chicago, where he continued his studies in the Drohitchin synagogue, Kehilat Yaakov. Later, he was hired as the rabbi of the Khomsk synagogue, and for a time he taught Talmud at the Tiferet Zion synagogue, where the great scholar from Lomza, Rabbi Yehuda Leib Gordon was the officiating rabbi. Rabbi Gordon admired R. Moshe Velvel greatly.

Rabbi Moshe Velvel died on 20 Shvat [Feb. 17], 1941 in Chicago.

Chava Leah Skolnick, wife of R. Moshe Velvel, was born in approximately 1864 on the Zasinov estate near Bereza. Her father, R. Aharon Kosovsky, was the estate broker. Besides her domestic tasks, he found the time to help others as well. She would frequently go door-to-door to collect money for charitable causes, help out widows and orphans, and take interest in the plight of the poor. In the United States she continued this work. Chava Leah passed away on 6 Nisan (March 24), 1931 in Chicago.

The Skolnicks had five children: Asna, Sarah, Hershel Zelig Skolnick (a well-known insurance broker in Chicago) and Shlomo Skolnick, a famous lawyer in Chicago.

Rabbi Shmuel Y. Kaplan

Born in Drohitchin, Rabbi Shmuel Yisrael Kaplan was a brother of Rabbi Avraham Yehuda and a son of Elyakim Getzel Kaplan. He spent many years in yeshivas, and was ordained by the great rabbis.

When he was at the Slobodka yeshiva, R. Shmuel Yisrael became the son-in-law of Rabbi Yechiel Michel Hovsha, the rabbi of Shkod, Lithuania. Shortly thereafter he received an invitation to serve as the rabbi of the Jewish community of Kolno, near Lomza, and spent the rest of his life there – until the Holocaust.

Rabbi Kaplan had two sons and one daughter. One son, a yeshiva student, died young, and the second son, Rabbi Yechezkel Kaplan, was a son-in-law of the rabbinical judge and rabbi of Lomza and became rabbi in the town of Podrozno, near Vilna. He was known as a great scholar and speaker. R. Shmuel Yisrael had yeshiva students and Talmudic scholars for sons-in-law.

Unfortunately, no one of this great rabbinical family survived. Everyone was killed. May G-d avenge their blood!

Rabbi Avraham I. Kaplan

Rabbi Avraham Yehuda *Hakohen* Kaplan

Rabbi Avraham Yehuda *Hakohen* Kaplan, a rabbi in Yanovo, was born in Drohitchin to a respected family. His father, Elyakim Getzel, admired rabbis and was one of the respected men in town. R. Avraham Yehuda was educated and ordained at the Heishishok yeshiva near Vilna.

After his wedding, Rabbi Kaplan headed a yeshiva in Bobroisk for 13 years. Afterwards, he was appointed officiating rabbi in Yanovo (near Drohitchin), where he devoted the next 28 years until he passed away in the 1930s. He lived through a horrific tragedy: his two scholarly sons died in their youth. R. Avraham was unable to get over this tragedy, which cut his life short. After he passed away, his son, R. Yosef, a son-in-law of Rabbi Blauweiss of Brisk, replaced him, but he was later killed with his family. May G-d avenge their blood!

[Page 153]

Rabbi Avi Aryeh Lewy

Rabbi Zvi Aryeh Lewy

Rabbi Zvi Aryeh Lewy was born on the first day of Cheshvan (October 19), 1876 in Drohitchin, Grodno gubernia. His scholarly father, R. Shmuel Lewy, provided him with an authentic Orthodox upbringing. R. Zvi Aryeh studied under the best teachers in town, and later he became close to the greatest scholars in the region, and studied on his own part-time in the House of Study. Among those who took him under their wing and studied with him was the chief rabbi of Drohitchin, Rabbi Menachem Reichman.

R. Zvi Aryeh later moved with his mother and family to Jerusalem (His father was in the United States.), where he studied at the Torat Chaim Yeshiva and became a main student of Rabbi Zvi Michel. R. Zvi Aryeh wrote his teacher's Torah commentaries in the evening until midnight when he recited the midnight penitential prayers, and then went to sleep.

When he was 18 years old, his teachers advised him to study to be a Torah scribe. He then became one of the best scribes in Palestine. At 24 he married the daughter of R. Aharon Cohen (who in those days became known for his miniature model of the Jerusalem Temple that he later sold to a museum in Berlin). Until a year after his wedding R. Zvi Aryeh remained devoted to his work as a scribe, though he didn't make much of a living doing it. Therefore, he started working as a senior instructor at the Talmud Torah School in Rehovot. During his time there, R. Zvi Aryeh published a large number of articles in *Chavatselet*, a journal published in Jerusalem.

When he left Rehovot, he was hired as a teacher in the settlement of Ekron. Due to his work, the Talmud Torah School developed and became famous throughout the region. Other settlements were jealous and asked him to establish similar schools for them. Rabbi Lewy later became the secretary of Ekron, and in 1908 he was appointed an emissary to England, Canada and the United States on behalf of the large Jerusalem institutions, Talmud Torah and Bikkur Cholim (Medical Assistance Society), and he was successful in establishing constant contacts between American supporters and the institutions in the Holy Land.

After World War I, Rabbi Lewy and his family moved to New York, where he became involved in education and single-handedly established Talmud Torahs, educated children, and a short time later, he succeeded in establishing the great yeshiva, Torah Me-Zion on Stone Avenue in Brownsville. During the next 10 years, the yeshiva was one of first to get Jewish children involved in Jewish studies.

When he realized that his own neighborhood of East Flatbush was a virtual desert in terms of Jewish education for children, he started teaching children in a basement and quickly attracted dozens of Jewish families who were happy to send their children to study under Rabbi Lewy. In a short time, he managed to collect funds to build a structure for a second appropriate yeshiva, which had been known as Yeshivat Rishon LeZion in East Flatbush. In 1935, R. Zvi Aryeh published a book of homilies called *Machaneh Shmuel*.

In his final years, unfortunately, he shared the same fate of many intellectual pioneers who devoted their entire lives to the welfare of the people but who themselves were overlooked. At the very end he was able to establish a Talmud Torah School and a synagogue, *Machaneh Yisrael* in Boro Park and a second Talmud Torah and synagogue, *Rechovot,* in East New York. As educator of young and old, R. Aryeh Zvi died on the 5th of Tevet (Dec. 19), 1936. He was buried in the cemetery of Agudath Achim Anshei Drohitchin [Association of Drohitchin Emigrés] in New York.

[Page 154]
R. Mendel Kaminetsky

R. Mendel Kaminetsky was born on 2 Elul (August 23), 1838 in Drohitchin and was endowed with great intellectual abilities. He never studied in any yeshiva and performed extremely well in his studies. Until he was 11 years old he studied and excelled under his father, R. Moshe Isser. Thereafter he studied on his own in the House of Study.

From right, R. Mendel and his father, R. Moshe Isser

R. Mendel once got involved in an academic dispute with R. Benzion, the rabbi of Belz in the home of Chaim Soloveitchik of Brisk. R. Benzion then commented to R. Mendel, "My son-in-law and your student, R. Yosef Valevelsky, said about you that you have an intellect comparable to that of the great 16th century Talmudic commentator, Rabbi Shmuel Eliezer Eidels. I just laughed, but now I see that he was right."

Besides being an illustrious Torah scholar, R. Mendel was also involved in general knowledge such as jurisprudence, mathematics, machinery and astronomy. He was also thoroughly fluent in Russian and Russian law, and even wrote a legal petition like a professional lawyer. R. Mendel could read complicated mathematical formulae understand the structure of complicated machinery, and he owned a collection of various devices which he worked on for many hours. He also had the ability to independently calculate the new moons and intercalation of the calendar.

There is a story of how the Rovno nobleman, Minkov, once went to court to force the Jews of the "new gardens" in Drohitchin to turn the gardens over to him. R. Mendel, as the defense attorney, took the case to the gubernia offices in Grodno and skillfully defended his clients. The result was that the famous and heroic General Minkov, who had conquered the Turkish fortress *Plevna* for Russia, lost the case. The Russian court ruled that the gardens, which had been developed by Jews for 99 years, should remain in their possession.

R. Hersh Beilin, the Genius of Pinsk, and a friend of R. Chaim Soloveitchik, once exclaimed, "Who can attain R. Mendel's mind?" R. Mendel died on the 3rd of Tevet (December 25), 1919 in Drohitchin. He had 11 children: Yossel, Motya

Leib, Lotsa Beila, Pinya, Yehoshua, Lana, Gavriel, Fradel, Shlomo, Miriam and Chana.

R. Asher Weitsel

R. Asher Weitsel, known as "R. Asher the government rabbi (*kozinyer rabbin*)" was the son of R. Mordechela Weitsel-Rosenblatt, known as "R. Mordechela Slonimer." We have no information about R. Asher's life, and especially about his youth. We only know that he got married in Drohitchin to R. Isaac's daughter and referred to himself as R. Asher Isaacs.

R. Asher Weitsel

R. Asher knew how to study well and learned the Russian language. Over the years before World War I, R. Asher handled the vital statistics documents of the Drohitchin which recorded the births and deaths of the residents of town, and, therefore, he was nicknamed "Asher the Government Rabbi."

R. Asher was a very quiet and modest man, and most of the time he was occupied in his shop located in the market. For a short time after World War I, he taught religious subjects to children at that Moriah school. He died in the 1920s and was survived by his son, Benzion, and daughter-in-law, Chana Gittel Valevelsky.

[Page 155]

Rabbi Dov B. Warshavsky
The Last Rabbi of the Last Community

As always, the sun shone brightly, and the whole town bathed in the sunlight. I walked through the streets of Drohitchin and noticed how nothing had changed. People were going and hurrying in various directions. I recognized faces with smiling eyes as they passed by and disappeared from view.

I turned in the direction of the rebbe's house. I opened the door of the house and saw how nothing had changed there either. Everything was just where it was before. In the living room of the rabbinical court the gray-haired rabbi sat at the large table and swayed while he studied a book. He didn't see me; I looked around in all the rooms; it was deathly quiet. It was weird, and then I realized I was dreaming.

This was the same dream I had every day and night ever since I left home, my parents, the rabbi, friends and the town with its Jews. It was a dream, and it was hard to believe that they were all dead. No! It couldn't be! It was impossible; it was unbelievable! It was just a dream. The sunlight disappeared, as did the bright images, while around me was a dark vacuum. The feeling was very bad, and my longing for them all broke my heart.

Just as how I saw him in this recent dream, I had seen R. Isaac Yaakov Kalenkovich 10 years earlier that very month when I came to meet him. At that same time, I had left the rabbi swaying over a Talmudic tractate; his eyes showed deeply hidden suffering behind his thick glasses.

I had the privilege from my earliest youth to be virtually a member of the rabbi's family. His house was a second home to me, and I had great pleasure from sitting in his house because aside from Torah study, visitors were able to discuss worldly issues with the rabbi. Even though his external appearance was gray and old (He aged prematurely.), his heart was young and fresh. People were able to consult him as they would their own father or intimate friend, and he made a person feel young again.

R. Isaac Kalenkovich, may G-d avenge his blood, was truly a hidden talent. He fled from honor and eschewed fame. Actually, he didn't know what honor was because his entire life studying Torah intensively.

Rabbi Kalenkovich rarely left Drohitchin at any time. I don't remember that he ever left town on vacation in the country for a few months as others did, even though his weak health demanded it. He was always available to answer halachic questions, listen to someone with a broken heart and offer advice and consolation. He served his community like a trustworthy guard.

When there were no halachic issues to be clarified, Rabbi Kalenkovich dove into his Talmudic studies. His health caused him to move slowly, but from time to time, he would let out a deep sigh together with a soft melody, chanting Talmudic passages.

Rabbi Kalenkovich never belonged to any party and stayed away from politics. Only now, as I realize the true face of parties and politics, am I able to value the rabbi's great trait. For this reason, Rabbi Kalenkovich attained a high level of truth and Torah, remaining undisturbed by party jealousies and hatreds.

Rabbi Kalenkovich was typical of rabbis of the previous generation, and was a thoughtful and logical scholar, acquainted with the entire body of Torah literature and G-d-fearing. He was friendly with everyone, maintained a good appearance, and was extremely hygienic. He hated watery empty speeches and rarely gave moralizing speeches. When he spoke, his words included some Torah teaching and his listeners had to pay close attention to understand his words. R. Isaac Yaakov *Hakohen* Kalenkovich, may G-d avenge his blood, was the last rabbi of the last Jewish community in Drohitchin!

[Page 156]

He lived together with his flock for more than 50 years, suffered with them, and departed this world together with them. They were together in life and in death.

I am writing these lines for the 6th anniversary, 5 Cheshvan (November 7), 1948, of the death of our murdered martyrs. It should be mentioned that in addition to being the rabbi of the community and intellectual guide, Rabbi Kalenkovich was the father of children and grandchildren. Who can express in writing the suffering of a child who watches his own parents being murdered? Who can describe that suffering of parents who watch their own children being killed.

What should be the result of our eulogies and commemorations of our martyrs? I strongly believe that it should not be lighting candles and praying for the souls of the martyrs, because the martyrs are so holy and great that even holy men cannot stand next to them. The martyrs stand even higher than others. We should plead for our own souls since we didn't do anything to save the martyrs from death. We still aren't doing anything to take revenge on their murderers, the Germans.

The commemoration anniversary for our martyrs will only achieve its purpose when we also remember their murderers, the Germans. We need to remember them at home, on the street, and at work. Anything connected to the Germans and Germany should disgust us and be considered unkosher and in excommunication – eternal excommunication of German.

London, 5 Cheshvan, 1948.

A group of Jews in Liekeva, near Shedlitz, that the Germans surrounded before they killed them. One Jew wears an undershirt tallith, and another wears a tallith. The Jew with the white beard standing behind the other Jew wearing the undershirt tallith was recognized by Mrs. Rubinschneider as her father. She received the photo by accident.

PART THREE

REBBES AND CHASSIDIM

[*Page 158 – unnumbered*]

Statement by the Editorial Board

This section about rebbes and Chassidim in Drohitchin was written by Zalman Shevinsky. Although the Drohitchin community was mainly composed of non-Chassidim, as a person raised in the Chassidic spirit, Shevinsky felt obligated to dedicate a special section to the Chassidic synagogue (shtibel) and Chassidim of Drohitchin. The special section is at his request and responsibility.

However small the Chassidic community in Drohitchin was, in Shevinsky's opinion, this special section deserves a few pages in the Drohitchin Yizkor Book. The Chassidic community in Drohitchin was small, but important in terms of quality.

When we use the term *Chassidim* in reference to Drohitchin, we are referring to the Kobriner Chassidic dynasty, of which the Drohitchin Chassidic synagogue was a branch. The Drohitchin community, of course, followed the Kobrin rebbes, who were the guides and spiritual leaders of Drohitchin Chassidim.

This answers the question of those who wonder what the connection is between Kobrin rebbes and Drohitchin. There **is** a connection. The Chassidic rebbe may have lived in Kobrin or perhaps further away, but his spirit hovered over the Drohitchin shtibel. The shtibel in Drohitchin exuded an exalted fear of G-d, joy and trust in G-d. The entire atmosphere was saturated with Jewishness, which wasn't confined to the four walls of the shtibel itself.

Through the doors and windows it flowed onto the street. The echo of Chassidic melodies also reverberated in the ears of non-Chassidim in town. Jews would come to the shtibel, especially on the winter Sabbaths, to warm themselves by the chassidic fire. Whenever anyone announced that the Kobriner Rebbe was coming to visit his followers in Drohitchin, the shtibel didn't have enough room to hold all the out-of-towners and curiosity seekers.

This is the Chassidic chapter in Drohitchin that never ended, and today is destroyed.

Zalman Shevinsky (Chicago)

The Chasidic Shtibel

My father, R. Nachum Shevinsky, was born in Kobrin and settled in Drohitchin after his marriage. In those days in Drohitchin, there was a small number of Kobriner Chassidim, and they didn't even have their own place to pray. They would gather together in private homes for services on the holydays and Sabbath. My father, a Chassid, didn't like go to different homes each time, and he decided to build a permanent shtibel for the Chassidim, so they would have their own place to pray all week long, as well as a location to host the Kobriner Rebbe on his Sabbath visits to Drohitchin. Since my father was an energetic individual, he started making his plans a reality. He met with R. Binyamin Moshe, the ritual slaughterer, R. Shimon Nahorier, R. Avrahamel, the cabinetmaker, R. Leizer Adler, R. Yitzchak Avigdor Telekhansky, R. Yaakov Eisenberg (Doboviyer), R. Yitzchak Binyamin Cooper, R. Aryeh Leib Gingold and Yossel Yitzchak Abramovich from the train station. They were all Kobriner Chassidim, and they purchased a place in an alley near the Old House of Study on the road to the Old Cemetery.

Construction of the shtibel began quickly. When the devoted non-Chassidim saw that my father's idea was no longer merely a dream but a reality, they started making various efforts to interfere with the work. Among these opponents were members of our own family on my mother's side. However, when they saw they couldn't stop the project, they resorted to their ultimate weapon: informing the government. In Russia in those days, there was a law that said that no synagogue could be built too close to a church, and the shtibel was being built not far from the town church.

The non-Chassidim, knowing about that law, went to the priest to ask him to stop the construction of the shtibel. They said that if he couldn't help them, they wanted him to go to higher authorities on their behalf. The priest immediately called my father to meet with him and ordered my father to stop construction. The reason the priest gave my father was the problem that the Chassidim shouted and made noise during their prayers, something which would disturb the Christian services. My father calmed the priest, and he proceeded to continue with the construction. However, he approached General Minkov, the Rovno nobleman to whom Drohitchin belonged, and asked him to tell the priest not to interfere with the construction work.

Near the end of construction, a decree arrived from Kobrin district police officer Rineyski to seal up the building and cease construction. The doors were covered with wood, but the Chassidim found a way to pray in the shtibel anyway – by sneaking in through the open windows.

One Friday night, when my father and my elder brother Zelig went to pray, they met the local policeman, Rothstein, who had converted to Christianity. He asked them whether they were going to the shtibel. My father responded that it was Rothstein himself who had sealed up the doors, so how could they go inside? The policeman responded, "Mr. Shevinsky, you can't fool me. I know that Jews figured out how to get in, and they are sneaking in through the windows." My father said, "Mr. Policeman, come with me and see that no one is praying in the shtibel." Father winked at my brother quickly ran off to the shtibel to tell the people there that the policeman was on his way. When he arrived at the shtibel, the policeman noticed the Jews leaving through the open windows. My father made sure that the policeman kept silent about it.

The same policeman told my father that the following week, the district police official from Kobrin would be arriving in town to measure the area through the alley right up to Sand Street, which was the main street in town, to determine how far the synagogue was from the church. He also advised my father to talk with General Minkov.

[Page 160]

Left: R. Shimon Eppelbaum, the custodian of the shtibel.
Right: R. Eliezer (Leizer) Adler, who died on Kislev 22 [Nov. 30], 1923.

The following week the official arrived in Drohitchin with the priest and Rothstein. My father also invited General Minkov to attend the proceedings. The priest began measuring through the surrounding gardens instead of through the alley itself. Doing it this way would help him justify not allowing the completion of the construction of the shtibel. My father then protested, and he insisted that the measurement be made through the alley, where people walk. His protest was helpful, although those present, except for the priest, had already been bribed. When General Minkov and the Kobrin police official agreed with my father, the priest had to give in. My father noticed, however, that they priest was using long steps during his measurements, and he reported this to the General, who told the priest that since he, the priest, was already elderly, and since measuring was too difficult for him, the General would do the measuring himself. The General started doing the measuring himself.

The Sabbath melody *She-Hashalom Shelo [Peace that is His]*, sung by R. Binyamin Moshe the ritual slaughterer of the shtibel.

The results were satisfactory, and the new shtibel was completed. The handful of lonely and persecuted Drohitchin Chassidim were overjoyed at the defeat of their enemies, and the Chassidim, including my father, started dancing for joy. During World War I, all the Houses of Study in Drohitchin, except for the chassidic one, burned down.

[Page 161]
Rabbi Moshele
The First Rebbe

R. Moshele was born in Piesk, near Kobrin, the son of a baker, and he was an outstanding person since his youth, as illustrated by the following story:

Moshele's mother was a very righteous woman who used to distribute bread to the poor for free. It happened that some of the poor people would insult her and thereby hurt her feelings. She suffered from this a great deal, and she would cry and complain why they were doing this to her. When little Moshele heard her, he said, "Mama, if the poor had praised and blessed you, you would have been happy. This would mean that you did your charity for a favor. However, if your good acts are repaid by suffering, this means that your actions were totally for the sake of Heaven."

R. Moshele often said that when he was small he was once playing with other children in the street during the month of Elul preceding Rosh Hashanah. His sister asked him why during such a holy period he was involved in foolishness, since even fish in the sea tremble during those days. Her words had their desired effect, and he started trembling too. This remained with him his whole life.

R. Moshele got married in Kobrin. His father-in-law provided him with a small meals and an apartment, where he spent his time in study and worship. There was an occasion when he became ill and refused to go to a doctor. Instead, he asked to be taken to R. Mordechale of Lechovitch. His father took him to R. Mordechale, and he recovered from his illness. From then on, he always went to Lechovitch.

R. Mordechale respected R. Moshele enormously. One Purim, R. Mordechale told his Chassidim that since on Purim one must give gifts to the needy, each person should indicate what spiritual level he wanted to achieve, and this would be granted to him. Everyone indicated his request except for R. Moshele, who said he hated gifts and that spiritual levels should only be attained by hard work.

He was asked why he doesn't write a book. R. Moshele responded that he already had, and it was written on the hearts of the Jewish masses. Many Chassidim, including R. Yehoshuale Ostrover attended R. Moshele's funeral. Upon returning from the cemetery, R. Yehoshuale went into R. Moshele's room and spent some time there in solitude. When he left, he said,

"I have heard Torah teachings *in* Kobrin, and now I will repeat it about Kobrin itself. With regard to the biblical verse *"You shall be holy for I am holy"* R, Moshele used to comment, *"You shall be holy* – this means that the Jewish People shall be holy without a choice to the contrary because they have a spark of divinity within. The words *for I am holy* then refer to a person saying that he knows and feels the holiness of the Creator, but does not have the means to verbally express what he feels in his heart." This is what R. Yehoshuale said about Kobrin Chassidism – that he knew and felt the holiness of Kobrin Chassidism but couldn't express it in words.

At the structure over the grave of R. Moshele, there is a framed copy of his will: "I will take revenge against any person who dares to exaggerate about me in a good way. However, anyone may say that I was a person who loved the Jewish people because I said that about myself too. Therefore anyone else may say the same thing."

R. Moshele was rebbe for 26 years. He died on 28 Nisan (April 30) 1851.

Torah Teachings of R. Moshele

The Soul and the Evil Inclination

"The soul tells the Evil Inclination what Abraham told his nephew, Lot: *If you go to the left, I'll go to the right. If you go to the right, I'll go to the left.* So the soul is saying, *if you want to take me to the left, I won't follow you, and I'll go to the right. And if you even advise me to go with you to the right, it'll be better for me to go to the left.*

Comments to the Shulchan Aruch (Code of Jewish Law)

My father thought there was a fifth part missing to the other four parts of the Shulchan Aruch. This part would be to teach a person how to deal with humans. I think there is a sixth part that is also missing: how to deal with inhuman people.

[Page 162]

Notes written by R. Moshe Kobriner to words of a song called *Yah Ekhsof (I desire G-d)* composed by the great Rebbe Aharon of Karlin.

The words were written by R. Baruch, the Kobriner Rebbe, and edited by Moshe Nathanson. From the book, *Horodetz.*

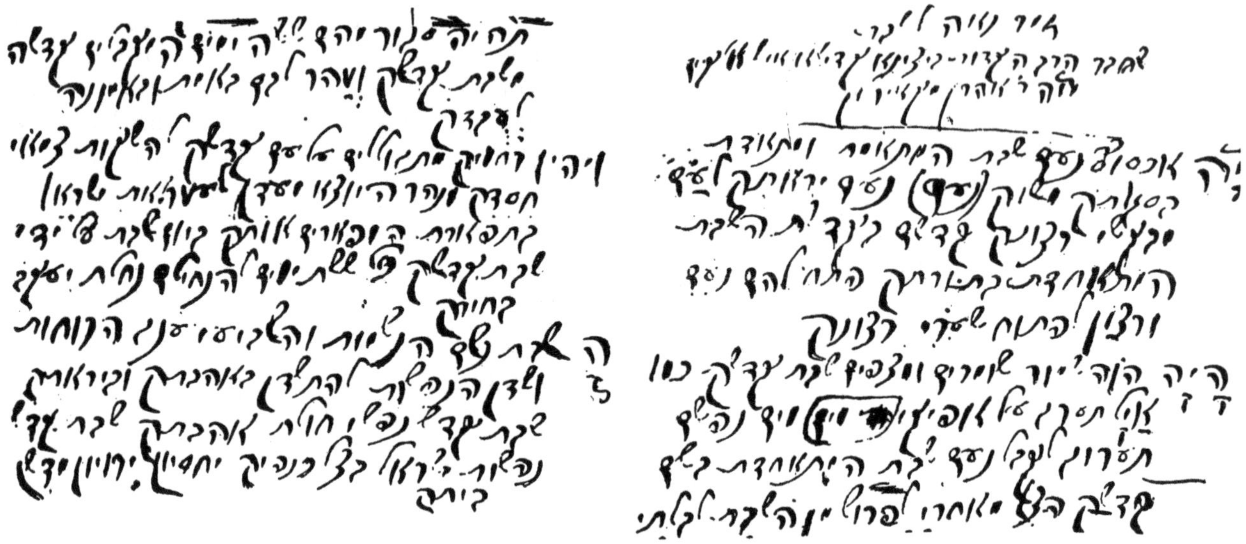

יה אכסוף

נאָטען פון ר' משה קאָברינער'ס אַ ניגון צו „יה אכסוף" פון ר' אהרן הגדול.
(פאַרצייכנט פון רי ברוך ז"ל „קאָברינער רבי" און בעאַראַבייט פון משה נתנזון).

אַרויסגענומען פון בוך „האָראָדעץ."

[The handwritten lines are very difficult to read.]

[*Page 163*]

Modesty

Someone once asked how it is possible that the opponents of Moses in the desert, Datan and Aviram, could say that Moses was trying to dominate them? The Torah itself says that Moses was the most modest person in the world. R. Moshele said, "When Moses sat on the chair of the tzaddik, he conducted himself like a leader, so they were able to think he was trying to dominate them. However, inside his heart he was the most modest person in the world. People who go around with bowed heads calling themselves modest are showing false modesty. True modesty is in the heart."

The Main Thing

After the death of R. Moshele, one of his disciples went to ask R. Mendel of Kotsk what the main thing was in the life of his teacher, R. Moshele. The student paused a while, and then answered, "Whenever he was involved in something, that 'something' was the main thing."

R. Noach Naftali

After the death of R. Moshele, his grandson, R. Noach Naftali, took over his role as rebbe. He served as rebbe for 35 years and died on 26 Av, 5649 (August 23, 1889) in the town of Kamen, Volhynia. His son, David Shlomo, took his place and died on 11 Cheshvan, 5689 (October 25) 1928.

*From Sefer Kobrin (*Book of Kobrin*)*

R. David Shlomo

R. David Shlomo, third Kobriner Rebbe

R. David Shlomo, Kobriner Rebbe, used to travel through the towns after the Sukkot holiday to visit his Chassidim. He used to come to Drohitchin for the Sabbath of the Genesis Torah portion, *Chayei Sarah* (the fifth portion after Simchat Torah).

The Rebbe would stay in the synagogue in the women's gallery, where he would have a table, chairs and a bed. He would meet his Chassidim and other visitors who came in large numbers to obtain a blessing from the rebbe.

The Rebbe would wear a long velvet coat and a belt, and white socks and a shtreimel (fur hat). A graying red beard surrounded his refined face. On Friday nights after prayer services, the local Chassidim ran home to eat their meal and then hurry back to the shtibel, where a long table covered with a beautiful white tablecloth, two large challah breads covered over by a small napkin, and a bottle of wine with a silver Kiddush cup for the Rebbe.

After the prayer services, he went to study in a room by himself, and later, when the Chassidim gathered together, the Rebbe left his room and came to the table to start singing *Shalom Aleichem*. Everybody joined the Rebbe in singing with tremendous enthusiasm. Then the Rebbe washed his hands and made the blessing over the large challah bread, and the custodian of the shtibel started serving the food.

[Page 164]

א בריוו פון דראָהיטשינער חסידים צו זלמן שעווינסקי וועגן
הילף צו פאַרריכטן דאָס חסידים־שטיבל.

Handwritten letter from the Drohitchin Chassidim to Zalman Shevinsky requesting assistance to repair the Chassidim shtibel. The stamp is of the shtibel, Drohitchin, Polesia.

[Page 165]

After the Rebbe tasted something of the first course, he distributed pieces of bread to his Chassidim around the table, and did this at every meal. At Sabbath morning prayers, the Rebbe remained in his private room until the end of the preliminary hymns, and then he entered the shtibel and served as cantor. He chanted all the prayers in a heartfelt and soulful manner, and from one word to the next he would start weeping. The congregants stood in amazement and waited for him to utter another word, which appeared as if he the Rebbe came back to life.

After the prayers, the Rebbe returned to his room, and the local Chassidim hurried home to make kiddush and eat the morning meal with the intention of returning to the Rebbe to hear him recite the after-meal blessing. As soon as the Chassidim returned to the shtibel, the Rebbe made kiddush and repeated the same ceremony as he had done the night before. He did the same thing at the third Sabbath meal.

The Saturday night meal (*Melaveh Malka* – Accompanying the departing Sabbath Queen) was conducted with great joy and enthusiasm until midnight. The shtibel custodian would then call out the names of the Chassidim who had purchased the bottles of wine for the meal, and the Rebbe would arrange to send the money off to Palestine for distribution among the needy. This fund was called the Kobriner Fund.

The Rebbe would give Torah discourses at every meal; the people would pay close attention to it, and there was a very large crowd around the Rebbe's table. People were practically standing on top of each other to be able to hear a few words uttered by the Rebbe as he spoke softly with his eyes rolled up. A word got swallowed, some crying, and nothing held back. The crowd thirstily swallowed every word he said, even though many people didn't understand his discourse. After he finished each part of the discourse, the Chassidim would break out into singing or dancing, which the Kobrin Chassidim were famous for.

The Rebbe's visit to Drohitchin was a happy occasion. Chassidim and other Jews in town would push their way into the shtibel to join the Chassidim. His visit provided excitement for the entire week.

Information is from the article by Shlomo Podelevsky from the book, *Horodetz.*

Rabbi Moshe Aharon

The last rebbe in the dynasty of R. Moshele Kobriner was the rebbe, R. Moshe Aharon Rabinovitch, who together with the remaining martyrs was killed in World War II by the Germans. May their names be obliterated! His face exuded high spirituality and fear of G-d. His eyes, always gazing heavenward, seemed to say 'I am ready to serve You.' R. Moshe Aharon was a meticulous person without any aspiration to rule, and he didn't offer anything new; he just continued the tradition of his parents.

Rabbi Moshe Aharon of Kobrin

He was an extremist and insisted that people serve G-d correctly and with love. He didn't allow for any compromise. His house was open to any bitter heart, but he didn't perform any miracles. However, whoever left his house was able to find a cure for whatever ailed him, carrying hope, comfort and an improved outlook for a better day.

The Rebbe never promised anything; he merely offered blessings and prayers for a sick person or a mother experiencing difficulty in childbirth. In the event of hardship, he would take a book that was handed down to him by his forbearers, and he would rest it on the head of the sick person. People believed in the beneficial effect of his book.

The Kobrin Chassidic Center was located on a muddy side street (Rotner) at the location of the Rebbe's house. It was an ordinary two-story building with a House of Study. It was symbolic that around that mud and dirt was a spiritual life full of cleanliness.

All year long, R. Moshe Aharon would visit his Chassidim in surrounding towns. The Rebbe didn't sing songs, but when it came time for Simchat Torah, no power on earth could hold him back as he danced with a Sefer Torah in his hands. Children in the House of Study impatiently waited a whole year for Yomtof – the week of Sukkot and then Simchat Torah – to be able to dance with the Rebbe.

R. Moshe Aharon was only the rebbe of the Chassidim in Kobrin and surrounding areas. Therefore he served as an example for everyone, and had an impact on everyone in town. This is the way the Kobriner dynasty existed and continued from generation to generation. It seemed that the Chassidim would always live and share the joys of their rebbe and shed tears with him too, to always be able to find comfort and forget their trouble while they sat at the Rebbe's table. However, as the saying goes: "Man thinks, and G-d laughs." The horrific and murderous hands arrived and completely uprooted the tree, destroying everything.

From Sefer Kobrin

Page 166]

R. NACHUM SHEVINSKY

R. Nachum Shevinsky

R. Nachum Shevinsky was born in Kobrin at Large *Zamukhovitz* (street name?). His father, R. Shlomo Zalman, an eminent Chassid was a tanner and involved in business. His mother, Fruma Mindel, was descended from a family of businessmen and scholars.

R. Nachum obtained his education in the cheder and under various teachers. When he was a teenager, he would help his father in the business. In 1887, R. Nachum married Bodya Shederovsky, who was part of the Volevelsky family and the famous Katzenelbogen family, and he went into the leather business. Throughout the years he lived in Drohitchin, he was in the tanning business, in which he processed various types of leather that was then sold throughout the country.

At the same time, R. Nachum was involved in community affairs. He was the founder of the only Kobrin chassidic shtibel in Drohitchin and was also its custodian for many years. He was also very close to the rabbi of Drohitchin, R. Eliyahu Mordechai Yudovsky, who he assisted in word and deed.

In 1912, R. Nachum Shevinsky emigrated to the United States and settled in Chicago, where he went into business. He was also one of the founders of the Kobrin-Karlin Chassidic shtibel on Washburn Ave., and later on Trumbell Ave. The Shevinskys had six children: Zelig, Zalman, Sheina Tsippa, Sarah Rachel, Toiba Gittel and Yaakov Mendel.

R. Nachum died on Kislev 13 (December 9], 1935 in Chicago and was buried in Waldheim at the Makarov Cemetery. R. Nachum's father, R. Shlomo Zalman, died on 26 Tevet, 5649 (December 30), 1888. The Hebrew year corresponds to 1888, not 1889, in Kobrin. R. Nachum's mother, Fruma Mindel, died in 1907 in Kobrin.

[*Page 167*]

(Handwriting difficult to read)

A bill of sale for two seats in the in the New House of Study on Great Zamakhovitz in Kobrin. The bill of sale was from R. Yitzchak Yaakov, great-grandfather of Zalman Shevinsky.

איש
תם וישר מורה
זלמן
בר יצחק יעקב ז״ל
נפטר כ״ו טבת
תרמ״ט ל׳ תנצבה

Gravestone of Zalman, son of Yitzchak Yaakov (father of R. Nachum, and grandfather of Zalman Shevinsky) at the Kobrin Cemetery. He died on 26 Tevet, 5649. Near the gravestone is beautiful Zelda Goldberg (Nachum's sister) of Kobrin. She lived in Zhelekhov and died in Palestine.

Gravestone inscription: An honest and just man, Zalman, son of R. Yitzchak Yaakov, died 26 Tevet, 5649.

[Page 168]

A bill of sale of two seats at the new chassidic shtibel in Lekhovitch. It was from R. Yitzchak Yaakov, great-grandfather of Zalman Shevinsky.

יעלה ויצמח כגן רטוב · ויפק רצון מהאל הטוב
ויאמר לדבם טוב · למזל טוב · מצא אשה מצא טוב

הכל שריר וקים

Дозволено Цензурою ршава 4 Марта 1881

Druk. i Litog. I, Lebensohnlica Franciszkanska № 27

כתובה פון ר׳ נחום און באדיע שעווינסקי, תרמ״ה, 1885, דראהיטשין

Engagement Document [*Tanaim*] of R. Nachum and Bodya Shevinsky,
1885, Drohitchin.

[*Page 169; Page 170 blank*]

PART FOUR

PERSONALITIES AND CHARACTERS

[Page 171]

Educators and Cultlural Activists

Professor Chaim Hochman

Professor Chaim Hochman

It was almost axiomatic among anti-Semites that the only thing Jews thought about was money and that they weren't involved in the exact sciences such as mathematics and physics. This "axiom" is false and baseless. Even in ancient times, Jews excelled in the aforementioned fields. The prominent Hebrew poet, linguist and biblical commentator, R. Avraham Ibn Ezra, was also known for his research in mathematics. R. Avraham Zacuta (1450-1510) was a prominent mathematician and astronomer in Saragosa, Spain. It was because of Zacuta's calculations and instructions that Colombus was able to discover America.

We can see traces of Jewish influence on higher mathematics sciences from the Hebrew letters that were used as certain mathematical symbols. In our time, great Jewish mathematicians are known the world over – especially the great Professor Albert Einstein, who is involved in the fields of physics and mathematics.

Although in Russia Jews were subject to oppression, and many obstacles were put in the way of Jewish scientists, they nevertheless had a major role in the development of the exact sciences. One of the prominent physicians and mathematicians in Russia at the end of the 19th century and early 20th century was Professor Chaim Hochman.

Chaim Hochman was born in 1851 in Drohitchin (Kobrin region). His father Yehuda and mother gave him a proper Jewish upbringing. When Chaim was older, he went off to study in Lithuanian yeshivas, where he studied the Talmud and commentaries. Young Hochman was, however, dissatisfied with Jewish studies and was drawn to worldly ideas. He quickly completed studies at the Kherson gymnasia (high school) in 1871. He was dissatisfied with the knowledge he had acquired in gymnasia and wanted to pursue higher mathematics. He was accepted to the Faculty of Mathematics at the University of Odessa (*Novorossisky Universitet*), and he ended his studies in 1876 with a gold medal for his scientific work in higher mathematics. Hochman remained at the university and continued his studies demonstrating enormous abilities and analytic intellect. In 1881, he was sent abroad to advance his knowledge further.

[Page 172]

Chaim Hochman was very disappointed when he returned to Russia. Based on his achievements, he was suited for a major position in a university. The Czarist government was willing to appoint him professor in a university on condition that he converts to Christianity. He responded resoundingly in the negative, but this didn't solve the day-to-day financial problems of Hochman and his family. In the meantime, he accepted a position as inspector at the Jewish teacher's institute in Zhitomir. He held this position until 1886, when the institute closed.

Although he was very involved in his work as inspector, Hochman found time to write a dissertation on an advance mathematics subject in which he solved various mathematical problems. His dissertation was recognized as extremely scientific, and in 1887, the Russian government – which wasn't so favorably disposed toward Jewish intellectuals – appointed him as a private instructor at the university in Odessa, where he gave lectures in mechanics and planning. Hochman didn't receive any payment for these lectures and did it out of his own devotion, because these sciences were very close to his heart. He only started receiving payment in 1894.

Meanwhile, Hochman continued his research, and thanks to his scientific work on steam and mechanics, he was awarded the title of PhD. in 1890. Nevertheless, he still made no money from it, and so he came up with a plan to open his own private school. In a short time his school became trade school entitled to all the rights of a government school.

For Hochman, a pioneer in the field of private middle schools, wide horizons were now open. Nevertheless, he was still confronted with the day-today financial problems. Then suddenly at that time Hochman published a few important works on the subjects of mathematics, physics and mechanics, which strongly impressed the scientific community. He became especially well known for his perpetual calendar.

Former residents of Drohitchin recall that Hochman also invented a device to measure the Black Sea; he based it on instructions in the Talmudic tractate of *Mikvaot.* The story goes that when he noticed that his device was not precise, he wanted to commit suicide. There is also the story that he invented a waterproof watch. In those days, this was a tremendous invention. Nevertheless, all of his scientific work created a lot of suffering because it didn't ease his financial situation. The climax was in 1905.

As is known, the year 1905 was when the first Russian revolution took place, and it was followed by pogroms. Odessa Jews also experienced a serious pogrom. Hochman's Christian friends advised Hochman to hang a crucifix in his window to spare him the wrath of the hooligans, but Hochman rejected this idea and preferred sharing the fate of his Jewish brothers.

The Russian pogroms affected Hochman very negatively. First, because his school, which was the source of his livelihood, was closed. Second, the pogroms broke him emotionally, and he suffered a major nervous breakdown. He quickly went abroad, where he recovered completely.

Upon his return to Odessa, Hochman continued to run his private school, which was very popular throughout southern Russia. The school provided him with a decent income, and he was able to return to his scientific activities. He wrote a series of treatises that he hoped to publish, but he overworked himself.

One of his projects at that time was to collect material relating to the exact sciences appearing in the Talmud. During this time, he was like his old self as a yeshiva student poring over his Talmudic tractates. Another project was his *Analysis and Synthesis of the Calendar.* He was supposed to give lectures about this topic at the Odessa Academy. Aside from complicated theoretical problems, Hochman was also interested in practical matters such as reforming middle schools in Russia and the question of a Jewish polytechnical school in Odessa.

[*Page 173*]

Hochman published a few articles on the aforementioned subject in the Odessa Russian press. He was also prepared to address the issues in the near future. Death, however, interfered with all his plans, and in the winter of 1916 Chaim Hochman died while Russia was involved in World War I, and the Jews of Russia were subject to a number of Czarist decrees.

Hochman died at a time when no one could even eulogize him properly. May his name be engraved in the hearts of his fellow émigrés, and may he never ever be forgotten!

Yoel Slonim-Slonimsky

Yoel Slonim (Slonimsky) was born in Drohitchin on October 24, 1884. When he was two years old, his parents and he moved to the United States, living mostly in Chicago, where he completed public elementary and middle school, and then attended university. He also visited Russian (Drohitchin – ed.), where he studied briefly in Jewish schools.

He began his literary career in English and published poems and public affairs articles in various English newspapers. Under the influence of his father, a follower of the Enlightenment, and a man educated in foreign languages who loved Yiddish, Slonim started writing Yiddish poems and started publishing in the *Yiddishe Velt* (Jewish World) newspaper. Thereafter Yoel continued publishing his poetry in various Yiddish newspapers and magazines in the United States, and he also wrote many critical articles about Jewish and general poets. He did a great deal to promote the Yiddish language and literature among assimilated circles.

Together with the prominent American attorney, Morris Rottenberg, Charles Zunser and Enny Shomer, Slonim organized a Yiddish club, where Yiddish was proclaimed the only national Jewish language. Slonim was one of the founders of the Yiddish Literary Association in New York, and together with A. Goldber, A. Litwin, Sarah Kestin and others, he was a co-founder of the Radical Zionist Association, one of the first Socialist Zionist organizations in the United States. The Association also published a quarterly publication, *Die Naya Shtimma* (The New Voice), which lasted for only one year until 1905.

One of the forerunners of the Jewish Artists Group in the United States, Slonim was a co-editor of the collection, *Literatur 1,* in which he published a treatise about Oscar Wilde; he did the same thing in the *Yiddisher Kempfer* (Jewish Fighter) in the nationalist *Dos Folk* (The People), in the collection *Troymen un Virklichkeit* (Dreams and Reality) and others. He wrote an article in that book about Edgar Allan Poe. Slonim was also known as a journalist and first-class reporter and interviewer and was active in the field as a contributor to *Mehrheit* (Majority) since 1906, and later to *Tog* (Day) under the pseudonyms of Lotshe Karmen, Y. Sanina, and others. He was especially popular for his reports and descriptions of Jewish gangsters in New York. As a poet, he excelled with his poems from New York City that express the powerful rhythm of the large metropolis, though they suffer from lack of focus. He published two books of poems and critical articles. (From Zalman Reisen's Handbook)

Yoel Slonim completed university with distinction, and served as an assistant district attorney for a while in New York. Some of Slonim's poems are publish in this Yizkor book. Yoel Slonim died on October 26, 1944 in New York (see p. 57).

[Page 174]
A Look at the Old *Kheder*
Radio, Warsaw, Nov. 15, 1935

If the rainy days in October are bothersome and unpleasant, for little Dovidel they were painfully unpleasant. They were the worst days of the year. Inside the classroom was the teacher flaying flesh with his whip, while outside the irksome rain and bitter cold penetrated the bones. Had it been summer, winter or even in freezing weather, Dovidel would have already found a solution: he would have snuck outside and spent his time running around the meadow or skating on the ice. Now, however, he couldn't even stick his nose out the door.

The rain continued outside without a break, and there was mud everywhere. You couldn't take a step anywhere. So little Dovidel had to stay in class the whole day. He remembered how good Yomtof was when he had a whole month off, living carefree and happy, without anything to worry about. But that vacation period went by quickly.

It was now only two weeks after Sukkot, though it seemed to him like months or years. He tried to find reasons to stay at home for a day. He wished he were sick, lying in bed with a fever. However, to his chagrin, he was healthy, and his mother sent him off to kheder. His tiny feet sank into the deep mud, and he could hardly move. He was wearing a pair of boots over his feet, since otherwise it would have been impossible to walk through the mud. Sometimes he stood there, sinking into the mud. Before he could pull out one foot, the other sank down into the mud. He barely managed to extricate himself from the swamp, but he was filthy and covered in mud.

He was close to school, and now Dovidel breathed easier. But he had a new problem: during the night, the rain flooded out the path to the kheder, and no ground was visible. Dovidel didn't have any time to think and tried to find a solution. He would get a whipping for every minute he was late. He made his way into the river with his boots and got to the other side. When he arrived in class, the teacher glared at him, and Dovidel started shaking from fear.

He had been studying under this teacher since Sukkot, and he already had the opportunity to experience him on his shoulders and bones. The Rebbe (teacher), a middle-aged man with a wide beard and large eyebrows, was known in town as an angry person. Everyone knew that any child who was in his class didn't taste honey from him. Under Shmuel (the rebbe's name), a student had to understand. Otherwise, he would be hit.

The classroom was a small room. Next to the window was an old table with a couple of benches seating 15 to 20 small boys, who followed the bible text with their fingers. Dovidel had a bit of joy during those mournful days when one morning the rebbe asked the boys to bring lanterns since they were going to begin studying into the evening. Dovidel was ready to forget all the "crimes" that the rebbe had committed against him.

That day Dovidel was very happy at home since he was going to get his very own lantern. That whole afternoon his studies didn't bother him, and he was anxiously waiting for the evening so he could use his lantern. The children were finally liberated and had their lanterns ready in hand. The Rebbe was trying to keep them in order outside, but as soon as the boys left his class, they forgot him, the kheder and everyone else. They were now the bosses in the dark night. The boys started making a real racket, yelling and pushing each other. Then suddenly someone slipped into the mud, and everyone broke out in laughter. The poor kid got up with a bloody nose. The rain buzzed slowly, in a monotone. The whole town was covered in darkness, and no one was visible, but this didn't bother the young boys.

Gradually the group got smaller as each one went to his house; Dovidel also separated from his friends and hurried home. He now had the strong feeling that he was all grown up. Here he was walking all by himself in the darkness, and he wasn't scared at all. He wasn't far from home when a wind gust blew out his lantern light. Dovidel became seized with fear and started running home. He wanted to shout because he felt that someone was chasing him, but he restrained himself. It wasn't right for him to do it so close to home. It was pitch black, and Dovidel's started imagining demons and ghosts. He was so scared he couldn't find his key, and he started sweating. Inside the house his family could hear rustling at the door as someone opened it. Dovidel rushed in breathlessly.

[Page 175]

It was bright and warm in the house. The sudden contrast from darkness to light impressed Dovidel as he saw his family and neighbors sitting and talking together. He felt like taking revenge on his family; his ego was hurt. He felt pressure on his heart and broke out in loud weeping. Everyone was quiet, but he didn't feel comforted. He went to bed feeling angry.

Dov B. Warshavsky

Eliyahu Zilbergleit

Eliyahu Zilbergleit, known as R. "Eliyahu Machles," was born in Drohitchin. His father, R. Binyamin Chaim Zilbergleit, was a prominent grain merchant who lived all his life in Nikolayev (Russia), and was scholarly in both Jewish and secular studies. His library, the largest in town, was renowned throughout the region, and it was in this home of religious and general knowledge that Eliyahu was educated. For a time, Eliyahu also studied under R. Menachem Reichman, the rabbi of Drohitchin.

R. Eliyahu was known to be both a scholar and a simple person. He wasn't too involved in business affairs, and his wife, Machle, was the breadwinner (which is why Eliyahu was known as Eliyahu Machles). Eliyahu always sat in the House of Study and studied, including kabbalah. He would immerse himself in the mikvah every day.

In his youth, R. Eliyahu had an olinitsa (oil factory?) not far from the church. The priest was very unhappy about this, and the peasants burned down the olinitsa, leaving R. Eliyahu and his family penniless. His father in Nikolayev sent him some money, and R. Menachem provided him with house and a store. Machle, R. Eliyahu's wife was the storekeeper and breadwinner, and R. Eliyahu returned to his studies.

It is told that one Sabbath R. Eliyahu was teaching a class on the weekly Torah portion in the House of Study. After he finished, a visitor approached him and said, "I really enjoyed your Torah lecture. I haven't heard a lecture like that in a long time." Later it was discovered that the guest was the prominent scholar, Rabbi Yisrael Meir Kagan, known throughout the world as the *Chafetz Chaim.*

R. Eliyahu's father, R. Binyamin Chaim, once printed a difficult passage of the Jerusalem Talmud in *Hamelitz,* and asked readers to explain the passage. R. Eliyahu was the person who explained it. *Hamelitz* sent someone to Drohitchin meet the talkative scholar. The representative of *Hamelitz* offered to take a photo of R. Eliyahu, but R. Eliyahu always refused to be photographed.

R. Eliyahu also supported Torah scholars. He aided the Kobriner Rebbe, R. Noachka, substantially and sent money to R. Nachumka of Grodno. R. Eliyahu gave the eulogy for the Osevitz Martyrs and mourned deeply for R. Sender Osevitzer, who had always been R. Eliyahu's guest whenever R. Sender came to town. There was also the occasion when R. Eliyahu gave the usual Sabbath lecture in the synagogue on the Sabbath between Rosh Hashanah and Yom Kippur when R. Menachem didn't feel well and asked R. Eliyahu to speak in his place. In his later years, R. Eliyahu taught children Talmud and earned a small living from it.

R. Eliyahu died suddenly from a stroke before World War I. His manuscripts on Torah subjects, unfortunately, were burned during the War. As mentioned, R. Eliyahu was a close relative of R. Zalman Sender of Maltsh.

Information from Gedaliah Kaplan

[*Page 176*]

Rabbi Shimon Tarasov

Rabbi Shimon Tarasov, a son of Rabbi Yosef Yehuda, was born in Brisk in 1885, and he studied at the Novardok Yeshiva, together with the esteemed scholar, Rabbi Yaffen. In approximately 1915 he married Fruma, the daughter of Shmuel from Volevel, near Drohitchin, and settled in Drohitchin, where he was a teacher until 1924.

די לויה פֿון סלאָנימער רב ה' מרדכי ווייצעל זצ"ל

Die Beerdigung des Slonimer Rabiners M. Weizel.

Funeral of R. Mordechale Slonimer, 25 Adar, 1916 [trans.: 1916 was a Jewish leap year, so there were two Adars that year. The text here does not specify which Adar the funeral took place on] (see p. 154, "R. Asher Weitzel)

In 1924, Rabbi Tarsov and his family emigrated to the United States, where they settled in Chicago. In Chicago Rabbi Tarsov served as a poultry ritual slaughterer, and he taught at the Beit Rachel-Leah Talmud Torah (St. Louis Street). At the same time, he served as rabbi of the Yavneh Synagogue (for three years), the Horodok Synagogue, and the Kobriner-Karliner Chassidic shtibel.

Rabbi Tarasov died on 24 Adar (March 13), 1950 in Chicago.

Yosef Shochet

Yosef Shochet

Yosef Shochet, or Yossel Tchernes, was born in Motele and married in Drohitchin, where he was always involved in teaching. He taught children Talmud and had a very analytical mind, like a philosopher. Unfortunately, there are no precise details about him. He died before World War I. R. Yossel had seven children: Avraham Shimon (Brisk), Reuven (Yanovo), Moshe (Palestine), Aryeh, Noachke, Hershel and Michel.

R. Yossel's grandson (son of Avraham Shimon) Yaakov was a professor of mathematics at the University of St. Petersburg. Afterwards, he became a full professor at the United States Navy Academy in Indianapolis, Indiana. He was also a professor at the University of Michigan in Ann Arbor and in Pennsylvania (Philadelphia). Yaakov died in the United States at the age of 77.

Shlomo Freidenberg

Shlomo Friedenberg was born in approximately 1880 in Drohitchin. His father, Berl, spent many years in yeshivas and was known to be a scholar. Later he got married in Bilien (a village near Drohitchin), and went into business, though he was unsuccessful. He moved to town and became a teacher. Until World War I he taught children Talmud and later taught it to older students at the Moriah School. Shlomo died in 1938 in Pinsk. His wife and children (except for one daughter in Palestine) were all killed. May G-d avenge their blood!

Shlomo Freidenberg

[*Page 177*]
Naftali Steinberg

Naftali Steinberg
(handwriting that is legible says 'Drohitchin')

Naftali Zechariah Steinberg, or Naftali the Teacher as he was called, was born in approximately 1863 in Pinsk. As a child he lost his father, Yitzchak, and had to spend his childhood and youth in poverty and under trying conditions. He studied in religious kheders and yeshivas and was certified as a teacher.

Naftali did not want to pursue a rabbinical career. He was attracted to secular culture and became a follower of the Enlightenment, specializing in pedagogy. He was self-taught, and studied intensively on his own as much as he could. After finishing his yeshiva studies, he would take a dictionary and study Hebrew and other secular subjects. He would also spend time reading book; even in later years he never let a book out of his hands. Naftali distinguished himself in his knowledge of both old and new Hebrew literature.

The gravestone of Naftali Steinberg, who died 24 Kislev [Dec. 5], 1921 [actually 1920]

Here is buried the outstanding man, enlightened in all sciences, who raised thousands of students, Naftali Zechariah, son of Levi Yitzchak Steinberg. He died on 24 Kislev 5681 (Decemeber 5), 1920.

Naftali was barely 17 years old when he married Chaya Sarah, a daughter of R. Motya Pinchas, the kheder teacher, a Jewish scholar from Drohitchin. In approximately 1880, Naftali began teaching in Drohitchin, but he was dissatisfied with the educational system and teaching methods of the old kheder, where the children would sit at long tables as their teacher would teach them the alphabet. Once they knew the rudiments of Hebrew, they then proceeded to study the weekly Torah portion with the Rashi commentary and Prophetic books. They also learned to write some Yiddish from a workbook. Later on, they started studying Jewish law, including Talmud and the commentaries. Girls studied Hebrew, prayers and basic Yiddish writing skills. There were special Jewish "writers" who were responsible for teaching Jewish girls how to write Yiddish letters. Naftali didn't approve of all of this, and he established a new educational system, reforming the study program and changing the teaching methods of the Kheder, which he re-named a *Class*.

Naftali's modernized education system was not approved of by the people in town. The parents didn't entrust their children to Naftali. So Naftali was forced to settle for a class geared only for girls, since there were some modernized families who were willing to entrust their daughters to Naftali to learn Hebrew. Some time later, Naftali managed to win over a few parents in town, and he was able to open a class for boys too. This class was the first modernized class in Drohitchin.

[Page 178]

In Naftali's modernized class there was a blackboard, and the children sat at desks. They studied the bible, Rashi, grammar and Hebrew. They read the works of Mapu and Smolensky and learned by heart the poems of Gordon and others. Later Naftali attracted the teachers Leibush Neiditch, Yitzchak Avramtshik and Ozer Lev. With their help he developed a network of modernized classes, and he had the major influence on them. He did this his entire life.

The Folk School under German occupation in 1917. Seated from left: Tordos Leib Milner, Naftali Steinberg, Moshe Beszhedsky and Yosef Wasserman. Standing, from left: Rossel Valevelsky, Pinsky (from Slonim) and Chana Steinberg.

Obviously, there were many kheder classes in Drohitchin having Talmud and other religious subjects as the main part of the curriculum while leaving secular studies in the background. Naftali was the undisputed leading pedagogue in town, and he was considered the "Rebbe" of the modernized community in Drohitchin.

Naftali died on Kislev 24, 1921 in Drohitchin. He had three children: Zeidel (who died in Chicago), Feigel (who was killed with her family in Pinsk) and Chana (who lives in Israel). Chana and Feigel followed in the footsteps of their father Naftali, and for years they worked as teachers of their own modernized classes in Drohitchin.

[*Page 179*]
Yaakov Sidorov

Yaakov Sidorov and his class before World War I

Yaakov Sidorov was born in approximately 1880 in Drohitchin. His father, R. Yitzchak was known as the "Old Cantor" or the "Grodno Cantor" and was a cantor and ritual slaughterer in Drohitchin. His mother was known as Chaya Gittel, "the Cantor's wife." Yaakov Sidorov, or Yankel the Cantor's as he was known, was a famous teacher and devoted person. From early childhood he excelled in his learning abilities. Most of his knowledge was acquired by self-study. From his youth he began to give lectures, and the money he earned was given to his parents to help them with their household expenses because there was little money at home. At the same time he studied on his own and learned Hebrew and Russian.

Sidorov later opened a school for girls, a Hebrew class for girls, which he ran successfully until 1915.

He spent the War years in the village of Motele (near Drohitchin), his wife's hometown. In Motele, Sidorov was involved in community affairs and served as mayor. After World War I Yaakov Sidorov and his family returned to Drohitchin, where he died in 1919 from typhus. His wife, Esther, and two daughters returned to Motele and apparently were killed there. May G-d avenge their blood!

Yaakov Sidorov was always an active Zionist and headed the movement in Drohitchin. Everyone in Drohitchin who knew him liked and respected him.

[Page 180]
Zvi Schwartz

Zvi Schwartz

Zvi Schwartz was born in Drohitchin in 1885. His father, R. Yossel Schwartz, was involved in business. Zvi studied in kheder and the House of Study in town and later in yeshivas in Pohost, Maltsh, Pinsk, Minsk, and others, where he excelled because of his good skills and dedication in his studies. Later on he studied secular subjects, including languages and Jewish and non-Jewish classics. He especially concentrated on the philosophies of economic and social sciences.

At 18 years of age, Zvi became active in community affairs. He established a library in Drohitchin, offered Yiddish and Hebrew courses, and had planned to build a modern school. For this purpose he traveled to Pinsk, Minsk, Brisk and Byalistock, where he collected material and studied methods to realize his dream, which he was finally able to carry out. A couple of years before World War I, Schwartz opened a modern model Yavneh School, which was a success. However, its existence was cut short because of denunciations to the authorities about it.

At that time, Zvi met his future wife, Leah Fanaberia of Brisk, a fiery socialist, who had been in hiding from the Czarist police in Kovel. Zvi taught her Hebrew, and under his influence she traveled to Palestine to the Herzliya gymnasia high school in Tel Aviv. She later became a Hebrew teacher at the settlement, Yavniel.

Before the outbreak of World War I in 1914 Schwartz went with Leah for a visit to Palestine. They then went to Russia with the intention of returning to Palestine to get married. The War, however, interfered with their plans and separated them. Zvi remained in the German-occupied area, and Leah went off to Vitebsk, and then to Odessa, where she studied to be a dentist at Novorossisky (New Russian) University. At the time of the Russian Revolution, Leah was in Moscow, where she worked as a teacher at the Tarbut School. She also worked at the Pedagogical Institute headed by the famous Professor Stanislav Teofilovich Shatsky.

In 1921 Zvi and Leah were reunited in Warsaw and got married and settled there. They remained there until 1936. During this period Zvi visited Palestine twice (in 1928 and 1934). He had previously been there in 1914. In Warsaw Zvi initiated the Palestine Produce Movement, which sought to strengthen and develop industry, agriculture, and business in Palestine. Zvi believed this would help attract millions of Jews to Palestine. He wrote articles in the Hebrew journal, *Business and Industry,* and he dedicated a special page to encouraging Jews to buy and use products made in Palestine.

In 1926, Schwartz started the Carmel society, the goal of which was to create consumers of Palestine wine. In May 1926, Schwartz and his colleagues, Dr. Klumel, Levi Yitzchak Kahanov of Warsaw and Yaakov Shapiro of the Vinyard Association in Palestine signed a contract that authorized them all to be representatives of the wine producers in the settlements of Rishon Lezion and Zichron Yaakov in Palestine. In 1927, Zvi and Dr. Y. Bagalyovsky published a book called *Wine as a Healer.*

In 1930, Schwartz put out a large anthology called *This is the Way,* in which he explained the importance of products from Palestine. Others who contributed articles were Ze'ev Jabotinsky, A. Khanin, A. Idelson, Dr. B. Feigin, H. Tcherniovsky, Dr. Yakovsohn, E. Zuckerman, M. Meirovitch, Engineer, S. Yaffe, Dr. S. Stavsky, B. Pinsker, Dr. S, Levenbaum, Rabbi M. Nissenbaum, S. Petroshka, S. Steinberg and others.

In 1937, Zvi and Leah arrived in Argentina to visit a brother and decided to remain there. The Schwartzes quickly became popular in Argentina, and their house served as a meeting place for writers, leaders and culture activists. Zvi spoke well, and interested his listeners in whatever he had to say. He decided he wanted to provide a good Jewish education for the children and a solution for parents who had become estranged from Jewish books. Zvi taught Torah, cited scientists and philosophers, and showed how Jews were different than other people. He argued that Jews should go against the stream, and as a result, a development movement would develop, intended to "improve Jews from inside out through economic productivity and intellectual elevation."

[Page 181]

In 1938, Zvi published a brochure, *Development,* in which he advocated his idea of a three-fold revolution in the life of the Jewish People: a socio-economic one; a national-psychological one, and a national-cultural one. Schwartz never belonged to any party; he was for a whole Judaism. He wanted a whole Jew, a whole people.

Schwartz over-exerted himself. Despite the warnings of doctors, he continued to speak and explain, dreaming of an organized Jewish community in Buenos Aires and a trans-national Jewish committee of South American Jewry. Some of his dreams were actually realized. He was a co-founder of the organized Jewish community in Buenos Aires and co-founder of the rabbinate; he organized courses on the Sabbath and Sunday. He was the senior co-founder of the YIVO archive and Central Library, to which he contributed a treasury of books and documents. For his service, the YIVO administration named a study room of the Central Library after him.

On the 900th birthday of the biblical commentator, Rashi, Zvi Schwartz and writers Yedidyah Efron, Nachman Gezang and Yosef Mendelson published the Rashi commentary in three languages: Yiddish, Hebrew and Spanish. The writer, Shachne Resnick, translated the book into Spanish. At Zvi's suggestion, the book of Jewish philosophy, *Kuzari,* was translated into Spanish.

In June 1942, Schwartz began publishing *Writings,* a monthly publication about "Integral Judaism," with a selection of classics of old and new Jewry. Each edition was 80 pages long, and was a fountain of Jewish teachings and knowledge. In his final years, Zvi Schwartz was very weak, suffered from heart trouble, and couldn't move. The destruction of European Jewry only worsened his health, and as he lay on his deathbed, Zvi wrote a will and testament about how to save the remnant of the Jewish People.

R. Zvi Schwartz died on January 7, 1945 in Buenos Aires, Argentina. Melech Ravitch writes: "At his funeral at the cemetery, his wife Leah eulogized him. It was a classic speech from a real Jewish Woman of Valor." Leah Schwartz continued publishing Zvi's *Writings* from June 1942 to the time of this writing, with the active collaboration of writers Avraham Golomb, Yisrael Efroiken and others.

(Information about the great Zvi Schwartz was taken from the monograph written by Pinchas Bizberg. Also see the reviews by Dr. Moshe Merkin in Die Yiddishe Zeitung, November 29, 1949, Argentina, and by Melech Ravitch in the Freie Yiddish Tribuna, December 1946, London, England.)

Kehat Kliger

The Ballad of the Death of R. Zvi

And when the Angel came for the heart of
the great Jew, R. Zvi Schwartz,
R. Zvi said: "In a minute, and his face was bathed
with the light of the Divine Presence.
The sun set; the summer evening played around
with *cherubim* and *seraphim* angels
on R. Zvi's unfinished book.
The entire room was enveloped in pink.
But R. Zvi smiled, his eye deep and wise,
drank down heaven like a blue jug.
R. Zvi smiled, his body and soul sang the prayer:
"The soul is Yours, and the body is Yours"
And Leah, R. Zvi's companion, the quiet dove;
understood his smile and heard his praise.
She didn't cry, but she saw. R. Zvi leaves this
earth, like the sun and final glow.
The angel says, "R. Zvi, let's go!"
And the angel rustles its white wings, like ivory,
its hand on his shoulder, the two of them as if
off to a family celebration.
But in *kheder*, with an open book,
R. Zvi's eternal light never goes out.
The light shines brighter in the morning blue,
and sings, "Blessed be He and blessed be his Name."

[*Page 182*]

TALMUD TORAH SCHOOL
TORAH VE-DA'AT (1934) IN DROHITCHIN
7 Iyar, 5694 (April 22), 1934
The Talmud Torah

The Talmud Torah, *Torah Ve-Da'at,* was founded with the money of R. Yitzchak Avigdor and Elka Telekhansky of Chicago (See p. 220).

This photo was taken in 1934. Seated, from left to right: Sender Shapiro (teacher), Zusha Warshavsky, Rabbi Kalenkovich, Zechariah Schmid (Committee), Shmuel Rock, Chaim Shulman (teacher) and two female teachers: Valevelsky-Charsel and another one.

Sender Shapiro

Sender Shapiro, known as the Odrezhiner Teacher, was born in Libeshei, near Pinsk. He studied in the House of Study following his wedding in approximately 1908 to Michla, the daughter of Nachum Pomerantz of Odrezhina (near Pinsk). Shapiro then settled in Drohitchin and opened a kheder for new Talmud students.

From 1924 until World War II, Shapiro was a teacher in the Talmud Torah. He and his wife had five children; however, no one survived. They were all killed. May G-d avenge their blood!

Shmuel Rock

Shmuel Rock was born in Kamenitz, and studied in the Slobodka and other yeshivas. He worked as a teacher at the Moriah School during his first stay in Drohitchin, but later left Drohitchin to become a teacher in Rozhinoy, where he also got married. He then returned to Drohitchin, and worked as an administrator of the Talmud Torah, where he also taught Talmud to older children.

Shmuel Rock was a capable person with a strong personality. He did a lot for the

[Page 183]

Mizrachi movement, and was an active member for many years prior to arriving in Drohitchin. He identified with the right wing of Mizrachi and was very sympathetic to the Revisionist Movement. In Drohitchin he was one of the leaders of Mizrachi.

Shmuel, his wife and daughters were all killed. May G-d avenge their blood!

Chaim Shulman

May G-d avenge his blood!

Chaim Shulman was from Motele, where he was in business and a leader of the Mizrachi movement. After World War I he married Reichla (a daughter of Shlomo Piasetsky from Lezitkevich) who died young, leaving him with two small children. Chaim had three additional children from a second wife.

Chaim Shulman tried going into business in Drohitchin. He opened a shoe business), but was unsuccessful, so he decided to become a religious teacher. Until the destruction of Drohitchin, he served as a teacher at the Talmud Torah while also serving as the secretary of Mizrachi, to which he was very devoted, belonging to its left wing.

In 1942, when the German murderers slaughtered the Jews of Drohitchin, Shulman and his family were in hiding out under the floor of his house. The hideout had been prepared earlier. Shulman was also able to smuggle his family out of Drohitchin together with a few other Jews and hide out in a trench in the Somenishcha Forest a few miles from town.

Winter arrived with bitter cold, and Chaim suffered from frostbite on his feet. Out of desperation to save himself, he warmed himself by a fire, resulting in gangrene and open infected wounds. He died from his pain and suffering in the ditch in the Somenishcha Forest. His eldest son and several other Jewish boys went to look for food to stay alive; he collapsed and died from fear.

Shulman's wife and the remaining four children died one after the other from exposure, cold, hunger and suffering at the hands of the enemy. The remaining Jewish boys buried Shulman and his wife and children in the Somenishcha Forest. May G-d avenge their deaths!

Shmuel Artshis Baum

R. Smuel Artshis (Baum)

Shmuel, son of Aharon Baum, or "Shmuel Artshis," was from an old Drohitchin family. He was a religious schoolteacher his whole life, teaching children mostly the basics of Hebrew and Torah. R. Shmuel was an expert in his field, and his work with the children had results.

R. Shmuel died on 13 Tishrei (Sept. 29), 1917 at the age of 85. His wife's name was Esther, and they had seven children: Hershel, Beila, Sheina Sarah, Aharon Asher, Yeshayahu and Breina.

Isaac Kolnick

May G-d avenge his blood!

Isaac Kolnick was from Libeshei, near Pinsk. During World War I he settled in Drohitchin, and married his wife, Miriam Itka, the daughter of Naches and Yoshpa Burstein. After the War he worked briefly as a teacher at the Moriah School, and later ran his own kheder at the Chassidic shtibel for beginning Talmud students, though officially it was affiliated with the Talmud Torah.

Kolnick and his wife and daughter Peshka were all killed. May G-d avenge their blood!

[*Page 184*]

MORIAH HEBREW SCHOOL, DROHITCHIN, 1937

A class from the Moriah School in 1937. Seated left to right: Moshe Bezdzhezsky, Miriam Epstein, Levi Feldman, Marisha Zilberstein, Betsalel Wolfson and Rachel Prishkulnik. Everyone except for Marisha Zilberstein was killed. May G-d avenge their blood!

Moshe Bezdzhezsky

May G-d avenge his blood!

Moshe Bezdzhezsky was born in approximately 1893 in Drohitchin. Until his Bar Mitzvah he studied in Pinsk, and then in a gymnasia in Brisk. Later he completed his studies at the Vilna Institute (Jewish Teachers' Seminar), authorizing him to be a gymnasia teacher or rabbi.

With his qualification, had Moshe been an aggressive and ambitious person, he could have had a good career. However, he wasn't this type, and was actually too modest and restrained, and (illegible) a lot in his life.

After he married Chana Zbar, the daughter of Simcha Lasintzer, Moshe settled in Drohitchin, where he took up teaching. He gave private classes and was briefly a teacher at the Yavneh School until the outbreak of World War I.

Under the German occupation, Moshe was the administrator of the Jewish school supported by the German authorities. From 1922 to World War II, Moshe was a teacher at the Moriah School, but he barely made a living.

Ideologically Moshe was a Revisionist Zionist, as were his two sons, Avraham and Yitzchak, who belonged to the Beitar movement in Drohitchin. Today Avraham (Avrasha) lives in Israel. Moshe, Chana and their children, Yitzchak and Nechama, were all killed. May G-d avenge their deaths!

[Page 185]
Chaim Betzalel Wolfson

May G-d avenge his blood!

Betzalel Wolfson was originally from Pinsk and was therefore known as the "teacher from Pinsk." He came to Drohitchin after World War I and was an exceptional person in town.

Wolfson knew how to study Talmud and regularly studied Talmudic tractates. He walked slowly and spoke softly and developed a good relationship with parents. Hhe always was held in esteem. Before World War I, Wolfson taught his own class and used modern methods with a Jewish flavor. From the establishment of the Moriah School until the bitter end, Wolfson was the main teacher.

Wolfson was a devoted Zionist his entire life and advocated Jewish control over all the historical borders of the Land of Israel according to G-d's promise to Abraham. He was a strong supporter of Jabotinsky, and in that spirit influenced his students and other young people in Drohitchin.

He, his wife Rachel and only daughter Alta were killed. May G-d avenge their blood! (See his picture on page 65).

Levi Feldman

May G-d avenge his blood!

Levi Feldman came to Drohitchin in his thirties as a teacher at the Moriah School. Levi was young and clever and was adept at his work. He was able to speak with young and old alike and succeeded with both.

Eventually Levi married Risha, the daughter of Chaim Zissel and Fradel Epstein of Drohitchin, and then became the director of the Moriah School. The principal of the school was Dr. Goldstein and others, but Levi was the last director of the last school in Drohitchin. He and Risha and their daughter were killed. May G-d avenge their blood!

Sheinka Feldman

Sheinka Feldman was born in 1907 on the Smulnik Estate near Drohitchin to her parents, Yudel and Chaya Feldman. She studied under Zvi Schwartz, Moshe Hershorn, Velvel Poliak, and others. Between 1922 and 1925, she took courses at the Preblistka School in Warsaw and studied to be a teacher. From 1926 to 1934, Sheinka worked as a teacher at the Moriah School in Drohitchin, and then she moved to Palestine, where she taught a class as well. Sheinka died in Palestine on the last day of Passover in 1945.

Sheinka Feldman and her Moriah School Class (The sign in the photo says "Moriah School party.")

[Page 186]

Ethel Goldberg

Ethel Goldberg, or Stella Black as she was known after her marriage, was born in approximately 1898. She was a quiet and charming girl and did well in school. When she was still young, she traveled to the United States and stayed with a sister in Indianapolis, where she worked in a hat shop and took evening English and secular classes. Shortly thereafter she started working as a schoolteacher.

In 1924, Ethel became interested in writing poetry. The poet Z. Bunin, who was married to a niece of Ethel, wrote the following:

"When Ethel found out that I wrote poetry, she became very influenced by my writing. Even though she didn't know Yiddish very well, she started writing and reading Yiddish so enthusiastically that in a short time I was way behind her. From the very beginning she was already recognized as a fine poet. Ethel published her work in various publications, and one of her poems appears on page 287 of the women's anthology published in Chicago in 1928."

Ethel's husband, Louis Black PhD., was the chief labor statistician of the state of California. During the war years, he held a senior position in the American government, and was also a university lecturer there.

Ethel suffered from a major illness and died in 1947 in San Francisco.

Ethel Goldberg

Over My Silence

Hours hang long and mute over my silence,
They pull about desolation and crookedness,
My hours, my days no longer want
to walk over desolation.
They remain trapped at night
standing at the head of my bed.
Over my silence
My hours, my days,
wait blind frightened,
with crooked dark patience,
until my silence finds a new way
for them, the difficult hours and days.

   Varheit

Shadows

On roads and streets,
shadows spread.
Already born,
like dark lived-through hours.
But the wind rejoiced
way out at noon with the early morning,
and through the shadows the sun shone
for a moment or two.
But you, my heart!
On whose muted blue wings
has my early morning dream ended?
You, bothered by waiting and longing,
it's still difficult to deceive the early morning.
You know that the moments rush to push
into the night.

   Varheit

[*Page 187*]
Zavel Averbuch

Zavel Averbuch

Zavel Averbuch, the eldest son of Meshel and Chava Averbuch, was born in Drohitchin, studied in yeshiva, and then attended university. He lived a very stormy life. His good abilities, and especially his effervescent temperament and revolutionary character, didn't allow him to limit himself to his own private world. Even as a teenager he developed a rare talent for speaking, and he traveled to cities and towns to give speeches pertaining to various Jewish issues.

Zavel then became involved in the revolutionary movement in Czarist Russia and fought against Czarist despotism. In Drohitchin, Zavel was the main founder of the S. S. (Socialist Zionists), and together with Yaakov Sidorov, educated and taught the working youth in town. They opened a library for the young people and offered evening courses and theater performances. Zavel traveled through towns and cities and gave revolutionary speeches. He railed especially against the Czarist pogroms against Jews. Following the Kishinev pogrom, Zavel gave fiery speeches against the Czarist regime in the central market and House of Study in Drohitchin under the watchful eye of the Czarist police. He was later a delegate to the Kiev Convention, which addressed issues relating to Jewish emigration.

In Polotsk (Vitebsk gubernia), Zavel was one of the leaders of the Jewish self-defense force and was wounded in the foot. He then had to go for treatment to Lousanne, Switzerland. Later, Zavel tried his luck in manufacturing in Byalistock, but he was unsuccessful. He lost his money and left.

After he married his wife, who was originally from Polotsk, Zavel opened a gymnasia in Semiatitz, but he didn't remain there long either. He traveled to Warsaw and began writing articles in the Jewish press. He accompanied the writer, Sholem Aleichem, on his reading tour, and Sholem Aleichem respected Zavel immensely.

During World War I, Zavel Averbuch traveled through Russia, but exactly what happened to him is unknown. Some say that he was a commander of a revolutionary unit in Astrakhan, was hit by the Russian White Guards in 1918 and buried there.

Zavel left behind a wife and three children. His two daughters currently work in journalism in Russia. His son held the rank of captain in the army, and is probably a higher officer today. (See pp. 188, 211).

Bashke Berezovsky
May G-d avenge her blood!

Bashke Berezovsky

Bashke Berezovsky, the daughter of R. Shimon and Lotze Weissman, was born in Drohitchin in 1887. She married Yosef Berezovsky of Yanova. Both were cultured people, and the whole time they lived in Drohitchin they were active in the cultural and community life of the town.

In January 1937, Basha arrived in Chicago, and remained there until July, 1939, when she returned to Vilna, where she married a second time. She died in the Vilna ghetto. May G-d avenge her blood!

Bashke's first husband, Yosef, died a few years before the war in Drohitchin.

[*Page 188*]

Menachem Averbuch

May G-d avenge his blood!

Menachem Averbuch, the youngest son of Meshel and Chava Averbuch, was born in Drohitchin. He studied in kheder and later graduated from a Russian gymnasia in Warsaw. In 1914 he was a student at the Conservatory in Poltava.

Ideologically, Menachem was a "Yiddishist" and a tended toward socialism, in contrast to the average person. He never married and assisted his parents some in their business. Menachem had a straight mind, spoke well, and knew languages. The town authorities often called on him as an advocate with outside authorities.

In 1919, the Poles arrested Asher Schwartzbard and sent him to Kobrin. During that frightful time, when the Poles suspected every Jew of being a communist, Asher was playing with his life. The community sent Menachem to Kobrin, where he exhibited self-sacrifice in working to free Asher.

Throughout his life, Menachem was affiliated with the Union of Jewish Cooperative Societies in Poland, and he would travel to many towns as an auditor to examine the books of the savings accounts. In this capacity he also served as a member of the administration of the Drohitchin People's Bank.

Menachem was also involved in writing. He wrote poems, collaborated on the *Pinsker Shtimma* (Pinsk Voice), and wrote articles in the Warsaw *Moment*. He was also an active collector of folklore for the Vilna YIVO office. In 1941, when the Russians were planning to send his family off to Russia, Menachem hid out in Lemberg. Later, when the Germans took over Drohitchin, he returned to town and worked with the Jewish Committee (See Yizkor Section).

Nothing specific is known about what happened to Menachem. According to reports, Menachem succeeded in breaking out of the Drohitchin ghetto and getting to Lemberg, where the German killers murdered him.

His brother, Avraham, wrote regretfully: "Menachem, who had so many friends and acquaintances among the gentile population and who owned so much gold and valuable assets, couldn't even find a hideout to save himself from death. May G-d avenge his blood!"

(See pp. 78, 187 and 211)

Moshe Sapozhnik

Moshe Sapozhnik, the son of Todres, was born in Drohitchin in 1897. Even before World War I he completed the Russian gymnasia in Warsaw and enrolled in the faculty of medicine at the University. Shortly thereafter the war broke out (1914), and Moshe became a student at the music school in Poltava, thereby remaining at home.

Moshe Sapozhnik

Under the German occupation, Moshe was the head of the regional hospital in Drohitchin, and participated in community affairs in town. He fought for Jewish honor, moral, and self-respect, and mocked the frivolous Jewish women who flirted with the Germans. For this he barely escaped being sent to jail by the German, but thanks to the head physician of the hospital, he avoided the punishment.

In March 1917, when the Germans took over Ukraine, Moshe enrolled the University of Odessa. With the outbreak of the Russian Revolution (1917), Moshe joined the revolutionary forces and was appointed commander of the Kherson garrison. He participated in the battles against the Black Hundreds: the *Varngeltsas, Hetmantsas, and Skoropodskys,* who made Jewish blood flow like water. During the battle near Sevastopol at the end of 1920, Moshe was killed; he was buried with full military honors as a hero of the people on the most beautiful boulevard in Sevastopol.

For 16 years, his brother Yonah hid the secret of Moshe's death from their parents.

[Page 189]
Tsippora Rovin

Tsippora Rovin, or Miriam Tsippa as she was known as a child, was born in Drohitchin. Her father was R. Shamai Hackman, and her mother was the daughter of R. Hershel Zelig from Brashevitch, who moved to Palestine in his old age.

In 1901, Tsippora and her husband left for the United States, where her father already lived for a long time, and settled in New York, where Tsippora began her writing career. Her first publication, a book of poetry called, *A World Unto its Own,* appeared in 1944. Thereafter she published poems and correspondence in various publications. In 1951 Tsippora put out a small book called, *A Land of Their Own – Independence Day,* in which she depicted her life in Israel between 1947 and 1949.

Tsippora Rovin

Tsippora was a strong support of Labor Zionism and visited Palestine three times. She now lives permanently in Israel.

(The Editors)

My maternal grandfather R. Hershel Zelig, was always a village Jew in Brashevitch, near Drohitchin. When he became wealthy, about 95 years ago, he started distributing charity, supporting many poor people in Drohitchin. He would send wagons filled with potatoes, flour, cabbage, beets, cucumbers, and vegetables for the needy of Drohitchin. Before Passover the poor Jews already knew that R. Hershel Zelig would, with G-d's help, provide them with what they needed for the holiday.

R. Hershel Zelig also helped build the old House of Study 95 years ago. I head that the old rabbi, R. Menachem used to say that if it weren't for the villager from Brashevitch, the old House of Study would never have been built. A few years later, R. Hershel Zelig traveled to Palestine. When the sad news arrived that he had died in Jerusalem, the congregants of the old House of Study studied Mishnah in his memory and said the Kaddish prayer on his behalf. In fact, the congregation observed his yahrzeit for many years.

I left Drohitchin a long time ago, but the pictures of the town are still fresh in my memory. I can still see the House of Study, where the Talmud Torah School that was supported by the rebbe's wife, was located, and where R. Mosher Isser's taught the children Talmud. At that time we lived in a store near Rivka Shepsel's that was next to the Street House of Study. I used to watch the children in kheder at the House of Study run over to the well in the courtyard and drink down fresh cold water.

I can still see the old wife of the cantor, who lived across from the House of Study, bringing cucumbers, carrots and lettuce from her garden for the children in the Talmud Torah. The religious wife of the cantor considered this to be a great mitzvah deed, to delight the children with some vegetables and thereby enable the children to make a blessing when they ate the vegetables.

I can remember that when I was a little girl my mother used to send me shopping for the house, especially to Motya Leib's store, where Motya Leib sold syrup for a kopek, and herring for a couple of pennies. Incidentally, in 1934 I had the opportunity to visit Motya Leib (R. Mordechai Leib Kaminetsky) in Jerusalem, where he lived with his wife Feigel in a tiny house on Sha'arei Zedek Street. When I met him then, he was 90 years old and was studying Talmud. His children were religious as well.

I can still see R. Mendel's father, R. Moshe Isser, who was known to be teaching a third generation of children. R. Moshe Isser was my grandfather's teacher, then my father Shamai's teacher, and finally, my brother's teacher.

I remember R. Moshe Velvel very well. He was a Talmud teacher who had a small house in the alley leading to Starasilia. I also remember Shmuel Artshis the Talmud teacher, who had his class at the synagogue courtyard near Binyamin Moshe Shochet. May these words of mine serve as a gravestone inscription for our destroyed hometown.

Tzippora Rovin

[Page 190]
Tordos Leib Milner

Tordos Leib Milner

Tordos Leib Milner was born in Drohitchin and was the eldest son of Moshe Mendel and Golda Hinda Milner. On his father's side, he was a descendant of the famous kabbalist and scholar, Rabbi Dovidel Yaffe.

He received his earliest education in the kheders and from the teachers in Drohitchin. Later he studied at the yeshivas in Yanova and Pruzhena. He also studied in Pinsk and Brisk, where he graduated from a dental technician school. At the same time he worked as a teacher.

Milner then established and ran a private school for girls and children in Drohitchin, and he was at the same time an active Zionist, especially as a member of the Labor Zionist party. During World War I under German occupation, Milner was briefly a member of the Jewish people's militia, and then the administrator of the typhus patients' hospital under the director Shimon, the doctor, and a German doctor. Later he was a member of the teaching staff of the Yiddish Folks School, which was subsidized by the German authorities.

In 1920, Milner emigrated from Drohitchin, arriving in Chicago in August. He was immediately accepted as a teacher at the I. L. Peretz Yiddish School (3322 Douglas Boulevard), and then served as a teacher at the Yavneh Talmud Torah and Douglas Park Workers' Circle School. In 1922 Milner began working as a correspondent of the *Tog* newspaper in Chicago as well as for *Kunds*. In 1930 he moved over to the *Morgen Journal* and *Amerikaner* newspapers, serving as their correspondent in Chicago and the Midwest until 1953.

From early 1953, Milner was the administrator of the Chicago division of the unified newspaper, *Tog-Morgen Journal,* and the weekly, *Amerikaner.* Todros Leib Milner was a skilled journalist whose reports and coverage of Jewish life in Chicago were published weekly in the aforementioned newspapers for several decades. Readers both in the United States and abroad knew him very well.

During all the years that Milner was in the United States, he was a member of the Jewish National Labor Union and participated in all Zionist, community, and Yiddish-Hebrew cultural conferences in Chicago. Todros Milner married Esther Altman (of Winnipeg, Canada), who was an activist in the Women's Pioneer Organization in Chicago. The Milners had only one child, a son Shimon Nachman, who was a student in the Faculty of Chemistry at the University of Chicago.

Dr. Goldstein

May G-d avenge his blood!

Dr. Goldstein was originally from Galicia and arrived in Drohitchin in the early 1920s. He was the first principal of the Moriah School, which was very successful under his administration. Dr. Goldstein was an educated and cultured man and was very popular in town because of his speaking abilities and his bearing.

Dr. Goldstein was the founder and director of the Beitar movement in Drohitchin, and he was a strong advocate of Vladimir Ze'ev Jabotinsky's ideas. Early in the 1930s Dr. Goldstein left Drohitchin, and no one ever heard from him again. In all likelihood, he and has family shared the same fate as the rest of our martyrs. May G-d avenge their blood!

See photographs on pp. 44 and 90.

Page 191]
Yisrael Baruch Eisenstein

Yisrael Baruch and Esther Eisenstein

Yisrael Baruch Eisenstein was born in Drohitchin on July 15, 1885. His father, R. David, was a religious Jew who traveled to the United States four times and returned to Drohitichin each time. He died on 16 Kislev (November 10), 1938. Yisrael's mother, Chaya Gittel, was a modest women who died on 26 Tammuz (July 22), 1930. She was a descendant of the kabbalist, R. Dovidel Yaffe.

Until he was 13 years old, Yisrael Baruch studied under the religious teachers and secular teachers in Drohitchin. Aside from religious subjects and Hebrew, he also diligently studied Russian. He then attended the Pinsk yeshiva, later transferring to study under R. Zalman Sender in Maltsh. Finally, he studied at the Mir Yeshiva, where the head of yeshiva was Rabbi Eliyahu Baruch Kamai. He remained at Mir until 1898, and then studied in the House of Study in Drohitchin and taught Hebrew to earn some money.

With the rise of Herzl's political Zionism, R. Yisrael Baruch became attracted to the Zionist movement. Together with others, he established a group of Zionist youth affiliated with the Enlightenment. They became involved with selling *Keren Kayemet* (Jewish National Fund) stamps and shares in the Zionist Colonial Bank. They also gave classes in Bible, Hebrew, history, etc. At the age of 23, Yisrael Baruch married the attractive Freidel,a granddaughter of Yizchak Kravetz. With the help of his wife, who was a real Hebraist, Yisrael Baruch opened a kheder and devoted himself to teaching.

In December 1912, Yisrael Baruch moved to the United States and settled in Chicago, where he ran a Hebrew-speaking Jewish School. He actually intended to make some money and return to Drohitchin, but in the meantime World War I broke out in 1914, and Yisrael Baruch was cut off from his family.

Immediately after the war, Yisrael Baruch undertook all possible efforts to save his wife and children. Before help became available, his wife Freidel succumbed to typhus and died a couple of days before Shavuot 1919, leaving behind two children. In the aftermath of the upheavals that made sending money to the suffering Jews of Drohitchin difficult, Yisrael Baruch convinced his brother R. Eliyahu Eisenstein to travel to Drohitchin to learn about the situation of the family in Drohitchin. At Yisrael Baruch's initiative, an extraordinary meeting of Drohitchin Jews was held in Chicago, where he was able to collect $5,000 for the war victims in Drohitchin. Eliyahu Eisenstein was the one who distributed the money in Drohitchin, and when he returned to Chicago, he brought back with him Yisrael Baruch's two small children as well as other Jews from Drohitchin.

In 1920 Yisrael Baruch found a partner and a mother to his children in his second wife, Esther, a cousin of his first wife, with whom he had two additional children. He then got involved in the clothing business and did well financially. Due to health problems, 12 years later he was forced to sell his business and move to Phoenix, Arizona, where he remained for seven years before returning to Chicago. Unfortunately, his asthma did not improve, and his great worry about his three sons who were serving in the US army on the battlefront. In addition, he had lost his youngest son, a lieutenant in the Air Force. This also had a negative effect on his health, forcing him to stop his community activity. In 1948 he moved with his wife to Miami, Florida.

R. Yisrael Baruch was renowned for his work on behalf of the community. He served as secretary of the Beit Avraham Synagogue for eight years. He was a member and strong supporter of the Anshei Drohitchin Synagogue, the Beit Midrash for Torah (House of Study for Torah), the Education Committee and the Parochial School in Chicago. Eisenstein was also a co-founder and first custodian of the Knesset Yisrael Synagogue in Miami Beach, as well as a member of the Miami Board of Education in addition to other activities.

[Page 192]

Yisrael Baruch was one of the co-founders and leaders of the Drohitchin Relief Fund in Chicago that dispatched large sums of money to Drohitchin for the needy. He collected money to rebuild the burned-down Houses of Study in Drohitchin and influenced R. Yitzchak Avigdor Telekhansky (Chicago) to contribute $2,000 to rebuild the Talmud Torah School in Drohitchin, and collected $3,000 for a charity fund in Drohitchin.

In April 1951, the Chicago Zeitshrift wrote the following about R. Yisrael Baruch Eisenstein:

"R. Yisrael Baruch Eisenstein is, as many people know, a religiously-devoted person, dedicated to practical good deeds, and has wonderful character traits. He has a good personality and is a friend to all. When he was healthy, he was always running to help and support the needy any way he could. People say that Yisrael Baruch did favors for them anonymously. The best example of his goodness and honesty was that he provided assistance to his relatives (What honor does one expect from helping one's own relatives?). R. Yisrael Baruch's dedication for those in need derived from his good heart and from Jewish law, which states that aiding those of one's one community and family is as big a mitzvah as aiding others, and possibly even bigger. Yisrael Baruch can serve as an example to many other community leaders."

Yisrael Baruch's wife, Esther Eisenstein, was born in Drohitchin and received a religious nationalist upbringing. She studied Hebrew and literature, and was proficient in the bible. As soon as she arrived in Chicago, she followed her husband's example and threw herself into community service. She worked extensively for the Kehilat Yaakov Talmud Torah School; she was very active in the Parochial School and brought aid to the Beit Midrash for Torah. She was a member of the Chevra Mikra Synagogue and others. In 1948 Esther continued hear work in Miami Beach, Florida when she and her husband moved there. In 1949 she was elected president of the sisterhood of Knesset Yisrael Synagogue, and in 1950 was re-elected. Esther was also a leading figure in the Mizrachi Organization, the Hebrew Academy, Pioneer Club No. 2, and belonged to Hadassah, the Geriatric Center and the Jewish Hospital.

Aharon Krivitsky

Aharon Krivitsky

Aharon Krivitsky, known as the Lechovich Teacher, was born in Motele. His father, Shmerel Yonah, sent him to both kheder and yeshiva. Aharon then began thinking about his future and decided that the best option was to go into teaching. For many years he was a teacher in Sarny, Dombrovitz and Berezhnitz in the Volhyn region.

After he married Yitzchak Lechovitcher's daughter, Kunya, in 1907, Aharon settled in Drohitchin and sought a teaching position, but since he was a newcomer, he faced many obstacles. Finally he managed to open a modernized kheder and continued in this work until the outbreak of World War I. Aharon and his family lived through the war at the Lechovitch Estate, where he worked in agriculture.

In 19420, when the Balakhov gangs rampaged around Drohitchin, Aharon and his wife lived through very fearful times. A gentile denounced them as communists to the Balakhov gangs, and terrorists then started looking for him. Miraculously, however, Aharon and his family were saved from certain death.

After these dreadful experiences, the Krivitskys didn't want to remain in the village and returned to Drohitchin. On August 1, 1921 they arrived in the United States. Aharon, his wife and children settled in Hartford, Connecticut, where he administered a Talmud Torah School.

[Page 193]

Yisrael Baruch Warshavsky

Yisrael Baruch Warshavsky was born in Drohitchin in 1882. On his father's side (R. Yeshayahu), he was a fourth-generation direct descendant of the great scholar and kabbalist, R. Dovidel Yaffe. His mother, Gittel, was housewife and upstanding G-d-fearing woman.

Until he was 13, Yisrael Baruch studied in kheder and the House of Study in Drohitchin, and then he attended the Pinsk yeshiva. In the summer of 1897, he traveled together with Avraham Asher Kravetz to the Vilna yeshiva, which was located in the Butcher's *Kloiz* [a synagogue usually frequented by people of a particular occupation). Warshavsky also studied briefly on his own in the House of Study in Kartuz-Bereza before studying together with Yisrael Baruch Eisenstein in Iveia, near Vilna, for an extended period.

Warshavsky was quite young when, due to economic conditions, he decided to learn an occupation; he chose teaching, and diligently spent his time studying on his own. He studied a lot of bible, grammar, Hebrew language and literature and became an enthusiastic reader of *Hamelitz* and *Hatzefira*. At the same time, he studied Russian intensively and became acquainted with the Russian literary classics. He also read the Russian newspapers constantly.

He briefly had his own class in Drohitchin but didn't enjoy teaching. So he went back to his studies and took up pharmacy; he then became a pharmacist. His skills and great diligence enabled him to break through all obstacles and achieve his goals. Shortly thereafter, he started working as a pharmacist and optician in Kobrin.

After he married Chaya Lieba from Pruzhena in 1913 She was a granddaughter of Yitzchak Kravitz of Drohitchin. Yisrael Baruch opened his own optician store in Dvin, near Kobrin. Later he moved his business from Dvin to Drohitchin (in Shimshon Goldman's place) and was on his way to achieve his life's ambition. However, World War I interfered with his plans, and in 1915 the results of all his work and effort went up in smoke.

During the war years and afterwards, Warshavsky suffered greatly (See his memoirs in this book, p. 79.), and experienced many difficulties until he got to the United States in 1923. For a while he was supported by his brothers Eliyahu and Yehoshua in Chicago (They had been the ones who sent him money for the trip.) until he got involved in teaching in Chicago. He was also a teacher in St. Paul, Minnesota, Rock Island, Illinois, and Vodoville. He finally moved to New York, and in 1930 he brought his wife and children from Drohitchin to New York, where he was hired by a synagogue and ran a Talmud Torah school. Sometimes he served as a cantor on the High Holy Days as well.

From his early youth, Yisrael Baruch belonged to the *Lovers of Zion* movement, and he was one of the founders of the Mizrachi movement in Drohitchin. He was also an active member of Mizrachi in the United States, collected for various Zionist funds, and assisted in building Palestine. Warshavsky was adept at writing, and he wrote frequently. He had a nice writing style and a literary sense.

The Warshavskys had one son and two daughters: Yeshayahu (who excelled as a US soldier in the war in the Pacific and who served in the Israeli army against the Arabs. Today he is the regional commander of the Ramat Raziel area in Israel); Chana Margalit (a high school graduate with a command of Hebrew, Polish, English and French, who lives with her husband and children in Louisville, Kentucky); and Frieda (a graduate in teaching with a government position in New York).

Hershel Baum

May G-d avenge his blood!

Hershel Baum, a son of Shmuel Artshis and a native of Drohitchin, spent his whole life as a religious teacher, though his kheder was a bit modern. In addition to bible and the Rashi commentary, he taught the children to read and write Hebrew and had a good reputation as a teacher.

Hershel, his wife and children (except for two daughters, Rachel Lozy in New York and Ahuva Becher in Israel) were killed. May G-d avenge their blood!

[Page 194]
Yosef Wasserman

Yosef Wasserman was born to his parents, R. Yaakov, the Ritual Slaughterer, and Chaya in 1896 in Obla, near Pinsk. He studied in kheder in Drohitchin, and then in 1908 in the Karlin Talmud Torah School in Pinsk, and with Motka Melamed in Yanova. In 1911 he arrived at the Mir yeshiva and then attended the Navarodok yeshiva for three years headed by the renowned R. Yozel. He also studied in a study group (kibbutz) in Lida. This group was led by Meitshet rabbi and Rabbi Rabinovich (a son-in-law of the head of the yeshiva, Rabbi Reines). R. Yosef Wasserman studied on his own in Slonim during World War I.

Seated from right: Yosef Wasserman (and his class, 1918 Drohitchin), Polia and Wertheim (Volhyn).

In 1917, Yosef came to Drohitchin, and for a while he was involved in teaching. In 1920 he married Solia, the daughter of Shimon and Lotsa Weissman. At the end of 1921, the Weissmans moved to the United States and settled in Chicago, where Yosef worked as a teacher (1922) at the Tiferet Zion Talmud Torah School. Between 1922 and 1923, he taught at Talmud Torah of Drohitchin. Starting in 1926, he went into business.

As a Zionist, Yosef Wasserman was a strong supporter of Ze'ev Vladimir Jabotinsky's ideas and of the Irgun in its battle for Palestine. He then became closely involved in the Herut movement here and in Israel. Yosef's wife, Solia, was an active member of Pioneer Women and Poalei Zion in Chicago. The Wassermans had four children: Miriam, Yaakov, Shimon and Chaya.

Shmuel Eppelbaum

Shmuel Eppelbaum was born in Drohitchin. When he was still a child he lost his father Aharon David (a son of Shimon Nahoriyer) and received his education from his mother who was known as Bobel, the candy store lady, and who was responsible for earning a livelihood for her six children.

Shmuel studied in kheder and under various teachers in Drohitchin. Afterwards he graduated from the Hebrew Teacher's Seminar in Vilna, and he became involved in teaching. Over the years, he worked as a teacher in various towns in Poland. In later years, he was a teacher at the Moriah School in Drohitchin.

When the Germans took away some Jews, including Shmuel and his family, from the Drohitchin ghetto to be killed in Brona-Gora, Shmuel jumped off the wagon. Despite shots fired at him by the Germans, he succeeded in disappearing into the forest, where he remained in hiding for a long time until he was able to join up with the partisans. Finally, he joined the Red Army and was one of soldiers who entered Berlin.

After the war, Shmuel ended up in a refugee camp, where he worked as a colleague and co-editor of *Dos Vort* and the Hebrew paper, *Netzotz* (Spark). From 1937 on, he lived in Palestine/Israel. Shmuel's mother and sister were killed. May G-d avenge their blood! For more details, see his articles in the yizkor section.

[Page 195]
Zalman Shevinsky

Zalman Shevinsky

Zalman Shevinsky was born into a Chassidic family in Drohitchin. His father, R. Nachum, was originally from Kobrin, and his mother, Bodya, on her mother's side was of the Valevelsky and Katzenelbogen families and related to R. Shaul Wahl. On her father's side, she was related to the Shedrovitskys. Zalman's parents provided him with a proper Jewish upbringing: he studied in a modernized kheder and privately with religious teachers and teachers Neiditch, Gedaliah Sacker, Moshe Velvel Skolnick, R. Yosef Shachat, Yaakov Sidorov, and others. In addition to Jewish subjects, Zalman also studied general subjects such as Russian language and Yiddish and Hebrew literature.

Just like the majority of young people before World War I, Zalman Shevinsky was an enthusiastic Zionist. He sold Jewish National Fund stamps and set out charity plates on the eve of Yom Kippur in synagogues on behalf of Zionist projects. In 1910, Zalman came to the United States, living briefly in Birmingham, Alabama. He then moved to Chicago where he married Chaya Simkin of Zhlobin, Russia, in 1916.

In the United States, he devoted himself to Zionist causes with his usual Chassidic enthusiasm, and this work filled his time both day and night. He patiently and stubbornly added one brick after another to building Palestine. In 1913, Shevinsky became secretary of *Techiya* (Rebirth), a branch of the *Knights of Zion*; he was a co-founder and secretary of Camp Nachum Sokolov of the *Bnai Zion Order;* he was one of the founders of the first Flower Days of the National Jewish Fund in Chicago; and he was an active member of the *Sholem Aleichem Branch* of the *National Workers' Union.*

Of special interest was Shevinsky's involvement in the "Drohitchin Branch" of the National Workers' Union, an organization that he helped establish. As the long-standing finance secretary of the Drohitchin Branch, Shevinsky did a lot of good work and was a person of action and purpose. He enjoyed carrying a burden. In addition to cultural activities in his role as cultural affairs chairman of the Drohitchin Branch, Zalman was published souvenir booklets, a monthly bulletin, and news announcements. He was also heavily involved in organizing yearly picnics, carrying the bags of food himself, and handling purchases in order to help the Branch pursue its work. Labor Zionism found a reliable and devoted friend in Zalman Shevinsky.

Shevinsky also worked on behalf of Jewish education. Leo Honor, professor of Education at Dropsie University, Philadelphia wrote the following about Shevinsky: "Zalman Shevinsky demonstrated his loyalty to his people, to the Hebrew language, and to Jewish culture with his daily work, energy and time that he devoted to those issues, as well as with his tremendous efforts on behalf of promoting the development of Hebrew and Yiddish literature. He was interested in Jewish education and showed that interest through his deep concern for educational institutions, as well as for the Board of Jewish Education during his years as president of the Friends of the Jewish Board of Education."

Shevinsky was a devotee of Yiddish and Hebrew books and was one of the first to purchase any newly published quality book. His library, which filled an entire room, included many books of historical value. Shevinsky was also president of the Kobriner Synagogue for 10 years, president of the Drohitchin Progressive Club, and was involved in relief efforts to assist the needy of Drohitchin. Zalman Shevinsky initiated the idea of the Drohitchin Yizkor Book, and for years patiently collected photos and material about his hometown of Drohitchin until he was able to see the realization of his dream.

In 1949, the Drohitchin Branch held a banquet in honor of Shevinsky for his work on behalf of the community. The Shevinskys have three daughters and one son: Fruma-Mindel, Eliyahu Leib, Bunya and Yehudit.

[Page 196]
Gedaliah Kaplan

Gedaliah Kaplan was born in Drohitchin in 1895 to his parents, Aharon David and Bobba. He received his education in the kheder, under R. Eliyahu Machles, Meir Kaplan and Mordechai Minkovitch. He also studied briefly in the Maltsh yeshiva until he became influenced by the Enlightenment movement, when he began reading books and studying on his own.

Kaplan then got involved in community activities, something that became part of his life. He helped poor people in need; he helped establish a library in Drohitichin even before World War I, serving as its librarian for five years and spreading Jewish culture among the young people. On the other hand, he also started a children's study group for poor children, teaching them Mishnah on the Sabbath.

When the typhus epidemic broke out in 1915, Kaplan worked as a volunteer medic at the German isolation hospital, where he helped saved the lives of many Drohitchin Jews until he came down with the terrible sickness himself.

Even before World War I, Kaplan was already a Zionist and sold Jewish National Fund stamps at Jewish celebrations. When the Balfour Declaration was made public, Kaplan started to increase his work on behalf of Zionism, collecting money for Zionist funds and preaching Zionism. In the beginning of 1919, Kaplan served as a policeman and deputy soltis under the Polish authorities. In that same year, the Poles lost Drohitchin to the Bolsheviks, and Kaplan was forced to flee Drohitchin because of his work for the Polish authorities. Eventually he made his way to the United States and settled in New York.

In the United States, Gedaliah Kaplan found enormous possibilities for his community work. He decided to start the National Workers' Union and helped build the Zionist movement in New York. In the last twenty years, Kaplan has been the recording secretary of Branch 401 of the National Workers' Union and an activist on behalf of the Jewish National Fund.

As secretary of the Relief Fund of Drohitchin émigrés in New York for 15 years, Kaplan succeeded in his work on behalf of needy Jews in Drohitchin before World War II and later on behalf of survivors in the German camps, sending money and food packages. He stayed in constant contact with the survivors of Hitler's hell and tried to console them.

Gedaliah Kaplan also published 42 poems in *Amerikaner,* and wrote articles there from time to time since 1934 about events and personalities. In

1952 Kaplan traveled to Israel, where he was greeted with great respect by Drohitchin Jews living there.

Kaplan worked faithfully on the Drohitchin yizkor book, collecting pictures, information and money that greatly assisted in the publishing of the book. Gedaliah Kaplan was married to Perl Piasetsky, a daughter of Shmuel Yudel, the Elder of Drohitchin. They had one son, Aharon.

Gedaliah Kaplan (right) and Moshe Aharon Zaretsky, a refugee, in Montreal in 1948.

A photostat of Gedaliah Kaplan's Polish passport, 1918.

[*Page 197*]

A Lively Newspaper

A Lively Newspaper

THE DROHITCHIN YAWN
No. 1: 9/28/1931
Humor, Satire, Sarcasm and other assortments

Table of Contents:

Translation of the Previous Page

[Page 198]

DOCTORS

Shimon Weissman

R. Shimon Weissman

Shimon Betzalel Weissman, or "R. Shimon the Doctor," as he was known, was born in 1845 to his parents Shmuel and Solia in Horodetz, where he received a solid Jewish education. He studied many religious texts such as Talmud, in addition to general subjects. He later studied medicine and decided to become a physician.

At the age of 20, R. Shimon came to Drohitchin and started working as a doctor. As a newcomer to Drohitchin, he encountered many difficulties, but over time he earned the trust and faith of the people in town and opened his own practice. Although Weissman was not a degreed physician, many doctors respected his medical knowledge.

Jews in Drohitchin made use of R. Shimon more often they did the official doctor of Drohitchin. First of all, R. Shimon didn't charge the visit tax for his visits. He always considered the financial situation of the patient. Second, R. Shimon was a talkative and warm individual as well as religious Jew. He would always spend time chatting with the patient and his family, and he liked adding some Torah anecdote, story or joke that always made his patients and their families feel better, thereby improving the health of the patient.

R. Shimon was also the doctor of the neighboring communities, including the Christians who had faith in him and his knowledge and followed his medical advice. During the war years 1915 to 1916, when the typhus epidemic was raging, R. Shimon was the person who was able to save the lives of dozens of people. In 1919, when the epidemic reoccurred, and hundreds of people – including my father – were bedridden, R. Shimon would come to visit our home every day and do everything possible to save us from the awful disease.

When he was asked about payment for his services, R. Shimon responded that this could be discussed after the patient recovered.

As mentioned earlier, R. Shimon was a religious and observant Jew. He had a seat on the second floor of the Old House of Study, where he spent many a Sabbath and weekday engaged in intensive study of a tractate of Talmud, humming a warm melody while he studied. Whenever he couldn't make it to synagogue, he would study at home.

How long ago was all this? It's as if it were today: I can still see him walking slowly, deeply engaged in thought, always exuding a refined, quiet and orderly image. Only the tapping of his cane gave away the fact that this person was R. Shimon the Doctor, a Jewish aristocrat.

[Page 199]

A few years later R. Shimon passed away. He died in November 1927, having served the people of Drohitchin as their doctor for 62 years.

Lotsa Beila Weissman, the wife of R. Shimon Weissman, was born in 1864 in Drohitchin. Her father, R. Mendel Moshe Isser's, provided her with a good traditional education, and she influenced her children and other people in the same spirit.

Lotsa Beila Weissman

Lotsa was a proud Jewish woman and ran a beautiful Jewish home. Her word was authoritative for everyone, family and friends alike, and everyone respected her. Lotsa Beila died in 1931 in Drohitchin.

The Weissmans had the following children: Avraham Yosef (died in Chicago); Naftali (killed in Brisk); Yehoshua (living in Chicago); Shmuel (died in Chicago); Dina, a dentist (died in Chicago); Yehudit (died in Drohitchin); Rivka Minkov (living in New York); Perl (living in New York); Bashka (killed in Vilna); Mordechai, Sula, Tzippa Miriam, (all living in Chicago); Ezra (died in Chicago), and Sarah (living in Israel). Tzippa Sidransky is active in the Pioneer Women organization and Poalei Zion in Chicago.

Dr. Mordechai Weissman

Dr. Mordechai Weissman

Dr. Mordechai Weissman was born in Drohitchin on March 11, 1887, to his parents R. Shimon, the Doctor, and Lotsa. He studied in kheder, and with private religious teachers such as R. Shmuel Artshis, Naftali Steinberg, Moshe Velvel Skolnick, and his own grandfather, R. Mendel Moshe Isser's Kaminetsky. Mordechai also studied general subjects, especially Russian.

At the age of 14, Mordechai went to study at the Maltsh yeshiva, where he remained for two years, followed by two years at the Slabodka yeshiva under R. Chaim Mishada and others. On July 13, 1906, Weissman moved to the United States and settled in Chicago. Like many other immigrants, he worked during the day – first in a shop, and then as a Hebrew teacher at the Winchester Synagogue – and in the evenings, he attended school to study general subjects and eventually entered university.

In 1912, Mordechai joined the Chicago College of Surgery (which later became part of Loyola University), where he studied medicine. After obtaining his degree in 1917, he worked for a time in hospitals, and in 1920 opened his own office specializing in heart disease. In later years, Dr. Weissman was involved with the tuberculosis sanitarium in Chicago, where he worked as a specialist in his field.

At the same time as he pursued his studies, Dr. Weissman was also involved in community affairs. Even as a child, he joined revolutionary movements that were spreading throughout Russia in those days. He was one of the founders and leaders of the Yiddishist Bund in Drohitchin, and fought for the rights of the working class. In Chicago he was a member of Y.L. Peretz-Shapiro Branch (6) since 1920, of the National Workers' Union, an active member of the Doctors' Union, and contributed frequently to medical journals. Dr. Mordechai Weissman's wife, Bessya (née Krasevitsky), whom he married in 1917, is a famous leader and former president of the Pioneer Women organization. The Weissmans had one daughter, Yehudit, who lives with her husband, Hugh Douglas, a well-known radio announcer and commentator, in Los Angeles.

[*Page 200*]

Naftali Weissman

R. Naftali Weissman

May G-d avenge his blood!

Naftali Weissman, a son of R. Shimon Weissman, was born in Drohitchin. In his conduct and attitude, R. Naftali was a carbon copy of his father, R. Shimon the Doctor. R. Naftali was a religious and observant Jew and made his living by healing the sick.

For many years, R. Naftali was the doctor of Horodetz, where he succeeded his grandfather, R. Binyamin, as doctor. His grandfather had served as a doctor there his entire life. R. Naftali was beloved and respected in Horodetz, where he lived as an honorable religious Jew. He attended services, studied

Talmud, and provided free medical services, including free medicine, to the poor.

R. Naftali was unsuccessful in earning a living in Horodetz, both because of the small Jewish population and because of competition from Christian doctors who treated all the non-Jewish patients. With help from his father, R. Naftali went to Warsaw to return to his studies. Some time later, R. Naftali returned to Horodetz as a dentist. He worked as both dentist and physician.

R. Naftali still didn't earn much of a living, so he returned to his studies once again. After a long period in Warsaw, R. Naftali returned to Horodetz as an eye doctor. Nevertheless, he still couldn't make a living. Then his wife, Dina, passed away, and he was left with several small children in a desperate financial situation.

R. Naftali was forced to leave Horodetz and settled in Kobrin, where he developed an excellent reputation among the Jewish population. After World War I, R. Naftali moved to Brisk, where he worked as an eye doctor, earning a good reputation as a doctor. In Brisk he resumed his religious studies as well, studying Torah and discussing Torah topics with his rabbi friends. He even authored a book of homilies, an encyclopedia of anecdotes and homilies of the sages of the Talmud, Midrash and Zohar.

R. Naftali was a model individual, combining Torah, wisdom and good character traits. Unfortunately, he and his family were killed in the Brisk ghetto. May G-d avenge their blood!

Information from the Horodetz Book

[Page 201]
Dr. Gershoni

Dr. Gershoni, the town doctor, arrived in Drohitchin around 1900. He studied medicine at the University of Odessa, where he married his wife, who was a midwife. There is no confirmed information about Dr. Gershoni's background, except that it is said he was a cousin of the great scholar, Rabbi Chaim Soloveitchik. Therefore, Gershoni apparently came from Brisk.

Dr. Gershoni, who was renowned as a good doctor, was a popular individual. He spoke Yiddish well and enjoyed chatting with people. He held the rank of colonel in the Czarist army, and during the 1905 Russo-Japanese War he served on the front for a long time. In World War I, Dr. Gershoni served as a medical colonel at the front and was wounded. He came to Drohitchin to recover and then returned to the army. Thereafter no one heard of him ever again. Rumors had it that he died in Odessa. His wife and two children, Yasha and Lola, currently live in Russia.

Doctors Shechter, Gloiberson and Lampa

May G-d avenge their blood!

Dr. Henrik Schechter, who replaced Dr. Gershoni, arrived in Drohitchin a couple of years after World War I. We know nothing about his background. People say that he was born in Galicia, and we know that his wife was a member of a fine Jewish family in Warsaw.

When he arrived in Drohitchin, Dr. Schechter was at the high point of his life (He must have been in his 30s.) and was extremely active and energetic. Ideologically, Schechter was a Zionist maximalist, a right-wing revisionist; he was actively involved in cultural, political and community life in Drohitchin. In the early 1930s, Dr. Schechter settled in Gdinia, where he practiced medicine and ran a Revisionist-Zionist organization called Zevulun for the fishing industry.

In Drohitchin, Schechter was replaced by Dr. Gloiberson of Pinsk (son-in-law of Y. and Sarah Meshel, daughter of Mordechai and Rivka Mirsky of Drohitchin). Dr. Gloiberson later returned to Pinsk, and was replaced by Dr. D. Lampa, about whose background we know nothing.

In the meantime Dr. Schechter fell victim to the Polish boycott movement in Gdinia, where he lost all his patients, and he returned to Drohitchin in 1937. Dr. Lampa was then appointed regional doctor, and Dr. Schechter resumed his position as doctor in Drohitchin, where he remained until the Germans took over Drohitchin in 1941.

Doctors Schechter and Lampa went through the living hell together with all the Jews in the Drohitchin ghetto. When the doctors found out about the murderous plans of the Germans for the Jews of Drohitchin, they poisoned themselves, thereby ending their suffering. May G-d avenge their blood! See references to them in the Yizkor section.

Dr. Schechter's wife and two little daughters, Yehudit and Halina, were also killed. Dr. Lampa was not married. Dr. Gloiberson and his family died in Pinsk. May G-d avenge their blood!

[Page 202]

Aharon Lasovsky

May G-d avenge his blood!

Aharon Lasovsky, the country doctor, was born in Pinsk. His father was involved in gardening and printing pamphlets. Aharon studied in Kiev, and was certified as an army surgeon. Aharon's wife Chaya (Chayka), born in Pinsk, was a very kind person. Her maiden name was Feldman, and she was a cousin of Leah Valevelsky, the wife Chaim the hardware store owner of

Drohitchin. Chayka's sister was married to the editor of the *Pinsker Shtimma*, M. Bolin. One of her brothers was one of the 36 martyrs of Pinsk who were accused of being communists and then shot by the Poles in 1920.

From right: Naftali Steinberg's house. Left in background: Lazer's windmill. This is the isolation hospital in 1915. From left to right: Solya Fideta, mayor; Rosenblatt (Russian-Jewish prisoner of war); German doctor; Todros Leib Milner, Gedaliah Kaplan, Shimon the Doctor, Pesach (Berel Rimmer's son-in-law), Dora from Pinsk, Moshe Perkovitsky, Meita Trashinsky, Aharon Lasovsky (army surgeon), Feiga-Rachel Warshavsky-Kotler, Reizel Baum-Shoshanov, Solia Weissman-Wasserman and a Russian prisoner of war. (See pp. 97-98).

Aharon Lasovsky came to Drohitchin during the 1915 typhus epidemic, and together with Shimon the Doctor and others was able to heal the typhus victims. After the death of Shimon the Doctor, Lasovsky took over his position, and he became the only doctor or army surgeon for Drohitchin and surrounding communities. Aharon Lasovsky was a nationalist Jew, a people's man, unassuming and traditional. He was also a Revisionist Zionist. Eyewitnesses report that until the last minute Aharon Lasovsky went from door to door, doing everything he possibly could to save the lives and spirits of despondent and sick Jews in the Drohitchin ghetto.

Aharon and Chayka had three children: Dinela, Hershela, and Moshela. They were all brutally killed by the German murderers. May G-d avenge their blood!

Dr. Avraham Yosef Weissman

Dr. Avraham Yosef Weissman, a son of R. Shimon Weissman, was born in Drohitchin. As a boy of 17 at the end of the nineteenth century, Avraham came to the United States and studied medicine. For many years he lived in Chicago, where he practiced medicine, especially delivering babies, and was renown for his work. Dr. Weissman died in November 1939 in Chicago at the age of 76.

[Page 203]

COMMUNITY LEADERS AND PERSONALITIES

Moshe Velvel Eisenstein
First Elder

Moshe Velvel Eisenstein was born in approximately 1840. His parents, Shmuel and Leah Eisenstein, were always villagers, residing in the village of Bulmak, near Drohitichin. Prior to his marriage, young Moshe Velvel also lived in Bulmak.

Later, Moshe Velvel Eisenstein moved to Drohitchin and became an office manager; he leased the office of the vodka monopoly, and his job was to collect the liquor and tobacco excise tax for the government. Over the years, the terms *office* and *office manager* came to be considered an autonomous Jewish business. In 1879, Eisenstein was selected the first elder of Drohitchin, and his job entailed representing the Jewish community with the Czarist authorities. He remained in that position for the rest of his life and was succeeded by Moshe Paritsker (Valevelsky), and finally by Shmuel Yudel Piasetsky, who was the last to serve in that role in Drohitchin. Eisenstein's second wife was named Zelda, and he had three sons: Khane Asher, Abba and Eliyahu.

Moshe Velvel had one brother and four sisters; Hershel Bulmaker, Chana (wife of Shmuel David Milner), Riva (Eliyahu Itsele's wife), Beila (wife of Shimon Gratch), and Perl (mother of Shmuel Eisenstein of Western United Dairies in Chicago).

A group of Jews near Sender Vinivker's house.

Moshe Pritsker-Valevelsky
Second Elder

R. Moshe Paritsker-Valevelsky

According to one story, Moshe Valevelsky, known as "R. Moshe Paritske," was a descendant of R. Mordechai Mordush of Paritsk (author of a commentary on the writings of Maharam Schiff) and was therefore called Moshe Paritsker. Another version says that he was called Paritsker because his parents lived in the village or estate of Paritsk, near Pinsk. Whatever the truth may be, the fact is that R. Moshe preferred to be called Partisker rather than Valevelsky.

R. Moshe's father, an eminent scholar, didn't earn much of a living, so his mother, Sarah Riva, became rather skillful in business. During the Turkish-Russian War, she made a lot of money. Sarah Riva was also the person who provided food products to workers building the rail line between Pinsk and

Brisk (known as the Warsaw-Terespol Railway). Sarah Riva and her family traveled from one village to the next along the rail line until they arrived in Drohitchin, where they remained. This is how Moshe Paritsker became a resident of Drohitchin.

[Page 204]

When he married Cherna, his second wife, Moshe was 18 years old. His two children from his first wife, Eliyahu and Rachel, went to stay with their grandfather, Leibka (which is why Eliyahu the tavern owner became known as Eliyahu Leibkas).

From the beginning, Moshe had in his home a store of produce and foodstuffs. Later he became involved in the timber business, dealing in plots of trees. Around 1890, when Elder Eisenstein of Drohitchin passed away, the community selected Moshe as Elder, and he remained in that position until 1901. He was then followed by Shmuel Yudel Piasetsky.

Cherna Paritsker-Valevelsky

From right to left: the rabbi's wife, Miriam, Chana Beila, Cherna (mother) and Ita – wife and daughters of Moshe Paritsker, 1923. See pp. 61, 130, 135 and 223.

R. Moshe, who admired rabbis, had rabbis for sons-in-law: R. Velvel the rabbinical judge and later the rabbi of Sernik, and Rabbi Mordechai Minkovitch. Moshe spent his last years in wealth and honor. He died on the first day of Rosh Hashanah in 1914. His wife, Cherna, died a few years later. The Valevelskys had around 14 children, but only nine of them lived to adulthood: Zelig (Alex Marcus), Shmuel, Hershel, Mordechai, Miriam, Chana Beila, Ita, and others.

Shmuel Yudel Piasetsky
The Last Elder

Shmuel Yudel Piasetsky was born in Drohitchin in 1859 to a respected family. His father, R. Yitzchak, provided him with a traditional upbringing. Young Shmuel also acquired a worldly education. Shmuel excelled in his study of Russian. In 1901, Shmuel Yudel was selected to replace Moshe Paritsker as Elder of Drohitchin. Shmuel was re-appointed to the position every three years, and he remained in the position until the Germans took over Drohitchin in 1915.

The functions of an Elder under the Russian regime were the same as those of a mayor. The Elder was the person who made decisions regarding the health conditions of the bathhouses, the firefighting department and its equipment, the roads, and unpaved roads. He had to make sure there was a doctor in town, and every year he had to provide the Russian authorities with a list of Jewish young men who had to enlist in the army.

[*Page 205*]

Drohitchin Jews in 1936

Shmuel Yudel (with a gold chain around his neck) would meet with the recruiting committee, reading off the names of Jewish recruits. For this work he was paid 300 rubles a years, and the money was provided by the town budget.

Shmuel Yudel also had to serve as mediator to alleviate Czarist decrees on the Jewish villagers, who were expelled from their villages. There were many nervous moments when the tax officials arrived in town, and Shmuel had to appeal to them to alleviate the taxes on the poor and waive penalties. His clever wife, Beila, frequently helped him out in this thorny work.

In 1905, when the Czarist police arrested Yaakov Goldberg, Avraham Yitzchak Lev, and David Goldstein for membership in the socialist party, Shmuel Yudel and Beila took them out of prison in the middle of the night and helped them escape. When Stolipin, the governor of Grodno, once passed through Drohitchin, the old rabbi, R. Menachem Reichman, and Shmuel Yudel and others welcomed him with bread and salt. Shmuel Yudel then took advantage of the opportunity to ask the governor to arrange to pave the streets of Drohitchin. The governor accepted Shmuel Yudel's request, and shortly thereafter the roads of Drohitchin were paved.

When the Germans occupied Drohitchin, Shmuel Yudel and his family moved to a village near Drohitchin. This sudden change in his stormy life evidently had a negative effect on his health, since shortly thereafter, in 1916, Shmuel Yudel passed away, thus ending the chapter of the Jewish Elders in Drohitchin.

Information from Gedaliah Kaplan

Moshe Leizer Gratch

Moshe Lazer Gratch was born in approximately 1862 in Drohitchin to his parents, R. Shimon and Beila. He learned in kheder and the House of Study, and also studied Russian, Polish, and English. In approximately 1882, Moshe Leizer married his wife, Hinda, a daughter of R. Shalom Goldschmidt of Drohitchin and started to earn a living. It didn't go very well, however, and in 1888 Moshe Leizer traveled to the United States with the intention of collecting some money to be able to move with his family to Palestine.

After spending five years in Chicago, where he also acquired US citizenship, he returned to Drohitchin. However, his plans to move to Palestine didn't bear fruit because his father and father-in-law decided to live out their lives in Drohitchin. With no other choice, Moshe Leizer got involved in a workshop manufacturing women's clothes because he always wanted to earn his own money. He was also a philanthropist in the community.

His cleverness and linguistic abilities, and especially his relationship with local gentile aristocrats and officials (his customers), enabled him to help his fellow Jews and develop a reputation to be able to become the head community leader.

R. Moshe Leizer was a long-standing trustee and administrator of the burial society, which in those days was one of the best-organized organizations and which carried a lot of weight in the community. He was also the treasurer of the Old House of Study, and he ran the Mishnah Study Group, Jewish Law Study Group and Psalm Reciters' Group. He also ran the organization responsible for providing room and board for poor visitors, and he was a councilor of the local council. R. Moshe Leizer was so involved in his community work that he neglected his own livelihood.

At the end of 1913, Moshe Leizer decided to move to Palestine, but by the time all his plans were ready to be implemented, World War I broke out in 1914, and he was stuck in Drohitchin. During the war years and the typhus epidemic, Moshe Leizer and his associates at the burial society worked night and day, preparing the dead for burial and helping the living. They were especially involved in assisting war refugees who came to

[Page 206]

From right, Shalom, R. Moshe Leizer (father), Nissel, Shmuel Velvel, Hinda (mother) and Sender

Drohitchin from the battle areas and who became the first victims of the epidemic. Over the years, R. Moshe was in charge of the Drohitchin Record Book, in which he would record the most important events in town. Unfortunately, no one knows what happened to the book.

Moshe Leizer finally realized his dream in 1923 when he departed for Palestine and Jerusalem, where he and his wife lived out their lives. R. Moshe died on the 8th of Tishrei (October 7), 1943, and his wife Hinda died on the 30th of Kislev (Dec. 30), 1940.

The Gratches had four sons: Nissel (arrived in the United States and became an active member of Poalei Zion. He died in Chicago on 29 Av [August 26], 1908); Shmuel Velvel (lives in Jerusalem since 1904, and attended the Torat Chaim yeshiva from 1904-1919); Sender (a Hebrew teacher. He arrived in the United States in 1920 and lives in Los Angeles), and Shalom (a respected businessman in Chicago).

[Page 207]

Zechariah Schmid

R. Zechariah and Pesha Schmid with their grandchildren

Zechariah Schmid, son of Zalman, was born in Drohitchin in 1865. He was known as a man of exceptional abilities, and under better circumstances had he spent time in studying, he would have become a great person. However, he didn't continue his studies beyond *kheder* and the Talmud Torah, and he took up a trade, helping his father with his blacksmith shop.

Zechariah's abilities, however, didn't limit him to his blacksmithing work, and he began to become involved in community affairs. In his youth, he was aggressive, battling against the revolutionaries of his time, i.e. the Brother and Sisters' Organization. This activity earned him many opponents, but as the years went by, he cooled off. His sharp intellect, deftness, and speaking ability forced everybody to pay attention to his words, and he eventually became one of the so-called tenured leaders of the community. He was also one of the advisors of the rabbi and attended all community meetings. He was one of the leaders of the burial society and many other Jewish institutions.

A special field of endeavor was his involvement in the cooperative savings bank, the Folks Bank, in which he served as a director and head manager for approximately 30 years (until he passed away), developing an expertise in finance. Educated bank directors would seek his advice about complicated financial issues. Dr. Shoshkes, the head of the Cooperative Society in Poland was one of his closest friends.

R. Zechariah was a member of the Talmud Study Group and a cantor in the Old House of Study. There is no confirmed information about the circumstances surrounding R. Zechariah's death. One story is that he died of natural causes in 1939, while another states that he died of unnatural causes under the Bolsheviks in 1940. A third version suggests that the Germans killed Zechariah in 1942. Unfortunately, we don't know which story is correct.

Zechariah was the brother of grandmother Chaya Ita. The Schmids had five sons: Yudel Schmid (killed with his family in Drohitchin in 1942); Yehoshua (the husband of Rasha Leah Lev) who died in New York; Yisrael (perished with his family in Drohitchin in 1942); Chaim Zalman (died in 1908), and Ephraim (who lives in New York).

Tuvia David Warshavsky

Tuvia David Warshavsky, a son of R. Shmuel Leizer and brother of R. Zusha, was born in Drohitchin. He received his education in *kheder* and with private tutors. He also studied under the great scholar, R. Pinchas Michel, in Antapolia, as well as in yeshivas. His wife, Sarah Leah, was the sister of R. Tuvia David Lev of Horbacha.

R. Tuvia David was a business partner with his brother, R. Zusha, though he was involved very little in the business itself. He was a quiet man who spent his time in study. Most of the time he was studying on his own and also taught those who attended the Old House of Study. As a good cantor, he would always lead the prayers (free of charge) for the Mussaf prayers during the High Holy Days in the Houses of Study in Drohitchin, and he was highly respected and admired in town.

In 1924 Tuvia David and his family moved to Palestine, settling in Rishon Le-Zion, where he owned his own hotel/guest house. He died in 1947. R. Tuvia David had four daughters and one son: Perl (who perished with her husband Zeidel and her children in the Drohitchin ghetto); Zlata (Yitzchak), who is in Canada; Eliyahu, Bashka and Rachel who are in Israel.

[Page 208]
Zusha Warshavsky

Zusha Warshavsky

Zusha Warshavsky was born in Drohitchin in 1868. His father, R. Shmuel Leizer, was one of the notables in town and was a great-grandson of R. Dovidel Yaffe. Zusha's mother, Basha, was also from a fine family. R. Zusha studied in *kheder,* Talmud Torah, and with private tutors; he also studied general subjects and languages.

Zusha served in the Czar's army for four years, and because of his linguistic knowledge he was able to do his military service as a writer in administrative offices. He never ate non-Kosher food and was able to bring money home. In 1894, Zusha married Chaya Frieda Pinsky in Motele, and they settled in the village of Horbacha, where his father Shmuel Liezer had a brick factory. He went into the lumber business with his brother, R. Tuvia David. R. Zusha was very adept in his work, and was very successful.

It didn't take too many years for Zusha and Tuvia David to become owners of their own large forests, lessees and owners of estates such as Klementova, Zamosh. They owned three beautiful houses in Drohitchin. R. Zusha was the business representative in dealings with army officials, generals, governors, barons and highly influential noblemen who valued Zusha's business skills and honesty as a Jew and as a person. They realized that R. Zusha was religious, and they forgave him whenever he had to excuse himself in the middle of an important meeting to pray. Zusha frequently made use of his important contact to do favors for other Jews.

In 1907, the Warshavsky brothers moved to Drohitchin. The "Horbacha brothers," as they were called, soon became renowned in Drohitchin for their fine Jewish homes that came to be the places where charity was distributed. In 1911, they bought Nachum Shevinsky's leather factory, built it up, and eventually became involved in marketing it in distant areas of the country.

When the German army occupied Drohitchin in 1915, they lost all their property. The houses and leather factory went up in smoke during the fires that broke out during the battles. The Germans confiscated all their timber from the forests as well as the remaining leather in the factory, and took over the estates, which they staffed with Germans. They stole everything and took it off to Germany. During the War, the Warshavsky brothers lived in Klementova and Horbacha.

In 1918, the Warshavskys got back their estate, and they started working on it again. However, things didn't go as well as they did under the Czarist regime because the Poles sought every opportunity to interfere with Jewish businesses. R. Zusha, who returned to Drohitchin, then became more deeply involved in community affairs. He was the advisor to Rabbi Kalenkovich and set the tone for all local meetings. R. Zusha also served as an arbitrator and mediator for various disputes pertaining to inheritances, and arranged marriages. He also interceded on behalf of those who got into trouble with the authorities. R. Zusha was a long-standing custodian of the Old House of Study, a devoted leader and contributor of the Polish Yeshiva Committee. He hosted visitors and provided charity anonymously. R. Zusha personified the typical Jewish intercessor and leader of the previous generations. His wife, Chaya Frieda, was the same way. She would always quietly assist the poor, anonymously sending them challah bread and other foods for the Sabbath. She taught this attitude to her children.

In July, 1941, the Bolsheviks exiled R. Zusha, his wife and children (Berl and Zlata Miriam and their families) to Russia, where his sick wife died in 1943 and was buried in a Christian cemetery. In May 1946, R. Zusha and his family were sent back to Poland. In December 1948, his daughter Rachel brought him over to the United States, and since July 1949, he lives in Israel, where he was well cared for by his daughter, Rachel, and son-in-law, Velvel Mazursky (of New York), who were prominent philanthropists.

In addition to Rachel, R. Zusha had two other sons and a daughter: Mordechai (Zissel) and Berl (Rachel) in Israel and Zlaata Miriam (Yeshayahu) in Canada.

[Page 209]
Shimshon Goldman

Seated from left: R. Shimshon and Henya Chaya Goldman. Standing, daughter Beila, son-in-law Aharon Volveler and child Rivka

Shimshon, the son of Meir Mordechai Goldman, was born in 1859 in Drohitchin. He studied in the House of Study from early childhood and earned a reputation as a good and religious young man. After he married Henya Chaya Shedrovitsky, R. Shimshon got involved in the lumber business. He bought plots of trees, processed the wood, and shipped it down the Dnieprovsk-Bug Canal. Unfortunately, that very year there was a flood, and all the wood was washed away. R. Shimshon saw this as an omen that he should be involved in the same work as his parents, so he opened a textiles store. At first business didn't go very well, since his money was washed away in the flood; however his good reputation earned him trust among customers, and the business prospered.

Despite the fact that R. Shimshon was very involved in his business, he still found time every day to study a page of Talmud between the afternoon and evening prayer services or after the evening prayers. He never sat at a table without a book in front of him. Until he reached middle age, he also used to recite the Midnight prayers as well, and there wasn't any religious author whose books he hadn't read. He had a large library of religious books, including books on kabbalah.

R. Shimshon was a strong opponent of Chassidism, and he would say that a Jew should serve G-d with prayers, study and acts of kindness, not with chassidic melodies or dances. Nevertheless, whenever R. Nachumka of Slonim came to Drohitchin, R. Shimshon would be there to welcome him. He would provide R. Nachumka with the best room in the house and serve him. R. Shimshon used to say that even though he was an opponent of Chassidism and rebbes, he respected R. Nachumka, because R. Nachumka was a scholar, and he had the greatest respect for a scholar. Indeed, R. Nachumka used to study night and day. R. Shimshon was involved in community affairs. For many years he was the custodian of the New House of Study and the burial society; he promoted shares in the Zionist Colonial Bank; he collected money for the Jewish National Fund. R. Shimshon raised his children to be religious, but he made sure they had general knowledge as well, imbibing them with a love of Zion and Jerusalem.

In his later years, R. Shimshon suffered a stroke, and the doctors forbade him from reading or studying. However, he refused to listen to them, and until his last day continued to study Mishnah, the *Eyn Yaakov Anthology*, and even a page of Talmud. R. Shimshon died on May 5, 1932.

Henya Chaya, R. Shimshon's wife, was born in 1854 in Drohitchin. For her engagement, her father, R. Yaakov Eliezer Shedrovitsky, bought a lottery ticket and said that the prize would be given to his daughter for her dowry. Indeed, he won 300 rubles, but the money was lost in the flood.

Henya Chaya was a virtuous woman, ran a large home, and even helped her husband in his business. She had tremendous respect for her husband, and he did for her too. Before he passed away, R. Shimshon stated that as long as Henya Chaya lived, she should always remain the owner of the house and business.

[Page 210]

Henya Chaya died on November 8, 1938. The Goldmans had 10 children – four sons and six daughters. Two sons died as small children. The eldest son, Aharon, died on July 6, 1943 in Kiryat Motzkin, Palestine. Sasha Rachel perished in Drohitchin together with her two sons and two daughters and her husband, Eliyahu, died in the ghetto. May G-d avenge their deaths! Arabs killed her son, Peretz, in Haifa in 1947 (One daughter lives in Haifa). Sheina Tzippa perished in Drohitchin together with her husband Yitzchak Goldman, and two daughters. May G-d avenge their blood! (One son lives in Canada). Malka Gittel perished in Brisk together with her husband, Mordechai Gillman, son and daughter. None survived. May G-d avenge their blood!. Bodya perished in Favorsk, Volhyn, together with her husband, Shlomo Fluss. May

G-d avenge their blood (Her son and daughter survived in the forest and fought with the partisans. The daughter was killed before liberation, and the son lives in the United States)! Beila perished in Lutsk together with her husband, Aharon Volveler, and three children. None survived. May G-d avenge their blood!. The Russians deported Shlomo Zelig to Siberia and he thereby survived; today he lives with his wife Rachel in Kiryat Motzkin, Israel. Yenta deported deep into Russia, today lives with her husband and children in Kiryat Motzkin, Israel.

Bodya Fluss (daughter of the Goldmans) and her children

Meir Kaplan of Lina

Meir Kaplan, or Meir of Lina, as he was known, was born in approximately 1865 into a scholarly family in Shavel, Lithuania. His father was a rabbinical judge in Shavel. Until he was around 16, Meir studied in a House of Study in town. In those days, there was supposedly a famine in the Shavel region, and many people left town to look for food to survive. Among the wanderers was young Meir, who after wandering for a long time arrived in Pinsk, where he enrolled in a yeshiva.

Some time later, a villager from the village of Lina, near Yanova, arrived at the yeshiva in Pinsk and asked the head of the yeshiva to recommend a young man to teach the children in the village. The head of the yeshiva pointed to

Meir, and thus the young man from Shavel ended up in the far-away Polesia village of Lina, where he got married and opened a store. R. Meir was a resident of Lina, and was nicknamed Meir of Lina.

Things changed in 1907, when the Czarist regime began to ruthlessly enforce the decree to move Jews out of villages. R. Meir was therefore forced to leave Lina, and moved to Drohitchin. For a brief period R. Meir taught Talmud to the older children at the Yaveh School and others as well. Later he gave up teaching and decided to study in the House of Study. For many years until he died, he taught Mishnah to the congregants at the Old House of Study, and he was also a cantor during the High Holy Days.

[*Page 211*]

R. Meir was a G-d-fearing person, and was known for his hospitality to visitors. Almost every visiting Torah preacher (magid), charity collector and other visitors stayed with R. Meir whenever they came to Drohitchin. He also frequently helped people with charity.

In 1939, when German airplanes bombed Drohitchin and everyone fled to hide in the fields and forests, R. Meir just remained at home, studying as usual. Bombs fell all around; windows broke and houses shook; but not a single window broke in R. Meir's house.

R. Meir died October 19, 1940, and was buried in the Drohitchin Jewish cemetery. The entire Jewish community attended his funeral (See photo on p. 52). He had five children: Sarah Eisenstein (perished with her husband Eliyahu in Drohitchin), Tzadok, Yosef (both died), Perl and Yeshayahu (living in New York).

Meshel Averbuch

R. Meshel Averbuch

Moshe, or Meshel, Averbuch was born in 1860 in Pruzhany. He studied in *kheder* and yeshiva and also studied general subjects and knew Russian well. When he was still a youngster, R. Meshel became the son-in-law of R.

Chatzkel Valevelsky of Drohitchin. With the assistance of his wealthy father-in-law and valiant wife, Chava, R. Meshel went into business and became very successful. He had the largest and wealthiest grocery business in Drohitchin. All the noblemen and officials in the region were his customers, and they considered him to be an honest businessman.

R. Meshel was renowned as a scholar, and was considered the wealthiest man in Drohitchin, but he was always extremely modest. He was never active in community affairs and never went anywhere. His only path was from his home to the House of Study, and then to his business. On the Sabbath and during the week between the afternoon and evening prayers when he had time, he studied Talmud in the Old House of Study.

In 1941 the Russians deported R. Meshel and his son Avraham with other Jews to Siberia, where he died on Dec. 19, 1943. He was buried in a Christian cemetery.

Chava Averbuch

Chava Averbuch, the wife of Meshel, was born in Drohitchin in 1864. Her father, R. Chatzkel Valevelsky, was from a wealthy family that was related to the Katzenelbogens and to R. Shaul Wahl. Chava Chatzkel's, as she was called, was a valiant woman with three advantages: she was educated, gifted and clever, and an outstanding businesswoman. Both Jews and gentiles had great respect for her. Chava had a fine sensitive personality, and she quietly helped to comfort the poor Jews in Drohitchin. Chava used to say, "A wagon driver in Drohitchin is greater than a rich person in Kobrin."

Chava, who suffered from ill health in her later years, died in Drohitchin in 1931. The Averbuchs had three sons and one daughter: Zavel, Avraham,

Menachem and Menucha. Avraham lives in Israel, and Menucha in Russia. (See pp. 78, 187, 188)

Eliyahu Eisenstein

Eliyahu Eisenstein was born in approximately 1875 in Drohitchin to his parents, R. David and Chaya Gittel Eisenstein. Gittel was a descendant of the famous kabbalist, R. David Yaffe, and hoped to make Eliyahu into a rabbi. Young Eliyahu showed good abilities in Talmud study and quickly learned a page of Talmud.

Eliyahu, however, couldn't continue in his studies for very long because there were already five younger children in the house. The financial situation of the family wasn't very good, so Eliyahu decided to travel to the United States to his father, R. David, who was already in Chicago. After an arduous journey, Eliyahu finally arrived in Chicago in 1891.

Eliyahu Eisenstein

Like any other immigrant, Eliyahu had to start toiling away to earn a living during his first years in Chicago. For a while he had a clothing store (1895) and then went into the real estate business, in which he flourished.

At first Eisenstein was involved in buying and selling. Later on he became a building contractor, building houses and offices. Between 1904 and 1916, he built dozens of large and fine buildings. From 1916 on, Eisenstein was involved in the coal industry, and briefly (1923) as a vice-president of the Community Bank on Rooseevelt Road.

At the same time, R. Eliyahu Eisenstein became involved in community affairs. He was the founding president of the first Drohitchin synagogue (1906) on Racine [sp?] Avenue and Clark Street. In 1915, he started construction of the large Drohitchin synagogue on Douglas-Hemlin, which is now the Kehillat Yaakov Synagogue and where he was its first president for three years. In 1924 he built the large Kehillat Yaakov Talmud Torah School, where hundreds of children went to school. Until the end of his life, Eisenstein was the president of the school.

In 1920, he traveled to Drohitchin as a representative of American émigrés from Drohitchin. Due to the war between Russia and Poland, the trip entailed great danger, and he made his way with great self-sacrifice to the war weary residents of Drohitchin, bringing along thousands of dollars sent by their relatives. He also contributed a sum of money to build a synagogue in Drohitchin.

In 1921, Eisenstein made a second trip to Poland. This time, however, he traveled not only on behalf of people from Drohitchin but of people from the entire region. He distributed approximately $300,000 to the Jews of Pinsk, Brisk, Drohitchin, Yanova, Motele, Antopolia, Bereza, and others. So many people came to see Eisenstein every day that they stood in line to get greetings he brought from relatives in the United States.

Eisenstein also worked to arrange visas for dozens of Jewish families whom he took along back to the United States. Today these families are indebted to Eisenstein for having saved them from hell.

In 1922, Eliyahu was entrusted with the task of building a yeshiva in Chicago.

[Page 213]

As chairman of the Building Committee, he built the current large Beit Midrash Le-Torah over a year and a half and served as its chairman of the board. Until he passed away, Eisenstein was the finance chairman of the Beth Midrash Le-Torah on Douglas Blvd.

Eliyahu Eisenstein was also one of the original founders of the Education Committee of the United Talmud Torahs. Through his initiative and assistance, and despite the opposition of some, the building on Wilcox Ave. was purchased and proved to be a success. Today the central offices of the Education Committee (headed by Eisenstein) are located at the building on Wilcox.

[Photo:] Standing, from right: B. Zissuk, Avraham Gratch, Shalom Gratch, Eliyahu Eisenstein, David Epstein, Menachem Averbuch, Itcha Goldman (seated) and Berele Vichnes. Lying, from right: Y. Zilberstein, Yosef Gratch, Ezra Weissman and Tevel Zbar, 1920, during Eliyahu's visit to Drohitchin.

In 1950 Eisenstein initiated the construction of the North Lake Shore Torah Center, and he contributed more than $50,000 to that project.

Chicago Zeitshrift, October 1951

Eliyahue Eisenstein died on December 20, 1953. He suddenly collapsed and died at a gathering at the North Lake Shore Torah Center. In his will, Eisenstein left almost his entire estate for religious educational institutions in Chicago and elsewhere, according to the decision of the trustees. Eliyahu Eisenstein left behind his wife, Chava (Eva) Eisenstein (who came from an illustrious family – her father, R. Moshe Salk, was the long-standing custodian of the Russian Synagogue in Chicago); four brothers and one sister: Lipman, Yisrael Baruch, Leizer, Avraham and Reichel Eisenstein.

Standing, from right: B. Zissuk, Avraham Gratch, Shalom Gratch, Eliyahu Eisenstein, David Epstein, Menachem Averbuch, Itcha Goldman (seated) and Berele Vichnes. Lying, from right: Y. Zilberstein, Yosef Gratch, Ezra Weissman and Tevel Zbar, 1920, during Eliyahu's visit to Drohitchin.

Chaikel Gratch

Chaikel Gratch was born in 1867 to his parents, R. Shimon and Beila, in Drohitchin. He studied in *kheder* and with private tutors, especially Rabbi Yosef Valevelsky, and was considered one of the best Talmud students. In 1890, Chaikel married Esther Yehudit, the daughter of R. Yeshayahu and Asna from Sporeva, near Khomsk. Chaikel also earned a livelihood and did so honestly. He traveled to the United States on two occasions. The first time was to New York in 1900. The second time, when he was planning to return home, he took ill suddenly and died on January 9, 1906. He was buried in the Drohitchin Cemetery in New York.

R. Chaikel was an all-round good person and liked by everybody. He used to teach classes to the congregation and knew how to tell anecdotes. He led prayer services well and was a public Torah reader. He knew Hebrew and Russian and was a supporter of the *Lovers of Zion* movement. He used his character traits for the benefit of the community, both in Drohitchin and in New York, where he was an active member of the brotherhood of the Drohitchin Synagogue. R. Chaikel had two sons, Avraham and Yosef.

[Page 214]
Esther Yehudit Gratch

Esther Yehudit Gratch

Esther Yehudit Gratch was born into a fine family in Sporeva, a village near Khomsk. Her father, R. Yeshayahu, son of R. Shalom Shachna Shapiro (died on the 8th of the second month of Adar), was involved in business. Her mother, Asna Devorah, was a daughter of Avraham Yehuda (died on 15 Elul). She received her education in Khomsk and also learned Hebrew and Russian.

In 1890, Esther married Chaikel Gratch and made her home in Drohitchin, where she opened a haberdashery and helped her husband in business. Esther Yehudit excelled as a businesswoman. Through her honesty she earned the trust and faith of the people in town and developed a clientele. After the death of her husband, Chaikel, in 1906, Esther became the sole breadwinner for her two wonderful children, Avraham and Yosef, who in addition to Jewish studies, received a general high school education. Later, when the children grew older, they helped their mother in business.

First row, from right: Mary Trubovitch, Chana Greenstein-Braverman, Avraham Gratch and Oska Lasovsky (grandchild). Second row, from right: Chaim (Herman) Grossman, Esther Yehudit Gratch-Greenstein, Kadish Greenstein. Third row: Zelig Grossman, Hertska Boff, Chayaka Lasovsky, Tanya Gratch, Malka Kaplan, and Gedaliah Grossman.

In 1912, Esther Yehudit married Kadish Greenstein of Liebeshy and was a devoted mother to his two young daughters, Bracha and Chana. In 1926, Esther Yehudit gave up her business activities and devoted herself to community affairs. She became the head of the visitors' hospitality organization, and co-founded and headed an orphan welfare organization called ZENTOS for many years in Drohitchin. She devoted a great deal of energy to these organizations, and she hosted meetings of the organizations in her home. She collected money, food, and provided assistance to the poor sick and lonely orphans. For her work with ZENTOS, Esther Yehudit acquired the title, "Mother of Orphans."

In 1938 Esther Yehudit came to Chicago on a visit with her children. She planned to return to Drohitchin but the War broke out in 1939, and she remained in the United States, surviving the German murderers. Her husband and daughter Chana and family perished. May G-d avenge their blood!

In Chicago, Esther Yehudit was also active in the Women's Auxiliary of the Kehillat Yaakov Synagogue and Talmud Torah, as well as of the Ateret Zion Synagogue. Her sons, Avraham and Yosef, live in Chicago. Avraham's wife, Tanya, who is from the eminent Goldhand family in Pinsk, practiced dentistry for many years in Drohitchin. Yosef's wife, Frieda, was born in the United States and is a grandchild of R. Yosef Shochet, known as R. Yossel Cherna's, of Drohitchin.

[Page 215]
Malka Warshavsky

Malka Warshavsky

Malka Warshavsky was born in approximately 1869 in Drohitchin to her father, R. Yitzchak Isaac, and her mother, Toive Leah Warshavsky, and was raised as a religious Jewish girl. In 1886 she married Yaakov Zvi Warshavsky, a son of Mordechai Warshavsky, who was a descendant of R. Dovidel Jaffe. Malka was energetic and clever and was a woman of valor to her husband, who ran an authentic Jewish home and had time to be involved in community affairs, helping the poor and needy.

In 1906, after a brief illness, Malka's husband, R. Yaakov Zvi, passed away at the age of 39, leaving Malka as a widow with seven young orphans. Malka took on the role of both father and mother to her children. She opened a food store and took care of her children in the spirit of Judaism.

During World War I, Malka and her children were in the village of Bilinka (near Drohitchin), where they worked in the fields. At the end of the war, Malka lived through the tragic death of her son, Yisrael Baruch, who moved to the United States in 1911 and was killed as an American soldier on the French front three months before the end of the war. Malka received the news of her son's death directly from the American government. Yisrael Baruch was the only casualty among Drohitchin Jews living in the United States in the World War I.

In 1920, Malka received official permission from the American government to come to the United States, where she settled with her children in Chicago. In Chicago Malka invested all her energy in community activities. She became involved in assisting new immigrants from Drohitchin who felt lonely and isolated when they came to the United States. Malka's house was always open for newly arrived immigrants from Drohitchin who found a warm welcome, a kosher meal, a place to sleep, and found in Malka a helping hand as they settled down in the United States.

Malka was particularly devoted to assisting war victims and the needy in Drohitchin who wrote her with requests for assistance. One of the requests was for aid to marry off a daughter; another asked for money to buy a cow, a third asked for food and clothing for orphans, a fourth requested help for patients in the hospital, surgery. Malka helped everyone.

R. Mordechai Warshavsky (Malka's father-in-law), who died in the 1920s. Mordechai's son, R, Yaakov Zvi Warshavsky (Malka's husband), died in Drohitchin at 39 years of age on 24 Shvat (February 19), 1906).

Malka was particularly involved in assisting new brides. She assisted a large number of poor Jewish girls and orphans in Drohitchin with their wardrobe, outfits and dowries so that they could get married and start a home.

Malka was also an active member of the Kehilath Yaakov synagogue and Jewish elementary school, House of Study and "parochial school," as well as other institutions in Chicago. There was almost no Jewish institution in the United States and Palestine that didn't appeal to Malka Warshavsky for assistance, and she accommodated all of their requests. Malka had in her possession a bagful of letters and receipts for contributions to dozens of institutions that she supported.

Malka Warshavsky had seven children: Moshe, Shmuel and Meir (killed with their families in Drohitchin); Israel Baruch (killed in World War I); Eliyahu David (killed in a car accident in Chicago); Toive Leah (Tilla) Kagan, Leizer Warshavsky, and Yosef Warshaw (living in Chicago).

**Sheina Warshavsky-Baum, the daughter of Moshe Shmuel's. She was killed.
May G-d avenge her death!**

Hershel Chaim, Khasha Levin

Khasha Levin

May G-d avenge her death!

Hershel Chaim and his wife, Khasha "the Bronner lady," as she was known, were rare individuals in Drohitchin. She never had any children, and therefore became involved in helping the children of others. Both Hershel and Khasha had the same view of life and worked harmoniously for the benefit of the public.

For many years R. Hershel Chaim was the treasurer and head of the Street House of Study and spent alot of time and energy on it. As the treasurer of the Sick Fund, he collected money to help the needy, visitors, and emissaries from institutions from out of town. He was particularly involved in Torah education for poor children and supported religious elementary schools. He was one of the main supporters of the local yeshiva that was located at the Street House of Study. When R. Hershel Chaim would finish his work and get into his Sabbath clothes, everyone knew that he was going to become involved in a charitable act. This occurred almost every other day.

His wife, Khasha, the daughter of R. Moshe Naftali Bronner Walinsky, was born in Drohitchin and acted in the same way as her husband. Even though she didn't appear to be in good health, Malka had a great deal of energy and fire within her. She didn't walk; she ran. She worked and spoke the same way, very quickly, and she never had enough time. She was always on the move and was always thinking about the shtetl.

Khasha used to visit the sick in Drohitchin to make sure they didn't lack anything. If it was needed, she would go and fetch a block of ice or fill a prescription. She behaved like a real nurse.

[*Page 217*]

Seated, from right to left: Hershel Chaim and Khasha Levin, Moshe Naftali Bronner Walinsky and Chaikel Milner. Standing from right to left: Dina Kharsel, Tenenbaum and his wife Golda; Feitsha Vichnes and Moshe Naftali's grandson. The children in front: Berele Vichnes and Chaikel's grandson. R. Moshe Naftali had 10 children: Yeshayahu, David, Yitzchak, Leib Chaim, Khasha Levin, Chava Milner, Sarah Kharsel, Liba, Golda, and Feitsha Vichnes.

Khasha worked with superhuman powers during the typhus epidemic during the World War I. She didn't worry about contracting the terrible disease and would sit day and night with patients in the hospital and private homes to try to alleviate their suffering. She showed the same concern for a poor bride to help her with her outfit or for getting food for a poor Jewish family.

A couple of years after the World War I, Hershel Chaim and Khasha emigrated to Palestine and settled in Rishon Lezion, where they continued their holy work. Rabbi Yisrael Halevy Beeri (Kolodner), the rabbi of Nes Ziona in Palestine, wrote us about Khasha's life and death in Palestine:

"On Wednesday, 26 Shevat 5713 (Feb. 13, 1953), the great righteous woman, Khasha Levin, passed away while she was carrying a glass of tea for a lonely woman in a nursing home. Khasha suddenly fell and died. She was a wonderful person who never lived for herself, but only for others. Anyone who knew her will praise her name. She'll be remembered by her nephews who she brought to Palestine and married off. She'll be remembered by yeshivas and charity institutions for collecting large sums of money; she'll be remembered by the synagogues in Rishon Lezion for her contribution for a Torah scroll and expensive Vilna edition of the Talmud; she'll be remembered by guests who used to come to Rishon Lezion and receive food, drink and lodging at her home."

R. Hershel Chaim died in Tevet (January), 1937 in Rishon Lezion. He was originally from the town of Khomsk.

Chaikel Milner

Chaikel Milner, a son of Yisrael David and Chana Milner, was born in Drohitchin in 1870 and was educated by religious tutors in town. In 1890, he married Chava, the daughter of R. Moshe Naftali Volinsky. Chaikel and his brother-in-law, Yisrael Eliezer Charsel, were the owners of a large steam mill, the first in the region. Chaikel was a member of the administration of the Folks Bank, the Community Council, the burial society and other organizations. Since 1934, Chaikel has been living in Tel Aviv.

The Milners had six children: Golda Wisotsky, Yosef, Ze'ev, Shifra Saratshik, Yitzchak and Shmuel. Yosef was in Renenkampf's Russian army when it entered East Prussia, and was killed in action.

[Page 218]
David Warshavsky

David Warshavsky was born in Drohitchin in approximately 1880 to his parents, Mordechai (Motya) and Tsippa. On his father's side, he was descended from the family of the kabbalist, R. Dovidel Yaffe. He attended *kheder* and studied under religious tutors in town.

After serving in the Czar's army for four years, David married Chaya Reizel Ratnovsky of Strelnoya (a village near Yanova). In 1905, he left for Chicago, where he stayed for three years before returning to Drohitchin. He then opened a hardware store (in Yoel Leib's store) and was on his way to an independent life when World War I erupted in 1914, leaving everything in a heap. David was drafted into the Russian army, and his store and merchandise were burned to the ground.

Other people were also drafted at that time (1915) together with David Warshavsky: Zelig Tennenbaum, Eliyahu Milner, Shalom the carpenter and Nahum "the truant." All of them were sent off to the front. Eliyahu and Shalom were wounded and sent home, but the retreating Red Army took away David (and the others). During the entire period of the German occupation, no one heard anything from him.

Eventually, when his family (who had been living under harsh conditions in the village of Bilinka during the occupation) had just about given up on him, David wandered through various war fronts with the Russian army. He passed through many areas and cities of Russia and finally served as a soldier in the revolutionary Russian army in Yekaterinberg, where the Czar and his family were shot. At that time, while at the fortress, the historic tragedy played out as David stood guard outside.

Seated, from right to left: Shepsel, Chaya Reizel (mother), David (father) and Alter Friedenberg (son-in-law). Standing from right: Bluma, Leizer, Reuven, Shmuel and Sheina Leah (Alter's wife). The children from right: Shlomo, Rivka and Yonah (grandchildren)

[Page 219]

In the beginning of 1919, David finally returned to Drohitchin together with Zelig Tennenbaum. Nahum "the truant", however, disappeared as if lost at sea, and to this day no one knows what happened to his remains.

David went back into his hardware business and became involved in community affairs. He was a member of the administration of the Folks Bank, medical assistance services, and charity funds, but he couldn't continue with his work for long. The war years, especially his wandering through the trenches, in the wet and cold caused his health to deteriorate. He suffered from blood poisoning, and his feet contracted gangrene. He repeatedly traveled to Warsaw to be treated by Dr. Soloveitchik. He underwent several operations, and was confined to the hospital for several months. Finally, Dr. Soloveitchik decided to amputate one of his feet (I lived in Warsaw in those days and witnessed the tragic operation. I was close by the patient). The last operation didn't help either, and the horrible disease spread to the other foot and then all over his body. After suffering terribly for several months, David passed away in Drohitchin on May 6, 1940.

His wife, Chaya Reizel, their sons Leizer, Reuven and Shmuel Warshavsky, daughter Sheina Leah Friedenberg, husband Alter and son Yonah, all perished in the Drohitchin ghetto in 1942. May G-d avenge their blood!

The survivors were: one son, Shepsel and his family, who were sent to Russia and who live in Haifa, and a daughter Bluma Gutov, husband Mordechai and children, who had left Drohitchin in 1934, and live in Chicago.

Drohitchin, June 1935

Aharon Drogitchinsky

Aharon Drogitchinsky, or "Arele the storekeeper," was born in Yanova. He spent most of his time studying Talmud in the House of Study and turned over earning a livelihood to his wife Khinele, an energetic and good businesswoman who was shopkeeper and breadwinner. Aharon would only be in the store on market days to make sure the gentiles weren't shoplifting.

In Volume 10 of *Hamelitz* of 1885, it is interesting to find that Aharon Drogitchinsky and Yitzchak Rosenkrantz were involved in establishing a Russian school for Jewish children in Drohitchin. This cannot possibly be our Aharon Drogitchinsky, but we have never heard of anyone else with his name.

R. Aharon Drogitchinsky

Aharon's son Meir had left for the United States long ago and prospered there. Later Meir brought over his sisters, Rachel and Tila, as well. In 1923, Meir and his two sisters went to visit their parents in Drohitchin and provided fine descriptions of conditions in town. Meir undertook the expenses for completing the New House of Study. Meir's son, Baron de Hirsh, an attorney in Florida, is a renowned banker and philanthropist. Meir died several years ago.

Aharon and Khinele passed away a long time ago, but their names are known to everyone. Aharon's daughter, Feigel; son-in-law, Yisrael Zelig Lev; and son, David and his family (Yaakov Sidorov's son-in-law) all perished. May G-d avenge their blood!

[Page 220]
Yitzchak Avigdor Telekhansky

R. Yitzchak Avigdor and Elka Telekhansky

Yitzchak Avigdor Telekhansky was born into a Chassidic family in Motele in 1865 and received a religious education. After his marriage to Elka, the daughter of Eliyahu Velvel Itsheles Kravetz, he became a resident of Drohitchin, where he helped build the Chassidic shtibel and contributed a new Torah scroll.

R. Yitzchak Avigdor traveled to the United States several times before he settled permanently in Chicago, where he went into a successful business. He contributed generously in the hundreds of dollars for the Talmud Torah School and religious institutions in the United States and Israel.

In the early 1920s, when R. Yitzchak Avigdor learned from a letter from Rabbi Kalenkovitch that Drohitchin needed a building for the Talmud Torah school and guest house, R. Yitzchak Avigdor wrote a check for $2,000 and gave it to Yisrael Baruch Eisenstein for that purpose. He later gave even more money. With the money contributed by R. Yitzchak Avigdor, Rabbi Kalenkovitch and merchants in town were able to purchase the house of Yehoshua and Rasha Leah Schmid (daughter and son-in-law of Yaakov Shimon Lev). The local Talmud Torah School, guesthouse, and charity fund were all located in that house.

Before he died, R. Yitzchak Avigdor wrote a will in which he donated a third of his estate for yeshivas in Palestine. He passed away on March 2, 1932 (1933 does not correspond to the Hebrew date of 24 Adar I). His wife, Elka, died on April 27, 1939.

The Telekhanskys had two sons and one daughter: Michel, Avraham and Meima Altman. They all live in Chicago. (See photo of the Talmud Torah School on p. 182).

Mendel Eisenstein

R. Mendel Eisenstein

Mendel Eisenstein was born in Drohitchin in 1872 into a Chassidic family. His father, Mordechai Ber, was a scholarly Jew. He spent all his years studying Talmud in the House of Study and was supported by his father, Hersh Leib. Mendel's mother was called Khamka.

Mendel received his education in kheder and from his father, Mordechai Ber. Later, Mendel married Bashka, the daughter of Yitzchak and Mindel Gutter. Yitzchak was known as "Yitzchak the Emperor" and was an eminent businessman in Antapolia. The Eisensteins ran a Chassidic home and sent their sons to study in yeshivas. Mendel helped build the Chassidic shtibel, where he was one of the eminent members. He was also an active member of the burial society.

Unfortunately, R Mendel didn't live very long. At the age of 43 he contracted typhus during the epidemic, and died on November 20, 1915. Upon his death, the burden of caring for and supporting his five small children fell to his widow, Bashka. She was a devoted mother and took on the responsibility with great dedication.

[Page 221]

In 1921, Bashka Eisenstein and her children departed for the United States and settled in Chicago. In her old age, Bashka was cared for with great honor by her children: Mordechai Ber, Hersh Leib, Shachna (Charles), Nachman (Norman), Henya Perl (Emma Wald) and Ada Match, who all live in Chicago.

Bashka Eisenstein

Nachman Weissman

Nachman Weissman was born in Khomsk in 1852 to his parents, R. Yaakov and Chana. He studied with tutors and later attended the yeshiva in Slonim (In those days there was a cholera outbreak in Slonim that took many young lives. Nachman also contracted the disease but managed to miraculously survive).

Weissman then married Feigel, the daughter of Yudel Milner's (Trashinsky) of Drohitchin. He helped his father-in-law for a short time in the horse's mill until he took over the lease for milk sales at the Rovin estate.

There was once a tragedy at the estate: a disease broke out among the animals, which died like flies. With the agreement of the landowner, Pavel Minkov, Nachman's wife Feigel traveled to R. Mordechele of Oshmany, known as R. Mordechele Slonimer, where she received a blessing that stopped the plague.

Some time later, (approximately 60 years ago), R. Mordechele's son, R. Asher, the official rabbi and a resident of Drohitchin (see p. 154), got into a dispute with the Czarist government because of an error that he made in the vital statistics records. He incurred a severe penalty, so R. Asher went to his father, R. Mordechele, for his advice. His father asked him the name of the most influential person in Drohitchin who could speak on R. Asher's behalf. R. Asher responded that it was Count Minkov, who had connections in high places, and he could be accessed through the agent of the estate, R. Nachman Weissman.

R. Mordechele then said that some time earlier a woman from the estate had come to him for a blessing. R. Mordechele gave R. Asher a letter of recommendation to Nachman Weissman to ask him to act on behalf of his son with the landowner. R. Nachman did speak with the count, and the whole case was dropped.

R. Nachman and Feigel Weissman

(As told by R. Nachman's son, Zeidel Weissman of Chicago)

In 1911 R. Nachman lost the Rovin estate, and he moved to Drohitchin, where he earned his livelihood from a store that he had in the market. R. Nachman, who was a quiet and honest man, died on April 29, 1919 in Drohitchin. His wife, Feigel, always a housewife, died on Yom Kippur (October 14), 1929 in Chicago.

The Weissmans had three daughters and one son: Chaya Karelitz who lives in Chicago, Rivka Deutsch who lives in New York, Bobtsha who died on April 30, 1931 in Chicago, and Zeidel, a businessman in Chicago.

[*Page 222*]

Left: Gravestone of R. Nachman Weissman, who died on April 29, 1919 in Drohitchin. Gravestone says: A pure and honest man who walked in a pure path. R. Nachman, son of R. Yaakov Weissman of the Rovin Estate, died on 11 Iyar 5779.

Right: Bobtsha Weissman (a daughter), died on April 30, 1931 in Chicago.

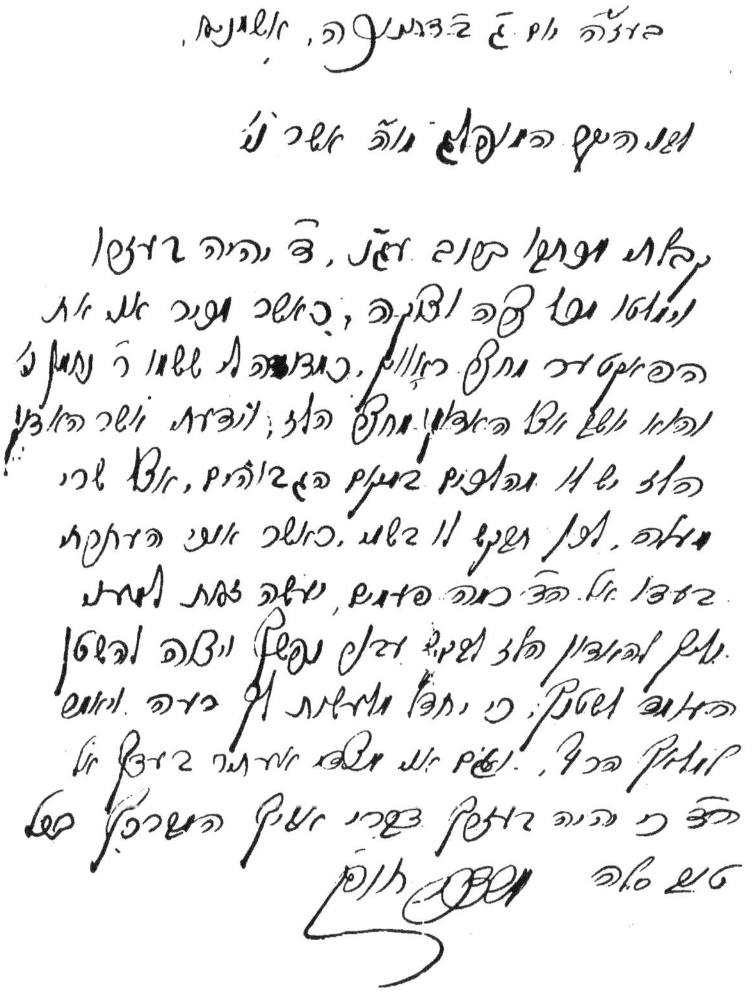

A letter from R. Mordechele Slonimer about Nachman Weissman:

Tuesday, the second day of Chanukah, Oshmany

To my dear son R. Asher:

I read your letter, which caused me great anguish. May G-d help you to escape from all trouble and distress! I know the agent at the Rovin Estate, whose name, I believe, is R. Nachman. He works for the landowner, who I know has connections in high places with senior officials. Therefore, ask him on my behalf, since I have prayed for his welfare a number of times, he should do it for me personally, i.e. to intercede on your behalf to confound the Satan who is troubling you and that he put a stop to what is troubling you. I will also pray on your behalf. May G-d help you!

Your father who blesses you with all good things,

Mordechai [illegible]

Gedaliah Grossman

R. Gedaliah Grossman

May G-d avenge his blood!

Gedaliah Grossman was born in approximately 1875 in Drohitchin. He was a friendly person and related to each person like a good brother. Gedaliah spent his childhood and youth in poverty. Therefore he decided that if G-d helped him prosper, he would help others in need as well. He did prosper, and he kept his word.

After he married Bobba, Gedaliah's economic situation began to improve. He traveled to the United States several times, and each time he returned to Drohitchin. He increasingly prospered financially and owned several houses. He was recognized as one of the preeminent businessmen in town.

Gedaliah was very concerned about his fellow man. If someone was in dire straits, or had a dispute with the authorities, he immediately turned to Gedaliah for help, and Gedaliah made sure that the person in trouble got out of his predicament. Gedaliah was very generous in giving charity, many times anonymously, and anyone in need was able to receive his assistance.

It's said that whenever Gedaliah would see some poor Jew hanging around in the market near peasant wagons to buy some wood, a bag of potatoes, or a pood of grain, Gedaliah would go over to the peasant and tell him to send the wood or potatoes to the poor Jew's home, and return to Gedaliah for payment.

Gedaliah was a friend to every Jew in Drohitchin. At every celebration (circumcision, engagement, wedding) Gedaliah would be a welcome guest, and of course, he brought along a generous gift. There was a saying in Drohitchin that whenever Gedaliah would be seen in town during the week wearing his Sabbath hat, it was a sign that he came to town for a celebration.

In later years Gedaliah became very active with the guesthouse and orphanage, covering many expenses. As mentioned, Grossman was one of the first immigrants in the United States from Drohitchin, and he was involved in building the first Drohitchin synagogue and community in New York, as well as the Agudath Achim Anshei

[Page 223]

Drohitchin (Drohitchin Immigrant Association), which still exists today.

Right: Bobba (daughter of R. Dov Grossman, wife of R. Gedaliah. She died at the age of 59 on July 27, 1935.

Left: At her gravesite are her children. From left, Yirmiyahu, Chaim Leib, and Zelig.

Gedaliah was a type of interesting person that doesn't exist any longer. His wife, Bobba, who followed in her husband's footsteps and who opened her home to all guests and people in need, died on July 28, 1935 in Drohitchin. R. Gedaliah perished in Drohitchin in 1942. May G-d avenge his blood!

The Grossmans had three sons. Yirmiyahu, who was deported by the Bolsheviks to Russia and lives in New York. His family perished in Drohitchin in 1942. May G-d avenge their blood! Chaim Leib Herman lives with his family in New York, and Zelig, who perished in Drohitchin. May G-d avenge his blood!.

Khomsk Alley. On left is the Grossman's wall.

Meir Yehuda Feldman

R. Meir Yudel and Chaya Feiga Feldman and children: Leiba (right), Peshka (grandchild), Bashka (May G-d avenge their blood), Yosef, today in Chicago.

Meir Yehuda Feldman was born in 1860 to his parents Michael and Heska in Drohitchin and received a religious-nationalist upbringing. In 1881, he married Chaya Feiga, the daughter of Yaakov Hersh and Pesha of the Kaminetsky-Mishovsk family, and went into business.

In 1892 Meir Yehuda went to the United States where he remained for four years in St. Joseph's, Missouri, and was deeply involved in community life. Among his achievements was the establishment of the Sha'arei Shalom synagogue, which still exists today.

When he returned to Drohitchin, Meir Yehuda and his family settled on the Smolnik Estate, which belonged to Count Kontorov. From 1897, Meir Yehuda was the lessee and agent of the Smolnik Estate, a position he retained until 1914, when, due to residential regulations, the Czarist regime forced him to leave the Estate. The Feldmans then returned to Drohitchin.

[Page 224]

Meir Yudel, who was descended from an old veteran Drohitchin family, died with his wife Chaya Feiga. May G-d avenge their blood!

The Revisionist Zionist Beitar movement of Drohitchin in military training.

The Feldmans had ten children: Avraham Mordechai came to the United States, married Rosa Boskov in Denver, Colorado, and has three children; Velvel married Sarah Gutter, a daughter of Yitzchak the Kaiser of Antopolia; Esther Beila married David Friedman, Yosel Itsher's son, in 1908 and lived in St. Joseph's Missouri since 1910 and died there in September, 1954; Sarah Leah arrived in the United States and married in St. Joseph's, Missouri in 1907; Bashka, whose first husband, Yoshka Schwartz of Lechovitch, died in 1932, together with her children died in the Drohitchin ghetto (May G-d avenge their blood!); Yosef has lived in Chicago since 1937; Leiba died together with his wife, Lieba, a granddaughter of Moshe Isser's, and children in Drohitchin (May G-d avenge their blood!); Sheinkam was a teacher in the Moriah School in Drohitchin and arrived in Palestine in 1934. She married there and died in 1947. Heska lives in Chicago since 1922, and married Sam Matz. Eliyahu died in Drohitchin in 1919.

Betzalel Hershenhaus

R. Betzalel and Ita Hershenhaus

Betzalel (Tzalka) Hershenhaus was born to his parents, Yehoshua Heshel and Malka Sarah in Dvien, near Kobrin and received a strictly religious education.

He later married Ita, the daughter of R. Moshe Poritsker, and was a resident of Drohitchin where he had a fabric and textiles store. Tzalka was actively involved in the construction of the Old House of Study, where he was also the treasurer, until he left for the United States in 1926. As a token of their appreciation, the congregants of the Old House of Study gave Tzalka a thank-you letter, which is printed below.

R. Betzalel died in Savannah on June 21, 1932. His wife Ita died on February 19, 1951. The Hershenhauses had three sons and two daughters who all live in the United States.

Goodbye Letter *(the first letters of each line spell out Betzalel, son of R. Yehoshua Heshel Hershenhaus, and then, House of Study)*
Blessing on your head crowned with jewels,
Your righteousness will endure forever, your rays will reach heaven,
To you, a public servant, thousands of blessings will be sent,
Because you were a cornerstone in our town,
Forever your memory shall be praised and glorified.
With self-sacrifice you were active when the crown fell down,
Your name is recorded among those who served faithfully.

[Page 225]
You set out to save a rocking ship at sea,
You were a saving angel when the battle began,
When the Balakhov gangs wanted to destroy us,
And you were there to rescue us.
He is the man who is beloved of G-d,
Because you were faithfully involved in the community at every stage,
May G-d bless you with a long life,
May the Creator give you a life of happiness and pleasure.
Of satisfaction and joy.
May He who gives and adds fulfill your every wish,
With purity forever, until your old age,
You were acceptable to us all as treasurer of the House of Study,
You helped us build the House of Study of Sinai,
You crowned the House of Study with all your strength,
Your acts were faithful, and you acted with wisdom and understanding,
You were also a member of the Talmud Study Group,
And joyfully provided charity,
May your successes shine like seventy suns,
And your memory crowned with jewels!
Our wish is directed to Heaven,
That He grant you a sweet long life, as well as your family,
And that your pure charity continue always.
He who chooses Zion and resides in Jerusalem
Shall fulfill all the blessings,
He did great things here in our town,
G-d saw and heard our prayers
that issued forth from the depths of our hearts.

These lines are few but great in quality. To R. Betzalel, son of R. Yehoshua Heshel Hershenhaus, we the undersigned express our goodbye blessings and the feelings of our hearts for the wondrous things you did here for the community, from the days of chaos until today. Thursday of the Torah portion recounting the construction of the Tabernacle in the Desert by Betzalel. Drohitchin, 1926.

Rabbi Isaac Yaakov Kalenkovitch, Yosef David, the Ritual Slaughterer, Aharon Leifer, Meir Kaplan, Betzalel Khatzkilevitch, Alexander Eppelbaum, Michel, son of R. David, Zvi Goldman, Shmuel Snitovsky, Meir Vigutov, Alter, son of R. Michel Cooperman, Yitzchak Zvi Wisotsky, Shmuel Berman,

Yehoshua Zovilovsky, Avraham Abba Leifman, Gedaliah Grossman, Yitzchak Levinovich, Chaim, so of R. Eliyahu Valevelsky, Feivel Katz, Yisrael Eliezer Kharsel. On behalf of everyone at the Great Synagogue and Talmud Study Group, Yosef David, Ritual Slaughterer of Drohitchin.

His children were: Feiga Rachel (perished with her family in Pinsk), Zeidel (Backsley, Georgia), Henya (Baltimore), Sarah, Leiba, Avraham (Miami), and Micheleh (Cuba).

Yaakov Shimon Lev

R. Yaakov Shimon Lev

Yaakov Shimon Lev, who was born in Drohitchin, was a quiet, scholarly, and refined person. He ran a large tailor shop and employed many workers. His business was high quality and always produced first class products. Most of his customers were noblemen and government officials.

Yaakov Shimon was a regular member of the Street House of Study, which he attended on the Sabbath and frequently on weekdays. When he had time, he spent it studying, and was respected in town.

In 1915, when the Germans took over Drohitchin, R. Yaakov Shimon and his family ended up in Horbacha (a village near Drohitchin), and it was there that he passed away at the age of 69 on August 5, 1916. His wife had died on August 1, 1907.

R. Yaakov Shimon had seven children: Fruma (died in Drohitchin), Avraham Yitzchak (died in New York); Rasha-Leah, Yoshka, Feigel, Rachel, Shmuel all live in New York.

[Page 226]
Zvi Reifuss

R. Zvi Reifuss

Hershel the Doctor, as he was called, was a tall man with a long white beard, thick eyebrows, and a long cane – which made him appear to be an angry person. Actually, however, Hershel had a soft and good heart and a crystal clear soul.

Hershel the Doctor loved to do favors and help poor and needy Jews. Whenever he heard that someone was in a tough situation, Hershel took him a couple of rubles as a loan. However, Hershel always forgot to collect the loan. His house was open for visitors and traveling emissaries of Jewish institutions.

On Fridays, his wife Fraida, always baked challah bread and distributed it to the poor, leaving it at their doors anonymously.

The poor people in Drohitchin always turned to R. Hershel for the Sabbath since they knew that Hershel's wife Fraida would provide them with a good meal. David Klepack of Khomsk would always stop by Hershel's house and offer him and his guests the best and biggest fish for the Sabbath. R. Hershel especially enjoyed having learned people at his table.

R. Hershel also healed the sick. He had a special room containing all kinds of bottles with medicine. It was like a real pharmacy. Hershel would mix prescriptions himself. For example, he had a known cure for swollen tonsils as well as a cough syrup. He could also make various preparations to heal wounds. R. Hershel and Fraida used cupping glasses to draw blood to the surface and leeches, and he considered his work to be a great mitzvah, a good deed.

R. Hershel treated both Jews and non-Jews. The peasants from the nearby villages would come to Hershel or bring him to their villages to cure them with his folk remedies, and they would pay him with bags of potatoes and grain. However, Hershel always distributed these items to the poor of Drohitchin.

Once R. Hershel applied cupping glasses to a village peasant woman. A couple of days later the peasant woman died. Her husband reported R. Hershel to the authorities, accusing him of having caused his wife's death. Hershel was heavily fined for practicing medicine without a license. Before he appeared at the district court, Hershel's wife went to the Slonim rebbe, R. Mordechele for a blessing. R. Mordechele promised her that her husband would be released.

The prosecutor in court demanded 30 years hard labor for R. Hershel. Then a young gentile girl spoke, declaring that she mistakenly gave the peasant woman carbolic acid, which killed her. Hershel was released immediately.

When Hershel returned from court a free man, he broke all his bottles and jars containing his medicines, and he devoted the rest of his life to community affairs. R. Hershel reached the age of 80 when he died on November 1, 1915. R. Hershel the Doctor was buried in the Drohitchin Cemetery.

Gedaliah Kaplan

Aharon David Kaplan

Aharon David Kaplan was born and raised in Khomsk. After he married Bobba, the daughter of R. Zvi Reifuss (known as Hershel the Doctor), he began to work in Drohitchin. All his life he earned his own living, and each summer he would travel to trade fairs in Balta and Yarmelinitz where he would purchase *krakols* for pumpkins from Pinsk, as well as his for own shop in Drohitchin. He also made hats for the peasants.

At the time of the great fire on the festival of Shemini Atzeret, 1905, Aharon David lost all his property. He then traveled together with his daughters Chana and Sarah to the United States. However, for religious reasons he could not remain there, and he returned to Drohitchi. Shimshon Goldman and David Valevelsky lent him some money, and he was thereby able to rebuild his business.

[Page 227]

At the same time, Aharon David was also involved in community affairs. He and his wife Bobba, supported Talmud Torah Schools, and he was the treasurer of the *Hayey Adam* and *Eyn Yaakov* study groups in the Old House of Study, where there was a custom to hold a festive meal upon the completion of a portion of study in the groups. His wife, Bobba, would cook and bake her very best for those occasions.

The Kaplans both died in the typhus epidemic in 1915. Aharon David died on Yom Kippur at the age of 63, and Bobba died on the eve of Sukkot, at the age of 54.

The Kaplans had several children: Morris, Eliezer-Moshe, Yehuda and Chaim (deceased); Enny was active in the Workman's Circle in New York and supported Yiddish literature; Flora and Sarah llive in Canada; Gedaliah Kaplan is in New York.

GK

R. Aharon David and Bobba Kaplan

Baruch Avraham Volinsky

R. Baruch Avraham Volinsky

Baruch Avraham Volinsky, or "Baruch Horlevitcher," as he was known, was born in Antopolia in 1804, and was fortunate to live to the age of 113 with great honor, enjoying five generations of offspring.

In his youth, R. Baruch had a cabinet-making business, but it was insufficient to support his large family. He moved to the village of Horlevitch (near Drohitchin) where he continued his business with the peasants, thus providing him with a livelihood.

Some time later, the landowner of the Horlevitch Estate visited the village, and was staying next door to R. Baruch. The landowner offered him an accounting job at his estate. Since Volinsky could write Russian and Polish, he took the job right away and eventually became the director of the entire Estate. This occurred later, when the landowner (a Pole) was forced to flee to Paris because of his involvement in an uprising of Poles against the Czarist regime.

R. Baruch Volinsky also persuaded the landowner to abolish lashings of peasants for any small misdeed, thereby earning the friendship of the peasants. This didn't last long, however, because as soon as the Czarist decree ordering Jews to leave villages was proclaimed, the same "friends" pillaged R. Baruch's house of all his possessions, leaving R. Baruch penniless.

Baruch Volinsky then visited the renowned rabbi of Antapolia, R. Pinchas Michel, for his advice. R. Pinchas Michel advised him to travel to the United States. R. Baruch responded, "Rebbe, only criminals go to America. How can I go there?" R. Pinchas Michel repeated his advice and promised R. Baruch that he would be successful there.

[*Page 228*]

R. Baruch followed the advice of the Rebbe, and in his 80s arrived in New York, where he prospered. He was the founder and secretary of the Khomsk and Antapolia Association, as well as of the charity fund in Brownsville. On his 102nd birthday, President Theodore Roosevelt sent R. Baruch a warm greeting and several 1804 coins as a gift.

On Yom Kippur, October 6, 1917, R. Baruch Volinsky died at the age of 113, leaving behind five generations of offspring, who are today organized as the Baruch Volinsky Circle with 125 members. The Baruch Volinsky Circle works on behalf of fellow émigrés and Israel, thereby keeping alive the name of their ancestor, R. Baruch Volinsky. Information provided by Gedaliah Kaplan

Leibetshka Michalsky

Leibetshka Michalsky was a personable individual with a good sense of humor. He worked as a drummer and director of a klezmer band that performed at Jewish weddings and celebrations. Leibetshka especially excelled in the skill of providing amusements at weddings. The jokes and rhymes he would tell when entertaining the bride and groom and during speeches at the wedding celebration caused people to both laugh and cry.

However, his primary source of income wasn't from entertainment but from his employment at the Rovin Estate near Drohitchin. The landowner of the Rovin Estate, General Minkov, liked Leibetshka very much because of Leibetshka's cleverness and sense of humor, making him his business agent. Leibetshka would make the purchases of all necessities in town and would sell the starch that was produced by the Estate's starch factory. Leibetshka was also the landowner's toll collector. In those days, the public baths of the entire town belonged to General Minkov, and the Jews would pay him fees.

Leibetshka Michalsky

Leibetshka would travel to town with the landowner in a carriage with six horses and watched both Jews and gentiles tip their hats to the landowner. Leibetshka would joke that he, Leibetshka, was a Jewish nobleman named Michalsky.

When World War I broke out, Mrs. Minkov called a meeting of the landowners. It was decided that all landowners should leave their estates and retreat deep into Russia. The landowners then asked Mrs. Minkov to ask Leibetshka his opinion about the situation. Leibetshka responded, "For 40 years the Germans have prepared for an attack on Russia, and the Russian regime has been preparing to expel Tuvia from the village of Osevitz because he didn't provide new shoes for the peasants."

When the Germans arrived in Drohitchin in 1915, Leibetshka was living at the Rovin Estate and became the leader of the Estate and surrounding area. He made use of his position to assure the supply of grain and potatoes for Jews in town.

On one Christmas night, a German officer had Chaim Ber Kravetz, the wagon driver, to take him to Rovin. When he arrived at Rovin, the German officer got drunk and started harassing Chaim Ber, accusing him of having "killed his God." The officer then beat Chaim Ber and brought him to the administrator, Leibetshka, who listened to the complaint and responded, "Officer, it wasn't this Jew who killed your God, it was the Jews of Lahishin." The drunken officer was satisfied with Leibetshka's answer and left Chaim Ber alone.

[Page 229]

After World War I Leibetshka and his children came to the United States, and Leibetshka missed home very much in New York. He missed the klezmer band and the weddings and celebrations and planned to return to Drohitchin. However, on January 27, 1924 he died at the age of 86 in York. His wife Leah had died on January 3, 1920 in Drohitchin. Their children were: Yudel (Chicago), Malka-Leah, Eliyahu, Mendel, Sheina and her husband Benny Tepper [live] in New York.

Information from Gedaliah Kaplan

Aharon Leib Schub

R. Aharon Leib Schub and Perl Schub

Aharon Leib Schub was born in 1867 into a large extended family in Antapolia and received his education there. His father was R. Moshe Eliezer Schub, and for a time Aharon Leib lived with his grandfather in the village of Tenevitch. In 1892 Schub married Perl, the daughter of Shimon the Doctor of Drohitchin, and remained in Drohitchin until 1906, when he and his family moved to Pinsk. In 1915, when the Germans took over the Pinsk region, the Schubs returned to Drohitchin, where they remained until the early 1920s, when they left for the United States. Aharon Leib, known as "Schub the Agent" was an insurance agent for the Grodno gubernia, and his professional society awarded him with a gold medal.

At the same time, Schub was active in community affairs, and he worked to alleviate the suffering of war victims, especially women whose husbands were in the United States. Aharon Leib was especially active in Zionism, collected funds for the Jewish National Fund, and gave speeches at Zionist meetings. Schub's two sons were among the first pioneers in Palestine. Schub continued with the same activities in New York, but he passed away there on August 15, 1930.

Perl Schub, Aharon's wife, was born in Drohitchin in July, 1875, and died on July 27, 1955 in New York. They had seven children: Penny, Shmuel, Binyamin, Leah, Noachka, Morris and Yosef. They all live in New York.

In Memory of Our Parents

Hinda-Matel   **Waldman**
Yosef Gratch's   **R. Shepsel**
Daughter   **Bery the Teacher's Son**

                       Died in Drohitchin
                       Feb. 13, 1937, age
                       69

1 Adar 1916, age 53 [1916 was a leap year and there were thus two Adar months. Thus this date is not clear, since it may have been another year, or one or the other of the Adar months in 1916]

                                        Chaim and Yehudit Hoffman, Chicago

[Page 230]

PHOTOS

The "grandmother," Beila Reizel Kaminetsky

The wife of Shepsel Leib Kaminetsky, she was always considered a "grandmother," a midwife. Whenever a child became sick, she would tie a red lace around its neck with a linen bag containing pepper as a good omen. Beila Reizel lived to the age of 105 and died in Drohitchin in 1915.

Chaya Gedaliah's

She was known as the "cheese maker." She would make certain cheese drinks and *gomelkas* that she would sell in town, especially to merchants from Pinsk.

Kaila, the Mail Carrier

A widow with eight small children, Kaila convinced the postmaster of Drohitchin to let her work as a mail carrier. She was able to make a living off of the gifts and tips she received. Incredibly, Kaila could not even read Russian. Because of an informer some 10 years later, the Russian authorities sent an official mail carrier to Drohitchin. The householders in town then appealed to the postmaster to let Keila deliver their mail. This arrangement continued until 1907, when Kaila and her children moved to the United States, where she died in New York in 1936.

Information from Gedaliah Kaplan

[Page 231]

Bobba [Grandma] Chaya Ita

Bobba Chaya Ita

Whenever you would walk down the street and meet a stooped-over woman of medium height wearing a red head-covering and dressed in a velvet coat and a wide dress colored in such a way that you couldn't decide whether it had been black or dark blue, you knew it was our local Bobba Chaya Ita.

Apart from the number of years borne by her stooped shoulders, her way of walking made her seem like a young woman; her sure steps took her over the streets and alleys, in rain or snow, thunder or storms, day or night. As far as Grandma was concerned, there was nothing around that could keep her from her tasks of helping to bring a new baby into the world.

Everyone – young and old – knew Bobba Chaya Ita. She was good-natured, good-hearted, and friendly to everyone. She had a kind word for everybody. She was everybody's "Grandma," and she was concerned about everyone's health; she would pray for each person's health.

She was always rushing around like she was scared of missing something. She came on time and had everything ready to bring the new baby into the world (which was her job). She acted as if two lives – mother and child – were her responsibility. When everything finally finished properly, she thanked G-d for having given her the strength and the opportunity of doing her holy work.

If, G-d forbid the birth was difficult and labor was arduous, she would shake the heavens and wake up the family to say psalms; she would run to the House of Study, open the Ark containing the Torah scrolls and start crying to G-d to spare the mother.

She considered everyone in town her grandchild, and these "grandchildren" would call her "Grandma," a name that she rightly earned. There was almost no expectant mother in Drohitchin for whom Bobba Chaya Ita didn't officiate as midwife. Her nickname "Grandma" made people forget her real name, Chaya Ita. Everyone knew who was meant by the mere mention of the word "Grandma." She was greatly concerned about her "grandchildren," and she did her job perfectly.

She continued her work until July 18, 1918. As usual, she was called to attend to a woman, an expectant mother, not far from Drohitchin. The mother was the wife of Leiba Hausman, the agent of the Tcheramcha Estate. Everything was fine, and the mother gave birth to a baby boy. Grandma spent a week there. At the end of the week, Lieba, the agent, traveled to Drohitchin, taking Grandma along with him. While they were passing the Dobavya Garden, Grandma told the agent that should wanted to stop off and buy some fruit, and he shouldn't wait for her. She said she would return home to Drohitchin on her own. So Lieba went on his way.

A few days went by, and Grandma didn't return. Her "grandchildren" were sick with worry, and people started looking for her everywhere. But she was nowhere to be found. No effort was spared to find her, but she couldn't be located. It was as if she had never even existed. To this very day no one knows what happened to her.

Zalman Shevinsky

Warshavsky – Moshe (son of R. Mordechai and Tsippa) and Beila (daughter of Bobba Chaya Ita Salever). They both died in 1915, Moshe on September 15 and Beila on September 20. The Warshavskys had five children: Feiga Rachel (who perished with her family in Drohitchin), Sarah, Bashka (living in Chicago), and Yaakov (living in New Jersey). See pp. 117, 215, 246 and 325.

[Page 232]
Alter Saratshik (Sraely)

Alter Saratshik, or Aharon Sraely, was a son of Eliyahu and Ita Saratshik, and was born in Maltsh near Pruzheny. He studied in yeshivas in Maltsh (under R. Zalman Sender Shapiro and R. Shimon Shkop), Mir (R. Eliyahu Baruch Kamai), and Volozhin (R. Rafael Shapiro). He also studied general studies and accounting.

From right in middle row seated: M. Bezdzhesky, H. B. Wolfson, S. Feldman, A. Eisenstein, School Director, a teacher, Alter Saratshik, Podolsky and S. Beich.

In 1917, Saratshik married Shifra, a daughter of Chaikel and Chava Milner from Drohitchin, where he settled and started a wholesale business. From 1898, A. Saratshik was active in community and Zionist affairs. In Drohitchin he was one of the leaders of the Zionist movement and its motivating force, gave Zionist speeches at every opportunity, and was an active fundraiser for various causes. He was a chairman of the Tarbut and Moriah Schools, a director of the Folks Bank, and Jewish representative in the municipal council, where he represented Jewish interests with the Polish authorities.

From 1933, Saratshik lived with his family in Ramat Gan, Palestine, where he continued his community work. He was a member of the Pioneer Zionists Associations, General Zionist Organization, co-founder of the General Zionists Labor Organization, Vice-President of the Bnai Brith lodge in Ramat Gan (a branch of the American Bnai Brith), and a director of the Religious Council of Ramat Gan, as well as secretary and accountant (since 1934) of the Sharon Cooperative Bank in Ramat Gan.

In Palestine Saratshik changed his name to Aharon Sraely. The Saratshiks had a number of children.

From Left: Bracha Kreines, Yaakov Ber Kreines, Yeshayahu, and Fruma-Gittel Warshavsky, 1932. The house belonged to Berl and Alta Lechovitsky.

[*Page 233*]
Shlomo Zelig Goldman

Shlomo Zelig Goldman, a son of Shimshon and Henya Chaya Goldman, was born on June 30, 1896 in Drohitchin and studied in the yeshiva of Rabbi Mordechai Minkovich. At the same time, he studied general studies, Hebrew, and Russian privately.

After he married Rachel Goldman, a daughter of R. Eliyahu Goldman of Brisk (a sister of Rabbi Yehuda David Goldman of Chicago), R. Shlomo Zelig opened a haberdashery and confectionary in Drohitchin. At the same time, he was active in community affairs, serving for many years as a member of the local municipality. He served as a director of the Folks Bank, director of the charity fund, vice-chairman of the Jewish community council, treasurer and director of the firefighter's association, president of the General Zionist Organization, president of the Tarbut School, president of the *Keren Hayesod,* and member of the Jewish National Fund.

In June 1941, Shlomo Zelig and his wife were sent to Siberia (Upper Berezovka, Altaic District) by the Soviet regime, and they worked in the forest. Following the Soviet-Polish (Shikorsky) Agreement, they were released from Siberia and worked in Sarakino, Russia as senior accountants.

When they returned to Poland in April 1946, Shlomo Zelig worked in Waldburg (Wolbzhich) as secretary of the Zionist Organization *Ichud (*Unity) and *Breicha* (an organization involved in helping Jews leave Poland).

In August 1946, he was smuggled into Munich, Germany, and from there, through refugee camps to Leifheim, near Olm. In the beginning, he was employed in Leifheim as the director of the historical commission involved in collecting material pertaining to German cruelty and murder. Thereafter he was elected to the camp administration and worked there as senior accountant. Shlomo Zelig was also the chairman of the General Zionist Organization, Jewish National Fund Commission, and representative of the Jewish Agency.

In April 1948, the Goldmans left Leifheim for Bergen-Belsen, where they obtained a certificate from the British occupation authorities, and reached the shores of Israel via Marseilles in June, 1948. The settled in Kiryat Motzkin.

Shlomo Zelig was the co-founder and chairman of the Drohitchin Association in Israel, as well as first treasurer of the large synagogue in Kiryat Motzkin.

From left, Rachel and Shlomo Zelig Goldman, Zvi and Yenya Weingarten and their daughters, Penina and Yaffa.

Standing from right: Alter Alberman, Leitshe Milner, Yitzchak Milner, Yenta Goldman and Khlavna Pisetsky. Seated from right: Yehudit Minkovich, Chana Epstein, ----, and Pessel Goldan. Below, from right: Esther Schwartz and Sheina Kreines.

[Page 234]

Rabbi Avraham Chaim Katzenelenbogen

Rabbi Avraham Chaim Katzenelenbogen of Svislotch (near Byalistock) descended from the famous Katzenelenbogen family, which is said to derive from the legendary R. Shaul Wohl, who was king of Poland for one night.

Approximately 175 years ago, Rabbi Katzenelenbogen came to Drohitchin looking for a son-in-law from among the family of Drohitchin Valevelskys, who were among the most veteran families in town.

It is believed the name Valevelsky is derived from the Valevel Estate near Drohitchin. Apparently, the first Valevelsky came to Drohitchin from Valevel.

The bride and groom were accompanied to the wedding canopy over a carpet of velvet that stretched from the house to the synagogue. The groom had received a large dowry for the wedding, and his father, the rabbi of Svislotch, also received a dowry.

Rabbi Avraham Chaim, who was called "the Rabbintchik" spent his entire life in study, and his wife, Bodya, was the breadwinner. Bodya was involved in the grain business and would shake hands with the noblemen using a glove.

Before his death, Rabbi Avraham Chaim asked for forgiveness from his wife for not having complied with the conditions of the wedding ketubba certificate, insofar as a husband is required to support his wife and children.

The Katzenelenbogens had four sons and two daughters: Zelig (his children: Sheina-Tsippa, Aharon, Yoel-Leib, Bunya and Sarah); Shimon (died together with his father. Feiga Motya-Liebs was a grandchild; Frank Volin of Chicago is a great-grandson); Freida (her children are unknown); Bunya (her husband was Zelig Kaplan of Brisk. Their children: Zalman, Shimon, Chatskel and Dvasha); Pinya (her children: Meir-Leib, Rabbi Yosef Valevelsky and Chatzkel Katzenelenbogen); Chatzkel (his children: Moshe-Leib, David, Sheina-Rachel, Leah, Sarah, Dina, Feiga and Chava Averbuch).

It's noteworthy that all of Rabbi Katzenelenbogen's children used their mother's last name, Valevelsky, and not Katzenelenbogen. The name of the great-grandmother Bodya was also very popular in the Valevelsky family until the present. Almost all girls born later into the Valevelsky family were named Bodya. The original Bodya lived for almost 100 years.

Information from Zalman Shevinsky

Bodya Shevinsky

Bodya Shevinsky

Bodya Shevinsky, a great-grandchild of Rabbi Avraham Chaim Katzenelenbogen, was born to her parents, Tsippa and Leizer Shedrovitsky, in Drohitchin. The Shedrovitskys had eight children: Feiga, Aharon-Yitzchak, Avraham-Shimon, Shlomo, Bodya, David-Leib, and Chana Reizel.

In 1887, Bodya married Nachum Shevinsky of Kobrin and assisted her husband in business. In 1912, the Shevinskys arrived in the United States, and Bodya became involved in her community service work. In her older years, Bodya and her children, Rabbi Nachum-Yitzchak and Toiba-Gittel Sacks, live in Chicago. See pp. 159, 166, 187, 188, 195, 209 and 211.

[*Page 235*]
Chana Reizel Shevinsky

Chana Reizel Shevinsky

Chana Reizel Shevinsky (sister of Bodya Shevinsky), the youngest daughter of Yaakov Leizer and Tsippa Shedrovitsky, was born in Drohitchin. At the age of 12, she lost her mother and had to help out her father in taking care of the family and in working in the tavern. Because of this she discontinued her studies in school, and then she married Aharon-Yosef Shevinsky of Kobrin. After the death of her husband in 1923, she moved to New York, where she lives today.

The Shevinskys had seven children: Sheina-Tsippa (New York), Zelig (Arizona), Toiba, Rivka, Yaakov (all in Israel), Shimon (died in Israel), and Michael (Chicago).

Chaya Ethel Valevelsky

Chaya Ethel Valevelsky

She was the wife of Rabbi Yosef Valevelsky, and over the years she ran a leather business in Drohitchin. Later she moved to the United States, where she lived with her children in New York. She was active in the area of philanthropy. Chaya Ethel died at the age of 97 on February 28, 1955.

Rabbi Yosef Valevelsky, who was a rabbi for a short time in a town and later a Talmud teacher in Drohichin, died on March 10, 1907 at the age of 39.

Aharon-Yosef Shevinsky

Aharon-Yosef Shevinsky

Aharon-Yosef Shevinsky was born in Kobrin to his parents, R. Moshe and Beila. He completed Russian high school with excellence, but because of the quota system in Russian academies, he could not pursue his studies and instead went into business.

Later he married Chana Reizel, the daughter of Yaakov-Leizer Shedrovitsky of Drohitchin. He followed his father R. Moshe and became a senior accountant and administrator of the Lifshitzes of Antapolia, major lumber merchants. For a time, he ran the Planter Forest near Kobrin and thereafter the Palushin Forest near Antapolia.

Like his father, he was a warm Chassid, hosted guests, and was known for his honesty.

Aharon Yosef died on February 3, 1923 in Zhobinka at the age of 52. His wife Chana Reizel lives in New York.

Aharon Goldman
Died in Kiryat Motzkin, Israel, July 6, 1943

358 Drohitchin Memorial Book

[*Page 236*]

Photos

באשקע   שעדראָוו   אברהב שמעון
כ״ה חשון, 1913   כ״ו אלול, 1926

שלמה   שעדראָוויצקי   ע הינ:
כ״ט תמח, 1927   1931 ,כסלו ׳ד

ﺵ

שעדראָוויצקי פֿאמיליע

שיינעציפּע   שעדראָוויצקי   יעקב־אליעזר
י״ד חשון, 1887   ב׳ אדר, 1900

שרה־הינדע   שעדראָוויצקי   דוד־לייב
ט״ז אלול, 1933   ה׳ אלול, 1914

רינהפֿריידע   שעדראָוו   אליהויבער
ח׳ אייר, 1939   י״ט אלול, 1950

דוד שעדראָוויצקי
ו׳ חשון, 1954

פֿייגע בערג
ל׳ כסלו, ת״ש — צו 95 יאר

אהרן יצחק שעדראָוויצקי גיטל
א.י. — מ״ז חשוו. 1913

See translation next page.

Translation of Captions of Previous Page

Avraham   Sherov
Shimon   Bashka
September 5,   Nov. 25, 1913
1926

Hinda   Shedrovitsky   Shlomo
Nov. 14, 1931   July 29, 1927

Shedrovsky Family

Yaakov-Eliezer Shedrovitsky Shaina-Tsippa
2 Adar 1900   Nov. 1, 1887

[1900   had   two   Adar   months,   so   English   date   is   unclear]

David-Lieb Shedrovitsky   Sarah Hinda Eliyahu   Ber Shedrov   Rina-
August   27,   Sept. 6, 1933 Sept. 1, 1950 Frieda
1914   April 27, 1939

Aharon   Shedrovitsky   Gittel   Feiga   Berg David Shedrovitsky
Yitzchak   Nov. 16, 1913 Dec. 30, 1940 – Nov 2, 1954
unknown   age 95

[*Page 237*]

Hausman Family

Top, from right: Moshe Ber and Feigel Hausman and children: Shmuel Greenberg (son-in-law), Chana (Shmuel's wife), and Raizel (below right), killed in Drohitchin in 1942. Son Shmuel, a petty officer in the Canadian Navy, died in action, August 30, 1945; Yisrael, died on 12 Adar, 1946 (In 1946 there were two Adar months, so corresponding English date is unclear.) in Argentina. Shmuel was a religious young man. When he went off to war, he left a will stating that if something should happen to him, his belongings should be given to charity.

Moshe Ber, a son of Alter the Magid's (Preacher's) and Charna Hausman, and Feigel (born in the village of Sokolovka) both died on the same day in the typhus epidemic on September 13, 1915. Moshe Ber was 39 and Feigel 41. They left behind 12 orphans. The daughter, Chaya-Ethel, reported that the funeral of her mother took place in the daytime, and her brother said the Mourner's Kaddish at the afternoon prayer. Her father said, "Say the Kaddish my son for your mother; later you'll say it for me." A while later her father died.

The two oldest sisters took care of the younger children. Chaya-Ethel had a grocery store and earned a living, while Chana ran the house until the children all grew up and went out on their own.

Sarah Devorah Nitovsky and Esther Leah Goldstein now live in Chicago; Freidel (Frieda) Gold lives in New York; Chaya-Ethel (Clara) Loffman lives in Los Angeles; Bodya (Beatrice) Faiman and Sheindel (Jennie) Steinberg live in Winnipeg, Canada; and Yankel (Jacobo) Gojzman lives in Argentina. (2014 edits by F. Schumacher, Jennie's daughter)

[Page 238]
Moshe the Ascetic

May G-D avenge his blood!

He was called Moshe "the ascetic." He was a short man with a pair of sparkling eyes that were set with a pair of broken eyebrows. He attended the Old House of Study, where he sat behind the Torah-reading platform, and he studied on his own day and night or taught a class in the classic anthology, Ein Yaakov, between the afternoon and evening services.

Moshe the Ascetic [illegible words] Drohitchin, summer 1935.

Every major businessman provided him with his meals. He never spoke about his family, and his life seemed to be a mystery to everybody. He would eat his Sabbath meals at our house. My younger sister would prepare dairy meals for him because he couldn't eat meat meals – only dairy.

One Friday evening, it was pouring rain and was impossible to leave the house. I asked him to spend the night at our home. On that occasion we happened to also discuss various Jewish issues, world politics, and our personal lives. I asked him to tell me about his life and why he became an ascetic.

He asked me to swear never to tell anyone what he said for as long as he lived. Now he is no longer alive, so I can recount the tragic story. "I lived in a village called Yuchnovitz, near Pinsk. I returned from yeshiva and married the daughter of a wealthy Jewish villager. My wife was very beautiful, and we earned a living from the store that my father-in-law opened for me. I was then blessed with two beautiful children, and we lived a happy life.

"The joy didn't last for long. As people say, 'no one knows what tomorrow will bring.' One morning my wife told me that she didn't feel well, and I should call the doctor. I immediately called the country doctor from Yanova who arrived quickly and examined my wife. He stated that she had typhus and provided us with various prescriptions. Like an arrow I shot off to Yanova to the pharmacy and ordered the prescriptions. The pharmacist gave me two bottles, one to drink and the other to spray around the house. It was like Lysol. When I got home I mixed up the bottles and gave my wife the bottle of Lysol to drink. Soon after she drank it, she started having convulsions and died.

" I was frightened and confused, but no one knew the reason. This awful mistake has broken my life forever. I didn't sleep at night and wandered around feeling that I was going to go out of my mind. I decided to give my children to my in-laws, leave my friends, and wander through cities and towns for a whole year until I came to Drohitchin, where I remained.

" Until today no one knows that I killed someone, my very best friend, by mistake. Therefore I am going to remain an ascetic until I die." He then ended his tragic story.

Gedaliah Kaplan

Memorial Boxes

In eternal memory of our beloved and dear parents

Berl   Lechovitsky   Alta
either 2/18/38
April 6, 1922
3/20/38 (There were two Adar months in 1938, not one as indicated.)

              Brother and Sister
              Meita and
              Yitzchak
perished with their families at the hands of the German murderers in 1942 in Drohitchin.

David Lakovitz,   Beila Levy,
Brooklyn   Chicago

              Tila Schwartzberg
In memory of my parents

Meir Yudel   Leah
March 24, 1939   Feldman   March 12, 1915

Chava Feldman

[Page 239]
Aharon Lashinsky

Aharon and Heska Lashinsky

Aharon Lashinsky, known as "Areh Falk's" was born in Drohitchin. His father was named Falk, and R. Aharon was a person from the old generation, and was renowned in Drohitchin.

In his youth, R. Aharon taught a *kheder* and studied the weekly Torah portion and Rashi commentary with the children. Later he became the custodian of the Street House of Study and remained in that position his whole life. R. Aharon was no ordinary synagogue custodian. He was totally devoted to his religious duties, and he was the cantor in the Street House of Study, Torah-reader and shofar-blower. Areh Falks' was the heart and soul of the Street House of Study and was respected by everyone.

When Areh Falks would lead the prayers during Rosh Hashanah and cry out *"The King"* during the prayers, the congregants in the synagogue would tremble. He would recite the prayers with loud wailing, and the same situation would occur during his recitation of the Ninth of Av eulogies commemorating the destruction of the Temple. Everyone felt the destruction in the synagogue. Areh Falks would also recite the midnight eulogies for the destruction of the Temple with the same intensity of feeling. In his private life R. Aharon was satisfied with little and happy with his portion. During World War II, when the Street House of Study was burned down, Areh Falks felt as if the Temple had been destroyed in his lifetime and that the source of his life's energy had run dry.

Areh Falks died in 1921 at the age of 85 on the Ninth of Av (Aug. 13), 1921. His wife Heska (a daughter of R. Gershon and Leiba) died in December 1913.

The Lashinskys had four children: Leizer Lashinsky, Aharon's son, lived in Chicago for many years and was a community leader. He was an active member of the Kehilat Yaakov Synagogue and the Talmud Torah School and Drohitchin Aid Association. Leizer died on December 9, 1950. His wife Mina died on July 18, 1935.

Leizer and Mina Lashinsky

Avraham Lashinsky, Aharon's son, also died in Chicago in 1947. Daughter Sirka died in Drohitchin in approximately April 1905. Daughter Esther-Yospa Drucker died in Drohitchin on December 27, 1917. Her husband Mordechai-Ber Drucker died in Drohitchin on September 30, 1928. The Druckers had eight children: Tsalka (who perished with his family in Drohitchin), Falk (died in Drohitchin), Lana (died in Drohitchin. Her family perished.), Chaytsha (perished with her family in Motele), Chaim Drucker and sisters Sirka (Resnick) and Lieba (Goldberg) and their families live in Chicago.

Zeidel (Meir Yitzchak) and Henya Steinberg and children (from right): Mordechai, Feigel, Hershel and Menachem (Dr.). Zeidel's yahrzeit is on the second day of Rosh Hashanah (1943). The rest, besides Zvi, live in Chicago.

[*Page 240*]
Zelig Hausman

R. Ezriel Zelig and Sirka Hausman
Ezriel Zelig Hausman, known as "Zelig the Preacher's" was born in 1858 in Drohitchin.
His father was known as "Leibe the Preacher."

The Hausman family was renowned in Drohitchin. Zelig's brother, Alter the Preacher's, was a scholar who owned a store (prior to World War I). Zelig's sister, Sarah Leah, was the wife of Meir Noach's (a brother of R. Binyamin Moshe, the Ritual Slaughter's wife). Another sister, Hendl, lived in Yanova.

R. Zelig studied in kheder and the House of Study. At the age of 19, he married Sirka, a daughter of the famous teacher, R. Motya Pinchas. Naftali Steinberg was R. Zelig's brother-in-law. R. Zelig, who was involved in business, was considered one of the esteemed businessmen at the Street House of Study and ran a dignified home.

During the German occupation in World War I, when the Polish rabbi, R. Noach Kahn, and Rabbi Yehudah David Goldman (today in Chicago) decided to repair the *eruv* (ritual Sabbath boundary) in Drohitchin that had been destroyed in the fighting, R. Zelig anonymously contributed the entire sum himself. He was always interested in charitable causes and enjoyed doing favors for Jews.

In 1922, R. Zelig and his family moved to Chicago, where he continued his membership in the Drohitchin community.

Alter, son of Zelig and Peshka Hausman, with his children.

From left: Freidel, Meir Motya, Pinya, Naftali, Nissel and Shmerl.

Sarah Leah, Meir Noach's wife (Lashinsky) is seated on right. They were all killed, May G-d avenge their blood!

[*Page 241*]

Standing, from left: Aharon Meir Oberman, Alter Hausman, Hershel Eisenstein, Moshe Levack and Moshe Kravetz. Seated from right: Hershel Levack (child), Hershel Hochman, head of yeshiva (see p. 44), Yisrael Kravetz, and unknown.

Picture was taken at the Street House of Study at the door under the inscription, "Established in 1920 and renovated with funds from the brothers Nehemiah and Yitzchak, sons of Yisrael Kravetz, in 1928. The treasurer was Zvi son of Moshe Eisenstein." Aside from Zvi Levack, everyone perished. May G-d avenge their blood!

The Hausmans had five children: Hendl (in Chicago with her husband David Eisenstein and children); Chasha; Esther-Rachel (in New York); Chana-Devorah (died in New York); and Alter (perished with his family in Drohitchin). R. Zelig died on March 5, 1928. His wife Sirka died on December 8, 1929.

Aharon Meir Oberman

May G-d avenge his death!

Aharon Meir Oberman was born in Kamenetz in approximately 1902 and became the son-in-law of Alter Hausman. Aharon Meir, who was a scholar, was a rare cantor and Torah-reader. He was the jewel of the family. Aharon Meir had a sweet lyrical voice and a good ear for music. His method of chanting the prayers was a mixture of ordinary praying and a cantorial style, and he was considered the best cantor in the region. People in the town and nearby area liked to have him lead the prayer services. In his final years R. Aharon Meir led the prayer services permanently in the Street House of Study.

Aharon Meir never received a penny for his Torah-reading. He earned a good living from his bakery, and was also involved in the export of eggs. His wife, Chasha Hendl, helped him in business. She, like her mother Charna, was a good businesswoman.

The Obermans had two children: Kalman and Leiba. R. Aharon and his family perished. May G-d avenge their deaths!

[Page 242]
Litman and Beila Eisenstein

R. Litman Eisenstein, Beila Eisenstein

Litman Eisenstein, a son of R. Hershel and Reichel and a close relative of Rabbi Avraham Eisenstein, was born in 1859 in Drohitchin and studied in the kheder. In approximately 1885, he married Beila, the daughter of R. Zalman and Rachel of Subot (a village near Drohitchin), and went into business.

In 1890, Eisenstein arrived in the United States, but he returned soon to Drohitchin. During the war years (1914-1919), the Eisensteins supported the needy, both relatives and others, with bread and potatoes. During the same period, Eisenstein was also active in the burial society, and he assisted with provide typhus victims with a respectable burial.

In 1920, Eisenstein and his family arrived in Chicago and settled there permanently. Litman, who was strongly influenced by the traditional way of life, lived out his life in the company of other émigrés from Drohitchin and at the House of Study in Chicago. R. Litman died on the first day of Rosh Hashanah in 1928.

Litman's wife, Beila, was respected and influential in her community and always lent a hand to the poor and oppressed. She was especially devoted to the education of her children and made every effort to raise them in the Jewish spirit. In later years, it was said that she left this world because of how much she missed her eldest son, Alter, who left for the United States at a very young age, and whom she hoped to see again. Her wish was fulfilled, and one year after she and the family arrived in Chicago, she and Litman accompanied Alter to the wedding canopy. Unfortunately, that same night Beila contracted a lung infection and died shortly thereafter at the age of 56 on February 17, 1922.

The Eisensteins had five children: Alter (Arizona), Avraham, David, Rachel, and Yosef in Chicago.

R. Litman also had two brothers, R. David and R. Yudel, plus a sister Chaya Dova. She died 13 years ago in Chicago at the age of 88.

[Page 243]
David Eisenstein

R. David Eisenstein

David Eisenstein, a son of R. Hershel and Reichel, was a close relative of R. Avraham Eisenstein and was born in 1849 in Drohitchin. After he married Chaya Gittel Warshavsky, he went into business. Unfortunately, he didn't make enough to support his family of six children.

Incidentally, a gentile landowner happened to come to buy something in the store of the aged Chatskel Valevelsky. When he left the store and got back into his carriage, he dropped a purse and went on his way. The Jews who were standing there and who knew about David's situation called him to get the purse. David ran home and counted out 85 rubles. The landowner was truly an emissary from heaven. The next morning the landowner returned to town to look for his lost purse. When the Jews told him that a poor Jew who wanted to travel to the United States had found his purse, the landowner responded that David should use the money in good health, and David in fact used the money for his departure.

David went to the United States and returned four times. His wife and all his children were already in Chicago, but he missed home, his House of Study and Jewish life in Drohitchin. After the death of his wife in 1932, R. David went back to Drohitchin for the fourth time with the intention of selling his house in Drohitchin and traveling to Palestine. However, he remained in Drohitchin. One Friday night after making the Kiddush David passed away at the age of 88. This happened on December 9. 1938.

Chaya Gittel Eisenstein, wife of David Eisenstein, was born in 1852 in Drohitchin. According to tradition, her father, R. Yisrael Baruch Warshavsky, was a grandson of the famous kabbalist, Rabbi Dovidel Yaffe. A modest woman, Chaya Gittel was very devoted to raising her children in the Jewish spirit.

In 1920, Chaya Gittel came to Chicago to be with her husband and children. Her daughter, Reichel, and her own children to her husband, Yitzchak Eisenstein, who lived here, accompanied her. Chaya Gittel, who enjoyed the great respect of her children and fellow-emigres, died at the age of 77 on July 22, 1930.

The Eisensteins had six children: Eliyahu (who died in Chicago), Lipman, Yisrael Baruch, Leizer, Avraham, and Reichel Eisenstein all live in Chicago.

Chaya Gittel Eisenstein

Daughter, mother and grandchild, Yitzchak

Toiba Kaplan-Kohn

Died at approximately 40 years,
on April 23,1919
(See p. 93)

Gittel Warshavsky

Died at approximately 80 years,
on January 30, 1916.
(See p. 88)

Yeshayahu, Son of Yisrael Baruch Warshavsky

Husband of Gittel, he died on 19 Tevet 1905 (This is an error and probably corresponds to the Hebrew year 5665 which fell on December 27 1904). See pp. 117, 193 and 247, Toiba's husband, Yeshayahu-Yossel, and children, Yitzchak and Eliyahu Kohn, Rachel Ehrman, and families are in New York.

Freidel Eisenstein

Freidel Eisenstein, a daughter of Chaim-Leib and Esther Kravetz, was born in Pruzhany in 1884 and received a nationalist-religious education. On August 10, 1907, she married Yisrael Baruch Eisenstein. Freidel was beautiful, intelligent, knew Hebrew and Russian, and helped Yisrael Baruch teach his class.

In December of 1912, Yisrael Baruch went off to the United States, and Freidel looked forward to the day when she could be reunited with her husband. Unfortunately, her hopes were not be realized as she was caught in World War I (1914). She lived under difficult circumstances, and by the time help was on its way, Freidel became ill with typhus and died in the flower of her youth, at the age of 34 on May 28, 1919, leaving behind two small children (Chaim and Leizer). Following her death, Yisrael Baruch moved to the United States with the children.

[Page 244]

Friedel Eisenstein

Freidel's father, Chaim Leib, a son of R. Yitzchak Kravetz of Drohitchin, had died in 1893. Her mother, Esther, a daughter of R. Eliezer Shmuel Yablonsky of Pruzhany, remarried. Her new husband was R. Feivel Greenberg of Narevki (near Grodno), who had a daughter, Rosa. The distinguished Rabbi Yisrael Rosenberg (long-time president of the Rabbinical Association in the United States) was a son-in-law of R. Feivel. After the death of R. Feivel, Rabbi Rosenberg supported Esther.

Freidel's mother, Esther, died on 23 Adar II, 1939 (This is an error because 1939 was not a leap year with two Adar months). Rosa and her husband and child perished. May G-d avenge their blood! Chaya-Lieba, wife of Yisrael-Baruch Warshavsky, and Freidel's only sister, lives today with her family in New York.

Chaim Leib Eisenstein

Chaim Leib, the eldest son of Yisrael Baruch and Freidel Eisenstein, was born in January 1910 in Drohitchin. At the age of nine, his mother passed away. In 1920, he arrived in Chicago and studied at the Beit Midrash Le-Torah and also studied journalism and wrote a book. Chaim was very talented and a devoted student. At the time he was serving in the United States army, he was about to obtain rabbinical ordination. However, he suffered a grave illness in the army and has not regained his health. We hope that G-d has mercy on him.

Eliezer Shmuel Eisenstein

Eliezer Shmuel Eisenstein, the second son of Yisrael Baruch and Freidel Eisenstein, was born on June 12, 1912 in Drohitchin. His mother passed away in 1920 when he was seven. He studied at the Beit Midrash Le-Torah from 1923 to 1930 and completed Marshall High School (1930) and Crane College (1932). He was drafted into the US army in October 1942 (until November 1945) and served with his regiment in Hawaii and Australia. In April 1944, he was in the 24th infantry division and participated in the assault on Dutch New Guinea. He was an insurance broker and was married to Gail. His children are Randy and Noreen.

[Page 245]
Peretz Goldman (Ben-Zahav)
May G-D avenge his blood!

Peretz and Zahava Goldman and children

Since childhood, the young Peretz Goldman had a strong interest in the Land of Israel. When he was 12 years old he assembled a group of Drohitchin children to tell them about the wonders of the Land. I was one of those children, and I remember how we went to the well-known teacher, Betsalel Wolfson (of Drohitchin), who Peretz asked to tell us more about Palestine and what we young people should do to help build the country.

We then heard our first lecture from Wolfson about Zionism and the ideas of Jabotinsky. Wolfson believed very strongly in the great Jewish leader, Vladimir Jabotinsky, whose teachings were about a Jewish Palestine on both sides of the Jordan River.

Shortly thereafter in 1927, Peretz organized the Betar (acronym for Brit Yosef Trumpeldor) organization in Drohitchin, and he was the cultural leader for eight years until he left for Palestine. Peretz was totally devoted to the work of Betar and Zionism. Day and night he organized Drohitchin boys and girls with whom he worked and whom he taught, inculcating them in the spirit of the Jewish State. Peretz prepared Drohitchin youth for Palestine, and he attended training camp himself to prepare for emigration to Palestine.

He arrived in Palestine in 1935, and his dream was partially realized. When I met Peretz in Haifa after his arrival in Palestine, he beamed with joy for being able to arrive in the Jewish homeland. "This only the beginning of our work to establish a Jewish State," he said. Peretz threw himself into his work and was a model of the idea of the "conquest of Hebrew labor."

Peretz began as a mailman in the Haifa post office, where only some of the workers were Jews. He worked to bring in as many Jews as possible to work there. Later he went to work in a village settlement, though Peretz was not up to performing physical labor in the settlements.

Some time later, Peretz was a worker in the Haifa port, where he was sent as a Hebrew laborer; still later became a fisherman. He and a dozen other boys were the pioneers who started to develop the fishing industry in Palestine. He was so happy to show me a fishing vessel anchored in the port of Haifa.

Peretz also worked in the rail line factory in Haifa until he became a mechanic in the Haifa refinery. He and a dozen other Jews worked there among hundreds of Arabs, while studying at night to obtain a degree from London as a locomotive engineer.

In his letter of November 1947, Peretz wrote about his friend who was in the process of settling in the Jewish homeland and building a home and community on Haifa Bay for his family.

[Letter:]

Embassy of Israel

Ref. 15/5/EB
March 29, 1950

To: Mr. H. Livak

RE: Date your friend was killed

Pursuant to our letter No. 5/5/EB of 2/17/50, your friend Peretz son of Yoel
(Goldman) Ben-Zahav was born in 1914 and was killed in an Arab attack at the Haifa
refinery on 12/30/47. He was buried in Haifa on 12/31/47. His wife's name is
Zahava, and her address is: 12 Hashalom St., Haifa.
I share your grief.
[illegible signature] E. Avidor Lt. Col. Army, Navy and Air Force
A letter from the Israeli embassy to Levak regarding the death of Peretz.

Peretz was one of the unknown soldiers who fought in the ranks of the Irgun under Menachem Begin to attain a Jewish State. Unfortunately, Peretz didn't live to see the establishment of the Jewish state. He wrote me that the Arab workers at the refinery were bragging that they would soon slaughter all the Jews but would spare Peretz because he was a "good Jew." The Arabs kept their word. On December 30, 1947, as soon as they got the order, the Arabs attacked the two-dozen Jewish workers with knives and slaughtered all of them, including Peretz, who died from an Arab knife, perhaps belonging to the same person who said he would spare Peretz.

[*Page 246*]

May 3, 1950, Los Angeles, California – Zvi Levack

Standing from right: Peretz Goldman, Menachem Steinberg, Shalom Warshavsky, Meir Motya Hausman, Yosek Siderov, Mordechai Gottlieb, and Yisrael Schmid. Seated, from right: Moshe Goldberg, Yosef Rubinstein, Zvi Levack – Instructor, Avraham Mishovsky, Kachler and Avraham Lev. Bottom, from right: Berl Vichnes, Berl Gottlieb. The Betar Group, 1933. Ten of them perished.

Yaakov Zvi Warshavsky

R. Yaakov Zvi

Yaakov Zvi Warshavsky, a son of R. Mordechai and Tsippa, was born in approximately 1864. On his father's side, he was descended from Rabbi David Yaffe. R. Yaakov Hersh was totally committed to Judaism and tradition and was involved in community affairs. He was a follower of the old rabbi, R. Menachem, and later Rabbi Kalenkovich. R. Yaakov Hirsh was impulsive and a bold activist. He would have eventually become a mayor. However, he passed away in the flower of his youth at the age of 39 following a brief illness, leaving behind his wife Malka and seven children.

The yahrzeits of Yaakov Zvi's parents: R. Mordechai, 10 Adar, and Tsippa, 4 Iyar.

[Page 247]
David, Feigel, Fruma-Gittel Warshavsky

From the right: David Warshavsky and wife Feigel. In the middle, from top, are Dov, Yeshayahu, and Fruma-Gittel.

My heart aches as I write these lines, which serve as a gravestone for my parents and young sister – a gravestone inscription on which so many tears and weeping are engraved.

My father, R. David, was born in approximately 1879 in Drohitchin to his parents, R. Yeshayahu and Gittel. On his father's side he was descended in a direct line from the renowned scholar and kabbalist, Rabbi Dovidel Yaffe. My mother, Feigel, was born in approximately 1888 in Motele (Pinsk) to her parents, R. Zelig and Fruma Antopolsky, who were descendants of a large Orthodox family in Motele, Yanova and Antopolia. My only sister, Fruma-Gittel, was born on January 15, 1924 in Drohitchin. When the German murderers killed her and our parents, she was only 17 years old, May G-d avenge her blood!

My father (May G-d avenge his blood!) had a strong character and yet was sensitive and G-d-fearing. You could say that he was able to observe and fulfill as many as is possible for a person to fulfill of the Torah's commandments. In order to keep the commandments, he faced many challenges. Fate ruled that my father serve in the Russian army for five years, and yet he never ate non-kosher meat. His sergeant beat him for not eating the food. However, he never gave in. For a time, he ate only water and bread and wouldn't touch non-kosher food until, with G-d's help, he was able to go into town (Berdichev) to find kosher food. When he would stand guard at night, he would recite psalms.

Many years ago, my father had lived for three years in Chicago. He struggled and didn't violate the Sabbath. He could have made a good living in the United States but instead returned home because he felt that it was impossible to raise children according to Judaism in the United States.

Father distributed most of his money for education. He hired the best and finest private tutors and Talmud instructors for my brother and me. Later, when we went off

[Page 248]

to study in yeshivas, he supported us as much as he could. Mother would go out in the worst blizzards in order to find opportunities to ship us food and other products by train.

My father never went to a workplace where he couldn't first pray with a quorum in a synagogue. The workers would lie down on the wagons and wait for him to return from synagogue. My father was an honest and dependable worker. In his work in construction (mostly at the estates of landowners), Father would work overtime, fearing misleading someone. Many a Friday Father would pay his workers, leaving him with very little for himself. He was always concerned about another person's money and was a very modest person.

On the Sabbath, Father never went anywhere besides to and from synagogue. He would spend the whole day with a book at home or study together with a group in synagogue. He was among the first to arrive at synagogue and among the last to leave. If there were ever a poor person who had nowhere to eat, father would invite him home for the Sabbath.

As far as I remember, Father used to fast every eve of a new month, and on Rosh Hashanah and Yom Kippur he remained standing throughout the services. He was also careful about gossiping, and was gentle. Almost every Sabbath, father had a guest at the table. In addition to the fact that the synagogue custodian would regularly send us someone carrying a note of introduction, father would also bring some other unexpected guest. Mother was happy to share whatever was left with guests.

My mother also always read the Yiddish translation of the Torah. She studied the Yiddish anthology, *Tseina Ureina,* and read prayers to women at home or in the synagogue. She was very observant.

Right after World War I, father wanted to sell our home and land and move to Palestine. However, he was over 35 years old and couldn't obtain a certificate from the Jewish Agency. In 1941, when the Russians sent a few Drohitchin families off to Russia, the Russians made an error and took father, mother and my sister (The Russians were looking for another David Warshavsky who was no longer alive). I was told that my mother cried uncontrollably, and Rabbi Kalenkovitch and some community leaders went to the Russian commissar on the Sabbath to appeal for their release.

As mentioned earlier, the German murderers took my parents and sister (as well as hundreds of other Jews) to Brona-Gora, near Kartuz-Bereza, to the limestone mines and killed them in awful ways. May G-d avenge their blood! The curse was decreed on July 25, 1942, but the actual killings occurred on Sunday, July 26, 1942. See pp. 117, 137, 305 and 307.

Finally, it should be mentioned that my only brother, Yeshayahu Warshavsky, who tried to get an emigration certificate for three years, finally arrived in Palestine in 1938.

(Abridged from Rabbi Dov B. Warshavsky's *Scroll of Ecclesiastes of the Third Destruction,* Chicago, 1952.)

(Free translation of verses from Ecclesiastes 1 and 2)

Arise in the night, at Midnight, pour out your heart before G-d. Turn your hands to Him in supplication for the souls of those who harmed you. Young and Old, young men and virgins lie on the ground, killed by the sword. Ecclesiastes 2

For these I weep. Tears flow from my eyes because my consolation is far from me to restore my soul. May all their evil come before You, because whoever harms him, harms You. Many are my groans, and my heart aches. Ecclesiastes 1

[p. 249 blank]

[Page 250]

PART V
INSTITUTIONS AND PARTIES

[Page 251]

RELIGIOUS AND CULTURAL INSTITUTIONS

The Burial Society - Chevra Kaddisha

The Chevra Kaddisha was apparently the first community institution in town. It was apparently as old as the Drohitchin Jewish community itself. It was also the last community institution. Even in the ghetto, the Chevra Kaddisha was the only entity to function officially until the Holocaust.

Like in many other communities, the Drohitchin Chevra Kaddisha/Burial Society had maintained a record book for hundreds of years. This book contained the events, rules and regulations of the community and could have served as a treasure house and fountain of historical material about the life of the Drohitchin community. Unfortunately, the book was lost, and we have no other source of information that was known elsewhere.

The customs and roles of the burial society in Drohitchin were more or less (according to law) the same as in many other towns. In those communities that didn't have an organized Jewish community, the Chevra Kaddisha was the independent and autonomous institution that functioned under its own responsibility and control.

The Talmud in Tractate *Moed Katan*, p. 27, describes the task of the Jewish burial society: "Rav Yehuda said in the name of Rav: In a town where a deceased is found, no one (even total strangers) may not perform any type of labor. Rav Hamnuna once came to a town where someone had just died. He noticed that the people in town were going about their business as usual, and because of this disgrace of the deceased, Rav Hamnuna wanted to excommunicate all the people in town. He was told that there was a special organization in town that cared for the dead. If so, said Rav Hamnuna, you may continue working." This is the provision of Jewish law: If there is no burial society, no one may work from the moment of death until the burial is completed.

For this reason, because the burial society members are involved with caring for the dead, a person may continue his activities. Caring for the dead is one of the greatest mitzvahs there is. It is a real true good deed and charity and is greater than the mitzvah of monetary charity (see tractate *Sukkah*, p. 49). This is why the society is called in Aramaic the Holy Association (Chevra Kaddisha). Therefore, I want to agree with the following statement: "The Association should be called Holy Association because they render themselves ritually impure by contact with the dead they are called by the opposite connotation, i.e. Holy."

According to the old practice in the towns in the old country, the burial society members never received monetary compensation for their work and undertook their sacred task on behalf of an entire community of Jews, who no longer are considered to have committed the sin of ignoring a deceased.

The task of the burial society was first of all to make sure the community had a cemetery surrounded by a fence. During the dedication of the cemetery or fence, the burial society members had to provide the deceased with what he deserved, namely water purification (which was performed, of course, in the house of the deceased), cover him with the burial sheets (including a tallith/prayer shawl according to Jewish law), and bury him. The deceased was transported to the cemetery in a wagon or a casket harnessed to a horse that the society borrowed from a wagon driver. I still remember how the children used to say that the horse that took the casket and the deceased suffered great pain because the demonic forces would be beating the horse mercilessly. This is why the horse was in front of the bridle.

The charity tin box was especially popular, and the synagogue custodian would bang the tin, announcing that charity keeps death away.

A deceased Talmudic scholar would be transported on a board the entire distance to the cemetery. The pallbearers would switch off during the procession. This would also take place for a funeral of anyone that occurred on the second day of Yom Tov. There was also a custom not to let the widow or her daughters accompany the deceased to the funeral.

No one was ever buried in a casket in Drohitchin. The gravediggers would place wooden boards in the grave by placing the deceased at the bottom of the grave and cover him up with the boards (as Jewish law provides for). There was also the custom of putting a small bag of earth from the Holy Land under the head of the deceased and to sprinkle it over his face. In addition, pieces of pottery would be placed over the eyes and mouth.

[Page 252]

A few elderly women were also members of the burial society, and they would handle the preparations and purification for deceased women. The burial society covered the expenses of maintaining the cemetery, holding funerals and other activities by selling plots. People would pay according to their financial ability.

R. Yisrael Baruch Warshavsky recounted that 50 years ago, there was a "rebellion" of the common people against the burial society. The "rebels" started their own small society that went to battle against the wealthy and those of illustrious pedigree who ran the burial society and who tore up the belts of the poor. The leaders of the small society were Chatzkel Pines, Hersh-

Leib the "Fence Builder" and others. The opposition referred to the
"insurrectionists" of the small society as the "linen pants." Nevertheless, the
rebellion worked, and the aristocrats of the burial society had to begin
considering the needs of the poor population.

According to Yeshayahu Warshavsky my brother, who heard from Chaikel
Milner and other elderly people in Palestine, the custodian of the burial society
was, as far as they could remember, R. Yitzchak Yoel's Simenovsky (see p.
110). After Yitzchak Yoel's, R. Moshe Leizer Gratch served as custodian, and
the following individuals worked together with him in the burial society:
Hershel Chaim Levine, Zechariah Schmid, Mordechai Ber Kreines (Kozack),
Avraham Yitzchak Boreisha, Chaim Goralsky, Mendel Eisenstein, Alter Itches
Burstein, Berl Friedenberg, Shmuel Hershka Snitovsky, Moshe Haneles,
Hershel Popinsky, Litman Eisenstein, Binyamin Toriansky, Aharon Begun,
and others.

**This photograph was taken at the funeral of Bobba Grossman on July 28, 1935. In the
front is the casket with the deceased. See pp. 53, 54, 222 and 223. From right: Fishel
Rimland, Alter Goralsky, Moshe Kravetz, Leibel Gurstein, Moshe Kravetz, Eliyahu
Shlackman, Berl Gottlieb, Yaakov Wermus, Yirmiyahu Grossman, Sarah Pisetsky, Chaim-
Leib and Zelig Grossman, Devorah Shlackman, Chaya-Beila Shushanov, Gedaliah
Grossman, Hershel Eisenstein, and others.**

After Moshe Leizers moved to Palestine in 1923, R. Zechariah Schmid was
chosen as the custodian of the burial society. Schmid's colleagues were: Zusha
Warshavsky, Chaikel Milner, Chaim Eliyahu Leibkes Valevelsky, Shmuel
Kolodner, Lipman Feldman, Aharon Gelstein, Aharon Begun and others. In
the final year, R. Moshe Prager the ritual slaughterer, also participated.
Shachna Ukrainetz and Yitzchak Berezovsky handled burials of the deceased.
Alter, the builder from Liebesha, was the gravedigger in the final years.

The annual dinner (following the fast) of the burial society took place on the 15th of Kislev at the home of R. Moshe Gratch, and later in the home of R. Zusha Warshavsky. R. Moshe Leizers was also responsible for the record book of the burial society. Thereafter, R. Zusha maintained it until 1941, when he and his family were exiled to Russia. The record book then was lost. The burial society functioned in the ghetto under the direction of R. Moshe Aharon Berg until the final Holocaust of Drohitchin. That was the end of it.

See pp. 22, 41, 53 and 54.   Dov B. Warshavsky

[Page 253]
The Talmud Torah School
(Letter is in Hebrew; note at very end of page is in Yiddish)

Eve of the Sabbath of the Torah Portion *Emor,* Drohitchin 1923 To the friend of G-d and my friend, the renowned Speaker and Preacher, Rabbi Yehuda David Goldman, Rabbi of the House of Study Beit Avraham in Chicago.

Greetings to you. Yesterday I received your letter dated the 13th of Adar. Thank you very much for not forgetting about me and the people of our city. Let me deal with each issue separately.

Although I do not know about the situation in the United States, I can tell you that the situation in our town is so bad I cannot even begin to describe it for you. Everyone is talking about the trip to Palestine. We don't hear about anything. Business is doing very poorly, and the situation in the large cities is even worse because all the businessmen have gone bankrupt, and even if aid from the United States were received, the situation wouldn't be any better than they were in the past, as you know.

You can understand and realize from what I have just described that R. Yosef David Schub was the head of the Talmud Torah building and school but has resigned. Bezdesky, the son-in-law of R. Simcha Lasintzer, has replaced him. You also knew who the committee members were. I realized that it was useless to fight with them because I had no help from people in town to make sure that the Talmud Torah provided both Torah and secular studies. Therefore I gave up. Gradually the Torah study was forgotten, i.e. Talmud with Rashi's commentary on the Torah. Only Gavriel Kamenetsky was teaching Talmud and Rashi. Then the businessmen were worried about the school's situation, and started to ask that we finish the building.

Then R. David Warshavsky decided to finish the school building. I only paid the amount of money according to the certificates that he sent me (from the money that I have from R. Eliyahu Eisenstein). Now we have a building, but we don't Talmud teachers, so what should we do? In the meantime, I received a total of 20 dollars for the school from R. Eliezer Adler who was a religious teacher in Drohitchin and who is now in the United States. I hired R.

Moshe Aharon from Khomsk for 150 dollars for the term. I got another 35 dollars from the charity plate on the eve of Yom Kippur, and the situation of the Talmud Torah improved. I am also able to fund two teachers from the money sent by Yehuda Milner.

There are now three Talmud classes at the school: a) one taught by Gavriel; b) one taught by R. Moshe Aharon of Khomsk, and c) one taught by R. Moshe Aharon. There is another group of five students who are studying Talmud with the *Tosafot* commentary: Eliyahu Ze'ev, of the widow Berezovsky, a son of R. Abba Laufer of Horbacha, a son of R. David son of Mordechai, and a son of R. Moshe Aharon. It took great effort for me to arrange all of this because of situation is extremely difficult. We still need money for two hours of independent Talmud study by the boys in the House of Study, but I have no way of doing it. It's hard to again request aid from the United States. My dear friend, R. Yisrael Baruch, writes that his brother, R. Eliyahu, will send us money, but this is only for the younger boys who study at the Talmud Torah.

Stamp of Rabbi Isaac Yaakov Hakohen Kalenkovitch, Rabbi of Drohitchin.

Recently Moshe Bezdzhesky resigned from his post as principal of the Talmud Torah, and through my efforts R. Shmuel Valevelsky replaced him and follows my advice. I also received 100 dollars from the United States. These two things gave me the strength to become responsible for the school. I used the 100 dollars from R. Eliyahu to pay the teachers.

There are more than 50 children of poor parents who do not have the wherewithal to pay tuition of $1.50 per child per month. The administration and members of the committee come to me on behalf of these poor souls to ask that they be admitted at no charge. I feel terrible about this. What should I do? There's no money left. Therefore, please approach our friends, R. Yisrael Baruch and R. Eliyahu Eisenstein about this. Please show them this letter, and also show it to R. Yitzchak Avigdor and R. Eliezer Adler so that they know what our situation is like here. I am not feeling well and must stop now.

Regards to everyone, and I end with blessings of the kohanim/priests. Isaac Yaakov Kalenkovitch

Note: Rabbi Isaac Yaakov Kalenkovitch writes in his letter to Rabbi Yehuda David Goldman (1923) regarding the Talmud Torah School in Drohitchin and his financial difficulties and ideological quarrels that he had.

Originally the Talmud Torah school building that had been built with the money that R. Eliyahu Eisenstein brought from the United States was a religious school. Later the secular Tarbut organization of Drohitchin took over the building and set up a modernized Moriah School instead.

The rabbi and his backers then open a separate Talmud Torah School with funds from R. Yitzchak Avigdor Telekhansky named the Torah Vedaat [Torah and Wisdom] Talmud Torah, which continued to exist until the War. See pp. 43, 44, 45, 182, 183, 184 and 220 (Editor)

[Page 254]

The New House Of Study
(Letter is in Hebrew; note at very end of page is in Yiddish)

Sunday of the Torah Portion *Mishpatim,* Drohitchin, 1925

Blessings and Greetings to my friend, the esteemed and praiseworthy Rabbi Yehuda David Goldman, rabbi of the Beit Avraham Synagogue in Chicago, and to the President who provides us with assistance, our dear friend who is totally devoted to public service for the benefit of his hometown, Yisrael Baruch Eisenstein. May G-d grant you both long lives in comfort and goodness together with your families until the arrival of the Messiah speedily in our days.

Greetings to you. With love, we the undersigned have the honor to hereby inform you that yesterday we received your letter together with the draft in the amount of 500 dollars that was sent from our fellow residents of Drohitchin who are in the United States with your assistance for the benefit of the new House of Study named after Rabbi Cohen, Mr. Zalman Kaplan and Mr. Aharon Dragitsinsky. On Saturday night, we found it necessary to call a meeting of all the congregants of the new House of Study together with the aforementioned individuals. After we heard a detailed report from the building committee about the building's history from the beginning through to today. The report was accepted by all those in attendance, who expressed satisfaction about the report. Those in attendance thanked the building committee, R. Zvi Eisenstein, R. Yozep Bezdesky, and R. Moshe Aharon Berg for their extraordinary devotion. Despite the lack of funds that is always a problem, they were able to complete construction up to the roof. Everyone remarked about the craftsmanship, and requested that the committee continue with their fruitful work until completion.

Among the decisions taken at that meeting regarding the beginning of the construction work, which had been interrupted during the winter, those in attendance stated unanimously to express their heartfelt thanks and appreciation to all of the residents of Drohitchin in Chicago who participated in the appeal on behalf of the House of Study. From what we heard, they did it themselves, and their names shall always be praised on our lips, i.e. R. Simcha Miller, R. Aharon Leib Motevetsky, R. Avraham Eisenstein and R. Yudel Tikotshinsky. The renowned community leader, the great woman Mrs. Malka Warshavsky, is also hereby thanked and acknowledged for her participation in the appeal. We also express thanks to Rabbi Goldman and R. Yisrael Baruch Eisenstein, who publicized and encouraged support for the building. Even though there is doubt that the amount will suffice to complete the building, and even though we already owe more than 200 dollars, nevertheless we believe that thanks to results of the appeal, we are that much closer to filling in the gaps with additional funds despite the economic crisis that exists in our country and especially in our town.

Rabbi Cohen of Drohitchin

Our dear brothers, we consider ourselves bound and tied to you for years, and will always remain so. We just need to encourage pure hearts to help us in our time of trouble. May G-d repay you for your efforts, and may you be blessed with the three-fold blessing of the Torah for everything good, and may you be able to go to Zion and attend the services at the Temple in Jerusalem to eat from the sacrifices.

My unending thanks to you, with great appreciation.

Signed: Noach, son of Rabbi Y.A., Zalman Kaplan, Shimshon Goldman, Chaim, son of M. Aryeh Valevelsky, Yozep Bezdzhesky, Moshe Aharon Berg, Aharon Shmuel Goldman – Drohitchin.

Note: Rabbi Noach Kohn and others in the letter to Rabbi Goldman and R. Y. B. Eisenstein speak about the new House of Study, which the former residents of Drohitchin living in the United States helped to build. See p. 41 (Editor)

**Yozep and Pessel Bezdzhesky and children (from right:) Reizel, Benzion and Nechama –
all perished. May G-d avenge their blood! Yozep was the treasurer in the House of Study.**

[*Page 255*]

People's Library

In approximately 1910, a Hebrew-Russian library was opened in
Drohitchin. The initiator of the library were the brothers Avraham and Yosef
Gratch, Zeidel Weissman, Sender Gratch, Menachem Averbuch, Yudel
Silberstein, Shmuel Epstein, Reuven Lev, Ezra Weissman, and others. Prior to
this, young people had access to reading material from the teacher Naftali
Steinberg for a small fee.

At the same time, another group of young people opened a Yiddish library.
Among the founders were Yehoshua Schmid, Rasha-Leah Lev-Schmid, Noach
Leifer, Berl Lopatin, Yitzchak Baum, Eliyahu Garber (Peshas), Shmuel Leifer,
Yudel Miller, and Gedaliah Kaplan.

Later the two libraries merged, and the Enlightenment Dissemination
Society was very helpful in developing the library by sending money and
books. Shalom Gratch and Moshe Kalenkovitch also belonged to the library.
The number of books increased daily. The library had three sections: a Yiddish

one, a Hebrew one and a Russian one. Gedaliah Kaplan ran the Yiddish
section. The Hebrew one by Yehoshua Schmid, and the Russian one by Rasha
Leah Lev-Schmid.

A. B. Drohitchin, Grodno Gubernia.

**A group of the founders of the Workers' Library: From right: Gedaliah Kaplan, Berl
Lopatin, Noach Leifer (murdered by the Balakhov gangs in Zakazalia in 1921), and Yudel
Miller. Yiztchak Baum and Eliyahu Poliak are missing from the photo. Above is the stamp
of the Workers' Library. The photo was taken in 1910.**

From the outset, the library was located in the house of Berl Kozack and was later transferred to the brick house of Chaim and Lieba Rimland. When World War I broke out in 1914, the library – which contained 1,500 Yiddish, Hebrew and Russian books as well as magazines bound in volumes – was located at the home of Alter Goldberg.

Due to the war, the library was abandoned and left without an administration or permanent location. After a meeting of a few culture activists, Hersh Leib Eisenstein took the initiative to run the library. At the end of 1915, he transferred the library to his own home, and during the entire period that it was there, Hersh Leib was the director and librarian. However, in May 1920, he moved to the United States.

All cultural and community activities of the youth focused on the library. The young people organized meetings, discussions, literary evenings, and amateur theatrical productions. During the war years, the library room at Eisenstein's home was used for meetings and conferences of various groups and societies such as the Visitors' Welcome Committee, Hebrew-Speakers Association, and Young Zion (this organization had S. Shiffman as chairman and H. L. Eisenstein as secretary). The celebration about the Balfour Declaration was also planned in the library room, as was the fundraising appeal of the Jewish National Fund and others.

[Page 256]

After Eisenstein left for the United States, Sheinka Feldman transferred the library to her home (Meir Feldman's house). Later the library was transferred to the home of Leah-Beila Mishovsky.

In 1925 the library administrative committee took over the entire second floor of Lieba Rimland's brick house, where there was not only the library, but also a reading room, and for the first time – a radio. Still later, the library was transferred to the home of of Chaytshe Epstein (her parents were Chaim Moshe Leizers and Sarah). Its last home was the Moriah school building.

Among the activists of the library were Hersh Leib Eisenstein, Sheinka Feldman, Yudel David Goldman, Feigel Epstein, Yitzchak Shuchman, Bluma Warshavsky-Gutov, Rivka Rosenszweig-Sertshuk, Esther Mishovsky, David Epstein, Chaytsha Epstein and others (see photo on p. 73). They were joined later by Reizel Milner, Risha Epstein-Feldman, Kobrinsky, and others. In 1931 the administration committee of the People's Library was made up of Menachem Kalenkovitch, Yaakov Mishovsky, Leiba Lievack, Beila Milner, Kalman Oberman, Sarah Slonimsky, Shmuel Milner, Mary Schwartzberg-Kalenkovitch, Shalom Beich, Leah Mazursky and others. New culture activists joined and the library functioned until the Holocaust.

For more information, see p. 49 and the photo there. Sources: Gedaliah Kaplan, Shalom Gratch, Hersh-Leib Eisenstein, Yosef Feldman and D. B. W.

Standing from right: Yudl David Goldman, Feigl Epshtein, Rivkah Rozenstvaig-Sertshuk, Itshe Pisetsky, Esther Mishovsky, Blume Varshavsky and her husband Mordechai Gutov.

Sitting from right: Baruch Katsman, Sheinke Feldman, Yitschak Shulman, Menuchah Rabinovitsh, Menachem Averbuch, and Sarah Kreines.

[*Page 257*]

People's House

פאָלקס־הויז – בית־עם

פאראייניקטער בוי־קאמיטעט
„בית-עם"
אין דראהיטשין פאל.

דראהיטשין פאל., דאטע פון פאסט־שטעמפל.

זייער חשובער פריינט

ווערטע האבן מיר דעם כבוד זיך ווענדן צו אייך, ווי צו א חשובן פריינט—לאנדסמאן, געבוירענער אין דראהיטשין וועגן דער א וויכטיקן ענין, וועלכער האט ארויסגערופן א ווארימע סימפאטיע און אפקלאנג ביי אלע קרייזן פון דער אָרטיקער באפעלקערונג.

דער ענין איז פאלגנדער:

אייך איז זיכער און גענוי באקאנט די אלגעמיינע לאגע פון די יידן אין אייראפא.

דער פאליטישער און ווירטשאפטליכער אנטיסעמיטיזם צעבערעכט טויזנטער עקזיסטענצן און ווארפט דער יוגנט־אן א פערספעקטיוו אין די ארעמס פון יאוש, אפאטיע און פארצווייפלונג.

דאריבער פאדערט זיך א אלוייטיקע, ברייט־פארצווייגטע קולטורעלע אויפקלערונגס־ארבעט דורך דער אינטעליגענץ און פראגרעסיווע כוחות.

כדי צו אונטערהאלטן דעם נאציאנאלן גייסט פון דער אונטערוואקסנדער יוגנט און שטארקן דאס געפיל פון זעלבסטווירדע און שטאלץ אלס מענטשן און יידן. דערפאר איז מיט באגייסטערונג געפאלן דער באשלוס פון אלע פראגרעסיווע, דעמאקראטישע פארטייען און יוגנט־ארג. צו אנגאזשירן זיך מיט אלע כוחות אין דער קאלאסאלער אונטערנעמונג צו בויען

א אייגענע פאלקס־הויז „בית־עם"

וווּ די אָרטיקע יידישע באפעלקערונג און יוגנט זאל זיך קענען צוזאמענטרעפן און אויסלעבן זיך גייסטיק, נאציאנאל און קולטורעל.

צו דעם צוועק האבן מיר פראקלאמירט א גרויסע געלט־אקציע.

די פאלקס־הויז קען געשאפן ווערן, ווען מיר וועלן אויפזאמלען בערך 6—7 טויזנט גילדן.

אלע כוחות זענען געווארפן געווארן אין דער גרויסער פאלקס־זאמלונג. כמעט יעדער איינער האט זיך מיט ענטוזיאזם אפגערופן אויף דער וויכטיקער אונטערנעמונג, באשטייערודיק זיך מיט 6—5 ארבעטס טעג, לויט דער מעגלעכקייט און פיל האבן געגעבן איבער דער מעגליכקייט. מיט פרייד קענען מיר גלייכצייטיק מיטטיילן, אז פאר די געזאמעלטע געלטער איז שוין געלונגען צו איינקויפן א שיינעם פלאץ פארן בנין און א טייל פון די בוי־מאטעריאלן.

ליידער, וועלן מיר אבער בשום אופן נישט קענען רעאליזירן אונזער לעבנס־וויכטיקן פלאן מיט אייגענע כוחות.

דעריבער ווענדן מיר זיך צו אייך אלס פריינד, פראגרעסיווער פערזאן, געבוירענער אין דראהיטשין פונקט ווי צו אונזערע פריינט און באקאנטע אין א"י און אין אנדערע לענדער מיט דער ביטע צו מיטהעלפן אונדז אין דער גרויסער אקציע דורך אייער שפענדונג לטובת דעם פאלקס־הויז.

מיר ווינטשן זיך, אז איר זאלט צוגלייך מיט אונדזערע געטרייע און איבערגעגעבענע עסקנים, פרייוויליק מיטהעלפן, מיט געמיינזאמע כוחות צו שאפן אין אונדזער שטעטל א נייטיקן נאציאנאלן ווינקל, וואו ס'זאל געשאפן ווערן א געזונטער גייסט צום נוצן פאר די יידישע פאלקס־איינוואוינער.

האפנדיק, אז איר וועט מיט דער גרעסטער ווארימקייט און פארשטענדעניש זיך אפרופן אויף אונדזער אפעל, וועט איר באוועגן אייערע פריינט, און באקאנטע, אז אייך זיי זאלן זיך אפרופן און באטייליקן אין דער אקציע.

איר קענט צוזאמען מיט אנדערע פריינט ארגאניזירן ספעציעלע פאראנשטאלטונגען, אימפרעזעס, פארוויילונגען, ביי־אוונטן א. א. וו., שאפנדיק דורך דעם א הכנסה־מקור פאר אונדזער אונטערנעמונג.

מיר זענען זיכער, אז איר וועט מאבליזירן אלע קרעפטן אין אייער רשות פאר דער ערפאלגרייכער דורכפירונג פון אונדזער אקציע, אנגעבנדיק זיך פערזענליך אלס ביישפיל פאר אנדערע.

און זייענדיק טיף איבערצייגט אין אייער מיטהילף, וועלכע וועט זיין ביי אונדז אנערקענט און מיט דאנקבארקייט אפגעשאצט, אלס אויסדרוק פון קעגנזייטיקער הילף און חברישער סאלידאריטעט, צייכענען מיר מיט

פיל אכטונג
פאראייניקטער בוי־קאמיטעט
„בית־עם"
אין דראהיטשין פאל.

אדרעס פאר געלד איבערווייזונגען:
Bank Ludowy w Drohiczynie Poleskim
dla „B E T - A M"
Poland.

22טן נאוועמבער, 1937

פאראייניקטער בוי־קאמיטעט
„בית־עם"
אין דראהיטשין — פאל.

זייער חשובע פריינדין,

בלומע וויגוטאוו!

מיר האבן דעם כבוד זיך ווענדן צו אייך, ווי צו א געוועזענער דראהיטשינער געזז. טוערין און ספעציעל ביי ביבליאטעק־ארבעט און אנדערע צווייגן פון קולטורעלער ארבעט אין אונזער שטאט, אז איר זאלט זיך פאראינטערעסירן מיט דעם אויפבוי פון א פאלקס־הויז אין דראהיטשין.

צו דעם צוועק לייגן מיר ביי אייניקע אויסגעפילטע געדרוקטע בריוו, אז איר זאלט זיי פונאנדערטיילן, ווי אויך צוגעבן אדרעסן אין די ליידיקע בלאנקעטן.

רעכנענדיק, אז איר וועט ווי ווייט מעגלעך, זיך פאראינטערעסירן מיט דער פראגע, דאנקען מיר אייך פאר־אויס און זיינען

מיט פיל אכטונג,

אין נאמען פון קאמיטעט:

'י. שוכמאן   פ. עפשטיין

•

פ.ס. ספעציעל שיקן מיר אייך אפ דעם בריוו, ווייל ער ליגט פון א לייענגערער צייט ניט קענענדיק פריער באקומען אייער אדרעס.

מיינע הארציקסטע און בעסטע וואונטשן פאר אייך,

פייגל

•

חשובע חברטע:

איך נוץ אויס די געלעגנהייט אויף א פערזענלעכן גרוס פאר אייך און מרדכין. איך בעט אייך, דערמאנענט זיך אן די אמאליקע יארן פון געזעלשאפטליכער צוזאמענארבעט. קאנענדיק אייך אלס אויפריכטיקע געזעל. טוערין ערלויב איך זיך צו זיין זיכער אין אייער מיטהילף. מיינע בעסטע גרוסן און וואונטשן.

אייער,

'י. שוכמאן

Following is the translation of the previous page.

United People's House Building   Drohitchin, Poland, date
Committee in Drohitichin, Poland   of postal stamp

Dear Esteemed Friends:

We have the great honor to you as a respected friend from Drohitchin regarding an important issue that engendered a warm and sympathetic reaction in all areas of the local population.

The issue is as follows:

You are surely aware of the social situation of the Jews in Europe. Political and economic anti-Semitism have hurt the lives of thousands of Jews and have cast the young people into arms of despair, apathy and desperation.

Therefore, a large-scale CULTURAL project has been undertaken by the intelligensia and progressive forces. In order to support the nationalist spirit of the next generation of young people and to strengthen the feeling of self-esteem and pride as men and Jews, therefore, the decision has been made by all progressive and democratic parties in young people to devote all our energies   to   develop   cultural   activities   through

OUR OWN PEOPLE'S HOUSE

so that the local Jewish community and young people can get together and derive intellectual satisfaction in both nationalist and cultural pursuits.

For this purpose, we are proclaiming a large fundraising campaign.

The People's House can be created if we can collect six to seven thousand gilders.

All our efforts are being devoted to the great People's Assembly. Almost everyone has responded enthusiastically to the important undertaken, and are contributing five to six workdays, depending on their ability. Many have given beyond their means. So we can now share with you that we have almost collected enough money to purchase a beautiful location for the building and some of the construction materials.

Unfortunately, it is impossible for us to be able to finish our life's work on our own. Therefore, we turn to you as a friend, a progressive person born in Drohitchin, just as we have turned to our friends and acquaintances in Palestine and elsewhere, with the request to assist us in this great endeavor by contributing on behalf of the People's House.

We hope you will be able to voluntarily assist us together with our faithful and devoted community leaders, and our joint efforts will be able to create an intellectual and nationalist center in our town that will serve as a healthy presence for Jewish interests.

We hope that you will respond to our appeal with the greatest warmth and understanding and will also encourage your friends and acquaintances to participate in our efforts.

Together with other friends, you will be able to organize special meetings, social events, entertainment, tea evenings, and the like to develop a source of funds for our project.

We are certain that you will mobilize all your energies at your disposal for the successful outcome of our project, serving as an example for others.

We deeply appreciate and value your cooperation. As an expression of our mutual assistance and friendly solidarity, we sign hereunder.

Yours truly,

Address for contributions:	Shlomo Goldman	
Bank Ludowy w Drohiczynie Polskim [most of rest illegible]		United Building
for BET-AM, Poland	P. Schiffman Y. Shuchman	Committee for BEIT-AM in Drohitchin, Poland

November 22, 1937

United Building Committee

BEIT AM

in Drohitchin, Poland

Dear Esteemed Friend Bluma Vigutov:

We have the honor of contacting you as a former Drohitchin activist, especially for the library and other areas of cultural life in our town. We would like to ask you to become involved in the construction of a People's House in Drohitchin.

For this purpose we are including several printed forms for you to distribute and to fill in addresses in the blank areas. Since we believe that you will do whatever you can about this issue, we would like to thank you in advance.

Yours truly and on behalf of the Committee,

Y. Shuchman, P. Epstein

P.S. We are sending the letter to you specifically because we didn't have your address previously. My very best wishes to you,

Feigel

Dear Friend:

I would like to take this opportunity to personally greet you and Mordechai. Please remember the old days of community cooperation. We know you as a sincere community activist, so I can be sure of your cooperation. My best wishes.

Yours,

Y. Shuchman

[*Page 258*]

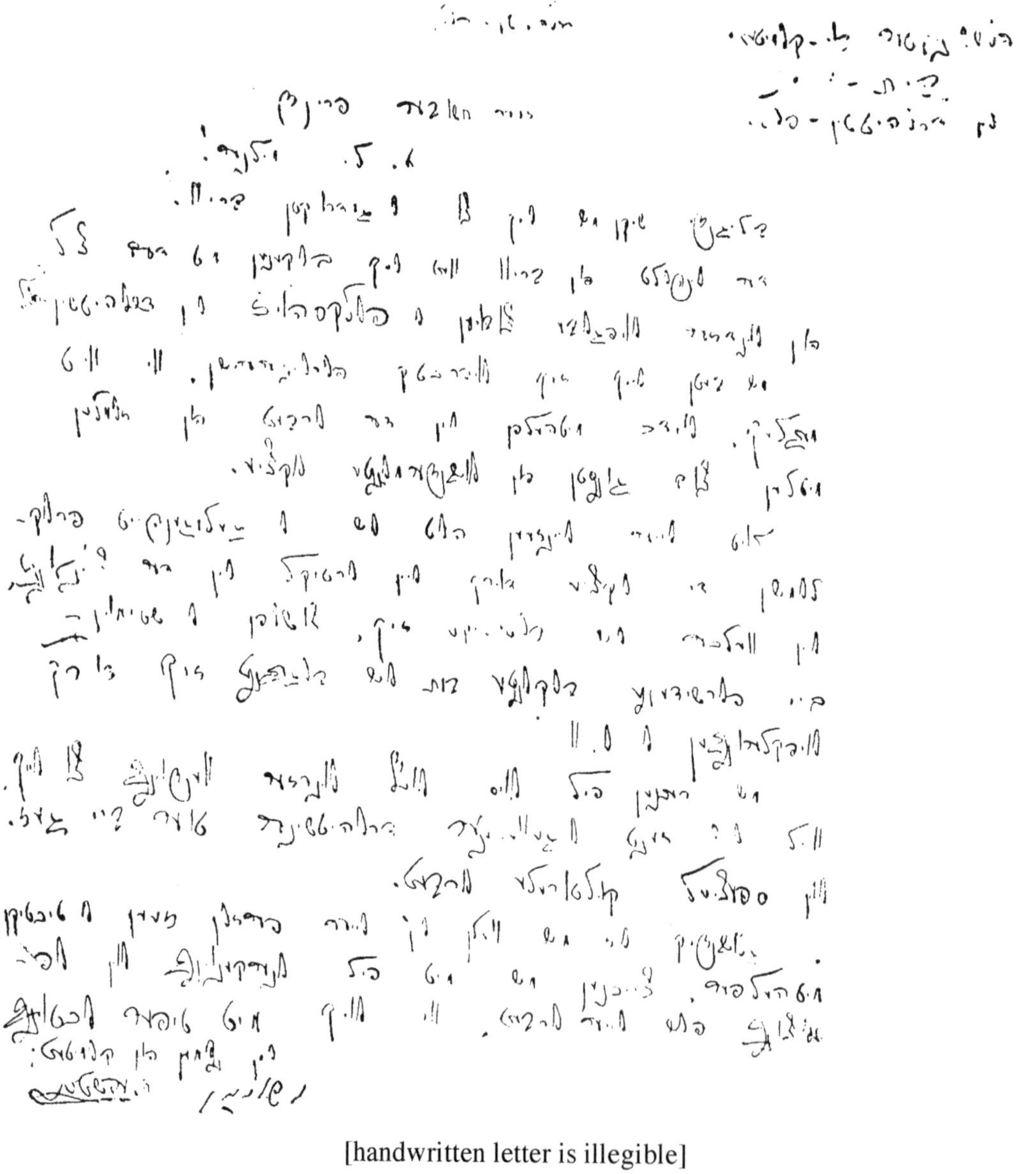

[handwritten letter is illegible]

Standing, from right: Esther Mishovsky, R. Zonschein, Feigel Epstein. Seated: Ze'ev Mishovsky, Beila and Aharon Volveler, and Chaytsha Epstein. Bottom: Y. Shuchman, S. Pisetsky, D. Epstein.

Beit Am – A Spiritual Center for the Youth

April 9, 1938

To all former residents of Drohitchin in Chicago:

We have the honor to contact you regarding an important issue – to assist us in building the People's House-Beit Am in Drohitchin.

In our last letter we sent you a receipt and thank-you for the 50 dollars that you sent us through Gedaliah Grossman.

Most of the Jews in Drohitchin are participating in building Beit-Am. We are employing every effort, both financial and physical. Among ourselves we have been able to collect the required sum to purchase the location, and 20,000 bricks and stones for the foundation. Unfortunately, we believe we won't be able to complete our project ourselves.

We know that in the United States you are now involved in collecting money for Passover for our brethren in Poland, which is a holy endeavor to enable people to prepare Passover. However, we believe that you will also have time and the possibility to contribute money to our project.

Some say that because of the circumstances developing in Poland, when many Jews don't even have a way to put food on the table and are looking to emigrate, this is not the time to build buildings and People's Houses.

However, we believe that this is an incorrect opinion. A community of three and a half million Jews cannot begin emigrating overnight. This entails many difficulties, and we therefore believe that we are tied to this country where we live, and that there is much for us to do and accomplish.

The younger progressive person in our town is in particularly difficult circumstances, and therefore there is a great need for a People's House, a spiritual place, where the cultural education in the spirit of Jewish nationalism can be offered our children so that they will be proud Jews and men.

We are hoping that you will take an active part in our project, and assist us to create a spiritual center in our and your town, Drohitchin.

The United Building Committee- Beit Am in Drohitchin

Signatures of the Building Committee are on the next page.

[*Page 259*]

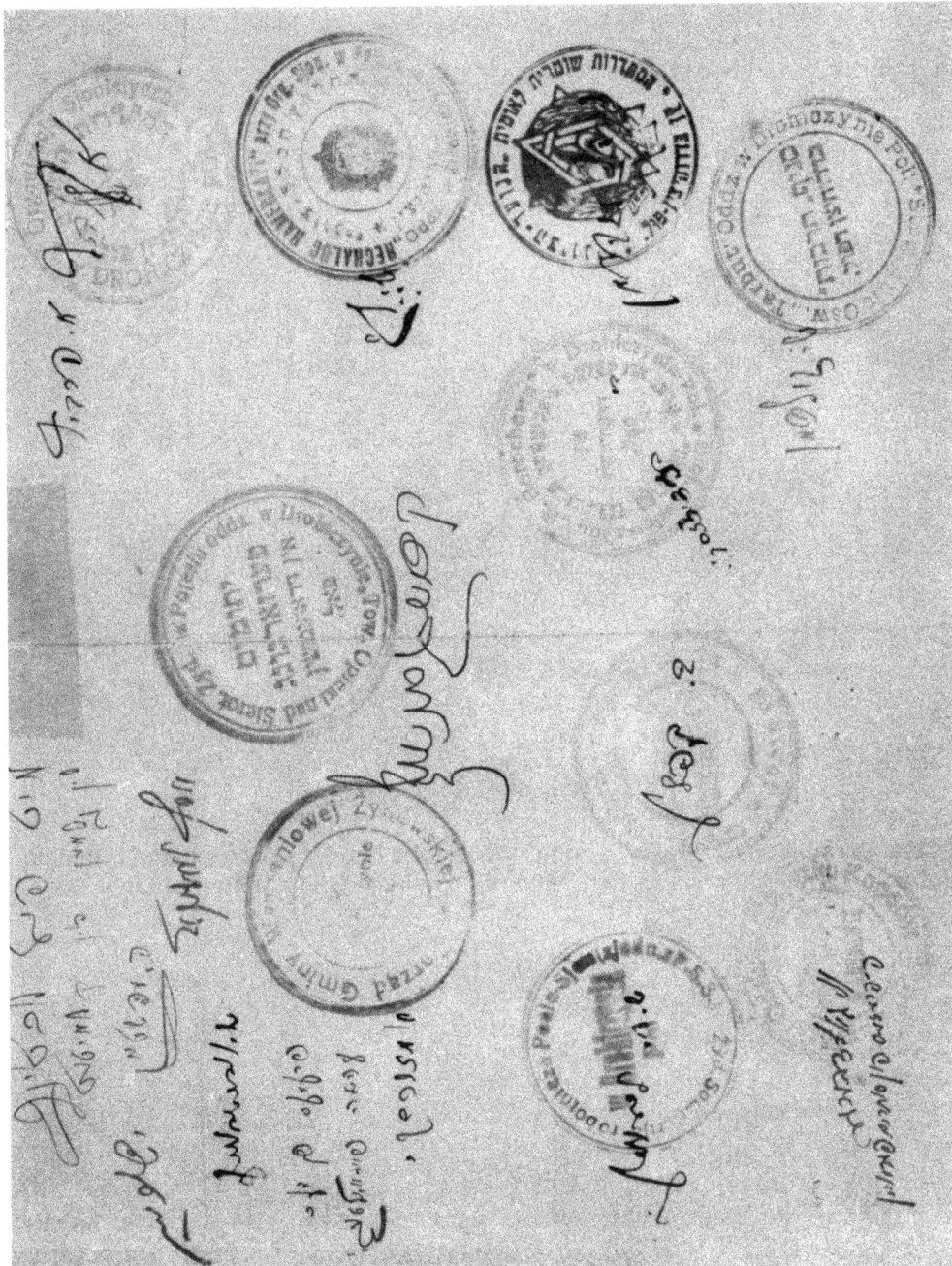

(Signatures and stamps of organizations)
Orphanage of Drohitchin
The Central Pioneer Organization
Zionist Youth of Drohitchin
Tarbut School
Borochov Group
(and others)

[*Page 260*]

Teachers of the Moriah School: Seated from right: Moshe Bezdzhezesky, Leiba Losinsky, Betzalel Wolfson, Levi Feldman, Esther Taluvna, Sheinka Feldmanand Shalom Beich, Treasurer

What the Youth of Drochitchin Seek

By Todros Leib Milner
Correspondent of *Morgen Journal*, December 3, 1937

Although this is almost a personal appeal, in any case, for a specific number of émigrés from this specific town, I would like to shake up towns with an appeal that we received because it is very characteristic of how Jewish youth are living, suffering, struggling and striving in the current emergency situation in Poland.

"At a time when political and economic anti-Semitism have hurt the lives of thousands of Jews and have cast the young people into arms of despair, apathy and desperation. This is now the time for a large-scale CULTURAL project to be undertaken by the intelligensia and progressive forces. In order to support the nationalist spirit of the next generation of young people, and to strengthen the feeling of self-esteem and pride as men and Jews, therefore the decision has been made by all progressive and democratic parties in young people to devote all our energies to develop cultural activities through our own People's House, so that the local Jewish community can get together and derive intellectual satisfaction in both nationalist and cultural pursuits. The People's House can be created if we can collect six to seven thousand gilders."

This is the request of Jewish youth and public in a town in Poland to their satisfied and secure brethren in the United States to help them "create an intellectual and nationalist center in our town that will serve as a healthy presence for Jewish interests."

This is my hometown of Drohitchin in the Grodno gubernia, which is now part of the eastern areas of Poland.

See p. 197 – a lively newspaper "Drohitchin Yawn", written by Chaim-Leib (Herman) Grossman, today in New York.

[Page 261]

ZIONIST AND SOCIALIST PARTIES

S.S. – Zionist Territorialists
By Gedaliah Kaplan, based on information from Yitzchak Cooper

The great revolutionary movement called the S.S., or the so-called Sisters and Brothers Organization, which spread across Russia in 1905-1906, had the goal of struggling against Czarist despotism and the improvement of the conditions of the working class. Naturally, it also swept up the young people in Drohitchin, who were the children of poor laborers, and was led by wealthy students.

The first battle signal took place when the two original founders of the S.S. in Drohitchin, Velvel Poliak and Godel Katzenelson, demanded that Yitzchak Cooper dismiss the workers at Kravetz's workshop. Yitzchak Cooper was then working as a tailor journeyman. In those days, a tailor employee had to work from 5 am to 10 pm. He also had to chop wood, carry water barrels, and take the animals into the field.

The leaders of the S.S. demanded an end to the long workweek (that ended on Friday afternoons before the Sabbath), shorter working hours, better working conditions, and more money.

A major conflict erupted between the Jewish employees and employers, and for a time there was a strike during which time the workers were assisted with money from the S.S. committee. One employee, Avigdor Tsipulnikes, who didn't want to leave his job with Yaakov Shimon Lev was beaten by the workers and forbidden from returning to his work. Yaakov Shimon's son,

Avraham Yitzchak Lev, was one of the leaders of the strike in his own father's workshop.

The businessmen in town didn't want to comply with the workers' demands, and the district police officer from Kobrin was called in, and several people were arrested. Finally, however, the workers won. Working hours were changed, reduced to 7 am to 7 pm. The protestors also won shorter working hours and better salaries for the straw workers.

After that struggle and because of the arrests, things remained calm for a while. However, the S.S. leaders continued with their work in secret. In the attic of Zalman Volevelsky, they had a printing press where they printed announcements in Yiddish, Russian, and White Russian, calling for a revolution against Czarism. The chairman of the S.S., Eliyahu Noach Mendelson, was planning to make the workers conscious of their situation.

In the slaughterhouse outside of town, classes for the workers were given in Russian, Arithmetic and Bible, together with socialism and Hebrew. The lecturers were from the young intelligentsia in town: Epstein, Yosef Halpern (from Pinsk), Yaakov Siderov, Rosa Shafit (Kobrin), A.N. Mendelson, and Todres Leib Milner. Milner was the treasurer of the movement, and was involved in putting out press *kripps*, new books and the Socialist Zionist publication, *The New Way*.

In addition, a lecture was held every Friday evening behind the old cemetery for the workers. On one occasion, Shmuel Deutsch from Pinsk came to speak. The lecturer explained the natural phenomenon of rainfall. Zechariah Schmid heard the lecture from his garden next door, and the next morning on the Sabbath he raised a ruckus in the synagogue, accusing the S.S. of preaching heresy. This caused a violent confrontation to break out, and Yitzchak Cooper was struck by his own father; Eliiyahu Leibkes did the same thing to his son Yisrael Baruch for listening to the heretics. The group, therefore, chose another location – behind the new cemetery. The businessmen in town, Schmid, and the elder spied on the group and interfered with the S.S.

Eliyahu Noach Mendelson then organized a group called *Tiferet Bachurim [Glory of the Young Men]* and pretended to study the halachic text *Mishnah Brura*. Under that book, they studied Jewish and general history and disseminated Zionist-Socialist ideas. Itka Valevelsky and Yonah Menashe's would give out paper and pencils to each participant.

Their opponents didn't stay quiet either. Someone told the police about the activities of the Sisters and Brothers. The district officer from Kobrin arrived in town with 50 policemen who interrogated all the members of the S.S. Fortunately Yitzchak Cooper buried the party stamp and illegal literature just in time. Rivka Valevelsky and her husband Zalman buried the printing press and all of the tools, and the police didn't find anything. Only Eliyahu Noach

Mendelson was arrested and sent to prison in Kobrin. He was soon released after his father provided some money.

[Page 262]

Moshe Shachat then brought a new printing press, and announcements in Yiddish were published at the cemetery building. These were distributed in all lecterns, pulpits, and tallith bags. Yitzchak Cooper and his friends would go around to nearby villages at night and put out announcements (in White Russian) calling on the peasants to join the struggle against Czarism. Moshe Warshavsky was one of the leaders of the S.S.

Zavel Averbuch was also one of the S.S. activists. After the tragic pogroms in Kishinev and Bialistock, Zavel called a protest meeting in the Old House of Study, where he fearlessly condemned Czarism and the Black Mahaidik pogromists. Velvel Poliak and A. N. Mendelson also gave fiery speeches. Rabbi David Yudovsky gave the eulogy over the murder victims, which evoked tears from everyone.

From right: Yosef Halpern (seated), Velvel Poliak, Moshe Horowitz, Eliyahu Noach Mendelson, Yitzchak Cooper, Moshe Warshavsky, and Shlomo Pisetsky. Below from right: Yonah Menashe's, Tordos Lieb Milner, and Avraham Yitzchak Lev. A group of leaders of the S.S.

Among the youngest people who participated in the work of the S.S., there were Gedaliah Kaplan, Yerachmiel Lopatin, and Aharon Neiditch. The opposition of the police to the S.S. members became even stronger. Many members of the S.S. were arrested, and some went off to the United States. Life continued, and the S.S. planted the seeds of the Zionist-Socialist movement.

[Page 263]

The First Zionist Youth Group

By Yisrael Baruch Eisenstein (Miami Beach)

After Dr. Ze'ev Herzl published his book, *The Jewish State,* in 1896, a movement to establish Zionist associations began in all cities and towns, including Drohitchin. At that time Drohitchin had a larger group of followers of the Enlightenment: educated teenage boys and young men, dreamers and fighters, who dreamt about Jewish redemption and world liberation. These young dreamers (over the age of 17) were the first to start spreading the idea of Zion in Drohitchin. Among the earliest founders of the Zionist Association were Yaakov Siderov, Zavel Averbuch, Moshe Zelig Goldman, David Goldman, Aryeh Shochet, Yisrael Baruch Warshavsky, the writer of these lines, and others as well.

The work of the Young Zionists Association was mostly focused on cultural issues. Several times a week, especially on Friday night and the Sabbath, they would gather together in synagogues or in a private home and listen to reports about Zionism, and learn Hebrew, Jewish history, and Bible.

For a while, the meetings of the Young Zionists were held at our house. My mother helped us a great deal and encouraged us in our work. Our group was also involved in selling shekels and shares in the Colonial Bank. Frequently visitors would come to our home and speak about Zionism and the Jewish Redemption. The Toshia Library in Warsaw sent us Hebrew books, which the young people read enthusiastically.

Our meetings were held at a high level and attracted a large number of local young people and the elderly, all of whom experienced spiritual satisfaction. I am talking about life in those years, in those fine moments of 55 years ago, and I am thinking about what subsequently happened to my hometown and the people who lived there whom I loved so dearly – people whose lives were snuffed out. Even my blind eye sheds a tear for the world that is gone, never to return.

See pictures on pp. 81 and 191 that are related to the article.

The First Zionist Organization

The Zionist Association of Drohitchin, Kobrin District

25 Sivan the first year of our Redemption*

Our Dear Brothers and Sisters from Drohitchin in the United States!

The bitter Exile that the Jewish People has been living in for 2,000 years puts its seal on us, the Jews of Russia, Poland, and Lithuania. During those generations, we have been situated here among fires, snakes, scorpions and hungry wolves. Our blood flowed like water, our lives and property were given over to strangers, and there is no one to even utter a protest against the great injustice that has been done to us in plain view of the whole world.

You in the Unites States are also Drohitchin residents, born into the Russian and Polish hell, and certainly feel the effects of the bitter Exile there in a free country. However, you cannot begin to imagine the kind of suffering and hardship we experience here. We suffered hunger and robbery during the war, but that is nothing compared with the emotional suffering we experienced every step of the way.

Yet from the darkness of the exhausted night, there was always a small scintilla of the sunshine of hope. As long as were looked to our holy east, the land of our forefathers and prophets, we were always strong in our hope and full faith that ultimately the day of redemption would arrive for our persecuted and suffering People, and the sun of charity would heal us under its wings by showing us the way in the dark until we got to our respite and inheritance.

Now, Hurrah! Our hope has been realized. Our great and wondrous dream that was dreamt of by forefathers over thousands of years, and for which they walked through fire and water, is now being realized in our own day. The Land of Israel has been returned to us – to the Jewish People, and the sound of the Shofar sounds throughout the Diaspora to have our People return to its borders. Come build the ruins; bring back the souls! We in Drohitchin are also listening to the great announcement, young and old alike; women and children are paying close attention. We also want to come in large numbers to embrace the earth of our land and soul, to water it with the sweat of our brow and the blood of our hearts.

Our Zionist committee, together will all the public officials here, has decided to organize a constant and organized emigration of the Jews of Drohitchin to Palestine, to help them as much as possible. For this purpose, we have established a Pioneer Association that numbers more than 40 men and women from among the best of our people and who have dedicated themselves to this purpose of being among the first to move to our holy land, and to devote the best years of their lives for the Land of Israel and the Jewish People.

[*Page 264*]

Unfortunately, however, we have very limited means, and we are unable to help our brethren, who are putting themselves out for our ideals during these serious times, and we cannot assist them adequately in their sacred task. The awful war has robbed us of all our property, and all we have are the clothes on our backs. We are unable to give them the money needed for them to be able to carry out their wonderful and great mission. Nevertheless, we are willing to give them our last few pennies solely in order to increase the number of settlers in the land of our hopes and future.

Therefore, we turn to you, our brothers and sisters of Drohitchin in the United States with a heartfelt call and urgent request: please act to assist your brothers and sisters of Zion who are venturing to raise the flag on the lovely Judean hills! May it be possible for the sons of Drohitchin to liberate themselves from Exile! Support our pioneers with funds so that we can offer sure and rapid assistance for the emigrants who wish to sacrifice their lives for the freedom of their People and the development of their Land.

It is a sacred duty for you, brothers and sisters, to take part in the building of our soul's Land! Don't withhold your money from those who give their all, their blood and souls for the resurrection of the eternal people in our eternal land! Each one of you must provide as generous a contribution as possible, and thus you too, across the sea, shall be among those providing assistance to the growth of our holy land.

Therefore, we are appointing our honored friend, Zvi Aryeh Eisenstein, as secretary of our committee. He has always been devoted to our great ideas here in Drohitchin with all his heart. He is now on his way to the United States to collect the funds for the pioneers who are traveling regularly to Palestine. We request that you welcome him and assist him as much as possible, and to request him to give you an official receipt with the stamp of the Drohitchin Zionist Committee. You can also send the money c/o our committee (address: Drohitchin).

We strongly hope that as soon as you receive this letter you will come to our aid and extend your hand, brothers and sisters.

We end with a blessing that has been on our lips for thousands of years – Next Year in Jerusalem!

We sign with feelings of respect and with the blessings for a rebuilt Zion and a complete redemption.

The Zionist Association of Drohitchin B, Chairman – Shmuel Fishman; Secretary – Zvi Shkolnick; Treasurer – Zelig Shochat. Members of the Committee: Yehuda Zilberstein, Gedaliah Kaplan, Miriam Weissman, Zvia Waldman and Y. Roshinsky.

The Pioneer Association of Drohitchin: M. Dov, Chairman; A. Valevelsky, Secretary; Y. Y. Khnovitch, Treasurer; M. Chazan, M. Zaretsky, members.

Standing from right: Rivka Burstein, S. Pisetsky, B. Torbovitch, F. Epstein, Goldman. Seated from right: H. Waldman, Goldman, Heska Feldman, Zvia and Chashka Waldman. Bottom, from right: Chaytsha Epstein, Leitsha Mendelson, Esther Mishovsky, Sheinka Feldman, and Sarah Kreines – 1922.

[Page 265]

NATIONAL REVIVAL AFTER THE BALFOUR DECLARATION
1919-1923
By Shmuel Fishman (Jerusalem)

Introduction

Unfortunately, I am not familiar with the situation of the Zionist movement in Drohitchin prior to the outbreak of World War I. When my family and I left the town of Libeshei (near Pinsk) as refugees at the end of 1916 and ended up in the abandoned village of Popina (near Drohitchin), I had the opportunity to work together with many young people in Drohitchin in German forced labor.

Shmuel Fishman

Together we chopped trees in the forest and placed the wood on the dirty roads and did other types of forced labor. Among these young people, I met real Jewish intellects, Hebraists and enthusiastic Zionists. We discussed the issue of the Jewish redemption among ourselves and expressed the hope that when the adversaries finally sat down at the negotiation table, they would also consider the situation of the suffering Jewish People and finally allow the Jews to return to their own land – Palestine.

In November 1917, when I and a few other young Jews worked in the fields, we saw a wagon with two Jews from Drohitchin. The Jews told us that Jewish merchants from Sedletz brought a Jewish newspaper to Drohitchin from Warsaw that wrote that England had made a declaration promising a Jewish National Home in Palestine. We couldn't believe our ears.

I returned home immediately, changed my clothes, and traveled to Drohitchin (In those days a person simply had to throw on his boots over his shoulder and walk barefoot into town.). We were more concerned about our boots than about our feet.

When I got to Drohitchin, I went directly to see the rabbi about the news. His son, Moshe, told me that he had read the article about the English declaration himself. The newspaper, which went from hand to hand in town, was currently at the Weissmans' house.

I met the entire Weissman family sitting around the table and discussing the news in the paper. I then suggested that we arranged a celebration or a mass meeting of all the Jews in Drohitchin in honor of the historic event. Yosef Berezovsky (R. Shimon Weissman's son-in-law) agreed with me, but we needed the permission of the German commander. We had to go to Yosef Zbar, who was very close to the Germans, and ask him to obtain the permit.

When we arrived at Zbar's home and told him about our plans, he stared at us and angrily shouted, "Idiots! Do you want to bring trouble onto the Jews of Drohitchin? Don't you understand that the British declaration about Palestine was an act against Germany? Do you think we can openly show our sympathy for England's declaration when we are under German occupation?" We understood his logic and correct arguments, and left feeling embarrassed.

A.

The tremendous revival and excitement that swept up the Jewish population of Poland and the entire world after the San Remo decision, when world government approved the Balfour Declaration, which recognized Palestine as the Jewish national home understandably infected the Jews of Drohitchin too.

[Page 266]

The large parade through the streets of Drohitchin that included young and old in honor of the meeting at San Remo will always remain in the memories of Drohitchin survivors. The rabbis marched in front carrying Torah scrolls. Yudel Zilberstein gallantly rode a beautiful white horse, and the members of the Zionist committee were adorned with white and blue armbands and other symbolic decorations. The large crowd proceeded in a stately and orderly manner until they arrived at the office of the Polish Commissar (I don't know his name), who was actually a very liberal person and friendly to Jews.

[The people who organized the celebration the Balfour Declaration were Yaakov Einbinder, Msohe Bezdzhesky, Gedaliah Kaplan, Naftali Steinberg, Betzalel H. Wolfson, a teacher, Hersh Leib Eisenstein, S. Fishman, Velvel Mishovsky, Hershel Shkolnick, Y. Zilberstein, Shmuel Schub, and others. See the picture on p. 96 – Editor)

The commissar came outside dressed in his uniform, and I greeted him in Polish on behalf of the large demonstration. I explained the meaning of the parade, expressing the hope that the Polish people, who had just been liberated from foreign rule, would also help the Jews to build historical Jewish land promised by G-d to the Patriarchs and Prophets. The commissar responded with very friendly words and stated that he would encourage Zionist activity in Drohitchin. He warmly greeted the Jews in honor of the historical act that took place in San Remo.

Tired and worn out, but with hearts filled with excitement and faith in the future of an independent and free Jewish People in Palestine and uttering quiet prayers to G-d for his mercy, the crowd dispersed. Each person in his own way started spinning dreams and hopes of how to take advantage of this auspicious time. Some decided on making their own personal link to the Holy Land, while the majority naturally just look for ways to help others to settle in Palestine as pioneers and builders.

German commander in Drohitchin (in Yaakov Polig's house), where Shmuel Fishman wanted to get a permit to celebrate the Balfour Declaration. The photo was taken in 1917.

[*Page 267*]

The *Poalei Zion [Workers of Zion]* Party and the *Freiheit [Freedom]* Youth Group in Drohitchin in 1934. [The board in the photo indicates the date to be 9/10/34.

B.

The next day, after the imposing and influential demonstration, the Drohitchin Zionist committees held a celebratory meeting and decided to begin recruiting pioneers among the young people and send them to Palestine as the first Drohitchin vanguard. A couple of dozen bright young people were called to be the first on the list. Our committee went over the entire list and chose 14 of them.

I was appointed to the Palestine Office in Warsaw to certify the 14. Unfortunately, I had to undertake great effort just to get seven of them accepted. Rabbi Yitzchak Nissenbaum, who was a member of the Palestine Office, demanded that at least 10 be approved, but Yisrael Mereminsky of the left-wing camp proposed to approve only five. He claimed that it was impossible to send such a large number of pioneers from one town.

However, everyone understood the real motive. Our boys all belonged to the General Zionists, who were interested in only one goal: to go to Palestine and help build the country for the entire Jewish people, without any other motives. Actually, there were no other parties besides the General Zionists in Drohitchin in those days. Therefore, the left wing didn't want to approve all the pioneers from Drohitchin.

There was great joy when I arrived home with certificates for seven people. The town started preparing to say goodbye to the first group of pioneers. Their names were: two Schub brothers, Isser Valevelsky, Ze'ev Milner, Yossel Kobrinsky, and Hershel Steinberg. I don't remember who the seventh was. I think I remember that the old Drohitchin businessman, R. Aharon Zbar (Areleh of Lidvinov), who then had a daughter and her family in Palestine. I believe that it was the famous Baruch Goralsky family who had opened the first furniture factory in Palestine.

[Page 268]

Aharon Zbar was going there to spend the rest of his life there, but unfortunately a year later he returned to Drohitchin because he didn't fit in with his daughter and her family.

The departing pioneers were sent off with a farewell evening party and music and singing. The next day the town accompanied them to the train station with blessings and tears. When the train pulled out of the station, the entire crowd spontaneously started singing Hatikvah, which even made a strong impression on the Christian onlookers.

C.

Strong and intensive Zionist activity then started in Drohitchin. We organized large fundraisers for the Jewish National Fund. Teenage boys and girls went around visiting Jewish homes to request people for a monthly contribution. Every opportunity was used to help the Jewish National Fund, which brought in relatively large amounts of money. From time to time, our committee would receive letters of appreciation from the central office of the JNF in Warsaw that emphasized that Drohitchin and its small Jewish population did better in its fundraising than other cities throughout Polesia.

After the London Zionist Conference, when the *Keren HaYesod* (Foundation Fund) was announced, Drohitchin was among the first communities to use the slogan of tithe contributions. Large sums of money were created, and the task of our committee was to keep the community excited and enthused. A group of friends including Shmuel Schub (now in the United States), Aharon Saratchik (now Aharon Yisraeli in Israel), the late Yosef Berezovsky and others would occasionally appear at meetings and synagogues to awaken the people to be prepared to act and sacrifice. Teachers and speakers from the central office in Warsaw would frequently visit us and speak on behalf of the development of Palestine.

I consider it my sacred task to mention as one example one of the ordinary Jews of Drohitchin, Hershel Dvinsky the Shoemaker, who with totally devoted with heart and soul to the Land of Israel. He would gather groups of Jewish artisans and merchants and preach to them about the love of Palestine and building it.

The right-wing Betar movement in Drohitchin: Standing on the left is Dr. Goldstein (with the revolver), former director of the Moriah school and founder of the Betar group in Drohitchin. See the pictures on pp. 44, 90 and 190.

[Page 269]

Since he was no simple Jew, he always used a verse from the Torah or the Prophets. On one Sabbath in the "Polish Synagogue," while Hershel the Shoemaker was listening to an emotional speech from one our speakers, he jumped on the platform and cried, "Jews, you should know that we are indeed in messianic days because the verse 'All trees of the forest shall sing' is being fulfilled. You are able to hear how a simple Jew, a shoemaker like me, can be so bold as to come up on a platform and speak to the public. This is a sign that the Redemption is near, and that we should move to Palestine. Let's not keep silent, Jews; we are in messianic times." It goes without saying that his entire brief speech had a strong impact on his listeners. All of Drohitchin treated R. Hershel the Shoemaker with great respect. Shortly thereafter he and his family moved to Palestine. These lines should serve as an eternal memorial for that Jew and our friend, R. Hershel the Shoemaker, who lived out his years in Jerusalem, the Holy City, and died in old age.

Hashomer Hatsair" from Drohitshin"

Standing from right: Mordechai Buder, Leizer Varshavsky, Bodie Fridenberg, Josef Buf and Shalom Baich

Sitting from left: Hershl Shmid, Valdman, Reuven Varshavsky, Ya'akov Rozenboim and Ya'akov Varshavsky

Below from left: Yisrael Shvarts, Ya'akov Orliansky and Miriam Tsirl's granddaughter

I would like to mention of the rare individuals in Drohitchin, Shachna the Synagogue Caller. He was a really poor person and made his living from working as a synagogue custodian and wood chopping. However, he was always among the earliest supporters of the JNF and the person who people turned to. When there was a tools project in Drohitchin on behalf of the kibbutzim in Palestine, Shachna was the first to bring his new axe and with a blessing offered it to the committee (See pictures on pp. 41 and 69 – Editor.).

D.

After San Remo, the central Zionist committee in Poland called on everyone to be ready for a post-war Zionist convention. Our committee decided to sell enough shekels to justify sending two delegates to the convention in Lodz. We couldn't even dream of being able to send more than two. Drohitchin sold more than 500 shekels and sent the two delegates: Shmuel Schub and Shmuel Fishman.

Both of us, the two delegates from Drohitchin, were surprised when Yitzchak Greenbaum announced Drohitchin as an example to the other delegates of a community, that proportionate to its population sold more shekels than any city or town in Poland. So we were the heroes of the convention, and many prominent Zionists warmly greeted us and shook our hand. When we returned home after the conference, we gave a report about it to a large audience.

In the beginning of 1922, the central committee appointed me as general secretary of the entire Polesia region, and with great regret my wife and I had to leave our beloved Drohitchin, where we lived and carried out our work together with many other friends, and we moved to Pinsk.

[Page 270]

Naturally, I remained in close contact with my Drohitchin and enthusiastically followed the growing Zionist movement.

In the summer of 1923, fate dictated that I give up my Zionist work in Poland and move to the United States. The first years there I still heard good news from Drohitchin from time to time, and I derived great pleasure from the Zionist activities that were growing there, as well as from the various Zionist parties that Drohitchin was blessed with, in the same way as all the other leading cities and town in Poland. I eventually lost contact with Drohitchin, and, unfortunately, I am unable to write about events after 1923. Hopefully, there are other friends who will expand on my review of the Zionist movement from 1923 until the Holocaust in 1942.

Note: Additional information about the Zionist Movement in Drohitchin is on pp. 46-49. Editor [box:] A sacred memorial to our dear and unforgettable

Mother

Batsheva Peshkovsky

Younger sisters

Feigel and Chasha Peshkovsky

who perished at the hands of the murderous Balakhov gangs

in Zakazelia, near Drohitchin

3 Cheshvan 5782 – [this corresponds to Nov. 4, 1921]

and our brother

Yehuda Leib Peshkovsky

died on 3 Cheshvan 5782

Sonia Feins
Meita Greenwald

See p. 101 and 102

A group of young members of *Freiheit* from Drohitchin

Betar. Standing from right: Peretz Goldman, ----, Leibel Kravetz, Berl Gottlieb, ---, and Avraham Mishovsky. Seated from right: Yosef Rubinstein, Zvi Levack and Menachem Steinberg. Below from right: Meir-Motya Hausman and Mordechai Gottlieb [see p. 246].

Photostat of the Drohitchin Betar seal

The left-wing *Hashomer Hatsa'ir [Young Guard]* of Drohitchin

Standing from right: Mordechai Buder, Leizer Warshavsky, Bodya Friedenberg, Yosef Buff and Shalom Beich. Seated from left: Hershel Schmid, Waldman, Reuven Warshavsky, Yaakov Rosenbaum, and Yaakov Warshavsky. Bottom: Yisrael Schwartz, Yaakov Orliansky and Miriam Tsirel's grandchild.

[*Page 271*]

First row, standing from right: L. Warshavsky, S. Warshavsky, B. Berg, M. Buder, P. Mazursky, L. Goldberg, H. Schmid.

Second row, from right: H. Eppelbaum, B. Z. Bezezhesky, R. Baum, R. Eppelbaum, Y. Goldman, Baum, Y. Beich, M. Kalenkovich.

Seated from right: T. Milner, Y. Schwartz, S. Feldman, Y. Mishovsky, A. Drucker, S. Zaretsky.

Below, from right: S. Feldman, Ch. Goldberg, D. Goldman, M. Valevelsky.

The group *Hechalutz* (The Pioneer) had members of all parties. 18 perished. May G-d avenge their blood!

Picture from left to right: Zechariah Sapozhnik, Hershel Steinberg (a woman) and Aharon Rosenzweig (Areleh Yankel Baruch's), former Bundists who fought for freedom and justice, sitting on the buggy. Their nature was to drive people on the right way. Zechariah and Areleh Yankel Baruch's perished. May G-d avenge their blood! Regarding Areleh Yankel Baruch's see p. 272.

Todres Sapozhnik who died in Drohitchin

Page 272]

THE BUND

In 1903, when the revolutionary movement called Sisters and Brothers was established, the youth of Drohitchin were also drawn into revolutionary ferment, and workers now began asserting their rights.

With the assistance of the Bund Central Committee in Pinsk, a local Bund party organization was established in Drohitchin. The leaders of the Bund in Drohitchin were Mordechai Weissman (the son of Shimon the Doctor) and W. Poliak (Kapulier's grandson). The secret Bund meetings were held in the Rovno and Brona forests as well as in the building next to the old cemetery. The Bund leaders always switched around their meeting places.

One day the leaders of the Bund Central Committee in Pinsk, Yaakov Gurin and Aharon Weinberg, came for a visit to Drohitchin. They were supposed to speak at the Old House of Study. However, the district police officer and his constables broke into the meeting and arrested almost everyone there. Only great effort and money made it possible to get the arrested people released from jail.

The first workers' strike in Drohitchin broke out at the shoemaker shop of Reuven Beita, who refused to accede to the demands of the workers. Areleh Rosenzweig (Yankel Baruch's son) pushed his way into meeting Reuven, kicked the workers out and demolished the shop. The Bund workers finally achieved an eight-hour day and higher wages.

At that time, Yaakov Goldberg (Yosef Nissel's son), who was a militant activist on behalf of the Bund, called a secret meeting in the Rovno Forest. The police were waiting for the meeting, and they arrested Goldberg, putting him in prison. He didn't remain there long, however. Khana Sarah Goldes the furrier and Areleh Yankel Baruch's the shoemaker dug a tunnel one night under the prison and freed Goldberg, who then got across the Russian border a few nights later and made his way to the United States.

On May 1, 1905, there was a large workers' demonstration in the central market of Drohitchin. Someone gave a strong revolutionary speech, and said, "Down with the Czarist regime. Long Live the Bund!" The result of this event was this person was arrested and sent for a period to Siberia. Following extensive attempts, he was moved from the prison in Siberia to one in Kobrin.

After the Czar's October manifesto of 1905, in which he planned to drown the Russian revolution in Jewish blood, the Czarist officials in Drohitchin used the excited peasant population to undertake a pogrom against the Jews. The event took place on December 9, 1905, at the Mikolai Fair. The Bund, however, was also ready, and on that day when the fair was supposed to take place, the Bundist young people went out very early to the roads behind town, and any peasant they found going to the fair was beaten severely and the sent back to his village. The fair didn't take place, and the Bund young people, therefore, saved the town from misfortune.

As became apparent later, the peasants had been intending to enter town with axes, scythes, and sacks. The same thing occurred in 1905, when young army draftee hooligans went on a spree against the Jewish population. The Bund proletariat attacked the hooligans and warned them not to start up with the Jews.

The Czarist officials, however, got the upper hand against the revolutionaries and through repression forced the Bundist leaders to flee to the United States. The Bund in Drohitchin, therefore, gradually faded away. But despite everything, the Bund in Drohitchin – like the Bund in all other towns – was responsible for writing its own page in Jewish history.

Information from Gedaliah Kaplan

Dr. Mordechai Weissman provided the following:

Yiddish announcements were mimeographed in the apartment of Gershon the shoemaker (a son of Kaila the mail carrier), who lived with his family of five children in one room in the home of Michel the gravestone engraver. Gershon also had his shoemaking shop in that same room.

Moshka Torbovitch was one of the most devoted Bundist activists in Drohitchin.

(Additional information about the Bund is on p. 49 – Editor)

[Page 273]

COMMUNITY INSTITUTIONS

Medical Assistance Organization and Hospice for the Poor
By Zvi Yitzchak Hoffman, 1890

When I returned to Drohitchin from the United States, Rabbi Menachem called me in and told me that there were many poor people in town, and whenever someone was ill, there was no one to help. Therefore, I came up with the idea to start a Hospice for the Poor.

I first bought fruit and berries and brought them to the rabbi's wife to be fried. She took a glass of preserves to every infirm person she visited. I then arranged that whenever someone became ill, I would send two people from opposite sides of town to keep that person company. Everyone had to participate, and even the rabbi had to hire a substitute when it was his turn to spend the night with a patient.

I would like to mention one event that gives an idea about the activities of the Hospice for the Poor.

On Kobrin Road, there lived a poor unmarried young man, a shoemaker, who was supposed to get married on a Tuesday evening. Since he had to complete all of his orders before the wedding, he worked Saturday night after the Sabbath until very late. He found he needed a certain tool, and he went to borrow it from another shoemaker. His mother waited for him to return, and when a long time had passed, she went out to look for him. She walked across a bridge and heard someone groaning below; the person turned out to be her son lying there in a ditch. She started screaming and people came rushing to get her son and take him home. Shimon the Doctor was called immediately, in addition to three other doctors from nearby towns. All of them gave up on the boy. Only Shimon claimed that they should try to wrap him up in sackcloth soaked in cold water as a way to help save his life. Shimon asked me to send to strong men who would change the wraps on the boy every ten minutes. I sent Moshe Handeles and Berl the Blacksmith. Moshe asked Berl to get some sleep; Moshe remained awake the whole night and changed the wraps every five minutes, and the wet wraps were thus continually changed for three straight days. Thank G-d the boy recovered and later got married.

In approximately 1898, before Shammai Hershel Dinas ran away during the Yom Tov, a cholera epidemic broke out in nearby towns. Shimon the Doctor instructed that hot water should be prepared and kept hot in tin cans as well as tubs for the patients, because it was feared that the epidemic would spread to Drohitchin. I prepared the tin cans and tubs, and the epidemic broke out 10 days later. We were prepared, however, and no one died during the epidemic.

To a certain extent, the containers were paid for by the sale of tickets during the second, two-day holiday at the end of Passover sponsored by Shmuel Hirsh, a brother-in-law of Chana Resha, and Markel, a cantor who had returned to Drohitchin from the United States. This money covered the costs of the tin cans and bathtubs.

The Hospice for the Poor also undertook another activity: since ice was needed for the patients, I hired gentiles to chop ice so that each person could take as much as he needed and contributed as much as he could afford to a charity box. When I returned to the United States, I gave the chairmanship of the Hospice to Hershel Chaim Lev, the belt-maker. The esteemed rabbi Zalman Sender provided the rules for the Hospice.

[*Page 274*]

Stow. „LINATH HACEDEK"
w Drohiczynie-Pol.

חברת
„בקור חולים"־־„לינת הצדק"
בדרוהיצין דפולסיה

№   שובר הכנסה

Otrzym. od

Zebrał

Ofjarował

SUMA ZI. 143 25 gr. פר.   סכום

Słownie   בפירוש

Dn. 22 m. 3   1937 תרצ"ז   יום בחדש   חתימת

Kasjer : הגזבר

Medical Aid and Hospice for the Poor
Drohitchin, Polesia
Receipt No.
Received from
For Sum of 25 dollars
March 22, 1937
Treasurer [illegible signature] [Stamp of Hospice]

Kholozhin Rebbe Requests Aid for the Medical Aid Organization

To our dear brothers and sisters, friends, and supporters of our organization Medical Aid and Hospice for the Poor who are in Chicago. February 1932.

Together with a report about our work in 1931, we are requesting you to become familiar with our work of last year, 1931. On behalf of the administration of the Medical Aid organization and on behalf of all the poor and needy, weak and infirm, who we support in their trying circumstances, we thank you for the $75.

As you can see from our report, we have limited our work, and the main assistance for the ill was for providing them with medical help (such as free doctor services, and prescriptions) as much as we could afford. In previous years, we provided support for the ill in the hundreds of zlotys, e.g. for transportation to a doctor in a major city, for surgery, *kinpetorins* assistance, country houses, fish oil for sickly children, and other various situations. We were able to save many lives.

We painfully regret that we are unable to meet the needs of many important dejected and suffering householders who approach us in their time of difficulty and to whom we can only respond with a small amount of money. Perhaps you know that we have on our conscience the cases of a number of victims who could have recovered from their illness had we been able to help them.

We turn to you, brothers and sisters, to request that you not abandon us as we face our awesome responsibility during these bitter times. Please help us to meet to meet the needs of your and our brethren in Drohitchin.

We extend our thanks to you, the esteemed activists in Chicago, Mrs. Malka Warshavsky, and all her colleagues for their efforts. May the Almighty make conditions better so that we can assist the needy.

Chairman: Yosef David Schub; Treasurer: David Warshavsky; Secretary: Alter Karelitz.

(This is a note from the esteemed Kholozhin Rebbe, R. Eliyahu Mordechai Levinovitz –Editor):

I bless all those who participate in assisting the holy organization of our town, Medical Aid organization. I, too, have their charity box for which I collect money for the organization. For G-d's sake, please do not abandon such a holy organization because if it can only maintain itself on a handful of coins, it will fail. Please accept my blessing that is offered from a heart suffering from the requests and distress of Jews. May you never know from such illnesses.

Eliyahu Mordechai Levinovitz

(His ink stamp with his name and "known as the Blacksmith of Kholozhin" handwritten: Eliyahu Mordechai Levinovitz, I ask that you read the letter in front of the congregation at the synagogue.)

[Page 275]

The handwritten report is the Report of the Medical Aid organization and Hospice for the Poor for 1931. It includes income (right column) and expenses (left column). The sources of income include membership fees, charity boxes, and other contributions. The total income is 3,185, and is matched by the same amount in expenses. The expenses include medical assistant for the infirm, supplies, financial aid, office expenses and equipment.

Medical Aid Organization and Hospice for the Poor in the Latter Years

To all émigrés from Drohitchin in the United States:

The charitable institution, Medical Aid organization and Hospice for the Poor, has existed for some nine years now and has sought to provide tangible assistance for the needs of the poor infirm population.

Since it has existed, the organization has increased in popularity in Drohitchin both among the poor infirm as well as among its supporters and members, such that today it is the finest and most important organization in town.

Those involved with the organization work quietly and modestly. They always face the difficulties in order to provide the poor of Drohitchin with as much help as possible. The organization has a rich history of service, and everyone can appreciate how such a Jewish aid organization must struggle in such stormy years of crisis so that it can earn the respect of the town.

With tremendous effort and dedication, the organization works and stands ready to provide assistance wherever help is required. We can most certainly take pride in our work, since more than once has someone been saved from death because of our assistance.

The economic situation in Drohitchin has become very difficult, and many of our members who financially supported our work now have no bread at home. Instead of providers, they are now themselves recipients. Therefore, it is no wonder that under such tragic circumstances, and in such a short a period, our account has become empty. Each month our income has fallen, and expenses have become much greater than before.

[Page 276]

We have no solution to offer from the tiny sums of money we collect here in Drohitchin.

Therefore, we have decided to appeal to you, former residents of Drohitchin in the United States, to assist us in carrying the burden of the many poor infirm, and thereby encourage the activists in their important work. There are three times as many of you, sisters and brothers, in the United States than there are of us in Drohitchin, and together we can save many suffering people. Our organization helps the unfortunate in their struggle, and saves many of them in cases of illness and need. By responding to the request of an unfortunate poor person who comes crying for help and frightens everyone, one feels that a stone has been lifted from one's heart.

We mention this to you, dear brothers and sisters, because of the approaching holidays when each of you is thinking about your hometown and relatives left behind there. Therefore, we appeal to you at this time to assure that our holy organization is able to continue to exist and save people.

Please send your contributions to the Medical Aid organization and Hospice for the Poor to the Drohitchin Fraternal Organization in New York, to the Drohitchin Aid Association in Chicago, or directly to the Hospice for the Poor in Drohitchin. We wish a good year to all our brethren from Drohitchin and their families wherever they may be.

חברת
לינת-הצדק
בדרוהישטין
דפלישא

[ink stamp of Hospice]

Management: Chairman, Yosef David Schub; Treasurer, D. Warshavsky. Additional information about the Hospice for the Poor is on pp. 42 and 50. (Editor)

Savings and Lending or Cooperative People's Bank established in Drohitchin in 1911

Seated, from left: Asher Siderov, Moshe Prager (ritual slaughterer), Zechariah Schmid, Lipman Feldman, Moshe Gingold, and Pinya Buder. Standing from right to left: Avraham Kravetz, Yonah Goldberg, Yirmiyahu Grossman, Feigel Epstein, Shepsel Warshavsky, Moshe Hochman, and Yaakov Beich. For additional information about bank, see p. 50.

[*Page 277*]

Interest-Free Loans

Leah's interest-free loan fund was established in Drohitchin in 1927. Aharon Eliyahu Zisuk gave 500 dollars. Fishel of New York bequeathed 1,000 dollars in his will. In total 3,000 dollars was collected for the loan fund in Drohitchin.

February 23, 1928.

(Handwritten signatures of the chairman and members)

Chairman: Isaac Yaakov Kalenkovitch (chief rabbi)

Members: Zalman Kaplan, Zusya Warshavsky, Moshe Shmuel Warshavsky, Moshe Prager-Schub, David Warshavsky, and S. Valevelsky, Secretary.

February 23, 1928.

Our totally devoted good friend, Yisrael Baruch Eisenstein in Chicago, greetings and good wishes to you and your family:

Many are those who love a rich man, (Proverbs, 14, 20*) and a brother to suffering will be born* (Proverbs 17, 17*).* There is a great difference between a wealthy good friend and a good friend who helps needy beaten down people. Such a person who helps the oppressed is called by King Solomon (author of Proverbs) "a brother."

We who are the living testimony to your work during the war and afterwards, on behalf of the poor of your hometown, and recently the best and greatest undertaking on behalf of the establishment of the popular free-loan organization that assists more than 300 poor families in your hometown.

How else can we describe you other than with the title of "brother" used by King Solomon? And even if we use that name to describe you, this is merely the tip of the iceberg, only a slight word of praise, because where is it even possible to find a brother as you are, who are so dedicated to assist his poor brother? How would our hometown look if not for your work? We thank you for your work and it goes without saying because such activists who are so devoted to community service ask for thanks. Our Sages have already spoken of people like you when they said, "He who lends money to a poor person in his time of need, it is said 'Call out, and G-d will respond' and 'G-d will pay them for their work.'"

We greet you warmly, your father and brother, Eliyahu Eisenstein. We also ask that you give our regards to Rabbi Y. David Goldman. May G-d grant you health and prosperity.

(Handwritten: signatures of the chairman and members)

Chairman: Isaac Yaakov Kalenkovitch (chief rabbi)

Members: Zalman Kaplan, Zusya Warshavsky, Moshe Shmuel Warshavsky, Moshe Prager-Schub, David Warshavsky and S. Valevelsky, Secretary.

R. Yisrael Baruch Eisenstein reports that Malka Warshavsky helped the Interest-Free Loan Fund in Drohitchin enormously. See the report of the Interest-Free Fund on pp. 50-51.

Invitation to an Interest-Free Loan Fund Meeting in 1939
Interest-Free Loan Fund in Drohitchin

We hereby have the honor of inviting you to the annual general meeting of the Interest-Free Loan Fund in Drohitchin, Polesia, which will be held on Sunday, August 6, 1939 at the Moriah School at 3 pm with the following agenda:

1. Introduction
2. Election of a Board
3. Reading the Minutes of the previous annual general meeting.
4. Financial report and activity report of the Free Loan Fund for 1938-39.
5. Decision about the budget proposal for the current year.
6. Decision about a new administration and auditors.
7. Suggestions.
Yours truly,
The Administration

[Page 278]

צענטאָס

געזעלשאַפט פאַר קינדער-שוץ
און יתומים-פאַרזאָרגונג אויף פּאָלעסיע
"צענטאָס"
אָפּטיילונג אין דראָהיטשין

193_ 30/_ דראָהיטשין, דעם ....

(הורצאָה)

וויר האָבאן עס קיין ווערטער ... וואָס ... צייק ... ... וייערד ... ...
און ... פאַביהונג ... ... ווענדאָ ... ...-לייענאָ ... ...
וויר ... אייער ... וויר ... ... 50 ... ...
... וואָלען ... פון ווענגער ... ...
... האָב וויר ... און ... ...
וואָס ... ...
און ... ...
... ... און ... ...
... ...
און ... ... בית ... ...
... ...
... ...
... ...
... ...
... ...
... ...

מיט ... גרוס פון צאַנק,

פאָרזיצער ...

סעקרעטער ...

Translation of Previous Page

Tsentos

Society for the Support of Children and Orphan
Care in Polesia

Drohitchin Branch	Drohitchin, September 30, 1937

Highly Esteemed,

We have no words to thank you for your good-hearted and warm attitude toward our poor and needy suffering brethren. We thank you for your support, i.e. the 50 dollars that you sent us care of our chairman, R. Gedaliah Grossman. This money arrived at the proper moment because there were many families who had nothing to eat for the holidays, and children who were going in tattered clothes. There were some who were even going barefoot. We distributed your monetary assistance for these purposes; our chairwoman, Mrs. Esther Yehudit Greenstein, will contact you about it. Not a single penny went for any unnecessary purpose.

We arranged the holidays in the large House of Study, where a blessing was pronounced for all of the contributors and officers of the associations. May the Almighty enable you to continue making your contributions in the future on behalf of our needy. You should never experience what we are currently going through. We are in the process of opening our winter kitchen for children and plan to provide them with warm clothing and shoes. We ask you to join us in this important work with your contributions.

Fraternal greetings and thanks,

The administration of the Tsentos Committee in Drohitchin

[*Page 279*]

THE WORK OF TSENTOS

Activity Report in numbers for 1936

Income

Member payments....................	263.88 zlotys
American contributions.............	241.50
Calendar sales........................	98.70
Summer colonies....................	179.00
Grants from Pinsk office of Tsentos...............................	747.50
Grants from Drohitchin authority.............................	150.00
Grants from mayor, Drohitchin....	100.00
Contributions for children's kitchen................................	75.72
Charity box from People's Bank....	16.31
Charity box from *Hortovnya*..........	1.37
Pre-Yom Kippur collection plates.....................................	7.08
Balance as of 1/1/1936.................	41.69
Total...............................	1,199.75 zlotys - approximately 366 dollars

Expenses

Clothing for 44 children............	352.55 zlotys
Seamstress training for an orphan girl.............................	52.95

Children eating outside of the "Tsentos" kitchen

[*Page 281 blank*]

[*Page 282*]

זעקסטער טייל

גרעלער „מגן-דוד", וואָס די דייטשן, ימ״ש, האָבן
געצוואונגען די ייִדן צו טראָגן אויף די בגדים

חורבן און אומקום

PART SIX

Remember what Amalek did unto you….

The yellow Star of David that the Germans forced Jews to wear on their clothes

DESTRUCTION AND DESTRUCTION

[*Page 283*]

YIZKOR
(REMEMBER)

With great sadness and wrath, we have begun to recite the mourner's prayers, Yizkor, for our families and all martyrs (approximately seven to eight million) who were brutally killed by the German murderers. May their names be obliterated!

The truth is that everything written thus far is a memorial, a yizkor! Almost 90 percent of all the pictures printed here, and especially wherever they include the term, "May G-d avenge their blood!" are pictures of our martyrs. The entire book is, therefore, a Yizkor book, a memorial book and nothing else. What is in this special section, "Destruction and Destruction," focuses on, and extensively expresses an entire Scroll of Lamentations or Scroll of Fire (and Ash) of a burned down city and its Jews. We feel their suffering and hear their weeping, especially their recitation of their final "Hear O Israel" and call for revenge!

While we were organizing and editing the Destruction material, we encountered repetition and many contradictions. We corrected some of them wherever possible, but in most cases we left untouched the testimony and accounts of those who went through the Destruction. We let them express their opinions, anger and feelings pro and con about the most painful subjects, such as the Judenrat (Nazi-appointed Jewish councils) and ghetto police, because each person saw and felt about things in different ways.

We must not forget that the Jews in the ghettos were dealing with a refined murderer who unique in history. The Germans cold bloodedly planned their murder of the Jewish People with devilish cunning and resorted to the most awful methods of extermination imaginable. They resorted to cynical and cunning behavior, and when necessary, to a smile to deceive their victims into going to the transports. Prior to extermination, the Jews went through seven levels of hell so that people eventually begged to die.

The German system of murder was to make one Jew control another so that the Jews in the sealed ghettos would quarrel and irritate each other, and then annihilate each other. Jews lived through terrible challenges, and many succumbed. Some grabbed onto someone else's hand or neck, like someone drowning, and pulled that person down as well.

Finally, the Germans attained their goal: their victims were tormented, and their divine image was crushed by the German devils who pulled the marrow out of their bones through slave labor, hunger, and cold. Thus, they no longer had any resistance or will to live. The German hangmen then liquidated everyone, and one thing is clear: an honest Jew could not remain alive.

Of course, the German hangmen carried out their murder mostly through others. They had their loyal collaborators among the Ukrainian, White Russian, Polish, Hungarian, Lithuanian nationalists, and other evildoers who relished Jewish property. We should never forget this! However, the top killers, the head butchers and hangmen who killed our loved ones were Germans! May their memories be blotted out!

Our loved ones left us a will and testament: To take revenge against their murderers, and the best way to fulfill the wishes of our martyrs is to always remember the hangmen, and never to have any dealings with them! Remember!

Dov Warshavsky

HOW CAN I FORGET MY BROTHERS AND SISTERS?

Can I forget my brothers in Poland
Who languished in frightful concealment?
Or the anguish of brothers who remained?
Or the horror of those who were expelled?
Can I forget the Jewish children
Who lost their childhood?
Or the Jewish youth who groan stooped over
With eternal pain over the years?
Who will warm them in the snow and cold?
And take pity on their suffering and despair?
No bread to eat, no water to drink,
Though there are toads in the swamps.
They are afflicted by savage suffering,
Like boats tossed about at sea,
Like birds feasting on sparrows.
How can I forget my brothers in Poland?
I think about the Jewish towns that look
With crying eyes and bent over backs,
The houses stand huddled from fear,
The synagogues stand cradled like in a dream,
Who will take pity on them from afar?
Surely there will come brighter days.
The rabbi next to the Holy Ark is in pain and in silence,
Surely Messiah will come.
Hitler will disappear with the swastika flags,
And will only be remembered with curses.
Jews in exile hiding out in princes,
Yet soon – the adversary with poisonous bullets.
How can I forget my brothers in Poland?
I now think about Poland and Hitler's country,
And my heart is aflame with a burning hatred,

Why, G-d, did you curse them alive,
My brothers, and gave them a new Scroll of Lamentations?
My Drohitchin passed before my eyes,
Which are filled with bitter tears,
In Drohitchin and other Polish towns,
A whip strikes the shoulders of brothers and sisters,
Every cruel dictator sings a song of prey.
I hear their prayer that death should come quickly,
And though they can be freed from shame and bondage.
And are covered silently in the grave,
How can I ever forget my brothers and sisters in Poland
through my tears and shudders?

Yoel Slonim, 1941. See pp. 57, 173

[Page 284]
Rabbi Dov Warshavsky*

R. Hillel Zeitlin
May G-d Avenge His Blood!

The martyr, R. Hillel Zeitlin, May G-d avenge his blood! (left), and Rabbi Yehoshua Shpetman of London, a friend who greatly respected R. Hillel and his family over the years. 1937 in Warsaw, see pp. 137-138.

R. Hillel Zeitlin was considered by everyone to be a mystic, and he certainly was. However, he was also a rational person. He was a visionary and a rebel, a deep thinker and a fighter, a conservative and a revolutionary, a builder and a destroyer, but above all, he was an openhearted, sincere, and honest Jew.

R. Hillel Zeitlin was considered a mystery by many and shone like a star on a dark night. However, not everyone could or wanted to take the effort to look at him in the eyes to be able to benefit from his light.

R. Hillel Zeitlin was a truth seeker and demanded justice. He sought truth and demanded justice from others and from himself. Zeitlin built buildings and destroyed them. He built organization and groups (*Bnai Levi, Bnai Yavneh, Bnai Hechala, 300 Individuals, All Israel*, but as soon as he felt that his colleagues were after their own interests, he threw away his buildings with the stroke of a pen.

R. Hillel Zeitlin always remained at home. He never traveled anywhere. Therefore, people would come to visit him at his home, where the doors were always open. Everyone came to him to ask a painful question, to ask for advice or assistance on some issue. They came to him when there was a rabbinical dispute in town, a dispute about kosher ritual slaughter, an issue relating to obtaining certificates for immigrants to Palestine or some ordinary personal problem. To whom would they turn if not to Zeitlin? He was visited by a provincial rabbi, a yeshiva student, a writer, a poet. Everyone came to meet R. Hillel Zeitlin and discuss things. His home at 60 Shliska Street was a meeting place for scholars. R. Hillel was undoubtedly the intellectual leader and rabbi of the Jewish people, and especially of the Jews in Poland, where he lived and worked for many years. Zeitlin was possibly the best-read writer, whose words penetrated every Jewish city and town in Poland.

Many considered Zeitlin to be someone who had returned to Jewish observance, but you can't say that he "became a penitent." R. Hillel Zeitlin was a penitent his entire life. He wasn't one those who had suddenly donned a Chassidic coat and become a religious person on the outside when he felt it was expedient for business. R. Hillel Zeitlin was a penitent his whole life and was never far away from a book. He was a very observant Jew who feared G-d and whose religious life was internalized in his immediate environment. In addition to observing all tangible commandments, he also observed the many prohibitions against lying, cheating, and exploiting, which are not always observed by religious Jews. Whenever I would visit R. Hillel Zeitlin at home (at 60 Shliska Street) in the morning or evening, I could hear his careful recitation of his prayers as I stood at the doorstep. He was like a scribe writing a Torah scroll. I frequently found R. Hillel, still wearing his tefillin (phylacteries) and tallith (prayer shawl), deeply engrossed in a book. He would go to his large library and take a book, continuing his reading for a full half a day. R. Hillel never allowed the words of Torah to escape his lips until the very end, and he completed study of the Talmud several times. From his earliest years, he was intensely knowledgeable about Jewish mysticism (kabbalah), and never stopped studying the ancient text called *The Zohar* (Book of Splendor).

[Page 285]

Today it is rare to find a penitent as profound as R. Hillel Zeitlin. R. Hillel never made any business out of his religiosity. The Agudath Israel, the Mizrachi, and other religious parties used to try to get him to join their movements, but R. Hillel rejected all their attempts. He was highly non-partisan and disliked back-room dealings and political machinations; he battled the parties' opportunism.

Even though R. Hillel was a mystic who aspired to reach the highest heavens, he was a person with both feet on the ground. He saw everything; his ears were always perked up; and he picked up even the smallest rustle in Jewish life. As a writer, he monitored the pulse of Jewish community life, and he reacted with his entire being against any misdeed or injustice committed by the strong against the weak. He never bowed before anyone and never pandered to anyone. He hated flattery as much as a Jew hates non-kosher meat.

R. Hillel Zeitlin said what he meant and meant what he said. He never showed favoritism. He stood like a tall oak tree (because of his height, wide shoulders and long beard and hair) planted deeply in the earth. No storm wind could move him from his place. He was a like a rock on the beach that remains unmoved by a wave, and there were many waves.

In his older years, R. Hillel Zeitlin didn't sing his songs in prose as he had in his youth and didn't write any kabbalistic meditations. He merely roared like a wounded lion, and he wrote with blood rather than ink as he poured his heart onto paper.

R. Hillel Zeitin the visionary, had seen the danger facing the Jewish People years earlier, and he yelled with all his bitterness, "Jews, save yourselves! Why do the Jewish leaders stay silent? Jews, get out of Europe!" He was the Jeremiah of our generation, and hurled the bitter truth in the faces of the Jewish party leaders, who were frequently more interested in their own party interests than in the good of the Jewish People.

There was no shortage of reasons why he couldn't speak directly to the Jewish masses in the newspapers he worked for, and Zeitlin published his won publications, brochures, newsletters and books (such as *Speak to the Nations; Silence and Voice; Librarian of Individuals; The Word; My Word; What should the Jewish People do in the pre-Messianic Times? The Speech of Prophet Jeremiah, son of Amotz, What He Would Have Said Today;* and *Alef)* in which he thundered and sought to awaken the Jewish people from their apathy. Zeitlin called meetings for this purpose where he would pronounce his dire warnings.

I can still see the picture of R. Hillel at a large gathering of his followers called *All Israel* on Zamenhoff Street in 1937. I was one of the organizers of the speakers who came to the meeting]. R. Hillel was so involved in the situation that he barely had any strength to cry out, "Jews, save yourselves!" and fell back onto his chair.

R. Hillel followed his own difficult and hard path, but he did so boldly and confidently together with his Jewish brethren right to the very end. It was a path of sanctification of G-d's name and bravery, of holiness and eternity. R. Hillel certainly had the choice and means to save himself, but he remained – like Jeremiah the Prophet who suffered self-inflicted punishment, dedication and reproof. But when the people went into exile, the prophet helped to bear the burden of that exile.

R. Hillel Zeitlin called on Jews to save themselves, and remained alone – that was how he was. A person like R. Hillel never abandons his role. He saw and felt the approaching danger and warned his brothers, who didn't listen. Zeitlin followed the same ancient and modern road of his brethren: the path of martyrdom, of self-sacrifice by sanctifying the name of G-d.

R. Hillel Zeitlin perished at the hands of the German murderers at the transport location in the Warsaw ghetto on the way to Treblinka on the eve of Rosh Hashanah, 1942. It is said that he traveled this last journey covered in his tallith and tefillin, holding a copy of the *Zohar* under his arm on his way to eternity. His wife Esther perished in a prior accursed *aktsia* of the Germans. May G-d avenge their blood!

They had two sons and one daughter: Aharon Zeitlin, a famous poet, writer and playwright, was born in February 1939. He visited New York (on the occasion of the performance of one of his plays), and remained there, thereby surviving the German hordes (Aharon today is one of the leading contributors to the Yiddish newspaper *Tog-Morgen Journal*). Aharon's wife, Tolia – Toiba Leah (Perlmutter) – and son Zvi-Dov (Hersh-Ber) died in Treblinka in 1943. May G-d avenge their blood! Elchanan Zeitlin, a famous writer, journalist and editor of *Unzer* (Our*) Express* died in the typhus epidemic in the Warsaw Ghetto on September 4, 1942 and was buried in the Gensher cemetery. Elchanan's wife, Renya (a sister of Polish parliament member Kirshbaum), perished. May G-d avenge her blood! Elchanan's only son, David, a very talented painter, participated in the Warsaw ghetto uprising, and he was later taken away with other Jews to various camps and finally to the Buzhin camp. David spent 13 months there in slave labor and three months after Germany's defeat, when the Russian arrived. David died from tuberculosis and was buried in the village of Gauting, Germany. May G-d avenge his blood! Rivka Hocherman, the only daughter, died in December 1938 in Warsaw. Her husband Nachum, who had a PhD in Philosophy, and their son Avrahamele (five years old), perished in the Warsaw ghetto. May G-d avenge their blood!

[Page 286]

After the war, Aharon Zeitlin set up gravestones on the graves of his brother Elchanan (in the Warsaw cemetery) and his nephew, David (in Germany).

R. Hillel Zeitlin, essayist, poet and thinker, was born in June 1871 in the Lubavitch Chassidic town of Korma (Mohilev gubernia) to his parents R. Aharon Eliezer and Cherna Bracha. He studied in yeshivas and under the Retchitz Rebbe (a grandson of the third Lubavitcher rebbe known as the *Zemach Zedek*), and he was influenced intellectually by Lubavitch Chassidic ideas. He was famous for his rare memory and dedication to study. He studied Talmud, rabbinical law, Chassidism, ethical teachings, homiletics, philosophical inquiry and kabbalah – whatever he could get his hands on. While a young person, he became renowned as a genius and expert in Torah knowledge. At 16 (his father had become impoverished), R. Hillel became a religious teacher in a village and suffered deprivation. He then became drawn to the Haskalah movement. He studied languages on his own and studied world literature. In 1896, he began writing his philosophical work, *Good and Evil.*

After he married Esther Kunin (a daughter of R. Avraham and Faige Traina of Uvaravitch, Gomel district) in 1897, Zeitlin began teaching Hebrew at Ratner's gymnasia high school in Gomel. In 1898, he published *Good and Evil* in a series in *Hashiloach* (The Dispatch), the publication of the writer Ahad Ha'am. Zeitlin briefly became involved in teaching in Roslavl and Kiev (1904). In 1905, he moved to Vilna and wrote in the Hebrew publication, *Hazman* (Time). In 1906 he first started to publish in Yiddish in the publication *Dos Yiddishe Folk* (The Jewish People).

In 1907, Zeitlin was asked by S. Yatzkan to serve as editor of *Dos Yiddishe Vachenblatt* (The Jewish Weekly) and also wrote for Yatzkan's *Heint* (Today). Zeitlin's "Letters to Youth" were highly acclaimed, and when *Moment* (1911) was founded he became one of its main contributors until he perished. May G-d avenge his blood!

FIRST LETTER ABOUT THE DESTRUCTION
The Forverts, July 19, 1945

Rabbi Shimon Tarasov of the Kobrin synagogue received a letter from his brother-in-law, Alter Mazursky, who is now in Siberia. The brother-in-law received the letter from Avraham Tcheromcher of Drohitchin, who describes the destruction of the town. The letter is as follows:

"My dearest friend Alter Mazursky! All nine of us Jews located currently in Drohitchin are healthy, thank G-d. May G-d allow us to hear from you. I don't know where to start. There is darkness and bitterness everywhere, and there are no Jews around. The German thieves cruelly murdered people. As soon as they arrived in Drohitchin, they shave off the beards of nine men: Shachna the Synagogue Custodian, Yisrael the Miller and other elderly Jews. Three days later a decree was issued that Jews were to wear a patch on their front and back. They were two large yellow patches.

Two weeks after they arrived, they divided all the Jews into two groups. One group were identified as "A" and the other "B." Group A couldn't enter the Group B ghetto, and Group B couldn't enter the Group A ghetto. If someone did go in, he would be immediately shot on the spot. Group A was called workers, and Group B was non-workers.

You had to turn the world upside down to be made part of Group A, and you needed connections. Your son, Shabsel, was happy to be part of Group A. They did hard work, and so did Shabsel. It was chaos and destruction. Thereafter, another decree was issued, saying that no Jew could walk on the sidewalk. All Jews, young and old, would have to walk on the street. Then came a decree specifying that the Group B ghetto would also be taken to work. On the Sabbath evening after the Ninth of Av, the Germans surrounded the town, grabbed 1700 men, and took them out to the Bereza Forest, where they dug trenches and got thrown in to the trenches alive, and then died horrible deaths. I escaped naked from a trench. Everyone was told to undress. I was unable to see how people were thrown alive into the trench. The Germans shot at me 12 times and missed.

There are many things to write about what the killers did to the Jews, how many dozens of Jews were shot on the street every day. A doctor, the female dentist, Zeidel the bathhouse attendant, and others poisoned themselves. Stay well everybody."

Avraham Adler of Tcheramcha

[*Page 287*]

Shmuel Eppelbaum

CHORBAN DROHITCHIN
(DESTRUCTION OF DROHITCHIN)
By Shmuel Eppelbaum (Israel)[*]

1.
People Were Warned. Why Didn't They Flee?

Sunday, June 22, 1941. The Soviet-German War had begun, and on Wednesday, June 25, Drohitchin was already occupied by the Germans, and Jews knew that Nazi rule meant extermination! They also figured that in the event of a war, Drohitchin, which was located only 105 kilometers from Brest-Litovsk (the border city between Soviet Russia and Germany), would possibly go back and forth, and eventually fall into the hands of the Germans. Yet almost no one fled. They waited for the tragedy. Why? Was it because no one believed there would be a war? No, we were sure that war would break out any minute following the occupation by Germany in April 1941.

Jews in Drohitchin saw unmistakable signs that the Soviets were preparing for war. The community Communist leaders were extremely nervous, and openly stated that the pause won through the Molotov-Ribbentrop Agreement in 1939 was approaching its end. Conscription of students and employees had begun. Military construction began; airports and highways were being built, and the so-called "unsafe elements" (former businessmen and Zionist activists) were sent to far-flung areas of the Soviet Union. People listening to the radio heard alarming reports from London about German demands and threats against the Soviets, and the Soviet press denied the London reports almost on a daily basis. Jews, however, would say that whenever a report was called a lie, this was a sign that the report was true.

In addition to the aforementioned signs, the Jews of Drohitchin also received warnings to move further eastward to the old Polish-Soviet border area. Moshe, the son of Yonah Goldberg, the oldest bookkeeper in Drohitchin, and other young people who had been captured by the Germans during the German-Polish War of 1939 wrote their parents that something was going to happen, and that it was worth moving further into Old Russian areas.

Jews understood the signs and hints and then didn't move away. Only on June 22, when the war broke out as the Nazis captured Brisk and approached Kobrin, did people in Drohitchin start talking about retreating with the Soviet army. Only a few people fled – those who were specifically connected to the Soviet authorities and the NKVD (formerly the CHEKA and GEPEO). These included the teacher Yachas (born in Svislotch), the photographer Yisrael Schwartz (son of Moshe Schwartz), the chairman of the shoemakers' workshop, Rubinstein, the printer, Orliansky, and Ukrainetz, and finally the daughter of Yeshayahu the Tailor.

No one aside from the aforementioned individuals left Drohitchin. Ezriel Pomerantz, the shoemaker, and a few others contacted the military commissariat to request to be drafted into the army so they could fight the German murderers. Unfortunately, the officials were in a panic and couldn't respond to the request of the population. On Monday, the second day of the war, all Soviet offices were closed.

[Page 288]

All officials fled in confusion, and the Jewish population remained helpless and desperate.

The confused retreat of the Soviet army made the Jews of Drohitchin feel that there was no one to flee with and nowhere to go. They said that the Germans got to Minsk before Drohitchin, and no one believed that Soviet Russia was so weak. People felt that in the event of war, the Soviets would immediately hit back at Germany, which was already exhausted for a lengthy war against many countries. The fact that the Soviets retreated and didn't resist pushed the Jews into despair.

If Soviet Russia was so weak, people thought, then it was quite possible that a strike from German could bring down the Soviet regime and restore the Czarist system with its tradition of pogroms and "Fight the Jews! Save Russia!" The German authorities would certainly support this type of new revolution. The distrust of Soviet power to resist, the fear of the restoration of Czarism, and the fear of being a refugee in faraway unfamiliar Russia prevented most Jews in Drohitchin from fleeing with the Soviets.

2.
Germans Occupy Drohitchin, and the First Victims Die

On Wednesday morning June 25, a German tank and an advance intelligence team went through Drohitchin firing machine guns in all directions. In the evening, the Germans took over the town with only a couple of exchanges of fire with retreating Soviet forces.

Jews, who during the gun battles were lying on the floor next to shaking windows, prayed that the battle should last as long as possible and hoped that perhaps the Germans might be chased out of town. The Jews started worrying when the shooting stopped and they heard German voices saying, "Hans come here!" and heard the sounds of marching soldiers. The Angel of Death had arrived!

R. Moshe the ritual slaughterer and Devorah Prager and their children, Beiltsha, Chaya, and Berl. On the right is Nechama and Binyamin Moshe (left) Schub, children of R. Yossel David and Mariasha Schub, sister of Devorah. All perished. May G-d avenge their blood! See pp. 149-150.

From right: Chanya Berg, Isser Zlotnick, Eliyahu Michaels, Elazar Lev, Avraham Drucker, Leizer Warshavsky and others. 1932.

[Page 289]

The first Jewish victims fell by nightfall, even before the Germans were in full control. R. Yaakov Vermus (brother-in-law of Rabbi Eliyahu Velvel Altvarg) and his eldest son died on Wednesday night in a tragic error. A group of retreating Soviet soldiers shot them in their home as they greeted the German's advance team, calling out "Communists are kaput!" It was a Polish neighbor of Vermus named Malish who greeted the tank crew and welcomed them with milk.

The Jews of Drohitchin mourned the tragic deaths of the Vermuses, but they were happy to learn that the Soviet soldiers were reporting that they had been able to hold off the Germans at Biala Podolsk (a few dozen kilometers from Brisk), and that they would soon liquidate the remaining Germans units that were around town. The breaking out of gunfire disappointed everyone. Many were feeling that they had made a tragic error in remaining in Drohitchin. This unfortunate impression soon proved correct.

The next morning, June 26, the Germans proceeded to take hostages in the middle of the market in Drohitchin, as was done in all other occupied towns. These several dozen hostages would be shot in the event something happened to the arriving German soldiers. In the meantime, groups of Germans checked Jewish homes (Drohitchin was populated exclusively by Jews, and the Christians lived in the outer areas of Starosiela and Zaritshka). The Germans went around in twos or threes to visit Jewish homes asking whether the residents had weapons. They would open money boxes, closets, table-drawers and would seize money, watches, leather coats, clothes, wallets, soap, and anything else.

The hostages were freed that same day, and the house checks and systematic theft continued. Some of those doing the checks would ask if a person were Jewish. If a person responded in the affirmative, they would begin packing large bags and ordering the owners to take the captured property with them to their camps. On the way, they would console the Jews by telling them to relax, because in six weeks they would capture Moscow and establish a Jewish state in Siberia.

R. Yaakov and Meita Rosenstein and their daughters. From right: Rivka, Chaytsha, and Tila. All perished, may G-d avenge their blood!

At the end of June a few days after the occupation of Drohitchin, a local government authority was set up, with the former Polish notary Chaplinski as mayor. Most of the officials in the government were Russian, and they plotted against the Polish mayor and the local police, which was made up of Poles.

The competing sides: the Pole Chaplinski and the Russian Kreiditch, who had many Jewish acquaintances before the war. They would assure the Jews that all inconveniences would be done the right way, and Jews should have no fear about their Jewishness. The Poles would make statements about how the Russian population hated the Jews, and the Russians would make the same statement about the Poles.

In the meantime, at a mass meeting in the market square, Mayor Chaplinski declared that Jews were outside of the law, and that they had to have yellow stars of David on their homes and clothes so they would be recognized. The Jews living in the nearby villages were ordered to move to Drohitchin.

Jews from Motele and Khomsk were killed with axes and scythes on the orders of the local priest.

In the village of Vietla the Christians didn't wait for the order and killed the Jewish families who had been living there for years. Only a few Jews succeeded in escaping to Drohitchin. No legal action was taken against the killers because the Jews were outside of the law.

[Page 290]

At the beginning of July, the Gestapo arrived in Drohitchin and captured the barber, Khatislavsky, the shoemaker, Litman Dolinsky, Shifra Schwartzberg (daughter of Asher the bricklayer), and a couple of Jewish refugees from Vietla, and sent them off to Brona (an estate four kilometers behind town), tortured them for a few hours and then shot them. They had all been accused of communist activity and were killed in connection with the anti-communist operation that took place in the entire region. A few days all the Jews of Khomsk and Motele were brutally murdered, as were most of the men of Brisk, Pinsk, and Yanova.

It was believed that the men from Brisk and Pinsk had been taken away somewhere for forced labor, and people waited for months to hear something about them. The Germans began their massacres in Khomsk and Motele after they obtained money from those Jewish communities. The German murderers claimed that the Jewish communists in Russia and their leader, Litvinov, together with the Jewish millionaires in the United States and their servant, Roosevelt, were responsible for the war, so the Jews around the world should have to pay for the costs and suffering of the war.

In Khomsk and Motele the slaughter lasted several days. The local Christian population looked for Jews, pulled them out of their attics, cellars, gardens, forests and swamps – wherever they were in hiding. They killed them with knives, axes, scythes, and blunt instruments. The priest of Khomsk was the person who led the anti-Jewish operations.

The first details about the aforementioned massacres arrived in Drohitchin around the ninth of the month of Av, and a few days after the first Judenrat was elected in Drohitchin. The Jews in town were worried and feared for their lives, and the Drohitchin Judenrat went about its work.

Yonah and Rachel Goldberg and their children, from right: Elka, Moshe, Milcha, Feigele, and Eliyahu. Aside from Feigele everyone perished. May G-d avenge their blood! Rachel was the daughter of Eliyahu Liebkas Valevelsky. Yonah came from Kobrin and was the senior accountant at the People's Bank in Drohitchin. Feigele and her husband, Herman Grossman, and children live in New York. See p. 203.

3.
Jews Elect a Judenrat and Hope It Will Help

Although the German commander had shortly after the occupation told the Jews that they had no recourse to civil or human rights, the Jews agreeably accepted the order to elect a Jundenrat, a Jewish council. Moreover, many went around with the illusion that the Jewish administration and a Jewish police force would somehow find a way to soothe the wrath of the beast and guarantee the status of the Jews of Drohitchin. Khomsk and Motele were already destroyed, and the men of Pinsk and Brisk were taken away to parts unknown. All the Jews were expelled from Shershev and Heinevka. Many refugees arrived in Drohitchin and said that the Germans had killed many of them during the expulsion along the road of anguish, while the Jews of Drohitchin believed that their fate would be better.

What did Drohitchin hope for? Had the Germans treated the Drohitchin Jews better than others? Never! From the earliest days of the occupation, the Jews of

[Page 291]

Drohitchin were robbed of such elementary human rights such as educating their children in school, reading a newspaper, listening to the radio news, going to a public bath, walking on the sidewalk, and traveling from one place to the other. In the second week an order was issued for Jews to wear a yellow patch on their chests and shoulders so they could be identified from a distance. The authorities did everything possible to show the Jews of Drohitchin that there was nothing to hope for. Nevertheless, the Jews kept hoping and went to vote for a self-governing administrative council to serve the interests of the Jewish population. They couldn't imagine that the Judenrat would be run by the Germans to function as an instrument for the implementation of their extermination plans.

At the election assembly that was held at the large House of Study, pharmacist Moshe Steinberg, mechanic Baruch Kaplan (born in Vilna) and many others refused to join the Judenrat and asked that no one do so. On the other hand, many others believed that it was appropriate to get involved because in any event, the Jews were under German control, and it was better to be a member of the Judenrat than to be an ordinary Jew.

The following were elected to the first Judenrat: Litman Feldman (chairman), Yaakov Siderov (vice-chairman), Velvel Goldberg, Yitzchak Levinovitz, Menachem Kalenkovitch, and Yosef Kobrinsky. Later on the following were co-opted onto the Judenrat: Avraham Kravietz, Hershel Kolodny, Leibush Sliep, Khlavna Pisetsky, and Shalom Morgenthaler. Two Jewish doctors served as advisors to the Judenrat, and the following positions were part of the Judenrat administration: secretaries, emissaries, and bookkeepers. The elder appointed a Jewish police force, which worked with the Judenrat.

The first activity of the Judenrat was to collect the first monetary contributions imposed on the Jews of Drohitchin – 10,000 rubles and 2 kilos of gold. The decree required it to be produced within two hours, and in the event of a delay, all the Jews were to be executed. On the very day of the decree, refugees arrived in Drohitchin from Shereshov who told of their misfortune. The sad news and fear of their own fate had their effect, and the Jews brought to the Judenrat gold watches, rings, bracelets, and the amount of money demanded.

From then on, the Judenrat would collect twice and three times the required amount whenever a monetary contribution was required so that they would have a reserve in bad times. They would do the same thing for mobilizing workers to work in town, outside of town or even in the labor camps. The Judenrat would always call for more workers than they needed and have them in reserve. They would operate the same way with household possessions and forced labor as they would with money. This was a daily occurrence, and the Jews wanted Judenrat members, police, and their relatives to participate and not simply be satisfied with relying on others, often coercively. The privileges of the Judenrat members and their relatives angered everyone against them. People who had lost their property, possessions, furniture, and especially their health over the number of months couldn't forgive the Judenrat members and the police who kept getting rich following each forced contribution, and who got fatter after every time of trouble. Jewish policemen would get drunk, enjoy themselves, and do business with the gentile policemen.

Sarah Kaplan Pisetsky, born in Ruzhinoy, graduated from gymnasia high school in a midwifery institute in Slonim. She married Shlomo Pisetsky of Drohitchin, where she practiced as a midwife her entire life. Shlomo died in 1915, and Sarah perished in 1942. Their son Izzy survived.

R. Velvel Leibetchkas and Rachel Lev and grandchildren, may G-d avenge their blood! R. Velvel's home was always open to guests, and he was very generous with charity. There were always guests in his home.

[Page 292]

On the left is R. Avraham Simcha, son of Yisrael Perkovsky, born in 1861 in Telyaki, near Kobrin. He was the custodian of the New House of Study. On the right is his daughter Freidka, the wife of Tevel Zbar. May G-d avenge their blood!

The community quickly came to feel that the Judenrat members and the police were nothing but trouble for the community. Of the elected Judenrat members, five were honest men who sought to alleviate Jewish suffering as much as possible. Unfortunately, their abilities were inhibited by other members who argued with them and who wanted to take advantage of the situation for their personal benefit.

At the same time as the Judenrat was established, Menachem Averbuch organized an aid committee in Drohitchin for the refugees from Shereshov, Khomsk, and surrounding villages who arrived without any possessions or money. Averbuch came from Lemberg after the occupation. He had been in hiding when the Soviets had exiled former merchants to Siberia. He was very familiar with Jewish suffering, and when he came home he claimed that Jews should only be concerned with self-help and that the Jewish administration should merely create organized chaos by doctoring the record books so that the Germans would never know exactly how many Jews there were or where they lived. The self-help committee included Eliyahu Eisenstein, Rabbi Kalenkovitch, Rabbi Altvarg, and the rabbi of Shereshov; the ritual slaughterers Moshe Prager and Yosef David Schub; teachers Wolfson and Rock; doctors Schechter and Lampa, and others.

The community liked the committee very much. In addition to the aforementioned institutions Drohitchin had another active organization: the burial society led by Moshe Aharon Berg.

4.
The Jews of Drohitchin are Herded into Ghettos

People started talking about a ghetto for the Jewish community as soon as the Germans arrived. No one had any idea of how large the ghetto would be or how life would be like in the ghetto, but everyone felt that the ghetto was going to be the beginning of the end.

The ghetto became overcrowded, and over a period of months the Jews gradually got used to the harsh conditions and didn't notice how bad the conditions were. The ghetto decrees started by moving Jews away from the Sand (the name of the street leading to the New Cemetery where many Poles lived) and from parts of Edward Dunin Markevitch Street (the Khomsk alley).

This decree only affected a handful of Jewish families. However, there was significant crowding because at the same time a few hundred Jews from Shereshov and Kolonia (a Jewish village not far from Drohitchin) were brought to Drohitchin, where there were also Jewish refugees from Khomsk and surrounding villages. The destruction of Khomsk, the expulsion from Shereshov, Kolonia, and other villages expanded the Jewish population in Drohitchin, and from the beginning of the ghetto decrees, there were approximately 4,000 Jews in Drohitchin.

Jews became deprived of resources. Where only one family had lived previously, there were now at the outset of the decrees two or more. Money, possessions, and furniture were handed over as contributions rather quickly. Most of the homes were emptied of practically everything they contained, so people didn't feel the crowding so much. They complained more about the unceasing demand for contributions, and especially about the order not to come into contact with Christians. Drohitchin Christians who lived on Zartishka and Starosilia streets didn't care about the decrees, and they would bring their Jewish friends flour, butter, chickens, eggs, and other food in exchange for clothes and shoes that Jews were now giving away so the Germans wouldn't take them as contributions. German supervisors and Judenrat policemen would severely punish anyone involved in such transactions. As long as the ghetto wasn't closed off, the Jews were able to get many more items than allowed according to official regulations (100 grams of bread a day, without shortening or sugar).

On Passover 1942, a sweeping transfer of the Jews into two ghettos took place: Ghetto A was for the "useful Jews" (artisans), and Ghetto B was for the "useless Jews" (former shopkeepers, employees, bookkeepers, teachers). A couple of weeks prior to the transfer, there was intensive activity to obtain working certificates. In exchange for gold watches and other valuables, Sielpuk, a Christian from Simenovitch (a village not far from Drohitchin) and the chairman of the workers' workshop, the Judenrat, and an employment expert from Kobrin obtained certificates for Jews attesting that they were tailors, shoemakers, carpenters, thereby enabling them to remain in Ghetto A in the meantime. A poor shoemaker such as Naska didn't get a certificate, and remained in Ghetto B, and many long-standing artisans who were not accepted into the workshops were forced to eventually move to Ghetto B to join the worthless Jews, those ordered to participate in all types of forced labor.

The certificate business and the subsequent transfer of the population into various ghettos exhausted and agitated everyone. A Jew who was always an artisan and who had a house now located within the confines of Ghetto A obviously made every attempt to be part of a workshop, so he could remain at home. However, this was not always successful, and as stated earlier, many artisans were ordered to Ghetto B, where life would be very bitter. The transfers took a few days, and many people with Judenrat certificates exchanged homes in the hopes of speedy redemption so they could return home.

Consolation from news about Budiany and Vorozhilov: At that time, reports circulated about the destruction of the Jews in Rovno, Kovel and Slonim. Jews in Drohitchin consoled themselves with false reports that they disseminated, saying that the Germans were already encircled, and that Budiany was already in Baranovich, and Vorozhilov was already in Brisk, and liberation was just around the corner.

[Page 293]

Moshe Shmuel and Perl Warshavsky and their children

From right: Sheinka, Teibel, Shalom, Yankel, Yisrael and Meir.

Except for Yankel, all perished. May G-d avenge their blood! Moshe Shmuel, a son of Yaakov Hersh and Malka Warshavsky, was a good cantor with a fine voice and a good ear for music. He played the fiddle and sang, and was deeply involved in community work. See pp. 215, 246, and 308.

In the meantime, Ghetto A was surrounded with a fence two and a half meters high, and many young people in Ghetto B were taken to labor camps in Petrovich (on the road from Kobrin-Brisk). Aside from that camp, voluntary labor camps were set up around Drohitchin in Yozefin and Radestov. If the Judenrat and police ever caught people on the road from Petrovich, they would forcibly send him to the labor camp. They would frequently arrest and torture relatives of a particular individual who went into hiding rather than go to work in the labor camp. This would easily solicit workers for Yozefin and Radestov.

[Page 294]

There were Jews in Ghetto A who would frequently approach Yoshka Volinetz, the organizer of the Radestov camp, to request being assigned to the camp because they preferred being there than in their own homes in Ghetto A.

In the aforementioned two camps, the Jews didn't work very hard in lumber work, and every week they would get food packages from Drohitchin. Jews didn't live so badly in Ghetto A. The chairman of the workshops, Sielpuk, made sure his workers didn't go hungry and smuggled in food in lumber wagons. Other Christians who did all types of work in the workshops also smuggled in food products.

Ghetto B was not fenced in and still had a greater possibility to obtain food from Starosilia Christians. Drohitchin Jews, therefore, didn't starve in either ghetto, though in Ghetto B people complained about the hard forced labor at the Nagoria station in Lipnik, and especially about the uncertain future of Ghetto B. The head of the Judenrat and the Jewish police would say that they would do everything possible to save Ghetto A. As far as Ghetto B was concerned, they said that it was already sentenced, and it was impossible to save it. At that time, the Jews in Drohitchin still didn't know what was meant by Ghetto B being sentenced, but they all feared being sent away to Petrovich or some other worse camp further away. They could never imagine that if they were "sentenced" to work in a "bad camp," they were sentenced to death.

So this was the way life was for days and weeks of forced labor in and around town. Days and weeks of torture, fear, insecurity and unlimited worry, until the day of July 25, 1942 arrived.

From right: Yisrael Schmid, Mordechai Sapir, A Kalenkovitch, Berl Goldberg, Baruch Schwartz, Naomi Wasserman, Hershel Steinberg, Zechariah Sapozhnik, Beila Milner, and others.

The Drohitchin market, where the Germans gather everyone from Ghetto B together for the Death March to Brona Gora

[Page 295]

5.
Slaughter of Ghetto B; 1,700 Jews Perished

Something was going on the Sabbath in Ghetto A. Menachem Averbuch and a few other members of the Aid Committee met with the Judenrat. The yelling could be heard in Ghetto B, but no one knew what they were arguing about. In the evening, the faint noise of German cars coming into town could be heard in Ghetto B and badly worried the people there. At 11 pm, the Jewish police announced throughout Ghetto B that everyone had to proceed to the town market, though no one knew what was going to happen an hour later. Some, however, had bad premonitions, and instead of going out to the market, they tried to escape through fields behind town and get into the forest. However, they found that all paths out had Ukrainian and Polish police assistants together with Jewish policemen pushing everyone out of the houses, attics and cellars toward the city market, under the watch of German police on horseback. Then they removed boots off of the feet of the Jews, their coats, and any valuables the women were carrying, and even struck a few over the head with the butts of their guns. The Jews then realized what was happening to them, and they started to mournfully recite, "Hear O Israel" (Shma Yisrael) and "G-d, have pity!"

The *aktsia* lasted for seven hours. The Jewish police zealously pulled people out of hiding, and took them to the market area, from where they were herded to the train station. Along the way, Chaim Ber Altvarg, the watchmaker, was killed, as were Pesach Lev the tailor, and a few others. At the end of the *aktsia,* the Germans found that approximately 100 men of the "worthless Jews" whose names appeared on the Judenrat list were missing, so as punishment, they took a few hundred Jews from Ghetto A, the Jewish police and the Judenrat. On Sunday, all of them, 1,700 people, were taken by train to Brona Gora (17 kilometers from Kartuz-Bereza) and put into open ditches, where they were all blown up.

The majority of Jews from Antapole and Kobrin were killed at the same place together with Drohitchin Ghetto B. Of the Judenrat, only three people remained alive during that *aktsia.* Two were in hiding, and they perished later.

My G-d, whoever heard the awesome recitation of "Hear O Israel" from the expelled people of Ghetto B and saw and experienced what I saw and experienced would never forget it and never know any peace. The most fiendish thing about it all was how Jews led other Jews to be sacrificed. A Jewish policeman and a lawyer led their own parents to the extermination spot. Another dragged Jews from the attics right to their deaths, and other such events took place regularly.

R. Moshe Mendel and Golda Hinda Milner. Golda Hinda, a daughter of R. Nisan of Khomsk, died on January 7, 1918. R. Moshe Mendel, son of R. Tordos Leib and descended from Rabbi Dovidel Yaffe, perished. The Milners had six children: Eidel-Chaya, Esther-Necha (perished), Sofia (California), Tordos-Leib, Nisan, and Aharon Yitzchak (in Chicago). See pp. 117 and 190.

Note: This frightening and horrible massacre of our parents and siblings at the hands of the German murderers actually took place on Av 12, 5702/July 26, 1942, but we have the custom to observe the yahrzeit (death anniversary) on the 11th of Av, which that year was the Sabbath following the fast day of the Ninth of Av, as the time when those hapless Jews were taken to the slaughter. May G-d avenge their blood! Editor

[Page 296]

6.
The Crying for the Dead Split Open the Heavens

The grief in Drohitchin the day after the *aktsia* was enormous, even though most of the residents at first did not know was happened to the people taken away to Brona Gora, where some believed there was a labor camp. Everyone grieved about the destruction that touched almost everyone. The men and women waited by the gates of the ghetto for their Aryan escorts to take them to work (No one would dare walk the streets without an escort.). They sobbed loudly and tore out their hair. Some cried over their friends and distant relatives, and others lamented about their parents or under-age children who were taken together with Ghetto B.

On Saturday night July 25, 1942, I experienced the worst misfortune of my life when I lost my mother, sister, many friends and students during that *aktsia.* I escaped from the market under a hail of bullets and automatic weapons fire, and hid out in the Rovno Forest for a few days until I was captured and sent to the Radostov camp. In subsequent years, I went through many more awful experiences. I was shot a few times, left for dead (once in eastern Prussia), and from 1942 to 1945, I wasn't alive or dead. The gruesome events of the recent past are unbelievable today, and even those who lived through them can no longer conceive of how such things could have happened, and how they could have survived.

The *aktsia* against Ghetto B lasted until 7 am. Those who were found hiding until then were shot. These included the teacher, Moshe Bezdzhesky, who had been hiding in a bean garden, and Zalman Kobrin, the ritual slaughterer from Kolonia, who was hiding in a garden and who tried to escape afterwards. Those who were found in hiding after 7 o'clock were allowed to go to Ghetto A and "settle down" there. These included Sender Shapiro the religious teacher and his family, who were found on Sunday in a cellar and transferred to Ghetto A, as well as myself, who was found a few days after the *aktsia* in a weak state in the Rovno Forest and transferred to Ghetto A.

In the meantime, the Judenrat and police got reorganized. The Judenrat got a vice-chairman, Bontsha Volovelsky (son of Chaika the pharmacist). Baruch Wolf of Lechevitch ran the police. It was proposed that I become a member of the new Judenrat and remain in town in my parents' home, or go to work in the Radostov camp. I chose the latter. In the meantime, the houses of Ghetto B were taken over by Christians in Drohitchin and the surrounding area. The new Judenrate in various warehouses collected the furniture and possessions belonging to the expelled Jews

The Moriah School of Drohitchin, Grade 1

From left, Moshe Bezdzhesky, Levi Feldman, director of the school, H. B. Wolfson, and other teachers. See on this page regarding the death of Bezdzhesky. May G-d avenge his blood!

[Page 297]

During the first few days after the tragedy, the Jews in Drohitchin hoped that following the great bloodshed the remaining Jews would be able to remain undisturbed for a longer period of time. However, their hopes were soon dashed, and the first destruction was just the beginning, and it was followed by subsequent massacres.

7.

Germans Hang Three Jewish Young Men

A few days after the destruction of Ghetto B, the young men of Drohitchin who had been working in the Petrovich camp (between Kobrin and Brisk) started escaping from the camp. Some made their way back to town through the forests and the Radostov camp, hoping to find out the fate of their parents and friends in Ghetto B. Others looked to join the partisan groups that were operating in the forests at that time.

Shalom Zavelovsky, a son of storekeeper Yehoshua Zavelovsky, came to Drohitchin from the Petrovich camp, At the same time, a few workers from Radostov came back to Drohitchin with a permit from the camp administration. Among these were the Tennenbaum brothers, sons of Sarah Chana Tennenbaum of the Sand, who said that they had to take revenge against the Judenrat for having sent away their mother. The Germans found out about this and ordered the Judenrat to hang the young men. Gallows were set up near the Old House of Study, and the Jewish police hanged the Jewish "rebels," Zavelovsky and the Tennenbaum brothers.

The executions had a terrible effect on the Jews in town and in nearby areas who now realized that their lives were cheap, not only to the Germans, but to the Jewish police and Judenrat as well. Ukrainian police in Drohitchin on the way to Radostov captured a few days after the executions eight Petrovich refugees. Yisrael Rimland, a grandson of the *Thundering Woman* (Dunertsch) and Abba Adelsky, son of the Grodno preacher, attacked the police with knives and made an uprising. They were shot on the spot. The other six were brought to Radostov, where they worked for one day together with the other Jews from Drohitchin, Vietla and Kolonia. The next morning they were separated and shot.

8.
A "Good German" Shoots a Jewish Girl

R. Yisrael and Esther-Rachel Kravetz and their children.

Shortly after the tragedy of the Petrovich refugees, a Jewish girl received some valuable items from her relatives in town that she hid away, hoping that upon liberation, she could use it to get themselves on their feet.

[Page 298]

Since the "redemption" was still far away, and everyone realized that they would need another redemption to get to that redemption, they were happy to fill the commander's "requests." They frequently gave him gifts of gold rings, watches, and anything else the owned, hoping that because of this the "friend of the Jews," Martin, would protect the lives of the camp workers just like he had supposedly done for Jews elsewhere.

9.
The Thief Bodanka and Local Russian Gentiles Help the Jews

In the meantime, the situation in Drohitchin worsened by the day. At the wink of the German authorities, the Christian population of Drohitchin and nearby communities made a request to have Drohitchin made *Judenrein* (free of Jews) by expelling the Jews from town.

Non-Jews in Drohitchin got along well with the Jewish community. In the first days of the German occupation, the Russian priest in town frequently intervened with the military administration on behalf of the Jews, and especially on behalf of Rabbi Isaac Kalenkovich. Once, when the Gestapo dragged the rabbi out of bed and threw him in their taxi to drive him out of town where they were going to shoot him, the priest ran out to appeal for the rabbi, thereby saving his life.

The Russian mayors, Kreiditch, and Borisiuk, who took over after the Polish mayor, Chaplinski, the Strapki family and others, would provide financial assistance (which many of the members of the Judenrat and the Jewish police wouldn't do) to help the Jews pay various contributions.

The local thief, Bodanka of Zaritchka, warned the gentiles: "Whoever touches a Jew will have to face me!" After the liberation, Bondanka told the Soviet NKVD that his sister handed Jews over to the Germans, thereby causing their deaths. The NKVD sent his sister to Siberia and gave Bodanka her property, though he refused to take it. A few days before the destruction of Ghetto A, Bodanka warned the Jews that death was imminent and they should flee.

In the wave of hatred toward Jews, Drohitchin was a happy little island where hatred didn't spread. Despite all the prohibitions, gentiles in Drohitchin would bring food products into the ghetto, and no Jews went hungry until the final Destruction.

Germans Shoot 16 Jews: an Omen of the Final Destruction

At the behest of the German authorities, announcements suddenly appeared on the streets of this same island of happiness stating that the town was to soon become empty of Jews, and that the population looked forward to becoming liberated of "Jewish filth." These announcements were like a death sentence for the Jewish community. Jews felt that an *aktsia* was going to take place. People thought it would be the same as what happened in Ghetto B, and that it would be limited, lasting for just a few hours, with those in hiding being saved. The entire community spent entire nights toiling away to build hideouts under floors, in attics, and behind double walls. There were a few Germans in Drohitchin who were responsible for the extermination *aktsias,* and the Judenrat paid them off enough to stop them from carrying out their vicious intentions.

Yaakov, Feitsha, and Berele Vichnis. All perished. May G-d avenge their blood!

[*Page 299*]

The terrorists liked receiving all types of gifts but did their work. One early morning they gathered together all the best workers and specialists from the workshops in Ghetto A, and sent them off to Kobrin to be together with the "worthy" Jews of the entire area.

This portended that those remaining behind were worth less, and, therefore, their lives were insecure. Just like the Jews from Ghetto B only a few months earlier had been jealous of their "lucky" friends in Ghetto A, those remaining behind were envious of those who were taken to Kobrin. Ghetto A – the island of work and life – now felt that just like Ghetto B it was now sentenced to death. The hope of surviving the troubled period and living to see the Redemption was now only with those who were taken to Kobrin. That's why everyone else was so envious.

The announcement of "Jew-free Drohitchin" and the transfer of the specialists to Kobrin worried all the Jews of Kobrin, and no one slept at night. They just melted from fear and worry. The only one who had less to worry about for their future was Bontsha Volovelsky, the vice-chairman of the Judenrat. He got along very well with the Germans involved in the *aktsias*, and he used to say, "If any Drohitchin Jew survives the war, it will be me."

It turned out that he was the first victim of the final *aktsia* in Drohitchin. In the Judenrat building, a German who knew him well shot him after a friendly discussion. On the same day, which was after Rosh Hashanah in 1942, the Germans shot another group of people in Ghetto A, confiscated their possessions, and ordered the Judenrat to sign an announcement about the fact that Bontsha Volovelsky and 15 other Jews died from heart failure. The chairman of the Judenrat had to sign that announcement.

Meir Leib and Dobka Gottlieb and their children

From right: Zvia, Berel, Mordechai, Shepsel, Chaya-Ita and others. They all perished except for Berel. May G-d avenge their blood! Meir Leib was considered a good professional and taken to Kobrin by the Germans. He was in a camp, and the German beasts murdered him there with many other Jews. Dobka was a sister of Yehudit Hoffman of Chicago.

Hertzka, Hoddes, and Sarah Buff; Esther Yehudit Gratch. Standing are: Shimon and Michele Buff and another. All died except for Gratch. May G-d avenge their blood!

[*Page 300*]

10.

Last Destruction of DrohitchinMassacre of Ghetto A – 3,000 Jews perished

Shortly after the death of the sixteen on October 15, 1942, Ukrainian police surrounded by Ukrainian police, and the entire community of Ghetto A were sent off to the train station not far from the old cemetery and shot. For several days thereafter, they searched for all Jews who were in hiding, and took them to the transport location near the train station. Old Gedaliah Grossman, who in fact regained his health shortly before the *aktsia* after having been very ill for a long time, was staying in a cellar together with his daughter-in-law Dora and granddaughter Bluma, the country doctor Aharon

Lasovsky and Alter Friedenberg (David Mordechai's [sic] Warshavsky's son-in-law). They were all taken away to the transport location and shot. Tuvia Zbar, who had been in hiding in a forest, came alone back to town and raised his hands to the police, asking them to shoot him. His request was fulfilled. In the meantime the Germans let Doctors Lampel and Schechter remain alive so they could work in the hospital. However, they rejected the Germans' mercy and committed suicide.

The Grossmans – R. Gedaliah (father), Zelig (right) and Bluma the grandchild perished. May G-d avenge their blood! Yirmiyahu (left) and Chaim Leib survived.

11.

Germans Incite Gentiles to Kill the Fleeing Jews

The local gentiles then received an order to bring any Jew they found to the police. They would receive 500 Ukrainian karbovantsys (50 German reichsmarks), a bottle of vodka, and a package of tobacco. By contrast, anyone hiding a Jew would be shot. They gentiles zealously carried out the order, and they would turn over poor Jews to the police, while they would kill wealthy Jews and rob them. Jews had nowhere to hide; everyone was mobilized against them, and death awaited them everywhere. No one recognized a Jew in his time of trouble.

Aharon Lasovsky and Alter Friedenberg, may G-d avenge their blood!

Benzion Bezdzhezesky, a young community leader, fled to his father's gentile friend in the village of Poyasi during the *aktsia*. They tied him up and brought him to the police, who shot him. The Bilinka "good gentile friends" did the same thing to Rivka Sertchuk (wife of Fishel the butcher) and many others. They were hunted like wild animals and couldn't find shelter or help anywhere. Partisan groups, who at that time were staying in the forest around Drohitchin, were mostly Ukrainian nationalists or ordinary bandits who would kill any Jew they met. At that time the partisan group of Dzhenkovsky operated around Khomsk. Those bandits systematically killed any Jews they got their hands on, hoping to erase any trace of the massacres the bandits had committed in Khomsk before fleeing to the forest presumably out of fear of revenge, and becoming partisans.

[*Page 301*]

At the beginning of 1943 the select "worthwhile Jews" of the region living in Kobrin, were killed. These included many people from Drohitchin.

From right: Y. Warshavsky, Sam Feldman, Sheinka Warshavsky-Baum, and Reuven
Warshavsky. The last two perished. May G-d avenge their blood! The photo was taken in
1932 on the Sand Street

Mordechai Milner, May G-d avenge his blood!

12.

Germans Kill the Rest of the Jews in Radostov

After the destruction of Ghetto A the camp in Radostov lasted for another three weeks. The camp commander, Martin Jefreiter, the so-called friend of the Jews, visited the camp workers a day after the destruction of the ghetto, handed out cigars, and consoled the Jews. He said that a million Jews worked for "us" in the camps, were important manpower, and that they would not let them be turned over to the German forces or Gestapo.

[*Page 302*]

The camp workers hardly believed these promises, and from day to day, Ukrainian workers arrived at the camp; the Jews realized that they were already "surplus workers" and that the work could already be performed without them. Everyone understood that they would be killed.

At that time, there was a department of German air force personnel camped out in Radostov. Jewish girls worked in the department as cooks and washerwomen. The soldiers confided to them that their department was being assigned for killing Jews. However, they didn't use the department, claiming that extermination work was not their area of responsibility but was to be done by the Special Department (SD) or the Gestapo. In addition, the Jews were needed for various types of work. After our departure the soldiers said that the Gestapo would surely arrive to kill us, so we should escape into the forest on time.

It was very easy to escape into the forest from Gorovitsa, the work site of the Drohitchin lumber workers in Radostov. Tthese people would tie together logs in rafts, sending them down river to distance locations. All you had to do was jump off of beams right into the forest. Jews, therefore, believed that even at the last moment, when the shooting would start, they could flee. Until a certain point, people didn't want to leave the camp, their home, and couldn't imagine living like hobos. Everyone was scared of the forest and the approaching winter.

It was understood that when the *aktsia* took place, all the gentiles in the area would be mobilized to hunt down the escapees, and it would be very hard for people who were unprepared to live in the forest to hide out there and survive. In addition, there were a few sick Jews in the camp: Kadish Greenstein, and the storekeeper, Yaakov Gorodetsky, and his wife, who could under no circumstances escape and who warned the others to wait until the last moment, since in the event that someone managed to escape, everyone else would be severely punished.

Fear of the forest and concern for the ill who could not escape and the hope that it wouldn't be too late to get to the forest prevented people from leaving. Everyone expected misfortune, and since the workers knew about the destruction of Ghetto A, the workers stopped sleeping at night. They spread around on the floors of the couple of buildings where they spent the night, and in the meantime, kept their ears perked up for the slightest sound outside, so they would be ready to escape to the unknown forest.

From right: Meir M. Hausman, Menachem Steinberg, Peretz Goldman, Henya Valevelsky, Zvi Levak, Asher Meshchanin, Mordechai Gottlieb. Standing from left, Berl Gottlieb and Moshe Goldberg. The Betar Organization.

Leiba and Liba Feldman. May G-d avenge their blood!

There were a few former village Jews in the camp – Leib Feldman (son of Meir Yudel Feldman), Avraham Adler (from Tcheromcha), Zalman Orliansky (from Lechevitch), and Jews from the village Vietla. In the evening, they visited their gentile acquaintances and negotiated with them about hiding out with them in the event things turned for the worse.

Misfortune struck on the morning of November 4, 1942. When the workers were leaving for work, they noticed Germans approaching them in cars. The Germans opened machinegun and automatic weapons fire on the workers, and yelled, "Stop, damn Jews!" Leib Feldman and Jews from Vietla and Dvoshka Spevak were the first casualties. Everyone started running without even knowing where he or she was going.

Of the 120 workers in Radostov, 40 managed to escape. The majority of them, however, shortly thereafter fell into the hands of gentiles and perished. Some died from the cold, hunger, and exhaustion during the winter of 1942-43 in their hiding places. Only 15 lived through the first winter in the forest in various hiding places, without even knowing about one another.

[Page 303]

13.
The Russian Army Saves the Jews in the Forest

In the spring of 1943, the lucky survivors found each other in the forest in Ozona, which was under the control of the Soviet partisans (near the village of Bilinka) and lived there in civilian camps (bunkers) until the beginning of 1944. In the beginning of 1944, with the approach of the battlefront, the partisans left for the "other side of the border" to meet the Soviet army. The Drohitchin Jews in the forest followed the partisans, and the elderly, the women, and children stopped in the liberated towns near Rovno. The younger people were drafted into the Soviet army, and they fought in their ranks, liberating towns and countries. They also took revenge on the German murderers while saving their own lives and not silencing their own suffering and wrath.

Almost all of the survivors visited Drohitchin after it was liberated, and absorbed renewed suffering and anger. The descendants of wicked Esau were sitting in the tents of his brother, Jacob, were dressing up in Jewish clothing, and burning the pages of Jewish books. The streets of Drohitchin were paved with Jewish gravestones from both the old and new cemeteries. Swine on four and two legs were rummaging through Jewish property.

It was awfully difficult for me to see all this. People seeking revenge and the liberator of Drohitchin were broken hearted having escaped their hometown, and they were only sorry that it wasn't devastated together with the good and bad "heirs" of the former Jewish community. The town of Khomsk shared the fate of its Jewish community, not leaving anything behind.

Drohitichin, my hometown Drohitchin – nothing of Jewish life remained with you. Drohitchin, why weren't you destroyed together with your Jewish children? Why?

WHERE IS YANKELE?

"Save yourself, my child. Escape to the forest," is what Leiba Feldman of Drohitchin told his nine-year old son Yankele when they dodged the German bullets that had left dozens of Jews of the Radostov camp dead. Leiba and his wife, Liba, were shot, but little Yankele listened to his father's last words and escaped into the forest (See pp. 223 and 302).

Yankele found other Jews in the forest. They had survived the German murderers and hid out together in an earth house in the forest and lived on one potato a day. When the elderly Jews would go into the forest to look for food, Yankele would look after the fire that had to be maintained day and night like a synagogue oil lamp because there were no other matches available to make a fire. So the little orphan Yankele suffered along with everyone else until 1943.

Later, when the Radostov survivors were admitted to the partisan camp, the situation of little Yankele improved. Chaya Reider of Drohitchin took little Yankele under her wing and was a mother to him. In the summer of 1943, a village peasant hired Yankele as a shepherd. He learned the White Russian language, gentile dances, and songs. He would perform dances and songs for the gentiles (who considered him one of their own), and looked forward to the time when he could go off to his uncle, Yosef Feldman, in Chicago.

Upon liberation in 1945, when all the Jews in the forests returned to their hometowns, they totally forgot about the little shepherd boy in the village. A Russian officer placed Yankele in an orphanage somewhere in Russia, and since then no one heard anything more about him. The Yankele affair was a terrible tragedy and heartrendering event for his uncle. Yosef Feldman complained about the fact that Drohitchin survivors forgot about his little Yankele. They could have taken him along with them. Yankele would have had a real home with Yosef, who would have been his mother and father. Now Yankele was gone. Yosef wondered why this had to happen. D. W.

[*Page 304*]

Dr. D. Lampel

Dr. Henrik Schechter

They poisoned themselves! May G-d avenge their blood!

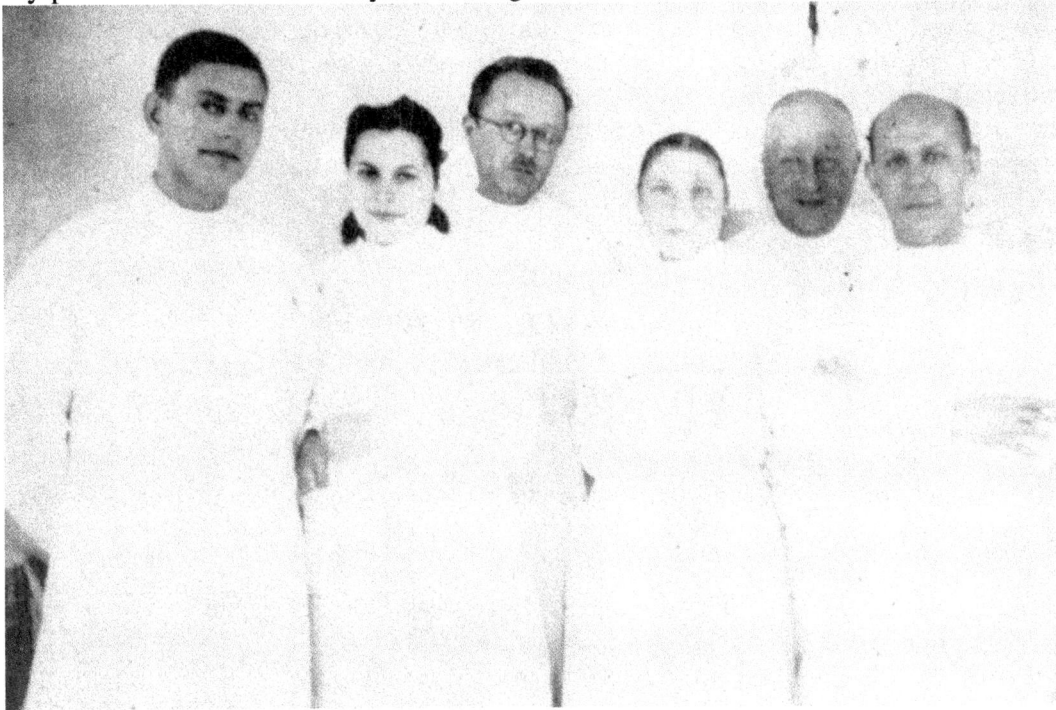

From right: Dr. Mirsky, Dr. D. Lampel, Dr. Belitsky, Beila Siderov, and a doctor from Shershev. The photo was taken in 1941 and provided by Zvia Tennenbaum of Kolonia.

The hospital – a Russian hospital – where Drs. Lampel and Schechter worked and poisoned themselves

When the German savages occupied Drohitchin, they set up a medical center under the direction of the Jewish doctors, D. Lampel and Henrik Schechter (city doctor) as his assistant. The job of the medical center was to provide medical assistance to Jewish workers who worked for the Germans.

A couple of days before the liquidation of the ghetto, Dr. Lampel called together his staff and told them the tragic news that the German murderers wanted him to stand next to the trenches and oversee the executions. Both doctors poisoned themselves. According to the Zvia Tennenbaum, when the Germans found Dr. Schechter half-dead, they shot him in the head. The next day partisans arrived to take the doctors with them, but they arrived too late.

[Page 305]

A MASSACRED TOWN
By Chava Feldman (Chicago)

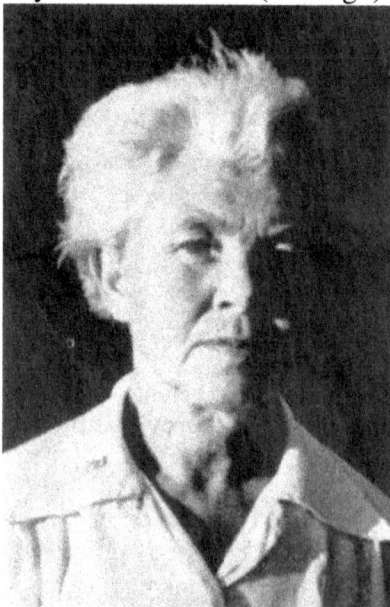

Chava Feldman

The Russian Army Takes Drohitchin, and the Jews are Pleased

As early as 1938, we Jews in Poland began sensing the danger that was moving in our direction. The first thing that was prohibited, both in Drohitchin and the rest of Poland, was ritual meat slaughter. Incited by Hitler, the anti-semitic Poles raised their heads. A Pole wouldn't dare enter a Jewish store, and a Jew with a beard was unable to walk on the street for fear of being harassed. We could tell that a large cloud was covering the horizon, and nothing good would come of it. We expected that war would break out any day, and this feeling remained until the end of the summer of 1939. The harvest had already been gathered, and only the potatoes still needed to be dug up.

I once went to the end of Starosilia and heard gentiles saying that Hitler had declared war on Poland. This was on September 1, 1939, and the very next day the Germans bombed Drohitchin. The air-raid sirens wailed the entire day to tell us that the terrorists were here. Everyone in town went to find somewhere to hide and thereby stay alive. The Polish police forced all the men to guard the roads and railroad with axes and mattocks. This lasted for an entire month.

We then heard that Poland was to be partitioned and that our section would be under the Russians. We were happy about avoiding German occupation because we had already heard about what the Germans were doing to the Jews in the areas they were occupying. Each one of us prepared some food and salt and hoped we'd get through the difficult period.

During Sukkot, 1939, the Russians arrived in Drohitchin. As was their custom, they requisitioned all the stock from the stores, and we had to stand in line for hours for bread and other food. There was no sugar or salt to be had for any money. We lived this way for 15 months. However, we hoped that things would eventually work out.

The Russians arrested Yirmiyahu Grossman, Nachum Spevak, Yasha Lev, and attorney Gilgore, and sent them to Russia. A few months later, the Russians sent off a number of people and their families to Russia: Zusha Warshavsky, his children Berl and Yeshayahu Warshavsky and their families; Meshel and Avraham Averbuch, Moshe Gingold, Shepsel Warshavsky, Shlomo Zelig Goldmann, Sender Vinocur, Alter Mazursky, Buder, David Warshavsky and their families. The entire town accompanied them mournfully. The last one, David Warshavsky, and his family were taken away through an error. He was confused with another David Warshavsky, who was deceased. The rabbi and businessmen in town testified on behalf of David to the Russians that the person they arrested was not the person they were looking for, so David was eventually allowed to return home.

Germans Arrive; Jews are in Danger

The aforementioned Jewish families were taken from town to Russia on the Sabbath, and the following day, Sunday, June 22, 1941, the war between the Soviets and the Germans broke out. Three days later, on Wednesday evening, the Germans were already in Drohitchin. The Germans got all the men together at the marketplace. The women and children cried and fainted, thinking that everyone was going to be killed.

However, G-d was there to help, and after one day under arrest all the Jews were released. The Germans demanded the Jews produce a few kilos of gold. The police of the Judenrat went from house to house and took whatever the Germans demanded. First it was gold, and when the gold was gone, they took cocoa, down blankets, cushions, men's suits, and ordinary merchandise. The Judenrat had to produce everything for the Germans, as well as men and women for labor. This produced tragic scenes between Jews and the Judenrat police.

[Page 306]

From right: Peshka Schwartz-Feldman, Yaakov Feldman, Chana Gingold, Meir Feldman, Yosef Feldman, and Motka Gingold. Everyone except for Motka perished. May G-d avenge their blood!

Later, the Germans ordered the Jews to wear a yellow path on their chests and shoulders, as well as to hang a Star of David on every Jewish home. It was forbidden to talk to a gentile or enter a gentile's home. The Germans hadn't yet taken away our animals, and we grazed them in the fields. What could we do? We brought together 16 families: Yaakov Feldman, Moshe Hochman, Meir Leib the stitcher, Lipman Feldman, Avraham Yitzchak Eisenstein, Zelik Feldman, Zeidel Lev, Simcha Perkovsky, Shmuel Snitovsky, and others, and together we pastured the animals in the field. Yaakov Feldman, Avraham Yitzchak Eisenstein, and Shmuel Snitovsky were once grazing the animals, and along the road were overtaken by some Germans who put bags over their heads and with rubber sticks pushed them along for a few kilometers until they fell into some manure. This is how the murderers tormented us for a whole year.

In the second year, around the festival of Shavuot, the Germans ordered that a ghetto be constructed. They built a high wall along the windows of the entire length of the road from the bridge to Zaritchka, the side facing the synagogue court. They surrounded it with barbed wire, and this was to be the ghetto. The other side of the road was outside the ghetto. When the ghetto was completed, the German S.S. terrorists arrived, which frightened the entire town. Whoever was able to, went into hiding. The SS went from house to house, but couldn't find any men. The Germans were going to start killing and arrested the rabbi as a hostage. His wife ran to the Russian Orthodox priest and the Polish Catholic priest to beg them to intervene and save her husband's life. The Christians went straight to the senior SS official and saved the rabbi from the savages.

The next morning the Jews started moving into the ghetto. The Germans only allowed healthy people and workers to enter the ghetto and human merchandise business then started. Overnight workers were no longer workers, and non-workers became workers. People with connections and money to pay went into the ghetto. Everyone else- poor workers and the weak stayed outside the ghetto, and were basically left defenseless. The Jews from the ghetto went to work in the "workshops." Women worked in the laundry, knitted sweaters and therefore had a right to get their allotted food ration.

[Page 307]

The Jews outside the ghetto didn't work and had no right to eat.

I was outside the ghetto, and I was together with my sister, Zelik Feldman, Avraham Yitzchak Eisenstein, Yaakov Feldman, Meir Yudel Feldman, Feivish Feldman and his son Moshe, Leizer Feldman, Zeidel Lev, Shmuel Snitovsky, and many others. They would all come to my house and we would discuss our bitter fate. We were defenseless against any hooligan or scoundrel, who could do to us whatever they liked. We knew very well that sooner or later something horrible would happen to us. We were like the poor sheep waiting for the slaughter.

First Killings – 1,700 Jews Taken to Brona-Gora

R. David, Feigel and Fruma-Gittel Warshavsky, May G-d avenge their blood! See p. 247

A neighbor, the Pole Yozef Romanovski who worked at the post office, lived in my home. He knew everything that was going on in town. One day – it must have been during the month of Av – my neighbor Romanovski came to tell me that there was going to be some news that same night because the SD had called together the police from all the surrounding villages, and in all likelihood they were going to take the Jews to live somewhere outside the ghetto. As soon as he finished speaking, Romanovski quickly returned to his job at the post office. On that occasion, Yaakov Feldman, Chasha Leah Eisenstein, my sister and a couple of other people were sitting together. Chava, they said, couldn't hear what he was saying, that he was an anti-Semite, which is why he was teasing us. Later that evening, all the neighbors went out, and I remained alone with my sister at home. Our men had long before been sent somewhere to a camp, and we hadn't heard anything from them.

Around 12 midnight, we heard a loud scream, and then someone started knocking on the door. I figured that it was executioners coming for us. I was resigned to my fate, and I opened the door. It was Romanovski, who told me to go into hiding as fast as possible. I didn't lose a single minute and ran out into the garden and hid in the grass. Romanovski locked the door and left. A half hour later we heard knocking at the door – it was the killers who had come for us.

We remained in our hideout all night. As soon as the crying and screaming stopped, my sister started pleading with me to let her go in and see what was happening in the house. She wouldn't listen to me and went in. As soon as she went into the street, a German saw her. Naturally, she resisted, and the Germans shot her twice and let for dead near the post office. I didn't know anything about this, but only first heard about it three days later, when I arrived in the ghetto, where I learned of the tragedy that befell my sister.

The murderers killed twenty-one Jewish men and women because they had been trying to hide from the executioners. Among the victims were Eliyahu Goldman (Shashka Shimshon's husband), Bezdzhevsky the teacher, Perl Lev, Zeidels; Peshka Hausman, Alters, and others.

The killers, however, weren't satisfied with the number of Jews left outside the ghetto because many Jews had escaped, and their numbers were less than they wanted. They then went into the ghetto and ordered the Jews to go outside, supposedly for a registration. The majority ignored the order, and only a handful of families came out of hiding. The savages thereby captured David Warshavsky and his wife and daughter, Meir Warshavsky and his entire family, some of the Judenrat, and many other Jews. They were all taken away to Brona Gora near Kartuz-Bereza, where they were all murdered.

[Page 308]

The 21 were later buried in the old cemetery. I was in my house with women and the children of Yitzchak Levinovitch (Kholozhiner), Lipman, and others whose husbands were taken to be massacred. We mourned over our catastrophe. A week later our rabbi, R. Isaac Yaakov Kalenkovitch died. He simply died from all the suffering and mistreatment and died suddenly. We all accompanied him to his eternal rest, and with broken hearts we sat on the ground as mourners and wept even though no one heard our weeping or saw our tears that made the ground wet.

Left: Meir Warshavsky. See p. 293

Right: Meir and Rivka Warshavsky and their children: Yankel, Chaytsha, and two others. All perished. May G-d avenge their blood! Meir was a son of Yaakov Hersh and Malka Warshavsky. See pp. 215, 246 and 293.

Germans Start Shooting People at Home

I went into the ghetto without a job. A few people signed up to go to the Radostov camp. However, since I had no connections, I had to remain in my dreadful situation in the ghetto. I then decided that I would take a broom and go with other women to clean off the cobblestone pavement. I shuffled along slowly until I got home and went inside. A policeman who lived nearby noticed this. He took me over to the police on the Sand Street. I was sure that I would be killed shortly, but they just locked me in a cellar. I spent a whole day there by myself, and then another day, without anyone showing up. I assumed I would die from hunger. On the fourth day a policeman appeared and brought me some moldy bread and a little water, and then closed the door. I then started wishing I would die instead of just lying around in a dark cellar. I spent eight days there, and I was given bread only twice.

On the eighth day the same policeman reappeared and told me that if I would wash the laundry well for the mayor, I would be released. Of course I was more than willing to do that just so I could get out of living grave. I was taken to the laundry and used all my strength to wash the laundry. It was good, but after the work was finished, the policeman returned me to the ghetto and warned me never to reenter a Christian house.

[Page 309]

Seated from right: Moshe David and Rashka Wasserman and children: Sheidel (daughter-in-law), Yoshka and Balinka. Standing from right: Naomi, Bontcha, Shalom and Shifra Morgenthaler, Leibel, Yenta. Below: Yankel and Hershel.

Gravestone of Moshe David, who died on January 11, 1936

Except for Bontcha (Chicago), Naomi, and Yankel (Israel), everyone perished. May G-d avenge their blood! (Note: the gravestone in the front appears to include the name of Aharon Drogitchinsky.)

(My own house was considered a Christian house). All the Jews in the ghetto asked me questions. They never expected to see me alive again.

The next day I went to work at the laundry workshop together with the remaining women in the ghetto. I worked with Tsippa Shimshons, a unmarried girl; Shlomo Beich's daughter Chana; Shifra, the daughter of Rashka Wasserman, and others. The workshop supervisor was a Russian Christian named Shelpuk (Today he lives in the United States.), and he liked my work. I received 100 rubles for my month's work in the workshop and a half-pound of bread per day. Later I was transferred to the post office. I cleaned, cooked, and did anything they asked me to do in order to stay alive. For one month as postal workers, we were allowed to go out of the ghetto. The postal official once told me that it would be a shame for me to die, but unfortunately there was an order from Hitler that no Jew should spend the night outside the ghetto. During the day I could work in the post office, but at night I had to return to the ghetto. This was bad news for me, but what could I do? After work the Germans would return me to the ghetto.

Once after work, I arrived in the ghetto to find chaos and confusion. Everyone was running to hide somewhere in cellars. I wasn't called, and so I remained at home with the small children. I soon discovered the reason for the tumult. A few German SD besieged Rashka Wasserman's house where there were 15 Jewish men, women, and children, and shot all of them. The dead were Rashka Wasserman and her son, Sheina Sapir's and family, Shifra's three children (Rashka's daughter), Yentel Sidorov (Rashka's daughter) and a young girl, Sapir's daughter-in-law and a child; Rachel, Chaim Kobrinsky's wife and Zelik from Partsev and his wife and two children. The only ones spared were Shifra and one of her young daughters and a child of Sheinka Sapir's, who were able to hide in the cellar. The picture was horrible – everyone was lying in a pool of blood.

I realized that it was a bad idea to stay in the ghetto overnight, and I told the Germans that I would like to go into the ghetto together with the workshop workers. However, the truth was that I would get away from them and hide out in my garden in a hole, where I would spend the night, very often in the rain and cold, since it was already around the time of the festival of Sukkot. Remaining in the ghetto carried the smell of death. The German bandits would always catch and murder a few Jews. One day the German SD arrived at the Judenrat office and demanded silk stockings. The only person there at the time was Bontcha Valevelsky, who told the murderers that there weren't any, and he asked where he should find silk stockings.

[Page 310]

Binyamin Valevelsky. Standing from right: Chaytsha Kobrinsky, Sheintsa Valevelsky, Manya Valevelsky. Seated from right: Sheinka Feldman, and Esther Taluvna. May G-d avenge their blood!

From top to bottom: Sheindel Valevelsky, Sarah Karzh, and Chasya Wisotsky. All perished. May G-d avenge their blood! The synagogue is in the rear.

The savage murderers shot Bontcha Valevelsky on the spot. Her mother, Chayka the pharmacist, came running wailing and weeping, asking what happened to her son. The beasts then shot Chayka as well.

In the latter period in the ghetto, there remained only women, children, and unskilled men. The Germans sent off all the tradesmen, such as carpenters, bricklayers, tailors, shoemakers, to Kobrin. We never heard or saw anything more from them. People in the ghetto started saying that the Germans were digging mass graves for the remaining Jews in the ghetto.

Last Massacre – a Mother and Two Children were the First

One morning, it must have been in the month of Cheshvan (October/November) when I left my night's lodging in the garden and went to my job in the post office; Romanovski came to tell me a secret that something was going to happen that night. He heard over the telephone that the Germans had called the police and ethnic Germans from the entire region to come to Drohitchin. These so-called ethnic Germans were half German and half Pole and were worse than the Germans. Romanovski warned me not to return to the ghetto at night.

I spent the entire day in worry and feverish terror. When I finished work, a German named Franz came to tell me that he had an order to take me to the ghetto. I now had a feeling of what was going on, but I had no choice. I couldn't get away, so I went with him to the ghetto. When I arrived in the ghetto, I couldn't restrain myself and started crying. They were going to kill us today. I told Jews what Romanovski told me, that if I wanted to get away from the hell, Romanovski would hide me. Dr. Schechter responded by asking me what kind of life I would have if I were all alone.

No one slept that night, and everybody stayed awake and alert, but resigned to the inevitable. It was quiet until midnight, and then in the middle of the night, the ghetto was flooded with light. We had never seen so much light in four months. We started imagining what was awaiting us. Then Germans and police started entered the ghetto.

The Germans started dragging people out of the houses. The first to go was Avraham Baum's daughter, Liba, and two children. Liba walked holding her children's hands, crying "Hear O Israel" and said to the others, "Jews, whoever remains alive must say that I and my children were the first to die for the sanctification of G-d's name!"

I immediately started looking for some way to escape from hell. I simply shuffled along, avoiding the light projectors. I crawled on all four, getting to the old cemetery. It wasn't easy for me to do, and I was often seized by fear and weakness. As I think about that moment, my pen falls from my hand as I write these words. After great hardship and crawling over holes and through water, I got to the cemetery. Rivers of water were flowing, and the cold sliced through my body. From the cemetery I crossed the gardens and bridge, and I got to Yossel Shinder's garden. From a distance, I could hear voices and crying from the ghetto. Today I wonder about myself, about how I had so much strength and courage to live through such tragedies.

[Page 311]

I was scared to remain in Shinder's garden because I noticed that there were people around there. I kept going in the dark until I got to the Krasna Ulitsa Gardens (Red Street Gardens). I jumped and crawled through deep holes filled with water and dragged myself to Zeidel Lev's garden, where Nachum Shevinsky's tannery used to be. There was a large straw stack. I crawled into the stack and stayed there for three days. I had arranged with Romanovski that if I were to survive the ghetto, he should look for me around straw stacks.

G-d helped me, and on the third day in the evening I heard someone walking around, and then a whistle. I wasn't sure it was Romanovski, but I decided to come out of hiding. How long could I sit in straw and not eat anything? In any case, I would die from hunger – so what difference would it make? I stuck my head out and recognized Romanovski. He told me to come and that he had a place for me.

From right: Rodia Rosenberg, Itka and Chaim Valevelsky, Miriam Tsirels. Standing: Leibush and Tsotka Sliep, Chaim's daughter. Left: Mordechai, Rivka, Chana Volveler, Shimshon's grandchildren. They all perished except for Rodia.

We walked slowly, staying close to the wall, and thank G-d we arrived at our stable. In the darkness, I could see a pit that Romanovski had prepared for me. I went down into it, and Romanovski covered it over with earth and boards. He placed a wooden crate on top. Next to the wall he left a small hole I could get air through, and through which he could pass food.

I Lived in a Pit for Three Years

I now started to live through a real hell. My heart was dark and bitter, and it was even darker in the pit, where at night I didn't have the slightest bit of light. I figured that I wouldn't survive. But gradually I got used to the suffering and no longer was bothered by the tarantulas and mice that danced and crawled over me, as long as they would let me survive. Romanovski would come and tell me that the Germans at the post office were grabbing Jewish property after the ghetto was liquidated, and the SD had caught them with Jewish property and sent them to the front the same day.

It was painful when Romanovski would come to the pit intoxicated and pour his wrath on me. "Why are you imposing on me?" he would scream. "I have already turned gray because of you. I can't sleep at night because of you. Go wherever you want!

[Page 312]

You can see that there's no end to the war!" He would open my pit a little, so I could come out. Without giving it much thought, I would quietly come up and go out into the street. My eyes would fill with tears – where should I go? There was a well in the courtyard; I thought about simply jumping into it and ending all my suffering. A while later, Romanovski would think things over and would swear to me that he would behave himself and act properly. He said he wouldn't drink anymore, fell at my feet to beg me to return to the pit. This scene repeated itself several times.

Germans built a ghetto for themselves in the municipal building because of fear of the partisans. Standing: H. Steinberg and L. Goldberg.

Some time later, some partisans wandered into the post office. Romanovski told them that he was hiding a Jewish woman. The partisans would frequently give him the Russian communist newspapers, Pravda and Izvetsia, for me to read, but the partisans didn't want me to join them. We then started to hear that the Germans were retreating from Stalingrad. Peasants and Germans were stationed at the rail lines to protect the roads. They chopped down all the forests around the lines, and every day the lines were torn up, and trains carrying Germans and food were blown up. The Germans moved the post office from my street to the municipal building on Sand Street, surrounding it with barbed wire like a ghetto because of their fear of the partisans. Romanovski told me that liberation was only three months away.

While we waited for liberation, winter arrived. Passover came and went, and so did the festival of Shavuot (Romanovski used to tell me the dates of the holidays), and thank G-d, the Soviets started bombing Drohitchin. This was a sign that the Russian army was close by.

The End of the German Murderers Approaches

On night Romanovski ran over to me and told me that we had to escape to the forest because the town was full of Germans and they could discover my hiding place. Romanovski quickly made off for a hamlet near Simenovitz and prepared a place there for me. He took his belongings and the animal that I had signed over to him. At night he had to come back for me. In the meantime, there was shooting and bombing in town, and I was sure I wouldn't leave my "grave" alive. G-d was there to help, and at approximately 12 midnight Romanovski arrived and took me out of my living grave. I started to walk but couldn't. I couldn't see anything; I was blind. What should I do? We had to leave quickly, and we didn't have a minute to spare. Romanovski* put me on his shoulders and carried me He took me a short distance until we arrived in a wheat field. I hid among the tall wheat stocks, and Romanovski brought me bread and water. I stayed there for three days. Romanovski left for the hamlet.

On the third day, not far from my new hiding place, a German transport came by and stopped there. As soon as it stopped, shooting broke out.
* Romanovski was half Pole and half Russian. It's possible he also had some Jewish blood. He came to Drohitchin right after World War I and worked as a mailman. He always smiled and was on good terms will all Jews (Editor).

[Page 313]

From right: Dvoshka Goldberg, Pinya Waldman. May G-d avenge their blood! Esther Eisenstein-Feldman and her Moriah School class May G-d avenge their blood! Sign held by child: Grade 1, Moriah School, Drohitchin, Polesia.

The Soviets struck with pitch and sulfur, shaking heaven and earth. When I saw how bad it was, I started crawling to the bunker on all four. When I got there, it was full of Germans. What was I doing there? I couldn't go back, so I moved into a corner and told myself that everything was up to G-d. As I stood in the corner, I heard people whispering "Hear O Israel." It was so close to my heart, and then I found out that these were Hungarian Jews who had traveled with the German transport. I was just so scared of being identified by the Germans.

Daybreak was approaching, and the German transport was stopped again because the bombing stopped, and the Russian airplanes went after the transport. I left the bunker and went back into the wheat field where I spent a few days without food or water because I was scared to move from my spot. Romanovski finally found me and brought me bread and water. The reason why he let me wait so long, he said, was that on his way to me the Germans shot at him, and he barely got away alive. So he was scared to come. He left me right away, and I was alone again. I was asking G-d when the redemption would come? Days and nights passed without end, and I remained in the wheat field for another two months.

Russians Liberate Drohitchin, Look at the Pit, and Cry

At night I suddenly heard loud shooting. I was scared to go into the bunker and remained in the field. The shooting lasted all night. When daylight arrived, I noticed Soviet soldiers running, and soon Romanovski came to tell me that news that I was now free!

There was a Russian transport not far from where I was lying. Romanovski went to the Russians and told them about me. All the soldiers in the transport came to look at me. I looked like a skeleton and broken apart. The Russians took me onto the transport and took me to my home in Drohitchin. My house was undamaged, but it looked like a horse stable because the Germans kept horses there. Soon a large contingent of Poles and Russians came to look at the amazing sight of the only Jewish woman who remained alive. The Jews in the forests arrived only a month later.

The next morning, the Russian NKVD arrived to see how I looked. They started crying when they looked at me and at the pit where I lived for three years in darkness. They couldn't imagine how I survived. A month later, the following arrived from the forest: Avraham of Tcheromcha and his daughter, Spevack's young daughter, Nachum of Bilina, Sheindel, Shepsel Zaretsky and his wife and child; Shalom, Avraham the merchant's grandchild, and a few other survivors.

[Page 314]

I will never forget the day when the murderers destroyed our city of Drohitchin. The last drops of blood that I possessed congealed. At night my savior told me with tears in his eyes that Drohitchin and its Jews no longer existed. He then asked me, "Chava, why has your people gone through such tragic destruction?" Unfortunately, the Jews with their bare hands were no matches for the weapons of the murderers.

Feivish Feldman and Motya Yachnes Akushevitz (above).
Both perished. May G-d avenge their blood!

I lived through the day when the murderers left our dead town, and after three years of suffering I recognized the light that had blinded my eyes. I was half blind the whole time, until I finally could see the illuminated world that had been dark for so long. However, my eyes went dark again when I discerned an entire community buried behind the priest's orchard. The fact that I survived made my heart turn to iron.

I left for Dobagenyev. My heart pained me when I saw the Polish peasants dealing in Jewish property. Young gentile women were re-stitching our mothers' clothes. Peasant houses were decorated with silver cups that our fathers had used to recite the Sabbath and festival kiddush. They used Sabbath candlesticks on their gentile holidays, and I couldn't watch the Polish storekeepers wrapping herring and pork in the holy pages of our volumes of the Talmud.

In 1950, after a long period of wandering and suffering, I arrived in Chicago, where I live now. The words of Dr. Schechter come to mind very often: "What will be if you survive all alone? What kind of life will you have if you survive, and all your loved ones are dead?" I feel now that it wasn't as valuable an experience to go through the suffering in the grave as what I went through and survived.

Rivers of water will flow from my eyes for the destruction of my People. My eyes will overflow and know no respite. May G-d avenge them according to their actions and chase them down in anger and destroy them from under the heavens of G-d. Lamentations 3.

[*Page 315*]

A CLARIFICATION
By Rachel Kravetz (New York)

Rachel Kravetz-Feldman and her husband Yosef

I was an eyewitness to the destruction of Drohitchin and was refined through fire, and blood. I saw and heard everything that took place in the ghetto of death, and I want to set the record straight as it relates to a few facts that don't correspond with reality. I have heard that people complain and accuse a few Jews of mistreating the Jewish community in Drohitchin. I categorically reject these accusations. Not everything is correct.

The Judenrat was established in my father's house (My father was Itsko Kravetz.). I know that all those at the meeting forced the leadership of the Judenrat on one of our neighbors, who then wept and begged them to leave him alone and select someone else. Finally he had no choice but to submit to community leaders and take the position. He was innocent! No one in his position would have done any better.

For example, when the German murderers issued a decree that every Jew give up his silverware, my mother called the elected Jewish leader to her house, opened to drawer, and told him to take as much as he needed. Others cursed and accused him of taking it for himself. Later on, when the Germans demanded gold, my mother tore out her gold teeth and gave them to him. He was, however, our community representative, and he had to carry out the orders of the Germans so that they wouldn't shoot a large number of Jews.

Take the example of the tragic case of the three Jewish young men – the Tennenbaum brothers and Zavelovsky – who escaped from the labor camp in Kobrin. The German savages demanded that the Judenrat hand these unfortunate Jews in the middle of the market. The Judenrat held a lottery to determine who should carry out the execution. The bitter outcome fell on a couple of men who complained and wept but had to do it. Otherwise, either another Jew would have to do it or else there would have been even more than three victims to die. The Judenrat head died together with all martyrs in a sacred death.

Through a crack in the roof of our house, my father, who lived for a short time after the destruction of the ghetto, saw Germans murderers take the Judenrat head together with Yisrael Zelik's wife Feigel to be killed.

Jewish Revenge!

"Let my soul die with the Philistines"

(Reported by the sisters Sarah and Rachel Kravetz, the daughters of Itsko the belt maker)

"The peasants from the village of Zaritchka, and many other villages turned over many Jews in hiding to the German murderers. The peasants received a reward of 500 marks for every Jew captured. The Jews in hiding were tortured to death, and the German beasts threw their bodies into a special pit at the Brona estate." This is how they turned over the Kravetz sisters.

The surviving Kravetz sisters reported that for a short time after the second massacre, when Drohitchin was already *Judenrein* (clean of Jews), "our entire family was hiding in the attic in the house of our neighbor Moshe Levack. However, seeing that the situation was deteriorating, and the murderers could to discover our hiding place at any time, we decided break through the German cordon and flee into the forest.

"On a dark November night and with a small child by the hand, we left our hiding place and headed in the direction of the forest. We crawled on all fours and succeeded in getting to Brona Forest, where we hid inside old trees. Later we encountered other Jews from Drohitchin in the forest. They had succeeded in escaping from the last massacre. We built earth houses in the ground, and with great fear of the murderers, we stayed in the dark for days and night and were tormented by hunger and cold.

At night we would go out to look for food in the nearby hamlets. Luckily we once found a pit full of potatoes that we gradually took over to our trees, and we were able to live on the potatoes for a while. Afterwards we started getting hungry again. Our limbs became swollen from hunger and cold, and our bodies were covered with wounds that hurt terribly, and some of the Jews who were with us in the pits died from cold and exposure.

Page 316]

On Left: from right: Rachel Kravetz, Rivka Lubashevsky, Rivka Rosenzweig, Sarah Lev, Epstein (Yitzchak's), and Eidel Epstein in 1939. Besides Rachel and Rivka everybody perished. May G-d avenge their blood!

On Right: Shimon Kravetz, may G-d avenge his blood!

Our brother Shimon (he was 17 years old) couldn't stand watching the suffering and torment of his loved ones. So one night he left for the village of Zaritchka to meet a certain peasant named Petruk, and he asked Petruk to give him his father's fur coat and other warm belongings that our father had hidden in his barn. Petruk told our brother to return the next morning. The next day when Shimon came for the items, Petruk shouted that he had captured a hidden Jew. The police, of course, arrived and arrested Shimon. Petruk was sure that he would get 500 marks and a bottle of vodka from the Germans as a reward.

The German murderers beat Shimon mercilessly and forced him to reveal the location of the other hidden Jews. Seeing that his fate was already sealed, and he wouldn't escape the killers alive, our brother Shimon, like Samson of the Bible, said 'Let my soul die with the Philistines.' He decided to take revenge against Petruk through his death.

Shimon 'admitted' that Petruk had hid him in his barn, and in order to convince the Germans, Shimon took them to the barn and showed them the possessions that had been hidden in the barn. The Germans arrested Petruk and his family of seven and prepared seven gallows in the middle of the market. They gathered all the peasants of the area and hanged Petruk and his family. This was the end of the low life peasant thief who was after Jewish property. The German murderers took our brother Shimon somewhere and we never heard from him again.

In hiding in the forest for approximately 14 months, the partisans discovered us and took us along with them. This is how we survived, and later, when the Red Army liberated us, we returned to Drohitchin. The peasants were amazed to see us alive again. We started crying from shame and pain, and we didn't find a single Jew in Drohitchin. We couldn't remain in Drohitchin any longer because the peasants were all poisoned with Hitlerism and hatred of Jews. We left our beloved hometown forever, and went on our way until we arrived in the United States." (See p. 183, Chaim Shulman. Editor).

Sarah Friedenberg, the Heroic Jewish Girl
This should be recorded as a memorial.

While the Germans took the first half of the community to be massacred in the Brona-Gora Forest (near Bereza), 25 Jewish wagon drivers and their horses accompanied the Jewish victims. When the death train arrived in the Valley of Tears, the German hangmen ordered the Jewish wagon drivers to graze their horses until the Germans completed their murders, and then return to town.

The brave Jewish girl, Sarah Friedenberg (daughter of Shlomo Friedenberg), stood on a wooden beam and yelled out to the Jewish wagon drivers: "Jewish brothers! How can you leave for home alone and allow us to be thrown into coal pits? Remember what you are doing! Your consciences will give you no peace your entire lives! Come with us! Let the Germans take the horses back to town themselves. Come with us and let's die together as heroes!" (See pp. 280 photo of Sarah. D.W.) These 25 wagon drivers remained with the Jews sentenced to death and shared their fate. May G-d avenge their blood!

[Page 317]

GERMAN MURDER
By Chaya Reider (Canada)

They Tied Jews to Horses and Dragged Them Across the Cobblestone Pavement

I was an eyewitness to the cruel murders of the Jews of Drohitchin at the hands of German killers. I saw how the German killers and their collaborators -- Ukrainians, White Russians, and others -- tore people away from their families and killed them. I bought my own life with money. For a time, I worked in a rope factory opened by the Germans to provide rope for their armies. I worked there in order to fall into the death pits. I couldn't buy my husband with money, and he perished.

Chaya Reider

I was born in Pinsk, a daughter of Burman. I arrived in Drohitchin for a visit with my cousins, the Mednitskys, who wouldn't let me return to Pinsk. In 1938, I got married to a young man from Drohitchin, Moshe Shinder, and I hoped to start a new life. However, my hopes ran out.

In 1939 the war started, and the Poles took my husband to the front, where he was wounded. When he came home, the Soviets were already in Drohitchin, and the Soviets arrested many rich Jewish families, sending them deep into Russia. The exiles were very scared of the possibility that they would be sent to Siberia. Some Jewish families asked the Russian officials for an exemption, claiming to be poor Jews, and they were able to remain at home. My husband and I, as well as our neighbors Liba Poretsky and her daughter Kraina, were exempted in a second survey. We were overjoyed to be able to remain in Drohitchin and not be sent to Siberia.

On June 23, 1941, Hitler's airplanes appeared suddenly over Drohitchin, and death and fire started raining on the town. Rumors circulated that the Germans were murderers, and that they were hanging Jews everywhere. But no one wanted to believe it. All of us neighbors gathered in Liba Poretsky's house and started to think about the situation. Each one believed that the rumors that the Germans were bad were untrue.

On June 27, a late Friday afternoon, the murderers showed up on their motorcycles. Nechemiah Zishuk was the first casualty. He happened to be in the garden when the Germans arrived, and they shot him immediately. The Germans soon issued an order requiring every person to register for daily work and requiring that every Jewish home display a Star of David. A Judenrat was set up, and it had to provide food for the Germans. We understood that life would be risky and we would get used to suffering. However, the situation got increasingly worse.

One early morning the Germans ordered the Jews to provide a few kilos of gold and a contribution of a hundred thousand rubles by the following morning. In the event the contributions were not provided on time, they would hang the rabbi of town, Rabbi Isaac Yaakov Kalenkovitch. May G-d avenge his blood. Confusion reigned in town, and each person provided whatever he had: wedding rings, earrings, watches, and even gold teeth were given away. We were thereby able to buy ourselves out of misfortune.

Then there was a new decree: The Germans demanded that Jews who had taken positions with the Poles and Russian be turned in. As a result, 10 Christians and eight Jews were arrested. The Germans stood these unfortunate people against a wall at Eisenstein's house.

[Page 318]

Nechemiah and Mirel Zishuk, their daughters and sons-in-law: Yospa, Ethel, Henya, Leiba, Moshe, and others. All perished. May G-d avenge their blood!

The Christian priest's house and garden, behind which the Germans murdered the Jews from Ghetto A, and buried them

The beasts then took Shifra Schwartzberg, Sarah Lindman, Litman, and other Jews, tied them to a horse, and let the horse run down the cobblestone street with its victims, who were broken and torn to pieces. The voices and screams of those poor Jews reached the heavens, and I can still hear them to this day. The German murderers took the surviving Jews to the Rovno estate and shot them with machine guns.

A couple of days later, the murderers came to my house, where the Russians had had their alcohol storehouse, and demanded we give them alcohol. I cried with bloody tears and told them that the Russians had taken everything along with them. The Germans whipped me and broke my husband's body. Finally, the Judenrat told my husband to take horses to the SS, but he never returned.

The Priest and a Russian Save the Rabbi and 30 Jews from Death

Shortly thereafter, the Germans imposed a second contribution on the town. However, since there was no more gold or money, the murderers took 35 Jews and the rabbi of the town as hostages. If we didn't give them the demanded sum of money, they would kill the rabbi and the 35 Jews. The mayor of Drohitchin interceded on behalf of the rabbi and the Jews, but it did no good. The wives of the arrested men and the rabbi went to beg the priest Palevski to save their husbands' lives. The priest Palevski quickly went to the SS commander and convinced him to release the rabbi and the 30 hostages. Five Jews were kept as hostages until the contribution was paid.

[Page 319]

Standing from left: Liba Kir, Mordechai Kolodner, Chana Schmid, Kraina Poritsky, Hershel Goldman, and Feigel Salever. Seated from left: Tsipka Salever, Asher Meshchanin, and Sheindel Zitch. Except for Asher and Hershel everyone perished. May G-d avenge their blood!

The murderers then ordered the Jews to move from their homes to the ghetto. Many Jews didn't want to leave their homes. At that time, I was home because I had paid a lot of money to be included in the group of agricultural workers. On the night when the Germans herded the Jews into the ghetto, I was hiding in the stable in the attic. Late that night, I heard the frightening voices of my neighbors: Chasha Isaacs (Vlodavsky) didn't want to leave her house so fast, and a gentile policeman from Lechovitch stabbed her to death with his spear. He did the same thing to Chasha's daughter, Hinda, who also died from being stabbed. A while later, I heard the groaning of the daughter of Alter from Socha, who was also stabbed. That gentile murderer from Lechovitch remained in town and did whatever he wanted with the Jews, because he got a salary increase for each dead Jew.

Before the Jews of Drohitchin were transferred to the ghetto, the Germans brought into town the Jews from Maltsh and Shershev. They arrived hungry and barefoot on two successive days. The Germans shot the small children and the weak along the way. Each person in town gave away his last piece of bread and cushion for the Jews from Maltsh and Shershev who were terribly hungry and exhausted. I myself took in a family of five into my barn (they were the Arinovskys of Shershev) and provided them with food and clothes until people were transferred to the ghetto.

The ghetto was divided into two parts: Ghetto 1 for the healthy, and Ghetto 2 for the weak and ill. In Ghetto 1 there were more than 3,000 Jews, and in Ghetto 2 there were around 1,600 people. Every day people were sent from Ghetto 1 to work in Lipnick or Radestov. I once pretended to be a gentile and wanted to escape from the ghetto. The Germans, however, recognized me because of my Jewish appearance and brought me back to the Judenrat, which, after the payoffs I made to them, assigned me to work on rope. Upon my return, I asked the Judenrat to give me some help in my work. I chose Yehudit Vinoker, Kreina Poritsky and other Jews, hoping I could survive this way since the Germans allowed me to take 15 people from the ghetto to work. However, my hopes ran out.

Germans Send Ghetto B to their Deaths, but She Saves Herself

Dina Milner, may G-d avenge her blood!

Once in the middle of the night, around 12 am, the SS invaded the ghetto and took all the Jews, including the Judenrat, to the Broma. I succeeded in escaping and hid out in our barn. I then escaped to the new gardens, from where I returned to the house of Dina, Shmuelik's wife, who had a hiding place. Unfortunately, the Germans found the hiding place, and I was saved from there. I fled from Dina Shmuelik's house, but a policeman caught me. Thanks to the fact that I had hid a little money, I bought off the murderer and continued fleeing along the dirt road to Socha, where I hid out with a Christian, Marusia Zatanska.

On the second night, I went in the direction of Dubovay to a hamlet where I had already hidden my possessions. The Christian woman, Balebushka, who kept my possessions gave me a place in her barn to hide. She also told me that the Germans had captured Kraina Poritsky as she fled and was shot. Later the Christian told me to leave the hamlet because her life was in danger.

[*Page 320*]

At night I left Dubovay and fled further into the darkness, wandering and searching for somewhere I could protect myself. During the day I hid in the bushes in the large forest. After it became dark I continued fleeing. I was hungry with swollen feet and managed to get to a village where I knocked on the door and asked for a drink of water. However, the peasants warned me to get out of the village. I continued on my way and encountered a peasant family who I knew previously. The old peasant wasn't at home, but I gave his wife a package of banknotes and dollars, and the peasant woman agreed to hide me under a heap on the condition that her husband didn't find out. Later, however, when her husband returned and discovered me lying there, he told me to leave his house. All my crying and begging had no effect. The peasant gave me a couple of berries, and I left his house. It was cold that night, and the snow and cold cut through my body like a knife. The Christians crossed themselves and told me to leave.

Two Years Living in a Heap

Before leaving I tried my luck with the old lady and promised to give her both of my houses if he would let me hide in her house. I convinced her, and she let me in. During the day I stayed in a heap under the oven, and my body was burning hot. I suffered enormously, but I stayed there for two years.

While I was in my hiding place, I would listen to the peasants talk about how happy they were that the Jews from Drohitchin had been eliminated. One day all the peasants in town were told to go to Drohitchin to see the peasant Petruk of Zaritchka be hanged in the middle of the market with his family for having hidden the Jew, Shimon Kravetz. Every peasant was promised liquor and a hundred marks as a gift for handing over a Jew in hiding to the Germans. I no longer had any tears to cry with. The source of my tears had already dried up.

When the Christian wasn't home, the old lady would let me out from under the oven and talk to me. She even taught me how to spin flax. I dressed like a gentile peasant woman and spoke the White Russian language well. The danger was reduced because of the fact that I wasn't recognized as a Jew.

Once two men from the SS came to the house, and I was the only one home. I didn't get flustered and told the Germans in White Russian that my aunt wasn't home. I gave them bread and butter, and they left. It was a miracle that they didn't discover who I was.

After a period of two years, when the Germans started retreating, a group of partisans happened to come by. They approached the old man to tell them where they had hidden Jewish property. I heard that and came out of my hiding place and stood before them and told them how the old peasant lady had saved my life. One of the partisans, a young man from Yanova, recognized me, and they took me along. Shortly thereafter the Russians arrived and liberated us from the awful German murderers.

When I returned to Drohitchin all I saw was a dead town with no sign of life. I continued my journey until I got to Italy. My relatives, the Weinsteins, brought me to Canada (Melville, Saskatchewan), where I found a place to live in peace.

Yaakov Yosef (died April 5, 1938) and Chaya-Leah Shinder May G-d avenge their blood!

[Page 321]

TO REMEMBER FOREVER
By Bashka Fialkov (New York)

Escaping with the Children to the Swamp from German Bullets
When I was a small child – eight years old – my late mother sent me to study under Feigel the teacher, who taught a class in Ezriel's home. I studied there for a few semesters and then advanced to a higher class taught by Yankel Siderov, the teacher. I studied there for four semesters, and his class was in Ita and Moshe Poritsker's home. Through another door in the classroom was where Leizer of Somonishcha lived. His wife would sell notebooks and various sweets such as candy and halvah. The children were avid customers, and I was especially pleased with the notebooks that had songs such as "A little letter to Mother" printed on the cover. There were others too that indicated that the notebooks came from the United States. The poems were very popular, and wherever you went, you heard children singing "A little letter to Mother." Mothers who had children in the United States shed buckets of tears when they heard the song. Mothers would especially start crying when they heard the words "A little Kaddish for Mother; don't let my son miss it."

Bashka Fialkov and her daughters

This is how life peacefully went on until the outbreak of World War I in 1914, which ushered in bitter times, and when we lived through a lot of suffering from war – hunger, epidemics, massacres by the Balokhov gangs, etc. My parents died during the harsh war years and awful experiences. My father was named Yudel Landman.

In 1925, I married my unforgettable husband, Avrahamel Fialkov, in the town of Sernik, near Pinsk, where Moshe Poritsky's son-in-law, R. Velvel, served as rabbi. My husband, our three children and I had a nice life. I was happy with my family life and gave my children a good upbringing.

Unfortunately, my good fortune didn't endure. When Hitler, may his name be obliterated, started to take over the world, our own world turned dark. From the first day – in June 1942 – when the Germans entered our towns and cities, they began beating us, torturing us, killing us, and incited the local anti-Semitic population, giving them the right to do whatever they wanted to us.

The German authorities issued an order for us to wear a Star of David on our sleeves, and a yellow patch on our shoulders and chests. Our sentence from the accursed Germans was that no one was liable for the death of a Jew. Killing a Jew was fun for them, and they therefore tortured us and caused us great suffering until they registered us and confined us in a dark ghetto surrounded by barbed wire. It was dark and bitter.

A rumor circulated that we were going to be deported to Treblinka. Some said that they would kill young and old, and those who could work would be sent to work in a concentration camp. We still held out hope even though we were in the ghetto. We were thinking that the bitter Hitler decrees would come to an end. We hoped that the world would find out how Hitler tortured us, and would intervene. Perhaps the world had already appealed to Hitler to stop the awful cruelty. Could the world stay silent while Hitler murdered us? This was our only hope. We fasted, recited psalms, and hoped for salvation. Unfortunately, our hope ended in a bloodbath (and the good world watched and kept silent. –W).

One early morning, the Gestapo and the police surrounded the ghetto, and at daybreak, they started sending us, half-naked, off to be massacred. I can still see before my eyes that tragic morning with the wailing and crying of our brothers and sisters.

[*Page .*]

The Germans herded us into trucks for the trip to mass graves that they had prepared for us, and where our loved ones recited their final "Hear O Israel" and left this world. Why did the bloodthirsty German murderers take my husband's life? Why did the German murderers take the life of my younger sister? Why? I will always demand an answer! Why?

I saw their tragic deaths with my own eyes, and I couldn't help them. The spirit of life pushed me on: Escape, save yourself from death and save the children who are still alive! The children fled from fire into the swamps. My unfortunate children sobbed, cried and said to me, "Mama, don't cry. We don't know what will happen to us. Maybe things are better for us." They no longer had anything to fear from death.

This is how my poor children, without hope for life – one was 14, the other nine – spoke to me. We fled into the deep swamps to hide. We found some dry land (a little island) and sat there. However, the Germans and the police started raiding the swamp areas and whenever they found Jews in hiding after escaping from the massacre, they shot the Jews on the spot.

Swollen from Hunger, Cold, and Wetness

Since I was fated to live, that fate accompanied me. There were times when my children and I would sneak around like little animals in the moss and would spend days and nights all wet, until the murderers would stop shooting and leave the area where Jewish bodies were lying around. We no longer feared death, and we even regretted having escaped death.

Hunger exhausted us, and when we got out we came across a peasant house, where we begged for a piece of bread, something that was risky. Many Jews lost their lives begging for bread from the peasants. The peasants would call the police, who would kill the Jews, and the accursed Germans would give the peasants money. I had no choice – either way we would die in the swamps.

One dark night, when it was raining very hard, the children and I left the swamps and went to look for a peasant house on a farm, far away near the forest, to ask for some bread to stay alive. I went in to a peasant I knew who always used to by from my store, and she gave us some bread.

Religious Peasants said that Jesus had Sent Hitler

This is how villages looked around Drohitchin. In front are some White Russian peasants, (*khokhols* as they were called). Many of them sold themselves to the German murderers, and hundreds of Jews were killed. Only a tiny minority of them demonstrated some humanity and helped to save Jewish lives, as described here (D.W.).

The peasant's husband looked at us angrily and said that it was a sin to give Jews any bread because Jews were sinners and suffer for their sins of having hanged the holy son, Jesus Christ, who had cursed the Jews and sent Hitler to kill them.

It was bad enough hearing the peasant tell us about our sins and why we were being killed. I went to another peasant who deplored our bitter lives and suffering.

[Page 323]

He told me that the day after the massacre of our town of Sernik, he passed by the area where the Jews from town were killed and went over to the mass grave. We started crying from his words, and his wife gave us bread and also started crying as she looked at us.

On the right are the former Russian offices. In their place the Poles later built the new municipal building. On the left in the background is the cemetery of the Drohitchin Christian population. Photo taken in 1917.

I fell at their feet, kissed them and started to beg them to let my children and me remain in the little forest on their farm. I had a gold watch and rings hidden on me, and promised to give it to them if they would let us stay in the swamp and would give us some bread to stay alive. If we remained alive, I would be forever grateful. The peasants showed some mercy as they looked at our dark fate, and they found us a place in the swamp not far from their farm. The peasant woman would bring us bread and a few potatoes, which was good enough for us. We now had a place to stay. However, even this joy didn't last long.

Five days later, the peasant ran out and told us to leave. He was scared that shepherds would see us there and turn us over to the Germans, who would kill all of us, including him and his wife. He said that the police had killed some Jews because shepherds had seen them hiding and turned them over to the murderers, and they would get money from the Germans for doing it.

At night the peasant took us away from the swamp where we were staying, and we started walking in the darkness. But where should we go? There was nowhere on earth for us to go, and if we didn't find somewhere to hide at night, we'd be found after daylight and be killed. My poor children and I wandered around the whole night until we came across peasant graves. We climbed over the fence and went into a mausoleum. We weren't scared of the "neighbors," the dead nearby. We were sure we'd stay alive among them. The next evening we heard bells ringing in the church, and immediately understood that there was no place for us at the cemetery. Of course, if a peasant died, he would be buried in the cemetery, so we had to get out of there. If we were found there, we would be turned over to the Germans and killed.

[Page 324]

At night we left there and headed in another direction. We dragged ourselves to a few marshes where there were haystacks and a constant source of water. The peasants only came there in the winter when the water froze. My children and I made our "home" under a haystack, and there were some berries growing on the moss stumps, which gave us nourishment. We couldn't remain there a long time because there were packs of wolves wandering around, and we were lying in water where there were various disgusting creatures.

We managed to get out of there alive two weeks later, swollen from hunger, cold and wetness. We couldn't stay there any longer, so we went further onto a dry field and lay down on the grass. It was a nice autumn day, and the air was fresh and the sun was shining. We remembered our home and my murdered husband and daughter. My children and I started crying over our dark fate.

Top, from right: Reizel Milner, Chaytsha Buff-Rosenbaum, Chana Braverman, Reizel Saratchik. Right: A. Shushanov, Beiltcha Sapozhnik. Everyone perished except for the two Reizels.

Shepsel, Eidel-Chaya (Milner) Kagan and two children were killed. May G-d avenge their blood! Sons Nissel, Meir and Gedal are in Israel. See pp. 295, 352.

Jewish Partisans Saved Us

A group of partisans passed by and noticed us. They saw a woman with two children who were exhausted and swollen from hunger, struggling to stay alive. We told them where we were hiding until now, and they felt sorry for us and said that near Yanova many Jews were killed in the forest. Those Jews had been fleeing the massacres. It was horrible to hear this tragic news.

The partisans brought us into the Svaritsvitch Forest where we met some other unfortunate Jews like us who were escaping from the massacres. There were already a few hundred Jews there, and more Jews were coming there every day to find a refuge from the destruction. There were trenches dug into the ground where they hid. Their lives were safe thanks to the Jewish commander, Alek Aguko, who is now in Israel, and Ephraim Bakaltchuk, who made sure there was food and clothes for the hapless Jews. It was a partisan zone there. When they came across a peasant to ask for bread and he provided it gladly, the situation improved. When the unit radio person, Melech Bakaltchuk (a teacher from Pinsk), would tell us the news about the Germans' defeat in Stalingrad and about the Warsaw Ghetto uprising, we felt a spark of hope. However, unexpectedly the situation turned bad.

[*Page 325*]

David and Feiga Rachel Kotler and their children: Beila, Moshe Leizer and Leah. They all perished. May G-d avenge their blood! Feiga Rachel was the daughter of Moshe, son of Mordechai and Beila Warshavsky. Her parents both died in the epidemic of 1915. Feiga Rachel was hidden somewhere, and the gentiles turned her over to the Germans, who murdered her. David was originally from Kolonia. See p. 231.

Ukrainian Nationalists Killed in the Forest

In 1943, the Ukrainian Bolbov gangs perpetrated murders in the forests. These Ukrainians had their impetus from the famous murderer of Ukrainian Jews, Taras Bolba. May his name be obliterated! These gangs attacked partisans in general, and Jews in particular. They would also kill peasants and Poles who were against the Germans. They didn't have many weapons so they used axes, scythes, and knives. They would actively cut off fingers, poke out eyes, and cut people up. So life again became unsafe, and they killed many Jews. The partisans had to bear large battles with the Germans and the Ukrainian gangs.

Around Passover in 1943, when the Germans surrounded the forests and attacked the partisans, the partisans undertook great battles against the

Germans. Then the gangs attacked our camp in the forest, where several hundred of us were staying. They savagely murdered 100 Jews and actively cut them up to pieces. When the partisans on the battlefield found out about their attack, Maxim Misora, the unit commander quickly ran back with the two Jewish commanders, Alek Agukov and Ephraim Bakaltchuk, and a group of partisans. They saved the rest of the Jews, including my children and me, from the murderers. Thanks to the partisan movement, we remained alive.

All of the survivors in the forest will never forget those dreadful days when the Germans murdered us in cities and ghettos, or the Ukrainian murderers who the Germans incited against us -- may their names and memories be obliterated-- and who murdered the survivors in the forests.

The year 1944 was very bad, and we had to deal with many murders at the hands of the Germans and the gangs in the forests. For us Jews it was an example of "great suffering is a partial consolation" because the Christian population was divided into two groups. The anti-Hitler Christians suffered along with us Jews, and those who sympathized with the Nazis and who helped them to kill Jews, were burning with hatred of Jews. There was friendship between Jews and some of the peasants and Poles, and therefore they murdered everyone, both Jew and gentile. They especially wanted to kill commander Misora, who was a friend of Jews and who developed friendships among people. His name was well known everywhere as a "Jewish father" because he would take revenge against those who helped the Germans kill Jews. May he be blessed!

[Page 326]

We were in the forest together with Russian and Polish families who were also in hiding. My children and I stayed in a cabin in the forest with the Polish family, Dzhalanzevski. We stayed there and bemoaned our bad luck. The Polish lady told me how her grandfather once suffered during the "mayotezh" – the Polish rebellion against Russia and had also hid out in the forest the way we were now. Suddenly, we heard Martsin Bambovski (a Pole) running toward us in tears, crying and telling us to escape to save ourselves. He said that the gangs had killed his wife and daughter, and chopped them to pieces. We started running deep into the forest and hid there. We then heard shooting – partisans attacked the gang and drowned many of them in the ditches.

Pinya and Mindel Siderov, daughter Friedel (standing), son-in-law Yisrael London (seated) and grandchildren: Yoel, Moshe, Yankel, Yudel, Sarah-Reizel, Chaya-Gittel and Yitzchak. A son of Pinya is standing on the left, and a girl in the middle of the top row. The German murderers killed the entire family! May G-d avenge their blood!

The Russian Army Liberates Us

This is how we suffered from the Germans and Ukrainian killers until liberation arrived. We had a twinkle of hope that we would live to tell the story of what we went through. We were going to be very happy after those tragic four years of suffering. The great day in history arrived when we were liberated from the Germans and their collaborators, the Ukrainians and other killers.

The air was now free, and the sun shone, though not, unfortunately, for everyone who had hoped to live to see it. We were liberated from the murders and came out of the dark Rovno, Svaritsevich, Azersk, Sporevo and Svorina Forests, which had been our places of refuge. After those tragic four years we returned to our abandoned and ruined homes. The town of Sernik was totally destroyed down to the ground. There was no hint that here had been a Jewish community there.

I came back to my hometown of Drohitchin, where I had spent my childhood. My eyes darkened, as I looked at all the destruction I encountered. There were no Jews in Drohitchin. The cemeteries were destroyed; animals grazed there; the gravestones were torn up, and the Germans had used the stones to build sidewalks leading to the Sand. I walked through the streets that were orphaned, empty and crying out over the destruction. I looked at the footpaths that our loved ones had walked along for generations. These footpaths are now soaked with Jewish blood. It seemed to me that I could see before my eyes living people with whom I spent time for many years, and who had built a future for their children.

I passed by the children's school, where our Jewish children had studied, where the little Moshes, Shlomos and Sarahs lived, danced and sang. These schools now stood ashamed and orphaned. They mourn over the great misfortune of the innocent little souls that the Germans had killed so cruelly. Anti-Semitic Christian children now took their places.

[Page 327]

I went over to the large mass grave that was next to the train, not far from the old cemetery, and where our brothers and sisters had died to sanctify the name of G-d. I fell onto the mass grave with a broken heart. I wailed, wept and spoke to the silent grave. Why were you torn away from this world? How did the Germans kill you? Who will come to visit your grave, mourn and shed a warm tear over your great misfortune? Who will take revenge for your innocent early deaths? No, my brothers and sisters, you are alive! You aren't dead! You will always live in our hearts!

Avraham, Sheina (Warshavsky) and Yitzchak Baum. May G-d avenge their deaths! See p. 293.

**Menucha Rabinovitch and her class of children from the Moriah Schhol of Drohitchin
They perished. May G-d avenge their blood!**

Soap from the Fat of Jews Distributed in Displaced Persons Camp

With a pained and broken heart, I said a permanent farewell to the mass grave, and left Drohitchin with my face covered in tears in August, 1945. We went to Lodz, Poland, where the survivors of all cities and towns had gathered. A Jewish organization called Ichud (Association) was created, and we joined it. With a bag over my shoulder and a staff in my hand, the children and I, together with a large group of war victims set out wandering through Poland, Czechoslovakia, Hungary, Austria and Germany.

With assistance from the Breicha (Escape) organization and the American Joint Distribution Committee, we got to a DP camp in Steier, Austria. The American organization UNRWA welcomed us and shared our suffering as they saw how tormented we were. They made us feel better and provided us with food, clothes and medical aid.

[Page 328]

I was ill and broken, and an ambulance from UNRWA took me straight to a hospital. Lieutenant Kaplan, an American Jew, took me to a German hospital in Linz, Austria, and put me in the care of a German doctor, telling him that I was a Jewish woman, a victim of Hitler. The doctor and his assistants looked at me pitifully.

After six weeks, I left the hospital in good health. I got better only because I lived through the fall of the Germans. I was taken back to the DP camp, and I cannot even describe the joy my children felt when they saw me. My children told me that there was stir in the camp when they found out that the soap we used in the camp that carried the letters "Riff" was made from human fat, from the fat of our tormented Jews (i.e. clean Jewish fat). Jews went to complain to UNRWA and went to the German store that sold the "Jewish soap" and tried to break the windows. UNRWA immediately ordered the German store to bury the boxes of "Jewish soap." (Is that all that the UNRWA personnel did? What a "humanitarian" action! W.)

R. Moshe Schwartz and his children: Baruch (top), daughter-in-law Rachel, Rivka, Avraham, etc. All perished. May G-d avenge their blood!

In 1946, the camp in Steier was transferred to Brona, where Hitler, may his name and memory be obliterated, was born. We would pass by the accursed empty house that stood next to the road not far from the camp where we stayed, and we would spit on the place where the biggest thief in history had lived.

One day we heard a report that the Red Cross would be distributing packages to us, and we should clean up our dormitories. An American commissioner came through with his secretary; he was the head of UNRWA. We all went to surround the secretary, who was dressed in a military uniform and who spoke to us in fluent Yiddish. She asked who had relatives in the United States. I said that I had a brother and sister in the United States. She took an interest in me and wrote down the address of my sister. A month later, I received a letter from my sister, who found out that we were living in a DP camp. My sister immediately sent off affidavits for my children and me.

In September 1946, my children and I arrived in the United States and settled in New York.

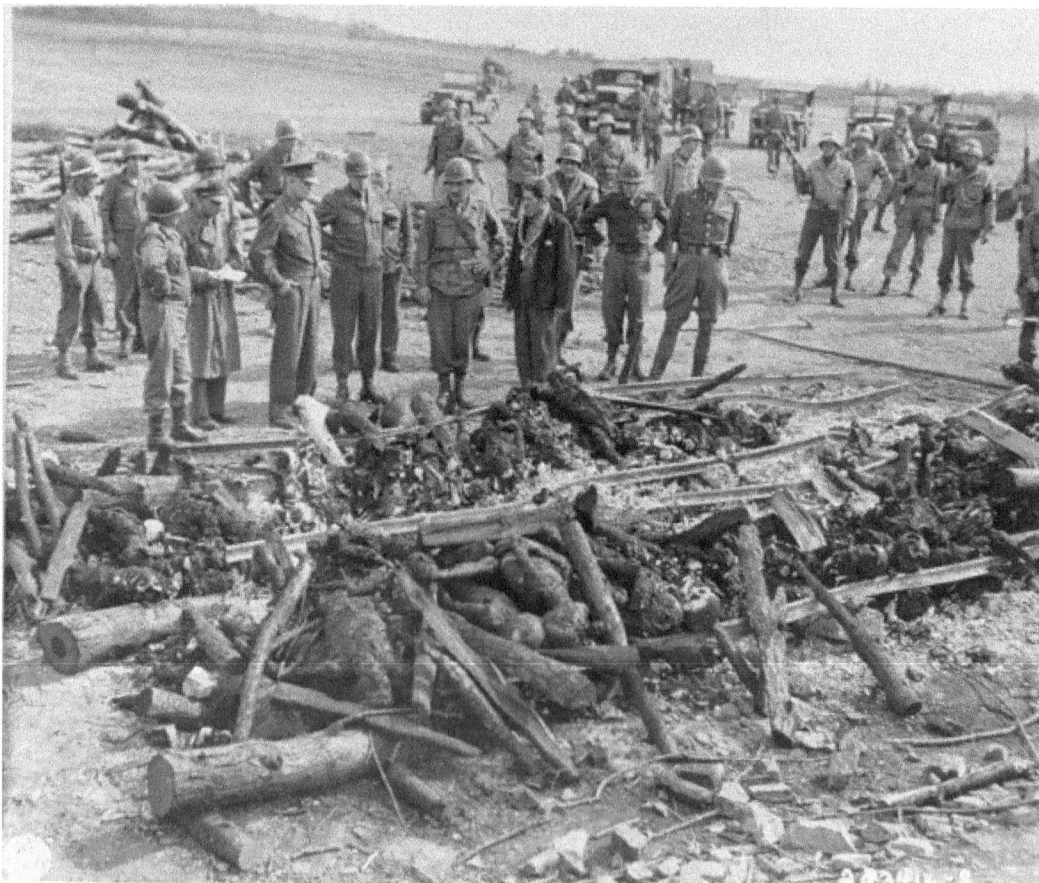

American and French soldiers at a mass grave in Germany

(Editor's note: General Dwight Eisenhower with Generals Bradley Patton and Eddy at the recently liberated Ohrdurf Cpncentration Camp.)

[Page 329]
Naftali Hoffman, May G-d Avenge His Blood!

Naftali Hoffman, a son of R. Binyamin Moshe the ritual slaughterer and Beila Hoffman, was born in 1896 in Drohitchin. He earliest education was in the *kheder* (school) and with his father. Later he studied in the Mir Yeshiva. Naftali learned ritual slaughter and practice it for a short time.

In 1918, Hoffman got married in Kovel, and became involved in the stock market. In 1925, he and his family moved to Byalistock, where he got involved in the wholesale fruit business on a large scale until 1939. Naftali, his wife Slava, two children and Beila perished. May G-d avenge their blood!

Left is Miriam (Mariasha), daughter of R. Binyamin Moshe and Sarah-Beila Hoffman, the wife of Rabbi Yosef David Schub, who died on the second day of Shavuot (May 24), 1920.

Right is Naftali Hoffman

Below: Miriam's children, Nechama and Binyamin-Moshe. Below right: Berl Prager, a nephew, and Naftali (above), and a brother. All perished. May G-d avenge their blood! See pp. 133, 149, 150 and 288.

[*Page 330*]

Leibe Hausman of Tcheromcha, perished. May G-d avenge his blood! Son, Yochanan, lost somewhere in Russia. A son, Chaim, lives in New York.

An eternal memorial to my dear father, Eliyahu the son of Tzadok Milner; my aunt Basha Milner and her children: Shifra and Leibel Ludvinsky and five children; Esther and Leizer Torniansky and three children.

Yudel Miller, New York
See photo below

From right: Shifra Ludvinsky, Basha Milner (mother), Esther and Leizer Torniansky, and children. All perished. May G-d avenge their blood!

From right: L. Goldberg, Chaytsha Andrinovsky, H. Steinberg, Avraham Schwartz, Baum, Schwartzberg, and others. May G-d avenge their blood!

An eternal memorial to my dear parents, Chaim-Sender and Rachel Devorah Zaretsky, brother Pesach Zaretsky, and family (Canada)

Hershel the Blind Goldberg chops wood next to his house.

http://www.jewishgen.org/yizkor/Drohichyn/images/250.gif

[*Page 331*]

Screams in the NIGHT

Reported by Zvia and Binyamin Wolf*

The Extermination of Ghetto B

Zvia reported that two weeks before Purim 1942, on the Sabbath, a group of Germans from Drohitchin (accompanied by someone from the Judenrat) came to Kolonia and confiscated all the silver of the Jews, their furs and other valuable property. The next day, Sunday, the Germans rounded up all the Jews in Kolonia, among whom were Zvia and her family, to send them somewhere. But where? No one knew. The Jews were sure that they were going to be killed. Luckily, the Jews were only frightened, and the Germans took them to Drohitchin and turned them over to the Judenrat. The Jews in Drohitchin welcomed them with open arms; they shared the last of whatever they possessed. Zvia, her husband David and child stayed in the home of Isser Kalekhovsky (David's brother).

Zvia and Binyamin Wolf

Until the ghetto was created, reported Zvia, people barely got by. The truth was that the Germans had robbed the Jews of all human and civil rights as soon as the Germans arrived. The Jews did not dare go onto the sidewalk, only in the street with the animals. They avoided even being in the street unless absolutely necessary so as not to become too obvious to the Germans. The only places where Jews would still meet each other were in the synagogues. Jews took risks, quietly and unnoticeably gathering in the synagogues for prayer and study. They also managed to purchase food products from the peasants without being noticed and would smuggle the food into town. They also occasionally brought in a quart of milk that was actually a kind of whey, from what the Germans had produced from the confiscated animals.

Their world turned dark.

After the creation of the ghetto, the situation turned harsh and bitter. Ghetto B (for young children, the elderly and the unskilled) was located on half of the synagogue street, from Leizer Radoshcher (at the end of Egypt Street) to the market. Ghetto A (for skilled workers and professionals) was concentrated on the other side of the street (toward the train), from Yaakov Siderov to the synagogue courtyard. Facing the windows of the houses in both ghettos, a high fence and barbed wire was installed. Both ghettos were in approximately one quarter of the area of the entire town, and in this small area the Germans squeezed in all the Jews in Drohitchin as well as a large number of Jewish refugees from Khomsk, Shershev, Kolonia, and many other settlements around Drohitchin. Fifteen and even more people were housed in a single home.

Some of the abandoned houses and stores outside the ghetto were taken over by the Germans themselves, and in the others they moved in Christian families.

[Page 332]

Tennenbaum family: Eliezer-Zalman, son of Avraham Zvi; Breina Mirel, daughter of Yisrael Aharon; daughter Zvia (standing); grandchild, and son Avraham Yaakov, left. Below: daughter Beila Miriam and Yisrael Polig. There was another daughter, Sheina-Rachel and Shmuel Kotler. All perished except for Zvia. The Tennenbaums cultivated their fields in Kolonia that they had inherited from their parents.

The Street House of Study was turned into a granary and a horse stable. The Germans prohibited any illumination or fire in the ghetto. In any event, there was nothing to use to illuminate the houses. People burned wood chips and resin wood on the chimneys, if such fuel was available. This kept people from living in total darkness at night. Women also used the resin wood for Sabbath candles, while water was obtained secretly from Chaim Moshe Lazer's (Epstein) well.

The terrorists made sure that no one sneaked out of ghetto. There were approximately 75 German police on white horses guarding the Jews of Drohitchin. If these guards ever showed up inside the ghetto, people would tremble like fish out of water. The Germans would round up the Jews for work in the forests or for chopping wood. Women would work in the train station, collect potatoes and perform other jobs.

A couple of hundred Jews, including Zvia's husband David, worked in the Yozafin Forest. Once partisans came along and advised the Jews to escape. This information got to the Judenrat, and Jews were no longer allowed to work in that forest. According to Zvia, a short time after Ghetto B was cursed out, the Germans called the Jewish ghetto police (10 to 12 men) told them to kneel in front of a mass grave and warned them that in regard to Ghetto B, if they said anything about the *aktsia* and did not round up all 1,600 Jews at the transport location in the market, the Germans would kill all of the police and their families by shooting them at the same ditch. Everyone remained silent and did not say a word about the plans.

Zvia also told a story about a Jewish policeman who was going around very agitated in the final hours. He dared let slip from his mouth to his own family that they should do what they could, since the next day he would not be with them any longer.

Beila-Miriam and Yisrael Polig
They perished. May G-d avenge their blood! See above.

[Page 333]

One Saturday night (July 25, 1942) the Germans and their Ukrainian and White Russian collaborators surrounded Ghetto B and started to round up the Jews at the transport location in the market. Of course, the Jewish police had to assist in the accursed *aktsia*. The hapless Jews were told that they were being taken to work, and that they should take food for the day with them. Many Jews went into hiding, and they were forcibly dragged out of the attics and cellars. The cries rose to heaven. Pesach Lev did not want to go. He said that he wanted to die in his own house. The murderers shot him on the spot. Pinya Waldman of Socha, Zalman Kalekhovsky and others from the market were shot; the hapless Jews were taken by foot to the train station in Nagoria. The weak and ill were taken by wagon.

At that time, frightful scenes of Jewish tragedy and sacrifice for the Name of G-d were played out. As a member of the Judenrat, Yitzchak Levinovitz had the choice to remain. However, he passed up this German "mercy", put his elderly mother in the wagon and accompanied her. He left behind his wife and children in Ghetto A. This was replicated by the Jewish policemen Zeidel Popinsky, Moshe Levinovitz (Kolonia), Pinya Khoyzman, Berg, and others. They did not want to benefit from their privilege to remain alive, and they went together with their families who had received the death sentence. Zeidel and Moshe also left behind their wives and children in Ghetto A.

At the station, the Germans confiscated the Jews' possessions, put them into freight cars, and took them away to Brona-Gora, near Kartuz-Bereza, and murdered them! May G-d avenge their blood!* The Germans took the clothes of the expelled Jews back to town to the Moriah School. They then ordered Jews from Ghetto A to sort them out; the good clothes were sent off to Germany, and the poor quality clothes were sold to the local gentiles.

Zvia, who was in Ghetto B, succeeded in escaping from the murderers and hid out in Ghetto A in the garden of Moshe Levack until Sunday night. This is how she stayed alive. Later on she got to Radostov (David was there.), and washed clothes in washtubs. After the destruction of the camp in Radostov, Zvia and David escaped into the forest. David perished, and Zvia got to the partisans of the Molotov Unit. She remained there until the liberation. (See pp. 301, 304, 337, 340).

Gedaliah Grossman and his grandson Oscar. They perished. May G-d avenge their blood!

Dora Grossman perished. May G-d avenge her blood! Her husband Yirmiyahu lives in New York. Previous page: Son Oscar and father Gedaliah. See pp. 222, 300.

[Page 334]
Former German Experts Used to Spread Anti-Semitism

The Germans were for a long time experts in spreading anti-Semitism, in taking advantage of Jewish tragedies for their political purposes, and they had conspired during good times in the Dreyfus Affair; they inspired blood libels, organized pogroms against Jews in Russia, Poland, Lithuania, and everywhere else. The Germans now also sought all possible disgraceful and awful methods to incite the Christian population against the Jews.

Binyamin Wolf said that the Germans hung posters in every open place, including in Drohitchin, showing hateful caricatures of Jews, and calling on the gentiles to murder Jews. Binyamin had seen one such poster himself. It showed a Jew wearing a Polish-Jewish hat and a revolver at his side. The Jew had two peasants harnessed to a plow, working the land. Under the picture were the words "Jewish commissar from Russia."

There were also pogrom-oriented inscriptions and slogans such as the following:

"Who eats the eggs of your hens? Who eats the butter of your animals? The Jew! Who takes your houses away? The Jew! Who takes away your jobs and livelihood? The Jew! Who rapes your daughters? The Jew! Help us, Christians, to destroy the Jews!" The gentiles listened to the advice and orders of the Master Race, the Germans!

Hundreds of Jews from Drohitchin, Khomsk, Kolonia, and Shershev worked in the Petrovitch camp near Kobrin, and they were tortured with hard labor and suffered from hunger and cold. They ate dead birds to calm their hunger. When the Jews in Petrovich found out about the massacre of the Jews of Ghetto B in Drohitchin, they revolted and made an uprising, fleeing to the forest. The partisans from Dzhenkovski's unit supposedly welcomed the Jews with friendship, fooled them into handing over their weapons and then shot all forty Jews.*

The following Jews were hiding out somewhere in the forest near Lechevitch: Shlomo Baum and his sister Reizel; Avraham Adler and his daughter Zissel; Sheindel Volansky; Shmuel Eppelbaum; Chana Feldman (Merim's); Zalman Orliansky; Ezriel Lev (Kolonia); Itche Lev (Avraham Berl's); Rivka Sertchuk-Rosenzweig; Chaya-Shifra Eisenberg; Avraham Tennenbaum (Kolonia); Yosef Kadishevitch, the ritual slaughterer from Koseva, and others.

Due to certain reasons the group split up. Itche Lev and Ezriel Lev went to look for partisans. They found the partisans, but unfortunately they met their own deaths as well. The partisans shot both of them.

From right: Moshe Yudelevsky, Binyami Valiansky, Shalom Warshavsky, H. Goldman, Y. Buff, A. Meshchanin, and Shepsel Mazursky.

Yisrael Elazar Charsel (left) perished. May G-d avenge his blood! Velvel, the son of Chaikel and Chava Milner, died. See p. 217.

[*Page 335*]

Rivka Sertchuk-Rosensweig, Chaya-Shifra Eisenberg, Avraham Tennenbaum, and R. Yosef Kadishevitch, the ritual slaughterer of Koseva went to Bilinok and asked a gentile for bread. The peasant closed the four Jews in his house and brought the police. The Germans took the four of them into the Bilina Forest and shot them.

Binyamin Wolf ended his story this way: Once when he was standing watch as a partisan at the Lechovitch Canal lock, a peasant approached him and told him about the four Jewish victims. Binyami went off to the specified location and found the four bodies that had already been eaten by wolves. Binyamin gathered the remains and buried them 100 feet from the Lechovitch Canal lock.

It should be noted that the following individuals were among those who hid out together with Zvia and David in a earth house in the forest: Paltiel Tennenbaum-Charsel, Baruch Baranchuk, Godel Shereshevsky, Yossel Lev, Sarah Spevak, Asna and Yaakov Feldman, Chana Gershenhaus, and others. Yarovsky died in the earth house. (See pp. 337-340, 360 and 361).

The sisters Chaya-Itka and Zvia Gottlieb of Drohitchin were among those in the Radostov camp. The sisters went to search for their parents and siblings. They sneaked out of the camp with the intention of going to Drohitchin. Unfortunately the Germans, who shot the sisters to death, caught them. The Gottliebs were nieces of Yehudit Hoffman of Chicago. On the left are Yehudit's two sisters and their children; daughters of Shepsel and Hinda-Matel Waldman.

Dov Warshavsky

[Page 336]

Digging Their Own Graves
Reported by Yehoshua Kapelushnick

Yehoshua Kapelushnick

The liquidation of Ghetto A

A month before the liquidation of Ghetto A, the Germans ordered the Jews to dig ditches between the priest's garden and the old cemetery. They told the Jews that these ditches were for protection in the event of bombings by

Russian airplanes. In fact, however, these were graves for the surviving Jews of Drohitchin.

For their own safety, Yehoshua and his two brothers avoided being in the ghetto and spent the night in the slaughterhouse located outside the ghetto. One Thursday, on October 15, 1942, around 3:00 am, there was loud shooting and screaming. According to Kapelushnick, he believed this was the end of the ghetto. The Germans and their Ukrainian collaborators attacked the ghetto and led the Jews to the slaughter. The Germans led groups of their Jewish victims, who were naked, to the ditches. They were then shot in the ditches. Suddenly, reported Kapelushnick, there was bitter wailing and recitations of "Hear O Israel" by the victims. This was followed by the clatter of machine-gun fire and then silence. Half an hour later we again heard screams of "Hear O Israel," the clatter of machine-gun fire and silence. This went on all night.

At daybreak, reported Yehoshua, through a crack in his hideout he could see Berl Laufer's daughter, Sarah-Itka, running from the ghetto. The Germans shot at her and killed her. Yaakov David Kozak, and Velvel Goldberg were hiding with the Christian Manya from the kiosk. The Germans found them and shot them.

"We stayed in our hideouts at the slaughterhouse," writes Kapelushnick "on Friday, Saturday and Sunday. From time to time, we would hear shooting and saw the gentiles carrying off Jewish property. On Sunday night, the six of us (my two brothers, a brother-in-law, a nephew of 15 years old, Binyamin Baum Vartsevich and I) left our hideout and headed into the Somenishch Forest, where we stayed the whole night and discussed our next move.

"Monday night Binyamin Baum left, heading in the direction of Vartsevich, and the rest of us headed for the forests around Pruzhany. This is how we lived until the following Sunday. We stopped during the day and moved at night. There was a truck of Germans traveling along the road near Ruzhinoy. Unfortunately the savages noticed us before we noticed them. They started shooting at us and killed my brothers Hershele and Simcha, Simcha's wife and Hershel's child. I had a machine-gun and shot back, and we were able to escape from the paws of the beasts."

Kapelushnick got to the Pruzhany ghetto. He joined up with a group of nine young men and made his way to the partisans. Later, he joined the Red Army and was wounded several times in battles against the Germans. In 1944, Kapelushnick captured four German soldiers. The Russian commander ordered him to take the Germans to a POW camp behind the front. He took them a short distance and shot them; he reported to his commander that he had carried out his order. The commander apparently realized that something had happened and started yelling at Kapelushnick that he would put Kapelushnick on trial at a military field court. However, Kapelushnick held his own and responded, "Comrade commander, I did this as revenge for my murdered parents, siblings and all Jewish victims." The commander understood and did not say anything further.

After the war, Kapelushnick arrived in Drohitchin. He found the mass grave was not fenced in, and without any sign that there were thousands of Jewish martyrs buried there. He could not remain in Drohitchin, and he wandered through the world until he got to Buenos Aires, Argentina. (See pp. 345 and 351).

Dov Warshavsky

[Page 337]

Hear O Israel
By M. M. Gershenhaus (Israel)

Moshe Mendel Gershenhaus

The Crying and Wailing of Jewish Children

In 1942, the Germans sent me to work at the Radostova labor camp (Radostova is a village about 10 miles from Drohitchin.). After spending six months at the camp, a confidential source told me that the Germans had killed our loved ones in Drohitchin. Shortly thereafter, the German murderers heard that there were still a couple of dozen Jews in the camp, and they came to kill us. One fine morning, German SS troops arrived in Radostova with

Ukrainian police, who cruelly outdid the Germans, and came to the house where my Jewish friends and I were living.

Suddenly, one of my friends cried out, "German SS are surrounding us!" Whoever had feet and strength headed for the forest. The Germans, however, had already surrounded us, and opened fire from all sides. Despite the hail of bullets, we kept running, thinking that whatever the case, it was better Red than Dead. If we were to die, it was better to die from a shot in the back than to be captured alive by the Germans.

As we got further into the forest, we didn't hear any more shooting, and I started looking around for my friends. Behind me were other Jewish children, among whom were my cousin, Shepsel Kravetz, and a married couple from Kolonia, David and Zvia. (Kolochevsky, Zvia's maiden name was Tennenbaum. W.) We all gathered together in one location and discussed what we should do next. We were 12 people, men and women. We appointed Shepsel and David as our leaders and spokesmen, and we headed further into the forest. Suddenly, we ran into two Christians on horseback; they asked us where we were going. We were all stood silent like rocks, and David worked us the courage to respond with a smile that partisans had attacked the Germans and were shooting at them, and that since we didn't know what to do, we decided to escape and hide in the forest. They gentiles left immediately, and we continued on our way.

Finally, we made started making plans how we would live in the forest. The first night we went into the home of a gentile, got something to eat and continued on our way. After two nights of wandering in the muddy, dark Lechovitch Forest, we came to an abandoned peasant hamlet (a farm in the middle of the forest) where we encountered six more Jewish girls. We were altogether eight people.

Death Hunted Them from One Place to the Other

This is how we spent eight days in the forest, suffering from hunger and cold, until the first snow started to fall. We then decided it was useless and dangerous to continue going further into the forest. We decided to make an earth house in the ground and remain there for the winter. After an entire night of digging and working, we dug out a ditch. The next day we rested, and the next night we placed a cover of branches and thorns on top, and placed fallen trees on top of that so that no one would notice that there were people living in the ditch. Inside we made ourselves a real palace.

[Page 338]

G-d helped us out some more, and we found two pits filled with potatoes in an abandoned hamlet. Some peasants had abandoned the potatoes and escaped because of fear of the partisans. We brought a lot of the potatoes to our earth house and dug another ditch where we kept a fire burning because we ran out of matches. This is how we spent our first difficult winter in the ditch, staying alive with three to five baked potatoes a day, and we finally got used to living there. We just prayed that no one would kick us out of our palace.

That dark moment finally arrived. We sensed danger in remaining in our hideout, and we fled deeper into the forest. We wandered in the forest for a few days and nights until finally we decided to return to our earth house and the potatoes. We walked silently in single file, and we suddenly noticed two sleds coming toward us. The men in the sleds saw us too. We all started running into the forest when we suddenly heard someone yell, "Stop!" in Russian. The noise of machine gun fire echoed in the air, and the bullets, which shone in the darkness with various colors (They were phosphorus bullets.), rang in our ears. However, we kept running and didn't stop. After we ran for a while, we stopped to see where the rest of our group was. I only saw one little boy named Tsadok and six little girls. The rest were lost somewhere. The eight of us continued running until we came to an open field where there were haystacks. We went to lie down in the haystacks and soon fell asleep from fatigue. (The people shooting were actually partisans in hiding. W.)

Drohitchin children by a haystack in Lasintsa

Help! A Little Water, I'm burning up!

Yisrael and Gershon Kan-Tsipor, perished. May G-d avenge their blood!

Children of Michla Kleinman-Kreines are in Israel

We continued sleeping for 24 hours, a full day and night. When we awoke the next night, we were frozen into pieces of ice. We had nothing to eat so we chewed pieces of ice. We stayed in the haystacks for one day, then another, and were scared to go anywhere. On the eighth day we felt that we weren't going to be able to survive much longer. We were totally exhausted from hunger and cold.

On the eighth night, Tsadok became delirious and started screaming, "Help! Some water! I am burning up!" He could be heard from one end of the world to the other. We were all very weak, and couldn't do anything for him. Then poor Tsadok passed away after suffering tremendously. He died from hunger and cold.

The next morning, with tears and wailing, I started asking the girls to let us leave that place since we would all die there. However, it was too late. The girls couldn't move from there. There were two sisters (I forget their names.). The younger one was half-dead, and the older one still had some strength to save herself. However, she said that she wanted to die there with her sister.

Only one girl, Esther, was able to be persuasive, and with her last bit of strength she got out of the ground. We took the clothes off of the dead Tsadok and put them on Esther, who was almost naked. We left the other girls, promising to come back to save their lives.

[*Page 339*]

Mordechai and Sarah Buder. Left: Yitzchak and Sarah-Itka Buder-Holtzman, Feigel and Yehudit. All perished. May G-d avenge their blood!

We wandered and rambled along in the dark, cold world. On or off the road, as long as our feet could move, we just hoped we'd get somewhere. We fell and walked, and fell and walked again. We helped each other get up again and continue crawling. We hoped we'd come across someone, anyone. Suddenly we came to a place we recognized, the place where we were being shot at. We just stood there for a while, amazed and not knowing what to do. However, we soon mustered up more courage and started going faster. It wasn't far from there to our earth house. We were on our way back "home" and hoped that no one would find us there. We were ready for anything and had nothing to lose.

Our hearts were pounding, and our minds were filled with all sorts of thoughts. Another hour, and then we were back "home" again at our ditch. I went in through the secret entrance in the ditch and suddenly heard a scream in Russian, "Who's there?" I recognized the voice of Yisrael Eliezer Charsel's grandson Paltiel from Drohitchin, and fainted.

When I came to, I found our "home" surrounded by the whole group, and told them everything that happened to us. The group told us to rest and eat something, after which we would all go out to save the five girls at the haystack. Asna, a girl from Drohitchin, ran outside, made a fire and cooked me some soup. She also baked a couple of potatoes to take along for the dying girls. In the meantime, my friends told me that David and my cousin, Shepsel, were also missing.

As I ate the potato soup that Asna cooked up for me, I felt that my boot was wet. My friends removed the boot, but they took off the boot together with some skin off my foot. My big toe on the right foot also came off. Ten minutes later I was lying there unconscious.

David Yudelevsky, Pelta Mazursky, Liba and brother Kir, Moshe Lasovsky (above), and others. All perished except for Pelta. May G-d avenge their blood!

Will you ever forget it? No. Never!

Later on, when I came to, my friends told me that I was talking with a fever, telling them to go save the girls, and even describing their location. My friends spent a whole week searching. Every single night they covered the entire area but didn't find the girls.

[Page 340]

Top: Esther Shushanov, Schwartzberg. Below: Epstein, Lev (Leizer's), Ukrainetz (Yeshaya's). They all perished. May G-d avenge their blood!

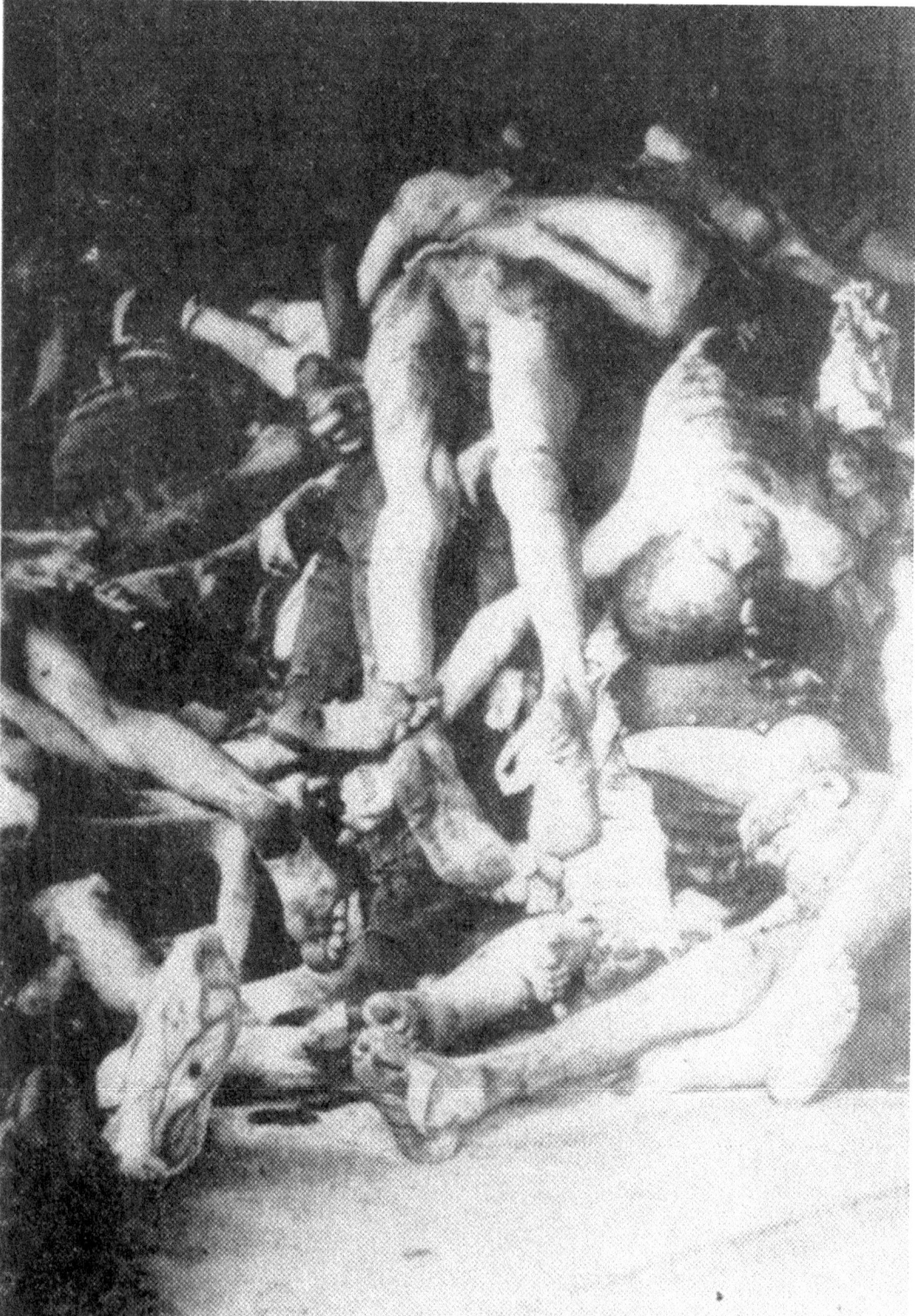

Well, will you ever forget it? Can you forget the tears and blood of our Jewish children? Will you forget the Jewish murderers? No! Never! Never! Never! D.W.

Esther, who survived together with me, suffered swelling all over her body, and she couldn't go off to help save the other girls. In any event, she didn't know the way, but she later recovered. I stayed in the ditch and was very ill. The aches and pains I suffered from in my feet are indescribable. The fact that I remained alive is thanks to a Christian, a "Subbotnik" (a Christian belonging to a sect that kept the Sabbath). He did a lot for all of us, especially for me. For an entire month, day and night, he brought me a bottle of milk, some bread, and pork fat to rub on to my feet until I could put my feet on the ground.

That same winter, thanks to two Christian partisans, we made contact with a second group of Jews from Yanova, among who was also Shmuel Eppelbaum of Drohitchin. The Yanova group took us with them, and we remained with them until the liberation. Six months before the liberation the Germans retreated as far as the Lechovitch Canal. The partisans received orders to move on to Kamin-Kashirsk, and we went along with the partisans.

After the liberation I found out that my two lost friends, David and Shepsel, wanted to get to Ogdemer, near Drohitchin, and the Germans captured them at the train station. David suffered a heart attack from fear and died on the spot. The Germans killed Shepsel and threw his body in a ditch near the train station, where all the Drohitchin martyrs are buried.

I also found out that the five girls were found dead in a haystack in the Lechovitch mud. They were all lying next to each other, having died in great suffering from hunger and cold.

[The names of the girls were: Freidel Zohn (Lechovitch), Mindel (Davidgrudok), Chayaleh (13), and Rivka (18) Tint – sisters from Drohitichin – as well as a few others who died at the hay stack: Zadok, 16, was from Yolitch (?) near Drohitchin. Esther was from Voldava. Asna worked for Averbuch. Moshe Mendel Gershenhaus is a grandchild of Chaim-Ber and Malka Kravetz. A gentile woman reported to Zvia Tennenbaum that she had passed by the haystack, and Rivka had asked her to save them, but the gentile was scared. The next day, the gentile and her husband arrived at the haystack, but it was too late. See pp. 333-335. W.]

[*Page 341*]

From right: Yonah Goldberg, Yankel Beich, Zechariah Schmid, Feigel and Risha Epstein.
All perished. May G-d avenge their blood! The Bank.

Blood Cries Out for Revenge!
By Dr. Chaim Shoshkes

In *Die Zeit* of December 22, 1943, London, England; Reprinted by *Morgen-Journal*, New York.

During those sleepy nights when the people, streets and houses of the now destroyed Jewish communities in Poland that I remember were still alive, I am starting to understand with great despair what we lost in recent years.

Despite all the poverty, the legal handicaps and economic situation of those communities, they were the wellspring of a pulsating desire not to give in to their bitter fate, and not to give our enemies the pleasure of seeing us give up.

For almost 50 years I have been traveling from community to community, from region to region. I was an inspector of the Jewish People's Bank, and my job was to set up and monitor banks, and to teach Jewish artisans and small businessmen how to improve their situation with loans, how to handle their poor finances, and especially how to stick together and not let themselves stay on their own.

I just recently read a brief notice in the radical underground newspaper, *To Arms!*:

"Since all Jews in central Poland have been killed, they are proceeding to kill off all the Jews in the Polesia region. There are mass murders in Brisk and Drohitchin; the Germans and Ukrainians are undertaking these murders. The Jews are first being used to dig their own graves, and right afterwards are being shot and thrown in and buried."

Brisk...Drohitchin. In that town of Drohitchin, near Kobrin, there lived Zechariah the blacksmith, a wonderful Jewish personality who is certainly remembered by almost everyone from Drohitchin living in Europe and the United States. He was a giant of a Jew who had steel hands and toiled for years banging away on his anvil. Many years ago, we appointed this simple blacksmith as an administrator of the People's Bank. He could have been an example to many people on Wall Street and in New York and London with his dedication in the way he worked as a banker, in the way he was careful with people's money and in the way, and in the way he dealt with his customers who were laborers like him. I remember when we once traveled with a wagon between Drohitchin and Khomsk and how the wagon tipped over, an event that in that bloody region was commonplace. Zechariah, the hero, turned the wagon back over and pulled the wagon and me out of the mud. Did his blessed hands also dig the large mass grave for the simple Jewish peasants and craftsmen of that secluded town?

Dr. Shoshkes ended his article of December 23, 1943 with a quote from a proclamation that appeared on the streets of Warsaw:

"Just a little more patience! The hour of revenge is approaching. The doors of the concentration camps will be open in Auschwitz, Belzec, Treblinka and all the other places of suffering. Our suffering brethren will be freed, and their places will be taken by the disgusting German lowlifes who we will let hang."

"This human blood, this innocent blood, seethes, sizzles and does not calm down! The murderers will not save any peace treatises! Millions cry out from their graves and demand revenge!

(This is how people wrote and spoke in 1943, and today? Today everything is ignored and forgotten. "Surely the People are grass...." Isaiah 40 - Editor).

[*Page 342*]

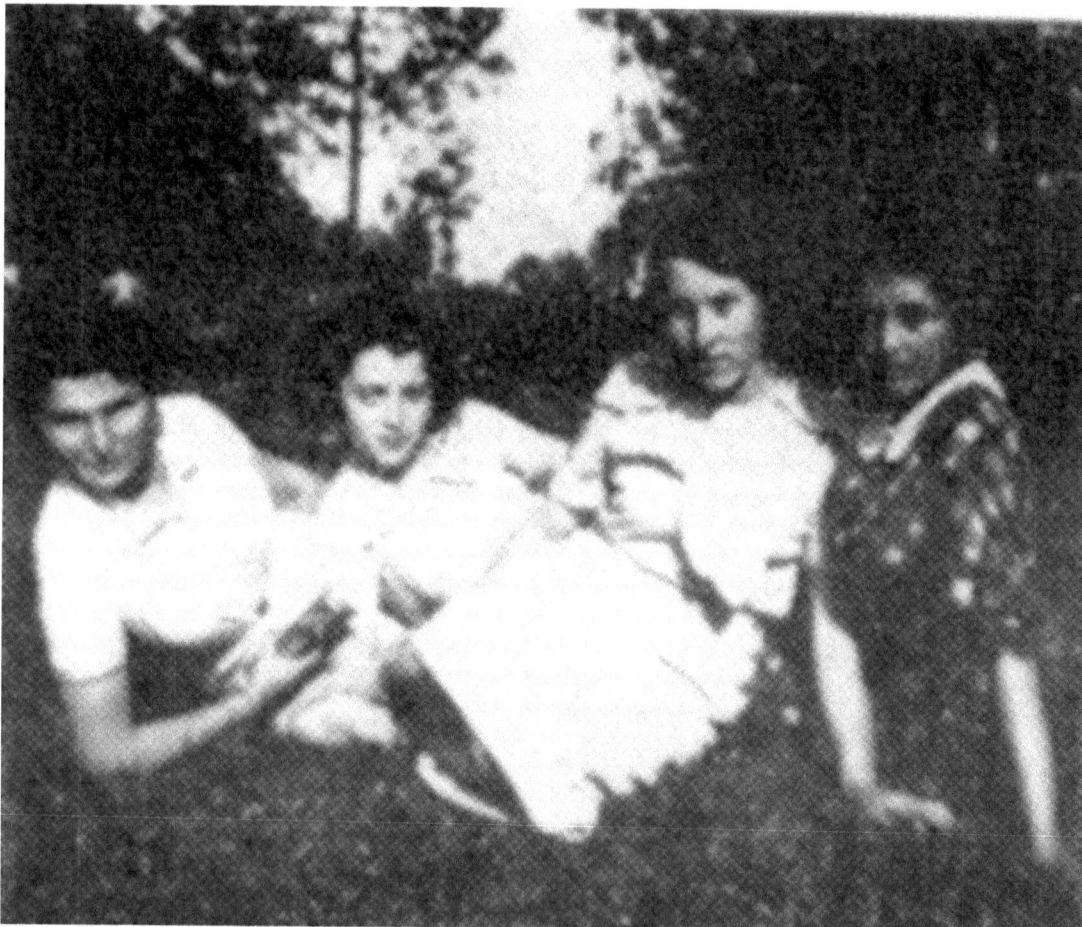

From right: Zelda Baum, Paya Buder, Sarah Pomeranetz, Chana Kravetz. Everyone except Buder perished. May G-d avenge their blood!

The kindergarten at the Moriah School in Drohitchin

The children and their teacher perished. May G-d avenge their blood!

An eternal memorial to our dear
Parents
Moshe-Leib and Chaya-Sarah Salever
Sister
Leah, her husband and four children
Brothers
Aharon Salever, his wife and four children
Chaim Salever
All perished, may G-d avenge their blood!
Liba and Eliyahu Salever-Trackman (New York)

An eternal memorial to our unforgettable
Parents
Eliezer, son of Yosef Halevi, died on March 12, 1919 at 39 years of age,
and Rachel, daughter of Shachna Yosef Schwartz, may G-d avenge their blood!
Brothers
Menachem and Itcha Schwartz
Avraham Schwartz (died in 1918)
Mother and brothers perished in Bereza, may G-d avenge their blood!
Hershel (Norvolk), Yisrael and Meir

Hershel the Blind Goldberg and his wife

They perished. May G-d avenge their blood!
Photo taken next to Hershel's house.

Standing from right: Bontsha Valevelsky, ----, Mazursky, Braverman, M. Kalenkovitch, Zaretsky. Seated from right: Schwartz, Steinberg, Yudelevsky, Goldberg, B. Wasserman. Below from left: Buder, Feldman, Milner. This is the Drohitchin sports group.

[*Page 343*]

From right: Shalom Morgenthaler, Nechama Schub, Bobtsa Berg, Mazurskys, Gendlers, and others.

Beginning class [First grade?] B of the Moriah School of Drohitchin, June 1939.
The children and teacher perished. May G-d avenge their blood!

An eternal memorial to my dear
Brother and Sister-in-law
Hertska (60) and Sarah (59) Buff
Brother's children
Chaytcha, Michlia, Shimon, Lotsa
All perished. May G-d avenge their blood!
Sima Yanov, Hodessa's daughter.

An eternal memorial to my dear
Father
Moshe-Yitzchak Volinitz
Sister
Elka, Miriam-Tsirel, Chaya-Esther, Shosha, Yehudit
All perished. May G-d avenge their blood!
Asher Volins (New York)

From left, Hershel Kaminetzky, Meir Lieberman, Moshe Berg, Yaakov Vermus (standing) perished. May G-d avenge their blood!

Standing from right: Liachovitsky, B. Ts. Bezdzesky, Popinsky, B. Berezovsky, -----, Gurstein. Seated from right: Liachovitsky, Siderov, Y. Goldberg, Tsizh, Shimon Kravetz. Bottom from right: Kapelushnik, Sherer. All perished except for Goldberg. May G-d avenge their blood!

[Page 344]

An eternal memorial to my dear Mother Feiga-Zissel Levinson (60), Sister Chana (32), Tzvia, husband Feivel Gurvitz

Sister's children: Natan (8) and Yaakov (10)

Brothers: Yisrael 27, Avraham 25, Levinson

All perished. May G-d avenge their blood!

Gershon Levinson Disappeared in Russia

All were from Osevetz

Ruta Levin (Savannah)An eternal memorial to our dear

Parents

Zechariah and Nissa-Beilal Salever

Sister Sarah, Ethel, Tsippa, Bracha, Chaya-Ita

All perished. May G-d avenge their blood!

Mirka Salever-Coleman (Hackensack, NJ) and Feigel (Israel)

Chaim Levinson sent the letter with the German swastika (above) to Yosef Feldman in 1941 from Warsaw and disappeared. See necrology.

Left: Fruma Schwartz, daughter Esther and son-in-law Shlomo Engel. May G-d avenge their blood!

Sirka Baum (in middle), the dressmaker, and her girls. From right: Kolodner, Lev, Sirka Lev, Gurstein, Yorinkas, and others. All perished. May G-d avenge their blood!

Rachel Shushanov (middle), P. G. Warshavsky, and two small Sendyuk children In front of Kapelushnik's house. May G-d avenge their blood!

[Page 345]

Partisans and Survivors
By Boris Baumovitch

Binyamin Baum

His name was Binyamin Baum. He was born in Vartsevich, about seven miles from Drohitchin. He lost his father when Binyamin was still very young, and his mother, Chava, became the breadwinner to support her five children. Later, when Binyamin grew older, he got involved in business and helped his mother earn a living. In 1937, after Binyamin returned from serving in the Polish army, the Baum family settled in Drohitchin (in the house of Meir Yudel Feldman). Binyamin got back into business and prospered.

When the German murderers started killing the Jews of Drohitchin, Binyamin survived the ghetto and joined the partisans in the forest. He was a fine soldier, knew how to hold and use weapons, and soon he became one of the leaders of his partisan unit. Binyamin then changed his name to Boris Baumovitch, and led large operations to take revenge on the German murderers.

One winter night, Boris and his partisans surrounded the Balkon estate (around three to four miles from Drohitchin), disarmed the Germans running the estate, and took the entire stock of animals (28 cows and horses). They forced the Germans to take the animals into the forest to the partisans. In the forest the partisans held a trial of the Germans and then shot them.

When Boris heard about the awful news about the deaths of the Jews of Khomsk, and how the gentiles, led by the priest, used scythes and axes to kill the Jews, he decided to take revenge against the treacherous peasants. Boris contacted the partisans and together they headed for Khomsk, where they used machine guns to kill all the guilty peasants, the priest and all the Germans in Khomsk (One exception was the priest of Drohitchin, Polevski, who helped the Jews. When the Germans imposed a huge tax on the Jews, the priest gave away his gold crucifixes to cover the amount of the tax).

Boris settled accounts with many other peasants who killed Jews or who helped the Germans. Whole families of peasants paid with their lives so that the people should hear and see!

On the left is Boris with the partisan unit

[Page 346]

Three Germans once captured Boris in a trap. He fought the three of them by himself and killed them. However, the Germans managed to shoot his horse and wound Boris in the leg. He remained alone losing blood, until a peasant wagon drove by. The peasant, seeing the three dead Germans, crossed himself and wanted to flee, but Boris was able to force him to take him to the partisan base. Boris later joined the Red Army, where he displayed great heroism as a commander, saw death and devastation in the German cities until the German murderers were destroyed. Boris was awarded the Orders of Lenin and Stalin for his heroic activities.

Simcha Feldman (right), may G-d avenge his blood, and Yosef Feldman of Chicago.

I received my first letter from Boris in 1946 in which he asked me to look for his sister Sarah and her husband Irving Farb in Chicago. Shortly thereafter, I received a letter from Boris from Prague, Czechoslovakia, in which he said that he was ill. Boris' sister traveled to Prague, but unfortunately she could not do anything to save him. A friend of Boris, A. Briland, wrote the following about Boris in 1947 in Lodz:

"We were in a battle with the Germans. We were few and they were many. A German bullet wounded Boris, and he fell down all bloodied. However, his desire for revenge did not weaken. I lifted him up and wanted to take him back to the partisan base, but Boris pulled away from me, and threw his last grenade at the Germans. I took him to the partisans' hospital some 15 kilometers away, but Boris responded, 'My heart is still uneasy because I couldn't shoot another couple of Germans.' Our experience cannot be put onto paper. Boris was both mother and father to me. My heart cries for him. I would like to engage G-d in a rabbinical court case. G-d had saved him from so many dangers, and now, when he could live, he took Boris away. Why?"

Boris himself wrote a letter dated July 15, 1945 in which he said the following: "I could never have enough paper on which I could write you everything. I was wounded five times in the battles with the Germans. I am now discharged from the army (the Red Army) as an invalid. On the outside I am all right, but inside I am not all right. If I have a home and take care of myself, I can still hope to recover completely. Emotionally I am very depressed because when I left the army, I didn't find any of our relatives. I am now alone in a foreign world."

As long as Boris held the gun of revenge in his hand, he was raging. His wrath and desire for revenge against the German murderers gave him strength and impetus to live through all physical and emotional suffering. However, as soon as he put down his gun, all of his physical and emotional wounds reopened. Boris passed away in the hospital in Prague, Czechoslovakia, in 1946.

Dr. Hershel and Liza Feldman. They perished. May G-d avenge their blood! Hershel was a cousin of Yosef Feldman.

[Page 347]

Shlomo Entin, May G-d avenge his blood!
Underground Fighter

Shlomo Entin

Shlomo Entin was born in Drohitchin in 1915. During World War I, his family joined the stream of refugees going to Yekaterinoslav (today known as Dneprpetrovsk), and in 1922 returned to Pinsk, where Shlomo's father had a haberdashery shop. Shlomo graduated from the Tarbut School and studied at the Tarbut High School. However, he did not complete his studies, and at 15 he was employed as a clerk at Luria's veneer factory. He was also a member and later one of the leaders of the *Noar Hatzioni* (Zionist Youth*)* in Pinsk.

Following the outbreak of World War II in 1939, Shlomo was active for a time in the underground in Pinsk. Later on he moved to Vilna and continued his Zionist pioneer work. After the Vilna ghettos were set up in the autumn of 1941, Shlomo became one of the main leaders of the Vilna *Noar Hatzioni*, as well as a member of the *Haganah Reshit* (Head Hagana)]. He represented his movement in the Zionist pioneer organization that existed in Vilna. Shlomo was a healthy, well-built, and courageous young man, and he was very popular among his friends during the time of the Underground. During the early period of the Vilna ghetto, he operated the public kitchen at 2 Strashun Street, and thanks to him the Jewish underground movement was able to use the kitchen for its meetings and preparing its plans for an uprising.

Shlomo was one of the first people to think of undertaking an armed resistance against the German murderers. During the *aktsia* on Yom Kippur 1941 in Vilna, when some 4,000 Jews were taken away to be killed at Fonar, Shlomo stood by the doors of the houses on Shavelsky Street and wrestled with the Lithuanians who were taking the Jews. He was able to save several victims from the hands of the murderers.

Shlomo was among the members of the Vilna youth delegation in Warsaw at the end of 1941 bringing the earliest reports about the destruction of the majority of Vilna Jews. He asked for money and weapons for an uprising. He returned to Vilna and continued his activities with the Underground.

In one of this missions, on the way to Warsaw from Byalistock to form a united partisan organization, Shlomo was arrested in April 1942 by the Gestapo at the Maklina train station (He was traveling with false documents under the name of Jan Stankevicz.), but the Germans already knew about the false documents of the Jewish underground, and were very cautious. Together with his colleagues Sarah and Khashka Zilber, Shlomo was imprisoned in Warsaw, and no amount of effort to save him from the hands of the Germans was of any use. During the transfer of the Jews of Warsaw in July 1942, Shlomo was murdered together with his colleagues. May G-d avenge his blood!

(From the book, *Destruction and Uprising of the Jews in Warsaw* by Melech Neistadt, 1948, Tel Aviv. Editor)

Moshe (Alters) and Fruma Warshavsky and children perished. May G-d avenge their blood! The children Chana and Esther live in Israel.

Avraham and Feigel Pinsky and children: Yosha, Esther, Anyuta (Naftali Steinberg's daughter). May G-d avenge their blood!

[*Page 348*]
Death Across Germany
By Y. M. Kerst
Forverts, April 28, 1946
Regarding Shmuel Eppelbaum

Life for Drohitchin Hebrew teacher, Shmuel Eppelbaum, proceeded normally. For years he was dedicated to educating Jewish children and to preparing them to becoming contributing members of society. Suddenly the war broke out, and his normal life was turned upside down, and several years of suffering and torment would now begin. The bloodthirsty Germans arrived and brought with them death and destruction. Shmuel saw his own fine young students being killed, and he saw his loved ones and neighbors, including his own mother and sister being carried away to be killed.

Shmuel slaved away at camps under the most dreadful conditions. He was among those who were taken away to be killed, but more than once he was able to escape from the murderers under a hail of bullets. The "good" Christian neighbors lay in waiting with scythes and axes in every nook and cranny. Shmuel had to hide from them in the forest and in ditches.

The difficult experiences brought the Hebrew teacher many disappointments, but did not break his courage. On the contrary, they transformed this quiet man, who could never hurt a fly, into a courageous fighter who fought bravely against the German beasts and who sought revenge for the innocent Jewish blood.

Shmuel Eppelbaum, who now lives in Lodz, is preparing to move to Palestine. He underwent a great deal during the bloody war years. His long and moving letter to the *Forverts* that he sent in his search for his brother, Yosef Eppelbaum, attests to this. He is also searching for Moshe Yosef and Leizer Dvoshkas from Drohitchin. He wants them to know that Chayatcha left behind a three year-old orphan, a child that she had had with her husband, a Warsaw doctor. A Christian in Drohitchin took in this child at the age of three months, and the child is still living there.

Here is a part of his letter:

"The German murderers occupied our town of Drohitchin on June 25, 1941. That day was the beginning of the most tragic chapter of our lives. The very next morning the soldiers started checking every Jewish home for weapons. However, instead they took good items such as shortening, shoes and other valuable items. They robbed and pillaged, claiming that it was because our American brethren had started the war against Germany.

"At the end of June, 1941, the notary Chaplinski, who became mayor, called together a town meeting in the market and declared that the Jews were no longer under the law, that they had no rights, and that they had to wear yellow patches, hang yellow Stars of David on their doors, participate in forced labor, and pay taxes to the German army and Ukrainian civilian authorities.

Alter and Dvoshka Goldberg and children: Chaytcha, Esther, Leizer. Apart from Leizer and their late mother, the rest perished. May G-d avenge their blood!

Massacres in Motele, Khomsk, Yanova, Pinsk and Brisk

"At the beginning of July, the gentiles in the village of Vetla killed the few Jewish families that had lived there and distributed their property amongst themselves.

[Page 349]

"The Germans then killed a few dozen Jewish men at the market in Khomsk. Thereafter, within a week, the White Russians used knives, scythes and axes to kill the entire Jewish community of Khomsk. The Christians did the same thing in Motele. They had permission from the Germans to get rid of the couple of thousand Jews who lived there.

"From Pinsk, Brisk and Yanova the Germans supposedly took Jewish men from 14 to 65 to perform forced labor at an unknown location in July 1941. Later, we found out that traveling to work meant leaving for the next world."

Shmuel continued his description of the dreadful situation of the Jews in Drohitchin during the time the Judenrat operated. This is a chapter in and of itself.

From left: Yitzchak Leib Kosack, Moshe Berg, Aharon Rosenzweig, Herman Grossman, Lieberman, Alter Goralsky (standing), Berg (child), and others. Except for Grossman, everyone perished. May G-d avenge their blood! Photos that are distributed are from H. Grossman.

"In the winter of 1941. a ghetto was established in Drohitchin. Jews did not dare go onto the street, and even when they went to forced labor, Aryans escorted them. The escort who took Jewish doctors to work in the hospital was a mere ten year-old boy. He would walk on the sidewalk, and the Jewish doctors would walk in the street. The Jewish population in Drohitchin numbered more than 4,000. There were some Jews who had escaped the destruction of Shershev and Kolonia. There were two ghettos in Drohitchin: one ghetto for tradesmen, community people and Jewish police; the other ghetto was for those without a trade or "worthless" Jews, which included our family.

"In the beginning of the winter of 1942, the Jewish communities of Rovno, Vilna, and Slonim were destroyed; in the spring of 1942, Kovel, Devin and Bereza. The Drohitchin Judenrat believed that it was because of them that the Jews of Drohitchin were still alive. They then stated that they could not save the ghetto of the unskilled Jews, who numbered some 1,600 people, and that their fate was already sealed. However, they hope that through their efforts, the other ghetto would survive the war.

Gentiles Awaited the Restoration of the Russian Monarchy and Killed Jews

"On the evening of Saturday, July 25, 1942, we experienced our greatest misfortune. The 1,600 people in the ghetto were taken away to the train station. They included my mother, Miriam and Avrahamele, Freidel's child (Rachel, Freidel and Natan were in the Pinsk ghetto. Meir Freidels perished in July 1941) and me.

Hausman, Aharon Kaplan, H. Wisotsky, S. Valevelsky. May G-d avenge their blood, and others.

Freidel Appelbloim, May G-d avenge her blood!

"Along the way, people were struck viciously over the head with guns. Zev Valevelsky, the engineer, had his head split open. In my case, they took my shoes and jacket. Avrahamele Freidels was struck over the head with a gun, and his brains were spilled onto the street. Mother was pushed inside the car where they put the weak, who could not make it to the annihilation location. Later, I found out that the place our loved ones were killed was in Brona-Gora, 17 kilometers from Kartuz-Bereza.

"I was filled with suffering and wrath when I pushed down the German who was walking next to me, and I ran off into the forest under a hail of bullets. On the third day, they found me after having fainted in the forest, and took me to Ghetto A, which still existed. Everyone realized that the days of the "worthwhile" Jews were numbered too. Suddenly the community administration was scared to keep me, one of the "worthless" ones, so I was sent to Radostov to a labor camp.

[*Page 350*]

"The lucky Jews of Camp A also perished at the end of 1942. The community leaders perished together with them, even though they thought that they would survive. Only a few managed to survive.

"When we found out in the labor camp that the Jews in Ghetto A perished as well," writes Eppelbaum, "we decided to flee to the forest. It was very difficult. The local population was attacking the Jews because they were promised 500 rubles for every Jew they turned in. The Christian partisans would also kill Jews, claiming that the Russian monarchy would be restored. They would cry out, "Kill the Jews, Save Russia!"

Taking Revenge on the Germans

"On November 4, 1942, our camp was shot at. I was able to escape under a hail of bullets. I hid out in the forest, and lived there in a pit for the entire summer. I lived off of rotten and frozen potatoes that I stole from faraway hamlets that were left over by the peasants.

"Later, when the partisan movement branched off and separated from the Russian army. They preferred working with Jews. I joined the unit in the Pinsk region and later joined the Red Army, where I carried out the most difficult tasks hoping to take revenge on the German bandits. More than once I risked my life, and I attained the rank of sergeant. I was at the Karel-Finnish front and was wounded several times. Therafter, I was sent to eastern Prussia, where I participated in attacks and capturing the city of Königsberg, where I received an award.

Zeidel (Yaakov) and Perl Lev. On the left is Zeidel's mother, Chaya-Mirel. The children from right to left are: Yosef, Rachel, Pesha, Bashka, and Binyamin Hershel. They all perished. May G-d avenge their blood!

Zeidel, the son of Tuvia David Lev from Horbacha was born around 1892 and studied in the Slobodka yeshiva under R. Baruch Ber Levovitz. In 1924 he moved to Drohitchin, and in 1942 Zeidel fled to Horbacha and perished there. Perl was a daughter of Tuvia David Warshavsky.

"Sometimes I wonder how I, someone who was educated in yeshivas and Hebrew schools and was a humanist, was able to could have been so wild and could have shed so much blood in eastern Prussia. I did not take any live prisoners. When the bloody hatred would say "Russia, good," I would slaughter them mercilessly. I went through the German towns and cities like a wild storm. My friends and I took death and destruction through eastern Prussia. Brothers, you may think that shedding the blood of the enemy might have calmed my rage consoled me. Unfortunately, it did not. There is no consolation for our suffering.

"After the demobilization I returned home to Drohitchin on the roofs of wagons. I found no one there. I found unknown gentiles taking over our home and all Jewish homes that remained standing. There were no Jews in Drohitchin, no Yiddish to hear or see. This was the same in Kobrin, Pinsk, and Brisk. There were a few 'passport Jews; from the eastern regions of Russian who did not even speak any Yiddish." See pp. 287.

The letter was sent from Lodz on December 27, 1945.

[Page 351]
Eight German Troop Trains Destroyed
By Yehoshua Kapelushnick (Argentina)

A letter to Yosef Feldman in Chicago, 1947

Dear Yosef:

I recently arrived in Lodz and am trying to establish connections with the rest of the surviving relatives and friends. After years of indescribable suffering and torment in the Drohitchin ghetto, in the forest with the partisans, and on the battlefield in the Red Army. I have a lot to tell and write about, and will describe some of the details to you now.

On June 25, 1941, the Germans occupied our town, and this introduced a period of suffering and murder! The German murderers would go around to the Jewish homes, robbing and beating people, claiming that the Jews were responsible for the war because they supported the communists with gold and weapons. The Germans rounded up all the Jews from all the villages and brought them to town. The local peasants from the village of Vetly started everything. They killed the Jews in their village, and gentiles of Khomsk and Motele did the same thing to the Jews living in those villages. They used knives, axes and scythes to kill the Jews. In Drohitchin itself during the first days of the occupation, the Germans killed those Jews who were known to be collaborators with the Soviet authorities. Then they started robbing Jewish property, tormenting, and sending the Jews to work in labor camps.

The Germans set up a Judenrat that would receive orders from the Germans. The Judenrat was responsible for collecting obligatory contributions, gold and personal possessions, as well as for sending people to work. This is how Jews themselves beat and plunder other Jews. During the first year, the Germans killed all the men in Brisk, Pinsk, Yanova, and other towns. Jews in Drohitchin were left alone for a while, though under tragic circumstances.

In 1942, the mass murder of Jewish communities in western Russia and Ukraine began. Jews in Drohitchin lived in two ghettos. One ghetto was for tradesmen, which is where I lived, and the other was for unskilled people, who were killed on July 25, 1942. Among the dead were my brother Mendel and his family.

After the unskilled were killed, we realized that the days of the tradesmen were numbered. I decided I didn't want to be slaughtered like a sheep but wanted to fight the murderers. I got some weapons and would spend nights hiding out in the outskirts of town with my brothers Hershel and Simcha. (See p. 336).

I remained alone with my indescribable anger and suffering, and I decided to take revenge for the spilling of Jewish blood, and fight against the German bandits with the last breath I had. I joined a partisan unit and fought against smaller German groups. I killed many Germans with my bayonet and chopped up eight German military trains carrying soldiers, who I wiped out.

Shoel and Devorah-Beila. Right: their parents: Chaim and Esther Khamsky. Left: Tsalka Feldman. All perished. May G-d avenge their blood!

[*Page 352*]

I also destroyed a tank and once was wounded. My thirst for revenge gave me courage to withstand the difficulties of partisan life. Many times I planned and carried out extensive operations. My greatest satisfaction was to hear a German moan, "Oh, my G-d." I would think to myself that this was a response to the millions of Jews reciting 'Hear O Israel.'"

Hershel, Esther-Necha Milner-Gurstein perished. May G-d avenge their blood! Sister of Todros Leib Milner, see pp. 295 and 324.

I got to the Red army together with the partisans, and in the Red army I had the opportunity to have an open assault and battle on the largest camps of the enemy until they were destroyed. We went through German towns and cities like a raging storm, and I admit that it was music to my ears to hear the cannons and the crumbling of German fortifications and buildings. The flames of the burning German houses, the destruction that my friends and I carried out made us feel great. Each one of us had a long score to settle with those cannibals. Until today I am still unsettled because I have still not settled all the scores I should with the murderers.

I grit my teeth and get agitated whenever I read about the trials of the bandits in Nuremburg and how politely the Germans are treated in the occupied zones. I know that any revenge against those beasts is too small for the six million tormented Jews in the concentration and extermination camps; for the babes who were killed by having their heads bashed against the wall until their brains poured out; for the tens of thousands of Jews who were buried alive up to their necks, and who were then killed when the Germans drove their tanks over them.

From left: Yosef, Sheina Feldman, Itcha Mishovsky, Levine, Esther Mishovsky, Velvel Mishovsky (below), Ungerman, and others.

You have no idea how cruel the Germans and their collaborators were to us! Don't let anyone say that it wasn't so bad! All of us who went through that suffering, starting from the Drohitchin ghetto and then with the partisans and in the Red Army, and who saw the Jewish catastrophe with our own eyes know that anything people say about it is only the tip of the iceberg of the gruesome destruction of our millions of brethren! It was terrible! It's impossible to describe!

Why are they going through those ceremonies for the German bandits, the Goerings, the Ribbentrops and the Rosenbergs? They killed millions of people! They are being treated too gentlemanly. Those criminals should be convicted! All Germans are criminals. None of them was innocent! According to law, we should carry out the decree of exterminating all of the German people as it is written, "Erase the memory of Amalek!"

[Page 353]

Left: Batcha Yanovsky and her mother Hanele Alberman.
May G-d avenge their blood!

Right: Moshe Mendel and Chava Perl Milner.
Moshe perished. May G-d avenge their blood!

Using Dynamite to Destroy Bridges
By Bashka Fialkov
Printed in the Amerikaner on November 22, 1946 by Gedaliah Kaplan

One day in June 1941, a dark cloud appeared over our town. The murderers had arrived. Their first order was that every Jew had to wear a yellow patch as a sign of shame. Soon thereafter, the Germans issued the awful decree that the Jewish population of Drohitchin had to bring the bloody authorities seven kilos of gold within three days. They took the elderly gray-haired Rabbi Isaac Kalenkovitch hostage and warned that if they did not receive the seven kilos of gold within three days, they would hang Rabbi Kalenkovitch in the marketplace.

People started weeping, and everyone took jewelry, rings watches and even gold teeth to the Judenrat, but unfortunately they were still half a kilo short. Jews started weeping and running to recite psalms in synagogue, begging for G-d's assistance to save their rabbi. The murderers were building gallows in the middle of the marketplace, and the next day they were planning to carry out their awful decree.

Suddenly in the middle of the night, the Russian priest, Palevsky, removed his golden crucifixes and gave them to the Jews. The next day they brought the half a kilo of gold, and the rabbi was released. Everyone was joyfully amazed that a Christian had helped to save the life of our rabbi, who was prepared to give up his life for the community that he loved so much. Their joy, however, did not last long.

One Sabbath morning, all the Jews were rounded up from Ghetto B, young and old, and were led away to Brona Gora, where they were all killed. Several months later, on October 15, 1942, the people in the second ghetto were taken away to be executed. The Germans took them to long pits that had previously been dug by the Jews of Ghetto A (every morning workers left, and in the evening the Germans shot the diggers). The Germans told every person to take off all his clothes and keep his clothes separated: the murderers sent the shoes and shirts somewhere else, and afterwards they hit the people in a hail of bullets with machine guns and threw them into the pits. Approximately 3,000 Jews were killed this way. Thereafter, the murderers got a board and wrote on it "Drohitchin is free of Jews."

At that time I was in a nearby town called Sernik, not far from Pinsk. The same murderers tormented us there, and took us to pits of death. It was in the early morning, and miraculously a policeman we knew saved my family and me. He was a Christian, and he told us to flee. My husband, children and I fled through the bushes and small trees. The murderers shot at us and killed my husband and small daughter. My other two children and I spent the night in a swamp. The next day my children and I made our way to a small abandoned house, but I was afraid to go out in the daytime to beg for bread. At night I knocked at the door of some peasants I knew, but they did not want to open the door. The peasant woman recognized me, crossed herself and said, "Fialkov! You were shot yesterday. Go away!"

[Page 354]

I started crying and told her that I was alive, begging her to save me from hunger. She threw out a loaf of bread, which calmed our hunger. We then spent the whole night in a forest and in the Pinsk swamps, where we were safe from the murderers but endangered by cold and hunger. We also had no water to drink, but we survived on red cranberries that grew around there. It was our "manna" from heaven. After weeks of torment, we made our way to the Sviren unit of partisans, who saved us from death.

As weak as I was, I somehow found latent strength within myself, and my children and I got guns and helped destroy the enemy positions. I laid landmines under bridges on which the murderers were supposed to pass over, or brought food from the villages until my children and I got to the Red Army and returned home to Drohitchin. I found a few Jewish survivors there, and everything was utterly destroyed. I found large mass graves; my heart was cold as a stone, and I trembled with pain. I could not look into the faces of the peasants who had taken the clothes of my brothers and friends. I could no longer live in the poisoned atmosphere of ruins and graves, so I went to live in the nearby town of Khomsk, where I did not find anyone. The peasants were living in the Jewish houses undisturbed. The Jews of Khomsk had been burned in the old synagogue that was destroyed except for four large walls. The awful Germans exterminated everyone up to the last Jews in town.

There were four Jews hiding out in Drohitchin, and the gentiles had handed them over to the German savages who bound the Jews hand and foot before police dogs tore them to pieces, limb by limb (It is said that Alter Goldberg of Socho, Moshe Perkovitsky, and others were killed by the German dogs. W.).

Standing, from right: Sisters Esther, Tila and Rachel Rosorovsky of Kremna. Seated from right: Reuven Burstein, Eliyahu Noach Ross, Rosa Goldstein, of Ozitch, and Gedaliah Kaplan in 1921. Esther (Morgan), Tila (Koppel) and Kaplan, of course, are now in New York. The others perished. May G-d avenge their blood! Rachel was the wife of Chaim Kobrinsky. See his memorial on p. 355, and a picture on p. 280.

[Page 355]

Fighting in the Red Army
By Shimon Lev (Israel)
a letter to Gedaliah Kaplan, March 1947

I was saved from the German brutes who brought this great misfortune on our Jewish People. This bitter fate was also visited on our town of Drohitchin (Polesia). When the Germans arrived in town, we were uprooted from the entire world, and put into the dark ghetto on the Vion, near the windmill. We were confined like criminals, without any means to survive or medical assistance. The country surgeon from Pinsk, Aharon Lasovsky, was with us and helped out as much as he could. Despair grew by the day, with 15 people being forced to stay in one bedroom. Various diseases broke out, and many people became swollen and died from hunger.

One Sabbath, on July 25, 1942, the weak and ill, together with the small children, were taken away to be killed in the lime pits in Brona Gora (Kartuz-Bereza). They knew where they were being taken, but they considered death better than suffering and torture. The German murderers destroyed the Jews with machine guns and mines. The small children were thrown into the pits alive. I am unable to describe everything, screams that rose to the heavens, and could be heard everywhere. Mothers cried as they watched their children being shot before their eyes while fathers cried out 'Hear O Israel.' As mentioned, this took place on the Sabbath after Tisha Be'Av, July 25, 1942. Half of the town was killed, and the second half, the so-called strong ones, continued to suffer until October 15, 1942.

I was also among those taken from Ghetto B to Brona-Gora. However, I managed to jump off the wagon and escape into the dense forest. The Germans shot at me wounded me in my right hand, but I was one of the lucky ones because I survived. I managed to make my way through the dense forest to the partisans, and was saved from death. I joined the Red Army and fought the whole time. I was wounded three times, but we bloodied the German bandits until they had no more blood, taking delightful revenge against them.

In 1945, I returned to my hometown, and unfortunately found no one left there. Of some 4,500 Jews, including my large family, no one remained. I saw how all the peasants from Starosila took over the Jewish houses, acted liked they owned them, and enjoyed our disaster. I was ashamed to go onto the street. The Christians would ask me what I was doing there, and whether I had come back from the dead.

I could not remain around there for long because the mass graves punctured my heart. I could not sleep for nights, and it appeared to me as if I heard voices from the mass graves where my parents, brothers, and sisters were buried. The side streets were paved with the gravestones from the New

Cemetery. With a grieving heart, I made a sacred oath to leave Drohitchin and move to Palestine. I wanted to go there no matter how difficult the road. There was no longer a place for me in my hometown, which had lost every trace of life. The Jewish community of my town, with all of its beautiful Jewish traditions and where the stones were saturated with Judaism and Torah, was uprooted. There were no more signs of it. Now I do not even have the words to describe this "Scroll of Fire" of my town of Drohitchin.

I took a last look at the streets of Drohitchin, said "Adieu forever," and headed for a camp in Frankfurt. I spent several months in a dark camp, watching the murdering nation enjoy itself after having murdered my parents. I was not able to breathe the muffled air of the country called "Germany," and my wife and I left by foot. We passed through high mountains and long roads until we arrived in Italy, from where we left by ship for Palestine.

> An eternal memorial to our unforgettable sister and brother-in-law
> Rachel (42) and Chaim (44) Kobrinsky
> Their children
> Mordechai (18) and Chaya-Beila (9)
> Sister
> Batsheva (45)
> All perished, may G-d avenge their blood!
> Esther Morgan (Ossining, NY) and Tila Koppel (New York)

See photo on p. 354.
[*Page 356*]

The Yiddish article here is virtually the same as the English one on page 357. The English article contains additional information that is not in the Yiddish one, which ends on another page not printed.

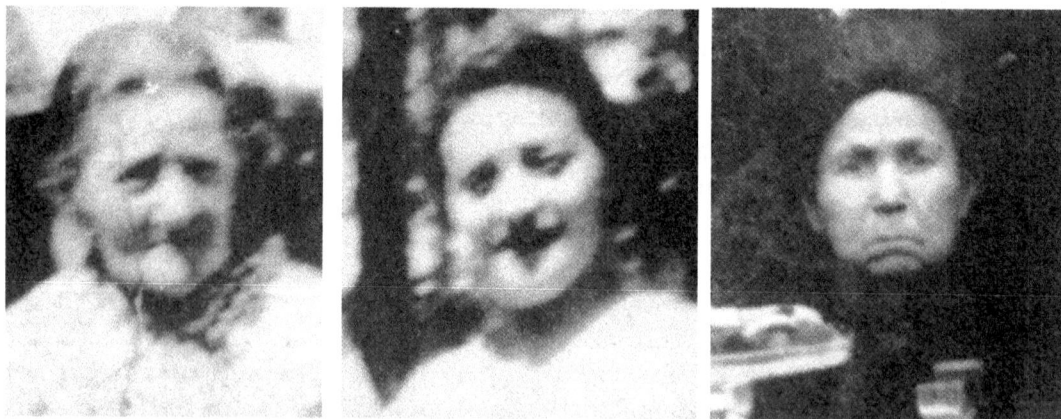

> An eternal memorial to our mother Basha (top, left) and sister Leah Mazursky, both of whom perished. May G-d avenge their blood!

The Mazursky children: Velvel (New York), Avraham, David (Argentina) and Pelta (Israel).

Eternal memorial: Our parents R. Zusha and Chaya-Frieda Warshavsky. Mother died on February 17, 1943 in Siberia, and father died on June 26, 1956 in Israel. See p. 208.

Warshavsky children: Rachel Mazursky (New York), Mordechai Berl (Israel) and Zlata-Miriam Warshavsky (Canada).

An eternal memorial to our and everyone's friends:
Moshe and Bodya Steinberg (pharmacist)
Their children: Esther and Khlavna
All perished, may G-d avenge their blood!
Yeshayahu and Zlata-Miriam Warshavsky (Canada)

Shimon and Chana from Horbacha, their children and grandchildren. All perished. May G-d avenge their blood! The photo was taken in Horbacha.

From left, Hershel Schmid, -----, Esther-Leah Lev, Bobtsa and Sarah Slonimsky (top). All perished except for Sarah. May G-d avenge their blood!

[*Page 357*]

R. Isaac and Khasha Valadavsky. Left: A neighbor, Leizer.

An eternal memorial to our dear parents, may G-d avenge their deaths:
Isaac, son of Shmuel, and Khasha Valadavsky
Brothers, may G-d avenge their deaths:
David Valadavsky and family
Meir Valadavsky and family
Sisters, may G-d avenge their deaths:
Reizel Grushevsky and Family
Hinda and family
Rachel and family
Laneh and Leizer Lev
Yehudis Novack
Nieces and Nephews (sisters' children), may G-d avenge their deaths
Yozep and Leah Lev and children, Moshe and Leizer
Toive, husband Moshe and children
Mother Toive Leah, daughter of R. Moshe – 22 Tevet
In sorrow: Malka Warshavsky, Chaya Goldman, Khasha Birnbaum, Feigel Kahn (Chicago), Yoshke and
Yudel Vladavsky (Cuba).

DROHICHYN LIBERATED

JULY 17, 1944

London. July 17.—Red Army forces, driving westward toward the twin German bastions of Bialystok and Brest-Litovsk, reached the Curzon Line today.

Other Soviet troops to the north pushed within a half mile of the Latvian border and widened their Niemen River bridgeheads for a direct attack into German-delineated East Prussia.

Stockholm reports said Soviet parachutists were descending in East Prussia and taht the Germans had ordered the eastern half of that province evacuated.

Gains Reach 16 Miles.

The five Soviet armies driving toward East Prussia and Warsaw scored maximum gains of 16 miles and liberated more than 410 localities today.

To the south Berlin reported a mighty Red offensive in southeastern Poland ha dcarried within 35 miles of the great rail junction and fortress city of Lwow.

There still was no indication

from Moscow that the Russians had driven into the Suwalki triangle of East Prussia which Germany annexed from Poland in 1939. But Moscow dispatches said the Russians were fighting in the "immediate neighborhood" of the border and Stockholm reported a wave of panic was sweeping taht breding ground of the German junkers military clan.

Drive for Bialystok.

The Curzon line was reached by a Russian column driving toward Bialystok, 78 miles north of Brest-Litovsk. That force took Velikaya Berestovitsa 35 miles east of Bialystok and on the Curzon Line which Russia has suggested serve as the basis for settling the Soviet-Polish border problem. The line was suggested by a commission headed by the Briton, Lord Curzon, as the Russo-Polish border after the last war but never was

The Russians took more than 300 towns in their double drives toward Brest-Litovsk and Bialystok, which form the main German defense wall guarding the entrance to the Polish plains and Warsaw.

One force descending on Bialystok captured Svislogh in a 10-mile gain. The other, pressing toward Brest-Litovsk from several directions, reached the closest to that city at the town of Shcherbovo, 30 miles northeast. Other towns captured were Shreshev, 37 miles northeast of Brest-Litovsk; Pruzhany, 45 miles northeast, and Drogichin, 60 miles east which was taken in a 16-mile spurt along the Moscow-Warsaw railroad.

North of Bialystok the Russians closed in on the old Lithuanian capital of Kaunas and front reports said Soviet artillery had begun shelling the Germans in that stronghold. Between Kaunas and Bialystok, the Moscow war bulletin said, the Russians widened their bridgeheads on the west bank of the Niemen River where they are two miles from the Suwalki triangle and 39 miles from pre-war East Prussia.

At the northern end of the 500-4mile front curving down from east of Latvia to the Pripet marshes the Russians overran the rail junction of Sebezh, on the Moscow-Riga line 10 miles from Latvia. North of Sebezh they took Stolbovo, half a mile from the Latvian border.

Yaakov Mishovsky, murdered, may G-d avenge his death!

From left: Zeidel Steinberg, Berl Kazack (with beard), Zechariah Kaplan Shinder, Kazack (child), deceased, and Steinberg (alive), next to Berl Kazack's house.

[Page 358]

THE RED ARMY IN DROHITCHIN
By Yoel Slonim

When I read that the Red Army had arrived in Drohitchin,
My heart beat with joy and I started to sing.
I looked at the words again and read them again,
I was absorbed by the words and read them again.
I heard some happy stories and saw some old men with happy glances.
Our shoulders became straight, our step proud and radiant,
Forgetting the days when hate was around.
Those days when Drohitchin was mourning in fear,
For many dark old months.
I saw children playing and laughing,
Running around the street, with young couples in embrace and smiling.
And Jews walking around with courage,
Without fear of the landlord's dogs, and the roads straight.
To the orchard keeper,
With apples and pears, and to the fields full of rye.
The air is filled with the sounds of heavy Russian songs,
And Jewish tunes of heartfelt longing, and intense romances
That are like bright flowers.
Oy, the years, Drohitchin's years, its childhood years,
When I got to Drohitchin from the streets of New York,
Possessed by my dreams.
Is this what I see an illusion that will pass
And disappear like the winds?
Or is this reality that ignites, where magical beams pass
Through tears of joy,
Where far away unknown people will come very close?
I read the light words again:
"The Red Army has arrived in Drohitchin."
And suddenly I forget about disputes and debates:
As to whether England or Russia is correct in the war?
I believe now and always want to believe that the Red Army
Will enjoy its victory for many jubilees,
And Hitler himself, with his regime of steel,
Will find himself crushed and defeated,
Yet stones and doubts fall again onto my heart,
Just like spears, I grit my teeth.
There's no salvation, how can we now hope?
My bright faith will run away in darkness,
Into the smoke of painful feelings and simple logic,
I go crazy, and want just to go up high,
To the pure blue, to the grass that is sunny,

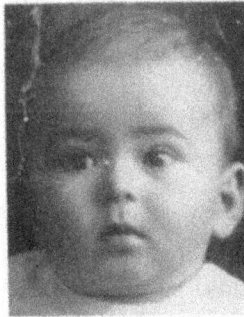

Aharon Shmuel and Beila Goldman and their grandchildren (top), who are the children of their daughter Pessel, and David Epstein
Second row, from right: Pessel and Miriam.

Third row: Pessel's child (right) and Miriam's little girl.

Fourth row: Esther and Yossel (died in the Polish army), Aharon Shmuel died on October 30, 1941. The others perished. May G-d avenge their blood!

[*Page 359*]

[Continuation of poem]

To large mountains, to a flying eagle,
To endless spaces in transparent light,
Then suddenly I hear the sound of trumpets,
"The Red Army has entered Drohitchin."
Scornful words glow and are believed,
And everything that was dusty, now becomes pure,
I see Yanova, Bereza, Khomsk and Kobrin,
The little houses of straw, and others of lime,
My grandfather's, my grandmother's, my father's home,
It seems as if my grandfather had risen from the grave
With his pipe moving around in his white beard,
And it seems as if I see my grandmother in her old clothes,
There she stands, next to him, as if hypnotized in her place.
There's the rabbi in his white garment, with his hands giving a blessing,
His beard and sidecurls ecstatic, his eyes aflame,
The rabbi's wife, a pure woman with extra charm,
Wraps herself in burial shrouds to go dance at a wedding.
In my fantasy I see under a linden tree
The march of the Red Army. I can see the martyrs,
The fighters, with fluttering flags,
Who died to sanctify G-d's holy Name,
Drohitchin – Berlin. The clouds move away,
The sun comes out,
"The Red Army has entered Drohitchin."
Is this what I see now, an illusion that will pass
And disappear like the winds?
Or is this reality that ignites, where magical beams pass,
With sparks of hope, to be reunited with my loved ones.

(Printed in *Tog,* New York, 1944. See p. 283)
(We have all felt what Yoel Slonim did, but, unfortunately, when the Red Army arrived in Drohitichin, only the "rabbi in his garment," his wife "in her shrouds" and thousands of martyrs wept in the streets. W.)

An eternal memorial to our dear parents and brothers:
Aharon, son of Yisrael; Sirka (daughter of R. Moshe Goldman); Lev, (top) and son Yaakov (right) and Avraham. The Levs were married in 1899, R. Aharon died on March 3, 1928 in Drohitchin. Sirka, Yaakov and Avraham perished. May G-d avenge their blood!

Relatives:

Chaim Moshe Leizer's and Sarah Epstein and children: Eidel, Berl, Chaytsha, her husband Berl and child perished. May G-d avenge their blood! Yitzchak and Sarah Epstein (of Tcheromcha) and children all perished. May G-d avenge their blood! The Lev children: Leizer, Mordechai, Khamka Kahn (Chicago), Shepsel, and Yitzchak (Haifa).

Khlavna and Leitcha Pisetsky and children, Yisrael-David and Shmuel-Yudel (left)
All perished. May G-d avenge their blood!
[*Page 360*]

Survivors of Drohitchin

They Survived after Being Sent Off to Russia

Rabbi Yehudah David Goldman received a letter from his brother-in-law, Shlomo Goldman from Liefheim, Germany dated August 10. In that letter, Shlomo wrote that on the 11th of Av a meeting had been held of survivors from Drohitchin and nearby areas. This date was the yahrzeit of the murders of their loved ones in Ghetto B in 1942 at the hands of the executioners. The people in Ghetto A were killed on October 15, 1942 – a total of 3,000 Jewish martyrs.

Following the recitation of chapter 79 of Psalms and a memorial, cantor Yosef Kaplan and Shmuel Eppelbaum, both of whom had survived the gruesome days in the ghetto of Drohitchin, provided all the details of their experiences and suffering. It was decided to make contact with émigrés from Drohitchin in the United States to request them to assist in the construction of the building in Israel to be called the Drohitchin Emigrés Building, where anyone from Drohitchin, Khomsk, and other nearby communities could rest up until he obtained a job and an apartment.

A committee made up of Shlomo Goldman, Hersh Greenberg of Liefheim, Shmuel Eppelbaum from Munich, and Shepsel Warshavsky from Einbing was elected to get in touch with the émigrés in Chicago and New York. The plan is to contact the appropriate Zionist institutions in the United States and Israel.

Here is the list of the Drohitchin survivors who participated at the meetings. The following are in Germany: Shlomo Goldman, Rachel Goldman, Hershel Weingarten, Yenta Weingarten, Perl Weingarten, Mordechai Goldman, Regina Goldman, Yitzchak Goldman, Shmuel Eppelbaum, Moshe Gingold, Leah Gingold, Malka Gingold, Motka Gingold, Berl Lev, Tsirel Lev, Eliezer Lev, Michela Lev, Meir Gendler, Esther Gendler, Chaim Gendler, David Gendler, Pesach Sandiuk, Zelda Sandiuk, Shepsel Warshavsky, Chaytcha Warshavsky,

Avraham Warshavsky, Yitzchak Pisetsky, Rachel Vinayoker, Yaakov Levin, Elka Levin, Yosef Levin, Lida Falk, Ignatz Falk, Feigele Falk, Alter Mazursky, Slava Mazursky, Chaytcha Mazursky, Chaim Mazursky, Pelta Mazursky, Ephraim Mazursky, Leah Mazursky, Adele Zissman, Pinchas Bider, Rachel Bider, Aharon Bider, Adel Bider, Nachum Bider, Hodem Bider, Shmuel Bidr, Paya Bider, Chaytcha Bider, Yenta Bider.

The following are in Poland: Avraham Averbuch, Sima Averbuch, Chaya Averbuch, Beila Averbuch, Zisha Warshavsky, Berl Warshavsky, Rachel Warshavsky, Avraham Warshavsky, Bashka Warshavsky, Yeshayahu Warshavsky, Zlata-Miriam Warshavsky, Breindel Warshavsky, Eliyahu-David Warshavsky, Nachum Spevak, Sarah Spevak, Sonia ?.

In Italy are Shepsel Zaretsky and ? Kravetz. In German are Yehuda and Opeda Feldman, Leah Eisenberg, Theodore Eisenberg, Moshe Bakaltchuk, Tsirel Bakaltchuk, Motel Dabrovsky, Nachum Eisenstein.

List of Survivors from Khomsk Now in Germany

Leibel Kahn, Hersh Greenberg, Pelta Greenberg, Chana Greenberg, David Greenberg, Meyers, Meyer Podorvsky, Paya Poderovsky, Chaya Poderovsky, Moshe-Aharon Poderovsky; Moshe-Hersh Simanovsky and Feiga Simanovsky are in Poland; Yitzchak Herlov and David Buff are in Italy.

Avraham and Sema Averbuch (top) and children: Chava and Bella (left). They were sent to Siberia by the Soviets, and returned in 1945. Today they live in Israel. The photo was

taken in Vraclaw, Poland in August 1949. See pp. 187, 188 and 211.

Rivka Rosenzweig-Karolinsky, husband, and child survived.

An eternal memorial to my dear sister and brother-in-law
Feiga-Rachel (daughter of R. Betsalel), and husband Moshe Garbuz
and five children. All perished. May G-d avenge their blood!
Louis Horsch (Miami Beach)

An eternal memorial to our dear parents
Leiba and Chaya-Sarah Sapir and children
They perished. May G-d avenge their blood!
Esther and Avraham Zelig Shedrovitsky

[*Page 361*]

Drohitchin Survivors
In Hiding in the Forest Around Drohitchin

A brief list from Jews surviving in Drohitchin, near Pinsk, and nearby towns who are now in Drohitchin. They can be written to at the following address: USSR, Pinsk Oblast, Drohitchin, USSR.

The note was received from Mr. David Kravitz, 504 Grand St., New York, NY.

Adler, Avraham from Drohitchin
Adler, Zissel from Drohitchin
Adrezhinsky, Yaakov from a village
Gerstenhaus, Moshe from Drohitchin
Goldberg, Nachum from Yanova
Zalinka, Chaya from Silna
Her child from Silna
Vanansky, Sheina from Drohitchin
Zaretsky, Shepsel from Drohitchin
Zaretsky, Sarah from Drohitchin
Zaretsky, Va** from Drohitchin
Lehrman, Shalom from Drohitchin
Spevak, Sarah from Drohitchin
Eppelbaum, Yenta from a village
Pakultsik, Moshe from Libeshei
Feldman, Chava from Drohitchin
Feldman, Yosef from Pohost
Kravetz, Rachel from Drohitchin
Rutsky, Itsik from Morly
Rutsky's brother from Morly
Schuster, Aharon from Adrizhna
Shinder, Chaya from Pinsk

Children from Drohitchin who are alive and serving in the Red army:
Arlansky, Zalman
Arlansky, Yankel
Berg, Shimon, Lev, Berl
Lev, Shimon
Lechevitsky, Leibel
Rubinstein, Itsel
Rubinstein, Yosef

Eppelbaum, Shmuel and others.

In the Red army there are also: Yirmiyahu Grossman (was in Russia), Izza Pisetsky, Reuven Goldberg, Mordechai Goldman, Yehoshua Kapelushnik, Baruch Baranstock, Binyamin Baum, Berl Gottlieb, Yossel Levin, Godel Shereshevsky, and others. The last two died in action.
Meshel Averbuch, Chaya Frieda Warshavsky, Chana Gingold, and Sender Vinovker died in Russia. See pp. 208, 211, 306, and 356.

A group of survivors from Drohitchin and Khomsk

The Bolsheviks sent them to Russia in 1941. They were photographed in Liefheim, Germany on July 28, 1947. First row, from left: ----- Gendler, Shmuel Eppelbaum, Zvi Weingarten, and others. Second row from left: Elka Lev, Shlomo Zelig and Rachel Goldman, Moshe and Leah Gingold, Yenta Weingarten, Shepsel and Chaytsha Warshavsky. Seated below: M. Goldman and others. See pp. 233, 333, 334, 335.

Meir Mordechai Hausman as a Polish soldier. He died in action in 1939.

Alter Kuperman (behind), may G-d avenge his blood, and Goldberg

An eternal memorial to our dear sister
Rachel Karzsh and family
Rivka and family
Brother
Alter Kuperman and family
All perished, may G-d avenge their blood!
The children of Michel Kuperman: B. Eisenberg (New York) and others.

[*Page 362*]

An Eternal Memorial for Our Drohitchin Martyrs

A group of Drohitchin émigrés from the United States and Canada:

Malka Grossinger, Yosef Warshaw, Tenenbaum Brothers, Samuel Lamasky, Harry Leiberman, Freida Miller, Meir Mishoff, Yonah Sapozhnick, Mr. and Mrs. Shatz, Schwartzberg, Annie Kronstadt.

These are those whom I shall remember, and my soul shall pour forth…because the wicked swallowed us without filling up…because in the days of Hitler there was no consolation for the Jews of Europe killed by government…The children of desolate Germany persecuted us and oppressed us worse than any other country. .Let everyone who hears tremble, and let our eyes flow with tears for the murder of eight million of our People.

אלה אזכרה ונפשי עלי
אשפכה... כי בלעונו זדים
כענה בלי הפוכה... כי בימי
היטלער לא עלתה ארוכה...
ליהודי אירופה הרוגי מלוכה...

יחתונו בני גרמניה השוממה...
הרעו לנו מכל מלכי אדמה...
רעדה תאחז כל שומע שמוע,
ותזלינה דמעות עינינו, בהריגת
שמונה מליונים מבחירי עמנו.

דאָס איז דער געלער מגן-דוד
מיטן וואָרט „יודע", וואָס די
דייטשן, ימח שמם, האָבן גע-
צוואונגען אונדזערע ייִדן צו
טראָגן, אַלס שאַנד-צייכן, אויף
זייערע בגדים, ווי אויך אָנצו-
קלאָפן אויף די טירן פון זיי-
ערע הייזער... דאָס האָט גע-

מיינט, אַז די ייִדן שטייען אוי-
סערן געזעץ, האָבן נישט קיין
שום בירגערלעכע און מענטש-
לעכע רעכט און יעדער איינער
קען טאָן מיט די ייִדן וואָס ער
וויל... טאַ לאָמיר עס געדיינקען
לדורות, וואָס דער דייטש האָט
געטאָן צו אונדז...! — [ד.וו.]

Jude
Remember what Amalek did to you.

This is the yellow Star of David with German word *Jude* that the Germans, may their names be erased, forced our Jews to wear as a sign of shame on their clothes. They also had to place them on the doors of their homes. This indicated that the Jews stood outside the Law, had no civil or human rights, and anyone could do as he pleased with the Jews. Let future generations remember what the Germans did to us!

DW

[*Page 363*]

Our Martyrs

Holy communities that sacrificed themselves for the sake of G-d's Holy Name...they were beloved and noble in their lives, and are together in death. Let the nations know before our eyes of the revenge of the blood of your servants...I cleaned their blood yet did not clean it. May G-d avenge their blood!

Perished at the hands of the German murderers in two massacres July 25, 1942 and October 17, 1942:

> Note: This list of names of the Martyrs is understandably incomplete. Certain names were omitted, but this was beyond our control. It was especially difficult to collect the names of the Jewish children of Drohitchin who were killed and who were among the thousands. We also do not have the list of the large number of Jewish refugees who were in Drohitchin and who perished together with the Jews of Drohitchin. May G-d avenge their deaths! Shlomo Zelig Goldman and Pinya Buder submitted some of the names. Yosef Feldman assisted us.
>
> *Dov Warshavsky*

Adler, Rachel-Leah
Adler, Yitzchak
Adler, Chaim
Adler, Sarah-Reizel
Adler, Chana
Adler, Yentl
Adler, Miriam
Avraham Tsheromkhers
Adelsky, Yosef, Magid
Adelsky, Bodya
Adelsky, Tsemach
Adelsky, Abba
Averbuch, Menachem
Oberman, Aharon Meir
Oberman, Khasha Hendel
Oberman, Kalman
Oberman, wife
Oberman, children
Oberman, Leiba
Oberman, wife
Oberman, children

Ukrainetz, Yeshayahu
Ukrainetz, wife
Ukrainetz, children
Ukrainetz, Shakhna
Ukrainetz, wife
Ukrainetz, daughter
Eisenberg, Chana
Eisenberg, Chaya-Shifra
Eisenberg, additional children
Eisenstein, Avraham Yitzchak
Eisenstein, Khasha Leah
Eisenstein, Tzvia, husband and children
Eisenstein, Eliyahu
Eisenstein, Sarah
Eisenstein, Hershel
Eisenstein, Leah
Eisenstein, Toiba
Eisenstein, three daughters
Eisenstein, Rabbi Asher
Eisenstein, his wife
Eisenstein, Shimon
Eisenstein, wife
Eisenstein, children
Eisenstein, Meir Leib
Eisenstein, Esther-Rachel
Eisenstein, Chaim Ber
Eisenstein, Rivka
[Page 364]
Eisenstein, a child Bobel Kleinman, mother
Altwarg, Chaim Ber
Altwarg, wife
Altwarg, Basha, husband Leibe Eppand, children
Altwarg, Rabbi Eliyahu Ze'ev
Altwarg, his wife
Altwarg, two children
Altwarg, a girl
Altwarg, Moshe
Altwarg, wife
Altwarg, children
Amstibovsky, Feivel
Amstibovsky, Esther
Amstibovsky, Reizel
Amstibovsky, Nisha
Amstibovsky, Friedka
Amstibovsky, Moshe
Andrinovsky, Freidel
Andrinovsky, Masha
Akushevitz, Matya (Yakhna's)
Akushevitz, Feigel
Akushevitz, children

Axenhorn, David
Axenhorn, Chayka
Axenhorn, three children
Axenhorn, Pinchas
Axenhorn, wife
Axenhorn, children
Arliansky, Yudel
Arliansky, children
Arliansky, Yenta, husband and children
Barenbaum, Wolfka
Barenbaum, wife
Barenbaum, Yossel
Barenbaum, Tsila
Barenbaum, Avraham
Barenbaum, Berel
Barenbaum, wife
Barenbaum, children
Barenbaum, daughter and family
Buder, Mordechai
Buder, Sarah
Buder, a girl
Buder, Moshe
Buder, Mendel
Buder, Shaina
Buder, Freida
Buder, Esther
Buder, Leibe
Baum, Yaakov Shimon
Baum, Avraham, son
Baum, Gittel
Baum, Zelda
Baum, Shashka
Baum, Meir
Baum, wife
Baum, Chava, Vartsevich
Baum, a girl
Baum, Toiba Hershel's
Baum, daughter
Baum, Chaim
Baum, wife
Baum, Yossel
Baum, wife
Baum, child
Baum, Shlomo
Baum, wife
Baum, 3 children
Baum, Meir
Baum, Sirka
Baum, Moshe
Baum, Massel

Baum, a girl
Baum, Motya
Baum, Rivka, sister
Baum, Esther, husband, children
Baum, Rafael
Baum, wife
Baum, a child
Buff, Hertska
Buff, Sarah
Buff, Shimon
Buff, Hinda
Burstein, Yosef, Yospes
Burstein, Rivka
Beita, Reuven
Beita, Basha
Beich, Shlomo
Beich, Lana
Beich, Meir
Beich, Yankel
Beich, Leizer
Beich, Nachum
Beich, a girl
Blankledder, Yitzchak
Blankledder, Yenta
Blankledder, Chaim
Blankledder Yossel
Blankledder, a girl
Bliach, Yudel
Bliach, wife
Bliach, Feivel
Begun, Aharon
Begun, wife
Begun, Moshe
Begun, other children
Begun, Meir
Begun, wife
[Page 365]
Begun, children
Bezdzhezesky, Yozep
Bezdzhezesky, Pessel
Bezdzhezesky, Benzion
Bezdzhezesky, Nechama
Bezdzhezesky, Reizel
Bezdzhezesky, Moshe
Bezdzhezesky, Chana
Bezdzhezesky, Yitzchak
Bezdzhezesky, Nechama
Becher, Yitzchak
Becher, Ethel
Becher, Avraham

Becher, Reizel
Becher, Malka
Becher, Feigel
Becher, Rachel
Berg, Binyamin
Berg, Bobtsa
Berg, Moshe Aharon
Berg, Tsippa
Berg, Malka
Berg, David
Berg, Fanya
Berg, four children
Berg, Motya
Berg, wife
Berg, children
Berg, Khonya
Berg, wife
Berg, children
Berg, Chaytsha
Berg, Moshe Gedaliah's
Berg, wife
Berg, children
Berezovsky, Sarah Rivka
Berezovsky, Bashka
Berezovsky, Baruch
Braverman, Leah (mother)
Braverman, Teibel
Braverman, Itsha
Braverman, Chana (wife)
Braverman, two children
Broffman, Bracha
Broffman, 3 children
Breindel, Shmuel
Breindel, Necha
Breindel, Beila
Breindel, two children
Breindel, Itsha, son
Breindel, Beila
Breindel, children
Breier, family
Gavrushin, Nechama
Gottlieb, Meir Leib
Gottlieb, Dovka
Gottlieb, Chaya Ita
Gottlieb, Tzvia
Gottlieb, Shepsel
Gottlieb, two girls
Gottlieb, a boy
Goldberg, Alter Socher
Goldberg, Esther, husband, Dr. Landau
Goldberg, Chaytsha, husband, Dr. Herring

Goldberg, Ovadiah
Goldberg, wife
Goldberg, children
Goldberg, Reizel Moshe's
Goldberg, Rivka
Goldberg, Bodya
Goldberg, Alter
Goldberg, Yehudis
Goldberg, three chidlren
Goldberg, Binyamin
Goldberg, Sarah
Goldberg, two children
Goldberg, mother
Goldberg, Berl
Goldberg, Sarah
Goldberg, a child
Goldberg, Baruch
Goldberg, Chana
Goldberg, Breina
Goldberg, Masha
Goldberg, Nassel
Goldberg, Hershel, Blinder [the Blind?]
Goldberg, wife
Goldberg, son-in-law Ezriel, his wife and two children
Goldberg, Velvel
Goldberg, Sheva
Goldberg, Teibel
Goldberg, Sarah
Goldberg, Yaakov
Goldberg, Zeidel
Goldberg, Fradel
Goldberg, 2 children
Goldberg, Zelig
Goldberg, wife
Goldberg, children
Goldberg, Yonah
Goldberg, Rachel
Goldberg, Moshel
Goldberg, Elka
Goldberg, Eliyahu
Goldberg, Milka
Goldberg, Yisrael
Goldberg, wife
Goldberg, a child
Goldberg, Meir Freidem
Goldberg, Shlomo
Goldberg, Avraham Yaakov
Goldberg, Sarah (wife)
Goldberg, Eliyahu

[Page 366]
Goldberg, Yudel
Goldberg, Motel
Goldberg, Moshe
Goldberg, Reizel
Goldberg, Moshe
Goldberg, wife
Goldberg, Yankel
Goldberg, Khama
Goldberg, Tamar
Goldberg, Moshe
Goldberg, Rivka
Goldberg, a child
Goldberg, Shimon
Goldberg, a wife
Goldberg, Pesha
Goldman, Eliyahu
Goldman, Shasha Rachel
Goldman, Yeshayahu 19
Goldman, Esther 13
Goldman, Yaakov 11
Goldman, Itsha
Goldman, Shaina Tsippa
Goldman, Nechama
Goldman, Beila
Goldman, Esther
Goldman, Miriam, husband Yitzchak and child
Goldman, Tsemach
Goldman, Devorah-Miriam
Goldman, Leizer
Goldman, Chaytsha
Goldman, Tsirel
Goldman, Yosef David
Goldman, Yehuda David
Goldman, Itka
Goldman, two children
Goldman, Hershel
Goldman, Elka
Goldman, Molya and husband
Goldman, Moshe Shlomo's
Goldman, Feitsha
Goldman, Yenta
Goldman, Yudel
Galitsky, Doctor
Galitsky, Manya
Galitsky, children
Gorodetsky, Yaakov
Gorodetsky, Chana
Gorodetsky, children

Gorodetsky, Malka
Gorodetsky, husband
Gorodetsky, children
Garbuz, Moshe
Garbuz, Feiga Rachel
Garbuz, five children
Gwirtzman, Yaakov
Gwirtzman, Esther Beila
Gwirtzman, Liza
Gwirtzman, a girl
Guralsky, Elka
Guralsky, Alter
Guralsky, wife
Guralsky, three children
Gurstein, Hershel
Gurstein, Esther Necha
Gurstein, three children
Gurstein, Leizer
Gurstein, wife
Gurstein, children
Gilgore, Albert Attorney
Gilgore, wife
Gilgore, daughter
Gillman, Mordechai
Gillman, Malka Gittel
Gillman, Yaakov 19
Gillman, Tsippa 16
Ginsburg, female dentist
Gloiberman, Shmerel
Gloiberman, wife
Gloiberman, children
Gelstein, Aharon
Gelstein, wife
Gelstein, children
Gershenberg, Bracha
Grossman, Dora, Yirmiyahu's
Grossman, Oscar
Grossman, Bluma
Greenberg, Yitzchak Noskes
Greenberg, wife
Greenberg, Shmuel Ber
Greenberg, Nassel
Greenberg, a girl
Greenberg, a boy
Greenberg, Shmuel
Greenberg, wife
Greenberg, two children
Greenberg, Yisrael
Greenberg, Moshe
Greenberg, others

Greenstein, Kaddish
Greenspan, Yitzchak Meir
Greenspan, wife
Greenspan Mattis
Greenspan, Menachem
Dolinsky, Litman
Dolinsky, wife
Dolinsky, a boy
Drucker, Betzalel

[Page 367]
Drucker, Chana Malka
Drucker, Fruma Leah
Drucker, Zlata
Drucker, Lotsa
Drucker, Tsalka
Drucker, Teibel
Drucker, two children
Drucker, Leibel an orphan
Drucker, Lotsa, husband, children
Drucker, Chaya, husband Aharon, children: Mordechai Ber, Meir and a girl.
Drucker, Yitzchak (Lipnick)
Drucker, Chaytsha
Drucker, four children
Hochman, Itsik
Hochman, Esther Rachel
Hochman, Shmuel Yudel
Hochman, Chaya
Hochman, Yaakov
Hochman, Lipman
Hochman, Fishel
Hochman, Avraham
Hochman, Yisrael
Hochman, Chana
Hochman, Gedaliah
Hochman, Chana
Hochman, three boys
Hochman, daughter
Hochman, son-in-law
Hochman, grandson
Hochman, Chaim
Hochman, Chasha
Hochman, Chana
Hochman, Chaya Ita
Hochman, Leizer
Hochman, Devorah
Hochman, Yitzchak
Hochman, wife
Hochman, children
Hochman, Moshe
Hochman, Sarah

Hochman, three children
Hochman, Chana, husband Breska and child
Hochman, Shlomo David
Hochman, wife
Hochman, children
Holtzman, Yitzchak
Holtzman, Sarah Itka
Holtzman, Yehudis
Holtzman, Feigel
Hammerstein, David
Hammerstein, wife
Hammerstein, Feivel
Hammerstein, Velvel
Hammerstein, Chaytsha
Hammerstein, Shepsel
Hammerstein, a boy
Hoffman, Naftali Schochet (probably profession of ritual slaughterer)
Hoffman, Slava
Hoffman, Beila
Hoffman, other children
Hausman, Alter
Hausman, Peshka
Hausman, Meir Mordechai
Hausman, Freidel
Hausman, Pinya
Hausman, Naftali
Hausman, Nissel
Hausman, Shmerel
Hausman, Leibka
Hausman, Gittel
Hausman, Rachel
Hausman, Chana
Hausman, Berl
Hausman, Pinya
Hausman, Chana, husband Shmuel Greenberg
Hausman, Reizel, husband Nissel Tsizh; children: Bluma and Feigel
Hausman, Berka
Hausman, wife
Hausman, children
Hausman, Zelig
Hausman, wife
Hausman, children
Hausman, Eliyahu
Hausman, wife
Hausman, children
Hausman, Berl
Hausman, wife
Hausman, children
Hausman, wife Yisrael's (possibly Yisrael's wife)
Hausman, Eliyahu
Hausman, a brother

Hausman, Yitzchak
Hausman, wife
Hausman, children
Hausman, Shimon
Hausman, wife
Hausman, children
Hausman, Aharon Shlomo
Hausman, wife
Hausman, children
Hausman, Mindel, mother
Hausman, Moshe
Hausman, wife
Hausman, two children
Hausman, Shayka
Hausman, wife
Hausman, grandchildren
Hausman, Chaim
Hausman, wife
Hausman, children

[Page 368]
Hausman, Zissel
Valiansky, Dobka
Valiansky, Tsippa, husband and three children
Valiansky, Shaina Milstein
Waldman, Pinya (Socher)
Waldman, wife
Waldman, Zvia
and family
Waldman, Henya
and family
Waldman, Chasha
and family
Waldman, Mordechai-Hersh
Waldman, Sarah Zlata
Waldman, daughter
Waldman, Dobka, husband and children
Volveler, Aharon
Volveler, Beila
Volveler, Mordechai 8
Volveler, Rivka 6
Volveler, Chana, 4
Volinetz, Yoshka
Volinetz, Menucha
Volinetz, Chana
Valevelsky, Rivka
Valevelsky, Zalman
Valevelsky, Mirka
Valevelsky, David
Valevelsky, Hersh

Valevelsky, Isaac

Valevelsky, Avraham
Valevelsky, Rosa
Valevelsky, Freidel
Valevelsky, Rachel, husband Malish and three children
Valevelsky, Chaim Eliyahu's
Valevelsky, Chana
Valevelsky, Eliyahu
Valevelsky, Shmuel
Valevelsky, Pessel
and children
Valevelsky, Chaim Meir's
Valevelsky, Itka
Valevelsky, Miriam Tsirel's
Valevelsky, Eidel, husband and two children
Valevelsky, Chayka and husband Shalom Halpern
Valevelsky, Bontsha
Valevelsky, Yisrael Baruch
Valevelsky, Feigel
Valevelsky, Sarah
Valevelsky, Moshe
Valevelsky, Yenta
Valevelsky, Leah Chaim's
Valevelsky, Binyamin
Valevelsky, Pessel
Valevelsky, Sheindel, husband and child
Valevelsky, Shmuel
Valevelsky, Breindel
Valevelsky, Zev, Engineer
Valevelsky, Shimon
Wolfson, Chaim Betzalel
Wolfson, Rachel
Wolfson, children
Volkovitsky, Meita
Volkovitsky, Tsippa
Volkovitsky, Moshee
Volkovitsky, Devorah
Volkovitsky, Feivel
Volkovitsky, wife
Volkovitsky, son
Volkovitsky, Michlia, husband Moshe Kronglass
children Chaya and others.
Volkovitsky, Itka, husband Chaim and child
Wasserman, Aharon
Wasserman, wife
Wasserman, two daughters
Wasserman, Rashka, Hershel and son
Wasserman, Yoshka and son
Wasserman, Sheindel
Wasserman, Esther
Wasserman, Rivka
Wasserman, Chaya

Wasserman, Nechama
Wasserman, Leibel, son
Wasserman, Chantsha
Wasserman, Nachman
Wasserman, Chaya
Warshavsky, David
Warshavsky, Feigel
Warshavsky, Fruma-Gittel
Warshavsky, Chaya Reizel
Warshavsky, Shmuel
Warshavsky, Leizer
Warshavsky, wife
Warshavsky, child
Warshavsky, Reuven
Warshavsky, wife
Warshavsky, child
Warshavsky, Moshe Shmuel
Warshavsky, Perl
Warshavsky, Shalom
Warshavsky, Meir
Warshavsky, Yisrael
Warshavsky, Teibel
Warshavsky, Meir
Warshavsky, Rivka
Warshavsky, Chaytsha

[Page 369]
Warshavsky, Yankel
Warshavsky, two children
Warshavsky, Moshe Alters
Warshavsky, Fruma
Warshavsky, children
Warshavsky, Sarah Leah
Warshavsky, Chaya, husband and child
Viganker, Chaya Sarah
Viganker, Bobel
Viganker, Tzvia
Viganker, Yaakov Eliyahu
Viganker, Perl
Viganker, Moshe, child
Vigutov, Meir
Vigutov, Sarah
Vigutov, three children
Vichnes, Yaakov
Vichnes, Feitsha
Vichnes, Berl
Vichnes, Zisel
Vichnes, a child
Vinovker, Mendel's wife
Vinovker, child

Wisotzky, Nachman
Wisotzky, Golda
Wisotzky, Velvel
Wisotzky, Khasya and others
Wisotzky, Moshe
Wisotzky, wife
Wisotzky, children
Wisotzky, Leiba
Wisotzky, sister
Waldavsky, Chasha
Waldavsky, Rachel, husband
Waldavsky, Hinda, husband and children
Waldavsky, Meir
Waldavsky, Motel
Waldavsky, children
Waldavsky, Paltiel
Waldavsky, wife
Venietsky, Yisrael
Venietsky, Minka
Venietsky, Yudel
Venietsky, wife
Venietsky, 2 children
Venietsky, daughter, husband and two children
Zavilovsky, Yudel
Zavilovsky, Yehoshua
Zavilovsky, Sarah Tila
Zavilovsky, Shalom
Zavilovsky, four children
Zavilovsky, Chaim
Zavilovsky, wife
Zaretsky, Rachel Devorah
Zaretsky, Pesach
Zaretsky, other children
Zaretsky, a daughter of Sarah Tila
Zbar, Tevel
Zbar, Friedka
Zbar, Nachman
Zbar, Teibel
Zbar, Zisel, Leah, Mother
Zishok, Nechemiah
Zishok, Mirel
Zishok, a girl
Zishok, Yospa, husband, child
Zishok, Ethel, husband, child
Zishok, Henya, husband Leiba Erlich and two children
Zistshok, Sarah
Zlotnick, Shlomo Chaim
Zlotnick, Sarah Leah
Zlotnick, Isser
Zlotnick, daughter
Zlotnick, Feiga Rachel, husband Yaakov and children:

Zlotnick, Eliyahu Yudel
Zlotnick, wife
Zlotnick, children
Khomsky, Chaim
Khomsky, Esther
Khomsky, Shoel
Khomsky, Devorah Beila
Khatskelovich, Tsalka
Kharovsky, Shalom
Kharovsky, wife
Kharsel, Yisrael Elazar
Kharsel, wife
Kharsel, Sheintsa
Kharsel, Sarah (a child)
Khinitz, Liber's son-in-law
Khinitz, wife
Khinitz, a girl
Tuller, Yisrael
Turniansky, Eliezer
Turniansky, Esther
Turniansky, three children
Turniansky, Baruch Pesach
Turniansky, wife
Turniansky, children
Turniansky, Berl
Turniansky, Rivka
Tint, parents
Tint, Chaya
Tint, Rivka

[*Page 370*]
Tint, others
Tenenbaum, Avraham
Tenenbaum, Ethel
Tenenbaum, Moshe
Tenenbaum, Sarah
Tenenbaum, Bracha
Tenenbaum, Yaakov
Tenenbaum, Eliezer Zalman
Tenenbaum, Breina Mirel
Tenenbaum, Avraham Yaakov
Tenenbaum, Rodya
Tenenbaum, Miriam
Tenenbaum, Beila Miriam, husband Shmuel Kotler, children:
Avraham, Hersh, Paya and Yenta
Tenenbaum, Zelig
Tenenbaum, Sarah Chana
Tenenbaum, Ezra
Tenenbaum, Pinya
Tenenbaum, a girl

Tenenbaum, Miriam
Tenenbaum, Rosa
Tchapotshnik, Aharon
Tchapotshnik, Leah
Tchapotshnik, Chaya Ita
Tchapotshnik, Shepsel
Cherniak, David
Cherniak, wife
Cherniak, children
Cherniak, mother
Cherniak, Sarah Leah
Cherniak, son
Yanovsky, Bobtsha and family,
Botsha's mother, Chanele Alberman
Yarenkes, Reizel
Yarenkes, children
Yudelevsky, Orele
Yudelevsky, Sarah
Yudelevsky, Moshe
Yudelevsky, Hillel
Yudelevsky, David
Yudelevsky, Lieba (wife)
Yudelevsky, two children
Katislavsky, Leizer
Katislavsky, wife
Katislavsky, six children
Katz, Binyamin
Katz, Chana
Katz, a boy
Lampel, D., Doctor
Lazarevitch, Sarah Leah
Lomasky, Esther
London, Aharon
London, Sarah Fruma
London, Avraham Leib
London, Yudel
London, Leizer
London, Rachel, husband and child
London, Bashkas, husband Avraham Fialkov and child, Esther
London, Binyamin
London, Hinda
London, Rachel
London, Hinda, husband Mordechai and children:
Chaim-Yudel, Rachel, Sarah, Reizel, Berl, his wife and child
London, Henoch
London, wife
London, five children
London, Toiba
London, Yeshayahu
London, Simcha
London, another two children

London, Yisrael
London, Freidel
London, Yoel Moshe
London, Yankel
London, Yudel
London, Sarah Reizel
London, Chaya Gitel
London, Yitzchak, wife and two children
London, Chava
Lasovsky, Aharon, country doctor
Lasovsky, Chayka
Lasovsky, Dintsha
Lasovsky, Moshe
Lasovsky, Hershel
Lasinsky, Leizer
Lasinsky, wife
Lasinsky, Leiba
Lasinsky, Yitzchak
Lasinsky, wife
Lasinsky, children
Lasinsky, daughter, husband and children
Lofman, Aharon
Lofman, Itka
Lofman, three children: Esther Leah Lev, Mother
Lopatin, Esther-Feigel
Lubatshevsky, Avraham
Lubatshevsky, wife

[Page 371]
Lubatshevsky, a girl
Lubatshevsky, a daughter, son-in-law Schlossberg, child
Lubatshevsky, Leizer
Lubatshevsky, wife
Lubatshevsky, two childlren
Lyubashevsky, Khamka
Lyubashevsky, Rivka
Lyubashevsky, Sarah
Lyubashevsky, children
Ludvinsky, Leibel
Ludvinsky, Shifra
Ludvinsky, five children
Basha Milner, Mother
Laufer, Berl
Laufer, Bluma
Laufer, 4 children
Laufer, Mordechai
Laufer, wife
Laufer, daughter, husband and children

Liakhovitsky, Avrham Yaakov
Liakhovitsky, wife
Liakhovitsky, children
Liakhovitsky, Falk
Liakhovitsky, wife
Liakhovitsky, children
Liakhovitsky, Shimon
Liakhovitsky, wife
Liakhovitsky, children
Liakhovitsky, Itsha
Liakhovitsky, wife
Liakhovitsky, children
Liakhovitsky, Leizer
Liakhovitsky, wife
Liakhovitsky, children
Lieberman, Meir
Lieberman, Esther
Lieberman, Yossel
Lieberman, Shlomo
Lieberman, Ezra
Lieberman, a daughter
Lieberman, Shaina Chaya
Lieberman, Reuven
Lieberman, Yankel
Lieberman, Golda
Lieberman, a child
Lichtenstein, Bashka
Lichtenstein, son
Linik, Aryeh
Lifshitz, Bobbel
Lifshitz, wife
Lifshitz, children
Lev, Eliezer
Lev, Rivka
Lev, Isaac
Lev, a daughter
Lev, Rachel, her husband and child
Lev, Ephraim
Lev, wife
Lev, children
Lev, Berl Shimon Nachums
Lev, wife
Lev, Dvosha
Lev, Manya
Lev, Sarah
Lev, Zlata and son-in-law
Lev, Velvel (Kirszner)
Lev, Yerachmiel
Lev, Binyamin
Lev, wife

Lev, child
Lev, Leibe
Lev, wife
Lev, two children
Lev, daughter, son-in-law and grandchildren
Lev, Velvel Leibetshkas
Lev, Rachel
Lev, Elazar
Lev, wife
Lev, children
Lev, Yerucham Lieb
Lev, wife
Lev, children
Lev, Zeidel Horbacher
Lev, Perl
Lev, Pesha
Lev, Basha
Lev, Hershel
Lev, Rachel
Lev, Yossel
Lev, Chaya Mirel, Mother
Lev, Temtsa Kalmans
Lev, daughter-in-law
Lev, four children
Lev, Yozep
Lev, Leah
Lev, Moshe
Lev, Leizer
Lev, another child
Lev, Toiba-Leah, husband Moshe, children
Lev, Yitzchak
Lev, son
Lev, daughter-in-law
Lev, children
Lev, Yeshayahu
Lev, wife
Lev, children
Lev, Yisrael Zelig
Lev, Feigel
Lev, David
Lev, Tsila
Lev, child

[Page 372]
Lev, Leizer
Lev, children
Lev, son
Lev, daughter-in-law
Lev, two children
Lev, daughter, son-in-law and two children
Lev, Sirka
Lev, Yankel
Lev, Avrahamel

Lev, Ezriel
Lev, family
Lev, Pesach
Lev, Gisha
Lev, Orele
Lev, Shmuel
Lev, Dovka
Lev, Fruma
Lev, Sarah
Lev, others
Lev, Shmuel
Lev, Itsa
Lev, Shaina Lotsa
Lev, Lana
Lev, Lieba
Lev, Beila
Lev, wife Shimons
Lev, Berl
Lev, wife
Lev, Reuven
Lev, wife
Lev, children
Lev, two unmarried boys
Lev, two daughters
Lev, Zvi
Lev, Chaim
Lev, Yenta
Levak, Moshe
Levak, Chaya Doba
Levak, Baruch
Levak, Zelig
Levak, Yenta, husband Isser and son, Binyamin
Levinov, Shammai
Levinov, Ethel
Levinov, five children
Levinovitz, Yitzchak
Levinovitz, Leah
Levinovitz, children
Levinovitz, mother, the Kholozhin rebbe's wife
Levinson, Shabtai
Lekhovitsky, Yitzchak
Lekhovitsky, Sarah Gittel
Lekhovitsky, Esther
Lekhovitsky, Nachum
Lekhovitsky, Michlia
Lekhovitsky, Yehudit
Lekhovitsky, Feivel
Lekhovitsky, a child
Lerman, Alter
Lerman, Sarah
Lerman, Chana

Lerman, Yisrael
Lerman, Nechemia
Mazursky, Basha
Mazursky, Leah and child
Mazursky, Shepsel
Mazursky, Michlia
Mazursky, child
Mandel, shoemaker
Mandel, wife
Mandel, three children
Morgenthaler, Shalom
Morgenthaler, Shifra
Morgenthaler, Beila
Morgenthaler, Chana
Meyerovitch, Moshe
Meyerovitch, Dovka
Meyerovitch, Nechama
Meyerovitch, Sprintsa
Meyerovitch, a girl
Milner, Avraham Meir
Milner, Kaila
Milner, David
Milner, Devorah
Milner, Sarah
Milner, Leiba
Milner, Lieba
Milner, Rivka
Milner, Mindel
Milner, two boys
Milner, Dina
Milner, Mordechai
Milner, Moshe Mendel
Milner, Chana
Milner, Moshe Mendel [sic]
Milner, Chava Perl
Milner, Chaya Chasha Lazarovitch
Milner, Zissel Lazarovitch, husband
Milner, Freidel, Freidel's husband
Millstein, Simcha
Millstein, wife
Millstein, four children
Mishovsky, Bobba, Mother
Mishovsky, Chana-Beila
Mishovsky, Velvel, son
Mishovsky, Peshka
Mishovsky, Itsha son
Mishovsky, Rachel
Mishovsky, Avrahm
Mishovsky, Tuvia
Mishovsky, Elchanan-Asher son

Mishovsky, Feigel
Mishovsky, a boy
[Page 373]
Mishovsky, Leah-Beila
Mishovsky, Velvel, son
Mishovsky, Chaytsha
Mishovsky, Tila
Mishovsky, Shepka
Mishovsky, Shual
Mishovsky, Leizer
Mishovsky, Devorah
Mishovsky, Mashka
Mishovsky, Yankel
Mishovsky, Avraham
Mishovsky, Dina, husband, and child
Melamed, Berl Silitshever
Melamed, wife
Melamed, children
Melamed, Lieba Naftalis, husband, three children: Yaakov, etc.
Mednitsky, Liber Kolonya
Mednitsky, wife
Mednitsky, Yaakov
Mednitsky, wife
Mednitsky, grandson
Mendelson, Shifra
Mendelson, Liza, husband Henoch, two children
Meshchanin, Aharon Eliyahu
Meshchanin, Ethel
Meshchanin, three children
Novick, Avraham
Novick, wife
Novick, two children
Saliver, Zechariah
Saliver, Nissa Beila
Saliver, Ethel
Saliver, Sarah
Saliver, Tsippa
Saliver, Bracha
Saliver, Chaya-Itka
Saliver, Chaya-Sarah
Saliver, Chaim
Saliver, Aharon
Saliver, wife
Saliver, four children
Saliver, Leah, husband, 4 children
Sapozhnick, Sarah
Sapozhnick, Zechariah
Sapozhnick, Beiltsha
Sapozhnick, Tsirela

Safir, Leib
Safir, Chaya-Sarah
Safir, Mordechai
Safir, Chana-Pesha
Safir, child David
Safir, Cherna, husband
Kapliss, two children
Sochavtshisky, Isaac
Sochavtshisky, wife
Sochavtshisky, children
Svetshnik, Yosef
Stricharzh, Mandel
Siderov, Asher
Siderov, Avraham
Siderov, Yentel
Siderov, Masha
Siderov, Yosef
Siderov, wife
Siderov, Chantsha, husband and children
Siderov, Yaakov
Siderov, Chava
Siderov, Beiltsha and husband
Siderov, Pinya
Siderov, Mindel
Siderov, children
Slomovitch, Yaakov Wolf
Slomovitch, Rachel
Slomovitch, Zelig
Slomovitch, Shaindel
Slomovitch Freidel
Slonimsky, Zelig
Slonimsky, Benzion
Slonimsky, Malya
Slonimsky, Shifra
Slonimsky, Bobtsa, her husband
Slep, Leibush
Slep, Tsotka
Slep, three children
Snitovsky, Chaim
Snitovsky, Avraham
Snitovsky, Pessel
Snitovsky, three children
Snitovsky, Shmuel
Snitovsky, Perl
Snitovsky, Rachel
Snitovsky, three boys
Segalovitch, Nechemiah
Sendiuk, father
Sendiuk, mother
Sendiuk, Hershel
Sendiuk, wife

Sendiuk, children
Sendiuk, Mordechai
Sendiuk, wife
Sendiuk, child
Sertchuk, Fishel
Sertchuk, Rivka
Sertchuk, Velvel
Sertchuk, Chaya
Sertchuk, Baruch
Spevak, Avraham

[Page 374]
Spevak, Dvosha
Spevak, Pesach
Eppelbaum, Bobbel
Eppelbaum, Miriam
Eppelbaum, Rachel
Eppelbaum, Friedel, husband, Meir, children: Avraham and Natan
Eppelbaum, Yaakov
Eppelbaum, wife
Eppelbaum, children
Eppelbaum, Sender
Eppelbaum, Elka
Eppelbaum, 2 children
Eppelbaum, Mordechai
Epstein, Chaim Zissel
Epstein, Fradel
Epstein, Shlomo
Epstein, Feigel
Epstein, Chana
Epstein, Rachel
Epstein, David
Epstein, Pessel wife
Epstein, three children
Epstein, Chaim
Epstein, Sarah
Epstein, Berl
Epstein, Eidel
Epstein, Chaytsha, husband Berl, children
Epstein, Yitzchak
Epstein, Sarah
Epstein, children
Erlich, Elchanan
Erlich, wife
Erlich, children
Erlich, family
(Yossel the Wagon Driver's)
Pomeranetz, Zeidel
Pomeranetz, Yehoshua

Pomeranetz, Asna
Pomeranetz, Tsirel
Pomeranetz, Sarah
Pomeranetz, Ezriel
Papinsky, Hershel
Papinsky, Elka
Papinsky, daughter
Papinsky, Shmuel, son
Papinsky, daughter-in-law
Papinsky, grandchildren
Papinsky, Motya
Papinsky, wife
Papinsky, four children
Papinsky, Zeidel
Papinsky, wife
Papinsky, children
Poritsky, Lieba
Poritsky, Kraina, husband Tsadok, child Feigel
Polik, Shimon
Pitkovsky, Sarah
Pinsky, Avraham
Pinsky, Feigel Naftalis
Pinsky, Yasha
Pinsky, Aniuta
Pinsky, Esther
Pisetsky, Beila
Pisetsky, Khlovna
Pisetsky, Leitsha
Pisetsky, Yudel
Pisetsky, Yisrael David
Pisetsky, Sarah the midwife
Pliss, Shlomo
Pliss, Bodya
Pliss, Rachel
Pester, Nechemia
Perkovsky, Simcha
Perkovsky, wife
Perkovitsky, Moshe
Perkovitsky, Tema
Perkovitsky, Reuven Meir
Perkovitsky, wife
Perkovitsky, child
Prager, Moshe, ritual slaughterer
Prager, Berl
Prager, Chaya
Prager, Beiltsha, husband and child
Prikladnitsky, Alter
Peretz, Leiba
Peretz, Yaakov
Peretz, others

Foxman, Isaac
Foxman, Chatshka
Foxman, children
Feinberg, Itseles
Feldman, Avraham
Feldman, Sender
Feldman, three children
Feldman, Levi
Feldman, Risha
Feldman, child
Feldman, Leib
Feldman, Esther
Feldman, child
Feldman, Meir Yudel
Feldman, Chaya
Feldman, Leiba
Feldman, Lieba
Feldman, a girl
Feldman, Yaakov nine (lost)

[Page 375]
Feldman, Schwartz Bashka
Feldman, Schwartz Peshka
Feldman, Yossel
Feldman, Feigel, daughter
Feldman, Tsalka
Feldman, Dina, wife
Feldman, child
Feldman, Hershel, Dr.
Feldman, Liza
Feldman, child
Feldman, Yankel
Feldman, Simcha
Feldman, Michael
Feldman, Hershel
Feldman, Hinda
Feldman, Chaytsha
Feldman, David
Feldman, two children
Feldman, Freidka, husband Noach Shapiro, 4 children
Feldman, Litman
Feldman, Peshka
Feldman, Zelig
Feldman, wife
Feldman, children
Feldman, Feibush
Feldman, Chaya-Lieba
Feldman, Moshe
Feldman, Peshka
Feldman, three children

Feldman, Avraham Yakkov
Feldman, Yankel
Feldman, Leizer
Feldman, Sender
Feldman, wife
Feldman, two children
Feldman, Zeidel
Feldman, Esther
Feldman, child
Feldman, Leizer
Feldman, Bracha
Feldman, Sarah
Feldman, Itsa
Feldman, two girls
Feldman, Rodka
Feldman, Shmuel
Feldman, two girls
Fruchtenberg, Ze'ev
Fruchtenberg, wife
Fruchtenberg, two children
Friedenberg, Moshe
Friedenberg, Chaya
Friedenberg, Yossel
Friedenberg, Nachum
Friedenberg, Rivka
Friedenberg, Rachel, husband Isaac
Friedenberg, Alter
Friedenberg, Shaina Leah
Friedenberg, Yonah
Friedenberg, Rivka Shlomos
Friedenberg, Sarah
Friedenberg, Berl
Friedenberg, Eliyahu
Friedenberg, Gittel
Friedenberg, Yenta
Tsizh, Yoel
Tsizh, child
Tsizh, wife
Tsizh, Yaakov Eliyahu
Tsizh, Bobtsha
Tsizh, 5 children
Tseshkes, Chasha
Tseshkes, Bashka
Tseshkes, Chana
Tseshkes, an unmarried boy
Kobrinsky, Traina
Kobrinsky, Chaytsha
Kobrinsky, husband and child
Kobrinsky, Chaim
Kobrinsky, Rachel

Kobrinsky, Mordechai
Kobrinsky, Eliyahu
Kobrinsky, Beila
Kobrinsky, mother-in-law
Kobrinsky, sister-in-law Batsheva
Kobrinsky, Yossel
Kobrinsky, wife
Kobrinsky, children
Kagan, Shepsel
Kagan, Eidel Chaya
Kagan, Ethel
Kagan, a son
Kadishevitz, Yosef ritual slaughterer
Kozack, Yitzchak Leib
Kozack, Feigel
Kozack, children
Kozack, Avraham
Kozack, Rachel
Kozack, child
Kozack, Yaakov David
Kozack, wife
Kozack, children
Kozack, Yitzchak
Kozack, wife
Kozack, two children
Kozack, Alter
Kozack, wife
Kozack, four children

[Page 376]
Kotler, David
Kotler, Feiga-Rachel
Kotler, Moshe-Leizer
Kotler, Beila
Kotler, Leah
Kachler, Pessel
Kachler, Yisrael
Kachler, wife
Kachler, children
Kachler, others
Kolodny, Hershel
Kolodny, Chaytsha
Kolodny, child
Kolodner, Shmuel
Kolodner, Guta
Kolodner, Getsel
Kolodner, Miriam-Ethel
Kolodner, Teibel
Kolodner, Dvosha

Kolodner, Dina
Kolodner, Frieda, husband Goldberg, five children
Kalechovsky, Isser
Kalechovsky, Bobel
Kalechovsky, Baruch
Kalechovsky, Moshe
Kalechovsky, Bracha
Kalechovsky, Avraham
Kalechovsky, David
Kalechovsky, son
Kolnick, Isaac
Kolnick, Miriam
Kolnick, Peshka
Kolnick, Yospa
Kalenkovich, Rabbi Isaac Yaakov
Kalenkovich, Michlia, his wife and son
Kalenkovich, Beila
Kalenkovich, Moshe Zvi
Kalenkovich, son
Kalenkovich, Menachem
Kalenkovich, Mary
Kalenkovich, children
Kaminetsky, Avraham
Kaminetsky, wife
Kaminetsky, children
Kaminetsky, Ephraim Alters
Kaminetsky, Binyamin
Kaminetsky, Beila
Kaminetsky, Sarah
Kaminetsky, Hershel (Beila Reisels)
Kaminetsky, Yosef Shimon and family
Kaminetsky, Yehoshua and family
Kaminetsky, Pinya and family
Kaminetsky, Fradel and family
Kaminetsky, Chana and family
Kaminetsky, Miriam and family, Mendels
Kaminetsky, Menachem
Kaminetsky, wife
Kaminetsky, Benzion
Kaminetsky, Berl
Kaminetsky, another three children
Kaminetsky, Necha Leizers, husband Avraham, son, daughter-in-law and grandchild
Kaminetsky, Elka
Kaminetsky, daughter and husband Malik and child
Kaminetsky, Sarah
Kaminetsky, two girls
Kaminetsky, Hesha son
Kaminetsky, Sarah wife
Kaminetsky, three children
Kaminetsky, Yitzchak

Kaminetsky, wife
Kaminetsky, child
Kaminetsky, Sarah [sic]
Kaminetsky, Yehoshua Hersh
Kaminetsky, Shifra
Kaminetsky, Shabtai
Kaminetsky, Shaina Leah
Kaminetsky, daughter,husband and child
Kaminetsky, Shabtai [sic]
Kaminetsky, wife
Kaminetsky, children
Kaplan, Dashka attorney
Kaplan, Malka, Zalman's
Kaplan, Fruma
Kaplan, Aharon
Kaplan, Moshe
Kaplan, Shalom
Kaplan, Chaytsha
Kaplan, Buntsha, husband and children
Kaplan, Zechariah
Kaplan, wife
Kaplan, three girls
Kaplan, Reizel and family
Kapelushnik, Lana, mother
Kapelushnik, Mendel
Kapelushnik, Chayka
Kapelushnik, Sarah
Kapelushnik, son
Kapelushnik, Hershel
Kapelushnik, wife
Kapelushnik, Shimon
Kapelushnik, Simcha
Kapelushnik, wife
Kapelushnik, children
[*Page 377*]
Karzh, Meir
Karzh, Rachel
Karzh, Yisrael
Karzh, Fishel
Karzh, a girl
Karzh, Michael
Karzh, Bobtsha
Karzh, children
Karzh, Shmuel
Karzh, Gittel
Karzh, widow
Karzh, children
Karelitz, Alter
Karelitz, Malka-Leah

Karelitz, Yisrael David
Karelitz, a child
Korn, Leizer
Korn, wife
Korn, daughter
Cooper, Shimon
Cooper, wife
Cooper, three children
Cooperman, Alter
Cooperman, wif
Cooperman, child
Cooperman, Rivka and family
Kier, David
Kier, Leah
Kier, Avraham
Kier, Sheintsa
Kier, Lieba
Kier, another three children
Kirzh, Mordechai
Kirzh, Shaina
Kirzh, Yaakov
Kirzh, Chaya Sarah
Klorfein, Zeidel
Klorfein, wife
Klorfein, children
Klorfein, Chaya-Sarah
Kan-Tsipor, Yisrael
Kan-Tsipor, Gershon
Kravetz, Yisrael
Kravetz, Esther-Rachel
Kravetz, Moshe
Kravetz, Leah, daughter-in-law
Kravetz, three chidlren
Kravetz, Leah, husband Leiba, 3 children
Kravetz, Peshka, husband Fishel Rimland and 3 children
Kravetz, Rivka Eliyahus
Kravetz, Chasha, husband Nissel Lisker and 2 children
Kravetz, Chaim-Ber
Kravetz, Malka
Kravetz, daughter, husband Gershenhaus
Kravetz, Itska, son
Kravetz, wife
Kravetz, Shimon
Kravetz, children
Kravetz, Mendel, son
Kravetz, wife
Kravetz, children
Kravetz, Avraham, son
Kravetz, Itka
Kravetz, Chana

Kravetz, two children
Kravetz, Sarah Senders and 4 children
Kravetz, Moshe
Kravetz, wife
Kravetz, Leibel
Kravetz, Reuven
Kravetz, Avraham
Kravetz, Elka and husband Yoel
Kravetz, Leizer
Kruptchisky, Yisrael Aharon
Kruptchisky, daughter
Kruptchisky, two grandchildren
Rabinsky, Simcha
Rabinsky, wife
Rabinsky, three children
Rosenbaum, Chana Malka
Rosenbaum, Yankel
Rosenbaum, Menachem
Rosenbaum, Chaytsha
Rosenbaum, Henya
Rosenzweig, Shmuel
Rosenzweig, Zlata
Rosenzweig, Aharon
Rosenzweig, Yenta
Rosenzweig, Zelda
Rosenzweig, Sima
Rosenzweig, Freidel
Rosenzweig, Yossel David
Rosenzweig, Yaakov Hershel
Rosenzweig, Chava
Rosenzweig, Yaakov
Rosenzweig, Tila, husband and children
Rock, Shmuel
Rock, wife
Rock, girl
Rubinstein, Alter
Rubinstein, Doba
Rubinstein, Sarah
Rubinstein, Chaya
Rubinstein, Eliyahu
Rubinstein, Asher
Rubinstein, David
Rubinstein, Baruch Leib
Rubinstein, wife
[Page 378]
Rubinstein, 3 children
Rubinstein, Yitzchak
Rimland, Lieba (Mother)
Rimland, Yankel
Rimland, Chamka

Rimland, Yospa
Rimland, Itsel
Rimland, Yisrael
Resnick, Aryeh
Resnick, Rachel
Resnick, Moshe
Resnick, another two children
Resnick, Berl
Resnick, wife
Resnick, three children
Resnick, Beila, mother
Shapiro, Sender
Shapiro, Michlia
Shapiro, Rachel
Shapiro, Shmuel
Shapiro, Shasha
Shapiro, Chaim
Shapiro, wife
Shapiro, children
Shapiro, Chana and her husband
Schub, Yosef-David, ritual slaughterer
Schub, wife
Schub, Binyamin Moshe
Schub, a girl
Schub, Nechama, husband and children
Schwartz, Moshe
Schwartz, wife
Schwartz, Avraham
Schwartz, wife
Schwartz, Rachel
Schwartz, Rivka
Schwartz, Shmuel
Schwartz, Tsippa, wife
Schwartz, Baruch
Schwartz, wife
Schwartz, children
Schwartz, Yenta
Schwartz, a child
Schwartz, Chana
Schwartz, Itka, husband Yudel Neiditz, children: Noyna and Zonya
Schwartz, Esther, husband Shlomo Engel
Schwartz, Rachel Leizers
Schwartz, Menachem
Schwartz, Itsha
Schwartz, Alter
Schwartzledder, Elka
Schwartzledder, Gresha
Schwartzledder, Yeshayahu
Schwartzledder, Hershel
Schwartzledder, Bracha, mother

Schwartzberg, Asher
Schwartzberg, Basha
Schwartzberg, Yitzchak
Schwartzberg, Shalom
Schwartzberg, Shifra
Schwartzberg, two children
Shuchman, Yehuda
Shuchman, Mina
Shuchman, Yitzchak
Shuchman, Avraham
Shuchman, Rosa
Shuchman, Sonia
Shulman, Chaim
Shulman, Reichel
Shulman, five children
Shulman, mother
Shuster, Yaakov, Rabbi
Shuster, wife
Shuster, children
Shuster, Hershel, Rabbi
Shuster, wife
Shuster, children
Shushanov, David
Shushanov, Reizel
Shushanov, Esther
Shushanov, Rachel
Shushanov, Miriam
Shushanov, a child
Shushanov, Chaya-Beila
Steinberg, Moshe
Steinberg, Bodya
Steinberg, Esther
Steinberg, Khlavna
Shinder, Chaya Leah
Shinder, Moshe son
Shinder, Mendel
Shinder, Mirel
Shinder, a son
Shinder, Nachum
Shinder, Perl
Shinder, three children, wife's mother
Shinder, Asna, husband Moshe and three children
Shinder, Alter
Shlackman, Eliyahu
Shlackman, Devorah
Shlackman, Shepsel
Shlackman, another two children
Schmid, Zechariah
Schmid, Yudel
Schmid, Elka

Schmid, Hershel
Schmid, wife
Schmid, Chana and husband
Schmid, Yisrael
Schmid, Breindel
Schmid, Chana
[Page 379]
Schmid, Melech
Schmid, Rachel
Schmid, two girls
Schmid, Yudel, Yankel's
Schmid, Bobtsha
Schmid, Sarah
Schmid, Yaakov
Schmid, wife, Moshe's
Schmid, children
Schmid, Yisrael
Schmid, Tsippa
Schmid, Shimshon
Schechter, Henrik, Doctor
Schechter, wife
Schechter, two children
Shereshevsky, Shmuel
Shereshevsky, Elka
Shereshevsky, Breina
Shereshevsky, Tema
Shereshevsky, Leiba
Shereshevsky, Godel
Shklyar, Yosef
Shklyar, Feigel
Shklyar, Shlomo
Shklyar, Shaina
Shklyar, Leiba
Shklyar, Aharon
Moshe the Pious
Local Preacher and his family
Kreina Dobes
Alter the builder from Lyubish, wife, three children, daughter, husband Berl and six children
Chaim Sherer, wife, two children
Itsa Mecher, wife and three children
Mindel, Davidgrudnik
Tsadok from Yolitsh?

Martyrs From Locations Near Drohitchin

Ogdemer
Lana and brother Avraham
Osevlan
Kleinman, Asher
Kleinman, Rivka
Kleinman, Baruch
Kleinman, Pesach
Kleinman, Zalman
Kleinman, Itka, husband and children
Kleinman, widow and children
Osevitz
Levinson, Moshe
Levinson, Feiga-Zissel
Levinson, Chana
Levinson, Yisrael
Levinson, Avraham
Levinson, Gershon, lost
Levinson, Tzvia, husband Feivel Gurvitz and children: Natan and Yaakov
Levinson, Malka
Levinson, Feigel, husband Yisrael Bregman and sons: Avraham and Lipman
Levinson, Shaina, husband Yossel Kaplan and children: Avraham and Breina
Levinson, Chaim
Levinson, Beila
Feldman, Chana
Feldman, Breina
Feldman, Malka
Feldman, Yenta
Feldman, Michael
Feldman, Avraham
Feldman, Chaytsha and husband
Balkon
Roitkopf, Yisrael
Roitkopf, wife
Roitkopf, children
Horbacha
Loffman, Alter Yosef
Loffman, wife
Lev, Shimon
Lev, Chana
Lev, Meir Lipman
Lev, Pesha, husband and child
Lev, Zlata, husband Pesach Zaretsky, children: Berl, Gitel and 3 others
Lev, Perl, husband Alter Wartsevitsky, children: Feivel 21, Gittel 19
Voulka
Yudelevsky, Zelig
Yudelevsky, wife
Yudelevsky, 2 children

[Page 380]

Valevel

Vladavsky, Shmuel

Vladavsky, Feitsha

Vladavsky, daughter

Vladavsky, Leiba

Vladavsky, wife

Vladavsky, children

Tcheromcha

Hausman, Leiba

Hausman, Fruma

Hausman, Moshe

Hausman, Yochanan

Hausman, Rivka

Hausman, Gittel

Yolitsh

Meshchanin, Moshe

Meshchanin, Chayka

Meshchanin, Pinya

Meshchanin, 5 children

Lechevitsh

Wolf, Lieba, Biyamin's

Wolf, Yaakov

Wolf, Hersh

Wolf, Baruch

Wolf, Chaim

Wolf, Chaya, husband Avraham Gordon, son Ze'ev

Wolf, Eliyahu

Wolf, Sarah

Wolf, Itka

Wolf, Baruch

Wolf, Yaakov

Barantshuk, Moshe

Barantshuk, Chana

Barantshuk, Leah

Barantshuk, Baruch

Zohn, Esther Leah

Zohn, Freidel

Zohn, Velvel

Zohn, Chaim

Svorin

Lyubashevsky, brothers and families

Simenovitch

Podorovsky, Velvel

Podorovsky, Tsippa

Podorovsky, Nissel

Podorovsky, wife

Podorovsky, 2 children

Podorovsky, Shmuel

Podorovsky, wife
Podorovsky, Kaila, husband and 2 children
Podorovsky, Gittel
Podorovsky, Pesach
Podorovsky, Rivka, husband and children
Podorovsky, Zalman
Podorovsky, Bluma
Podorovsky, Henya
Podorovsky, Fanya, husband Motel and son
Podorovsky, Peshka, husband Pomeranetz, children
Podorovsky, Moshe
Podorovsky, Peshka
Podorovsky, Dina
Podorovsky, Breina
Podorovsky, Shmuel
Podorovsky, wife
Podorovsky, 3 children
Podorovsky, Hersh Ber
Podorovsky, wife
Podorovsky, children
Podorovsky, daughter
Son-in-law, Shmerl, children
Blacksmith and family

Selitsheva

Goldberg, Meir, brothers
Goldberg, Esther
Toben, Isser
Toben, Dovka
Toben, Sonia, sister
Toben, Esther

Selishch

Volinetz, Moshe Yitzchak
Volinetz, Elka, daughter
Volinetz, Miriam Tsirel
Volinetz, Chaya Esther
Volinetz, Shosha
Volinetz, Yehudit
Blacksmith from Vortsevich
Antopolsky, Chaim
Antopolsky, a girl
Antopolsky, Freidel
Antopolsky, Golda, child
Zhabinsky, Yisrael-Lieb
Zhabinsky, Pessel
Zhabinsky, 3 children

[Page 381]

These Were The Murderers
By Rabbi B. Warshavsky[*]

On November 12, 1947, the former British minister for Germany, Lord Peckenheim, stated in the House of Lords that the German SS troops awaiting their trials would be freed on parole and that only a small number of SS, whohad been known as dangerous individuals would be held in the camps

("News Article" November 13, 1947, London England)

The liberal *Star* of London happily announced on December 4, 1947 that the decision of the American military authorities to end the trials at the Dachau concentration camp against the German murderers on December 31 was a welcome development.

"After more than two years of trials," wrote the *Star,* "the time has come to pay more attention to education rather than to punishment in Germany. All important war criminal held by the Allies were taken care of. If a few *small fish* escaped punishment, this should bother us less than the importance of teaching the Germans to live like civilized men. The time for punishment is over."

What this article was really saying was that all important German war criminals had been punished; all Germans guilt of shooting 50 English fliers had been uncovered under every rock, and have received their verdict; punishment for every possible crime by a German against a member of the armed forces of the Allies had been exacted; the Germans guilty of the single Christian *liditsa* had been seated at the defendant's bench (There were no additional *liditsas* because if there were, the gentiles would have made very sure that the world knew about it.). Even punishment for the crime of shooting a few hundred Italians was exacted against Field Marshal Kesselring, who was given the death penalty on May 6, 1947 and then had his punishment reduced to imprisonment prior to being released.

Thus who were just "small fish," and who were the victims that the "small fish" had devoured? If you are interested in it, then on the contrary, let's raise the curtain covering the screen and let's see the pictures – pictures from the dusty archives that have already been ignored and forgotten.

There is some evidence recorded matter-of-factly in a gruesome document about the Pinsk massacre that was found among the papers of the headquarters of the fifth German police regiment, the infamous SS troops.

Document from Pinsk Massacre*

"On October 27, 1942, our company received orders to head for Kobrin. On October 28, 1942, at around 9 pm, we arrived in Kobrin by truck, and from Kobrin we were ordered to march to Pinsk. The company arrived at the west end of Pinsk on October 29, 1942 at 4 am.

"A meeting was held with the regiment commander of Pinsk, and it was decided that two battalions (the second battalion of the fifteenth regiment and the second cavalry squadron) should remain on guard around the city while the 10th company, 15th police regiment and the 11th company of the 11th police regiment (except for two platoons) clean out the ghetto.

"The 11th company of the 11th police regiment (except for the first platoon) was ordered to protect the transport location, and the convoys heading for the massacre location located four miles from town. The execution location itself was cordoned off, and the cavalry was to be used for that purpose. Security measures were considered very important when some 150 Jews tried to escape. The guards captured all of them.

[Page 382]

"According to our orders, the cleanup of the ghetto was to begin at 6 am, but because of the darkness, it was delayed by half an hour. When the Jews of Pinsk heard about what was going to happen to them, large groups of Jews gathered out in the streets, and we were able to take several thousand Jews to the transport location during the first hour of the cleanup.

"When the remaining Jews realized what was happening, they voluntarily joined the Jews marching in columns, so the police, who were protecting the transport location, were unable to count the large number of Jews.

"We brought out 1,000 to 2,000 Jews on the first day. However, the result exceeded all expectations. The first cleanup action ended after 5 pm without incident. Some 10,000 Jews were killed on the first day.

"On October 30, 1942, there was a second cleanup of the ghetto, and a third on October 31. The fourth took place on November 1, 1942. Approximately 15,000 Jews were rounded up at the assembly location. Sick Jews and small children who did not leave their homes were killed in the ghetto itself. With only one exception, there were no incidents (and another 15,000 Jews perished –W.).

"In connection with that fact that Jews who gave up their gold were spared (a German swindle – W.), one Jew reported that he had hidden a lot of gold. One of our commanders accompanied the Jew to get the gold. The Jew lagged behind along the way, and he finally wanted the commander to climb up with him into an attic room. The commander took the Jew back to the assembly location. The Jew did not want to remain seated quietly like everyone else, and he suddenly gave a push at a cavalryman, grabbed his gun, and started beating him. A soldier from the company struck the Jew over the head, killing him.

"On November 1, at 5 am, the company was ordered to set up an outside cordon. There was no particular incident at that time. On November 2, 1942 at 8 am the company was released from Pinsk and sent to its posts. The company arrived in Kobrin at 1 pm, and over 17 hours it reassumed its position."

Notes

1. Axes and similar tools are to be used by groups involved in cleaning out and checking ghettos to open locked doors etc.

2. Even when there is no ladder or sign of stairs leading to the attic, we have to assume that there are Jews in hiding there, and all attics have to be checked carefully.

3. Even where there are no cellars, it has to be assumed that large numbers of Jews are in hiding in holes under the floor. These places have to be broken down, or else police dogs must be used. In Pinsk the dog Asta performed very good work in this area. Another idea is to throw grenades into suspected hiding places, where the Jews hiding there will be killed anyway, or be brought out of hiding.

This is an authentic horrific document from the German death factories, a photo from the crematoria of Treblinka, Maidanec, Auschwitz, Birkenau, Stutoff, Dachau, Bergen-Belsen, and others. In Auschwitz alone, where there were also six gas chambers besides the crematoria, the Germans would daily burn 24,000 Jews! The London *Star* of April 1, 1946 reported that in Auschwitz (headed by the executioner Rudolf Franz Ferdinand Hess), the Germans burned three million Jews! This type of death factory was also in Brona-Gora and Bereza.   DW

[*Page 383*]

4. The ground around the houses has to be inspected thoroughly and checked using strong iron bars because many Jews were hiding out in pits.

5. It is recommended that young Jewish children be offered to spare their lives in order to indicate where Jews are hiding."

This is the end of the Document about the Pinsk Massacre.

The "captain of the Police Guard-SS Troops and Commander SAUER signed this horrific document of German murder and cold-blooded killing! He was later the commander and chief butcher in Treblinka!

These are the Murderers!

In the same year, 1942, the same German police regiments (11th and 15th) massacred hundreds of thousands of Jews in one killing field on the Pinsk-Brisk train line because Polish Jews, who were temporarily held in Russian-occupied areas until the summer of 1941, must be taken into consideration.

The old Jewish communities of Pinsk, Motele, Drohitchin, Yanova, Khomsk, Antopolia, Horodetz, Zhabinka, Kobrin, and Brisk were wiped off the face of the earth. The horrific murders of Jewish men, women and children cannot be described. Many tens of thousands of Jews, young and old, were thrown alive into coal pits, in the coal ovens of Brona-Gora, and died with great suffering.

Here is the picture: The so-called small fish and their devoured victims. Here they are, the so-called small fish, who evade their punishment!

Germans bully their victims before they killed them. This is what they did to our families.

See p. 156.

[Page 384]

Why do they not hang these ugly German killers? The gentiles respond that it does not involve them. Of course not, because these victims were Jews, and maybe the gentiles are right. Why should the gentiles seek punishment when we Jews do not get involved?

I am speaking about the aforementioned Jewish communities, but I have in mind the Jews of all massacred communities. In our case, we have evidence, a document from the murderers themselves describing what they did to the Jews in that area. We know their names and who they are!

These are the murderers of the 11th and 15th German police regiments! Everyone from the top officer to the lowest soldier is guilty for killing our Jews! We appeal to our fellow émigrés and émigré organizations from Pinsk, Motele, Yanova, Drohitchin, Khomsk, Antopolia, Horodetz-Kobrin, Zhabinka, and Brisk who live everywhere! And we turn not only to those mentioned here, but to all redeemers of blood (of all murdered Jewish families, and especially to those who feel their own pulse and who still feel a responsibility to the dead).

Redeemers of blood, you have a sacred duty! If you want to be worthy to be considered the heirs of the martyrs, then fulfill the will and testament of your families who before their deaths called for revenge for their blood! The redeemers of blood must bring the killers of their families to justice! The murderers must be hanged!

This is the end of our Drohitchin. It is also the end of the Yizkor Book in memory of our tormented parents and siblings from whom there remains only ash and bones spread out everywhere, without having a proper Jewish burial. We tried to look for the bones of our martyrs, and after years of unceasing and difficult work we succeeded, thank G-d, to find those memories of the martyrs. We reattached one bone to another, joined one limb to the next, put a garment of fiery letters on them, and we resurrected Drohitchin and its Jews in writing and in photographs. We see a town with its streets and houses. We see people, parents, and children. It's as if they speak to us, but we hear no voices, no sound. They were silenced forever. This is all that remains for us: an eternal memorial for a dead community. The Germans, may their names be obliterated, squeezed out the last drop of blood from that town. I am sure, however, that G-d's punishment of Germany will come on time. But it will come eventually. It will be a bitter and frightful punishment.

First month of Adar 5717 (February), 1957, Dov Warshavsky.

[Page 386]

PART SEVEN

(One page is blank)

Drohitchin Around the World
A General Survey

In the Talmudic tractate Pesachim, p. 87, it says that G-d acted mercifully with the Jewish People by spreading them among the other nations. Were all Jews to live in the same country, their enemies could destroy them all. Anyone with any sense can see how true this is by what G-d did to hundreds of thousands of Jews in Europe at the same time he sent off and saved them from utter destruction. Had all Jews lived in one valley of death, the Germans would not have spared a single person of the Jewish People.

It was fortunate that a remnant of the decimated Jewish community of Drohitchin (Holocaust years 1940-1945) survived, and that Divine Providence created the causes and reasons to impel many Jews from Drohitchin to emigrate from Drohitchin from the 1880s on. As the verse says in Genesis regarding Jacob's meeting with his brother Esau, "And He divided the people, saying that if Esau attacks one part and destroys it, the remaining part should survive." Today there are many Jews from Drohitchin. May they continue to increase.

Emigration from Drohitchin

The first Jewish emigrants from Drohitchin started arriving in the United States in approximately 1880. Thereafter and until the outbreak of World War I in 1914, there was an intensive stream of emigration from Drohitchin to the United States. The world was not so "civilized" and "modernized" as today, and leaving and entering one country for another was accomplished without great difficulty. You simply made a decision and went.

During the war years of 1914 to 1919, emigration from Drohitchin ceased. In 1920 emigration from Drohitchin started again at a brisk pace. Hundreds of people from Drohitchin streamed to the shores of the free world. This continued until 1924, when the United States imposed heavy quotas, which brought Jewish emigration to the United States to a halt.

According to the American quota system, approximately 152,000 people were permitted to enter the country each year, and of those, approximately 108,000 visas were allotted to Germany, England and Ireland, while the remaining 44,000 were allotted to over 100 countries. It is easy to figure out how few visas were available for Jews in Poland, and especially for Jews in Drohitchin. The entire total for Poland was approximately 4,000.

Had the United States not closed its doors, the Jewish world would have been totally different, and hundreds of thousands of these Jews, including many from Drohitchin, would be alive today. So the United States is not entirely blameless for the large numbers of victims of German murder. After emigration to the United States stopped, many Drohitchin Jews looked elsewhere for a refuge – to Argentina, Cuba and Palestine. Emigration to Palestine was extremely limited due to the certificate system. A small percent managed to make their way to Canada and other countries.

Three centers: New York, Chicago and Palestine

Currently most of those from Drohitchin are concentrated in New York and Chicago. For some time, the New York community was the most dynamic and influential. Today, the Chicago community is the wealthiest and most stable. This is due to the fact that Chicago, which is a younger city with a developed industrial base and growing factories, is home to many people from Drohitchin who have had the opportunity to prosper economically.

Aside from Chicago and New York, there are people from Drohitchin in California, Florida, Missouri, Connecticut, and others. As mentioned, many Drohitchin émigrés are in Argentina, Cuba, and Canada. However, the third largest community of Drohitchin émigrés is in Israel, where the majority of survivors of the Drohitchin Holocaust found a refuge.

[Page 388]

The first emigrants lived mainly around the synagogue, which was the focal point of community life. However, life was never well established or rooted just in one spot. There was always a tendency to settle down and then move elsewhere, like the Jews in the Desert with Moses. Thus, they wandered from one place to the next, from one area to another, and wherever they settled, they found a new sanctuary for the Holy Ark.

The first Drohitchin emigrants were concentrated on the east side, around the Agudat Achim-Anshei Drohitchin (Brotherhood of People of Drohitchin) Synagogue on Henry Street. Today most of the Drohitchin community lives in Brooklyn, and some in Manhattan, the Bronx, and in the New York City area. In Chicago, the first arrivals from Drohitchin found their refuge in the southwest section – Clark and Holster. Later on, they moved further into the southwest, to Independence and Douglas. Today they are spread out throughout the city, from the most northern section, the west and south.

As long as the old émigrés from Drohitchin lived together in New York and in Chicago, and especially as long as the Yiddish language was spoken at home, in the synagogue, and on the street, there existed an emotional connection between the old country and the Drohitchin communities in the United States, where a warm atmosphere of good old-fashion comfort and Jewish life ruled the day.

Now, however, when the old generation has started leaving the scene and a new generation has arisen who have begun to get lost through distance, territory, and alienation, and especially with the demise of Yiddish in the home and synagogue, the emotional connection between the old country and the new has been broken, and continuity is in danger.

There are cases of children of Drohitchin émigrés, who are born in the United States and who attend the same schools, work together, and yet do not have the slightest idea of any connection between them. With the destruction of Drohitchin, the new American Drohitchin community is also disappearing because the source of the young Americans' nourishment has dried up. (DW).

Rabbi Yosef Kagan

Rabbi Yosef Kagan, son of Rabbi Aharon and Gittel Kagan, and grandson (on his mother's side) of the great Jewish rabbi, Yisrael Meir Hakohen Kagan, was born in Radin, attended the yeshivas of Radin (under his grandfather), Slabodka, Kremenchuk-Slabodka, Lukeshes-Vilna (under Rabbi Baruch Ber Lebowitz) and others. He also studied philosophy at the University of Basel. Since 1937, Rabbi Kagan has been the leader of the Drohitchin community synagogue, Kehillat Yaakov, located previously at Douglas-Hemlin and now at Devan and Londale. Rabbi Kagan is known for his deep scholarship and good character traits. He and his wife Rivka (daughter of Rabbi Shmuel and Chaya-Mina Shach) have one daughter, Ethel.

Chicago Drohitchin Community

The late R. Zvi Yitzchak Hoffman had sent us the following information about the Chicago Drohitchin community.

"In 1886 in the week of the Torah portion Nasah, 22 Drohitchin residents and I arrived in New York. One week later, in a group of seven men, we left for Chicago. Of course we were lonely and in despair. In Chicago we met a few individuals from Drohitchin – around seven or eight men who had no community life.

"Feeling lonely in a large foreign city (our families were still in Drohitchin), we all stuck together. The first thing we established was a free loan fund headed by Lamansky. Afterwards, we decided to get together every Sabbath in the new House of Study. Of course this weekly meeting was an important event and gave us pleasure.

[Page 389]

We would tell each other the news and the events we went through during the week and what we heard from Drohitchin. Those couple of hours that we met in the new House of Study made us feel better and cheered us up.

"Unfortunately, one of the heads of the synagogue, a certain Mr. Goodstein, could not understand our situation and could not stand that we were talking in synagogue. He sent a notice to one of our members, Kaddish Baum, telling him not to come to the House of Study anymore. Of course all of us were affected by this event, and during the week of Sukkot we left the new House of Study.

"Soon thereafter we set up our own small synagogue on Pacific Avenue with the name of "Agudat Shalom Anshei Drohitchin." The synagogue developed, and we could not remain there very long, maybe two years, because the location of the synagogue belonged to the mayor, Carter H. Harrison, and he sold all his properties, among them the synagogue.

"One Sabbath the mayor came to our synagogue and informed us that we had to move. He suggested that we meet on Saturday night with one of his representatives, and we could take care of the matter. So we did. We came to an agreement, and the mayor offered us $1,200 compensation.

"We used that money to buy land for a cemetery on Milwaukee Avenue. We also founded a second synagogue, "Agudat Shalom Anshei Drohitchin" at 393 South Clark Street, where we remained for several years until Jews in the area started moving to the West Side. Therefore, we closed the synagogue. When that neighborhood lost all its Jews, I returned to Drohitchin for a couple of years." See p. 390.

Kehilath Yaakov Synagogue

Aharon Asher Cooper (one of the oldest people from Drohitchin) and others reported the following:

When Cooper arrived in Chicago in 1898, he encountered a small Drohitchin synagogue at Clark and Harrison where there were around 30 Jews. In 1901, they moved to Kramer Street, where they turned a house into a synagogue. In approximately 1903, the Drohitchin community bought a synagogue from Yanova community at Jefferson and O'Brien. In 1905, when the number of arrivals increased, the Drohitchin émigrés bought a church at Racine and Taylor and turned it into a synagogue, which existed until 1915.

In 1915, the Drohitchin community started building the large structure at Douglas and Hemlin, and in 1917, they held the dedication of the Kehillat Yaakov-Anshei Drohitchin synagogue, which contained a sanctuary, House of Study, and a Talmud Torah School. From what we are told, the Kehillat Yaakov synagogue and House of Study had 1,800 seats, and for years was a place dedicated to Torah, service and charity. Five to six quorums of men attended prayer services there each day one after the other, and they had groups engaged in study of Talmud, Mishnah, Torah, and a group involved in reciting psalms. There was also a burial society and a free loan fund. The Talmud group of the synagogue was one of the largest in Chicago. Many scholarly Jews attended the lectures of the rabbi. When the Jewish community moved from the West Side to other areas of Chicago, the great Kehillat Yaakov synagogue, just like many others, had to close. It closed in 1955. In 1956, it reopened as Kehillat Yaakov Beit Shmuel at Devan and Londale.

Rabbi Shmuel Shach

Rabbi Shmuel, son of R. Shraga Feivush Shach, was born in Khvidan near Kovno. He was one of the finest students in the yeshiva for married men under Rabbi Yitzchak Elchanan Spector in Kovno. In 1907, Rabbi Shach arrived in Chicago, and a year later he was appointed rabbi in the Drohitchin synagogue, previously at Racine and Taylor, and later at Douglas and Hemlin as the Kehillat Yaakov synagogue. Rabbi Shach, who was considered one of the major rabbis of Chicago, was famous for his sharp understanding and expertise in Talmud. He was loved by all, and died on December 16, 1937 at the age of over 70. His wife, Chaya-Mina, daughter of R. Zvi Aryeh (Hersh Lieb) of Kovno, died on August 21, 1945.

[*Page 390*]

The Talmud Torah School

As mentioned, the Kehillat Yaakov Talmud Torah school began operations in 1917 in the building of the Kehillat Yaakov synagogue, which contained a special wing for the elementary school. Eventually, however, the place became too small for the large number of students who came from far away streets to the school. Then the community started to think about a new building, which was built in 1924 on Hemlin Avenue. This was the large modern Talmud Torah School that became a jewel for the entire region.

Eliyahu Eisenstein was the chief architect and chairman of the building committee for the construction of both the Kehillat Yaakov Synagogue and the new Talmud Torah school. The Kehillat Yaakov Talmud Torah School, which was renowned throughout Chicago, had two divisions: a division for teaching Hebrew in Hebrew, and another division for teaching Hebrew in Yiddish. Each division had eight classes, for a total of 16. At its height, the Talmud Torah had 800 students, and during the period it operated the school saw thousands of Jewish children pass through its doors to receive a five-year education in elementary Jewish education. The educational program included Yiddish and Hebrew, Bible with Rashi's commentary, the Prophets and Writings, Talmud, Jewish law, Jewish history, and music.

This continued until fairly recently, when with the move of the Jewish population to the West Side; the Kehillat Yaakov Anshei Drohitchin Talmud Torah School – together with many other Jewish institutions – closed its doors in 1955.

The Cemetery

As early as 1894, the first immigrants from Drohitchin bought land for a cemetery on Milwaukee Avenue to be called the Morton Grove Cemetery. Several émigrés from Drohitchin were buried there. However, there were many problems with this site because it was located far away from the Jewish neighborhood. In approximately 1906, the officers of the Drohitchin synagogue on Racine Avenue bought a parcel of land on Waldheim Street for $7,500 to be dedicated as a cemetery, which is still used today.

The sacred ground on Waldheim is managed by a committee of people originally from Drohitchin, and is headed by a superintendent, who directs all cemetery activities. Over the years the office of superintendent has been held by: Hershel Hackman, Yaakov Guter, Hershel Skolnick, Eliyahu Eisenstein, and Reuven Deutsch, in that order. Today Abraham and David Eisenstein hold the position jointly.   DW

Left: R. Simcha Miller, son of R. Dov and Rachel Miller

He was born in Drohitchin and arrived in the United States in 1921. For ten years, he was the vice-president and then the last president of the Kehillat Yaakov synagogue on Douglas Street. Today he is the vice-president of the Kehillat Yaakov Beit Shmuel synagogue on Devan Street. This photo was taken at the Kehillat Yaakov Street next to the Holy Ark in 1956.

Right: R. Zvi Yitzchak Hoffman was born in Drohitchin and was one of the oldest residents of Drohitchin living in Chicago. In his final years, he lived in San Francisco and died at the age of 106.

See pp. 273 and 388.

[Page 391]
The New York Drohitchin Community

The first Jewish immigrants from Drohitchin who arrived in New York experienced great difficulties during their early years in adjusting to their new homeland. In addition to their problems and worries about livelihood, they also suffered emotionally because they missed their homes and the friendships of the old country. They missed having a place where after working hard all week, they could get together on the Sabbath or holidays, pray communally and enjoy each others company in their free time. After several meetings, the Drohitchin immigrants decided to try to organize an association of émigrés from Drohitchin. This resulted in the creation of the well-known association in New York known as the Agudat Achim Anshei Drohitchin.

The organization was started in the home of Moshe Aharon Goldberg. Among the main founders of the organization were: Yaakov Pollack, Moshe Aharon Goldberg, Gedaliah Grossman, Shmuel Eliyahu Grossman, Yaakov Shmuel Aremland, Shimon Berman, Meyer Levy, Yechiel Peer, Ike Levy, Henech Miller, Shaul Koch, Moshe Isser Rosen, and others. On February 17, 1900, a charter was issued to the organization in the name of Henech Miller, and the Agudat Achim Anshei Drohitchin thereby came into existence on February 17, 1900. That very same year the organization, which consisted of bout 20 members, moved into its own location at 158 Eldridge Street. In addition, the organization bought a piece of land for burials at the Mount Zion Cemetery, but the dedication of the fence of the sacred site took place only in 1906.

Due to the increase in the Organization's membership, it was forced to move into larger quarters at 156 Henry Street in 1908. In 1910, the Society celebrated its tenth anniversary. At that event, the Society's first written constitution was distributed, and in 1915, a second parcel of land was purchased in the Mount Zion Cemetery.

In 1919, one of the most important funds of the Organization was created – the Medical Assistance Fund. This Fund was enhanced in 1926 by a $900 donation from Abraham Cooper, and eventually other funds were established such as the Free Loan Fund in 1920 (the first $1,000 of this fund was contributed by Fishel Dov Rosenberg); the Old Age Fund was established in 1922, and the Endowment Widow and Orphan Assistance Fund was established in 1928.

The Organization celebrated its 25th anniversary in 1924 with an impressive banquet that raised a sum of $3,500. Yaakov Pollack gave the first $1,000, with the express purpose of buying for the organization a home of its own.

(This article continues on p. 392)

For an eternal memorial to our dear parents
Rabbi Mordechai son of R. Shalom Shachna the Levite Minkovitch
Died on August 14, 1955
Chana Beila, daughter of R. Moshe, Minkovitch
Died on May 8, 1939
Sarah, Yisrael, Yehudit, Michael and Esther
(See pp. 16, 135, 203 and 204. W.)

Aharon Asher Cooper

Aharon Asher Cooper, a son of Yitzchak Binyamin and Hendel Cooper, was born in 1878 in Drohitchin. He studied in the *kheder* (school) and in the Talmud Torah School. In 1895 he married Toiba (Tila) Buder, a daughter of Ephraim and Chaya Buder of Drohitchin. He moved to Chicago in 1898 and for a long period served as the owner and director of the A. Cooper Shoe Company, a wholesale shoe business.

He was also involved in community activities. He was the president of the Drohitchin synagogue on Racine and Taylor from 1905 to 1908; he was a co-founder and vice president (1926), and president (1929) of the Kehillat Yaakov synagogue on Douglas and Hemlin; he was a co-founder and longtime member of the board of the Kehillat Yaakov Talmud Torah School and the Drohitchin cemetery on Waldheim Street. In addition to time and work, he covered many expenses.

In his final years, Cooper lived with his children. Aharon Asher's wife, Toiba died on November 13, 1949 in Chicago. The Coopers had seven children: Hendel Michaels, Pinchas, Yitzchak-Binyamin, Frieda Fishman, Perl, Yaakov, and David. DW

(Page 392)

In 1925 the Agudat Achim Anshei Drohitchin organization moved into its own building at 158 Henry Street, and in 1930, the Society bought a third parcel of land at the Mount Lebanon Cemetery in New Jersey. In 1932, yet another piece of land was purchased at the House of David Cemetery.

With the assistance of Shaul Koch, the Drohitchin Ladies' Auxiliary was established in 1933, and in 1930 and 1934 the organization held two balls, the profits of which greatly helped to improve the situation of the organization's new home. In November 1935, the organization celebrated its 35th anniversary with great fanfare, and in 1936 the organization initiated the Drohitchin Relief Society, which helped to support hundreds of families back in the hometown of Drohitchin.

In 1950, The Society celebrated its 50th golden jubilee anniversary. Currently, the organization has paid off and owns the building at 158 Henry Street in New York, where it still houses the famous Drohitchin Synagogue and all of the community organizations and groups that the Organization still actively operates for various activities. However, the most important function of the Organization was to support those who were spared from the last holocaust with money and advice. DW

The synagogue building of the Agudat Achim Anshei Drohitchin in New York
It was purchased in 1928 at 158 Henry Street. The synagogue continues to exist today.

The New York Drohitchin Branch 401
Jewish National Workers Union

This organization was founded in 1944 on the initiative of Yosef Kollen, Benny Tepper, Efraim Shmid, and Asher Volins. In addition these men, Herman Grossman, Gedaliah Kaplan, Yudel Miller, Garber, Zlotnick, and others also attended the first meeting. The branch started operating officially with Yosef Kaplan as chairman. During the festival of Shavuot of that same year, the Union helped support a holiday celebration for émigrés from Drohitchin, where the participants were motivated to help build the new organization.

In October 1945, a banquet was held for the purpose of the officially inauguration of the branch of the Workers' Union, which received its charter under the number 401. At that time, the Branch decided to take an active role in the Union's orphan adoption campaign. Herman Grossman adopted an orphan and paid $300 to the branch. In March of 1946, a large executive committee was elected. In addition to the aforementioned, the following members also joined: Yosef Schub, Yosef Birnbaum, Alfred Gray, Mrs. Stauber, Carl Sheinbaum, Itche Pisetsky, and Shmuel Levi, elected as chairman.

[*Page 393*]

In May of 1946, under the leadership of Gedaliah Kaplan, the branch participated in the "cares package drive" for refugees from Drohitchin. In the autumn of 1946, the branch participated in the care package campaign for refugees in Germany. In January, 1947, the branch participated in the Union campaign on behalf of the Israeli Histadrut Trade Union, and in the spring of 1947, the branch took part for the first time in the Jewish National Fund Campaign. In 1948, in conjunction with the Drohitchin Relief Society, the Branch initiated a joint aid campaign to assist those who had come from Drohitchin but who were now in Germany, Poland, Italy, and Cyprus.

In 1948 and 1949, the chairman of the branch was Asher Volins. The branch was on the "honor roll" several times because of its dedicated efforts in building up the State of Israel. The branch holds regular meetings, organizes literary evenings and lectures, and organizes annual banquets (in conjunction with the Israel Guarantee campaign). The energetic businessman community activist Benny Tepper, the chairman of the Drohitchin Aid Society in New York, heads this branch, which had more members from Drohitchin, today.

DW

Information from Shmuel Levy

Hershel Schwartz

Hershel Schwartz, a son of Eliezer and Rachel Schwartz, was born in Drohitchin in 1906. In his early youth in 1921, he left Drohitchin and moved to Norwalk, Connecticut, where he attended high school. On December 21, 1930, Hershel married Bertha, a daughter of Zvi-Hillel and Sarah. Zvi, a successful businessman in Connccticut and was connected with large supermarkets for many years, until 1955. He was also the pioneer of self-service businesses in Connecticut.

At the same time, Schwartz was very active in Jewish community life in Connecticut. He was the former chairman of the Israel Bonds campaign since 1951, the former treasurer of the Jewish Center, the former president (until this year) of the synagogue there. Since 1948, Schwartz has been the chairman of the United Jewish Appeal, vice president of the Community Council, member of the Zionist Club that puts on performances on behalf of needy individuals and organizations.

The Schwartzes have a daughter Ronni and a son Leonard.

Chicago Drohitchin Branch 294
Jewish National Workers Union
By Zalman Shevinsky

As a member of the "Sholom Aleichem Branch" of the Jewish National Workers Union and being familiar with their programs and activities, it occurred to me to establish a special Union branch of Drohitchin émigrés whose agenda would be first, to address for the needs of the Jews in Drohitchin; second, to work for Jewish national interests in this country; third, to address the fraternal and cultural needs of the branch members; and fourth, to actively help in the building of the state of Israel in any way possible.

The first founders' meeting of a small group of Drohitchin émigrés took place, with the participation of B. Frimer, in February of 1941, when the foundation of the Drohitchin branch was laid. After obtaining the legal quorum needed for a meeting, the official installation of branch officers took place on June 29, 1941. Louis Segal, secretary of the Union made a special visit from New York to lead the installation ceremony, and the Drohitchin branch was admitted to the Union as a full-fledged member, thereby coming into official existence.

Many Drohitchiners became members of the Branch, which, in time, grew substantially and gained a reputation in Jewish Chicago as well as in Union circles across the country. The work of the Branch concentrated on the following areas:

1) Israel Funds: Through its annual fund-raising events, the Branch raised tens of thousands of dollars for Israel's trade union (Histadrut) campaign, the Jewish National Fund (Keren Kayemet le-Yisrael), the Combined Jewish Appeal, Zionist Workers' Fund and other organizations.

[Page 394]

2) Relief Work: The Branch runs several fundraising campaigns to contribute to various Jewish philanthropic organizations and institutions throughout the country.

3) Aid for Drohitchin émigrés: The Branch supports and helps needy émigrés from Dohitchin, wherever they may be, with food packages and cash.

4) Cultural Work: For a long time the Branch published a monthly bulletin called *Yediot* (Information) as well as souvenir booklets (eight) containing informative material that was distributed among all the members.

(Continues from p. 394 of last installment)

Miriam Gingold

Miriam Gingold, a daughter of R. Shimon and Lotsa Weissman, was born in Drohitchin. She studied in the gymnasia high school in Pinsk and was active in community affairs in Drohitchin. In 1927, Miriam and her husband and children moved to Chicago, where she became very involved in the Zionist Labor movement. For 25 years, Miriam was connected with the Pioneer Women's Organization, where she served in various important positions. Today she is a member of the national executive there. She was also a member of the World Federation in Israel, and she was appointed as a delegate to the Zionist Congress in 1946 and to the last Congress in 1956.

In addition to her Zionist activism, Miriam Gingold is also active in the Jewish education in Chicago. She is the chairwoman of the Central Synagogue Committee of the Zionist Labor movement and member of the Board of Education. Miriam is a gifted speaker and frequently delivers speeches at various community events. Her husband, Bernard Gingold, is a well-known businessman and is also active in the Zionist Labor movement, especially in the National Labor Union, where he has served as Chicago vice-president for many years. The Gingolds have two daughters. W.

Left: The Drohitichin Branch 294 of Jewish National Workers Union organized in 1941.
Right: The Drohitichin Proressive Club Emblem

The Progressive Club

In 1937, a group of men and women who originated from Drohitchin organized the Progressive Club in Chicago. The Club works in tandem with the general Aid Association, sending monetary assistance to the impoverished Jews in Drohitchin. The Club was especially involved in assisting Tsentos, the society for aid for children and orphan assistance and in the construction of the cemetery in Drohitchin. The Club existed until 1941, when members helped to create the Drohitchin Branch, resulting in the Progressive Club being disbanded.

Drama Club

At the end of World War I, a few new young arrivals from Drohitchin organized their own drama club to help raise money for the Aid Association through putting on performances. The Association then sent the funds to Drohitchin. Ben Kest was the director of the Club, and one of its actors.

[*Page 395*]

Banquet photo of the 35th anniversary of the New York Drohitchin community "Agudat Achim-Anshei Drohitchin" in 1935.

From an old Minutes Book in 1917

The Chicago Relief Committee sent $2,152.72 to Drohitchin. The committee was made up of Zvi Hackman, chairman; Zalman Eisenstein, treasurer; Leibel Barenbaum, secretary; Yisrael Baruch Eisenstein, Lana Goldberg, Yisrael Baruch Warshavsky Malka's. The Club Association donated $300. The Club committee was made up of Tsippa Shevinsky, Yisrael-Baruch Eisenstein, Moshe Gratch, and Lana-Reizel Goldberg, secretary

New York Aid Association

During its lifetime, the New York Aid Association provided material assistance to the community living in Drohitchin. One document sent from Drohitchin to chairman Benny Tepper indicated that the Aid Association had sent to Drohitchin 4,291 zlotys that were distributed among 204 families.

DW

Yaakov Warshavsky

Y. Warshavsky in the hospital

Yaakov Warshavsky, a son of Moshe Shmuel and Perl Warshavsky, was born in Drohitchin. In 1934, he moved to Palestine and served in the police. In 1940, he came to Chicago and was drafted into the army in March, 1942. He participated in many battles on the battlefronts of northern France, Germany (Rhineland) and Austria. In the last week of the war, he was badly wounded and spent the next six months in the hospital. Yaakov was awarded the following medals and awards: a Bronze Star, a Purple Heart, three Battle Stars, a European-African-Middle East Service medal, a World War II Victory medal, and others. Today he is in the auto parts business. (See photos on pp. 269, 293, and 301. W.)

[Page 396]

Caption for next page:

A Group of the Drohitchin Branch – Administration and Executive in 1949 First row, seated from right: Dovka Gold, Adel Kohn, Leizer Warshavsky (chairman), Sheindel Dvinsky, Nechama Dvinsky and Ida Kohn.

Second row, standing from right: Chaya Shevinsky, Lana Lambert, Binyamin Shederov, Frieda Warshavsky, Chana Goldberg, Lana-Reizel Goldberg, Meita Eisenstein, Frieda Myers, Yehudit Hoffman, Beila and Morris Levy (vice-chairman).

Third row, from right: Zalman Shevinsky, (finance secretary), Baruch Gold, Bluma Gutov (protocol secretary), Berl Lopatin, Alter Dvinsky (Histadrut chairman), Sam Kohn, Louis Myer, Chaim Hoffman (vice-chairman).

Last row from right: Sam and Heska Match (vice chairwoman of the National Jewish Fund branch), Yosef Feldman, Mordechai Gutov, Yitzchak Yonah Goldberg, Hersh Leib Eisenstein (organization chairman), Sender Dvinsky, Aharon Kohn, Neiten Lambert.

Missing are Morris Dubin (treasurer), Yisrael Aharon Tennenbaum (Jewish National Fund chairman).

(Page 397)

Chicago Aid Association

The first Drohitchin Aid Association in Chicago was created at the beginning of World War I under the title of Aid Committee. Thousands of dollars were sent to Drohitchin after the war to assist the community and needy individuals. American dollars made possible the reconstruction of the burned-down town, Houses of Study, Talmud Torah School, public bath and ritual bath/mikvah. People in need of food were fed, and businessmen and workers who lost their income were assisted in meeting their needs.

In the mid-1920s, the economic situation of the Jews in Drohitchin improved significantly, and thus there was no need, except for unusual cases, to offer assistance from the United States. So the American Relief Committee was disbanded. However, with the onset of Nazism and Hitler's anti-Semitism in Germany, Polish anti-Semitism also began to raise its ugly head socially and economically. Polish government bodies in Drohitchin and everywhere else in the country started breaking the economic position of the Jews. Government taxes applied the screws and extracted the last bit of income from the Jewish worker and merchant. Jews in Drohitchin then started alerting their relatives and friends in the United States regarding the catastrophic economic situation.

In 1933, there was an extraordinarily large meeting of émigrés from Drohitchin held in the Kehilat Yaakov synagogue, which established the Chicago Drohitchin Support Association to be headed by David Eisenstein as president. During its lifetime, the Aid Association sent thousands of dollars to Drohitchin to be distributed for Passover and the High Holidays among hundreds of Drohitchin needy and many former businessmen who lost their businesses. This money supported the Houses of Study, the hospital, the Talmud Torah School, the Health Assistance Fund, and Hospice program. Orphans were fed and clothed, and poor brides were helped with expenses. Wood for the poor was also provided in the winter.

The Support Association later changed its name to the Aid Society, and continued to exist until the destruction of Drohitchin.   DW

On the next page is a photo of the Aid Society banquet honoring David Eisenstein in 1940.

HONOR BANQUET
FOR MR. &MRS. DAVID EISENSTEIN
FROM DROHITZINER AID SOCIETY ON
SUNDAY MARCH 17, 1940

[Page 398]
David Eisenstein

From Right: David and Hendel Eisenstein, Rabbi Yehuda-Leib, and Freidel Saks and son and Rabbi Menachem Benzion and Chana Saks

David Eisenstein was born in Drohitchin to his parents R. Litman and Beila. He studied under Yitzchak Avramchik, Naftali Steinberg, the Obler, Halpern, as well as in the yeshiva of Rabbi Mordechai Minkovitch in the Street House of Study. Later he became involved in business. In 1918, he was one of the leaders of the Self Defense Group in Drohitchin. (See p. 99).

In 1919 David married Hendel Hausman, a daughter of R. Zelig and Sirka Hausman, and in 1920, he took his family to Chicago in the United States. In Chicago, David found wide opportunities for community work. He served for many years as a Board member and trustee of the Kehilat-Yaakov synagogue and Talmud Torah School at Douglas and Hemlin. Today he is the honorary chairman of the Board of Directors of the new Kehilat Yaakov and Beit Shmuel synagogue; he is president of the Anshei Drohitchin Cemetery; a Board member of the Agudat-Achim South Shore synagogue; a member of the Board of the Knesset Yisrael synagogue in Miami Beach, Flordia, and a member of the Apollo Masonic Lodge. He is also a member of the Shomrim Zionists and other organizations.

A special chapter in its own right is Eisenstein's activity on behalf of the Drohitchin Aid Association in Chicago, where as president (from 1933 to the Holocaust) he worked devotedly to send large sums of money to assist Jews living in Drohitchin. As a successful businessman (president of A. D. Motors Sales), Eisenstein is a great supporter of Jewish religious and nationalist institutions such as the Yeshiva, the Education Committee, Combined Jewish Appeal, and Israel Bonds.

David Eisenstein is also chairman of the Drohitchin Yizkor Book Committee. The Eisensteins have three children: Freidel (Frances) Saks, Harold, and Bernard (See pp. 99, 240 and 242. W.)

Rabbi Menachem Benzion Saks

Rabbi Menachem Benzion Saks, a son of R. Dov-Ber and Yocheved-Devorah Saks, was the fourth generation born in Jerusalem (1897). His great-grandfather, R. Zadok Saks from Saksen, Germany, was the first person of his family who had settled in the Holy Land 175 years ago and founded the first courtyard of homes in the old city of Jerusalem. The great scholars R. Avraham Yitzchak Kook and Rabbi Zvi Pesach Frank ordained Rabbi Saks, a student of the Etz Chaim Yeshiva and Rabbi Kook's yeshiva in Jerusalem. Since 1922, Rabbi Saks and his family have lived in Chicago. He was thedirector of the Jewish community in Chicago. Today Rabbi Saks serves as executive director of the Education Committee, is chairman of the Synagogue and Public Division of the Combined Jewish Appeal; he is chairman of the administrative committee of the Religious Zionists (United Mizrachi and Poalei Mizrachi), and is director of the Rescue Fund.

[Page 399]

Mrs. Chana Saks, the wife of Rabbi M. B. Saks, is the daughter of the chief rabbi of Jerusalem, Rabbi Zvi Pesach Frank. Rabbi and Mrs. Saks (married in 1915) have four children: Rabbi Yehuda-Leib Saks, Chava Swirsky, Naomi (wife of Dr. Yitzchak Landes) and Avraham Yaakov (a manufacturer in Colombia).

Rabbi Yehuda Leib Saks

Rabbi Yehuda Leib Saks was born to his parents Rabbi Menachem Benzion and Chana Saks in Jerusalem and received a religious upbringing. At 11 years old, he studied in a yeshiva in Jerusalem. In 1922, his parents and he moved to Chicago, and he continued his studies at the Beit Midrash LaTorah and attended Marshall High School, where he graduated with distinction and a scholarship.

After receiving ordination from the Beit Midrash LaTorah, Rabbi Saks attended the University of Chicago and received a doctorate in philosophy. In 1946, Rabbi Saks married Freidel Eisenstein, a daughter of R. David and Hendel Eisenstein, and went into the rabbinate. His first pulpit was in Indiana Harbor. Later he became the rabbi of the Beit Eliezer synagogue and Humboldt Blvd. Temple (both in Chicago). Since 1952, Rabbi Saks has been the rabbi of the Edmonton Jewish community in Alberta, Canada, where he has been very active in the religious and cultural areas. Rabbi Saks has three doctorates – in philosophy, theology and Hebrew Literature (the last was obtained from Dr. Schechter Seminary). He is a professor at the University of Alberta, the head of the Hillel Foundation, chairman of the Jewish-Christian

Friendship Association, and is the religious preacher on a Canadian radio program funded by the government, which enjoys an audience of thousands of listeners.

Mrs. Freidel Saks, a clever and educated woman, is also very active in community affairs, and is very involved in community life in Edmonton. The Saks have two children, Zelig-Dov and Yocheved Devorah.

From Left: Rabbi Yehuda Leib Saks, David Ben Gurion, and Freidel Saks

[*Page 400*]

Dr. Dov Eisenstein

Dr. Dov (Bernard) Eisenstein, a son of David and Hendel Eisenstein, was born in Chicago in 1926. In 1947 he graduated as a medical doctor from the University of Chicago. He married Esther in 1954.

From 1951 to 1953, Dr. Eisenstein served in the American army and saw action in the Korean War. He was a captain and commanding officer of naval troops who landed in Korea from Japan. He also served with distinction in the 14th Field Hospital. Dr. Eisenstein is a recognized practicing physician with five offices in Chicago. He is a member of the American Medical Society and staff physician at the Michael Reese Hospital and elsewhere.

Zvi Aryeh Eisenstein

Zvi Aryeh (Harold) Eisenstein, a son of David and Hendel Eisenstein, was born on October 19, 1921 in Chicago. He studied at the Talmud Torah School and studied with private teachers. He graduated from high school and attended Wilson's College simultaneously. He married Dorothy Silver on June 22, 1943. During the war years (1943 to 1945), he served as a technical sergeant in the American 13th Air Force in the South Pacific, and he was stationed with his division in Admiraltes, New Guinea, Maritea, and elsewhere.

For his military service, Harold was awarded a flight medal and four Oak Leaf Clusters, six battle stars, and twice was cited in the President's List of Excellence. Zvi and Dorothy have three children: Linda, Robert, and Gary.

Esther Rachel Silverman, a daughter of R. Zelig and Sirka Hausman She died in 1956 in New York and was survived by her husband Yonah and two children, David (a doctor) and Sam Silverman.

[*Page 401*]
Morris Eisenstein

Morris Eisenstein, a son of Avraham and Malka Eisenstein, was born in Drohitchin in 1918. He came to Chicago with his parents at the age of 1. He graduated high school and studied business at Roosevelt College. During World War II Morris served three and a half years in the 42nd Rainbow Division of the 7th American Army. He was heavily involved in battle and earned four medals and many ribbons and stripes. Lieutenant General Edward P. Witsell of the Defense Department sent Eisenstein the following document together with a Silver Star:

"I am very honored to inform you that on the orders of the President of the United States, you are receiving the Silver Star. It took place on April 29, 1945 near Dachau, Germany, when under a hail of bullets from every direction, you, Corporal Eisenstein, jumped onto a jeep and grabbed a machine gun lying next to a dead soldier. When the gun failed to work, you crawled over to a truck abandoned by our fleeing soldiers, and you started shooting with an anti-aircraft gun at a German airplane. After you used up all the ammunition, and under a hail of bullets, you crawled back to a box at the back of the truck, got fresh ammunition, loaded the anti-aircraft gun and started shooting at the enemy without stopping.

"Your heroism enabled our soldiers to occupy the enemy's position and capture 150 men who had presented a large obstacle in the way of our division."

Major General Harry G. Collins, Eisenstein's commander, reported in a document why Morris received the bronze medal Oak Leaf Cluster.

"On April 20, 1945, Eisenstein was with a patrol of two soldiers near Furth, Germany. From barracks, the Germans shot heavily at the patrol and other American soldiers following them. Under a hail of bullets, Eisenstein crawled to the barracks and sneaked inside, where he found a German major and three soldiers. Morris pointed his loaded gun and ordered the major to order the German garrison of 15 men to surrender.

"Afterwards, Morris took the major to a nearby hospital and ordered him to tell the entire staff and patients to surrender. During the same day, Morris returned with the major, who gave the order to another 120 officers and soldiers to surrender. Corporal Morris Eisenstein's heroism played an important role in the successful capitulation of the German city of Furth."

Morris received the Purple Heart for the wounds he received in all the battles he was in. (Information from *Forverts*, written by S. Regensberg). Morris, who was discharged with the rank of staff sergeant, now works with his father in the car business.

Morris was commander of the Chicago Jewish War Veterans Post. Today he is the vice-commander of the Jewish Veterans of Illinois and was chairman of the Israel Bonds Campaign and other projects in 1957.   DW

Harry Eisenstein

Harry Eisenstein, a son of Avraham and Malka Eisenstein, was born in 1915 in Drohitchin. In 1920 he came to Chicago. In World War II he served for two and a half years in the U.S. Army, and earned the rank of sergeant. Today he is in business, and he and Rota Eisenstein have two children, Susan and Sandra.

[Page 402]
Eliyahu Eisenstein

Eliyahu (Elik) Eisenstein, a son of Yisrael Baruch and Esther Eisenstein, was born on the first day of Rosh Hashanah in 1923 in Chicago. He studied at the Talmud Torah School, the Yiddish Folks School and later at the University of Michigan at Ann Arbor. In 1942, he was drafted into the American Air Force and served at the rank of lieutenant (navigator). He flew 10 times with his bomber squadron over German territory to bomb the enemy's positions. On his eleventh mission, he was shot down somewhere over Italy. Eliyahu jumped out of the burning airplane, but unfortunately his parachute failed to open, and he fell into the Adriatic Sea (between Italy and Yugoslavia). Eliyahu was the only casualty of the Drohitchin community in the United States during World War II. He died on the fifth of Elul (August 24), 1944.

Yitzchak Eisenstein

Yitzchak Eisenstein, a son of Yisrael Baruch and Esther Eisenstein, was born on August 24, 1921 in Chicago. He studied at the Talmud Torah School, the Yiddish Folks School, and at Roosevelt University. In 1942, he was drafted into the United States Army, returned two and a half years later, and went into business. Yitzchak was a successful home building contractor and contributed greatly to philanthropic causes. Yitzchak died suddenly in the flower of his youth on 18 Tishrei (September 23), 1956. He left behind a wife and three children. See p. 191.

Yitzchak Eisenstein

Yitzchak Eisenstein, a son of R. Hershel and Chana, was born in Drohitchin. In approximately 1904, he married Reichele, a daughter of R. David and Chaya-Gittel Eisenstein. In 1912, he arrived in Chicago and brought over his family in 1920. R. Yitzchak, a religious and moral Jew, died on 7 Iyar (May 5), 1957. He was survived by his wife Reichel and three daughters: Pessel (Morris) Rosenberg, Chana (Yosef) Geneles, and Leah (Bontcha) Wasserman. See p. 243.

Yeshayahu	Weinstein	Pesha
11 Nisan (March 23), 1945		9 August 1911

Yehuda Leib Barenbaum

Yehuda Leib (Leibel) Barenbaum, a son of R. Aharon Shmuel and Chaya, was born in Drohitchin and received a religious upbringing. In 1906, he moved to the United States and was a co-founder of the Kehilat Yaakov synagogue and Talmud Torah School. He was involved in the Drohitchin Relief Committee. Yehuda Leib, a Sabbath observer, died on 1 Adar (February 24), 1936 at the age of 53. He left behind his wife, Chashka, and three children: Moshe (Washington), Zvi-Hirsh and Shoshana (Chicago). Chasha is the daughter of R. Isaac Vladavsky of Drohitchin. (See p. 357 DW)

[Page 403]
Eliyahu David Warshavsky

Eliyahu David Warshavsky, son of R. Yaakov Hersh and Malka Warshavsky, was killed in an automobile accident on the second day of Sukkot in 5700 (October 1, 1939) at the age of 40. He left a wife and two daughters, Irene and Lucille Green. *See pp. 215, 216, 246, 293, 308, and 357.*

An eternal memorial to our beloved mother
Malka Warshavsky
12 Tishrei 5718 – October 7, 1957
Tila Kagan, Leizer Warshavsky and Yosef Warshaw

An eternal memorial to our beloved parents
Eliezer   Tenenbaum   Pesha
20 Adar 5712 – March 17, 195220 Av 5701 – August 13, 1941
Frieda Toiva WarshavskyNorton Avraham Tenenbaum

Yisrael Baruch Warshavsky

Yisrael Baruch Warshavsky, son of R. Yaakov Zvi and Malka Warshavsky, arrived in Chicago in 1911. He was active in the Drohitchin Relief Committee and other similar organizations. In 1916, he was drafted into the American army and fought against the Germans in France. He was killed there on 21 Tishrei 5679 (September 27), 1918 at the age of 24. He was the only casualty in the First World War from among Drohitchin émigrés in the United States. See p. 215.

An eternal memorial to our dear parents

Eliyahu	Warshavsky	Chaya-Tsirel
(Son of Yeshayahu and Gittel)		(Daughter of Leizer-Shlomo and Chaya)
3 Elul 1955 – August 21, 1955		16 Av, 1941 – August 8, 1941

Esther and Bernard Goodman, Chicago See p. 243.

[Page 404]
David Steinberg

David and Gesha Steinberg

David Steinberg, born in Brisk, settled in Drohitchin after his marriage in approximately 1902, and for a while ran a tax office. Later, he moved to the United States. He was one of the most active members of the Drohitchin synagogue in Chicago. He died on 22 Shvat (February 19), 1941 at the age of 90. Gesha Steinberg, a daughter of R. Yosef and Chaya-Ita Gratch of Drohitchin, and wife of R. David, came to Chicago with her family in 1910. She and her husband were known for their religiosity and charity. She was an active member in the Sha'arei Tikvah (Gates of Hope) Anshei Ma'arav (Men of the West) synagogue and the Drohitchin synagogue for 40 years. She also supported yeshivas and people who lost their businesses or jobs. Gesha died on September 19, 1955 at the age of 92.

The Steinbergs had four children: Shlomo (Washington), Bobel, Harry, and Zeidel (Chicago).

Moshe (Tanna) son of Pinchas Lev (Levy)
perished in a tragic death on 14 Adar (March 8), 1955 in Chicago.
He was 56 years old, and had been a co-founder of the Progressive Club.
He was a co-founder and vice-chairman of the Drohitchin Branch, and
raised money for the Histadrut, Jewish National Fund, etc. He left behind
a wife, Beila, and three sons.

Yaakov Gratch

Yaakov and Sarah Gratch

Yaakov Gratch was born in Drohitchin in 1874 to his parents, R. Shimon and Beila. He studied in a *kheder* and then in the Maltsh Yeshiva. In 1903, he arrived in the United States and then returned to Drohitchin. In 1907, he returned to the United States, to Chicago, to settle. In 1912, he brought over his family.

R. Yaakov was an active member of the Kehilat Yaakov synagogue, of the Drohitchin Aid Association, and the Free Loan Association. He also read from the Torah at the Rodfei Zedek synagogue. R. Yaakov died on 5 Av (August 2), 1946.

Sarah, daughter of Simcha and wife of R. Yaakov Gratch, was born in 1873. She was a housewife and took great interest in the newly arriving immigrants from Drohitchin. The warm welcome that she gave the lonely immigrants made them feel at home back in the old country. She gave them encouragement in their struggle for a new life.

Sarah died on 20 Cheshvan (November 12), 1949. The Gratches had five children: Zlata, Sima, Shimon, Chaim-Simcha and Leibel. All live in Chicago. R. Yaakov had four brothers and two sisters: Moshe Leizer, Chaykel, Yossel, Shmerel, Chana-Itka, Hoddes, and Gisha. (See pp. 55, 205, 206, 213, 214 and 299. D. W.)

In eternal memory of our dear
Mother, Esther Yehudit Gratch
11 Cheshvan (October 16), 1956
Avraham and Yosef Gratch

See pp. 213-214.

[Page 405]

Photo from right to left:

Devorah	Hoffman	Leizer	Avraham-Chaim	Goodman	Ethel
1 Adar 1955			12 Elul 1941	21 Cheshvan 1956	3 Av 1956
4 March 1955			4 Sept 1941	26 October 1956	11 Jul 1956
	Children:			Children:	
Malka, Itka (Chicago), Miriam (L.A.)			Esther Feigel (Cleve.)	Binyamin Moshe (Ind.)	

Dvosha	Hoffman	Yisrael-David
Lives in Chicago		13 Tammuz 1948
		20 July 1948
	Children:	
Chaya Gitel, Miriam (Chicago), Reizel (NH)		

Leizer, Ethel and Yisrael David are the children of R. Binyamin-Moshe the Ritual Slaughterer and Beila Hoffman of Drohitchin. Their only brother, Chaim Hoffman, lives in Chicago. See pp. 133, 149, 150, 288, and 329. W.

Hersh-Leib	Miller	Chaya-Esther
22 Av		12 Sivan

Rachel Miller died on 5 Iyar (24 April), 1939 at the age of 94. She had four sons: Hersh-Leib, Zelig (died), Simcha and Yudel Miller, who live in Chicago. See p. 390

Bashka Eisenstein

Bashka Eisenstein, the wife of R. Mendel Eisenstein, and the daughter of R. Yitzchak and Mindel Gutter of Antopolia, left Drohitchin with her children for Chicago in 1921. She died there on 7 Cheshvan (1 November), 1957 at the age of 82. She was survived by four sons and two daughters: Mordechai-Ber (Morris), Hersh-Leib (Harry), Shachna (Charlie), Nachman (Norman), Henya-Perl Wald, and Ida Match, 11 grandchildren and 10 great-grandchildren. See p. 220.

[Page 406]
Zelig Shevinsky

Zelig Shevinsky, a son of R. Nachum and Bodya Shevinsky, was born in Drohitchin. At the age of 13, he joined his uncle in August, Georgia, and became a peddler. Later he moved to Birmingham (Alabama), where he opened a successful clothing business in 1917. He had a reputation as an honest businessman and became involved in community life. He made a major contribution to the development of the Jewish community of Birmingham.

Shevinsky was the president of Temple Beth El; a former president of the Hebrew School; former campaign chairman and co-developer of the new large school building that cost $175,000. He provided bus transportation for the school children of the Hebrew School as well as for the elderly congregants so that they would be able to pray at the synagogue. Shevinsky was also the person who arranged for the rabbi and cantor to have their own homes.

Shevinsky was the chairman of the Zionist Organization and a co-founder of the Permanent Country Club for the young people. He was a former board member of the United Jewish Appeal. In September 1939, his wife Rivka-Rachel Sorosen, who was born in Jerusalem, passed away. Shevinsky thus had to serve as both father and mother to his children, who he raised in the spirit of nationalism.

Rivka-Rachel Shevinsky

Shortly before his death, Shevinsky visited Israel and returned with enthusiasm for plans for helping the new state. However, this was interrupted by his sudden death. Zelig died on 12 Tishrei 5717 (17 September), 1956, leaving behind a daughter Marjorie, and a son Harold.

Yehuda Matthew

Yehuda, the son of Levi, Matthew was born in Matsev, Volhynia, into a Chassidic family. Young Yehuda received a strictly religious upbringing and studied at the Kolev yeshiva and other places. He also studied Hebrew. In 1912, Matthew moved to Chicago and eventually became a successful manufacturer and industrialist. As a true Sabbath observer, Matthew always closed his factory on the Sabbath and holidays. Today as well, after his death, the factory maintains its principles with regard to the Sabbath and the Jewish holidays. In addition to his private activities, he also remained active in community affairs in the area of religious and nationalist education.

Matthew was a co-founder of the popular Adath Bnai Yisrael (an organization of religious young people), where he taught for the public on the Sabbath and holidays. He also helped found the Young Israel chapter in Chicago and St. Louis.

As a totally devoted Zionist, Matthew had been active in the Ahavat Zion association, which he established in 1914 in the building of Adath Bnai Yisrael. Later he served for many years as the president of the Chicago religious Zionist organization, Mizrachi, and also assisted religious people in Palestine.

Matthew was known as a person who admired rabbis, and therefore provided much assistance to rabbinical scholars, yeshivas, and Hebrew parochial schools. Matthew owned a beautiful library with many books and scheduled time each day to study. In his later years, Matthew lived in Miami Beach because of his health and was involved in community affairs there as well.

[Page 407]

Matthew had plans to move to Israel, but he died too soon to realize his plans. He passed away on 9 Nisan (21 March), 1956. He was survived by his wife, Sheina-Tsippa (daughter of R. Nachum Shevinsky of Drohitchin) and three children: Yaakov-Aharon, Beila, and Avraham-Yosef.

Mordechai Mirsky

Mordechai and Rivka Mirsky

Mordechai Mirsky, a son of Rafael and Mina, was born in approximately 1857 and studied in the *kheder* (school) and the Slonim yeshiva. Later he moved to Drohitchin where he married Rivka, a daughter of R. Velvel and Devorah, and went into business.

The Mirskys ran a bakery and sold flour, which earned them the name of "wholesalers." Rivka was involved in *podraden* with her own hands and was the sponsor of food supplies for the workers who build the highway between Brisk and Kartuz-Bereza. The Mirskys were also involved in community affairs, and belonged to *Chovevei Zion* (Lovers of Zion), Bikkur Holim (Medical Assistance Service), and other community institutions.

During the war years of 1914-1918, the Mirskys lived in Pinsk, and then in Kobrin, later returning to Drohitchin. In October 1921, they moved to the United States and were briefly in business. They lived out their final years in New York. R. Mordechai died at the age of 86 on 12 Tammuz 5703 (1943, not 1934-14 July 1943). Rivka died on 2 Av (16 July), 1942 at the age of 80. Rivka was the aunt of the writer, Yoel Slonim. The Mirskys has six children: Abba, Reuven, Sarah, Eliezer, Velvel, and Leah Lubin.

In memory of my dear parents and brother

Shlomo	Goldman	Vichna-Devorah
20 Kislev 1940		15 Adar 5688
20 December 1940		7 March 1928
David Goldman 7 Adar 1940		

(There were two Adars that year – so English date was either Feb. 16 or March 17.)

Sarah		
Yaakov	Cooper	Feigel
11 Adar 1942		21 Shvat 1936
28 February 1942		14 February 1936

Far Right: Elmer L. Shevinsky, son of Zalman and Mrs. Shevinsky
Middle: Major Harold Shevin, son of Felix and Mrs. Shevinsky
Far Left: Holtzman brothers: from right: Corporal Hayman, Lloyd L. (Engineer) and
Lieutenant Jack Holtzman – sons of Lena Holtzman.

[*Page 408*]

DROGITCHINSKY FAMILY TREE
(2014 edits, F. Schumacher)

Parents

Aharon Drogitchinsky, Chana D Drogitchinsky

Children	Married	Grandchildren	Great-Grandchildren	Great-great-grandchildren
Rosa	Shmuel Goldfarb	Sarah G. Blumenfeld	Harriet B. Kahnweiler	Susan Kahnweiler
				Jill Kahnweiler
		Evelyn G. Levinson	Norman S. Levinson	Lena Rabin Levinson
			Patty L. Schwartz	
			Donald Levinson	
		Frances G. Citron	Phillip N. Citron	Joanne Citron
			David Citron Jr.	Leslee Citron
				David Citron, III
			A. Robert Citron	
		Marion M. Eskow		
		Esther G. Stone	Helene S. Lane	Richard Lane
				Lisa Lane
		Hazel G. Rogers	Rodger L. Rogers	Ronald Rodgers
				Howard Rodgers
				Thomas Rodgers
		Alger David Goldfarb		
Shlomo		Morris Mayer		
Hinda	Gershon Strangin	Two daughters		
John Mayer	Sarah Yaskulka	Leah Mayer	Shirley Rosen	Norma Rosen
				Richard Rosen
		Eva Mayer		
		Baron de Hirsh Mayer		
Feigel	Yisrael Lev	Eliyahu Lev	Carolinia Lev	
			Michael Lev	
		Edward Lev	Alan Lev	
			Richard Lev	
		David Lev		
Elka	Yisrael Goldman			
Sarah	Pakov	Leonard Pakov	Violet Pakov	
		Faye		
Tila	Binyamin Zucker	Hazel T. Steiner	Benjamin Steiner	
			Joseph Steiner	
			Lisa Steiner	
		James Zucker		
Tsippa	Schreibman	2 children		

Baron De Hirsh Mayer

Major Baron de Hirsh Mayer

Baron de Hirsh Mayer

Baron de Hirsh Mayer, a famous attorney, banker and philanthropist in Miami Beach, was born on April 12 to his parents John and Sarah Mayer in Prairie du Chien, Wisconsin. He went to law school at the University of Wisconsin and Harvard. On August 22, 1951 he married Paula Lax, a daughter of Pauline and John Lax of Pittsburgh, PA. Baron de Hirsch Mayer, who was a leading personality in Miami Beach, was a trustee of the University of Miami Beach and of Mount Sinai Hospital. He was a member of the Board of Directors of the Jewish Federation and of the home for the aged there.

[Page 409]

John Mayer

John Mayer, a son of Aharon and Chana Drogitchinsky, was born in 1872 in Drohitchin. His wife, Sara, was a daughter of Yaakov Yaskulka and was born on December 9, 1871 in Brisk. John Mayer, who was a businessman, died on August 27, 1942. The Mayers had three children: Leo Mayer, Eva Mayer, and Baron de Hirsh Mayer.

Photo right top is of John Mayer. Left top is of John and his wife Sarah Mayer, who live in Miami Beach.

Photo in middle is Tila Zucker, a daughter of R. Aharon and Chana Drogitchinsky. She lives in Miami Beach (see pp. 66 and 219. DW)

On the left is Meir Paykov, a family member who died at the hands of the Germans in

Europe during the War.

Shmuel Goldfarb

Shmuel Goldfarb, born in Kobrin, was a businessman and died on January 20, 1934. Roza, a daughter of R. Aharon and Chana Drogitchinsky, was from Drohitchin and was Shmuel's wife. She died on July 29, 1933. The Goldfarbs had seven children: Sarah Blumenfeld (San Diego), Evelyn Levinson (Detroit), Frances Citron (Chicago), Marion Eskov (Miami Beach), Esther Stone (St. Joseph, Missouri), Alger D. Goldfarb (Highland Park, Illinois), and Hazel Rogers.

Shmuel and Roza Goldfarb

[Page 410]

Heska Match

Heska Match, a daughter of R. Meir Yudel and Chana Feiga Feldman, was born in Drohitchin. She studied under private tutors in Drohitchin and at the Smolnik Estate, where she spent part of her youth. She was an active member of Zionist youth organizations and helped in building up Palestine.

In 1922, Heska moved to the United States and married Shmuel Match in 1930 in Chicago, where she became involved in Zionist activity in various organizations and associations. Shmuel Match, a son of Ezra and Miriam Match, and husband of Eska, was born in the village of Aziat, near Dvin. He lived in Chicago since 1921 and was a successful businessman in the home real estate business.

The Matches have three children: Sarah Leah, Yisrael Ezra, and Morry. Sarah Leah was married in 1954 to Rabbi Avraham-Mordechai (Milton) Kantor. Rabbi Kantor, who was born in Chicago in 1929 is a graduate of the Beth Midrash La-Torah and has a master's degree from the University of Chicago. Since 1956, Rabbi Kantor has served as rabbi at a synagogue in Skokie, Illinois. (See pp. 67, 223, 306. W.).

Esther Beila Friedman

Esther Beila Friedman, a daughter of R. Meir-Yudel and Chaya-Feiga Feldman, was born in Drohitchin in 1889. In 1907, she married David Friedman and moved to the United States with her family. Esther-Beila died in St. Joseph, Missouri on 27 Elul (25 September), 1954. Her husband, David, lives in St. Joseph. Their children are: Yaakov, Helen (Denver, Colorado), Leah, Pesha, and Yosef, a physician (in St. Joseph).

Pesha Kaminetsky, wife of Yaakov-Hirsh, died on September 29, 1915. Her children were: Chaya-Feiga Feldman, Rivka Volinsky, Leah-Beila Mishovsky, and Avraham Stone.

This photo was taken at the home of Sarah and Willy Feldman at the wedding of their daughter Esther in St. Joseph. In the photo are: Abe Feldman, his wife and daughter; Heska and Sam Match and children; Abe and Willy Stone; Sarah and Benny Forman and family; David Friedman and family; Harry Baskov and family, Rivka Wolinsky and daughter Yetta Wolinsky-Kalman, and others.

[Page 411]
Avraham Mordechai Feldman

Avraham Mordechai Feldman, a son of Meir-Yudel and Chaya-Feiga Feldman, was born in Drohitchin in 1883. In 1904, he arrived in the United States, and he died in Denver on April 2, 1956. Avraham Mordechai's wife Roza (née Baskov) lives there. The Feldmans had three children: Margaret Kotler (California), Lucille Rinsky (Cincinnati, OH), and a son who is a lawyer in Denver.

Avraham-Yehuda Stone (seated), his son Willy, and Willy's daughter, Helene S. Lane, and her son, Richard, and the grandmother, Pesha. See p. 410 – five generations.

Rivka Volinsky

Aryeh Leib and Rivka Volinsky, and daughter Y. Kalman

Rivka Volinsky, a daughter of R. Yaakov Hersh and Pesha Kaminetsky, was born in 1879 in Drohitchin and received a religious upbringing. In 1894, she married Aryeh-Leib Volinetz (Volinsky) from Selishch, near Drohitchin.

In 1896, Rivka and her husband arrived in the United States and settled in St. Joseph, Missouri, where they went into business. Rivka became the chairwoman in St. Joseph of the Ladies' Auxiliary of the Sha'arei Shalom synagogue from 1925 to 1940; she was the vice-chairman of the Talmud Torah School from 1928 to 1930; former chairwoman of the Jewish National Fund from 1930 to 1940; board member of Hadassah from 1930 to 1945; and a member of the board and administrator of the Aid Committee that undertook to assist the Jewish needy in town. She was also one of eight women nominated by the mayor to lead the public school bond drive in St. Joseph.

In 1944, Rivka was awarded the title of Outstanding Woman of the Year for her outstanding community service in St. Joseph. Rivka died at the age of 72 on 22 Tevet (14 January), 1947. Aryeh-Leib, son of R. Yeshayahu and Devorah Volinetz was born in 1878 in Selishch. For a while, he was a trustee of the Sha'arei Shalom synagogue in St. Joseph. Aryeh-Leib Volinsky died on Purim (March 8), 1936. The Volinskys had two daughters: Helen Mayerson (Council Bluff, Iowa) and Yetta Kalman (DW). Yetta, her husband, Eliezer (Louis), and son, Shraga-Aryeh (Lorne), live in Chicago. They are active in community affairs.

[Page 412]
Eliyahu Milner

Eliyahu Milner, a son of R. Tsadok and Shifra, was born in 1876 in Drohitchin and studied in the *kheder(* school) and Talmud Torah. After he married Ethel, a daughter of R. Shmuel and Liba of Pruzhany, he opened a bakery and a confectionary in town. His wife, Ethel, was especially good in business, and the Milners' bakery products were famous in town and the surrounding area. Eliyahu was the first person to bring a matzo-making machine into town to make "machine matzos," and was also the first person to manufacture ice cream for sale in Drohitchin. When World War I broke out in 1914, as a reservist, Eliyahu was drafted into the Russian army and sent off to the front.

Once on a dark night, Eliyahu was sent on a reconnaissance mission to spy on the German positions. He came up with an idea, and shot himself in the foot with his gun. As a result, he was sent to the hospital in Kazan. Not long thereafter, his wound healed and he had to return to the front. He sat in the synagogue in Kazan and recited psalms. A well-dressed man approached him, greeted him, and started to ask where he came from as a Russian soldier. This was the beginning of an amazing story.

When Eliyahu served as a new conscript in the Russian army in Astrakhan, he spent his free time working in a tailor shop owned by a Jew. There was another employee there by the name of Motel Nechamkin, with whom he got along well. One day Motel received a telegram that his wife was ill and needed money. Motel had no money, and Eliyahu lent him 25 rubles, which Motel sent to his wife. The years passed, and Eliyahu forgot about the whole story. Now, twenty years later, Eliyahu was standing face to face with his old poor friend Motel Nechamkin, who eventually became wealthy and a supplier of military clothes for the army, which brought him great success.

The now-wealthy Motel Nechamkin wanted to thank Eliyahu for the favor he did for him years earlier. Motel brought Eliyahu home and was quickly able to arrange Eliyahu's discharge from the army. Eliyahu then went home to his family a happy man. (Information is from G. Kaplan in the *Amerikaner*).

In 1920, Eliyahu arrived in New York with his daughter Feigel. In 1927, he also brought over Ethel and the other children. Eliyahu died on 19 Shvat (21 January), 1938. Ethel lives in New York with her children: Feigel, Shifra, Yudel, Tordos, Sarah, and Devorah. A son, Yisrael, lives in Cuba.   W.

Shlomo	Fishman	Esther-Chaya
29 Nisan		25 Adar
David Wolin	Liba Klein	

For a memorial, the Broners

Choneh Greiber

Choneh and Chaya-Sarah Greiber

Choneh (Chonya) Greiber, a son of Mordechai and Riva Greiber, was born in Drohitchin and arrived in Chicago in 1911. He worked in a kosher meat store removing the sciatic nerve from beef. He was the first contributor to the free loan society of the Drohitchin Progressive Club. He died on 18 Adar (There were two Adars that year – one date was February 19, and the other March 21), 1938.

Chaya-Sarah, a daughter of Velvel and Yochna Yarenkas of Drohitchin, was Chonye's wife. She supported Torah scholars, the Motele synagogue, and the home for the aged. She died on 5 Tevet (14 December), 1950. The Greibers had six children: Dova-Reizel, Avraham-Yaakov, Shmuel, Meir, David, and Golda. Their son-in-law was Yisrael-Zalman Amilinsky.

[Page 413]
Sender Dvinsky

Sender Dvinsky, a son of Hershel Dvinsky of Drohitchin, moved to Palestine after World War I and was one of the people who built the Mekor-Chaim neighborhood near Jerusalem. Sender was one of the leaders of the Haganah in his neighborhood. During the day, he worked, and at night he guarded the area from Arab attacks. In 1929, during the Arab pogroms, Sender and his friends prevented a tragedy in Mekor-Chaim. He had to leave his family many times to go to defend other settlements. In 1938, Sender came to visit Chicago and remained there. He and his family here got along well, and he was an active member of the Drohitchin branch, serving as its chairman for a time. Sender died young in 1952 and left behind his wife, Sheindel (daughter of Hershel Goldwirth of Mekor-Chaim) and two daughters in Chicago.

Ezra Weissman

Ezra Weissman, a son of R. Shimon and Lotsa Weissman, was born in Drohitchin. He studied both Jewish and secular subjects, loved music and art, and was active in community affairs in Drohitchin. After World War I, he arrived in the United States and quickly became accustomed to the country. Unfortunately, he died tragically in Chicago in 1949.

Avraham Yitzchak Lev

Avraham Yitzchak Lev, a son of Yaakov Shimon and Sarah Lev, was born in Drohitchin in 1890 and studied in the *kheders* in town. Even in his youth, he was active in the Socialist Zionist movement and brought this spirit into his efforts to convince the workers of his father's workshop. He joined the self-defense group in 1905 and was hunted by the Czarist gendarmerie. At the age of 18, he left for the United States, where he became an active member of the

Poalei Zion and a cultural activist. He was also one of the first supporters of the Drohitchin yizkor book. Avraham Yitzchak died suddenly in 1944, leaving behind his wife, Yehudit (daughter of Yaakov and Chava Pollack of Drohitchin) and two daughters.

My Memorial
With a broken heart I am memorializing my dear and beloved husband and son, Yehoshua and Reuvele, who loved their Drohitchin so much.
With eternal grief,
Rasha Leah Schmid, New York

For an Eternal Memorial to my dear parents

Yehoshua	Warshavsky	Michlya
(Son of R. Yeshayahu and Gittel)		(Daughter of R. Moshe Kushner)
born on July 10, 1867		born on July 14, 1866
	died	
21 Tammuz, 1952		4 Sivan 1936
14 July 1952		25 May 1936
	Sister	
Chaya-Rachel Warshavsky		11 Cheshvan 1929
		14 November 1929
See p. 243	Bessya Warshavsky, Chicago	

See p. 243

[*Page 414*]

Binyamin Michel Eisenstein

Binyamin Michel Eisenstein, a son of Leizer and Bluma Eisenstein, was born in Chicago in 1909. After graduating from the Kehilat Yaakov Talmud Torah and high school, he went to work at city hall, and in 1937 was appointed a court bailiff. During the war years, Eisenstein uncovered and disrupted a spy cell of the German Bund in Chicago. Eisenstein died tragically; he was a guest at a party of his friend, Albert Fineberg, whose house was broken into by two robbers, and Eisenstein shot one of the robbers. However, the second robber shot back and killed Fineberg and Eisenstein on the spot. This took place on May 9, 1947.

Eisenstein's wife, Ethel/Ella (a daughter of Meir and Chaya Beila Grossband), and three children: Chaya-Gittel, Mardy, and Eileen survived him (See p. 243. DW).

Avraham Feldman

Avraham Feldman (Avrahamel from Yolitch) lived for many years in the village of Yolitch, near Drohitchin, and was a hardy villager from the old days. It was said that Avrahamel was attacked by a large wolf, but grabbed the wolf by the tongue, sat on it and rode it around, chasing away peasants from the village. In 1906, Feldman moved to New York and then to Chicago in 1908, where he lived out his years with his children, Leizer and Bluma Eisenstein. He died at the age of 60 on July 20, 1914. The Feldmans had 10 children: Feiga-Rivka, Chana, Charna, Yaakov-Yossel, Moshe-Zalman, Meir (deceased), Yechiel-Tordos, Fanny Rotenberg, Bertha Miller, and Bluma Eisenstein live in Chicago.

[Right:] Captain Dr. Yosef Friedman, son of David and Esther-Beila Freidman. See p. 410.
[Middle:] Sergeant Philip (right) and Corporal Henry – sons of Louis and Frieda Mayers.
[Left:] Fred, son of Hersh and Mrs. Kotock

[Page 415]
Mordechai Ratnovsky

Mordechai Ratnovsky, a son of Shalom Moshe and Reiza, originated from Kolonia, near Drohitchin. Early in his youth, Mordechai moved to Chicago and was vice president of the Meat Cutters Union, Local 596. He was a member of the Drohitchin Chapter and others. He died at the age of 46 on 10 Tammuz (17 July), 1948. His wife Beila and six children survived him: Yisrael-Lipa, Shabtai, Chaim-Henach, Henya-Leah, Necha, and Zvia-Reizel. Mordechai's brother and sister, Leizer, Sarah and Gruntcha, died under the Germans in 1942. Beila's father, Chaim Yarinkas, died on 29 Av (12 August), 1931, and her mother Zvia, died on 10 Tevet 1940 (This date only corresponds to December 22, 1939). Beila's grandfather, Yaakov Yarinkas, died on January 21, 1949. Beila's grandmother, Sarah, died in 1916.   DW

| Feigel Mayers | -- | 25 Kislev (29 November) 1956 |
| | Wife of Neiten | |

Chaim Henach Ratnovsky

Chaim Henach Ratnovsky, a son of Mordechai and Beila Ratnovsky, was born on May 10, 1937 in Chicago. His father died early in his youth, and after he completed his studies in the Talmud Torah and high schoo,l he decided to assist his mother financially. He was a very devoted son and strove to take care of this mother and sister. On the evening of March 17, 1957, two detectives came into the shoe store at 112 S. State Street where Chaim worked, and Chaim thought they were thieves. The detectives made the same mistake, and Chaim started to run. As a result, the detectives shot him. He managed to survive for a couple of days, but died on March 21, 1957.

Hershel	Mayers	Mirel
25 Shvat 1905		18 Shvat 1911
31 January 1905		16 February 1911

[Left:] Bernard Berezovsky, [Center:] Leonard Berezovsky [Right:] Ben Kest

Sons of Herman and Mrs. Berezovsky

[*Page 416*]

Shlomo Shederovsky

Shlomo Shederovsky, a son of Yaakov-Eliezer and Tsippa, was born in Drohitchin. Shlomo was self-educated and a follower of the Enlightenment. He taught himself Russian, read the Russian classics, and was proficient in Hebrew literature and the Talmud.

Shederovsky had progressive inclinations and modern ideas. He was one of the founders of a Russian elementary school in Drohitchin and brought a pharmacist to Drohitchin. He was, therefore, called a heretic in Drohitchin. Subsequently, when Shederovsky lived in Lodz for a time because of his business activities, he was also involved in social and cultural affairs.

Due to the fact that he was a Zionist from his early youth, Shederovsky realized his life-long dream in 1913 by emigrating with his family to Palestine, where he settled in Petach Tikvah. He purchased land and worked in agriculture. As a courageous and fearless speaker, Shederovsky eventually became well known by those around him; his home was open as a guest house to new immigrants and travelers. A hot samovar was always standing on the table, and Mrs. Shederovsky spent her entire days providing for the guests. People came to Shederovsky for advice about living in Palestine, and others asked him to serve as an arbitrator in disputes.

Shederovsky was a strong supporter of unlimited mass immigration into Palestine and investment of private capital in Palestine. He also participated in many Zionist congresses and briefly served as a representative of the Palestine Citrus Society in Egypt. Shederovsky was also the senior school inspector of Petach Tikvah and was involved with educational issues there. Shlomo occasionally wrote for the publication *Doar Hayom* (Daily Post) and *Voskhod* (Russian = Sunrise). He started to write a book called *The Conception of the Talmud* and a second book about *Jewish Ideas and Knowledge,* but neither book was ever published. Shederovsky died on 29 Tammuz (29 July), 1927 in Petach Tikvah.

Information is from his son Yaakov (Petach Tikvah) and Dr. Shudron (Johannesburg, South Africa).

Velvel and Esther Kreines died in Palestine.

Hershel Dvinsky

Hershel Dvinsky in his final days

Hershel Dvinsky was known for his simplicity and honesty and was one of the first immigratsto Palestine. Right after World War I, he moved to Palestine with his family. Hershel Dvinsky, Hershel Goldwirth, Mordechai Ratner, and others were the pioneers and builders of the Mekor-Chaim neighborhood, five kilometers from Jerusalem. (Ratner's son, Yosef, is a member of the Drohitchin Chapter). Their houses were built from large hard stones that they dug out of the mountains. Each one of the people living in the community had one or two cows, would sell the milk in Jerusalem, thereby managing to eek out a living. In his last years, Hershel Dvinsky lived in a home for the aged, and died at an advanced age.

[*Page 417*]

Shmuel Lev

R. Shmuel Lev, founder of the Visitors' Hostel in Jerusalem

R. Shmuel Lev, a Talmudic scholar and community leader, was born in
1856 in Drohitchin. In his youth, he studied under the great scholar, R.
Pinchas Michel of Antapolia, and after his wedding, R. Shmuel settled in
Antapolia and went into business. Later he returned to Drohitchin, where he
taught Torah classes to the community.

When his children grew up, he decided to travel to Palestine. It is told that
the great rabbis Eliezer Moshe (Pinsk), Pinchas Michael (Antapolia), and
Mordechaileh of Buten told him to visit the United States before traveling to
Palestine. R. Shmuel Lev therefore traveled on to Chicago, where he
established a Talmud study group at the Agudath Achim-Anshei Drohitchin in
memory of Rabbi Lesser. From Chicago, R. Shmuel went on to Paris, where he
established a Talmud study group and a *Chayei Adam* study group in memory
of Rabbi Labetsky. He then traveled on to Jerusalem, and with the assistance
of Max Neiten, a philanthropist in Chicago, he purchased a large estate of
houses, where he set up a visitor's hostel for rabbinic scholars, an orphanage
called Tiferet Zion Ve-Yerushalayim, as well as a synagogue called Zoharei
Chama for old-timers who always prayed at sunrise. R. Shmuel devoted his
whole life to this huge project, and dozens of scholars and lonely children were
supported with everything they needed in these houses. Together with Rabbi
Chaim David Spitzer, R. Shmuel was able to obtain support from the United
States government for his charitable undertakings through the offices of the
American consulate in Jerusalem.

Years later, when he came to New York on a visit, he established a Tiferet
Zion Ve-Yerushalayim Society, as well as the Yeshiva Torah Mi-Zion in
Brownsville, Brooklyn. R. Shmuel died in Jerusalem on 21 Tevet 5683
(January 9), 1923. (See p. 153. W.)

Yehuda Leib Eisenstein

R. Yehuda Leib, son of Asher Eisenstein, was born in 1865 in
Drohitchin. At the age of 18 (in 1883), he moved to Palestine, where he studied
in the Agrarian School of Baron Rothschild in Zichron Yaakov. R. Yehuda-Leib
was one of the pioneers and founders of the Bat Shlomo settlement (seven
kilometers from Zichron Yaakov), where he worked in agriculture. He was a
talented agriculturalist, and his fields provided enough food for his own needs
as well as for others.

R. Yehuda Leib was a religious Jew, and studied extensively in his free
time. R. Lieb was also the rabbi of the famous agronomist, Aharon Aronson
(who had earlier been part of the Nili movement in Palestine during World War
I. – DW). R. Yehuda Leib died on 23 Elul [September 13], 1938 in Bat Shlomo.
All his male grandchildren born in Bat Shlomo in the year he died were named
Leib.

R. Leib was survived by five sons and two daughters. Freidel Volansky, a granddaughter of R. Chaim Ber Altwarg, was one of his daughters-in-law there.

R. Yehuda Leib Eisenstein (second from right, with the hat) with members of the Bat Shlomo community.

[*Page 418*]
Yeshayahu Warshaw

Yeshayahu Warshaw, a son of Rabbi Yisrael Baruch and Chaya Liba Warshaw (Warshavsky) was born on 15 Shvat (7 February), 1917 in Horbacha near Drohitchin. He later lived for a while in Drohitchin and in Pruzhany, where he attended the Tarbut School. In 1930, he moved to New York and continued his studies. At the same time, Yeshayahu joined Ze'ev Jabotinsky's Betar movement, where he became a leading figure. From June 13, 1941 to the end of 1945, he served in the 112th cavalry unit of the US army. He spent three years in the South Pacific and participated in five military campaigns on the islands of Woodlark, Itape, New Britain, Lyete, and Luzon. Warshaw was one of the first and only men to land on the island of New Caledonia, where he served as a French interpreter and helped organize the French guerrilla forces and strengthen the defenses there. He also served many times as chaplain. In Luzon, Warshaw spent a month behind enemy lines, and as an outstanding shooter, shot thirteen Japanese soldiers himself; among them were two officers, and he captured their swords.

On the beach of Arawa in New Britain (where he was one of the first to land), Warshaw's patrol was ambushed. His sergeant, T. M. Yensa, was badly injured, and Warshaw crawled on all fours to the sergeant to bandage his wounds. The Japanese shot him at three times, and every time he was able to shoot back and hit the target. He killed the Japanese and took the enemy's positions. Warshaw also served in the intelligence services, and was discharged on September 14, 1945 with more than 100 points (*Yank,* February 18, 1944; *Forverts,* December 2, 1945).

After the war Warshaw returned to join the battle for a Jewish state. He was taken to court in May 1948 for having sent arms to Palestine, and on June 11, 1948 without telling his parents, he secretly left New York. On June 22, 1948 he arrived on the historic ship *Altalena* in Tel Aviv. On Ben Gurion's orders this ship was shot, and Warshaw had to swim away to save his life. Two weeks later he joined the ranks of the [continues on lower half of p. 419] Irgun against the Arabs around Jerusalem. He and his friends got into the Old City and held the forward positions on Mount Zion from July to September, until the ceasefire. After leaving the organization in September, Warshaw joined the Israeli army as an officer and held the positions at Kastel Mountain, Kaslon, among others.

Warshaw was one of the main founders of the Betar kibbutzim, Ramat Raziel (November 1948), and Mevuot Betar (April 20, 1950). In June 1950, he came to New York to recruit Betar pioneers for those kibbutzim. On August 12, 1951, he returned to Israel, and in the winter of 1952, he completed a commander's course in the Israeli army.

Warshaw today lives with his wife Margalit (married on July 22, 1953) and two daughters, Varda and Esther in Ramat Raziel, where he is a regional commander and is responsible for protecting the area. Warshaw is connected with the army and the police and has the ranks of police sergeant and army lieutenant (second). See pp. 193 and 244.

Yeshayahu Warshavsky

Yeshayahu Warshavsky, a son of R. David and Feigel Warshavsky, was born in Drohitchin. He received his early education under private tutors and in the Moriah School in Drohitchin. Afterwards he studied in yeshivas in Grodno (1924 to 1927) under Rabbi Shimon Shkop; in Kobrin (1927 to 1931) under Rabbi Pesach Pruskin, and in Kaminetz (1931 to 1933) under Rabbi Baruch Ber Leibovitz. At the end of 1932, he joined the *Hechalutz Hamizrachi* (Religious Zionist Pioneers) and became one of the people who developed the organization in Drohitchin. From 1934 to 1938, he worked in the central committee of the Torah Ve-Avoda (Torah and Labor) organization in Warsaw (at 6 Rimarski Street), where he worked a great deal on behalf of religious Zionism. On March 8, 1938, Yeshayahu moved to Palestine, where he became affiliated with Ze'ev Jabotinsky's revisionist movement. In the summer of 1938, he joined their Nationalist Labor Federation.

From 1940 to 1946, Warshavsky served as a conscripted soldier from Palestine with the British air force (RAF) and spent all the bitter war years at the battlefront. He traversed all the routes, starting from Egypt, Libya (Tobruk), all the way to Benghazi, and then back via Al-Lamein and the last assault up to Tunis. He was blinded and burned from the hamseen sandstorms and soaked and frozen in flooded trenches; worst of all, he lived through days and nights of bombardments from German Messerschmidts and had his life hanging by a hair. After the war, Yeshayahu received an offer from his officer to settle in England and benefit from all veteran privileges. However, he passed on the privileges, so he could live in Israel.

Yeshayahu was active in the War of Independence in Israel and had participated earlier in the uprising of the Irgun. Finally, he became a soldier in the Israeli army. In 1949, he joined the Herut part, and became a committee member and secretary of the northern branch of Herut in Tel Aviv.

Yeshayahu and his wife Tova (married December 1945) live in Tel Aviv.

See pp. 21, 117, 137, 247, 305 and 307.

[*Page 419*]

SUPPLEMENTS
Drohitchin is 500 Years Old

The historian Dr. Yitzchak Schiffer mentions a very important date in his book with regard to Drohitchin. This date is not mentioned in historical articles at the beginning of the Yizkor Book.

Therefore, we contacted historian Rabbi Dr. Katriel Lipman Mishkin in Chicago, who after a long and exact investigation stated that the Drohitchin mentioned by Dr. Schiffer is none other than our Drohitchin. Based on this statement of Rabbi Dr. Katriel Lipman Mishkin, we are including here a few paragraphs from Dr. Schiffer's book that clearly indicate that our Jewish community of Drohitchin is more than 500 years old. On page 267 of his book, Dr. Yitzchak Schiffer writes the following:

"In the documents of the Grand Duchy chancellery (the so-called Lithuanian metric records) from 1463-1494, we find quite a few pieces of information indicating that Jews were leasing almost all of the significant customs offices in the Duchy. We find them as lease arrangements for the customs tariffs in Byalistock, Bryansk, Drohitchin, Grodno, Kiev, Litovitch, Minsk, Novogrod, Putivel, Zhitomir, and Zviahl. We find the same picture in Red Russia and Volhyn (Volhyn then belonged to Lithuania).

"The financial opportunities in leasing were no less in Lithuania than they were in Red Russia, because the business route leading to Danzig went through Lithuania. Danzig was one of the most important arteries of Polish-Lithuanian business contacts with other countries.

"Just like in Red Russia, in Lithuania the customs leases had the stature of large capitalist enterprises. For example, in the 1480s and 1490s the annual lease tax of the customs in Berestetchko, Drohitchin, Beilsk, and Grodno were around 1,100 shok groshes (more than $7,000); in Lutsk it was 1,512 shok groshes; in Putivel, 1,100 shok, and in Minsk, 250 shok."

Our fellow émigré, Shmuel, son of Tuvia-Daid Lev of New York, also made us aware of this document of Dr. Schiffer. We thank everyone very much! DW)

Sadie (daughter of Rabbi Ze'ev Miler) and Norman Mirsky.

[*Page 420*]

Over a cup of tea of chapter 401 of the Drohitchin Émigrés Association, September 28, 1947 at the New York Drohitchin Chapter 401 at a party in 1947. See p. 392.

Because most of the people in the photograph are standing in this way, it is difficult to indicate in writing who is who; especially because we didn't know many of the names, we left off all the names, even those names of people we know, so as to avoid any arguments. Please forgive us.   **DW**

[*Page 421*]

Mrs. Rachel Spetman, wife of Rabbi Yehoshua Spetman of London, England, and daughter of Rabbi Yehuda-Noach and Chana Braver (for 30 years he was the rabbi of Barnov near Lublin, and died in Jerusalem in 1939). She died on 2 Tammuz (15 June), 1953 in London. She was survived by a son Yisrael (Bessya) Spetman and two daughters: Sarah (Rabbi Ezriel) Tarshish (London) and Chana (Dov) Warshavsky, Chicago. 284.

During those Fateful Days

By Mrs. Etka Kohn, Baltimore

It was in October, 1920 when we were fearful about the partnership between the Poles and the murderous Balakhov gangs who were coming to Drohitchin. One early morning, I took a look through my window (We were then living in David Eisenstein's brick house.), and I saw two Balakhov thugs tormenting and beating our neighbor Shmulik Milner into telling them where the rabbi lived. Later on, the two thugs banged on my door and ordered me to bring them the rabbi. One of them showed me a knife and said, "There is a whole train-full of Balakhovists waiting at the Nagoria station for our orders."

I felt deathly scared. My husband, Rabbi Noach Cohen, was not at home at the time; he was hiding somewhere. With no choice, I went over to my husband and told him about the threats from the Balakhov thugs and prayed that the merit of my saintly father, Rabib David-Mordechai, would protect us from the terrible danger.

When my husband came out of the cellar, he was white as chalk from fear. However, he worked up the courage and greeted the thugs, who welcomed him with a cigarette and with a smile. The officers told him that if he wanted to save a town full of Jews, he should go with them. So he went along, but they would not allow me to accompany him.

An hour later my husband returned carrying a sheet of paper with writing on it. The thugs ordered the town to present them with 25 calves, 10 cows, 25 cases of cheese and five bags of salt by the next day at 10 am. They said that if these items were not provided, they would massacre the town.

My husband and some businessmen in town (with the approval of the terrorists) went around all night and were just barely able to come up with what they could get. The animals were brought over to our courtyard, and they waited for the executioners. It was almost 10 am, then 11, and then 12 noon, and the thugs had not yet appeared. At 1 pm, someone riding a horse arrived from the Zakazelia estate and told us the terrible news that they had killed 17 Jews in Zakazelia. Those thugs had kept their word and quenched their thirst with Jewish blood elsewhere, not in Drohitchin. The train with the Balakhovists left for Pinsk after their massacre was completed.

(See pp. 128, 131. DW)

Hershel Steinberg, a son of Meir-Yitzchak (Zeidel) and Henya. He was born in Drohitchin and moved to Palestine in 1922. In 1930, he arrived in the United States and died in Chicago on March 27, 1943 at the age of 40. Hershel left behind a wife Beatrice and two children, Leon and Bernie, in Chicago. Steinberg was a Zionist all his life and provided alot of assistance in the development of Palestine. See pp. 239, 294, 312 and 330.

A group of pioneers from Drohitchin before their departure for Palestine in 1926

When Jews Were Vulnerable
By Leizer Lev, Chicago

It was during those bitter days during the Polish-Bolshevik war of 1920. The town was burned down, and there was no food. So people had to plant in gardens and fields, and they lived on whatever the earth would give them. Of course, to cultivate the land you needed a horse, and my cousin, Chaim (Moshe Leizer's) Epstein, and I traveled to Yanova to buy a horse. After traveling a couple of miles, we noticed from a distance that two Polish soldiers were coming toward us. This stabbed me in my heart, and I said to my cousin, "I have a feeling we aren't going to get away easily from the Poles."

I was not wrong. The Poles checked us out thoroughly, and not finding any money, they took our permits. Then they ordered us to stand at a distance while they started rummaging through our wagon. We were sure they would not find anything suspicious in the wagon. However, we were absolutely amazed when the Poles found five unshot bullets that they supposedly found in our wagon. "Aha!" they said, "You are communist spies!" Our hands and feet started trembling, and we were sure we were finished. Who would believe us that the Poles had planted the bullets?

We fell to our feet and begged the Poles to take us back to Drohitchin, where they would find out the truth about us. The fact that I was speaking Russian (I did not know any Polish) only made matters worse. I was most certainly a communist spy, and none of our crying and begging did any good. The Poles took us to Yanova with swords drawn. It did not look good for us.

Suddenly I had an idea. Maybe money would help. We had some money hidden away, and my cousin Chaim started crying and begging the Poles that because he was a father of children, they should take the money and leave us alone. After many hours of suffering and torment, the Poles took the money and let us go. We came home and thanked G-d that we had been saved from death. (See p. 359. DW)

Avraham Bezdzhezesky, Sergeant Major (in the right-hand photo, from right, with the little hat and in the left-hand photo on the left) is together with a group of Irgun fighters who attacked Jaffa on 16 Nisan (25 April), 1948 and captured it on 4 Iyar (13 May), 1948. Avraham is a son of Moshe and Chana Bezdzhezesky. See p. 148.

Leibe Peretz, killed, son of Moshe from Kobrin Street

Left: Avraham Michel (Milton) Luria died on 24 Adar 1948. (This year had two Adars, one being March 5, and the other April 5). He was survived by his wife Tila, a son Jerry, and two daughters, Ethel and Sheindel.

Right: Fruma Leah Michalsky, wife of Chaim the Teacher.

http://www.jewishgen.org/yizkor/Drohichyn/images/423.gif
[Page 423]

Yosef Heftman (Emanuel), writer, columnist, publisher of the publications *Hatsfira, Hayom, Doar Hayom, Moment* (Warsaw) and editor-in-chief of *Haboker* (Tel Aviv). He was born on July 23, 1888. He died on January 18, 1955 in Tel Aviv. See p. 138, column 2.

Gravestone says: Here is buried Chana, daughter of R. Chaim. She died on 17 Adar 5690 – March 17, 1930.] Liba (Argentina), Yaakov (New York) and Yenta (left) at the grave of their mother, Chana Goldberg, in the Drohitchin cemetery.

As an eternal memorial to the Martyrs of Drohitchin
From a group of émigrés from Drohitchin in Chicago:
Mordechai Ber and Mrs. Eisenstein; Shmuel and Janie Eisenstein; Morris and Mrs. Leison; Mrs. Potolsky; Yaakov and Mrs. Kohn; Eliyahu-Meir and Mrs. Shedrov.
As a memorial to Henach, son of Aharon-David Miller, New York.
Wife Chaya, and daughters Freida and Etcha Miller.
As an eternal memorial to the Martyrs of Kolonia
Binyamin-Yehuda and Esther Teplitsky, Chicago.
In memory of Pinya and Minda Siderov, brother and sister; May G-d avenge their blood!
Sons David-Mendel and Velvel Bloom, New York. See p. 326.

Left: Jews at prayer at the Western Wall in 1943
The soldier is Yeshayahu, brother of the draftsman.
Right: Meir Lieberman. May G-d avenge his blood!

(DW)

Kaddish

On the road between Pinsk and Brisk,
There was once a little town,
A name, a dot on the map of Russian Poland,
My town of Drohitchin, was one.
Today there are no more Chassidim or non-Chassidim,
Shopkeepers, workers, young and elderly Jews,
No more scholars or businessmen,
Wealthy merchants, small ones, traveling to fairs.
Like a tearful mourner, with head bowed,
During the first thirty days of mourning,
I stand with my eyes filled with tears,
And say the Kaddish prayer for the martyrs.

Shepsel Lev, Haifa, April 1951.

Table of Contents of the

Original Yiddish Drohitchin Yizkor Book

Drohitchin Worldwide
Part Seven: pp. 385-424

Note: We have included as much as possible in the Table of Contents. There was no room to include group photos. The asterisks indicate that in addition to the written material, the raw material is also the work of D. B. W.

INDEX